INSIDE

3D STUDIO MAX 2

VOLUME III

ANIMATION

GEORGE MAESTRI

DENNIS BRADSHAW

JAN-ERIK SJOVALL

JEFFREY ABOUAF

ANNA HENNEQUET

JACQUES HENNEQUET

ANGIE JONES

New
Riders

New Riders Publishing, Indianapolis, Indiana

Cover Art by Todd Sheridan of GlyphX, Inc.

Inside 3D Studio MAX 2 Volume III: Animation

By George Maestri, Jeffrey Abouaf, Dennis Bradshaw,
Anna Hennequet, Jacques Hennequet, Angie Jones, Jan-Erik Sjovall

Published by:
New Riders Publishing
201 West 103rd Street
Indianapolis, IN 46290 USA

Printed in the United States of America 1 2 3 4 5 6 7 8 9 0

Library of Congress Cataloging-in-Publication Data: **97-80887**

ISBN: **1-56205-865-7**

EXECUTIVE EDITOR
Alicia Buckley
ACQUISITIONS EDITOR
Laura Frey
DEVELOPMENT EDITORS
Julie MacLean
Jennifer Eberhardt

PROJECT EDITOR
Katie Purdum
COPY EDITOR
Michael Brumitt
TECHNICAL EDITORS
Paul Hormis
David Marks
Larry Minton
SOFTWARE PRODUCT DEVELOPER
Adam Swetnam
TEAM COORDINATOR
Michelle Newcomb
BOOK DESIGNER
Louisa Klucznik
COVER DESIGNER
Dan Armstrong
PRODUCTION TEAM
Carol Bowers
Mona Brown
Ayanna Lacey
Gene Redding
INDEXER
Greg Pearson

Warning and Disclaimer

About the Authors

Jeffrey Abouaf is a fine artist, designer, and instructor, whose experience includes television animation and design for print and online media. He was a contributing author for *Inside 3D Studio MAX 2 Volume I* and follows industry developments in 3D graphics, animation, and virtual reality as a conference reporter and product reviewer for several publications. He holds BA, MFA, and JD degrees. He teaches 3D Studio MAX in San Francisco State's Multimedia Studies program, recently authored online tutorials for Kinetix for inclusion in the 3D Studio MAX R2 upgrade, and spends substantial time exploring 3DS MAX as a fine art tool. He can be reached at jabouaf@ogle.com or www.ogle.com.

Dennis Bradshaw majored in Philosophy at UCLA. One day, deep in philosophical contemplation, he had the revelation that he would much rather be creating 3D computer animation than go to law school, and thus his saga began. He taught himself 3D modeling, texturing, animation, and 2D design in the wee hours of his spare time. He designed his own 3D Animation class at UCLA, while going to school full time and working for UCLA Advertising, doing computer graphics for video, and digital editing. Before long, Dennis was hired as Lead 3D Artist/Animator for a Los Angeles-based game company and put in charge of all the art direction and production for an entire real-time 3D game. Two years and many models later, he began his own company, 3Dstorm. He does freelance work, producing beautiful 3D models and flowing animation. Dennis has extensive experience in many different aspects of the field, from non-linear digital and audio editing to 3D visualization work for architectural firms, commercial products, and entrepeneurial marketing, 3D logo design and animation, every aspect of video game design, character design and animation, and animated 3D movies. Visit the 3Dstorm Web site at 3Dstorm.com or e-mail Dennis at den@3Dstorm.com.

E. K. Anna Hennequet was born in Seoul, South Korea. She moved to New York in 1980. She has a degree from New York's Parson School of Design in Graphic Design. Anna also has formal training as a fine artist. She has worked as a Designer and Art Director for large companies such as Jim Henson Productions, Bally of Switzerland, Simon & Schuster, and Geoffrey Beene. In 1993, Anna joined Gotham Digital, Inc., a company specializing in high-end computer graphics and animation, with clients including CBS, CNBC, TNT, TBS, and The Discovery Channel. Her design work has since earned her two International BDA (Broadcast Designer's Association) awards. She left Gotham Digital in 1996 to move to Seattle and create Dreamtek, LLC, a company specializing in 3D CGI.

Jacques Hennequet was born in Paris, France. He moved to New York in 1981. He was first hired by Image Factory, a CGI production company where he performed as an animator, then as producer for clients such as Amblin Entertainment, 20th Century Fox, as well as a number of large corporate clients (Kodak, Polaroid, and so on). He then went on to become a freelance director/producer. His work received several national and international awards (Clio award, New York International Film Festival award, Houston International Film Festival, and others). Jacques was the cofounder and vice president of Gotham Digital, Inc., a company specializing in high-end computer graphics and animation, with clients including CBS, CNBC, TNT, TBS, and The Discovery Channel. He left Gotham Digital in 1996 to move to Seattle and create Dreamtek, LLC. He is now art director for Strategic Simulations Inc. (subsidiary of Mindscape), a Novato-based game company. Jacques holds a degree in Film and Animation from New York University. He has taught Animation at the New York School of Visual Arts.

Angie Jones is a 3D animator with 5 years experience with 3D Studio MAX, specializing in character animation. She worked as a successful freelance animator in Atlanta, Georgia, after graduating the Atlanta College of Art in 1994. After moving to San Diego from Atlanta, she has kept busy the past 3 years working for The Lightspan Partnership, Inc., on over 25 educational software products released for the PC and Sony Playstation. She has also worked on the childrens' educational TV show *Reality Check* for Mindflex, Inc., New Line Home Video and Conduit Communications, that aired on both NBC and CBS affiliates. Other credits to her career include Coca-Cola USA McDonald's Worldwide and Majority Stock Presentations, AT&T True Experience On-line Interface, Castleway Entertainment Film Trailer, and the "Cyberdillo" 3DO Game by Panasonic. Her freelance work continues in San Diego under the name Spicy Cricket Animation. For more information about Angie Jones and Spicy Cricket Animation, visit the Web site at www.spicycricket.com.

George Maestri is a writer, director, and producer. His credits include a number of shows, including *Rocko's Modern Life*, and *South Park*. He has written numerous articles on computer animation for magazines such as *Digital Magic*, *CGW*, *DV*, and *Publish*. George is also the author of *[digital] Character Animation*.

Jan-Erik Sjovall is a successful freelance 3D Animation Designer. By heart and birth a Utahan from Salt Lake City, he is currently living and working in Hamburg, Germany, mainly on game projects and for advertisement and news media agencies. You can contact him on the Net at je.sjovall@hammaducks.com.

Trademark Acknowledgments

Contents at a Glance

Part IV: Video Post Effects

Table of Contents

Introduction

Inside 3D Studio MAX 2, Volume III: Animation *is the third book in a three-volume set. Due to the robust nature of 3DS MAX, New Riders is dedicated to bringing users detailed, top-quality information on all of the features and functions of the software.* Inside 3D Studio MAX 2, Volume III *is a complete tutorial and reference on animation. It includes coverage of the many different animation techniques used in the industry—from animation with transforms to character animation to animating the environment. Also included is expert coverage of MAX's powerful Video Post module. Learn how to use the Video Post module for compositing and editing animations, as well as for creating special effects.*

The previous volume in the *Inside 3D Studio MAX 2* set is *Volume II: Advanced Modeling and Materials*. Like this book, it is presented in the *Inside* style, packed with detailed tutorials and valuable tips and techniques from industry experts. Look for *3D Studio MAX 2, Volume II: Advanced Modeling and Materials* in your bookstore.

Organization of the Book

Inside 3D Studio MAX 2, Volume III: Animation is organized in four sections:

- Part I, "Animation Techniques," Chapters 1 through 4.
- Part II, "Character Animation," Chapters 5 through 10.
- Part III, "Animating the Environment," Chapters 11 through 14.
- Part IV, "Video Post Effects," Chapters 15 and 16.

Part I covers animation techniques in MAX 2. The tools are not explained; instead, the techniques that are best served by MAX 2's tolls and plug-ins are described. Animation tutorials take you through the steps needed to animate with transforms, controllers, expressions, and multiple modifiers.

Part II takes you through the unique world of character animation. From creating a character to animating it with MAX tools and plug-ins, this section teaches the best methods of animating for a variety of situations.

Part III explores animating the environment. These chapters cover how to animate cameras, light, and atmosphere to achieve the feel you are looking for in your animation. Also covered is how to animate with particles and space warps to generate a number of effects.

Part IV covers the powerful Video Post module within MAX. This section extends your knowledge of Video Post by teaching you how to create special effects and how to compose and edit your animation within Video Post.

How to Read the Exercises

Unlike most tutorials you read, the *Inside 3DS MAX 2* exercises do not rigidly dictate every step that you perform to achieve the desired result. These exercises are designed to be flexible and to work in a wide range of situations. This approach provides you with the following benefits:

- *A better understanding of the concepts.* You must think through the example rather than blindly follow the minutiae of many steps.

- *The opportunity to apply the examples to your own work.* The flexibility built into the exercises enables you to experiment with the effects until you achieve the results you want.

Most exercises begin with some explanatory text, as shown in the following sample exercise. The text tells you what the exercise should accomplish and sets the context for the exercise.

SAMPLE EXERCISE FORMAT

You might encounter text such as this at the beginning of or in the middle of an exercise when one or more actions require an extended explanation.

1. Numbered steps identify your actions to complete the exercise.

    Indented text adds extra explanation about the previous step, when needed.

The word *choose* in an example always indicates a menu selection. If the selection involves a pull-down menu, you are told explicitly where to find the menu item. If the selection is from another part of the user interface, you are told which component to click and the location of the interface. Setting the Hemisphere option for a Sphere object, for example, requires clicking the Hemisphere check box in the Creation Parameters rollout (you would have been told previously whether you were accessing the rollout from the Create panel or the Modify panel). The word *select* always refers to selecting one or more objects, elements, or vertices. Select never refers to menus or other user interface components.

Because this book is designed for people who already have some experience with 3DS MAX 2, some exercise steps are implied rather than explicitly stated. You can, for example, find yourself instructed to "Create a smooth, 20-segment Sphere with a radius of 100 units," rather than reading all of the steps required to create the object.

Exercises and the CD-ROM

Most of the examples and exercises use files that are included on the *Inside 3D Studio MAX 2, Volume III* CD-ROM, which ships with 3D Studio MAX 2, or you are shown how to create the necessary geometry. Sample files are located on the accompanying CD-ROM. Instructions on how to use the CD-ROM files or to install them on your hard drive are described in the following section.

Using the *Inside 3D Studio MAX 2, Volume III* CD-ROM

Inside 3D Studio MAX 2, Volume III comes with a CD-ROM packed with many megabytes of plug-ins, scenes, maps, and other sample software. The sample files can be used directly from the *Inside 3D Studio MAX 2, Volume III* CD-ROM, so "installing" them is not necessary. You might want to copy files from the CD-ROM to your hard drive or another storage device. In that case, you can use the Install routines found with some of the sample programs, or you can copy the files directly to a directory on your hard drive.

Installing the Exercise Files

All exercise files not included with 3D Studio MAX 2 are contained in a single subdirectory on the *Inside 3D Studio MAX, Volume III* CD-ROM: \I3DSMAX. You can access these files directly from the CD-ROM when you execute the exercises, or you can create a directory called \I3DSMAX on your hard drive and copy the files there. Some of the exercise files require maps from the CD-ROM that ships with 3D Studio MAX 2. You must copy these files to a subdirectory that is referenced in the 3DS MAX Map-Paths parameter.

3D Studio MAX automatically looks for map files in the directory from which a scene is loaded. If you copy the exercise files to your hard drive, make sure that you keep the mesh files and map files together, or at least put the map files in a directory where 3D Studio can find them at rendering time.

A number of sample scenes, animation files, and maps are provided on the *Inside 3D Studio MAX 2, Volume III* CD-ROM for your use. These are licensed free for your use. You cannot, however, resell or otherwise distribute the files.

Registering Shareware

Most of the sample programs on the accompanying CD-ROM are either demonstration programs or shareware programs. Shareware programs are fully functioning products that you can try out prior to purchasing—they are not free. If you find a shareware program useful, you must pay a registration fee to the program's author. Each shareware program provides information about how to contact the author and register the program.

Using CompuServe and the Web

The CompuServe Information Service is an online, interactive network that you can access with a modem and special access software. The most important feature of this service (at least as far as this book is concerned) is the Kinetix forum.

The Kinetix forum is an area of CompuServe that is maintained by Kinetix for the direct support of 3D Studio MAX and other Kinetix software. Hundreds of people from all over the world visit this forum daily to share ideas, ask and answer questions, and generally promote the use of 3D Studio MAX. If you ask a question on the forum, you are likely to receive an answer from any number of other 3D Studio MAX artists. Every question, from the most basic to the most mind-bending puzzler, receives the same quick and courteous treatment.

Kinetix also maintains a site on the World Wide Web where you can get the latest information about 3DS MAX 2, future software releases, and plug-in development. You can also send questions and feedback directly to Kinetix and download software. The Kinetix Web site is www.ktx.com.

New Riders Publishing

The staff of New Riders Publishing is committed to bringing you the very best in computer reference material. Each New Riders book is the result of months of work by authors and staff who research and refine the information contained within its covers.

As part of this commitment to you, New Riders invites your input. Please let us know if you enjoy this book, if you have trouble with the information and examples presented, or if you have suggestions for the next edition.

Please note, however, that New Riders staff cannot serve as a technical resource for 3D Studio MAX or for questions about software- or hardware-related problems. Please refer to the documentation that accompanies your software or to the application's Help systems.

If you have a question or comment about any New Riders book, there are several ways to contact New Riders Publishing. We respond to as many readers as we can. Your name, address, or phone number will never become part of a mailing list or be used for any purpose other than to help us continue to provide the best books possible.

You can write to us at the following address:

New Riders Publishing
Attn: Alicia Buckley
201 W. 103rd Street
Indianapolis, IN 46290

If you prefer, you can fax New Riders Publishing at the following:

317-817-7070

You can also send electronic mail to New Riders at the following Internet address:

abuckley@mcp.com

New Riders Publishing is an imprint of Macmillan Computer Publishing. To obtain a catalog or to purchase a Macmillan Computer Publishing book, call 800-428-5331, or visit our Web site at http://www.mcp.com.

Thank you for selecting *Inside 3D Studio MAX 2, Volume III: Animation*.

Part I

ANIMATION TECHNIQUES

Chapter 1

ADVANCED TRANSFORMATION ANIMATION

Transformation animation describes the use of simple changes in position, rotation, and scale over time to achieve a desired Motion effect. Although this chapter deals with rudimentary principles, it applies these principles in an evolved form to achieve sophisticated results. The goal of this chapter is to teach you various principles for applying the most basic and powerful tools in MAX 2—the Move, Rotate, and Scale tools—in additional ways. Instead of merely transforming objects, you'll experiment with more complex animation derived from the use of Helper objects, sub-objects, vertex, and spline animation.

You will learn about Nested animation, Linked transforms, transformation inheritance, creating a Walk cycle, and deformation of lofted objects.

This chapter demonstrates the following advanced Transformation methods:

- Transform animation and non-linear animation
- Positioning Ranges and Out-of-Range values
- Grouping, instancing, and offsetting an animation
- Complex rotations using dummies
- Sub-object animation
- Transforms along surfaces
- Animating using multiple object instances

In this chapter, you explore advanced Transform animation by animating a UFO. First, the UFO flies into view and you use Linked dummies to create the spinning and banking effect as it comes to a halt. The UFO hovers above the ground and panels open on the body, letting out long, spidery legs. This is achieved by using the Scale feature combined with specific Inheritance assignments. At the end of the legs, small spheres morph into boots by using the new capability of MAX R2 to animate base vertices of an object.

Then the UFO begins walking forward, using a series of Linked transformations. Eventually the UFO reaches into a glass of water that comes into view. The UFO stops and a hatch opens at the top of the UFO. A hose snakes out of the UFO, making use of the new capability of MAX R2 to animate spline vertices and handles. The hose finds its way over the edge of the glass and down to its bottom, and the water then lowers until the UFO is satisfied.

Working with Dummy Objects

Careful and proper preparation of your models will ensure a smooth animation process. By taking the time to strategically place pivots, as well as Helper objects like dummies, you reduce the chance of unpleasant surprises when you begin the animation process.

Dummies are objects that do not show up for rendering. Their primary purpose is to link objects together, or to be linked to other dummies. Dummies are essentially aids for animation, and when used properly are extremely powerful in expediting complex Transformation animation.

Instead of adjusting the pivots of every object or group of objects, you merely link the objects to a dummy and position it. The dummy serves as a more permanent, reliable, and malleable way to define origins and axes of transformation. This is helpful because you are then free to construct objects in any orientation without concern for the position of their axes. It is also a permanent way of ensuring that pivots remain where you want them, regardless of modifications to objects.

However, unlike an Object pivot, you can always animate the position of a dummy if you want. Furthermore, if you need an object's pivot aligned with the orientation of the object for scaling purposes (as you will) yet need to perform your rotations using an alternate axis orientation, dummies are your simplest solution.

To set up the UFO leg for animation, you will use the 01max01.max file from the book's accompanying CD. The leg boxes, joint-cylinders, and feet have already been created and positioned for you. You must create the dummies and link the leg together. You then learn to create and strategically place the dummies, and how to effectively link them up in the following exercise.

PLACING DUMMIES

1. Load 01max01.max from the accompanying CD.

2. In the Create Command panel, click the Helpers icon and click Dummy.

3. In the Front viewport, create four dummies, as illustrated in Figure 1.1. Place one dummy centered on the left end of the far left box, one centered at the base of the far right box, and two centered on the cylinders between the boxes. It may be helpful to use the Align tool with the local axis checked to achieve this proper placement.

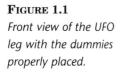

FIGURE 1.1

Front view of the UFO leg with the dummies properly placed.

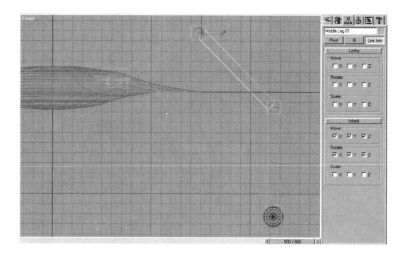

4. Beginning with the dummy on the far left (at the base of the leg), name the dummies Upper Leg Z Rotate 01, Mid Leg Z Rotate 01, Low Leg Z Rotate 01, and Foot Rotate 01.

Linking Objects Together

Now that the dummies are in place, let's link the dummies and the leg together. Once they are all linked, you'll use them to control the leg's animation through multiple planes. But first, you will experiment with backwards key-setting and scaling the legs of the ship so that they seemingly expand from nowhere.

LINKING THE DUMMIES AND SHIP LEGS

1. Select ShipFoot01 and link it to the dummy named Foot Rotate 01.

2. Link the dummy named Foot Rotate 01 to Lower Leg 01.

3. Link Lower Leg 01 to the dummy named Low Leg Z Rotate 01.

4. Link the dummy named Low Leg Z Rotate 01 to Middle Leg 01.

5. Link Cylinder 01 to Middle Leg 01.

6. Link Middle Leg 01 to the dummy named Mid Leg Z Rotate 01.

7. Link the dummy named Mid Leg Z Rotate 01 to Upper Leg 01.

8. Link Upper Leg 01 to the dummy named Upper Leg Z Rotate 01.

Inheritance Properties

Seeing what it takes to disable a link gives you a better idea of what it takes to be a link. A Hierarchical link is simply the "passing on" from one object (the parent) to another (the child) its changes in position, rotation, and/or scale using the parent's Coordinate system. These changes are referred to as the child's inheritance. A child inherits its parent's transforms, adds its own transforms to its parent's, and passes the sum of these transforms on to its children.

To properly animate, it sometimes becomes necessary to disable or sever this inheritance of linked objects, as in this next exercise. You'll want to scale the legs without scaling the joints that connect each leg segment and without scaling the feet at the end of the legs. You may even decide to first scale the upper leg, then the middle leg, and finally the lower leg. If link inheritance isn't turned off, when you scale the upper leg, everything beneath it is scaled at the same time and to the same degree. Because this is not the desired result in this situation, you will disable link inheritance.

SEVERING INHERITANCE

1. Select any of the dummies.

2. In the Hierarchy Command panel, click the Link Info button.

3. In the Inherit rollout, uncheck all three Scale axes.

4. Repeat this process for each of the dummies, leg boxes, cylinders, and the sphere at the end of the leg.

5. Save the scene as **UFO1_1.max**.

NEW TO R2

You can also use the Link Inheritance (Selection) utility that is new to MAX R2 to disable one or more axes of multiple objects at once. This utility works exactly like the Inherit rollout, except that the inheritance adjustments you make are applied to every object in the current selection set. Thus, you can select all the dummies at once and uncheck all three Scale axes in the Link Inheritance utility.

By removing the checks from each axis under the Inherit tab, you sever the hierarchical inheritance of scale from each object's respective parent. Now when you decide to scale the legs of the UFO, scaling any part of the leg does not affect any of the objects beneath it (its children). This works equally well for disabling the inheritance of rotations or position. If position, rotation, and Scale inheritance are disabled for every axis, the link is fully disabled.

Now that the first leg is linked, you will position it. Proper positioning of the leg is essential to a "believable" animation. The leg should be coming out of the front right hatch on the UFO (your right when looking at it from a Front viewport). The leg should not intersect the body itself; it should also be at an angle, rather than perpendicular to the Front viewport. You can't start animating the legs until they are properly positioned, because the position affects just how far forward and backward the legs will reach when they walk. So let's position the leg now.

POSITIONING THE LEG

1. Continue working with the previous scene.

2. Select the Top viewport, select the Rotate tool, select Local axis, and select the dummy named Upper Leg Z Rotate 01.

3. Rotate this dummy -15 degrees on its y-axis. It should now be aligned over Leg Panel 01 (see Figure 1.2). There is only one problem—there is a missing dummy that you need if you are to properly animate the leg. Thanks to a new feature in the MAX 2 Align toolbox, as you'll see in step 5 of this exercise, properly placing this new dummy is very easy.

4. In the Top viewport, create a slightly larger dummy surrounding the dummy named Upper Leg Z Rotate 01. Name this dummy Leg Base Y Rotate 01, and with it still selected, click the Align tool and select Upper Leg Z Rotate 01.

FIGURE 1.2

Top view of the UFO, with the leg properly positioned.

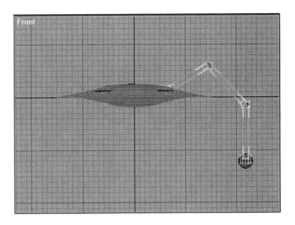

5. Check the boxes next to X, Y, and Z positions and leave the Current object and Target objects set to Center.

6. MAX 2: Instead of having to manually rotate the dummy -15 degrees to align its orientation with the other dummies, you may simply check the box next to Z Axis under the new Align Orientation panel in the Align toolbox. (Do this now.) This may seem trivial when it's just one simple rotation off, but for more complicated disparities, it comes in very handy!

7. Save the scene as **01max02.max**.

Copying Linked Geometry

Copying the leg saves you the trouble of linking this whole thing up three more times. You will copy this leg once, work out the animation for the right side of the UFO, and then create an instance of that animation on the other side of the UFO. You will use the Copy feature instead of mirroring the selection. This is because Mirroring the selection also mirrors the pivots of the objects, which vastly complicates animating such a simple Walk cycle. Instead of dealing with the pain of tweaking pivots and axes, and the other problems inherent in mirroring linked selections, you simply create your copy using the Shift-Move feature.

COPY THE LEG

1. Continue working with the previous scene, or load 01max02.max from the accompanying CD.

2. Under the Edit pull-down menu, select Select All.

3. Select the World coordinate system. Select the Top viewport as your active view.

4. Select Move, Constrain to Y Axis, hit the Spacebar to lock the select, and move 125 units to the top.

5. Select Copy and accept the new name. Unlock the selection.

6. Select Leg Base Y Rotate 02 and rotate it 30 degrees on the local y-axis.

7. Save the scene as **01max03.max**.

So far you have prepared your UFO for its Walk cycle animation. You created and positioned animation controllers (dummies), and once created, you copied the entire leg structure from the front to the rear. Next you animate the Walk cycle for the two legs, and then instance the animation to the opposite side of the craft.

Transformation Animations and Non-Linear Animation

Now that you've prepared your model, you will perform your first transformation animation. The final result will have impossibly long legs growing out of little doors on the UFO's body. This Scaling procedure requires each of the three leg segments to fully scale out before the next one begins scaling, which is why you disabled the Scale inheritance. With Scale inheritance disabled, you can scale each leg segment independently of its parents or children.

NOTE

You disabled the inheritance of the scale because scaling a parent transfers the scale to its children. Although this may seem to be what you want, it, in fact, is not. You want to scale each leg segment only along *its* local x-axis. By scaling the parent, each child would also be scaled along its parent's x-axis. This would be acceptable if the objects were all in an aligned orientation, but they are not. It is in circumstances like this that the capability to sever specific inheritances is very valuable. If you are curious what would have happened had you not disabled Scale inheritance, feel free to try the next step in this tutorial with Inherit Scale enabled (see Figure 1.3).

FIGURE 1.3
Improper result of scaling the parent without disabling Scale inheritance for the children.

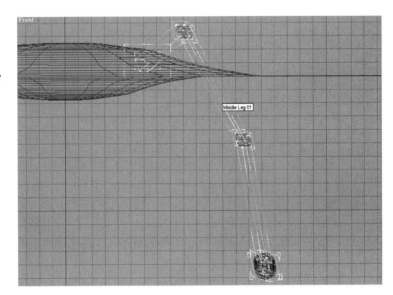

Non-Linear Animation of Transformations

Often, with complicated animations, it is easier to animate in reverse chronology (that is, backwards) than it is to animate chronologically. Instead of starting with minuscule legs and scaling them up, you start with the legs at the scale and position where you want them to end up. You then move backward in time and scale them to where they start. This is often a useful and important technique in computer animation.

Think of it this way: If you had to do a film of 50 rubber balls bouncing *into* a jar, wouldn't it be easier to film the jar falling and spilling the balls out, and then play it backward, than to try to make all the balls end up just where you want them? This concept is often the same in the world of 3D animation. It is often easier to take structured order and turn it into chaos, than vice versa. Because you have exact control over the Time slider, this is not a problem.

ANIMATING ROTATE AND SCALE TRANSFORMS IN REVERSE CHRONOLOGY

1. Load 01max03.max from the accompanying CD or continue to work with the model you designed in the previous exercise.

2. Be certain that you are at frame 0. Select every object in the scene (except for the objects that are hidden or frozen).

3. Right-click the Time slider and click OK. This opens the Create Key dialog box.

4. Enter a Destination time of 100. The Source time should be set to 0. Click OK. This creates a Position, Rotation, and Scale key for every selected object at frame 100. These keys are called *Null* keys, because they create Animation keys that don't animate the object. Instead they serve as placeholders, keeping the object from being affected at the Null key time by any animation before or after the Null key.

5. In the current frame field, enter 30 to go to frame 30.

6. Select the Rotate tool, select Local Axis, make certain the Angle Snap Toggle and the Percentage Toggle are turned on, and click the Animate button.

7. Press the H button to access the Select by Name dialog, and select objects Mid Leg Z Rotate 01 and 02.

8. Press the Spacebar to lock the selection, select the z-axis, and rotate 75 degrees.

T IP

Making use of MAX's "Hot Keys" or keys that have been assigned to specific tools can save vast amounts of time. It is wise to become familiar with these keys and customize them if you wish. For example, to select the z-axis in this step, you merely need to strike the F7 key. The x-axis is F5, y-axis is F6, and to toggle between any two axes, hit F8.

9. Select Low Leg Z Rotate 01 and 02, and rotate 45 degrees on the z-axis.

10. Select Lower Leg 01 and 02, select Non-Uniform Scale, and right-click the Scale icon. Type in 1 under Absolute Local X to scale the legs to 1% of their current length on the x-axis.

11. Repeat this process for Middle Leg 01 and 02 and Upper Leg 01 and 02.

12. Select Uniform Scale and right-click the Scale icon. In the Scale Transform Type-In, under Offset: Screen, enter a value of 1%.

NOTE

From this point forward, this book will not reiterate procedures and help tools you have previously been shown. It's up to you to explore the tools you have been shown and use them when you think it is appropriate!

13. Turn off the Animate button, hide the dummies (under Display, Hide by Category, Helpers), and play the animation.

14. Save your file as **01max04.max**.

The legs now magically "grow" into place starting at frame 30 and ending at frame 100. This is only one example of the types of Scale transforms you may apply to objects to achieve a desired animation effect.

Animating a Walk Cycle

The Walk cycle is one of the most common, and therefore one of the most important, of all animations. There are many different means for achieving a believable Walk cycle, including Motion capture, Inverse Kinematics, and Transformation animation.

Because this is a simple animation, and a rather mechanical one, (and because this chapter is on Transformation animations), it makes sense to use transforms to achieve your walking UFO. Transformation animation is generally the best choice when animating something mechanical, because it yields very precise control over the motion of the animated objects. Transformation animation doesn't tend to produce the slight imperfections and variations that Inverse Kinematics does, which is ideal for living creatures as opposed to using Transformation animation for robots. To see more in-depth information on animating Walk cycles and using different tools to animate characters walking, see Part II of this book, "Character Animation."

ANIMATING HORIZONTAL LEG MOVEMENT

1. Load 01max04.max from the accompanying CD or continue working with the previous file.

2. Advance the time to 115 and turn on the Animate toggle.

3. Select Leg Base Y Rotate 01 and rotate it -30 degrees about its local y-axis.

4. Advance to frame 130. Rotate the same dummy 60 degrees about its local y-axis.

6. Advance to frame 145. Rotate the same dummy -60 degrees about its local y-axis.

7. Return to frame 115, select Leg Base Y Rotate 02, and rotate it 30 degrees about its local y-axis.

8. Advance to frame 130. Rotate the same dummy -60 degrees about its local y-axis.

9. Advance to frame 145. Rotate the same dummy 60 degrees about its local y-axis.

You have animated the back and forth motion of the legs. If you play the animation, however, you will notice that the motion doesn't look quite right. The feet of the UFO drag along the ground in an unnatural manner. To correct this, you must animate vertical motion for the legs when they move forward, leaving them planted on the ground as they slide backwards.

ANIMATING VERTICAL LEG MOVEMENT

1. Advance to frame 100. Select Upper Leg Z Rotate 01 and 02, and set keys for them at frames 100, 115, 130, and 145.

2. Select Upper Leg Z Rotate 01, move the Time slider to frame 105, turn on the Animate toggle, and rotate the dummy 5 degrees on its local z-axis.

3. Advance to frame 138, and rotate the dummy 15 degrees on its z-axis.

4. Select Upper Leg Z Rotate 02 (for the other leg), advance to frame 123, and rotate the dummy 15 degrees on its z-axis.

5. Turn off the Animate button.

Play the animation. It looks pretty good, but to the astute observer there is something slightly wrong. Select Unhide By Name under the Display command panel and unhide GroundTest. Switch to the Right viewport and play the animation. The pseudo-ground shows us that the legs are going through the ground plane (see Figure 1.4). This is because there is interpolation going on between the keyframes. The default setting in MAX is to ease in and out of each keyframe. This brings up a feature you will very often use in MAX: the Key Info dialog (see Figure 1.5). This dialog allows you to adjust the Interpolation In and Out values for any keyframe. Because you are animating a mechanical object that probably should have uniform motion, you can set all the keys to Linear In and Out values.

FIGURE 1.4

UFO legs going through the ground plane because of Key interpolation.

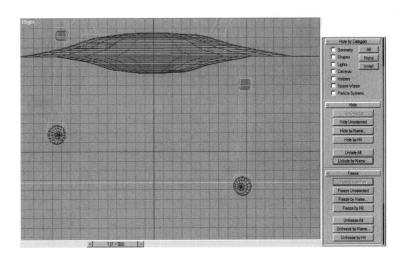

ADJUSTING KEY INFO

1. Select each of the two Upper Leg Z Rotate and the two Upper Leg Base Y Rotate dummies. The Select by Name dialog will come in handy here!

2. Open Track View, and with the four dummies selected, click Filters. Select Show Only: Selected Objects and Visible Objects, and uncheck Show: Transforms: Position and Scale.

3. You must make the Key Tangent In and Out Curve types for each Rotation key Linear.

FIGURE 1.5

*The Key Info dialog,
with Linear In type
selected.*

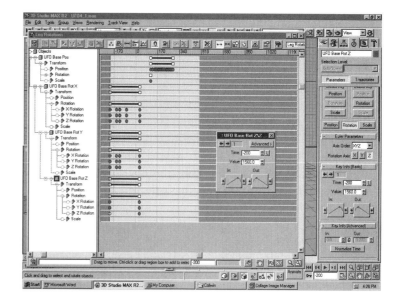

TIP

Altering the Tangent types of multiple keys is easily achieved by turning on the Modify Subtree button at the top of the Track View dialog. Then select all the keys in a given track, right-click any key in the track, and change its Tangent Curve type. By doing this, when you adjust the In and Out Tangent types for any one key, it changes all the other selected keys in the same track to that type.

4. Turn on the Modify Subtree button at the top of the Track View.

5. Select all the Rotation keys for any dummy. Right-click any key in each of the three Euler Rotation tracks. Change the In and Out type to Linear. Repeat this process for each of the other three dummies.

6. Now play the animation. The UFO "walks" on the ground. Save your file as **01max05.max**.

Positioning Ranges and Out of Range Values

Now you will adjust the Out of Range values to loop your Walk cycle animation. Out of Range values control the animation of objects before the first and after the last keyframe you set. The default setting is Constant, which leaves the objects in their last keyframed position.

You select the keys that you would like to have repeated by positioning the Range bar for the pertinent track over those keys. This defines, on a track-by-track basis, which keys are active. By selecting the keys you would like to loop and altering the Out of Range selection, you can take this little snippet of animation and have the UFO walk indefinitely. The different types of Out of Range Type curves control the way in which the selected keys are repeated. The best way to get a feel for what each of these types does is to assign each type to the animation and see its results.

DEFINING ACTIVE KEYFRAMES AND ASSIGNING OUT OF RANGE TYPE CURVES

1. Load01max05.max from the accompanying CD or continue working with the previous file.

2. Select the four dummies you've been working with here and open the Track View.

3. In the upper-left corner of the Track View, select the Filters button.

4. Under Show Only, check next to Animated Tracks and Selected Objects. Click OK.

5. In the right corner of the Track View, type in Leg Transforms. In MAX 2, you may name and save your Track View and recall it whenever you want.

6. Click the Position Ranges button on the Track View toolbar. By positioning the ranges, you tell MAX which keyframes you want to include in the Out of Range animation.

7. Adjust the left side of the ranges for each rotation axis for each of the dummies, so that the left side of all the ranges lines up at frame 115.

8. Press the Ctrl key and select all the Rotation tracks for each of the four dummies.

9. Click the Parameter Curve Out of Range Types button and a Param Curve dialog opens (see Figure 1.6). The arrow pointing to the left should remain on Constant. Click the arrow pointing to the right under Loop and click OK.

FIGURE 1.6

View of the Track View in Position Ranges mode and the Parameter Curve Out-of-Range Types menu active.

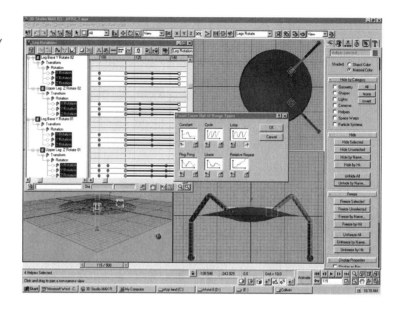

10. Save your scene as **01max06.max**.

Assigning the Loop Out of Range Curve type tells MAX to loop (or play repeatedly from beginning to end) the keys you've selected with the Range bar. You will experiment with other Out of Range Type Curves later in this chapter.

Grouping, Instancing, and Offsetting the Walk Animation

Now you'll create the other two legs and offset their animation so that the leg animation is staggered. If you ever watch a dog walk, you will notice that as the front left leg moves forward, the front right leg moves back, and the two rear legs move in opposition to the two front legs. This is the model you will use for your animation.

To quickly achieve the animation described, you will group all the leg objects and instance them to the opposite side of the UFO. Grouping takes your current Selection set and turns it into one selectable object. You can always ungroup a group into its constituents. Grouping is useful when you want to duplicate and transform a number of objects simultaneously.

Groups also help simplify scenes. By instancing the group, you copy linked objects as well as the animation applied to them. Thus, one set of animating legs becomes two sets. Finally, you will offset the animation so that as the legs on one side of the UFO contract, the legs on the other side expand. This adds a touch of realism to the walk.

GROUP, COPY, AND POSITION THE INSTANCED ANIMATION

1. Load 01max06.max from the accompanying CD or continue with the previous scene. Select all and move to frame 126. Be certain the Animate button is turned off.

NOTE

You have moved to frame 126 because this places the two legs parallel to each other when viewed in the Top viewport (see Figure 1.7). When at this orientation, the dummies for both legs are in the same orientation they were in when created. By grouping the legs in this orientation, the rotations applied to the two legs remain the same. If you group the two legs at any other time, for example at frame 0 or at frame 100, which perhaps seem like more natural times to group the legs, additional rotations are applied to the Leg Base Y Rotate dummies of each leg. This is a problem inherent in MAX 2. For linked objects, it is generally ideal to group them at the time when their local axes are aligned with the world.

FIGURE 1.7

Top view of the UFO at frame 126 with the legs parallel to each other and with their pivots aligned with the world.

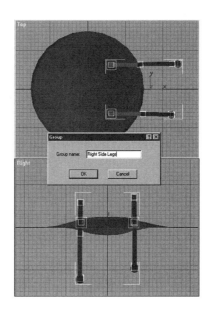

2. Group the objects and name the group **Right Side Legs**.

3. Press the Spacebar, and while holding the Shift key, drag to your left along only the x-axis.

4. Select Instance and name the group **Left Side Legs**.

5. Rotate the group 180 degrees on the z-axis and position them across from the other two legs.

Play back the animation. From a top view, the UFO appears to be swimming the breaststroke. You need to offset the animation for the left legs from the animation for the right legs. Because the total Walk cycle animation is 30 frames long, you should offset by 15 frames. Also, the front and rear legs have been reversed, such that when they move forward, they remain in contact with the ground, and when they move backwards, they leave the ground. This is obviously the opposite of what you want but is easily corrected. In the following exercise, you will offset the legs and tweak the leg lift animation.

OFFSETTING THE ANIMATED TRACKS

1. Continue from the previous exercise. Open the Leg Transforms Track View. Select Edit Keys mode.

2. In Track View, under Left Side Legs, move the Transform ranges for the four dummies for the two new legs 15 frames to the left, with the keys on the far left lining up at frame 85.

T IP

It is helpful, when positioning ranges, to select one of the keys at the beginning of the range before positioning the Range bar (in this case at frame 100). With the key selected, its time is shown at the bottom of the Track View, even as the range is positioned. In this way, you can monitor the exact frame position of the beginning of the range.

3. Select Upper Leg Z Rotate 03, and in the Track View, select the rotation keys at frame 123. Slide these keys back to frame 108.

4. Select Upper Leg Z Rotate 04, and in the Track View, select the rotation keys at frame 108. Slide these keys forward to frame 123.

5. Save your scene as **01max07.max**.

Play the animation. Through effective use of Range bars, Position keys, key easing, grouping, instancing, and Out of Range values, you've achieved a nice Walk cycle. Instancing animation and using the Range bars to offset animation is a very valuable tool. It is useful not only for Walk cycles, but for creating groups of identical objects that perform the same animation out of synchronization with each other. Examples of such groups would be flocks of birds flying, a bunch of balls bouncing, a group of animals walking, or insects buzzing.

Measuring Strides and Creating Keys from Out of Range Curves

To complete the Walk cycle, you just need to link the legs to the UFO and then move the UFO itself, so that it's not doing a Wally Gator. (For those who don't remember, whenever Wally Gator would begin running, he would spend several seconds with his legs spinning and his body not moving.) It is important that you move the UFO the right distance. If you don't move it far enough, the legs will look like they are sliding on the floor, and if you move it too much, it will look like the whole UFO is sliding forward as it walks. Either mistake will make the animation completely unbelievable. This can be avoided by taking careful account of the distance the legs travel with each step.

In the following exercise, you will measure the stride length of the UFO and then animate movement for the UFO to match its stride.

LINKING THE MODEL AND MATCHING MOTION TO STRIDE LENGTH

1. Continue from the previous exercise or load the scene 01max07.max from the accompanying CD. Move to frame 115. Open the two groups using the Open command under the Group menu.

2. Unfreeze the UFO body named Circle02.

3. Select the four Leg Base Y Rotate dummies.

4. Link the four selected dummies to Circle02 body. You may find it helpful to save this as a Selection set. Merely type in a name in the Named Selection Sets bar and the selection will be saved.

5. Now that the bases of the legs have been linked to the UFO body, the groups no longer pertain. Select the two groups, named Right Side Legs and Left Side Legs, and delete these two groups. They have served their purpose.

6. Move to the Right viewport and maximize it. At this time, the legs are at their extreme positions. You can measure the distance between strides at this frame.

7. Under Create, Helpers, select Tape. Measure from the front right leg's "foot" to the front left leg's "foot." It measures 155 units. This is the stride length, and thus the distance the UFO must move every 15 frames to keep its "feet" from appearing to slide along the ground (see Figure 1.8).

FIGURE 1.8

Side view of the UFO with a tape measure object measuring the stride from the front leg maximum position to its minimum position.

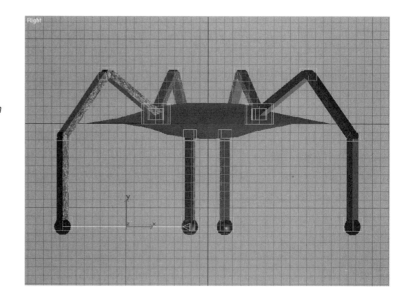

8. Unhide and select the dummy UFO Base Pos, and under the Motion Command panel, set Null frames for position, rotation, and scale at frame 115. These Null frames ensure that the starting position of the walk is not affected by any animation you choose to add prior to or after this time.

9. Turn on the Animate button. Move the time to frame 130 and move UFO Base Pos -155 units along the Local y-axis.

I find it easiest to use the Offset: Local section of the Move Transform Type-In dialog when you know you want to move an object a specific number of units along specific axes. This dialog is accessed by right-clicking the Select and Move icon in the toolbar.

10. Advance to frame 145 and again move UFO Base Pos -155 units along the y-axis.

11. MAX 2: Open a new Track View and name it UFO. This is a new feature in MAX 2. You may name and save any Track View you want. These named Track Views are accessible via the new Track View pull-down menu.

12. In Track View, delete the first position key for UFO Base Pos, located at frame 0. This key is unnecessary, and by deleting it, you don't need to position ranges to select the keys you want for Out of Range Type curves.

13. Adjust the key info for the three new keys so that the In and Out interpolations are set to linear.

14. Select the Position Track of UFO Base Pos and set the Out parameter of the Out of Range Type curves to Relative Repeat. Relative Repeat repeats the motions of the keys, beginning each new iteration from where the last key left off.

15. Save your scene as **01max08.max**.

Now your UFO will walk as far as you'd like it to. For every 15 frames, it travels 155 units. It repeats this animation until the end of the active time segment because the Relative Repeat Out of Range type takes any animation and repeats it. Unlike the Loop Out of Range Type, however, Relative Repeat begins each new iteration of the selected keys from where the last key left off. Thus, because your selected animation consists of moving the UFO forward 155 units, Relative Repeat continues to move it forward 155 units every 30 frames, each time beginning its motion from where the last key left off. This Out of Range Type is most useful for Position keys, as it allows you to take the movement of an object and project it forward any amount of time (like a ball bouncing down stairs).

Converting Out of Range Type Curves to Keys

What if you want the UFO to stop and take a break? In the past, you would have had to use different copies of the model, one with Out of Range types turned on, and one without Out of Range types assigned for when the model is stopped. You would then have to splice between these models with either different camera angles or using Visibility tracks and precise positioning. MAX 2 has an answer to this problem. All you need to do is decide how long you want the UFO to walk and how many keyframes you'd like to interpolate that motion.

The animation cycle you've created takes one second or 30 frames right now, and there are no more than four keys in the range of any one track to which you've assigned Out of Range types. Once you determine this information, you merely need to access the Create Out of Range Keys tool in the Track utility. With the Create Out of Range Keys tool, you can create a specific number of keys for a specified number of frames for the selected Out of Range–animated tracks.

CREATING KEYS FROM OUT OF RANGE TYPE CURVES

1. Load 01max08.max from the accompanying CD or continue to work with the model you designed above.

2. Select the four Leg Base Y Rotate dummies and the four Upper Leg Z Rotate dummies. Open a new Track View.

3. Under Filters, select Show: Hierarchy, Objects, and Transforms (with all options under Transforms checked), and Show Only: Selected Objects and Animated Tracks.

4. Select all 24 of the Rotation tracks for all eight dummies that you've been animating (Leg Base Y Rotate and Upper Leg Z Rotate dummies), as well as the Position track for UFO Base Pos. These are all the tracks to which you've assigned Out-of-Range Type Curves.

5. Click the Track View Utilities button (with the hammer on it) and select Create Out of Range Keys. The Create Out of Range Keys dialog appears (see Figure 1.9).

FIGURE 1.9

*The Create Out of
Range Keys dialog.*

6. In Before, type 0. (This is unnecessary because this utility only creates keys for non-constant Out of Range types, but it's good to get in the habit of being specific.)

7. In After, type 150. This creates Out of Range keys for the next 150 frames. In Samples, enter 20. This generates four keys every 30 frames for the next 150 frames.

8. Select Apply.

9. With all the tracks still selected, go into the Parameter Curve Out of Range Types dialog and select the right arrow under Constant.

10. Play the animation. The UFO takes a step and then slides along. What went wrong? When you adjusted the Range bars for the Rotation keys for the legs, you told MAX that those keys were the only ones you wanted to work with. That was OK when you had Out of Range types active for those tracks, but now that there aren't, you must adjust the Range bars for each track.

11. Click the Position Ranges button at the top of the Track View.

12. Instead of manually adjusting the Range bars for all 24 tracks, you can have MAX automatically extend the ranges of the selected tracks to include all active keys by simply clicking the Recouple Ranges button. This button is only visible when in Position Ranges mode.

13. Switch to Edit Keys mode and delete the last key of the UFO Base Pos animation.

T IP

To make the animation look a bit smoother, set the Key Info dialog's In curve for all of the last Rotation key's interpolation to decelerate. This technique is generally useful when you want an object whose motion is stopping to gradually slow to a halt.

14. Save your scene as **01max09.max**.

The Walk cycle animation is now complete. Through careful use of the Out of Range Type curves and Track utilities, you have taken a simple 30 frame animation and turned it into a 180 frame animation. Now with Animation keys in place for the walk, you can animate the keys leading up to the Walk cycle. In the next section, you will perform complex rotations to give the impression of the UFO flying into the scene.

Complex Rotations Using Dummies

Up until now, you have limited your rotations to very simple rotations on one axis. Objects like a UFO, a frisbee, or a wheel have much more complicated "nested" rotations. The word "nested" refers to the concept of one object contained within another object, much like eggs are contained within a nest. Here it refers to rotations within rotations. These nested rotations occur when objects spin on one axis, while the axis they spin on—and thus the plane they spin in—also rotates on other axes. When a wheel turns, for example, the wheel rotates on its z-axis along its XY plane, and that XY plane then rotates when the wheel turns. Thus, the wheel maintains its plane of rotation.

Most terrestrial objects that roll or spin rotate in this manner. Things that don't are objects that float in space (like a satellite), objects that are thrown or dropped (like a baseball), or objects that do not maintain contact with another solid object during their rotation (like a planet). You simulate these nested rotations and conservation of Rotational planes by linking the object you want to rotate to a hierarchy of dummies that are centered within each other. Each dummy is assigned one axis. The axis that the object spins on is assigned to the dummy lowest in the hierarchy. Each dummy is then rotated about its assigned axis (see Figure 1.10).

FIGURE 1.10

Rotations along two axes directly applied to the object (top) and applied individually to linked dummies (bottom).

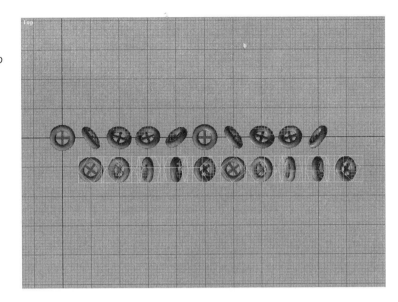

PREPARING FOR NESTED ROTATIONS

1. Load 01max09.max from the accompanying CD or continue to work with the model you designed above.

2. Click Time Configuration and make the animation start time begin at -200. MAX is very forgiving and doesn't care if the time is before zero. Accept the changes by clicking OK.

3. Unhide the dummies named UFO Base Rot X, UFO Base Rot Y, and UFO Base Rot Z. The dummies are made for you, but it is important that you pay careful attention to their layout so that you can use this same technique in the future. These dummies are placed within each other and within the dummy named UFO Base Pos.

4. Link the dummies, linking the UFO to Z, Z to Y, Y to X, and X to UFO Base Pos.

NOTE

It is important that Z be the hierarchically lowest dummy because it is the axis upon which the UFO spins. The other two dummies control the pan and tilt of the plane the UFO spins in as it lowers to the earth. The dummy that controls the UFO's spin must be at the lowest level. This is because it is the dummy that rotates over 360 degrees. This one dummy will constantly be spinning, whereas the other two dummies will not rotate more than about + or - 30 degrees along either of the other two axes.

If the Z or Spin dummy ends up as the parent of one of the other dummies, they inherit its rotation and add theirs to it, making the UFO gyrate out of control. What you want is for the spinning Z dummy to add and subtract the small rotations of the other two dummies to its own rotation, making it roll and tilt slightly. For this to work, it must be the child of the other two dummies. The Z dummy may only have the UFO as a child, controlling the total rotations of the UFO itself.

5. Go to frame 30. This is the frame where you want the UFO to stop spinning. Set a Null key for the Z dummy at frame 30. Leave the Rotation keys for the X and Y dummies at frame 0. These keys serve as your Null keys, allowing the UFO one second to hover and spin before the legs expand outward.

6. Return to frame -200, select UFO Base Rot Z and turn on the Animate button.

Now that your model is set up to receive nested rotations, you may proceed with setting keyframes. You must first determine the number of rotations per second you want from your UFO. When this is determined, you set keys for the rotations and adjust the Key In and Out curves. There are 230 frames, or about 7 2/3 seconds where the UFO should be spinning. The simple equation:

(seconds * 360)*(rotations per second)

tells us the number of degrees that the Z dummy should spin in the selected time period to yield the desired number of rotations per second. Thus, if you want the UFO to rotate about one time every two seconds, simple math tells us to rotate the dummy (7 2/3 * 360) * 1/2 degrees, or 1380 degrees on the z-axis. This equation simply multiplies the number of seconds in the desired animation (here 7 2/3) by the number of degrees in a circle (360), and multiplies the product by the number of rotations desired per second (one-half, or divide by two).

Once you have the UFO rotating, you can set a few position keys to bring it down from the heavens. The combination of the complex rotations with the simple positioning yields a very compelling animation of a UFO landing. In the following exercise, you will place a keyframe for the spinning effect of the UFO. Then you will animate the positional change of the UFO flying in from off-camera. Finally, you will add banking effects to the animation by rotating the other two rotational dummies.

SETTING ROTATION AND POSITION KEYS FOR THE UFO'S LANDING

1. Continue working with the previous example. Rotate the UFO Base Rot Z dummy 1380 degrees, as described in the previous paragraph.

TIP

I find it best to enter any Rotation values over 359 degrees manually under the Motion Command panel or in the Rotate Transform Type-In: Offset Local dialog, (accessed by right-clicking the Select and Rotate tool). This is because often when using the Rotate tool directly on an object, MAX 2 resets rotational values every 360 degrees. Thus, even though the Rotation degrees at the bottom of the screen may read 1380 degrees, when you check the Key Info for the key you just set, it often reads 360 or 0. By manually entering the value you desire, you force MAX 2 to rotate the object exactly the number of times you want, no questions asked (see Figure 1.11).

2. Move to frame -200. Rotate UFO Base Rot Y -30 degrees on the local y-axis. Move to frame -150. Rotate UFO Base Rot Y 10 degrees on the y-axis. Advance to frame -125. Rotate it 20 degrees on the y-axis. (When a dummy is named with a certain axis, from now on, that is the local axis upon which it should be rotated.)

3. Move to frame -200. Select UFO Base Rot X and set a key with no rotations. Move to frame -150 and rotate it 15 degrees. Then advance to frame -125 and rotate it -25 degrees. Finally, advance to frame -75 and rotate it 15 degrees.

4. Go to frame -75. Select UFO Base Pos and move it upward on the local Z axis 85 units.

5. At frame -125, move it to 100 on the X and 75 on the Z.

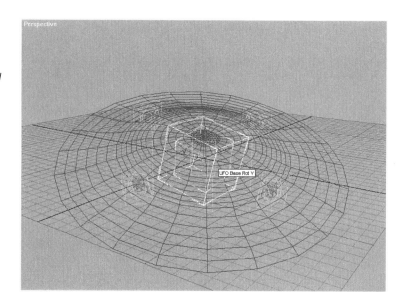

FIGURE 1.11
View of the UFO with the rotation dummies in place, rotated on all three axes.

6. At frame -150, move it 75 on the X, and 50 on the Z.

7. At frame -200, move it 375 on the X, and 375 on the Z.

8. Make the Key Info key Interpolation *Out* values for the second to last Rotation keys Linear, and make the Key Info key Interpolation *In* values for frame 0 decelerate when the UFO stops spinning. This helps make the animation come alive.

9. Make the Interpolation In and Out values for the Position key at 0 Linear, and the Interpolation Out value for the Position key at frame -75 Linear.

10. Save the scene as **01max10.max**.

Play around with the In and Out curves for the keys. The rotations and Position curves should all decelerate coming into frame 0.

You have now animated the UFO gracefully flying into the scene, hovering, scaling out legs, and walking along the ground. The animation makes use of the major animation Transformation tools: the Scale, Position, and Rotate tools. Next you will learn about sub-object animation, which is a new feature of 3D Studio MAX R2.

Sub-Object Animation

Sub-object animation is an extremely powerful new feature in 3D Studio MAX 2. It allows the user to animate the vertices and handles at the base of splines, and the edges, faces, and vertices at the base of Editable meshes. MAX 2 provides this feature with the mere click of the Animate button without having to set up complicated XForm or Linked XForm modifiers. The ease and power provided to the animator by this new feature is remarkable and is well worth becoming familiar with. Although all sub-object parameters of an object are now animatable, two of the most common animation situations you encounter will be the need to animate the vertices of a mesh or patch and animating the vertices of splines. We will explore both of these situations in the following exercises.

Animating Vertices, Faces, and Edges of an Editable Mesh

You now explore animatable vertices, faces, and edges of Editable meshes. In the next example, you will work only with vertices for simplicity, but the same principles apply to animating faces and edges.

Previously when animating individual vertices (or faces or edges) in an object, the only option was to select the desired vertices one by one and apply a separate XForm modifier to the object for each vertex you want to move independently of the other vertices. Animating the motion of many different vertices in different directions, would have required the use of separate models and morph targets; the only other option would be to use XForm and Edit Mesh after XForm and Edit Mesh in the stack of the object you were animating. Not only was this a selection nightmare, but it also took a lot of memory, and therefore, a lot of time.

MAX 2 provides an elegant solution: You can now independently animate the Mesh vertices (or faces or edges) of any base object. You merely need to collapse the object to an Editable mesh, turn on the Animate button, and begin setting keys. You explore this further in the following exercise by animating the vertices of a sphere to make it inflate like a balloon to the shape of a boot. This boot is then instanced within the Track View to replace the spheres currently at the base of the UFO legs. Then you explore sub-object spline animation to give your UFO a straw-like hose and to make that hose come alive.

ANIMATING THE VERTICES OF THE UFO'S FEET

1. Load 01max10.max from the accompanying CD or continue to work with the model you designed in the previous exercises.

2. Hide everything in your scene and move the Time slider to 50.

3. Create a sphere with a radius of about 8 and click Generate Mapping Coords. Name the sphere Foot.

4. In the Modify Command panel, click Edit Stack and select Convert To: Editable Mesh.

5. Turn on Animate and select Sub-Object: Vertex.

6. Sculpt a shoe-like shape from the sphere, pulling vertices wherever you like (see Figure 1.12).

FIGURE 1.12
The final sculpted sphere, shaped like a boot.

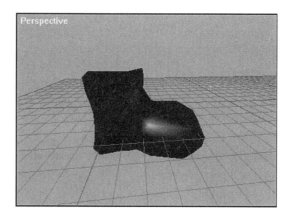

NOTE

You may, of course, change the sub-object type to Face or Edge at any time, and do your sculpting at the Face or Edge level. The power of this new feature in MAX 2 is that you can animate any of the sub-object types of any base object at any time with the mere click of a button.

7. When you are happy with the shape of your shoe, turn off Animate and preview your animation. Make any final adjustments, remembering to turn on and off Animate.

8. Open Track View and Slide the Range bar for Foot so that its beginning time is at 50 and its ending time is at 100.

9. Unhide the UFO and its children. Select Foot and Ship Foot 01 through 04. In Track View, right-click Objects and select Expand Objects.

10. In Track View, select the Object Level track for Foot and click the Copy Object button in the upper left.

11. Now select the Object Level tracks for Ship Foot 01 through 04 and click the Paste Object button.

12. Select Instance.

NOTE

It is very important that you create instances and not copies of the foot. Copying the object merely makes an exact duplicate of the selected geometry at that frame and discards any animation applied to the object. Thus, all the vertex animation is lost. By instancing the foot, the vertex animation is preserved for each instance of the foot. Likewise, any subsequent changes you make to one instance are applied to all, maintaining symmetry within the model.

You may need to manually adjust the positions of the feet so that they are all attached to the bottom of the legs in proper orientation. Simply switch to a Top viewport and change the time to frame 105. This is a good frame to adjust the feet in because all the legs are at roughly the same angle in relation to the body (see Figure 1.13).

FIGURE 1.13

A top view of the UFO with its new feet properly aligned at frame 105.

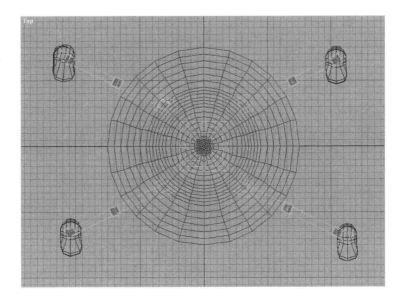

13. Save your scene as **01max11.max**.

Play your animation. You now have boots on your UFO that seemingly inflate from tiny spheres. This animation is easy to create, without bothering to place morphs and morph targets. It's also a very fast way to achieve simple Vertex Deformation effects.

Animating Spline Vertices for Loft Objects

Previously i n MAX, the only way to animate the vertices of a spline was to set complicated Linked XForms for every vertex you want to move. If you are only animating two vertices of a spline, this is not a big problem. However, when you must animate a spline with 10 or 20 vertices, it is a different story. Setting up even just 10 Linked XForms can take quite a bit of work, and for every Linked XForm in your stack, you need a separate Edit Spline modifier to tell MAX which vertex or vertices you want controlled by each individual Linked XForm (see Figure 1.14).

FIGURE 1.14

Spline animated at the Base Object level (top) versus a spline animated using a separate Linked XForm for each of its 10 vertices (bottom). (Note the number of modifiers in the Stack to achieve this one effect using Linked XForm.)

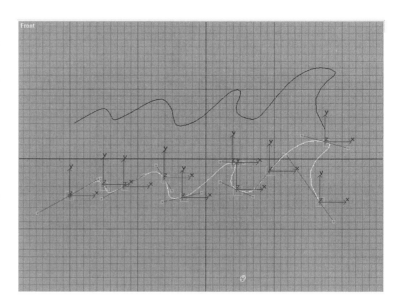

Also, the previous version of MAX had no way to animate the handles of the splines, which control the continuity of the segments between the vertices. This means that it was impossible to take a curved line like the one in Figure 1.14 and make it straight. With the new capability in MAX 2 to animate Spline vertices and handles in the base object, animating any spline into any shape is quite easy. In MAX 2, you have a new level of control over the subtle nuances in animation, while at the same time being able to animate splines more easily and intuitively.

To round off your animation, you animate a straw-like hose coming out of the UFO and entering into the glass. This straw is a Lofted object that has been linked, along with the spline that controls its shape, to the UFO's body.

Loft objects rely on two things for their creation: a path and 2D shapes that are lofted (similar to being extruded) along that path. By changing the position of the vertices, and the curves between them, you easily control the shape of the Lofted object. Objects like hoses, snakes, or really any Loft object are easily and smoothly deformed as one contiguous mesh. The following tutorial shows you how to easily breathe life into any Lofted object without needing an expensive plug-in skeletal deformation program like Physique or Bones Pro, and without having to set Morph targets.

ANIMATING THE LOFTED UFO HOSE

1. Continue from the previous exercise or load 01max11.max from the accompanying CD. Advance to frame 325.

2. Unhide the line named StrawSpline and the loft named Hose. StrawSpline is a spline that controls the shape of the lofted hose you will use for the UFO. Both have been linked to the UFO for you.

3. Unhide the objects named Drink and Cup, and turn on Animate.

4. Select StrawSpline (using the Select by Name feature), and in the Modify/Sub-Object menu, select Vertex.

5. Move all the vertices of the spline, except for the lowest one, up over the UFO. The highest vertex should be slightly higher than the edge of the cup with each additional vertex evenly spaced beneath it.

6. Advance to frame 350.

7. Move the highest vertex directly over the center of the cup, and place the other vertices to make a curve from the UFO up over the rim of the cup and over its center.

8. Advance to frame 400.

9. Move the highest vertex near the bottom of the inside of the glass.

10. Position the other two vertices so that the straw goes up and over the rim of the glass and down inside it (see Figure 1.15).

FIGURE 1.15

View of the UFO with its hose up, over, and into the glass by frame 400.

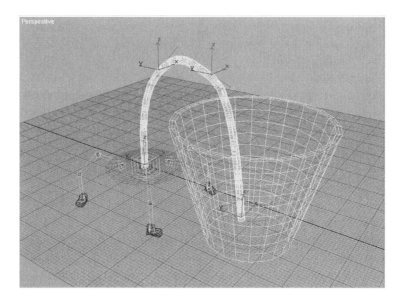

11. You may add more keyframes to further elaborate this animation.

12. Turn off the Animate button. In Track View, adjust all key In and Out values for the StrawSpline vertices to Linear. Grab the first keyframes for every vertex of StrawSpline (found under Object(Line)), and slide them up to frame 300.

13. Play back your animation and save the scene as **UFO6**.

The straw should now scale up out of the UFO, snaking over the rim of the glass and down to the glass's bottom. You may add extra keyframes if you want, having the hose "look" around before entering the glass, or perhaps have it re-emerge from the drink like a periscope. This example is merely to show you one example of how this tool may be used. Take some time to explore this technique and think of other applications for it, like animating a snake or any other lofted object.

At the moment, the legs of the UFO scale directly out of the UFO's body and the hose seems to push right through the metal shell of the UFO's dome. Little doors or panels have been created by exploding specific faces of the

UFO to separate objects, with Angle Threshold set to 0. These panels are then linked to the UFO and each object's pivot is placed where the door hinges would be. Keyframes should be set 30 frames before the doors are wide open, and then keyframes are set with the doors wide open on the frame when the legs or hose begins scaling outward.

Now that you've finished the UFO tutorial, you can choose to go back through your final project and refine the animation you have produced. There always seems to be room for more detailed animation on almost any project, and only your deadlines and patience determine when the project is truly finished.

When you feel content with your project, be sure to save it, and then render out a final AVI, like the one included on the CD. You might choose to add animated lights and cameras to add to the drama of the scene. File 01max12.max on the accompanying CD is a copy of the UFO scene, with the UFO panels opening for the legs and hose, and the water disappearing.

Combining Animated Spline Vertices and Linked XForm Animation

Despite the power of being able to animate at the Sub-Object level in MAX 2, Linked XForms still serve a purpose. Take, for example, a case where you need to have separate objects move along with the loft (such as a separate hose nozzle or Particle controller moving with the end of a lofted hose). You will explore this special case by creating an animated fire hose. You can animate the central vertices of the fire hose using the Vertex and Handle animation technique reviewed above.

However, your fire hose needs a nozzle and a Particle gizmo attached to the vertex at the end of the hose; and you cannot link an object directly to the spline's vertex. If you link an object to the spline itself, it only moves as the entire spline is moved. You need the nozzle and the Gizmo to exactly track just one specific vertex at the end of the hose. The only way to achieve this is by assigning a Linked XForm modifier to the last vertex of the spline, linking this vertex to a dummy centered around this vertex, and then linking the nozzle and the gizmo to this same dummy. Then when you move the dummy, the transforms applied to the dummy are inherited by both the nozzle and gizmo, and by the end vertex of the spline.

For simplicity, the models in the next exercise have been created for you. First you will animate the hose, being careful not to animate the vertices at either end of the hose. The nozzle end of the hose will be animated with a Linked XForm modifier, and the hydrant end of the hose will remain exactly where it is, keeping the hose connected with the fire hydrant at all times.

NOTE

When applying a Linked XForm to a spline that you will also animate at the Sub-Object level, you always want to directly animate the central vertices of the spline first, because they may only be animated at the Base level of the line. If you apply the Linked XForm and animate the end vertex of the line *before* animating the other vertices, you have to go back down to the Line level of the stack to animate the other vertices anyway, and will therefore not be able to see the results of your Linked XForm animation.

This may not seem like a problem, but the Linked XForm actually gets in the way of animating the other vertices unless you disable the modifier completely. Because there is no benefit to animating the end of the hose first, and it may potentially confuse the animation process, you begin by simply animating the other vertices of the hose, estimating approximately where you want the nozzle to be. You then learn how to set up the Linked XForm and animate the end of the hose, its nozzle, and its Particle gizmo. You can view a completed animation off the CD, titled 01avi01.avi.

COMBINING SUB-OBJECT SPLINE ANIMATION WITH LINKED XFORM ANIMATION

1. Open 01max13.max from the accompanying CD-ROM.

2. Select Line01. This is the spline that controls the deformation of the lofted hose.

3. Select Sub-Object: Vertex and turn on the Animate button.

4. At frames 30, 60, 90, and 120, place keys for all the vertices except the vertices at either end of the hose. Make the hose snake around to your liking, adjusting the Vertex handles to fine-tune the tension among the vertices.

5. With Sub-Object: Vertex still turned on, select the last vertex on the nozzle end of the hose.

6. Under Modifiers, click more and scroll down until you find Linked XForm. Then select Linked XForm.

7. Under Parameters, click Pick Control Object. The button will highlight.

8. Press H or click the Select by Name button at the top of the toolbar, and select the dummy named Nozzle XForm Dummy.

9. Select Nozzle XForm Dummy, and with Animate still turned on, place the keyframes for it at frames 30, 60, 90, and 120. Try to place the dummy in the same general area as the second to last vertex, so there is not an exaggerated deformation at the end of the hose. Be sure to play with rotating the dummy as well as moving it.

10. Save your scene as **01max14.max**.

FIGURE 1.16

View of the animated hose with Nozzle and SuperSprayer attached via Linked XForm.

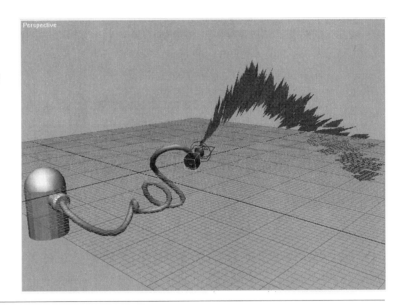

Using an Animated Spline as a Path

Now that you can animate splines so easily, not only do you have simple control over Loft objects, but you can use the same spline as a path for other tools, like the Displace space warp. Using the Displace space warp, you can assign Displace gizmos to a path, forcing the gizmo to travel along the path and deform anything along its way. This is ideal for creating traveling lumps within a Lofted object, like a snake digesting its meal, or cartoony bulges of water traveling through a hose. In the following exercise, you add bulges to the animated hose you just created.

ASSIGNING A DISPLACE SPACE WARP TO AN ANIMATED PATH

1. Load the hose project from the previous tutorial. You can load the same version of this project from the CD. The file is titled 01max14.max.

2. Select Displace01. This is a Displace space warp gizmo that has been created for you. Feel free to explore the different settings and their effects on the final project.

3. With the Displace gizmo selected, go to Motion: Parameters: Assign Controller.

4. Select Position and click the Assign Controller icon.

5. Select Path.

6. Under PRS Parameters, select Position and then click the button labeled Pick Path.

7. Using the Select by Name dialog, select Line01.

8. Select the Displace Gizmo, lock the selection by pressing the Spacebar, and holding Shift, drag to copy the gizmo.

9. Select Instance and accept the name. Under Path Parameters: Path Options: % Along Path, enter **10**. This places the gizmo 10% of the way down the path.

10. Repeat the above, creating separate instanced gizmos for 20 to 100% of the path.

11. Select Loft01. Click the Bind to Space Warp button at the top of the toolbar.

12. Using the Select by Name dialog, select Displace 01. (You may only bind an object to one space warp at a time.)

13. With Bind to Space Warp still highlighted, select each additional Displace space warp, one by one until Loft01 has been assigned to every space warp (see Figure 1.17).

FIGURE 1.17

View of the animated hose with Displace space warp applied to the spline as a path.

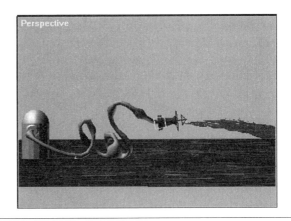

Save your animation and play it back. A completed version of this project, named 01max15.max, can be found on the CD. The gizmos now travel along the path, within the hose, while the hose itself animates. You can easily apply this animation to the UFO animation if you wish to show the fluids pumping up the hose and down into the UFO.

Transforms Along Surfaces

All animation will not be like our UFO, flying through space and walking on a flat plane. Sometimes you will find that you need to animate one object in respect to the orientation of another object. The technique of performing transforms along surfaces takes advantage of the capability of MAX 2 to enable you to transform an object along the surface or along a selected axis of another object.

There are several ways to move an object along a surface (as you may occasionally want to do). The "simplest way" really depends on the animation situation. Sometimes it is easiest to "eyeball it," trusting your ability to place things where they need to go. Sometimes you need more precision for your animation. When this is the case, you will often find that using the Pick Reference Coordinate tool in conjunction with Helper objects is especially useful for this purpose, because Helper objects are easily created and do not render.

Moving objects along a Grid or other Helper object that has been aligned to a surface gives you the ability to easily animate one object sliding along the surface of another object, like a drop of rain morphing down a windshield. The local axis of a Tape Helper object can also be picked as the path of motion for any object.

NEW TO R2

If the object whose surface you need to move along is a Parametric object, such as a torus, cylinder, or sphere, you can use the new Surface controller. The Surface controller lets you pick any Parametric object as a Target surface along which you can move any other object.

Using Grid Objects as Transform Paths

To use a Grid object as a Transform path, you first create a Grid Helper object. Then you use the Align tool to place the Grid object coincident to the surface you wish to move along. Then select your object. After the grid is in place, you can use the Pick Reference Coordinate command to pick the grid as the surface on which you want your object to move. In practice, you would constrain the axis of movement to the axis on which you want to move.

Using Tape Objects as Transform Paths

Tape measures are excellent tools for animating projectiles. You simply use the tape measure to draw a line from the source position to the destination position. Tape Measure objects are good not only because they are easy to work with, but because, being Helper objects, they do not render.

You select the tape measure as the Transform path in much the same way as you selected the Grid object as a Transform path. Once you create the Transformation path using the Tape object, you select the object you wish to transform along that path, select Pick from the Coordinate Reference system, and select the Tape Measure object as the object along whose axis you move your selected object. For the tape measure, you want to move your object along the tape's local Z axis. For example, if you wish to make photon torpedoes shoot from the UFO, you could use a Tape object to define the line of fire and transform the torpedoes along the tape.

Animating Multiple Object Instances

The Shift key, when combined with applying any transform to a selected object, allows you to create instanced clones of that object that maintain its animated properties. Likewise you can create instances of objects or groups of objects using the Mirror tool or the Create Array tool. These instances can be placed anywhere, and their animation can easily be offset using the techniques you learned for adjusting Track ranges. This is extremely useful when creating groups of animated objects or just when needing several identical clones of animated objects, as with the UFO Foot.

You can experiment with these different techniques for creating animated instances on your own. One possible application would be to group all the UFO parts, advance to frame 300 when it is in front of the cup, move the group's pivot to the center of the cup (when viewed from above), and create an array of six UFOs around the cup (see Figure 1.18). The possibilities are truly endless!

FIGURE 1.18

An array of instanced UFOs descending upon the soda.

In Practice: Advanced Transformation Animation

- **Non-Linear Animation.** It is helpful to create keyframes or even whole segments of animation in a non-linear order.

- **Linked Transforms.** When you need complicated animation without setting up Inverse Kinematics or extremely precise control over multiple axes of motion, Linked transforms are exceptionally powerful.

- **Instanced Animation.** You can save much time and trouble by "recycling" your animation using cloned instances.

- **Keyframe In and Out Curves.** Learning to effectively adjust the In and Out tension between keyframes quickly and efficiently allows you to make any animation more believable.

- **Out of Range Type Curves and Create Out of Range Keys.** These two tools, when combined, let you take any existing animation and quickly create many different, lengthy, and/or complicated series of animations.

- **Sub-Object Mesh Animation.** By animating the faces, edges, and vertices directly in the Base object, you can quickly create intricate, morph-like effects without ever applying an XForm modifier.

- **Animating Splines.** By taking advantage of MAX 2's capability to animate the vertices and handles of any line at its Base Object level, you can very quickly create extremely intricate Loft and Deformation animations.

Chapter 2

ANIMATING WITH CONTROLLERS

3D Studio MAX provides animators with an extensive toolbox for applying animation to their scenes. The data for every animation within a scene is handled by a group of plug-ins called controllers. These controllers store and interpolate all animation data values within 3D Studio MAX.

For every animated track, MAX assigns a default animation controller, which handles the keyframe information, function curves, and procedural animation data. These controllers also handle interpolating between animation key values, calculating the frames between keys based on user definable parameters. Most animation is handled by the Bézier controller, which is the default for position and scale tracks. The other controllers provided with MAX yield alternative animation solutions and allow for special animation techniques.

This chapter explores the following topics:

- Path controllers

- Euler Rotation controller

- List, Noise, and Bézier controllers

- Ease curves

- Expression controller

- Controlling visibility

- Animatable Link controller

- Look At controller

- Surface controller

- Instancing controllers

To help illustrate the various applications of animation controllers in 3D Studio MAX, you will adopt the project of animating a water-ski boat picking up and towing a skier. You will build on a basic boat animation, adding waves, a jump, and a parametrically animated propeller. Then you'll add a tow rope and a skier who will watch the boat and, eventually, be picked up by the boat. This project will introduce various different animation controllers and special animation techniques made possible by the creative use of these controllers.

Before you begin, open 02avi01.avi on the accompanying CD-ROM to watch the final animation and get a feel for what you will accomplish in this chapter.

Working with Path Controllers

Paths are extremely powerful tools for creating complicated but smooth animation. Path controllers replace the position controller and are especially useful for applications like animating boats, flying objects, and rolling objects. A path controller accesses its positional information for an object from a user defined spline. The spline serves as the guideline for the object's trajectory, and may be adjusted and tweaked interactively at any time in the animation process.

Assigning a Path Controller

The Path controller is assigned either from within the Track View dialog's Assign Controller dialog or from the Parameters: Assign Controller section of the Motion control panel. The Path controller is assigned to the object that you wish to move along the path.

In the following exercise, you will assign the boat to the path (the path has been provided for you). Then, in the following exercise, you will explore the Follow, Bank, and Constant Velocity options. The Follow feature forces the animated object to remain parallel with the trajectory at all times. With this option unchecked, the animated object maintains its original orientation while it moves through the path. The Bank feature allows the object to bank (roll) as it negotiates the curves of the path. The Constant Velocity option forces the animated object to travel along the path at the same velocity. Finally, you will adjust the path key in and out curves to smooth the animation.

The boat will be assigned to a generic path, which you will later adjust to your liking.

ASSIGNING THE BOAT TO A PATH

1. Load 02max01.max from the accompanying CD-ROM. This file contains a boat on water, a path, and some objects that have been prepared for your scene.

2. Select Boat Body and open the Motion panel.

3. Under Assign Controller, click Transform, and under the Transform controller hierarchy, highlight Position.

4. Click on Assign Controller. Select Path and click OK.

5. Under Path Parameters in the Motion panel, click Pick Path.

6. Select the boat path. The boat is now assigned to the path, and placed at the beginning of the path.

What if, however, you want the boat to begin at the other end of the path. The boat travels along the path in the order that the path spline vertices were created. You can remedy this situation in one of two ways: either reverse the key values of the Percent track for the path controller, or select the last vertex of the path, and under an Edit Spline modifier, click Make First. The latter only works on open spline shapes.

7. Select the Boat Path spline. In the Modify control panel, turn on Sub-Object, and select Vertex.

8. Select the vertex at the other end of the path, and click Make First.

The boat is transported to the start of the spline path. If you press the play button, you will see the boat travel along the path. This is the quick fix for interactively changing the direction an object moves along a path.

However, there is still work to be done. The boat is facing backwards at the beginning of the path and drives in reverse. Also, the boat doesn't follow the contours of the path in a very boat-like manner, maintaining its original backward orientation as its position changes along the path. This is because you need to assign the Follow function to the boat to make it remain parallel to its trajectory. Likewise, you want the boat to gently roll along the path as it goes, and thus you need to apply the Bank function.

Bank and Follow

The Follow feature of the Path controller forces the boat's orientation to remain aligned to the trajectory as it follows its contour. Thus, as the path curves, the boat is rotated to remain parallel to the path. This powerful feature makes it very easy to create extremely complicated paths that an object like a boat or a plane will follow in a realistic manner.

The Bank feature of the Path controller makes the object that is following the path rotate (roll) along the axis of the path (along its trajectory) as the object goes through curves. The sharper the curve, the greater the angle of rotation. This is very useful in mimicking the motion of objects like airplanes, boats, and motorcycles, which all either "lean" or "roll" in toward the center of their turns.

In the following exercise, you will adjust the boat's orientation, tell it to follow the path, and adjust its banking values.

CHANGING THE BOAT'S DIRECTION

1. Continue from the previous exercise. Check Follow. The boat lines up with the path but is backward.

2. With Boat Body still selected, under Path Parameters: Axis check the Flip option. This flips the selected axis, making the boat face the proper direction relative to its trajectory.

3. With Boat Body still selected, check Bank.

4. Increase the Bank Amount value to 1.0. This increases the angle that the boat will bank as it goes around the curves (see Figure 2.1).

FIGURE 2.1

The top view shows the boat going through a turn without banking applied. The bottom view shows the boat going through the same turn with banking applied.

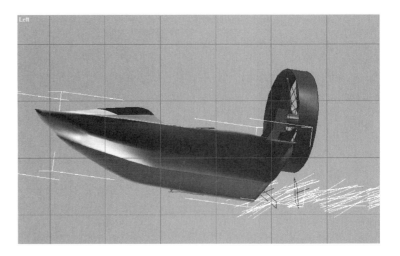

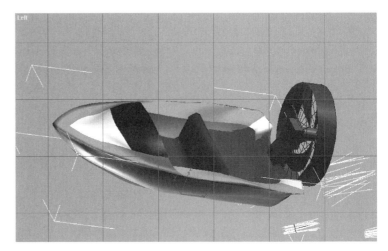

5. Decrease the Smoothness value to .4. This makes the interpolation between maximum and minimum Bank amounts more abrupt.

6. Check next to Constant Velocity (covered in detail in the following section).

7. Save your file as **boat01.MAX**.

You can play with the Bank Amount and Smoothness values to your liking. By increasing the Bank Amount value, the turns appear sharper and the boat seems to dig deeper into the turns, as if it were traveling faster. By lowering the value, you get the illusion of a slower, less aggressive boat. Furthermore, you may roll an object outward as it moves through the curves by making the bank value negative. Smoothness controls the rate of change in roll angle as the object moves through the turn. Decreasing the Smoothness value makes the banking increasingly jerky, whereas increasing it gives the illusion of a smoother and more stable ride.

Constant Velocity and Key Tangents

By placing a check next to Constant Velocity, you tell 3D Studio MAX that you want the object (Boat Body, in this case) to travel at a constant velocity along the path.

Perhaps you are thinking that boats don't travel at constant velocities. You would be correct. There's an easier way to very directly affect your boat's speed and acceleration: keyframe In and Out curves.

By strategically setting and adjusting the Bézier tangent types of specific keyframes, you can have the boat accelerate, decelerate, or travel at a constant speed. 3D Studio MAX has an intuitive tool specifically designed to facilitate this process: the Key Info dialog. Using the Key Info dialog, you can access the tangent curve data for any key in any track and adjust each key's In and Out curves.

The default tangent type is set to Smooth, which creates smooth interpolation through the key. You have the added choice of Linear, which creates linear interpolation at the key like a Linear controller. This tangent affects the curve only near the key. Full linear interpolation is achieved by making the adjoining In and Out tangents of two consecutive keys both Linear. The Step tangent provides binary interpolation from one key to the next. Slow causes deceleration around the key. Fast causes acceleration around the key. Custom allows the user to adjust the tangent handles at the key in Function Curves mode.

In the following exercise, you will adjust the tangent curves for the keys on your boat's path to make the boat accelerate up to speed and decelerate to a stop at the end.

ADJUSTING KEY TANGENT TYPES

1. Continue working with the previous scene. Select Boat Body.

2. Open Track View and expand the Boat Body track, Transform, and Position.

3. On the Percent Track, right-click the first keyframe at frame 0.

4. Select Slow for the Out Tangent for this key. This tells 3D Studio MAX to gradually accelerate Boat Body from a stopped velocity up to its full speed.

5. Click the right arrow at the top of the dialog to advance to the next key. This is the last key on the path, at 100%. Select Slow for the In tangent for this key (see Figure 2.2). This tells 3D Studio MAX to gradually decelerate Boat Body from full speed down to a stop.

FIGURE 2.2

View of the Track View, with Key Info Dialog and Slow Out tangent selected.

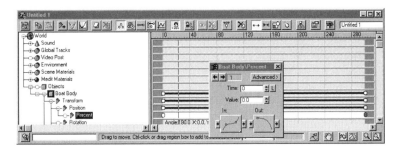

6. Save your file as **boat01_1.MAX**.

The boat now accelerates at the beginning of the animation, and decelerates to a stop at the end of the animation. These nuances of detail combine to give the animation a professional appearance in a very short amount of time.

Assigning Path Controllers to Cameras, Targets, and Lights

Paths are also very useful for animating complicated camera fly throughs, moving or flying lights, or simply matching camera targets to the paths of other objects. Take, for instance, your boat animation. You will soon be adding secondary animation to the boat to make it bounce up and down as if it were striking waves, and to make it jump off a ramp. If you set a camera to simply look at the boat itself, using a Look At controller, the camera would jitter up and down with every oscillation of the boat. Unless you want to keep the boat in the center of the frame and have the horizon leaping up and down, this is an unacceptable solution.

You could also set individual keyframes for the camera's target, but this is very tedious and time consuming and not exceptionally accurate. Instead of tracking the boat by hand-animating the camera target to approximately match the boat's position, you can simply assign the Camera Target to the same path that the boat is assigned to (see Figure 2.3).

FIGURE 2.3

View of Camera01 with its target assigned to the same path as Boat Body.

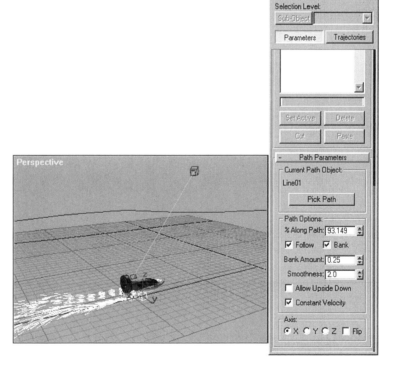

If you wanted the camera to follow behind or look back from the front of the boat throughout the entire course, you could simply assign the camera itself to the boat's path. Of course, in either of these situations, it may be necessary to match the Path Percentage key tangent In and Out values for the camera and its target to those of Boat Body, so that they accelerate and decelerate at the same rate as the boat. Cameras, Lights, and Targets are treated the same as geometry by the Path controller. Therefore, the same options are available for them, and the same techniques apply to them as apply to geometry animated with the Path controller.

Assigning Secondary Animation Effects

Now that you have a nice basic path created for your boat, you can begin to add secondary animation effects to the boat. The Path controller tells the boat along what trajectory to move, and how to move along that trajectory. However, if you want to add a bit of noise to the boat's path, to simulate the chaotic effects of striking waves, you cannot simply turn on the animate button and start moving the boat with your transform tools.

The boat is very strictly limited to the path you have created by the Path controller. You could theoretically make the path extremely complicated, with many vertices, and create the waves in the path itself by hand. This, however, would be an extremely time-consuming and arduous task, and if the waves are even a little bit too big or too small, every vertex would have to be hand adjusted. Fortunately, there is an easier way to add waves to the boat: The List controller. Using the List controller, you can combine other forms of animation with your base path animation.

Using the List Controller and the Noise Controller

The List controller is a compound controller that combines several controllers into one effect. It works much like the Modifier Stack, in that it allows you to layer controller upon controller, and interactively select which controller is the active controller for editing. This extremely powerful controller also allows you to rearrange the order of the controllers within the list. Using the List controller, you can add easily adjusted parametric waves to your boat's animation with very little effort at all. The following exercise uses the List controller to add a Noise controller to your boat body's preexisting controllers.

ANIMATING SECONDARY POSITIONAL NOISE WITH THE LIST CONTROLLER

1. Continue working from the previous exercise. Select Boat Body. Open the Track View.

2. Expand the Boat Body track, and expand Transform and Position. Select the Position Track.

3. Click the Assign Controller button on the Track View toolbar.

4. Select Position List controller and click OK.

5. Expand the Position Track. The Path controller still exists but has been placed under the List controller. There is now a new track beneath the Path controller called Available.

6. Select Available track.

7. Click the Assign Controller button, and select Noise Position.

8. Right-click the Range bar for the Noise Position track. This is the same as selecting Properties and opens up the Noise Controller dialog (see Figure 2.4).

FIGURE 2.4

View of the Noise controller dialog.

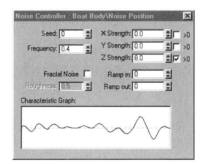

9. Select any value for Seed. This generates a random starting point from the number you set. Under Frequency, enter **.2**. This determines the number of oscillations per time period.

10. Deselect Fractal Noise. This smoothes out the curve that will be used for the boat's upward and downward motions.

11. Check the effects of the Noise controller by playing the boat animation. Unfortunately, the boat jumps every which way, and you only want it to move up and down on its z-axis slightly.

12. Under X Strength and Y Strength, enter **0**. This removes the effect of the Noise controller from all axes except for the z-axis. However, the jumps are still too big for such calm waters, so change the Z Strength value to 8.

13. Place a check next to the Greater than Zero box for Z strength. This constrains the motion along the z-axis to only positive values, keeping the boat from dipping too far below the water's surface.

14. Save your file as **boat01_2.MAX**. Play the animation.

As the boat moves along the path, it bounces slightly, as if it were striking small waves. Secondary animation like this adds much realism to your work. It is the small inconsistencies and slight chaos that can turn a good animation into a truly believable one. Only in an absolute vacuum do objects move perfectly and evenly, without friction or chaos.

You can add even more realism to this animation by adding rotations to the boat as it moves up and down, simulating the effect that striking the waves has on the boat's hull. Every time the boat hits a wave, it forces the front end of the boat up, and as the boat lowers back down into the water, the angle of the hull's rotation lessens. You can easily create this complicated effect by using the same Noise controller you used for the boat's position, only this time applying it to the boat's y-axis rotation. By using the same seed and frequency settings, you can make the boat rotate in unison with its striking the "waves."

ANIMATING SECONDARY ROTATIONAL NOISE WITH THE LIST CONTROLLER

1. Load 02max02.max from the accompanying CD-ROM, or continue working with the file from the previous exercise.

2. With Boat Body selected, open the Track View, expand Objects, Boat Body, Transforms, and Rotation.

3. Select the Rotation Track. Click the Assign Controller button.

4. Select Rotation List and click OK.

5. Expand the Rotation track. Select Available under TCB Rotation, and click the Assign Controller button.

6. Select Noise Rotation, and click OK.

7. Right-click the newly created Noise Rotation track, and select Properties. This opens the Noise Rotation Controller dialog.

NOTE

It is very important that you enter the same Seed value for the Noise Rotation controller as you entered for the Noise Position controller. MAX uses the Seed number to generate the characteristic wave that will animate the position or rotation changes. For the rotation of the boat to exactly match the up and down positioning of the boat, which is necessary for a real-istic wave effect, the wave, and therefore the Seed, must be the same.

8. Enter the Seed value from Noise Position. Under Frequency, enter **.2**. This determines the number of rotations per time period.

9. Deselect Fractal Noise. This smooths out the curve, which will be used for the boat's tilt rotations.

10. Check the effects of the Noise controller by playing the boat animation. The boat rotates every which way, whereas you only want it to tilt, or rotate on its y-axis slightly.

11. Under X Strength and Z Strength, enter 0. This removes the effect of the Noise Rotation controller from all axes except for the y-axis. The values under Strength represent the maximum angle degrees that the Noise Rotation controller will rotate the given object at the highest peaks and lowest troughs of the wave. Enter a Y Strength of 15, for 15 degrees.

12. Place a check next to the greater than zero box for Y Strength. This con-strains the Y rotations to only positive values, from 0 degrees to 15 degrees. If you left this unchecked, the boat would nose-dive into the water unnaturally.

13. Save your file as **boat02.MAX**. Play the animation.

The boat now rotates, tilting its bow up and down as it strikes the waves.

Applying Multiplier Curves

Next, you will take your boat animation and make the boat go off a jump. The first thing you need to do is remove the effects of the Noise controllers on the position and rotation tracks for the duration of the jump. The jump will go from frame 130 to frame 155. There are various different ways of disabling the effects of the controllers, some which you have explored previously (adjusting Key Info values and tangent curves). However, you can also use a Multiplier curve to accomplish this.

In 3D Studio MAX 2, you may assign an Multiplier curve to many different animated tracks while in the Edit Function Curves mode. The value of a Multiplier curve is a scale factor applied to the value of its superior function curve. The Multiplier curve is a curve that scales the value of the selected function curve. So, by assigning a Multiplier curve to the Noise Position and Rotation controller tracks, you can reduce the value of the Noise controllers to zero, so that their values remain constant for the duration of the pertinent frames.

You have already assigned Noise controllers to both the position and rotation tracks of Boat Body. However, you don't want the noise controller to affect Boat Body while it's sliding up the jump ramp, or while it's in mid-air. So in the following exercise, you'll disable the Noise controller for those keys.

USING EASE CURVES TO DISABLE THE NOISE CONTROLLER

1. Load file 02max03.max from the accompanying CD-ROM.

2. Select Boat Body, and open Track View.

3. Expand Boat Body Transforms, showing the List Position and List Rotation sub-tracks.

4. Click the Function Curves button to enter edit function curves mode.

5. Select and expand Noise Position, and click Apply Multiplier Curve.

6. Click the Multiplier Curve track to view the Multiplier Curve assigned to Noise Position.

7. Select the Multiplier curve itself. The keys at the beginning and end of the "curve" appear. (The curve appears as a horizontal line at a constant value of 1 right now.)

8. Click the Add Keys button. Add a key at frame 130, a key at 150, and a key at 155.

9. Right-click the key at frame 130. In the Key Info dialog, change the key value to 0, which multiplies 0 times the parameters for the Noise Position controller when it is at frame 130, thus eliminating all effects.

10. Change the In and Out Tangent types to Step for the key at frame 130.

11. Set the key value for the key at frame 150 to 0. Set the In Tangent type to Step, and leave the Out Tangent type set to Smooth. Change the Out Tangent type for frame 155, and the In Tangent type for the last frame to Linear. Your Ease curve should now look like Figure 2.5.

FIGURE 2.5

View of the Multiplier curve used to disable the Position Noise controller.

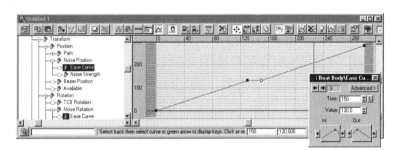

12. With the Multiplier Curve track still selected, click the Copy Controller button.

13. Select the Noise Rotation track and expand it. Click the Apply Multiplier Curve button.

14. Select the Multiplier Curve track under Noise Rotation, and click the Paste Controller button. Select Instance and click OK.

Using the List Controller with the Bézier Position Controller

List controller allows you to utilize any combination of controllers you desire. This expands your power to harness the very fast and efficient capability of 3D Studio MAX to create procedural animation, while maintaining the capability to hand tweak the resulting animation to your liking. This means it is easy to make your boat go off the jump. Now that you've eliminated the effects of the Noise controller for the pertinent frames, you can add the jump itself. (Because the boat is fan driven, as opposed to propeller driven, this is actually not so far-fetched.)

You can simply add a Bézier Position controller to the Position List, make this the active controller, turn on animate, and start adding keys. With a few refinements, you will make your animation rather sophisticated, without necessitating a complicated animation process.

ADDING A BÉZIER CONTROLLER TO THE POSITION LIST

1. You can continue working with the previous scene, or load the equivalent scene, named 02max04.max, from the accompanying CD-ROM.

2. Unhide the object named Ramp (this is the jump). Select Boat Body and, in Track View, expand the Transform, Position track. Select Available.

3. Click the Assign Controller button on the Track View toolbar.

4. Select Bézier Position, and click OK.

5. In Edit Keys mode, right-click the Position track to display Properties. The List controller dialog appears (see Figure 2.6). Select Bézier Position, and click Set Active. By setting this as the active controller, any position changes you make will be stored by the Bézier Position controller and added to the sum Position animation.

6. Select the Rotation track for Boat Body, and set the TCB Rotation controller as the active controller. Now you are also free to adjust the rotational value of Boat Body independent of the Noise Rotation controller. Any rotations you perform will now be stored by the TCB Rotation controller, and added to the sum Rotation animation.

FIGURE 2.6

*View of the List
Controller dialogs for
Position and Rotation.*

7. Move to frame 130, and turn on the Animate button. Position the Front viewport to show the boat and the ramp.

8. Adjust the position and orientation of Boat Body so that it is just beginning its ascent up the ramp (see Figure 2.7).

FIGURE 2.7

*View of the boat at
the base of the ramp.*

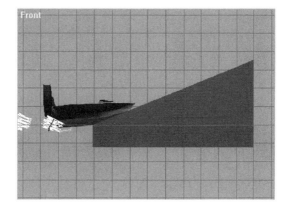

9. Advance to frame 133, and position the boat halfway up the ramp.

10. Advance to frame 138, and position the boat at the top of the ramp, ready to jump off.

11. Advance to frame 150, and position the boat just above the water.

12. Advance to frame 155, position the boat in the water, and rotate it to a level orientation, so that it is parallel to the water.

13. Adjust the key tangents for the Bézier position keys in the following manner:

Frame 0: Linear In, Linear Out;
Frame 130: Linear In, Linear Out;
Frame 133: Linear In, Smooth Out;

Frame 138: Smooth In, Smooth Out;
Frame 150: Smooth In, Smooth Out;
Frame 155: Smooth In, Linear Out.

14. Save the file as **boat03.MAX**.

You may, of course, continue to tweak the animation to your liking. You could easily fill this whole book with nothing but instructions for making small adjustments to the animation so that it is perfect. Instead, these exercises just show you the tools you need to make the refinements you want to make and let you explore.

Using the Expression Controller

The Expression controller is an extremely powerful tool for generating complex parametric animations using mathematical functions that return single values. For every frame of an animation, the Expression controller is evaluated by 3D Studio MAX. The Expression takes user-designated input values from your scene as variables, and outputs values from those equations that control the parameter the expression is assigned to.

The input variables may come from any of the different time measurements (seconds, frames, ticks, normalized time), or almost any animated parameter in your scene. The output of any expression is a single value that animates the parameter the Expression controller was assigned to. You will experiment with one example of a relatively simple expression in this chapter.

Euler Rotations and the Expression Controller

Your boat is powered by a large fan, but as of yet, that fan doesn't turn. This is obviously a problem. The use of an Expression controller is one way to easily solve this problem. You will create an expression that takes the current frame number as its variable input, and outputs a rotation value for the Z axis of the fan's main cylinder, Cylinder01.

This is a prime example of an advantage of using the Euler XYZ controller versus the TCB controller. You want to control the rotation angle of one axis of the fan's main cylinder using the Expression controller. This would be impossible using the TCB controller, which averages all three rotation values into one final orientation for each frame.

The Euler XYZ controller separates each rotation axis into a discrete track and provides the option of assigning a Float Expression to each rotation track. This option is unavailable for TCB rotations. Also, with the Euler XYZ controller, you can view and adjust rotation values in the Function Curves mode of Track View (see Figure 2.8).

FIGURE 2.8

View of Euler XYZ controller curves in the Function Curves mode of Track View.

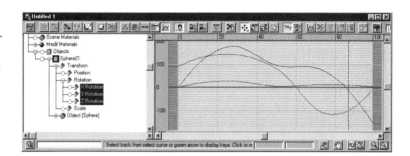

TIP

I highly recommended that, for most situations, you use the Euler XYZ controller instead of the default TCB controller. The Euler controller is much more powerful and flexible, and affords the animator more specific control over the individual axes of rotation. You can set Euler as the default controller by choosing Make Default in the Assign Controller dialog.

NOTE

Occasionally, the Euler XYZ controller has its own set of problems. Notably the most common among these is a phenomena known as gimbal lock. In any system of Euler angles, orientations exist for which two Euler angles are undefined. When a mechanism is rotated into such a singularity, it locks up along the two axes. When this occurs, either the offending angle must be avoided, or a different rotation controller, like TCB, must be used. However, this phenomenon is relatively rare.

The cylinder that controls the spinning of the fan has already been assigned and positioned using a Euler XYZ controller. You will now assign a second Euler XYZ controller using the List controller. This is necessary because the cylinder has been positioned using the Euler XYZ controller, and by assigning an Expression controller to one of the axes, the resulting animation will not follow the axis you intend. After assigning the second Euler XYZ controller, you will assign an Expression controller to the Z axis of the fan's main cylinder and make it rotate parametrically.

MAKING THE FAN ROTATE

1. Continue working with the previous example. Select Cylinder01. Open Track View, and expand and select Rotation track of Cylinder01.

2. Click the Assign Controller button, and select Rotation List. Click OK.

3. Under Rotation, select Available, and click the Assign Controller button. Assign the Euler XYZ controller. Click OK.

4. Select and expand the new Euler XYZ controller. Three tracks, one for each rotation axis, should appear beneath the Euler controller track.

5. Select the Z Rotation track. Click the Assign Controller button, and assign the Float Expression controller to the Z Rotation track.

6. Select the Z Rotation track, and right-click it. Select Properties. This will open the Expression Controller dialog (see Figure 2.9).

FIGURE 2.9

View of the Expression Controller dialog.

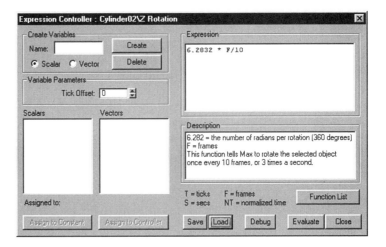

7. Select Load to load a function called 02xpr01.xpr, which will do the job for you. In the Description field of the Expression Controller dialog, there is a description (which the user creates) of what the function does.

8. Click Evaluate, and close the dialog.

9. Preview your animation and save the file as **boat03_1.MAX**.

The following is a brief explanation of what the function, 6.2832 * F/10, does:

This Expression controller has been assigned to the rotation value for the Z axis of Cylinder01. That means that whatever value is output by the function is the number of radians (or degrees, depending on the function) that the object is rotated. The number 6.2832, at the beginning of the function, is the number of radians in one revolution, or the equivalent to 360 degrees. The letter F is a default variable that references the frame number. Here, F is divided by 10 and multiplied by the number of radians in one revolution. Thus, for every 10 frames (or one-third of a second), the cylinder will complete one revolution along its z-axis. For example, at frame one, the output value will be 6.2832 * 1/10, or .62832 radians. On frame 10, the output value will be 6.2832 * 1, or 6.2832, and on frame 100, the output value of the function will be 6.2832 * 10, or 62.832 radians.

TIP

Three rotations a second may not seem very fast for a fan. However, for rotating or spinning objects, it is sometimes more effective to make the object rotate a little slower and add a good Motion blur to it. This often gives the appearance of an object rotating much faster than the same object simply spinning faster.

The Expression controller is very useful for generating parametric animation in a multitude of situations.

Assigning Controllers to the Visibility Track

 A new feature in 3D Studio MAX R2 is the capability of the Visibility Track to smoothly animate the visibility of any object. Previously in MAX, the Visibility Track could only use a binary controller—either it was on or it was off. Now, you may smoothly animate an object's visibility by simply assigning a Bézier controller to the Visibility Track, setting keys and adjusting Tangent values.

In the following exercise, you will work with this new feature to add a hoop to your scene that materializes as the boat moves up the ramp, and disappears after the boat jumps through it.

MAGICAL HOOP ANIMATION

1. Continue working with the previous scene.

2. Unhide Hoop. Open Track View, and make sure you are in Edit Keys mode. Advance to frame 130.

3. Select the Hoop track, and click the Add Visibility Track button.

4. Select the newly created visibility track, and click the Assign Controller button.

5. Select the Bézier Float controller and click OK.

6. Add keys in the visibility track at frames 135, 140, 148, and 158.

7. Make the In tangent of the key at frame 135 linear.

8. Change the value at frames 135 and frames 158 to zero.

9. Save your scene, and play the animation.

By assigning a value of zero, you tell MAX to make the object invisible. A value of 1 makes the object 100% visible. Any percentage of the number 1 makes the object visible by that percentage (.25 makes the object 25% visible). By leaving the default Smooth tangents between keyframes, you tell MAX to apply Smooth interpolation between the visibility keys for the hoop.

Using the Link Controller

The Link controller enables you to animate the transfer of hierarchical links from one object to another. This new feature in 3D Studio MAX R2 is very helpful for animation where you want one object to become attached to, or released by, another object at a specific time.

NOTE

The Link controller is only predictable when applied after the parent's animation is completed. It is important that, if you need to tweak the parent's animation, you either do so before the Link controller is assigned, or you delete the Link controller before tweaking the animation. For simplicity, the parent's animation for this scene has been prepared for you.

In this next example, you'll open a file that's been prepared for you. It involves the ski-boat from the previous example. This time, there's a generic water-skier floating in the water, and a tow rope attached to the boat. The tow rope is worth looking at just to see how it was set up.

The tow rope is essentially a lofted spline, with a Linked Xform applied to the vertices at either end of the spline. Each spline end is linked to a dummy that is placed over the vertex at either end of the rope. Then, both dummies are linked to a third dummy that is located at the base of the boat, which is linked to Boat Body. Thus, as the boat is moved along the path, it drags the tow rope behind it. The effect of the end of the rope whipping around the corners is simply achieved by turning on the animate button, grabbing the dummy that controls the end of the rope, and moving it out to the side and rotating it.

ANIMATING HIERARCHIES WITH THE LINK CONTROLLER

1. Load 02max05.max from the accompanying CD-ROM.

2. Play 02avi02.avi from the accompanying CD-ROM to get a feel for what your completed project will look like.

3. Select Skier, and open the Motion panel. Under Assign Controller, select the Transform track and click the Assign Controller button.

4. With Skier still selected, select Link Control and click OK. The Link controller panel will now replace the old controller panel under Motion: Parameters (see Figure 2.10).

5. Select and link Skier to Skier Dummy. If you play the animation, you will now see that Skier is being moved by its parent, Skier Dummy6. Advance to frame 95. Note that the tow rope handle lines up with the little skier's hands on this frame. This is the frame at which you will sever the link between Skier and Skier Dummy, and you will animate a new link between Skier and Rope Handle Dummy.

FIGURE 2.10

View of the Link controller panel.

6. Under Link Parameters, click the Add Link button. This button will highlight and will link Skier to the next object you select.

7. In the Select by Name list, select Skier Dummy.

8. Under Link Parameters, Start Time, enter **0**. This begins the Link at frame 0.

9. Once again, click the Add Link button, and this time, select Rope Handle Dummy. You want this new attachment to begin at frame 95, so be certain that **95** is entered in the Start Time field. Deactivate the Add Link button.

10. Save your file as **skier02.MAX**, and preview the animation.

The skier now becomes attached to the tow rope partway through the animation. There are many powerful uses for the Link controller that previously required complicated work-arounds. It is now very easy to animate the exchange an object from one parent to another, whether it be a robot arm handing a ball to another robot arm, or a character drawing a sword from a sheath; this tool has many different applications.

Using the Look At Controller

The Look At controller is a very useful controller for making one object "look at" another object. The Look At controller replaces the entire Transform track of an object. It orients the designated axis of the selected object to always point at the pivot point of the target object, and maintains that orientation regardless of where either object is moved.

The most common use for the Look At controller is to force either a camera or a light (a spotlight) to track the motion of an object in a scene. This is very useful if you want to perform complicated animation with the certainty that your target will remain centered in the viewport throughout the sequence, or if you want to guarantee that a specific object is lit at all times. The Look At controller is built into the motion attributes of a target spotlight and target camera. You can also, of course, assign a Look At controller to make one object look at another, or just to make one object rotate along one axis to attempt to track another object. The beauty of the Look At controller is the ease with which it creates a complicated tracking animation.

Creating Spectators

You can use this controller to create a group of other water-skiers in the water who watch the boat as it speeds by. By applying the Look At controller to one skier, and adjusting his orientation so that he's looking at the boat, you can then instance that skier anywhere in your scene, and every instance will look at the boat.

MAKING A SPECTATOR WITH THE LOOK AT CONTROLLER

1. Load 02max06.max from the accompanying CD-ROM, or continue working with the previous file.

2. Select Skier. Using the Select and Move keys, hold down Shift, and make a copy of the skier. Accept the name Skier01.

3. Position Skier01 inside the curved path (see Figure 2.11).

FIGURE 2.11

Instanced skier placed within path.

NOTE

It is very important that you properly orient the pivot of any object you assign a Look At controller to. The Look At controller uses a designated axis to point at the object's target. The default is set to point the negative z-axis at the object's target.

4. With Skier01 still selected, open the Motion panel, and under Assign Controller, select Transform and click the Assign Controller button.

5. Select Look At and click OK. This replaces the previous Link controller.

6. Under Look At Target, click the Pick Target button. This button will highlight when active. Select Boat Body. Leave Axis set to the default of Z. This points the negative z-axis of Skier01 at Boat Body.

Now, as the boat rounds the turn, the skier floating in the water rotates to watch the boat go by. You can now duplicate this skier and place instances anywhere in the scene, and create a whole slew of water-skiers watching the boat. Each new instance of Skier01 will track the progress of the boat (see Figure 2.12).

Assigning a Look At Controller to a Dummy

You can also use the Look At controller in more sophisticated ways. By assigning the Look At controller to a dummy, and limiting the rotational inheritance of the dummy's children, you can force an object to look at another object along only one axis.

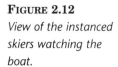

FIGURE 2.12

View of the instanced skiers watching the boat.

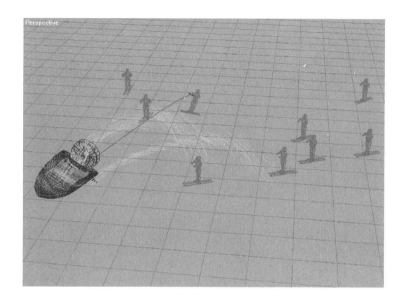

In the following exercise, you will experiment with this concept by flying a helicopter over a stranded water-skier. You'll assign a Look At controller to a dummy that will make a camera on the bottom of the chopper look at the skier at all times. Then you'll assign a Look At controller to a dummy that the helicopter will be linked to, and you'll change the helicopter's link inheritance so that it only pans to face the skier.

TARGETING THE CAMERA

1. Load 02max07.max from the accompanying CD-ROM. In this scene, you will find a model of a helicopter flying above a blue ocean, with a swimmer floating in a life preserver.

2. Select Camera Lens, and link it to Camera Dummy.

3. Select Camera Dummy, and link it to Chopper.

4. With Camera Dummy still selected, open the Motion panel. Under Parameters: Assign Controller, select the Transform track.

5. Click the Assign Controller button, and assign the Look At controller.

6. Under Look At Parameters, highlight Pick Target, and select Skier. Note that, for the Camera Dummy, the negative z-axis will be the one you want to use to Look At any target.

Now, no matter where you move the helicopter, the camera turret will always look at the water-skier. You can grab the helicopter and move it around to verify this (see Figure 2.13).

FIGURE 2.13

Camera turret tracking the skier.

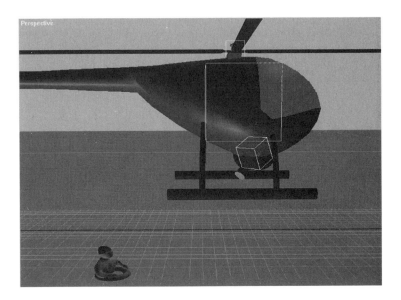

You can assign the same kind of Look At controller to the helicopter itself, to make it always face toward the skier. However, in the following exercise, you will limit the link inheritance of the helicopter to limit the effects of the Look At controller on it, so that it only makes the helicopter pan, but not tilt or roll.

CONTROLLING THE HELICOPTER

1. Continue working with the previous scene. Select Chopper. Under the Hierarchy panel, select Link Info. Under Inherit, uncheck the boxes next to the Rotate X and Rotate Y axes.

2. Link Chopper to Chopper Dummy. This is the dummy that will control the helicopter's panning.

3. Select Chopper Dummy. Note that its pivot has the x-axis facing away from the nose of the helicopter. This will be the axis you use for looking at the skier. Open the Motion panel.

4. Under Assign Controller, select the Transform track. Click the Assign Controller button. Select Look At, and click OK.

5. Highlight the Pick Target button under Look At Parameters, and select Skier.

The helicopter doesn't look at the skier like you would expect. This is because you still have to tell MAX to point the negative x-axis at the skier, instead of the default negative z-axis.

6. Under Look At Parameters: Axis, select the x-axis.

NOTE

When using the Look At controller, it is important to be careful of your hierarchical links. Earlier, you linked one object with a Look At controller, the Camera Dummy, to the Chopper. You then linked the Chopper to the Chopper Dummy. It would seem that you could have as easily just linked Camera Dummy to Chopper. However, had you linked one Look At controlled object to the other Look At controlled object, the animation of the camera lens would have been distorted. This is why it is important to use dummies as mediators for the animation links.

Wherever you move the helicopter, it will always face the skier in the water (see Figure 2.14). As you move the helicopter up and down, it remains level with the horizon, but the camera lens on the turret adjusts up and down to track the skier. You can turn on the animate button and move the helicopter around to achieve your own animation. The same Rotation Expression controller you applied to the boat fan earlier has likewise been assigned to the helicopter propeller.

Using the Surface Controller

Another new feature in 3D Studio MAX R2 is the Surface controller. The Surface controller positions an object across the surface of another. By adjusting spinners that show the X, Y, and Z coordinates, the limitation of this controller is that the target surface must be a parametric object. This limits you to either a sphere, cone, cylinder, torus, quad patch, Loft object, or NURBS object. Any parametric object that has been converted to a mesh will not work with this controller. The Surface controller is applied just like any other Position controller.

FIGURE 2.14

Helicopter tracking the downed skier.

Instancing Controllers

3D Studio MAX provides the animator with a very efficient set of tools. One great time-saving feature is MAX's capability to instance a controller across multiple tracks. This allows you to take the time to set up a complicated animation controller, then copy it to the Track View clipboard, and paste it into other tracks of the source object, or to tracks of different objects.

By instancing controllers, you could save valuable time by copying the Expression controller from the boat's fan to the helicopter's rotor, or you could copy the Noise controller from the position track of the boat to the rotation track of the boat. When many objects call for the same animated effect, instancing the animation controllers is the logical choice.

In Practice: Animating with Controllers

- **Controllers.** Understanding what controllers are and how they store animation data in MAX will help you to better utilize the right controller for the right situation.

- **Path controllers.** The Path controller is an extremely powerful compound position controller. The Path controller is a wise choice for creating complicated, flowing animation not only because of the ease of path generation using splines, but because of its unique capability to interactively follow and bank along any given trajectory.

- **Euler XYZ controller.** The Euler XYZ controller is a useful alternative to the standard TCB Rotation controller. The Euler XYZ controller enables the user to view and adjust the Rotation values of individual axes in the Function Curves mode of Track View.

- **List controller.** A parametric controller, the List controller is a user-defined compound controller used to combine the effects of multiple controllers.

- **Noise controller.** Another parametric controller, the Noise controller is useful for creating an amazing variety of irregular animated effects, such as buzzing wings, rustling leaves, flashing lights, and other effects.

- **Ease Curves**. Any animated controller in a scene outputs data that changes with time. By applying and altering an ease curve track to a controller, you can change the timing of the time for any animation.

- **Expression controllers.** Expression controllers allow the animator to generate animation using functional equations that output singular values to an animatable parameter. Expressions can utilize equations that are simple or extremely complex to achieve parametrically generated animation.

- **Controlling Visibility.** MAX 2 provides the capability to smoothly control the visibility of any object in a scene.

- **Animatable Link controller.** Animatable hierarchies are now easily defined using the Link controller. Objects can change parents and children at any time with the mere click of a button.

- **Look At controller.** This controller is a compound controller that combines the output of an object's Position, Roll, and Scale controllers. It completely replaces the standard PRS (Position/Rotation/Scale) controller and forces the source object to constantly point a user-defined axis at a target object.

- **Instancing controllers.** An efficient tool for reproducing complex animation is to instance controllers among tracks.

Chapter 3

ANIMATING WITH EXPRESSIONS

Expression controllers provide the user with the capability to generate animation from mathematical equations. An expression is a mathematical equation that returns a single value as a function of user-defined variable inputs. 3D Studio MAX enables the user to define variableinputs based on constants, time measurements, or the parameter value of another animated object within the scene.

This chapter explores the following topics:

- Transforming animation with Expression controllers

- Animating modifiers

- Establishing functional relationships

- Using Parametric animations

- Using the Expression controller for accuracy

Understanding Expression Controllers

Expression controllers are one of the most powerful and simultaneously difficult tools to master in 3D Studio MAX. They require the animator to have a deeper understanding of the relationships within and among the animated objects in their scene. Expressions don't do anything on their own, but they provide the user with the tools to perform very complicated animation and establish relationships among objects very easily. To effectively use the Expression controllers, the animator must be aware of when an expression can more efficiently and realistically generate procedural animation than key-based controllers. Furthermore, the animator must have a grasp on how to generate equations that provide the desired animation results. In this arena, people with experience in math and logic are at an advantage.

Although the Expression controller is probably the most difficult controller to master, it is also one of the singularly most powerful tools in your animation arsenal. Spending time learning how to properly use and apply this tool provides you with the capability to quickly generate parametric animation and realistic effects.

Despite their flexibility and power, Expression controllers are not a cure-all. They are merely a tool that enables you to control the animation of existing controllers and establish functional relationships within your scene. To achieve more than this, you will want to become familiar with the MAX SDK and the Script controller.

Expression Controllers for Transformations

An Expression controller is always used to control the animation of one animated track. This might be a transform track, a modifier track, an object creation parameter track, or almost any other animated track in your scene. In this section, you will explore different applications of the Expression controller for transform animation. Before beginning, it is crucial that you understand the way the Expression controller works and the rules for using it.

An Expression controller can provide two different types of value outputs. These value output types are determined by the kind of controller the expression is assigned to:

- A Float Expression outputs a singular floating-point scalar value. A floating-point scalar value is always a single numerical value at any given time—for example, 4.372. Take for example, the Z rotation axis of an object. This can only take a singular value that tells it how many degrees (or radians) to rotate along the selected axis. Likewise, for a modifier parameter value, like a bend angle, the modifier makes use of only one numerical input at any given time.

- Position, Scale, and Point3 expressions output a vector. The vector is made up of three components. For example, a vector output of [3,7.5,–2] would be used by the position track to place the object at 3 units on the x-axis, 7.5 units on the y-axis, and –2 units on the z-axis.

The format of an expression is extremely important. Using the Expression controller is akin to using a very smart calculator. It can do very complicated tasks for you, but you have to give it instructions that it understands by using the proper format. When creating expressions, remember the following:

- One of the easiest mistakes to make is improper use of the parentheses (or brackets). A good rule of thumb is that there must be as many left parentheses as there are right ones. Parentheses are useful for separating different sections of an expression and for forcing the order of operations, which always starts within the deepest nested parentheses and works outward, from left to right. In Appendix A of the *MAX 2 User's Guide*, there is a very useful review and reference section that goes over the basic operators, functions, and predefined variables.

- Expressions must also be mathematically and logically valid statements. To help you create valid statements, try separating different parts of an expression with parentheses and use ample "white space." Spaces between components of an equation facilitate the readability and editability of your code.

- Variable names are case-sensitive and might not contain spaces. Although they can contain numbers, they must start with a letter. The variables themselves are always isolated to the track they are used in. An expression only has access to default variables and the variables defined within its particular dialog.

Transforms as a Function of Time

Using the Expression controller, you can set up parametric animation as a function of animated controllers in the scene, animated modifiers, or of time. Expressions work by taking inputs that vary over time and outputting a single varying value based on those inputs. The output value is what controls the animation of the track that the Expression controller is assigned to. In the first example, you will experiment with a default variable that uses the current time as an input to power simple transform animations.

NOTE

The Expression controller works only with the individual XYZ tracks of the Euler Rotation controller. You cannot assign an expression to any other type of rotation controller. For this section at least, you will find it helpful to set the default rotation controller to Euler (I recommend permanently). The default is set within the Assign Controller dialog box.

Parametrically Animating Object Expressions

This project harnesses the power of the Expression controller to parametrically animate object rotations. You will take the clock model (see Figure 3.1) and assign Expression controllers to the pendulum, hour, minute, and second hands. These objects will all be animated to move accurately with the actual time.

FIGURE 3.1

View of the grandfather clock.

ANIMATING THE CLOCK

1. Load the file 03max01.max from the accompanying CD-ROM.

2. Select Second Hand. Open Track View and expand the Second Hand Transform: Rotations tracks.

3. Select the Z Rotation track.

4. Click the Assign Controller button and assign a Float expression.

5. Right-click the Z Rotation track and select Properties. This opens the Expression Controller: Second Hand/Z Rotation dialog box.

6. Select Load and load 03xpr01.xpr from the accompanying CD-ROM. The equation is loaded into the Expression Controller dialog box (see Figure 3.2).

FIGURE 3.2

View of the Expression Controller dialog box with the second hand Rotation expression.

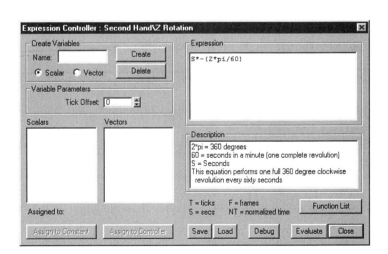

7. Click Evaluate and play the animation in real time. The second hand moves around the clock in perfect time.

We will now dissect this equation to understand what its constituent parts are doing.

NOTE

You can also get a brief description of this by loading 03xpr01.xpr and looking at the information in the Description dialog box. This box is provided for the user to enter helpful notes about the expression he is generating. I have entered these notes for your edification.

Analyzing the Second-Hand Rotation Equation

It is very important at this point that you have a clear understanding of how the Expression controller works and what all the different parts of the equation are doing.

Let's analyze the elements of this particular expression to get a feel for exactly what it is doing.

- **S (Seconds).** This is a default variable. When you enter the S variable, MAX inputs the current second in the animation after time 0 and provides fractions down to five decimals. Thus at 30 frames, if the time setup is set to 30 frames a second, S has a value of 1, and at frame 65, S has a value of 2.16667.

- **2*pi.** There are 6.283 radians, or 2 times pi (3.1415), in one rotational revolution (360 degrees). This by itself gives a steady output value of 360. By multiplying this value by the number of seconds, MAX rotates the designated object of 6.283 radians (360 degrees) every second. This makes your equation to this point (S*6.283).

- **/60.** This divides the 2*pi, or 360 degrees, by 60. Because there are 60 seconds in a minute, you want the second hand to rotate 1/60 of a revolution every second.

At this point, your equation is (S*6.283/60) or (S* .10471667).

NOTE

The number 3.1415 is merely an approximation for pi, which in mathematics is the symbol for the ratio of the circumference of a circle to its diameter (π). Its value is approximately 22/7; the approximate value of pi to seven decimal places is 3.1415926. The true ratio is actually an irrational number, so the decimal places go on infinitely without repeating or ending in zeros. Thus, it is best to not use 3.1415/60, as it is not only messy (producing a product of .1047166... to be multiplied by S) but also inaccurate. Although the small degree of inaccuracy might not be apparent in a small number of rotations, after several thousand frames, your clock would be running slow. It is much easier and faster to just use pi and let MAX do the math!

Animating the minute hand and the hour hand is now very easy. All you need to do is assign Expression controllers to both hands and slightly modify the equation from the second hand.

ANIMATING THE MINUTE AND HOUR HANDS

1. Continue working with the previous scene.

2. Select the minute hand.

3. Assign a Float Expression to the z-axis of the minute hand.

4. Open the Expression Controller dialog box.

5. Load 03xpr.01.xpr from the CD-ROM.

6. Alter the expression to read **S*–(2*pi/60)/60**.

7. Click Save and save this expression as **03xpr02.xpr**.

8. Because the previous equation produced one rotation every minute and you want this one to produce one rotation every 60 minutes, you must divide the previous equation by 60.

9. Select Hour Hand.

10. Assign a Float Expression to the z-axis of the hour hand.

11. Open the Expression Controller dialog box.

12. Load 03xpr02.xpr, which you just saved.

13. Alter the expression to read S*–(2*pi/60)/60/12.

14. Click Save and save this expression as **Hour Hand**.

The Minute Hand expression rotates the hand once every 60 minutes. You want Hour Hand to rotate once every 12 hours, so you can simply divide the Minute Hand expression by 12.

TIP

If you want, you can always simplify your expressions by doing the math yourself. For example, the Hour Hand expression is equivalent to "–S*pi/21600." However, I think it's helpful to leave in all the multiplication and division, because it is easier to analyze the equation and reuse it for different things. The number 1/21600 seems arbitrary, while 1/60/60/12 is obviously seconds divided by minutes divided by hours, or the number of seconds in 12 hours.

ANIMATING THE PENDULUM

1. Continue working with the previous scene.

2. Select Pendulum.

3. Assign a Float expression to the z-axis of the minute hand.

4. Open the Expression Controller dialog box.

5. Load 03xpr03.xpr from the CD-ROM. This loads the equation (sin(360*S)*pi*Swing (see Figure 3.3).

6. Select the Scalar variable Swing, and click the button labeled Assign to Constant. Enter a value of **.1**. Click OK, and select Evaluate.

7. Play the animation. The pendulum swings back and forth once every second. Save your scene as **Clock01.max**.

Analyzing the Pendulum Swing Equation

Let's analyze what the constituent parts of this equation achieve:

- **sin (360*S).** This equals sine of 360*Sec. The sine function is a trigonometric ratio that varies in numerical value from 0 to 1 as the angle increases from 0 to 90 degrees (or pi/2 radians). It returns from 1 to 0 as the angle goes from 90 to 180 degrees, from 0 to –1 as the angle goes from 180 to 270 degrees, and from –1 back to 0 as the angle goes from 270 degrees to 360 degrees. So by using sin (360*S), you get an output that ranges from 1 to –1 and back every second.

FIGURE 3.3

A view of the Expression Controller dialog box with the pendulum swing expression.

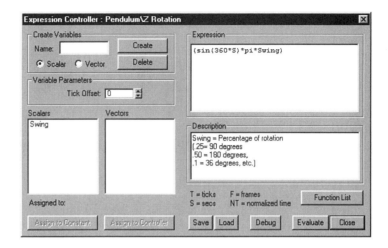

- ***pi*Swing.** The purpose of this section of the equation is to turn the equation into something easily editable for future use.

By multiplying sin (360*S) by pi, you make the output of the equation oscillate from pi to –pi and back. Thus, the pendulum (with this alone) oscillates a full 360 degrees and back every second.

Now by multiplying *this* equation by a decimal, you can determine what percentage of the rotation you want your pendulum to swing. Your decimal is represented by the user-defined scalar variable named Swing. If you assign a value of 1 to Swing, the pendulum continues its current rotations. By making Swing equal to .5, the pendulum only oscillates through a total of 180 degrees. This is still far too much for your clock. A Swing value of .1 yields a nice pendulum swing through 36 degrees of motion.

NOTE

The sine and cosine functions are extremely useful in defining animation expressions. The sine and cosine are identical except that their phases differ by 90 degrees. These functions can be used for any kind of oscillating animation, such as the pendulum here, windshield wipers, and so on. They are well worth the time to learn!

You can now play your animation and watch the clock tick away in real time. If you advance to frame 162,000 (which is 5,400 seconds or an hour and a half), you see that exactly an hour and a half have passed on the clock.

The capability to build a clock on your computer might not change your life, but the capability to apply the lessons you've learned here about using expressions and trigonometric functions for parametric animation very well might! It is always helpful when beginning an animation to determine if you can save time by letting MAX generate parametric animation for you by using Expression controllers.

Animating Tornado Rotations with Float and Position Controllers

In this section, you will take a Tasmanian devil and animate it so that it moves like a tornado. This entails the use of a Float Expression controller for the devil's rotation and the Position Expression controller for its position.

The devil has already been animated sliding across the screen by using the default Bézier Position controller. You combine the Bézier Position controller with a Position Expression controller by using the List controller. (For a more detailed description of the List controller, refer to Chapter 4, "Animating with Multiple Modifiers.") You can view the completed animation, titled 03avi01.avi, from the accompanying CD-ROM.

Setting the Rotation

The first order of business in animating the Tasmanian devil is to set up his rotations. This is very similar to the expression used previously for the clock rotation except that you want the devil to rotate much faster!

ROTATING TAZ

1. Load 03max02.max from the accompanying CD-ROM.

2. Select Taz, open the Track View, and expand the Transform and Rotation tracks.

3. Assign a Float expression to the Z Rotation track.

4. Right-click the Z Rotation track and select Properties to open the Expression Controller dialog box.

5. Click Load and load 03xpr04.xpr from the accompanying CD-ROM. This loads the following expression:

   (S*(–2*pi)* Rotations)

6. Select the variable Rotations, and assign a constant value of 2. Click Evaluate and close the dialog. Then play the animation. The devil rotates two times per second. Save your file as it moves across the screen (see Figure 3.4).

FIGURE 3.4

View of Taz rotating along the Bézier trajectory.

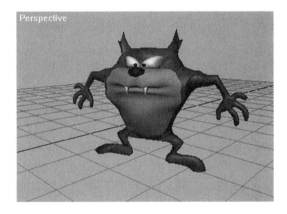

Analyzing the Tornado Rotation Equation

This equation is very similar to the Rotation expression used to drive the clock's hand mechanisms, so we will pass over it only briefly:

- **S (Seconds).** The degrees of rotation are multiplied by S to yield the number of rotations per second.

- **–2*pi.** –6.2832 radians of rotation—360 degrees, or one complete revolution.

- **Rotations.** This is a user-defined scalar variable that determines the number of rotations per second. The number entered for the scalar variable is multiplied by –2*pi, or one revolution, to yield a user-definable number of revolutions, which is then multiplied by the default variable S to yield the number of rotations per second.

Animating with Position Expression

Now that you have our Tasmanian friend rotating, you need to give him a slightly more interesting path. Something random and tornado-like is in order. You use the existing Bézier Position controller as the basis for your position animation and simply add to it by using the List controller.

NOTE

You must use a List controller if you want to combine the effects of more than one controller for a given track. Merely assigning the Position Expression controller to the Position track simply replaces the Bézier Position controller. The only way to combine the effects of both controllers is by using the List controller.

MOVING TAZ

1. Continue working from the previous exercise.

2. Open the Track View and expand the Transform, Position track for the Taz object.

3. Select the Position track and click the Assign Controller button. Assign the Position List controller.

4. Select the track named Available under the Bézier Position track. Open the Assign Controller dialog box and assign the Position Expression to the track.

5. Open the Expression Controller dialog box for the Position Expression track.

6. Load Devil Position. Set the value of Leaves to 4. Set the value of Radius to 100. Set the value of Repeat to 1.

7. Click Evaluate and view the animation. Select Taz, click the display dialog, and under Display Properties turn on Trajectory.

    Displaying an object's trajectory is an excellent way to interactively view the effects of tweaking the expression on the object's path. Try changing the Repeat value to 2 and observe the change it makes in the path (see Figure 3.5).

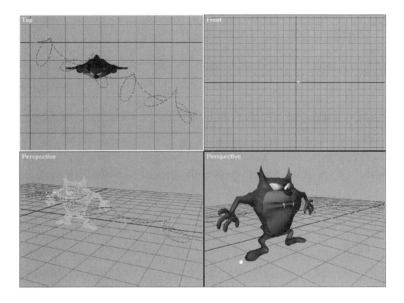

FIGURE 3.5

View of the new trajectory, created by combining the two controllers.

---

8. Save your file and play the animation back.

Analyzing the Rose Curve Equation

The preceding expression is a curve known as a Rose curve. In the Polar coordinate system (r, Θ), it is described by the equation r = a*sin(n*Θ). By substituting a*sin(n*Θ) for r, you can convert the following equations for x and y from the Polar coordinate system to the Cartesian (x, y, z) coordinate system.

X = r*cos(Θ) = a*sin(n*Θ)*cos(Θ)

Y = r*sin(Θ) = a*sin(n*Θ)*sin(Θ)

These equations determine both X and Y positions, given the angle, Θ. n determines the number of leaves on the Rose curve. Varying the angle of Θ from 0 to 360 traces out the curve in X and Y. To vary Θ in this manner, replace Θ with 360* NT. NT or Normalized Time progresses from 0 to 1 from the beginning of the active time segment to the end of the active time segment. Thus throughout the active time segment, this equation steadily builds from 0 to 360. If you wish to repeat the pattern, you simply multiply the equation by a variable named Repeat. By varying the Repeat value, you vary the number by which Θ is multiplied. In other words, if Repeat is 2, Θ varies from 0 to 720; if Repeat is 3, Θ varies from 0 to 1080, and so on. Replacing Θ with (n*360*Repeat*NT) yields the following equations:

X = a*sin(n*360*Repeat*NT) *cos(360*Repeat*NT)

Y = a*sin(n*360*Repeat*NT)*sin(360*Repeat*NT)

Notice that the first two terms of each expression are the same. Put this into vector format for the Position expression, collecting those shared terms and replacing the variable name a with Radius and n with Leaves:

Radius*sin(Leaves*360*Repeat*NT)*

[cos(360*Repeat*NT),

   sin(360*Repeat*NT),

   0]

As a final experiment, you might want to try different values for Leaves in the first sin() function to vary the number of leaves in the pattern. Any even integer value of n produces a rose with 2n leaves. Odd values create roses with n leaves. Non-integer values produce unpredictable results.

TIP

You can view the results of the Position expression on the trajectory of the object by opening the List Controller dialog box, selecting the Bézier controller, and selecting Cut. Then click the Go To Start button and the new trajectory sans Bézier controller appears (see Figure 3.6). You then need only click Paste to add the Bézier controller back in.

NOTE

You must paste the Bézier controller back into the list before closing the List Controller dialog box. If you fail to do so, the controller is permanently deleted. You may continue working with your file with the List Controller dialog box open, and you can even open and tweak equations in the Expression Controller tracks (see Figure 3.7). Therefore, there is no reason to close the List Controller dialog box before pasting the old controller back in. (Of course, in the worst case scenario, you can undo cutting the controller.)

FIGURE 3.6

The view of the trajectory, created by the Expression controller alone.

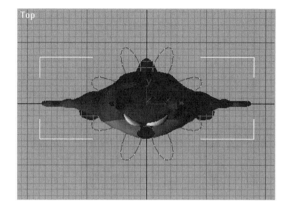

FIGURE 3.7

The view of the Expression dialog box, open while the List Controller dialog is also open and the Bézier controller is ready to be pasted back in.

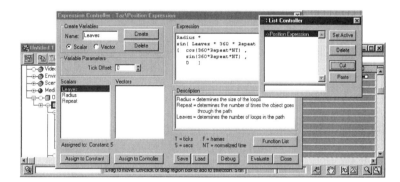

Establishing Functional Relationships

Expression are not just used to apply complicated transformations to objects. Although expressions are very effective tools for generating raw parametric animation, they also provide the animator with the capability to develop a level of structured interactivity in the objects in a scene. Expressions are very powerful tools for establishing functional relationships among and within objects and their transformations, modifiers, creation parameters, and so on.

There are so many different ways to apply the Expression controller that one chapter could never do it justice. It is a tool that, once you have the basics down, must be explored and experimented with to truly capitalize on its power. You can use the Expression controller to create an interactive relationship between the transformation of one object and the parameter of a modifier applied to another object. An Expression controller can also establish a relationship among an object's creation parameters and that same object's transforms.

Base Object Parameters and Transforms

For example, if you have a torus rolling along the ground and you modify the radii of the torus, you should want the degree of rotation and the Z position of the torus to change as a function of its radius, to keep it connected with the ground and rolling the right distance along the ground at all times.

This type of functional relationship is easily established by using the Expression controller. In the next example, you will take a torus linked to a dummy and assign a Float expression to make it roll as a function of the distance the dummy is moved along one axis. Then you will assign a List controller to the dummy and add a Position expression to it, such that as the torus' radii increase or decrease, the position of the controlling dummy above the ground adjusts accordingly. This keeps the bottom of the torus from sinking into the ground as it scales up.

ROLLING A GROWING TORUS

1. Load 03max03.max from the accompanying CD-ROM.

2. Select Torus01. Set null keys for Radius 1 and Radius 2 at Frame 50 and Frame 250. The value at these keys should be 35 for Radius 1 and 10 for Radius 2. Advance to Frame 150, turn on the Animate button, and change the value of Radius 1 to 70 and the value of Radius 2 to 5. Turn off Animate.

3. Open the Track View and expand the Euler Rotation tracks for Torus01. Select the Y Rotation track and click Assign Controller. Assign the Float Expression controller.

4. Right-click the Y Rotation range bar to open the Expression controller dialog box. Load 03xpr05.xpr from the accompanying CD-ROM. This loads the following equation:

    (position.x) / (radius1 + radius2)

5. Select Radius1. Click Assign to Controller. The Track View Pick dialog box opens (see Figure 3.8).

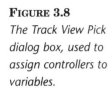

FIGURE 3.8

The Track View Pick dialog box, used to assign controllers to variables.

6. Expand the hierarchy to Torus, expand Object (Torus), select Radius 1: Bézier Float, and click OK.

7. Assign Radius2 to Radius 2: Bézier Float under the Track View Pick dialog.

8. Select the Vector variable named position. Click Assign to Controller to display the Track View Pick dialog box. Expand the hierarchy to Dummy, expand Transform, select Position: Bézier Position, and click OK.

9. If you move the dummy along its x-axis, the torus rotates exactly the right degree for the distance it is traveling.

Analyzing the Rolling Torus Equation

The circumference of a circular object is determined by the formula 2*pi*R, where R is the radius of the object. For every 2*pi*R units that the object travels, it should rotate 2*pi radians, or 360 degrees. Thus, the formula for the number of rotations an object should make given a distance traveled is

Rotations = Distance / 2 * pi * Radius

Since one complete rotation (or 360 degrees) is equivalent to 2 * pi radians, you must multiply Distance / 2 * pi * Radius by 2 * pi to convert it from rotations to radians. The equation is now

Radians = 2 * pi * Distance / 2 * pi * Radius

The 2 * pi in the numerator and denominator cancel out and you are left with the formula

Radians = Distance / Radius

Positioning the Torus Based on Radius

In this section of the exercise, you will generate a simple expression to keep the torus touching the ground at all times by making its Z position a function of its radius.

POSITIONING THE TORUS

1. Continue working with the previous example. Select Dummy, open Track View, and expand the Transform track. Then select the Position track.

2. Assign a List controller to the Position track. Right-click the available Range bar and assign a Position expression to the track.

3. Right-click the Range bar for the Position expression track. Click Load and load 03xpr06.xpr.

4. Assign the Radius1 variable to Object (Torus): Radius 1. Assign the Radius2 variable to Object (Torus): Radius 2.

5. Click Evaluate. Now as the torus grows, the Z position of the dummy adjusts accordingly to keep it in constant contact with the ground.

6. Save your file.

Analyzing the Position Scaling Torus Equation

This equation is very simple. The three parameter structure is that of a vector. Any controller assigned to a vector must have three discreet outputs, which are assigned to the XYZ parameters.

In this equation, you want the Z position to vary on a one-to-one relationship with the radius of the torus. Thus, if the torus's radii total 50 units, you want the center of the dummy to be at a height of 50 units on its z-axis. This equation leaves the X and Y positions set at 0 and adds the two radii of Torus01 to ascertain the Z position of the dummy.

Controlling Object Modifiers and Conditional Statements

Expressions are very useful for establishing interdependent relationships between Object Transforms and Object Modifiers. This can be very useful in many different ways. For example, you can adjust the complexity of a model as it gets further from the camera, or you can taper an object as it gets closer to a black hole. The relationships that you can establish are almost unlimited.

Using the if() Function

In this section, you will also begin to learn how to establish conditional arguments. Constructing arguments is akin to writing rudimentary computer programming and is achieved by using the if() function. With the if() function, you can set up controllers so that they do one thing if a certain condition is met and another thing if that condition is not met. By nesting these if() functions within one another, you can achieve a very complicated and powerful set of instructions. You will use it in the following exercise to bend the board twice as much when the spheres bend it down than when they bend it up.

There are specific rules for using the if() function and the format is very important. Let's say you want to create a function that is the logical equivalent of "if the value of X is greater than 50, then output 50; if it is not greater than 50, then output 0." You would write it like this:

if((X > 50), (50), (0))

Thus, the argument to follow the "if" is the conditional argument. In this case, the conditional argument is ((if) X > 50). The next item, separated by a comma, is the result to be generated if the first statement obtains. Thus, if the statement X > 50 is true, then (50) is the result. The last item, separated by a comma, is the result to be generated if the first statement does not obtain, namely, (0).

Bend as a Function of Position

In this example, you will learn how to assign Expression controllers that change the value of a Bend modifier assigned to one object as a function of the position of another object. By setting up a system of expressions, you can easily animate two balls bending either end of a plank. As one ball goes up, the other goes down and the plank bends accordingly.

BENDING THE BOARD

1. Load 03max04.max from the accompanying CD-ROM.

2. Select Board. Apply Mesh Select and in the Front viewport select the faces on the left half of the object (see Figure 3.9).

FIGURE 3.9

Board with the
faces on the left half
selected.

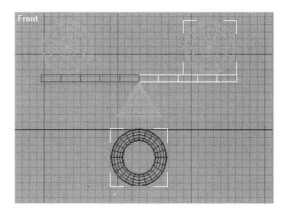

3. Apply the Bend modifier to the object. Position the Bend gizmo so that its center is at the center of the board. Under Parameters: Bend Axis:, make sure the x-axis is selected.

4. Repeat this process, selecting the faces on the right half of the object and applying a Bend modifier to them.

5. With Board still selected, open the Track View dialog box and under Board, expand the Modified Object hierarchy. Expand the Bend tracks and select the Angle track from the first Bend track (see Figure 3.10).

6. Click the Assign Controller button and assign a Float expression to the track.

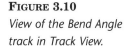

FIGURE 3.10

View of the Bend Angle track in Track View.

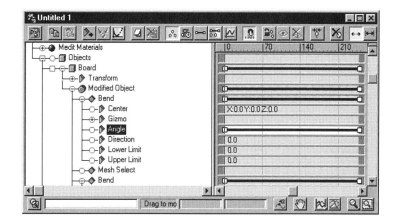

7. Enter the following equation:

    if

    ((P.z) < InitialZPos),

    ((InitialZPos - P.z) * 2),

    (InitialZPos - P.z)

    or load it off of the accompanying CD-ROM. It is titled 03xpr07.xpr.

8. If you didn't load the equation off the CD-ROM, create a Vector variable named P. Now, either way, select the variable P, and click Assign to Controller.

9. In the Track View Pick hierarchy, expand Objects: ControlSphere: Transform. Select Position: Bézier Position.

NOTE

In the equation you just entered, instead of merely entering the variable P, you entered P.z. This is because the variable is assigned to a Position controller, which is a vector. Vectors provide you with three scalar values—one each for the X, Y, and Z axes. However, you can only perform if() functions with scalar variables. By writing P.x, P.y, or P.z, you tell MAX to isolate the X, Y, or Z axis parameter of the designated position vector. Thus, you are using only the Z scalar value of the ControlSphere position vector in this equation.

10. If you didn't load the equation, create a scalar variable named InitialZPos. Otherwise proceed to step 11.

11. Select either sphere. With the sphere selected, right-click the Select and Move button. This expands the Move Transform Type-In. If you look at the bottom left of the dialog box, you see the absolute z-axis position of the selected sphere. This is the initial position of the sphere and is the value that should be assigned to the scalar variable InitialZPos.

12. Select InitialZPos under Scalars and click Assign to Constant. Enter the sphere's initial z-axis position (in this scene, 109).

13. Click Save and save the expression as **03xpr07.xpr**.

14. In Track View, select the second Bend modifier under Board and expand it. Select the Angle track.

15. Click the Assign Controller button and assign a Float expression to the track.

16. Load 03xpr07.xpr. Click the Vector variable P and click Assign to Controller.

17. Assign the controller to the object named Effect Sphere. Select IntitalZPos under Scalars and assign the value of 109 again.

18. Click Evaluate and close the dialog box.

19. Save your file as **SphereBounce.max**.

You have now established a functional relationship between the position of the spheres and the bend angle of the board. If you move either of the spheres on their z-axis, Board bends accordingly (see Figure 3.11).

Analyzing the Equation

if

((P.z) < InitialZPos),

((InitialZPos - P.z) * 2),

((InitialZPos - P.z))

This equation takes the relative change in the z-axis position of the spheres—in units—and bends the board an angle of two times the change in Z units when the spheres are below the center of the board and an angle equal to the change in Z units when the spheres are above the center of the board.

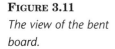

FIGURE 3.11

The view of the bent board.

The conditional argument, if ((P.z) < InitialZPos), sets the condition for all sphere positions greater than the initial Z position, (in this scene, 109 units). Thus, if the sphere is lower than 109 units, this condition is true and the first argument following the conditional is used:

((InitialZPos - P.z) * 2)

If the sphere is higher than 109 units, this condition is false and the second argument following the conditional is used:

(InitialZPos - P.z)

This is a quick way to determine if the sphere is going above or below the level of the board.

Both spheres are placed at a Z height of 109 units. This number is arbitrary. The important thing is to know how to take account of the position of objects in your scene when they don't happen to be at the origin. You want to use the change in Z units, not the absolute Z unit position of the spheres. By using the variable P.z, you pull the absolute z-axis position of the sphere. In order to get the relative change in position from the sphere's initial position, you must take the sphere's current position (P.z) and subtract its initial position (InitialZPos).

Let's say that the current position of the sphere (P.z) is equal to 64 units on the absolute z-axis. You already know that InitialZPos is set to 109. If you plug these values into the equation, you will see that 64 is less than 109, so the conditional argument is true. You know that if the conditional is true, then MAX uses the second argument and discards the third argument.

If you plug these values into the second argument

  ((InitialZPos - P.z) * 2)

you get ((109 - 64) * 2), or 90. Thus, for a Z position of 64, your equation outputs 90, which is used by the Bend: Angle controller to bend the board 90 degrees downward.

For instance, let us assume the current position of the sphere (P.z) is equal to 173 units on the absolute z-axis. If you plug this value into the equation, you will see that 173 is greater than 109, so the conditional is false. You know that if the conditional is false, MAX discards the second argument and uses the third argument.

If you plug these values into the third argument,

  ((InitialZPos - P.z))

you get (109 - 173), or -45. Thus, for a Z position of 173, your equation outputs -45 degrees to the Bend modifier, bending the board upward 45 degrees.

Using Nested Expressions

After you set up one object or parameter to control the controller of another object or parameter, you have not exhausted your expressional resources. You can assign expressions to your Controller object, to the object(s) that control it, and so on. In this way, you can create a nested system of expressions that generates intricate and complicated animation very easily.

For example, say you want to set up the previous scene so that when you move ControlSphere up or down along its z-axis, EffectSphere moves in the opposite direction along its negative z-axis. You can very easily animate the position of EffectSphere as a function of ControlSphere by assigning a Position expression to EffectSphere's Position track. Then by moving ControlSphere, not only do you affect the right side of the board, but you move EffectSphere also, effectively bending the left side of the board.

Positioning EffectSphere

1. Continue using the previous scene.

2. Select EffectSphere. Assign a Position expression to the Position track of EffectSphere.

3. Open the Expression Controller dialog. Enter the following equation:

    [(InitialXPos),

    (InitialYPos),

    ((2 * InitialZPos) - Pos.z)]

    This equation can also be found on the CD-ROM, under the name 03xpr08.xpr.

4. Create three scalar variables, named InitialXPos, InitialYPos, and InitialZPos. Create one vector variable named Pos.

5. With EffectSphere selected and time set to 0, right-click the Select and Move button. This opens the Move Transform Type-In, which provides you with the absolute World coordinates.

6. For each of the scalar variables, click Assign to Constant and enter the X, Y, and Z values respectively.

7. For the vector variable Pos, click Assign to Controller and assign it to the Position controller of ControlSphere.

8. Click Evaluate. Save your equation and the scene.

Now when you move ControlSphere along its z-axis, EffectSphere is moved equally along its negative z-axis. You have established a mathematical relationship between the positions of the two spheres. You can now set several keyframes with the spheres moving up and down, bending the board.

Control Objects, Scaling, and Limits

One of the problems presented by the Expression controller is that you cannot assign a variable to a Scale track. For example, if you want to control the scale of one object as a function of the scale of another object, you can't just establish a direct functional relationship between the two. This relationship can be established, however, through the use of a Control object. A

Control object is simply a third object that is used to mediate between the other two. In the following example, you will make the scale of one object the inverse of the other by using a Control object.

A sign of a wise animator is one who knows her limits and using the Expression controller is no exception. Knowing when to set limits is an important aspect of properly using the Expression controller. If you make the rotation of a see-saw a function of the scale of an object, you don't want the see-saw to rotate through the ground plane if the object gets too big. To avoid this, you need to build limits into your expression equation so that when the see-saw hits the ground plane, it stops rotating no matter how big the object gets.

Control Objects and Scaling

There are going to be times when an animator has a system of objects they want to animate in an interrelated way. A good animator often sees various windows of opportunity to combine the animation tools in their arsenal to facilitate otherwise complex scene animation. One such powerful combination is the use of Animation Control objects with expressions. By assigning expressions to various objects, parameters, and modifiers within a scene and sourcing one control object as the variable controller, you can simultaneously and precisely animate various aspects of your scene interacting with one another.

For example, in the next tutorial, you will animate an apple and an orange on a balance. Your final scene will have the apple scale up as the orange scales down and the balance will tilt accordingly. You might think you can just assign a Scale expression to one fruit and create a variable in that expression that sources the Scale controller from the other fruit. In this way, you could make an equation that scales one as an inverse function of the other's scale. However, you cannot assign a Scale controller to a variable in MAX.

The solution to this problem is to assign Scale Expression controllers to both fruit and pick a third object to assign the variable to. The rotational angle of the balance is likewise assigned, using an Expression controller, to the same Control object. In this way, you need to animate only the Control object and everything else in your scene will animate accordingly.

SCALING WITH A CONTROL OBJECT

1. Load 03max05.max from the accompanying CD-ROM.

2. Select Orange. Open Track View. Expand the Orange Transform track.

3. Select the Scale track for Orange. Assign a Scale Expression controller to the track.

4. Open the Expression Controller: Orange/Scale dialog. Load 03xpr09.xpr or enter the following equation:

    [1 + (Control.x / 100),

    1 + (Control.x / 100),

    1 + (Control.x / 100)]

5. If you didn't load the equation, create a Vector variable named Control. Select Control under Vectors.

6. Assign the variable named Control to the Position controller of the Dummy named Controller.

7. Select the Scale track for Apple. Assign a Scale Expression controller to the track.

8. Open the Expression Controller: Apple/Scale dialog box. Load 03xpr10.xpr or enter the following equation:

    [1 - (Control.x / 100),

    1 - (Control.x / 100),

    1 - (Control.x / 100)]

9. If you didn't load the equation, create a Vector variable named Control. Select Control under Vectors.

10. Assign the variable named Control to the Position controller of the Dummy named Controller.

Now if you grab the Dummy controller and slide it to either direction along its local X axis, the fruit you move it toward grows and the fruit you move it away from shrinks, respectively. The Dummy is controlling the scale of both objects simultaneously.

Analyzing the Functional Scale Equation

The Scale expression requires a vector format, as it requires parameters for the X, Y, and Z axes. Within the Scale Expression controller, an output value of 1 on any axis is equivalent to 100 percent of the object's scale on that axis. Thus, an output vector of [1, 1, 1] is 100 percent of the object's size. Any fraction or multiple of 1 is likewise that fraction of 100 percent. Thus, [.25, 1.23, 62.1] is equivalent to 25 percent of the x-axis, 123 percent of the y-axis, and 6,210 percent of the z-axis.

[1 + (control.x / 100),

1 + (control.x / 100),

1 + (control.x / 100)]

This equation for the scale of the orange starts each scalar value of the vector at 1 (100 percent) and adds the X position of the Control Object controller divided by 100. Because you start Controller centered over the scale at an X position of 0, the initial output of this equation is [1, 1, 1]. As you move the Control object left toward the orange, its X position increases. At a position of 50 units, the equation has three arguments that all read 1 + (50 / 100), which is equivalent to 1.5, or 150 percent of the original scale. As the Control object is moved to the right toward the apple, the X value diminishes into the negatives. When the controller is at an X position of -75, the equation has three arguments that all read 1 + (-75/100), which is equivalent to .25 or 25 percent of the original scale.

The equation for Apple is identical to that for Orange, except that the change in X position is subtracted from 1, instead of added to 1. This means that when the equation for Orange reads 1 + (50 / 100), or 1.5, the equation for Apple reads 1 - (50 / 100), or .5. Thus, as the scale of one of the objects changes, the other varies in inverse proportion.

Expression Controllers and Limits

Now say you want to assign an expression to the board that the fruit is sitting on that makes it rotate as the fruit scales. This is a simple task to perform. You simply assign a Float Expression controller to the board's Z Rotation track and control it with the Control object.

CONTROLLING ROTATIONS

1. Continue working with the previous scene. Select Balance Board.

2. Expand the Transform: Rotation tracks of Balance Board. Assign a Float expression to the Z Rotation track.

3. Load 03xpr11.xpr from the accompanying CD. This loads the following equation:

    degToRad(–Controller.x/2)

4. Select the Vector variable controller and assign it to the Position track of the dummy named Controller.

5. Click Evaluate.

Now as you move the Dummy controller to either side and the fruits scale, the board rotates accordingly, balancing the two objects. If you move the dummy too far, however, the board goes right through the ground plane (see Figure 3.12). This is obviously unacceptable, so we'll have to assign limits to the expression to keep this from happening.

FIGURE 3.12

View of the board going through the ground plane.

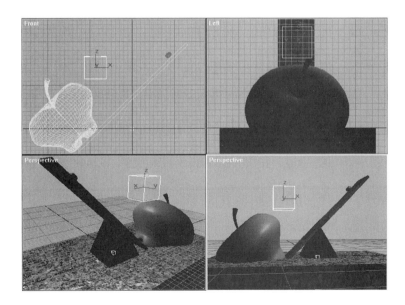

If you move the controller 50 units to the right, (toward the orange), this equation rotates Balance Board – 50 / 2 degrees (the output is converted to degrees instead of radians because of the use of the default function degToRad). Thus, at 50 units, the board rotates –25 degrees, which just puts it into contact with the ground. To keep the board from sinking into the ground, you want the board's rotation angles to remain between 25 and –25 degrees. You can guarantee this by creating an equation that uses the if() function.

SETTING LIMITS

1. Continue working with the previous scene.

2. Open the Expression Controller dialog box for the Float expression assigned to BalanceBoard's Z Rotation track.

3. Load the equation 03xpr12.xpr from the accompanying CD-ROM. This loads the following equation:

    if ((Controller.x < –50),

        (degToRad (50 / 2)),

        (if ((Controller.x > 50),

            (degToRad(–50 / 2)),

            (degToRad(–Controller.x/2)))))

4. Click Evaluate and close the dialog box.

Now when you move the Control object more than 50 units in either direction along the x-axis, Balance Board stops rotating at the ground plane. Once you understand how to apply limits to your expressions, they are easy to do and can make animating a scene a fun, interactive process instead of a painstaking, tedious task. Right now, if you move the Control object more than 100 units in either direction, the fruit inverts and scales negatively. Using the if() function, try placing limits on the Scale functions assigned to the apple and orange to keep them from inverting.

Analyzing the if() Function in an Equation

The function shown in the last exercise is just one of several ways to assign upper and lower limits to a function. In the previous function, you use the if() function to set up the conditions for the object's rotation. Each if()

function can handle one distinct limit. To place multiple distinct limits in one function, you must nest if() functions.

For example, in the previous equation, if the value of Controller.x is any value less than –50, then the output value is locked to (degToRad (50/2)) degrees, or 25 degrees. However, if it the value of Controller.x is not less than –50, the third argument is evaluated. So far, this appears to provide you with only one limit. However, the third argument happens to be another if() function. This if() function provides that if the value of Controller.x is any value greater than 50, then the output value is locked to (degToRad (–50/2)) degrees, or –25 degrees.

So by adding another if() function to the equation, you can add another limit. If it is false that the value of Controller.x is any value greater than 50, (and you already know that it is not a value less than –50), then the last argument of the second if() function is used. This argument is the argument you initially used for your function. It makes BalanceBoard rotate as a function of the motion of Controller along its x-axis, but thanks to the limits you have imposed, the board stops rotating at any value above 25 degrees or below –25 degrees or right at the ground plane (see Figure 3.13).

FIGURE 3.13

The view of the board rotated with limits applied. Note that the Control object is well beyond 50 units, but the board is not below the ground plane.

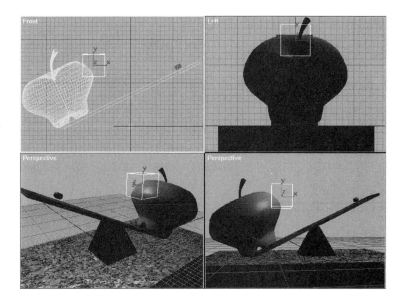

Animating by Proximity

Another useful function built into the Expression controller is the length() function. The length() function can provide you with the distance between any two points—A and B. You merely assign the variables A and B to the position controllers of two distinct objects, and subtract A from B or vice versa (it doesn't matter which, because it is a relative distance). Thus, the length between the objects assigned to A and B would be determined by the formula length (A–B).

The length() function is not that difficult to master and there are many different applications you will find for it. The following are a couple of examples of how you can use the length() function.

Altering Object Width with the Length() Function

In this exercise, you will see how you can set up a scene to control the width of a box by simply moving two Dummies.

USING THE LENGTH() FUNCTION TO DETERMINE WIDTH

1. Load the scene 03max06.max from the accompanying CD-ROM.

2. Select Box01. Expand the Object parameters in Track View. Assign a Float expression to the Width track.

3. Open the Float Expression dialog box. Enter the following equation:

   length (a–b)

4. Create two Vector variables, named a and b.

5. Assign **a** to the Position controller of Dummy 01.

6. Assign **b** to the Position controller of Dummy 02.

7. Click Evaluate. Save your file.

Now move to a Top viewport and move either dummy around in the scene. As the dummies move further apart, the box widens. As the dummies get close together, the box shortens (see Figure 3.14).

If you turn on the Expression Debug Window dialog box, you see the output of the function (the width of the box) vary as you move the dummies around (see Figure 3.15).

FIGURE 3.14

When the dummies are close together, the box is narrow. When they are far apart, the box is correspondingly wider.

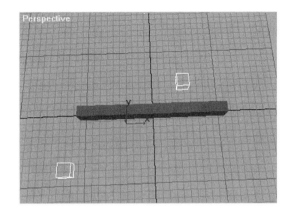

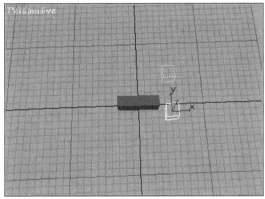

FIGURE 3.15

The View of the Expression Debug Window. Compare the Expression value with the Box Width (which is grayed out under the Modifier Stack).

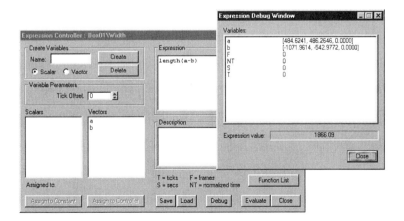

Animating Modifiers by Proximity

A useful application of the length() function is to use the proximity between two objects to animate a modifier. In the following example, you control the angle of a Bend modifier assigned to a "wind measuring rod" by the proximity between the measuring rod and a fan in the center of a bull's-eye.

The fan and the rod both have Look At Position controllers assigned to them so that they constantly face each other, and the fan already has a Rotation expression assigned to the fan blades. All you need to do to finish up the animation is define an expressional function that bends the rod as it nears the fan and has an upper and a lower limit to keep it from bending backwards when it is too far from the fan, or from bending through the ground plane if it is too close to the fan.

THE WIND-MEASURING DEVICE

1. Load 03max07.max from the accompanying CD-ROM.

2. Select Rod. Open the Track View and expand Modifiers: Bend: Angle.

3. Assign a Float Expression controller to the Bend Angle track.

4. Open the Expression dialog box. Enter the following equation:

   if (((200-length(fan-rod)/4)<0),

       (0),

       (if (((200-length(fan-rod)/4)>135),

           (135),

           ((200-length(fan-rod)/4))

5. Create the Vector variables Fan and Rod.

6. Assign Fan to the Position controller of Fan Grate.

7. Assign Rod to the Position controller of Rod Position. Click Evaluate.

8. Move Rod Position around on its local x- and y-axes. Set keyframes for it sliding around the fan.

9. Save your file.

When you move the Rod Position object around the scene, as the rod nears the fan, it bends further and further backward until it just touches the ground. When the rod is off the bull's-eye, it stands straight up, unaffected by the fan. You have created the illusion that the fan is blowing the rod backward (see Figure 3.16).

FIGURE 3.16

The wind-measuring rod: straight at a distance, bent when close to the fan.

Analyzing the Bend by Proximity Equation

Much like the equation you used for the apple and orange scene, the equation in the previous exercise uses a nested if() function to assign an upper and lower limit to the bend angle of the rod. As you learned in the apple and orange exercise, the last argument of the equation is the one that powers the animation when it is within its limits.

In this equation, the argument that powers the animation is the function (200–length (fan–rod) / 4). This equation takes the distance between the two objects (Rod Position and Fan Grate), divides it by four, and subtracts it from 200. You want the rod to bend over a range of 135 degrees. If you leave the distance between the two objects on a one-to-one ratio of units to degrees, it bends through its full spectrum in only 135 units of distance, but the bull's-eye has a 1,000-unit radius.

To expand the distance over which the angle increases to its apex, divide the length() function. By dividing length (fan–rod) by 4, the units over which the rod bends are expanded to four times 135 degrees, or 540 units.

The distance/4 is then subtracted from 200. If you merely had the distance(fan–rod)/4, then as the distance between the two objects increased, the output value (and thus the angle) would increase. This would bend the rod more as it were further from the fan, the opposite of the effect desired. You want the angle to increase as the rod approaches the fan. One way to do this is to start with a number that is higher than the highest bend angle you would want the rod to have, such as 200. Then subtract the equation length (fan–rod) / 4 from 200. As the distance between the two objects increases, the number being subtracted from 200 increases, and thus the final output value decreases.

You then simply limit the equation just like in the apple and orange scene so that when the function value is above a certain angle output, it only outputs 135 degrees, and when it is below a 0 degree angle output, it only outputs 0 degrees.

Rolling: Parametric Rotation Generation with Paths

One problem you probably have or will encounter when using expressions for object rotations is the dilemma of making an object roll the right number of degrees for the distance it is traveling. It is simple to assign a Float Expression to a Rotation track and make the distance it travels a function of its radius. This is what you did in the very first exercise in this chapter. However, that is only useful if you are animating an object rolling forward and backward along a straight line.

If you want the object to follow a curved path, there's never been a way to calculate the distance the object has traveled along its curved trajectory, and thus no way to calculate the exact number of rotations needed. Until now, the only way to make a wheel accurately roll around corners and up and down hills has been with the help of third-party plug-ins. 3D Studio MAX R2 has a solution for this problem.

NEW TO R2

There is a new tool in 3D Studio MAX R2 that allows you to measure the length of a line. This is the Measure tool, found under the Utilities panel (see Figure 3.17). Using this tool, you can immediately ascertain the exact length of any line, no matter how curvy.

FIGURE 3.17

The Measure tool, located under the Utilities control panel.

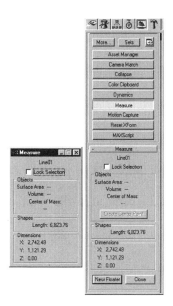

Paths with Expressions: Solving the Wheel Puzzle

The capability to measure a line might seem insignificant, but it provides you with the solution to the puzzle of the rolling wheel. You simply create a line that resembles the approximate trajectory you want the wheel(s) to roll along. Use the line as a path to control the trajectory of a dummy that the wheel will be linked to. You then apply a Float expression to the Z rotation track of the rolling object.

The formula for determining the number of radians an object must rotate to cover a certain distance is described by distance divided by radius. In this situation, the current distance is described by the current percentage along the path multiplied by the total path length, or (pathpercentage times pathlength). Finally, since you want the wheel to roll forward, the final equation needs a negative sign somewhere in it. The final equation should be in the following format:

(pathpercentage * pathlength) / radius

In the following exercise, you will apply this roll function to the wheels of a motorcycle that has been linked to a dummy that moves along a path. You will take into account the particular radii of each wheel, measure the path, and assign Expression controllers to both wheels. To view the final movie, play 03avi02.avi off the accompanying CD–ROM.

APPLYING A ROLL FUNCTION

1. Load the scene 03max08.max from the accompanying CD-ROM.

2. Play the animation. Dummy 01 has been assigned to the path. It follows the path and banking is turned on. The motorcycle has been linked to the dummy and, thus, follows its motions (see Figure 3.18).

FIGURE 3.18

The motorcycle, linked to the dummy, which is in turn assigned to the path.

NOTE

It is very important that Constant Velocity is turned on for the path of the wheel. Constant Velocity maintains an accurate correlation between %AlongPath and the distance the object has traveled along the path. When this is disabled, the object's velocity varies, depending on the distance between the vertices on the path.

3. Turn on Constant Velocity under the Motion control panel.

4. In the scene, select the path named Line01. Open the Utilities control panel and select the Measure tool. Click the Create New Floater button to open a floating window with the measurement information on it.

5. Select FrontWheel. Assign a Float expression to the Y Rotation track. Open the Expression dialog box.

6. Load the expression 03xpr13.xpr. This loads the following equation:

   $-((\text{pathpercent}*\text{pathlength})/(\text{radius}))$

7. Select the scalar variable path percentage. Assign it to Dummy01: Position: Path: Path Percent.

8. Select the scalar variable radius. Assign it the constant value of 53, which is the approximate radius of the front wheel.

9. Select the scalar variable pathlength. Assign it the length of the path, as listed in the Measure tool's Float window.

10. Click Evaluate.

11. Select Rear Wheel and repeat this exact process, assigning the Float expression, loading the expression, and assigning the variables. The only difference is that the scalar variable radius needs a constant value of 60 instead of 53, because the rear wheel is larger than the front wheel.

If you play the animation, you will see that the wheels rotate the proper amount for the distance the motorcycle travels. You can make the motorcycle speed up and slow down by adding keys and adjusting the key tangents for the Position: Path: Percentage track of the dummy that follows the path.

You may also apply an Edit Spline modifier to the path and tweak the path in any way, adding hills and curves. You then merely need remeasure the length of the path and enter the new path length for the pathlength scalar variables in the Expression controllers for the two wheels.

Using this simple process, you can make any object roll along a path easily and accurately.

In Practice: Animating with Expressions

- **Expressions for Transforms.** Expressions are useful for many different Transform applications. They can be used to add parametric animation to any scene and can generate very complicated animation when used in conjunction with the List controller.

- **Transforms as a Function of Time.** Expressions can generate parametric output by using any of a number of different time-based inputs as variables. This is particularly helpful for expressions based on functions.

- **Establishing Functional Relationships.** One of the most powerful uses of the Expression controller is to establish interactive relationships among and within objects in a scene. By properly setting up a scene with expressions, a very complicated animation can be achieved easily by a savvy animator.

- **Conditional Statements.** By learning to harness the power of using conditional arguments in expression equations, the animator can create very complicated systems in any scene that animates precisely and easily. Conditional arguments also allow for the imposition of limits on expressions. Limits provide the animator with precise control over the ranges of motion, angle, position, and so on.

- **Animating by Proximity.** The length() function allows an animator to create an interrelationship among objects in the scene. Using this function, the animator can alter any parameter value(s) based on the distance between any objects in the scene.

- **Parametric Rolling Using Paths.** Using the new Measure utility included in MAX R2, it is relatively easy to make an object roll precisely and accurately along any specified path.

Chapter 4

ANIMATING WITH MULTIPLE MODIFIERS

Modifiers in 3D Studio MAX enable the user to shape, tweak, sculpt, and otherwise deform geometry without committing to any changes. At any time, the animator can tweak the parameters of, deactivate, delete, or add modifiers to the selected geometry. MAX R2 even enables you to cut, copy, and paste modifiers within the stack, which means you can change the order of modifiers.

This chapter explores the following topics:

- Animating Object Modifier parameters
- Animating modifiers
- Layering multiple modifiers
- Navigating the Modifier Stack

Animating Object Modifier Parameters

Every object in 3D Studio MAX R2 has a Modifier Stack associated with it that contains the sum history of that object. This history includes the creation parameters of the object and the modifiers assigned to the object. Almost every entry in the modifier stack has animatable parameters. At the most basic level, the creation parameters of an object can be animated, such as the number of height segments in a box.

The Modifier Stack is organized chronologically, with the modifiers first assigned to a model at the bottom of the stack, and the modifiers assigned last to the model placed at the top of the stack. MAX uses the stack's order as an order of operations. Because of this, you must be careful of the order in which you assign your modifiers to an object. For example, if you want to take a rectangular box, twist it, and then bend it so that it looks like a bent screw, you first must assign a Twist modifier to the box, and then, after twisting it, apply a Bend modifier to the box. If you applied the Bend first and then the Twist, the result would be a mangled box (see Figure 4.1).

FIGURE 4.1

On the left is the mangled box, with the Bend applied first, and on the right is the correct box, with the Twist applied first.

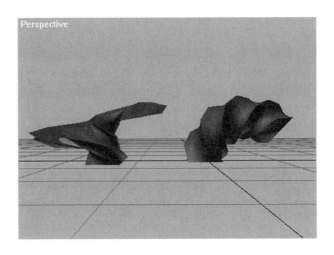

NEW TO R2

In MAX R2, you can now rearrange, cut, copy, and paste and add Object Modifiers from within the fully redesigned Edit Modifier Stack dialog (see Figure 4.2). This new feature provides you with the capability to completely reorganize and add to any object's creation history without limits. Furthermore, MAX R2 enables you to copy part or all of an object's Modifier Stack to a different object. This flexibility enables you to creatively explore different combinations of modifiers easily and also provides an easy means of correcting any problems throughout an object's history.

FIGURE 4.2

The new Edit Modifier Stack dialog.

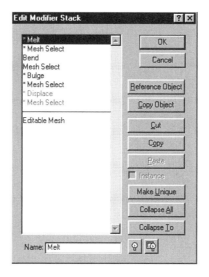

As you add Standard modifiers on top of an object's creation parameters, you may choose to animate different parameters of those modifiers. The gizmos that control the placement of effects like Bends, Skews, Twists, and Tapers can be animated over time. Furthermore, the strength and angles, as well as other attributes, can be animated. Many of the different modifiers you use to model your scenes are also excellent tools for achieving beautiful animation. By layering multiple modifiers, you can achieve very complicated and sophisticated animation with minimal work.

Your test subject will be a little devil (see Figure 4.3), which you will put in several different scenarios and explore the different possibilities afforded by modifier animation. In this chapter, you will also be working with a series of free plug-ins—the Ishani MAX; Form Object Modification Tools. These extremely useful Object Modifier plug-ins are provided compliments of Ishani Graphics and their creator Harry Denholm. Before you begin work on this chapter, it is recommended that you install the plug-in set from the accompanying CD-ROM. Follow the installation instructions found within the file. These plug-ins are designed to work with Max R2. For updates or versions compatible with Max R1, check out the Ishani Web site at http://www.max3d.com/~ishani/index.html. After the plug-ins are properly installed, continue with this chapter.

FIGURE 4.3
The model of Taz!

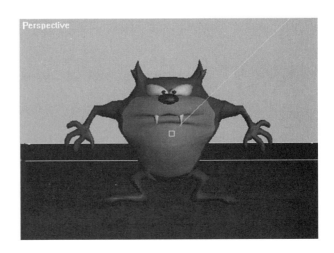

Animating Taz's Heart

In this first scene, you will take a model of Taz and get him all excited. First you will make his heart come pounding out of his chest like a cartoon, and then you will breathe some life into him, and finally you will make him swoon and melt into a swirling puddle. Before you begin, open 04avi01.avi from the accompanying CD-ROM to view the final animation and get an idea of what you're working toward.

Using the Displace Modifier to Displace Taz's Heart

When you wish to push or pull certain sections of an object's geometry, using Displace on the geometry is a viable option. Displace comes in two flavors: as a modifier and as a space warp. Although the space warp is extremely useful, it is not technically a modifier and will be covered in Chapters 13 and 14. The Displace object modifier has two different modes of application.

It can deform geometry by using a Displace gizmo (planar, cylindrical, spherical, or shrink wrap), which is animated along with the Strength and Decay settings, or it can deform object geometry by using the luminance of a greyscale bitmap to determine the displacement value and position of selected geometry.

Before moving on, you should orient yourself with the Displace modifier's parameters (see Figure 4.4):

- By adjusting the Strength and Decay values without assigning a bitmap, the Displace gizmo directly affects the mesh. By assigning a bitmapped image for displacement, the lighter areas of the image create the highest areas on the selected mesh, and the dark areas the lowest.

- By adjusting the animatable Strength value to anything other than 0, you activate the Displace modifier. For values more than 0.0, the geometry is displaced away from the gizmo. Values less than 0.0 displace geometry toward the gizmo.

- By assigning a value other than 0 to the animatable Decay parameter, you cause the displacement Strength to decrease proportionately to the distance from the Displace gizmo.

- Luminance Center enables you to adjust and animate the median luminance value at which geometry is displaced either inward or outward. The default of 0.5 is at 50% gray (greyscale value of 128). Values above 128 greyscale are displaced outward, values below 128 are displaced in toward the gizmo. By adjusting the spinner, the median is raised or lowered.

- By adjusting the animatable Blur value of an image, you cause MAX to "smooth" out the image used for displacement, helping to eliminate jaggies.

- The Map section of the modifier works just like UVW mapping for textures, with most of its parameters animatable. The Bitmap button allows you to select a bitmap whose luminance will be used to displace object geometry.

FIGURE 4.4

View of the Displace modifier control panel.

Using bitmaps to displace object geometry is a very useful technique when you want quick, detailed control over the deformation of geometry. It is useful for modeling random terrains (using blurred noise as the source image), generating embossed patterns or pictures on a mesh that are beyond the scope of a bump map, or animating mesh bulges. In your first manipulation of Taz, you will experiment with displacing object geometry by using bitmap luminance. With this technique, you will give Taz a beating heart.

USING BITMAP LUMINANCE TO GIVE TAZ A HEARTBEAT

1. Load the scene 04max01.max from the accompanying CD-ROM.

2. Select the model of the devil, named Taz.

3. Select the Modify panel and observe the Mesh Select modifier at the top of the Object Modifier Stack.

NEW TO R2

The Mesh Select modifier is new to R2. It is similar to its cousin, Edit Mesh, in that it enables you to pass sub-object selection up the stack to subsequent modifiers. It also provides you with the capability to get selections.

The Get Selection option makes a selection set of the designated sub-object type (face, vertex, or edge) based on the current sub-object selection. For example, in Sub-Object Face mode, Get Vertex Selection selects all faces shared by the vertices in the current vertex selection. Mesh Select provides more selection capabilities than Edit Mesh does, without providing the capability to transform the sub-object selection, which saves a lot of overhead. In short, Mesh Select is the choice for pure selections, as it takes less memory and provides more advanced selection options.

4. Select Sub-Object Face, and under Named Selection Sets, select Tazheart. This loads the selection of faces we will use for the displacement.

5. Add a Displace modifier to the stack.

6. In the Parameters rollout, under Image: Bitmap, click None, and select the file Heart.tga from the accompanying CD-ROM.

    Select sub-object Gizmo. Choose the Scale tool and reduce the gizmo to about 70% of its original size. In the Front viewport, click View Align. This aligns the gizmo with the viewport. Still in the Front viewport, rotate the gizmo about 5 degrees clockwise. Compare your work to Figure 4.5.

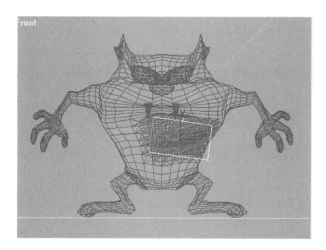

8. Turn on the Animate button. Advance to frame 10. In the Parameters rollout, under Displacement, enter a Strength value of -20.

9. Open the Track View and expand Objects, Taz, Modified Object, and Displace. Select the Strength track and then click the Parameter Curve Out-of-Range Types icon. Depress both icons under Ping-Pong and click OK.

10. Save your file as **04max02.max**.

If you now play back your animation or render it out, you will see that Taz's heart has a steady pulse (see Figure 4.6). If you're feeling wild, you can see what results you get by loading different bitmaps in place of his heart. After you get that out of your system, you can save the file and move on to the next exercise.

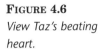

FIGURE 4.6
View Taz's beating heart.

Using Bulge to Animate Taz's Breath

If you know anything about Taz, you'll know he's a heavy breather (and not just on the phone). You can make Taz seem to breathe by using the Displace modifier, placing a spherical gizmo inside of his chest, and then animating the strength values. However, this is the perfect opportunity for you to experiment with a new plug-in, one of a series of free plug-ins provided for this chapter. These extremely useful plug-ins are provided compliments of Ishani Graphics and their creator, Harry Denholm. The first Ishani plug-in you will use is the Bulge modifier (see Figure 4.7).

FIGURE 4.7

View of the Ishani Bulge Modifier Control panel.

Bulge is an advanced Spherify modifier used to map object vertices onto a "virtual sphere." Unlike Spherify, which offers only a Percent parameter, Bulge provides many more controls to tweak and animate the bulge effect. There are two main control panels. The Axis and Controls enable you to adjust Bulge percent, individual axis Bulge values, and Confine to Gizmo.

■ **Bulge%** is the main bulge operator, and works as a "universal" value. Bulge% is fully animatable; when its value is positive, it explodes the object, and by the maximum of 400, the object becomes a sphere. Negative values implode objects. Each axis also has a selector and Bulge value that enables you to affect individual axes for non-linear spherification.

- **Confine to Gizmo**, when checked, forces the modifier to affect only the selected surfaces inside the gizmo. When unchecked, the modifier is applied to the entire selection set.

The second main control panel, the WaveForms panel, enables you to apply sine wave noise to the effect by adjusting the Frequency, Wave Size, and Phase.

- By adjusting the animatable Frequency spinner, you adjust the wave-length of the Wave Form, or how compact the wave will be.

- By adjusting the animatable Wave Size spinner, you adjust the intensity of the waves to be applied.

- Adjusting the animatable Phase spinner sets the phase of the WaveForm, which is used for animating the effect.

By simply applying a modifier like Bulge to a character, you can quickly give the impression of a living, breathing entity without even touching a character animation program. This technique is also useful for adding life to inanimate objects. For instance, if you want to give the impression that a model of a toaster or a shoe were alive, assigning a Bulge modifier would be a quick way of achieving this.

BREATHING LIFE INTO TAZ WITH THE ISHANI BULGE MODIFIER

1. Continue working with the previous scene or load 04max02.max. Select Taz and move to the Modify control panel.

TIP

You might find it easier to work with the model if you first temporarily disable the first Mesh Select modifier and the Displace modifier. Do this with the Active/Inactive Modifier Toggle. This will make the animation play more smoothly without having to render out the scene to test individual results. You can reactivate the modifiers when you are ready to render the scene.

2. Apply another Mesh Select modifier to the Taz mesh. Select Sub-Object, Face, and then select all the faces of the model.

3. Switch the selection type to Fence Selection Region, and deselect the faces of the lower legs (see Figure 4.8).

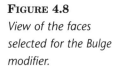

FIGURE 4.8
*View of the faces
selected for the Bulge
modifier.*

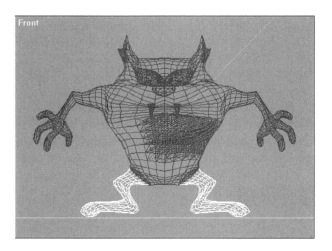

4. Apply the Bulge modifier to the Taz mesh.

5. Uncheck Confine to Gizmo. This makes the modifier ignore the constraints of the gizmo and applies the modifier to the entire selection.

6. The Animate button should still be turned off. Under Bulge% enter a value of 4. You will notice Taz's chest bulging outward. Because you want Taz to have a cartoon-like breathing effect that makes him look like he is growing as he breathes, leave all three axes selected.

NOTE

Instead of animating the Bulge% value up and down to create the breathing effect, you will apply a WaveForm to the effect. This will make the effect increase and decrease cyclically.

7. Under WaveForm Noise, enter a Frequency value of 10. Under Wave Size, enter the maximum value of 15.

8. Turn on the Animate button, and advance to frame 300. Under Phase, enter a value of 50. This makes Taz "breathe" about 8 breaths in a period of 10 seconds. Turn off the Animate button.

9. Now you can tweak the Axis values to your liking. The number you enter under each individual axis bulge percentage is added to the value listed under Bulge. Try entering a value of 4 to the x-axis %, -8 to the y-axis %, and 2 to the z-axis %. This gives the x-axis a total of

8 percent, the y-axis a total of -4 percent, and the z-axis a total of 6 percent. Taz will therefore expand the most on the x-axis and will contract on the y-axis. This produces a nice cartoon-like breathing cycle.

10. Experiment with other values if you want. Save your file as **04max03.max**.

If you make certain all the modifiers are turned on, and render out the animation, you will see that the modifiers you've applied to the Taz mesh have been layered on top of one another. The Bulge modifier is added on top of the Displace modifier, with their individual effects added together. Now you've given Taz a heart and brought him to life, but you're not done with him yet!

Bending Taz with the Bend Modifier

The Bend modifier is an extremely useful tool for animation. You can give a character or an object a lot of life by simply assigning a bend to part or all of the object and playing with the parameters. The Bend modifier takes the existing selection and bends it up to 360 degrees about a single axis. Once you designate the effect axis from the Bend Axis section of the controller, you can determine the axis position by positioning the gizmo. You can control the Angle and Direction of the bend along the selected axis, and you can also assign an Upper and Lower Limit to the effect (see Figure 4.9).

BENDING TAZ

1. Continue working with the previous scene or open 04max03.max. Select Taz and make certain that you are at the top of the Modifier Stack.

2. Apply another Mesh Select modifier to the model. Select Sub-Object, Face, and select *all* of the model's faces.

3. With Taz still selected, apply a Bend modifier to the stack.

4. Be certain that under Bend Axis, Y is the active axis. Advance to frame 80, and turn on the Animate button.

5. In the Parameters rollout, under Bend, enter an Angle value of **25**.

FIGURE 4.9

View of the Bend modifier.

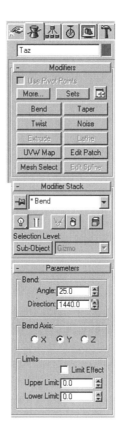

6. Move to frame 300. Enter a Bend Direction value of 1440.

7. Move back to frame 50. Enter a Bend Angle of **0** and a Bend Direction of 0.

8. Turn off the Animate button. Select Sub-Object, Gizmo. Move the gizmo about 65 units down along the local y-axis.

9. Under Parameters, Limits, check the box next to Limit Effect. Enter an Upper Limit value of 190. Your model should now look like that in Figure 4.10.

10. Open Track View and for all the Bend modifier keys, convert the Key Tangent types to Linear. Save your scene as **04max04.max**, and play the animation.

FIGURE 4.10

View of the Bend modifier gizmo properly positioned on Taz with Upper Limit set.

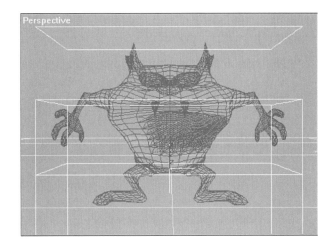

By leaving the Lower Limit at 0, the Bend modifier has no effect upon any mesh located below the gizmo's center. Setting an Upper Limit of 190 ensures that all geometry within 190 units above the gizmo's center is included in the bend.

Taz now begins swooning at frame 50 (see Figure 4.11). He looks rather overcome with love, but you're still not done with Taz yet. If you ever watched cartoons as a kid, (or perhaps this morning?), you might remember that when a character is overcome with love, they sometimes simply melt. Say that you want Taz to do just this type of cartoonish effect. Normally, this would be a very difficult effect to achieve and would require the use of various modifiers and tools. However, thanks to the Ishani Melt modifier, melting ice cubes, wicked witches, or any object in 3DS MAX R2 is a snap!

FIGURE 4.11

View of Taz with the bend applied.

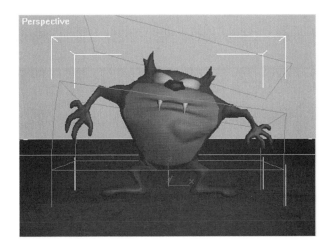

Melting Your Models

The Ishani Melt modifier, provided by Harry Denholm, is designed to do nothing less than melt objects in your scenes. Melt is an Object Modifier that simulates the gradual decay of any geometric mesh. Melt has several user-animatable parameters that let you control how any object melts over time (see Figure 4.12):

■ The animatable Melt parameter controls how much the object has melted from its original form.

■ The animatable Spread parameter controls what percentage of the original melt is spread out.

■ The animatable CutOff parameter provides a lower limit for the Melt effect, making it possible to melt only a portion of an object.

The user can also specify a preset or custom Viscosity setting that adjusts the modifier melt curve and thus the attributes of the melt. The Axis to Melt section enables the user to define along which axis the melt occurs.

FIGURE 4.12

View of the Ishani Melt Object Modifier.

In a few simple steps, you can turn Taz into a puddle! You will also set a few keyframes to make the Melt begin halfway through the animation.

TAZ MELTDOWN

1. Continue working with the previous scene or load 04max04.max. Select Taz and be certain that you are at the top of the modifier stack.

NOTE

Because you will be melting all of Taz, you can continue to work with the face selection set you made for the Bend modifier. This selection set is passed up the stack through the Bend modifier to any subsequent modifiers.

2. Assign the Melt modifier to Taz.

3. Turn on the Animate button, and advance to frame 300. In the Effect section, enter a Melt value of **180**. In the Spread section, % of Melt, enter **50**.

4. Go to frame 275 and enter a Spread: % of Melt value of **20**.

5. Go to frame 145 and enter an Effect: Melt value of **0**.

6. Make certain that the Viscosity is set to the default of Ice.

7. Turn off the Animate button and set the Axis to Melt to Y.

8. Open Track View and expand the tracks for Objects, Taz, Modified Object and Melt. For all the Melt modifier keys convert the Key Tangent types to Linear. Save your file as **04max05.max**, and preview the animation.

Preview the melt animation. There are enough modifiers assigned to Taz now that the animation might be playing very slowly on your computer. Every modifier you add takes up more of your computer's overhead, making the animation playback slower (or making it skip many frames, depending on your viewport settings). One workaround for previewing the effects and parameters of a modifier is to disable the effects of the other modifiers in the stack.

NEW TO R2

Previously, the only way to disable a group of modifiers was to disable each modifier individually, selecting them one at a time. This is a time-consuming process, as MAX had to load each particular modifier before you could disable it, often after clicking through seemingly endless Warning dialogs. Then, when done previewing, you would have to re-enable the modifiers in the same fashion.

Now, in MAX R2, it's very easy to temporarily disable the effects of a group of modifiers by using tools found in the Edit Modifier Stack dialog (see Figure 4.13). The Edit Modifier Stack provides you with the capability to select any number or combination of modifiers from the stack, and disable their effect on the model within the viewport by simply clicking on the Active/Inactive in Viewport button. This disables the effects of the selected modifiers on the mesh in the viewports, but still enables them at render time. The old option of disabling the modifiers entirely is still available, but the new option is the best of both worlds, providing the efficiency of disabling the modifiers at build time, and still being able to render them without having to reactivate them.

FIGURE 4.13

View of the Edit Modifier Stack dialog, with the Active/Inactive in Viewport button selected.

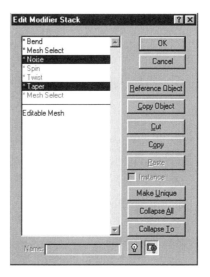

The capability of the Edit Modifier Stack dialog to enable and disable multiple modifiers at once makes it very easy to test the effects of just one or several of the modifiers upon the mesh, and also enables you to tweak the parameters of a modifier and preview the results at a much smoother, more accurate frame rate. This technique saves a lot of time compared to rendering out a preview animation to see the effects and test the parameters of a single modifier.

Taz now melts into a puddle at the end of your animation (see Figure 4.14). For some people, that would be good enough—but not you. You want to see Taz turn into a *swirling* puddle of love. Sound difficult? You're wrong!

FIGURE 4.14

View of Taz melting.

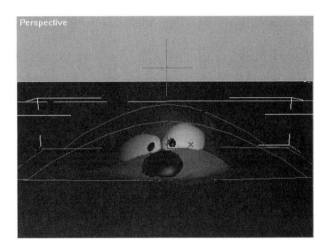

Spinning the Mesh

Thanks to the crafty coding at Ishani Graphics, spinning an object or making it swirl and twirl is just a click away. Provided for this chapter is a free plug-in called Ishani Spin. The Spin Object Modifier twirls an object around its axis point, basing the twirl on how far away from the center the vertex is so that parts farther from the axis will move faster, and those nearer the center move slower. Spin has several user-definable parameters that let you control how the object spins:

- The animatable X/Y/Z Spin controls define how much the effect will appear on each of the axis planes.

- The animatable Multiplier value is a global control for how much the effect appears on all three planes.

- The animatable Bias value controls how strong the effect is manifested.

- Confine to Gizmo makes sure that only geometry inside the object's Gizmo object will be affected by the effect. Default is off.

NOTE

Spin works around the axis point defined before the modifier is applied. To change this point, you can go to the Hierarchy: Pivot panel, choose Affect Pivot Only, and then click Center to Object, or you must remove the modifier and adjust the axis' position manually.

Spin is a useful tool for many different types of twirling effects. Whether you're creating a tornado or animating water going down a drain, Spin provides you with the capability to create a complicated animation effect with very little effort.

SPINNING THE TAZ PUDDLE

1. Continue working with the previous scene or load 04max05.max. Select Taz and be certain that you are at the top of the modifier stack. If you disabled any modifiers, now is a good time to open the Edit Stack dialog and re-enable them.

2. Because you will spin all of Taz, you can continue using the previous face selection. Click More and select the Spin modifier.

3. Change the Multiplier value to 2. Change the Bias value to 8. Play with these values. You will notice that by changing the values in these two boxes, you change the appearance of the spin, how tight it is, how complicated the mesh is, and so on.

4. Advance to frame 400, and turn on the Animate button. Enter a Y Spin value of 250.

5. Go to frame 250, and enter a Y Spin value of 0.

6. Turn off the Animate button. Convert the Y Spin keys to Linear Tangent Types. Save your animation as **04max06.max**.

It's as simple as that. Now as Taz finishes melting, he begins to swirl around (see Figure 4.15). You can play with the individual settings for this plug-in until you are happy with the result. You can also add some finishing touches such as scaling Taz from frame 350 to frame 400 so that it looks like he's going down a drain, or adding a visibility track and making him seem to dissolve into the earth at the end of the melt. Then render the final complete animation, making certain that all the modifiers are enabled.

FIGURE 4.15

View of the spinning Taz puddle.

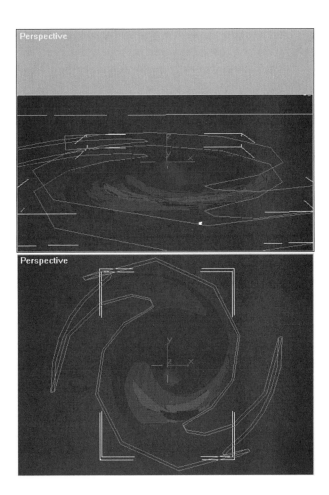

Animating a Taznado

In the next scene, you will create a more rambunctious Taz, using nothing but Object Modifiers to animate him. You will begin by modifying a static Taz model to look like the lower half of his body is a tornado, and then you will animate different parameters of the modifiers to give the impression of him moving like a tornado.

To create the impression of a tornado, you need to apply several different modifiers to parts of Taz's body. First you will taper his legs to give him a tornado-like shape. Then you will apply a twist modifier to wring him like a true twister. Next, you will add noise to roughen up his profile. Then, you will add a Bend modifier to animate his tornado mid-section snaking around. At the end of the animation process, you will set keyframes that will null out the effects of the modifiers between frame 100 and frame 125 so that Taz appears to come out of his spin at the end of the animation.

Finally, you will give Taz's eyes some character by animating them with FFD and Linked XForm modifiers.

Before you begin, open 04avi02.avi from the accompanying CD-ROM to view the final animation and get an idea of what you're working toward.

Tapering Taz with the Taper Modifier

Probably the most obvious attribute of a tornado is its conical shape. If you're going to turn Taz's lower body into a tornado, it is going to have to be tapered. The Taper modifier, as its name implies, takes the selected mesh and gradually scales one end of the geometry to a user-defined girth. The Taper modifier is a tool that is equally useful for modeling and for animating (see Figure 4.16).

FIGURE 4.16

View of the Taper modifier control panel.

Taper has several user definable parameters that enable you to control how the object tapers:

■ The animatable Amount parameter controls the degree to which the selection is tapered.

- The animatable Curve parameter applies either a positive or negative curve to the taper.

- You can select any of a combination of Primary and Effect axes and can set an animatable Upper and Lower Limit to the Taper's effect.

TAPERING THE TAZ TORNADO

1. Load 04max07.max from the accompanying CD-ROM.

2. Select the Taz mesh. The first Mesh Select modifier has already been assigned, with the proper faces for the animation selected. Turn on Sub-Object: Face to see this selection. The torso and legs should be selected, as shown in Figure 4.17.

FIGURE 4.17

View of the selection for tapering.

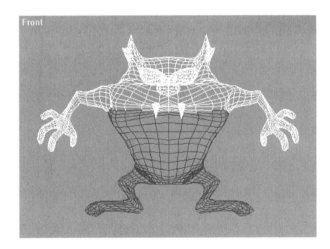

3. Assign the Taper Object modifier to the mesh.

4. Make certain that the Primary Taper Axis is set to the y-axis, and the Effect Taper Axis is set to XZ. Leave Symmetry off.

5. Turn on the Animate button. At frame 0, enter a Taper Amount of 0.75.

6. Advance to frame 125, and enter an Amount value of 0.

7. Go to frame 100 and enter an Amount value of 0.75. Turn off the Animate button.

8. Turn on Sub-Object, Gizmo, and move the gizmo until its center is just above the top of the selected faces (see Figure 4.18).

FIGURE 4.18
View of the properly positioned Taper gizmo.

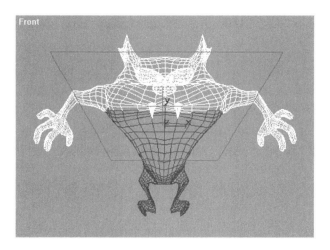

9. Open Track View and for all the Taper modifier keys, convert the Key Tangent types to Linear.

10. Save your file as **04max08.max**.

Taz now has teensy little legs that look pretty silly. The keyframes you set will reduce the taper from frame 100 to frame 125, when Taz comes out of his spin. This is the first step toward turning Taz into a Taznado. The next outstanding attribute of twisters is that they're twisty. MAX has a modifier that is just right for the job, and not too surprisingly, it's called Twist.

Using Twist to Animate the Taznado

3D Studio MAX R2 has tools to help you create and animate just about anything you can imagine. The variegated concoctions of modifiers you can mix is staggering. The Twist object modifier is just one example of these tools. It creates a twist in an object's selected geometry akin to wringing out a wet rag (see Figure 4.19).

FIGURE 4.19

*View of the Twist
object modifier control
panel.*

Twist has several user-animatable parameters that let you control how the
object twists:

- The animatable Angle parameter controls the animation on any of
three axes.

- The animatable Bias parameter compresses the twist effect relative
to the pivot point.

- The animatble Upper and Lower Limit parameters limit the twist to
a portion of the selected geometry.

The Twist modifier is perfect for creating a Taznado! All you need to do is
assign it to the pertinent portion of Taz and adjust the parameters. You will
set up the Twist and adjust the Bias value, and then set keyframes toward
the end of the animation so that Taz untwists out of his spin.

USING TWIST TO ANIMATE THE TAZNADO

1. Continue working with the previous scene, or load 04max08.max.
Select Taz and move to the Modify control panel.

2. Apply the Twist modifier to the Taz mesh. In the Parameters rollout,
under Twist Axis, select the y-axis.

3. Under Twist enter an Angle value of 750. This twists the gizmo 750
degrees along the selected y-axis (see Figure 4.20).

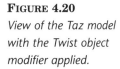

FIGURE 4.20

View of the Taz model with the Twist object modifier applied.

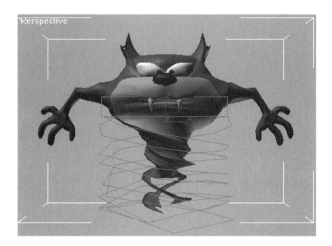

4. Enter a Bias of 20. This bunches the twist 20 percent more at the bottom of the twist than at the top.

5. Check the box next to Limit Effect, and enter a Lower Limit of -130.

6. Advance to frame 125, and turn on the Animate button. Enter an Angle of 0.

7. Go to frame 100 and enter an Angle of 750. In Track View, give the three keys for the Angle track Linear Tangent Types.

8. Turn off the Animate button. Save your file as **04max09.max**, and preview the animation.

Taz is looking more and more like a tornado every minute. You can tweak the Angle and Bias values to your liking, and then continue to the next part of the project.

The Twist modifier isn't being used here to animate the spinning effect of the tornado. It's just being used to create a twisty feel to the lower section of Taz. Adding the Bias value to it makes it twistier at the base than at the top, which is how a real tornado appears. The Twist modifier could be used to provide a spinning-like effect by increasing the Twist Angle throughout the animation. Although this gives the appearance of the mesh spinning, it also necessarily makes the twist tighter, and while you may want this effect, you do not want to be limited to it. Animating the Twist gizmo rotating about its y-axis has no effect on the mesh whatsoever. This might seem like an obstacle, but as earlier stated, through proper combination of different modifiers, you can achieve almost any effect you desire.

Animating the Tornado Rotation with Spin

The solution to the rotation problem lies in the Ishani Spin modifier. The Spin modifier is useful for more than just whirling puddles. The Spin modifier moves the selected mesh vertices closest to the center axis at a higher velocity than those further from the center. This is how an actual tornado would work because the center of the vortex is where the highest wind speeds occur.

The Spin modifier not only adds a nice tornado effect to the existing mesh topology, but it automatically spins around each affected axis, without increasing the strength of the modifier or animating the gizmo. This is exactly what you need to solve the Twist modifier's rotation problem.

TAZ SPIN-OFF

1. Continue working with the previous scene or load 04max09.max. Select Taz and move to the Modify control panel.

2. Assign the Ishani Spin modifier to the mesh.

3. Enter a Y Spin value of 300 (the maximum). Enter a Multiplier value of 6 to amplify the Spin value and a Bias value of 8.

4. Advance to frame 100, and Shift Right-click on the Y Spin value spinner. Shift-right-clicking is a new feature of Max R2 that sets a key equal to the value currently on the spinner.

5. Advance to frame 125, turn on the Animate button, and enter a Y Spin value of 0. Again, in Track View, make the key Tangent Types for these keys Linear.

6. Turn off the Animate button and save your file as **04max010.max**.

Taz is looking more and more vortical, with his legs spinning like a blender (see Figure 4.21). However, he still looks a little too controlled and linear. The tornado section of his body appears to remain directly beneath him. To make the animation more believable, you will want to make Taz's rotations more dynamic. You want to add a little noise to those predictable spinning twists.

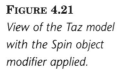

FIGURE 4.21

View of the Taz model with the Spin object modifier applied.

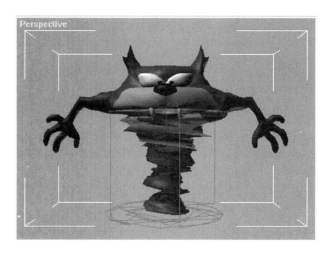

Adding Noise to the Animation

What Taz's legs are lacking is some distortion. There are a number of ways you can distort his "twister" section. For example, you can assign a Bend modifier to the selected region and apply random bends at random intervals. However, setting keys for all the bends at all the different intervals would be a somewhat time-consuming task. A much more efficient way to achieve the effect you want is to simply assign a Noise modifier to the selected region (see Figure 4.22).

The Noise modifier randomly modulates the position of an object's selected vertices along any combination of three axes. The Noise modifier is an extremely important tool, as it can be used to generate random variations in any object's shape.

- The animatable Seed value affects the random seed used to generate the noise.

- The animatable Scale value sets the size of the noise effect, with larger values producing a smoother effect, and lower values a more jagged effect.

- The Fractal option with animatable Roughness and Iterations creates random, rippling patterns.

- The animatable Strength values allow the user to adjust the amplitude of the Noise effect.

FIGURE 4.22

View of the Noise object modifier control panel.

- The Animation section provides Frequency and Phase spinners that vary the regularity of the Noise effect by adjusting the shape of a sine wave that controls the effect.

RANDOMIZING THE TAZNADO

1. Continue working with the previous scene or load 04max010.max. Select Taz and move to the Modify control panel.

2. Assign the Noise modifier to the mesh.

3. Under Parameters, Strength, X, and Z, enter values of 75. Be certain to leave the Y value at 0. This limits the noise to the horizontal plane. If it were applied to the y-axis, the tornado would jut up into Taz's face and below the ground.

4. Place a check next to the Animate Noise option.

5. Advance to frame 125, and turn on the Animate button. Enter Strength, X, and Z values of 0. This can be achieved by right-clicking the X and Z Strength spinners. Right-clicking a spinner sets its value to 0.

6. Go to frame 100 and enter Strength, X and Z values of 75. Open the Track View and convert the Key Tangent Types for the Strength keyframes to Linear.

7. Save your changes to the scene as **04max011.max**, and play the animation.

Now the tornado section of Taz moves around beneath him randomly. You can vary the randomness of this effect by altering the Seed value, and watch the gizmo change its shape (see Figure 4.23). You can also alter the Animation curve's Frequency and Phase values to vary the effect, but for this example, the default values function very well. The default scale of 100 is also appropriate for this scene, but you should play around with the controls to see how they alter the model with different values.

FIGURE 4.23

View of the Noise gizmo assigned to the Taz model.

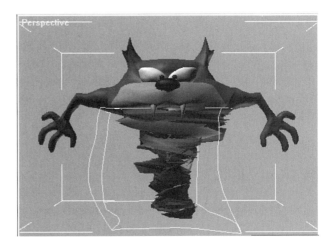

Bending for Secondary Motion

Taz's lower body looks pretty good now, but his upper body has been neglected. His whole upper torso remains static and unaffected, which doesn't look at all believable. Even just a little motion will aid the animation. Small secondary animation of Taz's body can easily be achieved by assigning an animated Bend modifier to the mesh. By assigning a small Bend angle and animating the direction, you can give a very subtle feel of motion to the mesh. Any living creature, no matter how still it is trying to be, always moves at least a little bit. Your characters, even when they are just standing still, should have some sort of animation applied to their frames to give them a subtle sense of realism.

The Bend modifier is not new to you, so you can jump right in and just assign it to Taz.

ADDING SUBTLE BENDS FOR REALISM

1. Continue working with the previous scene or load 04max011.max. Select Taz and move to the Modify Control panel.

2. Apply a Mesh Select modifier and exit the Sub-Object level. This selects the whole mesh.

3. Apply a Bend modifier to the Taz mesh. Enter an Angle value of 10.

4. Advance to frame 140, turn on the Animate button, and enter an Angle value of 0. Enter a Direction value of 1080.

5. Go to frame 125, and enter an Angle value of 10.

6. Save your scene as **04max012.max** and preview the animation.

Now when you view the animation, you will notice that Taz's head and arms sway in a slightly circular motion, like a gyroscope. This is perhaps what you'd expect if he had a tornado for his lower body. You can play around with the bend angle and direction controls. If the Bend angle is much higher, however, you will notice that it severely distorts Taz's hands and arms. When you're done, you can move on to the next section, where you'll put on the finishing touches on your animation.

Animating Taz's Eyes

The life of the character always shines through his eyes. By adjusting the shape and focus of the eyes, you can alter a character's mood and intention. Using a few tools new to 3D Studio MAX R2 and a few old tools, you can quickly give Taz beautifully animated cartoon eyes. This is no simple task because his eyes are not spherical—you can't just rotate them. Instead, you need to deform them. After deforming the shape of the eyes themselves, you can assign Linked XForm modifiers to each iris, and animate the irises independently.

Selecting the Eyes and Irises for Deformation

Before you can do anything, you need to select both the eyes and the retinas for the deformation. Because the eyes and retinas are recessed into the model of the actual body, the best way to select the relevant faces is by using Select by Material. Once the faces are selected, and undesired faces are de-selected, you are free to deform the eyes.

USING THE EDIT MESH AND MESH SELECT MODIFIERS

1. Continue working with the previous scene or load 04max012.max. Select Taz and move to the Modify control panel.

2. Assign a Mesh Select modifier to the stack. Turn on Sub-Object: Face. Enter a value of 3 in the Material ID box, (the Material ID for the eyes and teeth), then click the Select by Material ID button.

3. Click the Select by Material ID button, enter 4 (the Material ID for the irises and nose). Uncheck the Clear Selection box and then click OK.

4. Using the Selection tool with the Alt button depressed, move to a Left viewport, zoom in on Taz's head, and de-select the tooth and nose faces.

5. Using the Named Selection box in the upper-right area of the toolbar, save your face selection set as **Taz Eyes**.

6. Save your file as **04max013.max**.

You now have the eyes and retinas selected, but selected under a Mesh Select modifier (see Figure 4.24). Now you're ready to animate the deformation of the eyes.

FIGURE 4.24

View of the final eye selection.

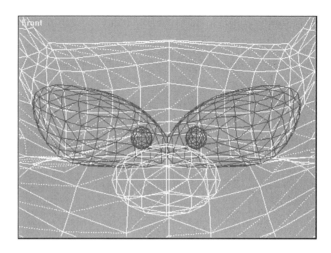

FreeForm Deformation Modifiers

The FreeForm Deformation *Box* and *Cylinder* modifiers are new to 3D Studio MAX R2. The FFD modifier places a lattice box around the selected geometry. The lattice has Control points that, when moved, deform the relevant geometry. The geometry closest to the Control point is affected the most, the farthest the least.

The FFD (box) modifier is preferable to the original 2×2×2, 3×3×3, and 4×4×4 FFD modifiers because it can be adjusted to any resolution along each of its axes. The FFD (cyl.) modifier provides the new ability to deform with a cylindrically shaped gizmo. The All Vertices option deforms all vertices, whether they are inside or outside of the source volume. The Only in Volume option only deforms vertices that lie within the source volume.

You will use the FFD modifier to deform Taz's eyes. By pulling the Control points, you sculpt his eyes into different shapes, giving him different expressions.

DEFORMING TAZ'S EYES

1. Continue working with the previous scene or load 04max013.max. Select Taz and move to the Modify Control panel.

2. Assign the FFD (box) Modifier to the stack. An orange rectangular lattice appears around the selected eyes. Click the button that says Set Number of Points. Set the Length to 3, the Width to 3, and the Height to 2.

3. Turn on the Animate button, and click the Sub-Object button.

4. You can now deform the eyes by simply grabbing the Control points on the lattice and dragging them around. Advance to frame 50, and position the control points to look like the lattice in Figure 4.25.

FIGURE 4.25

View of the first eye deformation.

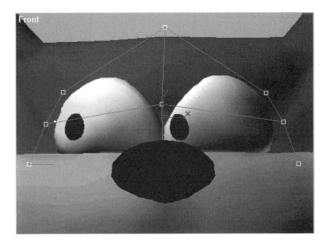

5. Advance to frame 110 and position the Control points to look like Figure 4.26.

FIGURE 4.26

View of the second eye deformation.

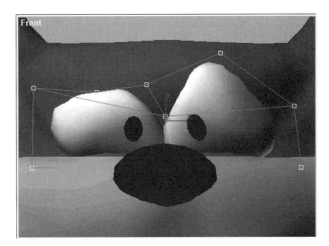

6. Open the Track View, expand Taz, expand Modified Object, and expand the FFD modifier track. Select all the Control point keys at frame 0, and copy them to frame 145.

7. Save the changes to the scene as **04max014.max**, and play the animation.

Taz's eyes now deform through several different expressions. This effect adds a lot of character to your scene, and livens it up quite a bit. The final refinement is to animate the retinas themselves. This is easily achieved by using the Linked XForm modifier.

Linked XForm

The Linked XForm modifier enables you to assign any geometry selection to another object, which is referred to as the Control Object. The selected vertices follow the Control Object when it is moved. Linked XForm has only one option, which is to pick a control object.

The scene has been prepared with two dummies that you will utilize as control objects. They are named LEye Control and REye Control.

LINKED XFORM EYE ANIMATION

1. Continue working with the previous scene or load 04max014.max.

2. Switch to the Display control panel, and remove the check next to Helpers in the Hide By Category rollout.

3. Select Taz and move to the Modify control panel. Be certain that you are at the top of the Stack.

4. Apply a Mesh Select modifier to the mesh, and turn on Sub-Object: Face. Click the select by Element button, (the button with a cube on it below the Sub-Object button). This allows you to select by entire elements.

5. Click on Taz's left iris. When you click on it, the entire iris becomes highlighted.

6. Assign a Linked XForm modifier to the mesh.

7. Click the Pick Control Object button. Press the H key to display the Select By Name dialog, and select Dummy01.

8. Open the Edit Modifier Stack dialog, and select the Mesh Select modifier and the Linked XForm modifier at the top of the stack.

NOTE

The new capability of MAX R2 to copy and paste modifiers can save you substantial time, especially for modifiers like Linked XForms, which require an independent selection modifier and Linked XForm modifier for each control object. Look for opportunities to apply this new feature, and it's sure to save you time!

9. Click on the Copy button. Select the modifier at the top of the Stack, (in this case, Linked XForm), and click Paste. The two copied modifiers are pasted in at the top of the stack.

10. Click OK. Select the new Mesh Select modifier, and click the select by Element button.

11. Click on Taz's right iris. When you click on it, the entire iris becomes highlighted.

12. Move up the stack to the Linked XForm Modifer. Click on the Pick Control Object button, and select Dummy02 as the Control Object.

13. Turn on the animate button. Advance to a later frame. In a front viewport, with the View: XY constraints turned on, use the Move tool to place the eyes wherever you want them. When you are finished, turn off the Animate button and save your scene as **04max015.max**.

You are now free to animate the eyes to look wherever you like. You will want to adjust the key In and Out Tangent Types and might need to spend some time tweaking the animation. You can look back at the 02avi02.avi included on the accompanying CD-ROM for direction.

In this chapter, you have walked through some substantial modifier animation, and learned how to effectively combine modifiers to achieve sophisticated animation results. Your stack should now contain 14 modifiers. When you really get animating, you will probably find that your modifier stack will go *off the screen*! That's OK! Don't be afraid of mixing and matching different modifiers, and exploring new ones. One of the great new features of MAX R2 is its capability to let you reorganize the entire stack by using the Edit Modifier Stack tool, and eliminate modifiers you don't really need without having to re-create the animation history. Placing your modifiers in different order can subtly or substantially alter the animation. Now that you understand how the stack functions in applying a modifier history, you are armed to produce beautiful animations!

In Practice: Animating with Multiple Modifiers

- **Modifying Geometry.** Modifiers are the primary tools for manipulating geometry in 3D Studio MAX. They are a suite of tools, each designed to deform geometry in a different manner.

- **Animating with Modifiers.** Every modifier provides you with a different animation option. For almost any animation need, there is a modifier that can animate a different type of geometric manipulation.

- **Layering Modifiers.** The order in which you apply your modifiers affects the end result. Careful attention must be applied to the chronological order of the Stack History. However, this history is now easily rearranged thanks to new features in MAX R2.

- **Editing the Stack.** You can save valuable time by knowing how to properly navigate and manipulate the stack. Disabling modifiers or cutting, copying, and pasting modifiers can add up to substantial time savings.

Part II

CHARACTER ANIMATION

Chapter 5

SETTING UP CHARACTERS FOR ANIMATION

Setup is one of the most important tasks a character animator faces. It involves not only building the character so that it looks nice but also tweaking the models and adding elements, such as skeletons and expressions, to help the animation process along. If a character is solidly built and easy to animate, the process goes faster and the animator's creative flow isn't interrupted by frustrating problems and system delays.

Setting up a character also enables it to move naturally and realistically. If the character is modeled, boned, and manipulated properly, this comes about naturally. If the character is modeled improperly, you will be fighting your models to get them to look right.

The rule of thumb in setting up characters for animation is to "animate light, render heavy." This simply means that you should devise methods within the MAX framework to animate with the minimum mesh detail and render at the maximum mesh resolution required to keep your characters smooth and lifelike.

You should also create your characters so that the software does all the "busywork." That way you can spend time on the slight movements that bring life to your character. For example, if you set up a dummy as a Control object on a finger's bone structure, you can rotate that dummy and it affects all the bones in the finger at once, causing the finger to curl.

Types of Characters

When modeling characters, you can take a number of approaches. You can create your character using individual objects, or segments, for each joint, or you can create a seamless mesh that is deformed. The models can be constructed using any of the geometry types supported by MAX. These include Polygonal models, Patch models, and NURBS models. At render time, of course, even patches and NURBS are tessellated to polygons for the renderer.

Segmented Characters

The easiest way to animate a character is by constructing the body out of individual objects, or segments. Picture a segmented character as the classic artist's mannequin, constructed of wood and fitted together with pins at the joints. Robots and other mechanical types of characters lend themselves quite well to this method. Figure 5.1 shows an example of a segmented character and Figure 5.2 shows the same figure with an exploded view of the segments.

FIGURE 5.1
This is a good example of a segmented character.

FIGURE 5.2
This exploded view shows his body is composed of multiple objects.

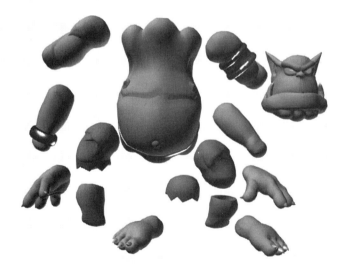

Segmented characters are pretty much required for applications such as video games because deforming a mesh requires too much overhead (although as machines get faster, more and more games are using deformable characters). The same is true for MAX; it will animate segments faster because deforming a mesh requires extra calculations.

The many parts of a segmented character are put together via a hierarchy. This hierarchy can then be animated using Forward Kinematics or Inverse Kinematics (IK for short.)

There are, of course, downfalls to creating segmented characters. First, segmented characters do not look as natural as seamless ones because the segments themselves are rigid and do not deform. Second, seams always find a way to show themselves, no matter how hard you try to hide them. You can always turn this pitfall to your advantage by purposely designing your character with exposed seams. Pixar's Buzz Lightyear is a good example of such a design. Insects are also naturally segmented and make good candidates for this technique.

Polygonal Mesh Characters

A character can also be constructed out of a solid polygonal mesh. In the past, this has proven to be problematic for MAX users because the level of detail required to obtain a smooth surface creates a huge number of polygons. This creates problems in a number of areas. First, the extra detail tends to bog down the system when it is deforming the mesh. Second, the additional detail also causes a higher incidence of unwanted crimping and tearing of the mesh.

With new modifications to Meshsmooth, however, these problems have evaporated. Polygonal models can now be created at a low mesh resolution, deformed using a mesh deformation plug-in, such as Physique or Bones Pro, and then have extra resolution added to the model using Meshsmooth. This circumvents problems with tearing and crimping and allows for extremely organic polygonal models to be created and animated.

Low Res Polygonal Models

In gaming, the low resolution polygonal model has become the standard way to create characters. Modeling a low res character is really just an exercise in simplicity. Most modelers start with simple objects, such as cubes or spheres, and then extrude faces as needed to create the appropriate detail.

In this form of modeling, operations such as Booleans become a major faux pas. Although they are used quite often in a number of areas of animation, Booleans inevitably add more detail to a model than they are worth. If you observe the seam created from a Boolean operation, you'll notice a huge amount of tiny faces used to bridge inaccuracies in the fusing of the models (see Figure 5.3). These polygons add very little to the model but can nearly double the weight.

FIGURE 5.3

The left object has a cylinder attached to a sphere using Booleans. The right object is created by extruding faces of the sphere.

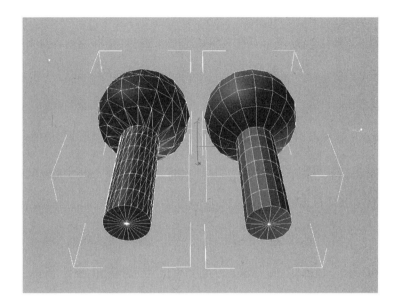

When Meshsmooth is applied, the object with the Boolean breaks up at the seams. This is because Booleans create extra unseen detail at the seams. The extruded cylinder is clean, light, and smooth (see Figure 5.4).

FIGURE 5.4

Meshsmooth applied to the objects. Notice the breaking up on the left (Boolean) object.

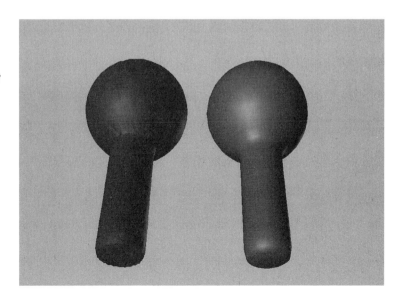

TIP
Instead of Booleans, smart polygonal modelers rely on tools such as face extrude. These can accomplish many of the same results as Booleans but with a much cleaner joint, which lightens the model considerably and speeds animation as well.

Low Res Models and Gaming

One of the reasons low res modeling is so attractive to gamers is because it animates as fast as you can push the joystick. The same goes for MAX. The small number of vertices in a typical low res model does not bog down the system, and animation can be authored in real time.

The problem with models this light is that, although they may work perfectly in a gaming environment, they do not work as well in other environments—such as film and video—because they are not perfectly smooth. Low resolution models tend to look blocky on the big screen, but this can be solved with Meshsmooth.

TIP
The Tessellate modifier Tessellate modifier is very similar to Meshsmooth in that it can add detail to a low resolution mesh. Meshsmooth rounds sharp edges off the mesh, approximating the surface of a patch. Tessellate does not round off edges, which may be desirable at times.

Using Meshsmooth at Render Time to Add Resolution

From a character animation standpoint, one of the best additions to the 3D Studio MAX version 2 toolkit is one of the simplest. As of version 2, Meshsmooth retains mapping coordinates (see Figures 5.5 and 5.6). This may not sound like much, but it turns Meshsmooth from just a simple modeling tool into a powerful animation tool as well. The new Meshsmooth allows polygonal models to gain resolution and smoothness much like patches or NURBS.

FIGURE 5.5

A low res polygonal model with a texture applied.

FIGURE 5.6

When Meshsmooth is applied, the mapping is retained. This gives animators the ability to animate the low-res mesh and render at high res using Meshsmooth.

Because it retains mapping, Meshsmooth can now be placed at the top of the stack, after the UVW Mapping modifier and also after any Mesh Deformation modifiers. This allows you to interactively switch off Meshsmooth to gain speed while animating and then switch it on at render time to make the model organic and smooth for the camera. As you will see later, this technique can make polygons as much of an organic modeling and animation tool as spline patches or NURBS are.

TIP

The best way to get good results with Meshsmooth is to use the Quad Output option. This eliminates all triangular polygons in the mesh and provides for a much smoother surface.

Using Patches to Construct Characters

Patches are terrific for modeling and animating characters, though the tools may be a bit tough to master. Many people use patches to create heads and faces, but patches also work quite well for bodies. Patches can create very smooth and very realistic characters. Because they are defined by only a few control vertices, animation of patches is reasonably fast.

To aid in the creation of patch-based models, some people use Digimation's Surface Tools plug-in. This has given animators an easy-to-use and serious tool for animating Patch surfaces. The plug-in gives animators a much better way of creating a Patch surface by defining the outline with simple Bézier curves, much like UV lofting in NURBS.

Creating Characters Using NURBS

 New to R2 is the addition of NURBS to 3D Studio MAX. NURBS is an acronym for Non-Uniform Rational B-Splines. A NURBS surface is similar to a patch but with a much greater degree of control over the curvature of the surface. NURBS have been used extensively in other packages to create very realistic and organic characters. MAX can now join this elite crowd, because its integrated NURBS modeler has the tools to create very organic characters (see Figure 5.7).

The NURBS technology used by MAX provides for quick and easy animation. The Control vertices of the NURBS object can be animated directly or they can be controlled like any other vertex using Physique or other plug-ins.

FIGURE 5.7

Characters made from NURBS can be extremely flexible and organic.

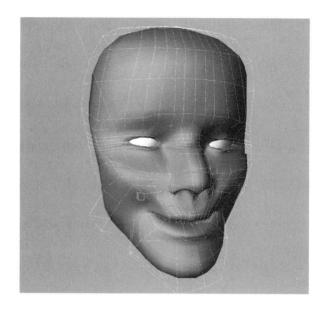

Constructing Characters with Metaballs

One final way of creating characters is with metaballs. Two competing plug-ins are available that provide MAX with the most sophisticated metaballs technology on the market. REM Infografica's Metamuscles and Digimation's Clay Studio Pro enable you to create and animate metaballs that emulate the behavior of real muscles under skin. These programs create a mesh that represents the skin which covers the muscles, and by animating the muscles you can animate the skin (see Figure 5.8).

The muscles created in either of these packages can be attached to skeletons and can be infused with properties that allow them to bulge, stretch, and flex like real muscles (see Figure 5.9). Not only that, but both of these implementations allow you to apply textures to the muscles so the textures stick to the surface no matter what shape the character takes.

FIGURE 5.8

These muscles can then be assembled in a skeleton to create highly realistic characters.

FIGURE 5.9

This Metaball object, created using Digimation's Clay Studio Pro, can bend and flex like a real muscle.

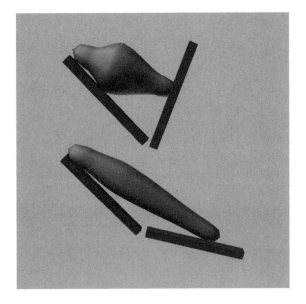

This technology also lends itself to quick and easy animation because the calculated metaball surface can be turned off until rendering time. This affords the animator the speed and interactivity needed and the heavy calculations needed to create the metaball surface are postponed until rendering time.

Creating Hybrid Characters

Because MAX can mix and match geometry types on-the-fly, there is no reason you cannot mix and match any of the previously mentioned methods when building your character. A spline head on a segmented polygonal body with metaball hands might work best for a particular application, while other combinations of techniques may work for others. MAX has many capabilities, so be sure to consider them all when building your characters.

Creating Skeletons for IK

Whenever you build a seamless mesh character, you need to deform that mesh in one way or another. For very simple characters, simple modifiers such as Bend, Twist, or an FFD might work, but typically this is not enough. In most cases, you want to create a skeleton and, along with Physique or Bones Pro, use it as a way to deform the mesh.

NOTE

Physique is sold by Kinetix and a demo version is on the MAX R2 CD. Bones Pro is sold by Digimation. A demo version of the plug-in is available on the accompanying CD.

The skeletons used by these plug-ins are very similar to the bones in a human body. Most digital characters built in this way have thigh bones, shin bones, spines, necks, shoulders, and hips to name a few. Of course, digital skeletons are merely a simplified approximation of the real thing. The human body has dozens of vertebrae in the spine, but a digital skeleton may only have three or four.

Skeletons are put together in much the same way as segmented characters. They are merely objects linked together into a hierarchy. You can build your own skeletons out of MAX's bones or out of simple geometry, such as boxes.

TIP

If you are building a two-legged creature, owners of Character Studio can use the pre-built skeletons supplied with Biped (see Figure 5.10). Building your own skeleton, however, allows you to customize its behavior.

FIGURE 5.10

A biped is a good example of a skeleton, although there are many other ways of building skeletons in MAX.

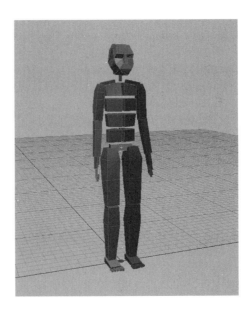

Types of IK

With the introduction of R2, Inverse Kinematics in MAX now comes in two separate flavors:

- **Calculated IK:** This is the same as the previous version of MAX. It enables you to apply IK solutions to hierarchies of linked objects. This is enabled by pressing the IK button on the Button bar. When this button is pressed, the rotational values of the IK solution are put into Track View as rotational keys.

- **Real-time IK:** This is new to R2 and allows for real-time IK solutions needed for professional character animation. Real-time IK is implemented as a controller and the IK button does not need to be toggled in order for the IK solutions to be calculated.

When Real-time IK is used, only the end effector is animated, saving the animator the headache of plowing through rotational keys. Key data is positional, which makes better sense from an animation standpoint. Real-time IK is so ideally suited for character animators that it is the absolute best choice to use when building skeletons.

Types of Skeletons

There are four types of skeletons you can create in MAX:

- **Bone-based skeletons:** Those created using MAX's bones.

- **Object-based skeletons:** Those created by linking objects (typically boxes) hierarchically.

- **Biped skeletons:** As found in Character Studio.

- **Hybrid skeletons:** Any combination of the above methods.

Working with Bone-based Skeletons

MAX's built-in bones are a system of Helper objects that are linked hierarchically. By themselves, they do not deform meshes. In order for that to happen, they need to be linked to the mesh through a plug-in or series of modifiers (explained in the next chapter).

For those wanting to use Real-time IK, bones are required because Real-time IK is implemented as a controller assigned to the bones at creation time. In fact, for character animation, Real-time IK is a necessity, making bones much more of a necessity as well. Although in version 1, most functions of bones were duplicated simply by linking objects hierarchically, Real-time IK sets bones apart from linked objects.

A bone is a tetrahedral Shape object linked hierarchically to other bones in the chain (see Figure 5.11). Any bone can have an effector tied to it, represented by a jack-shaped object. The effector can affect position, rotation, or both and is assigned upon creation or any time later using the IK Controller rollout in the bone's Motion panel.

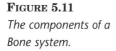

FIGURE 5.11

The components of a Bone system.

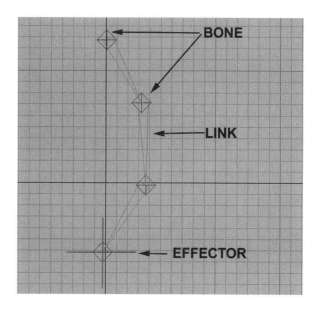

Creating Bones

Bones can be found in the Systems panel. Because of the new features, this panel has changed considerably:

- **Assign to children:** This assigns the IK controller to the children of the chain. Toggling this off makes the bones behave as they did in MAX version 1.x.

- **Assign to root:** This assigns the IK controller to the topmost bone in the chain. The default for this is off.

- **Create end effector:** This creates an effector at the end of the chain, which can then be animated.

The one caveat with the IK controller is that you cannot use it to keyframe a bone's position, rotation, or scaling. This can only be accomplished by linking the bone to another object that has a controller which allows for such keyframing. The next series of exercises illustrates this important point. In the first exercise, you create a simple system of bones to familiarize yourself with the tools.

CREATING BONES

1. Under the Create panel, select Systems.

2. On the Object rollout, select Bones.

3. Make sure Assign to Children, Create End Effector, and Assign to Root are all toggled on. You are now ready to create the bones.

4. Click once in the Left viewport to create the base of the chain.

5. Once the base has been set, move the mouse. As the mouse moves off the base of the chain, a triangular-shaped bone appears and follows the pointer.

6. Anchor the second bone by left-clicking below the first bone.

7. Click again below and to the right of the second bone to anchor the third bone. See Figure 5.12 for a reference. Right-click to end the creation.

FIGURE 5.12

The completed bone chain.

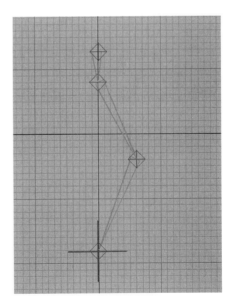

8. You can continue adding bones simply by moving the mouse anywhere in the viewport and left-clicking.

Youshould now have a completed bone chain with an effector at the end, ready to be manipulated. Manipulation is very straighforward. Selecting and translating the effector moves the bone chain. If you translate the top bone, the effector stays in place and the rest of the chain "reaches" for the effector. If you pull the bone linkage far enough away, you see that the chain "tries" to reach the effector.

Keyframing Bone Chains Using the IK Controller

Keyframing the system is simply a matter of toggling the Animate button and moving the effector, which you do in the following exercise.

ANIMATING BONES

1. Continue from the previous exercise. Toggle the Animate button on.

2. Select the effector at the end of the chain.

3. At frame 0, move the effector to set a key.

4. Select the topmost bone (Bone01) and move that to set a key.

5. Move the Time slider to frame 10.

6. Move the effector again to set a second key.

7. Move the Time slider to frame 20.

8. Select the top bone (Bone01) and move that to set a key.

9. Scrub the animation.

If you did this right, you'll notice something wrong. The end effector moves as it should, but the top bone does not accept keyframes and does not move. At first, this may seem odd, but it shows explicitly how the Real-time IK system is set up.

Real-time IK is set up as a controller, like all other controllers, accessible from the Motion panel (see Figure 5.13). If you look in the Motion panel, however, you'll notice this controller operates a bit differently. As mentioned previously, it does not accept position, rotation, or scale keyframes. Its only function is to calculate and solve the IK for the entire chain.

If you turn off Assign to Root when the bone is created, then this is not a problem. Another issue presents itself: The first bone in the chain does not have the IK controller assigned and is not affected along with the rest of the chain by the end effector.

FIGURE 5.13

The IK Controller rollout.

In order for the top of the chain's position to be keyframed, it needs to be linked to an object that has a standard Position/Rotation/Scale (PRS) controller applied. This can be accomplished by linking the top of the chain to an object, such as a dummy. The dummy's position can then be keyframed normally, allowing the top of the chain to be animated.

This problem can also be circumvented when creating the chain by toggling the Assign to Root button in the IK Controller box and adding one extra bone at the top of the chain. This simply assigns a PRS controller to this topmost bone of the chain and places the IK Controller on the rest.

CREATING BONES WITH A KEYFRAMABLE ROOT

1. Under the Create panel, select Systems.

2. On the Object rollout, select Bones.

3. Make sure Assign to Children and Create End Effector are toggled on and Assign to Root is toggled off.

4. Click once in the Left viewport to anchor the first bone.

5. Anchor a second bone immediately below the first.

6. Add a third bone below and to the right of the previous bone.

7. Add a final bone to the chain below and to the left of the previous bone.

Now go back and repeat the previous exercise (on animating bones) with this new chain. This time, the topmost bone is able to be keyframed. The bone can be animated because it has a standard Position/Rotate/Scale controller applied because Assign to Root was left unchecked at creation, allowing for standard keyframes to be set.

As you will see, the bones created in the previous example could be used as a leg bone for the character, with the end effector at the ankle and the top of the chain at the hip. Keyframing the end effector moves the ankle. Keyframing the top of the bone chain raises and lowers the character at the hip while keeping the feet locked.

Building a Basic Skeleton with Bones

The next series of exercises will show how to use MAX's bones to create an animatable two-legged skeleton. The object is to make the skeleton move naturally yet be easy to animate.

One of the things to remember is that skeletons can be assembled in a wide variety of hierarchies and topologies. This particular skeleton is not the only way to build a skeleton, but it will cover most of the major tools.

Creating Legs and Feet

The first thing to do is to create a hierarchy of bones for the legs and feet.

BUILDING LEGS AND FEET FOR A TWO-LEGGED SKELETON

1. Open the Bones Creation panel.

2. Make sure Assign to Children and Assign to Root are toggled on. Toggle Create End Effector off.

3. In the Left viewport, click once to anchor the first bone, then click four more times to create a thigh, shin, foot, and toe bone similar to the shape shown in Figure 5.14.

FIGURE 5.14

The basic leg and foot bone shapes.

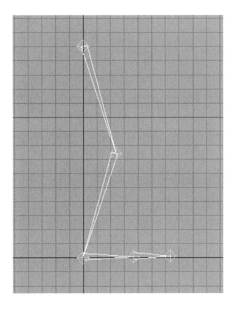

No effectors were created, so moving the bones does nothing but resize them. In order to make the joints bend, effectors need to be added. This can be done through the Motion panel.

4. Open the Motion panel.

5. Select Bone03. This bone ends at the ankle, which is the perfect place for an effector. From the Motion panel, open the IK Controller Parameters rollout. Within the End Effectors box, press Create for both Position and Rotation. The effector appears.

6. Select the effector. Moving the effector bends the leg at the knee. Rotating it rotates the foot.

7. The toe also needs to bend, but it does not need to translate. Select Bone04, at the ball of the foot. From the Motion panel, create an end effector for rotation only.

You now have the basic workings of a leg. The leg can be moved at the ankle, using IK to solve the position of the knee. The foot is manipulated using Forward Kinematics rotating both at the ankle and at the ball of the foot. If you rotate the ankle, notice how the toe retains its direction. This is because of the rotational effector at the ball of the foot that attempts to maintain the direction of the toe.

TIP

For those with an aversion to Forward Kinematics, another popular option would be to delete the rotational effectors at the ankle and toes and add a positional constraint to the end of the foot at Bone05. This locks down the position of the toe, keeping it pinned to the ground as the ankle lifts. When animating, however, keeping the position of the toe and the ankle synchronized can be tricky, so this method is not for everyone.

Rotational Constraints

Oncethe leg is built, it is a good idea to limit the joints so that they behave naturally. The knee, for example, only bends along one axis for about 120 degrees. Similar limits need to be added to the toe and ankle as well.

Rotational constraints are set by selecting the IK button in the Hierarchy panel. This gives you a series of rollouts that allow you to constrain the behavior of the individual joints, as well as bind bones so that they follow other objects, such as linking a character's hands to a steering wheel, for instance. The following exercise steps you through adding limits to the joints.

ADDING ROTATIONAL LIMITS

1. Continue from the previous exercise. Open the Hierarchy panel then select the IK button.

2. From the Left viewport, select Bone02, which represents the knee.

3. Open the Rotational Joints rollout (see Figure 5.15). From here, you see that the joint is active only along the x-axis. Toggle the Limited box so it is checked.

FIGURE 5.15

The Rotational Joints rollout.

4. Adjust the From: and To: spinners so that the knee bends naturally. The exact values vary depending on how the knee was created, but the general range should be from about 150 to 180 degrees. Notice how the limits are displayed graphically in the viewport.

5. Move the effector at the ankle to test the motion of the knee.

6. Select the Ankle (Bone03) and adjust this joint so that it moves approximately 30 degrees on either side of center.

7. Do the same for the toe (Bone04). This joint should bend up to 45 degrees above center and perhaps 15 degrees below.

8. Rotate the ankle joint. Notice what happens when the joint hits its limit—the rotation actually moves the foot.

You now have a fairly operational leg. The knee can be bent by moving the top of the leg at the hip, or the bottom of the leg at the ankle. The ankle tries to maintain its orientation to the ground and is keyframed by rotational values only. On the CD is a version of this basic leg. The file is named 05max01.MAX.

Finishing the Lower Body

The next step is to duplicate this leg to create the left leg and add some hips to finish the lower body.

ADDING HIPS

1. To keep track of things, the bones should be renamed to reflect their position and function. Rename the bones using the following table.

Bone01	R_Hip
Bone02	R_Knee
Bone03	R_Ankle
Bone04	R_Ball
Bone05	R_Toe

2. From the Front viewport, select all the bones and duplicate them by holding down the Shift key and dragging the bones to the right.

3. One thing you will notice is that when you drag this new left leg, the ankle effector remains in place under the right leg. This is because the effector is not an object, but a controller. It is copied with the associated bone but does not translate until it is reselected. Select and move this effector so that it is placed under the left.

4. Go through the bones in this leg and rename them according to the scheme outlined above, substituting the letter L for the letter R.

5. Now add some hips. For this skeleton, a simple dummy will suffice. From the Create panel, select Helpers and then Dummy. Click and drag halfway between the hips of both legs and create a Dummy object. Name this object Pelvis. The skeleton should look like Figure 5.16.

6. Next the hips need to be linked to the Pelvis. Select R_Hip and L_Hip; then press the Select and Link button from the Button bar. Drag the pointer over the dummy and release.

FIGURE 5.16

The lower body skeleton.

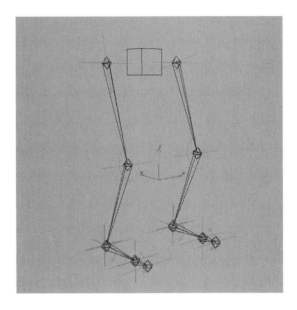

7. Select the hips and, from the front view, move them to the left and right. Notice how the legs do not bend at the hips and the feet slide. This is because, by default, bones are limited in their motion to only one axis.

8. To fix this, simply go to the Hierarchy panel and select the IK button. In the Rotational Joints rollout, toggle the x-, y-, and z-axes all on.

Now, when you move the hips, the feet remain in place. If you want to further tweak this, you can add X, Y, and Z limits to the hip joints. Unless your character is doing gymnastics, this is probably not required.

Creating the Bones for the Upper Body

Now that the legs and hips are in place, it's time to create the upper body. The big decision for the upper body is whether to manipulate the spine via Inverse Kinematics or via Forward Kinematics. The choices depend to a great extent on how you plan to animate. The IK Spine is easier to manipulate, while the Forward Kinematic spine gives you a much higher degree of control and, with a couple of expressions, can be reasonably easy to manipulate. To satisfy everyone, the next exercise discusses how to create both.

BUILDING AN IK SPINE

1. To make the spinal column, three bones should suffice. From the left view, draw three bones to represent the spine. For a more natural pose, put a slight forward arc in the backbone as in Figure 5.17. Be sure to draw these away from the skeleton so they don't become automatically attached.

FIGURE 5.17

The spine should have three bones and bend forward in a slight arc.

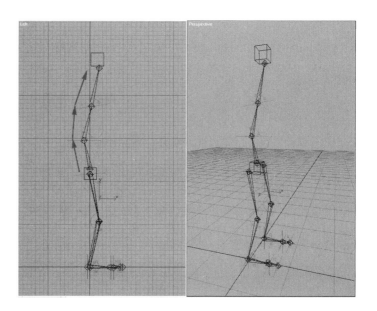

TIP

If you anchor a bone chain near the base of another bone chain, MAX tries to connect the two as one hierarchy. To avoid this, draw the chain away from the skeleton, then move the bones into place after they are drawn.

2. Go through the chain and rename the bones Spine_01, Spine_02, Spine_03, and Spine_04.

3. Select all the bones in the spine and move the chain so the base is centered on the hips.

4. Select and link the base of the spine (Spine_01) to the pelvis.

5. Create a dummy and position it at the top of the spine. Rename the dummy Spine_Top.

6. Select and link Spine_Top to the pelvis.

Now comes the trick. The top of the Spine needs to be controlled via IK, so you'll use the Dummy object Spine_Top as the controlling object using IK Bind.

7. Select the top of the Spine (Spine_04) and open Hierarchy/IK. In the Bind To Follow Object box, select the Bind button and from the Front viewport, drag the pin to Spine_Top and release.

8. Since the Dummy object Spine_Top is linked to the pelvis, it moves with the body. It can also be repositioned to bend and manipulate the position of the spine. Select the dummy and move it from the Left viewport to test this out.

9. From the Front viewport, move the dummy Spine_Top left and right. Notice how the spine does not follow, which is because the joints are limited.

10. First, it's a good idea to lock down the motion of the base of the spine. In real life, the lower vertebrae of the back move less than the upper vertebrae. The easiest way to simulate this is by completely limiting the rotation of this joint. Select Spine01 and from the IK panel make all the joints inactive by deselecting the Active button in the Rotational Joints rollout.

11. Next, limit the upper motion of the spine. The spine needs to bend forward and back, and also from side to side. From the bone's IK panel, select Spine02 and limit its motion in the x- and y-axes. Again, the exact numbers depend on how the spine was originally drawn, but limit the joint so the spine bends forward in X about 30 to 40 degrees and back by five to 10 degrees. On the y-axis, it should move 30 degrees to the left and right.

12. Once these are set, you can copy these values to Spine03 simply by using the Rotational Joints Copy and Paste buttons. You may need to adjust these, depending on how the skeleton was built.

The spine is now complete. After manipulating the dummy, the spine bends to match (see Figure 5.18). Since the dummy is linked to the hips, it moves with them, allowing the spine to retain its posture even as the character moves.

FIGURE 5.18
Manipulating the
dummy bends the
spine.

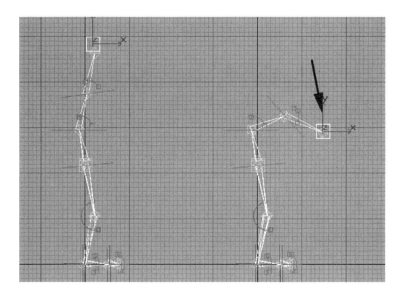

For those who need more accuracy in posing a character, Forward Kinematics is a good alternative. Forward Kinematics simply means animating the joints through rotation. In this case, the spine is simple.

The easiest way to build and visualize this form of spine is with boxes. This also goes to show that objects other than bones can be incorporated seamlessly into skeletons with MAX. Any type of object from bones to teapots can be used as the structure with which to deform a mesh.

BUILDING AN FK SPINE

1. Create a simple, narrow box that is approximately one-third the distance from the pelvis to the shoulder. Call this object Spine01.

2. Since this is going to be a bone, it does not need to be rendered. It is a good idea to turn it off to the renderer at this point. This is done from the Properties menu. Right-click Spine01 and select Properties. In the Rendering Control Box, toggle Renderable, Cast Shadows, and Receive Shadows all off.

3. With Spine01 selected, from the Hierarchy panel select Pivot.

4. Toggle the Affect Pivot Only button on and reposition the pivot at the bottom center of the box.

5. Press Align to World to orient the pivot to World space. Toggle Affect Pivot Only off.

6. Position Spine01 immediately above the Pelvis object.

7. Duplicate Spine01 by shift-clicking and dragging up along the y-axis. Name this Spine02.

8. Position Spine02 directly above Spine01.

9. Copy Spine02 to create Spine03. Place this above Spine02.

10. Assemble the hierarchy. From the Button bar, toggle Select and Link on. Select Spine03, drag the link to Spine02, and release.

11. In the same manner, link spine02 to Spine 01, and Spine01 to Pelvis.

This completes a basic spine (see Figure 5.19). As you probably have noticed, it is simply a hierarchy of boxes that act as bones. These boxes can be animated directly simply by selecting and rotating them to position the spine correctly.

FIGURE 5.19

A Forward Kinematic spine can be made out of a few simple boxes.

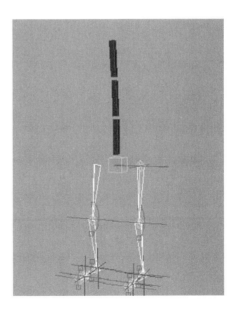

Using Sliders to Control a Spine

When you have a series of joints, such as this spine, keyframing each individual joint can become tedious. Typically, the spine bends evenly along its length. You can use this little tidbit to write a series of expressions to help control the spine with expressions and make it bend evenly.

This next exercise makes the process less tedious. The exercise sets up three sliders that each control the X, Y, and Z rotation of the spine evenly. First, you need to make the slider objects—Text objects make good sliders. Because they're splines, they don't render and the text automatically labels them.

CONTROLLING THE ROTATION OF THE SPINE

1. From the front viewport, create a Text object named Spine_X_Rot. In the Text field, type the letter **X** in 20 point type to give it a label.

2. With the object Spine_X_Rot still selected, open the Motion panel. Under Assign Controller, select the position controller and assign the Position XYZ controller.

3. Copy the object Spine_X_Rot twice, naming the resulting objects **Spine_Y_Rot** and **Spine_Z_Rot**. In the Text fields of these, replace the text with **Y** and **Z**, respectively.

4. Select the object Spine01. From the Motion panel, under the Assign Controller rollout, select the Rotation controller and change it to Euler XYZ by pressing the Assign Controller button. Euler XYZ simply segments the vector (XYZ) value of the rotation into three separate X, Y, and Z scalar values (see Figure 5.20).

5. Repeat this operation for Spine02 and Spine03.

6. Starting with Spine03, enter the expressions. Open Track View and select the X Rotation Controller for Spine03. Assign a Float Expression Controller.

7. Open the Properties panel for this controller, which brings up the Expression Controller dialogue.

8. Create a scalar variable named Xrot. Assign this to the controller Spine_X_Rot/Y position.

9. Enter the expression **Xrot/100** (the expression is divided by 100 to give a bit of play in the slider).

FIGURE 5.20

Three Text objects con-
trol the motion of the
spine.

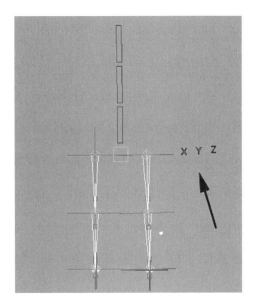

10. Manipulate the slider in Y. The Spine03 bone should now rotate around X.

11. This is the basic expression for all the bones. Since the Expression controllers for all the Rotation parameters in the spine links are the same, you can use the Copy/Paste functions available in Track View.

12. While in Track View, expand the Spine01 object.

13. Under Transform, select the Rotation field.

14. Click the Copy Controller button.

15. Now expand the Spine02 and Spine 03 objects and select the Rotation field for each object.

16. Click the Paste Controller button, and the bones now have the same controller.

Once this is done, manipulating one slide will move three bones.

17. Repeat steps 5 through 16 for the Y rotations of all three bones, substituting Spine_Y_Rot for the controlling object.

18. Do the same for the Z rotations with Spine_Z_Rot.

When complete, there should be a total of nine expressions, three for each of the three bones. When animating, this set of expressions reduces what was originally nine sets of keyframes down to three, which simplifies the animation process considerably—the goal of a good setup.

Building Shoulders and Arms

However you build the spine, the shoulders and arms can be built in the same manner. The shoulders will be simple boxes, while the arms will be bones that use the IK controller. In between the shoulders and tops of the arms, dummies are used to aid in keyframing the position of the upper arms.

CREATING SHOULDERS AND ARMS

1. Create a narrow box for the right shoulder. The box should be long enough to place the edge of the shoulders past the edge of the hips. Name this object **R_Shoulder**.

2. From the Hierarchy panel, select Pivot and toggle Affect Pivot Only. Adjust the pivot of R_Shoulder so it rests on the edge of the box closest to the spine.

3. Duplicate this object and rename it **L_Shoulder**. Position it on the opposite side of the spine.

4. From the Hierarchy panel, select Pivot and toggle Affect Pivot Only. Adjust the pivot of L_Shoulder so it rests on the edge of the box closest to the spine (see Figure 5.21).

5. Select and link both R_Shoulder and L_Shoulder to the object Spine03 (or for those using IK - Spine_Top).

6. Create a dummy named R_Arm_Top and position it at the outer edge of the right shoulder. Create a second dummy named L_Arm_Top and position it at the outer edge of the left shoulder.

7. From the Creation panel, select Systems/Bones. With Assign to Children toggled on and Assign to Root and Create End Effector toggled off, draw a two-bone chain in the Left viewport to create a similar arm. Use Figure 5.22 as a guide. The arms should be long enough so that, when fully extended, the wrists are at waist level.

FIGURE 5.21

The shoulders are positioned so the arms hang just outside the hips.

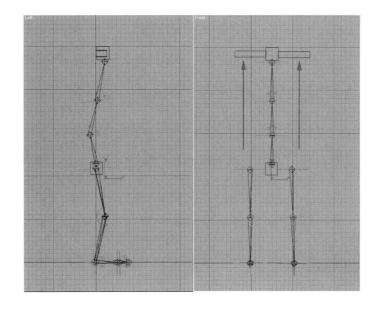

FIGURE 5.22

The arm bones are drawn with a slight bend.

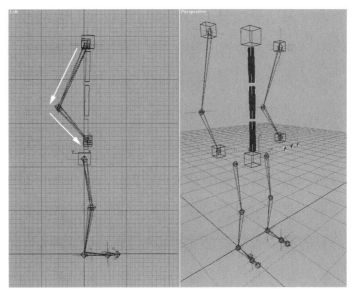

8. From the Front viewport, position these bones at the edge of the shoulders.

9. Duplicate these bones to make the left arm.

10. Select and link the top of the right arm to R_Arm_Top. Do the same for the left arm and L_Arm_Top.

11. Select the bone that represents the right forearm. From the Motion panel, create a Position End effector for the arm.

12. Repeat the previous step for the left arm.

13. The skeleton is almost complete. Select the pelvis and move it. Notice how the ends of the arms stay locked in space. The arms should probably move with the body. To accomplish this, the end effectors need to be linked to a point on the body so that they move along with it.

14. Select the end effector for the right arm. From the Motion panel, toggle Link and select the top of the spine. Do the same for the left arm. The arms now move with the spine as it is bent. The pelvis is another point to which these can be linked. Figure 5.23 shows the final skeletons.

FIGURE 5.23

The finished skeleton on the left is the IK-controlled skeleton, on the right is the Expression-controlled skeleton.

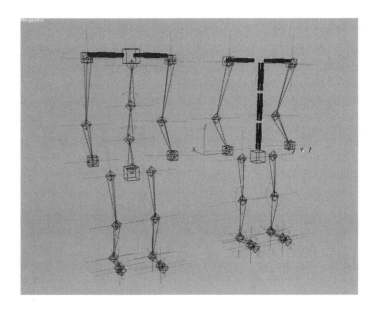

On the CD are two skeletons, one with an IK-controlled spine named 05max02.MAX, and another with an Expression-controlled spine named 05max03.MAX.

Creating a Four-Legged Skeleton

The four-legged skeleton is actually similar to the two-legged skeleton in that it can be built with a combination of bones and boxes. The actual configuration of the bones is a bit different than humans. While two-legged creatures walk on their heels and toes, four-legged creatures walk on their toes. The heel becomes a major joint of the leg, giving the limb three joints. The front legs are similar in that four-legged creatures walk on their fingers, making the wrist a major joint as well. Figure 5.24 shows the bone structure of a quadruped.

FIGURE 5.24

The limbs of a four-legged creature.

The center of gravity is also slightly different for a four-legged beast. Instead of being located at the hips, it is further up on the body, roughly centered between the front and back legs. This may cause you to set up the hierarchy of a quadrupedal skeleton slightly differently. Because both the front and back legs move equally, the hierarchy can be set up with the center of the spine as the parent. The following exercise walks you through building a basic skeleton that can be adapted quite easily to most four-legged creatures, such as dogs, cats, and horses.

BUILDING A QUADRUPED

1. From the Create panel, select Systems/Bones. Turn on Assign to Children, Assign to Root, and Create End Effector.

2. From the Left viewport, create a back leg skeleton. This is done by drawing a simple three-bone skeleton in the shape shown in Figure 5.25.

FIGURE 5.25

Back leg skeleton.

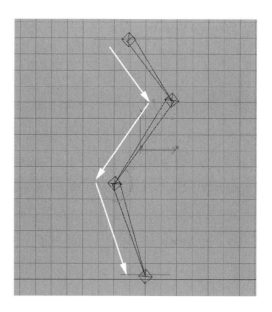

3. Rename the bones according to the following list:

   Bone01   R_Rear_01

   Bone02   R_Rear_02

   Bone03   R_Rear_03

   Bone04   R_Rear_04

4. Set the joint limits from the IK menu in the Hierarchy panel according to the table below.

	X from/to	Y from/to	Z from/to
R_Rear_01	active	inactive	active
R_Rear_02	60/-30	inactive	inactive
R-Rear_03	-120/20	inactive	inactive

5. Select all the bones and copy them using Shift-drag from the Front viewport. Position these as the left rear leg. Rename these bones **L_Rear_01**, **L_Rear_02**, and so on.

6. Create the front legs. From the Left viewport, draw a three-bone skeleton in the shape shown in Figure 5.26. If you notice, this shape is a mirror opposite of the back leg.

FIGURE 5.26

Front leg skeleton.

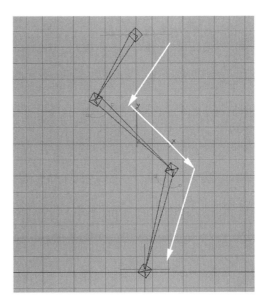

7. Rename these bones **R_Front_01**, **R_Front_02**, and so on.

8. Set the joint limits for this set of bones according to the table below.

	X	Y	Z
	from/to	from/to	from/to
R_Front_01	active	inactive	active
R_Front_02	60/-40	inactive	inactive
R_Front_03	60/-40	inactive	inactive

9. Duplicate this to make the front left leg. From the Front viewport, position these in front of the left rear leg bones. Rename these bones accordingly.

10. Make some shoulders by creating a long, thin box that bridges the gap between the top of the front legs. Rename this **Front_Shoulder**. Copy this to create an identical bone named **Rear_Hips** and position that between the tops of the back legs.

11. Select and link the tops of the front legs to Front_Shoulder and the tops of the back legs to Rear_Hips.

12. From the Left viewport, create three thin boxes for the spine. Name these **Spine_Rear**, **Spine_Cent**, and **Spine_Front**, respectively. When finished, the hips, spine, and shoulders should look like Figure 5.27.

FIGURE 5.27

The basic skeleton for the body.

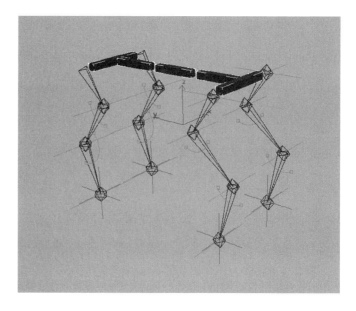

13. Select and link Front_Shoulder to Spine_Front, and Rear_Hips to Spine_Rear.

14. Select and link Spine_Front and Spine_Rear to Spine_Cent. This is different than in a two-legged skeleton, which has its parent at the hips—near the center of gravity for most two-legged characters. In a four-legged skeleton, the center of gravity is usually halfway between the shoulders and the hips.

15. This is the basic skeleton. If you want to add some bones to make a tail, you may do so by copying the spinal bones.

16. A neck may also be created by copying one of the spinal bones. A head may also be a bone, or the actual geometry of the head, depending on your animation requirements.

An example of this skeleton is found on the CD (05max04.max) and is illustrated in Figure 5.28.

FIGURE 5.28

The finished skeleton.

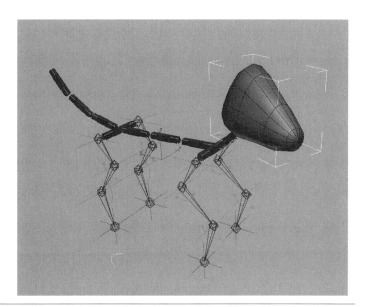

Six-Legged Skeleton

Keyframing six legs can be quite tedious, so the procedure can be sped up quite significantly using MAX's expressions. Expressions allow you to create mathematical relationships between objects. In the case of insect legs, the rotation of one leg can easily control the actions of the other five.

The key to making an expression-driven insect work is that insect legs follow a very predictable pattern. As described earlier, the rotations on each row of legs simply mirrors the rotations of the row in front of it. Additionally, the left side of legs mirrors the rotations on the right. These simple rules make it quite easy to set up a series of expressions that can make one leg drive many.

For the following exercise, load the file BUGEXP01.MAX. This file contains a very simple "bug." The body is a simple box, as are the legs. This particular bug only has one leg, which needs to be duplicated to create the other five. Before the leg is duplicated, however, it needs to be properly positioned and aligned to the world.

POSITIONING LEGS ON A SIX-LEGGED CHARACTER

1. Position the leg so that it is slightly bent with the "knee" slightly above the body of the insect. A bent knee gives the insect a more relaxed and realistic pose (see Figure 5.29).

FIGURE 5.29

The proper positioning of the leg and the pivots.

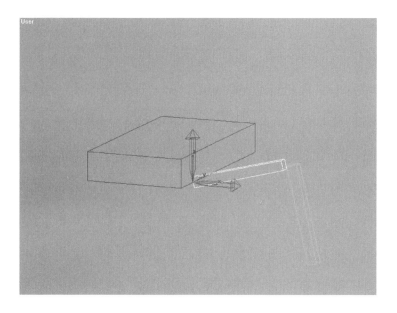

2. In the Hierarchy panel, select Affect Pivot Only and press Align to World. This simply puts the pivots in World space, which makes each leg movement work along the same axis as the body.

Rotations around the leg's local z-axis move the leg forward and back. Rotations along the local y-axis lift the leg off the ground and also plant it. Local X rotation twists the leg. The two primary rotations used in walking are the Y and Z rotations. The legs must move back and forth along Z to propel the insect forward. Additionally, legs must rotate along Y to lift and plant the feet.

Since Y and Z rotations of the leg need to be isolated to create the expressions, the leg must be assigned the Euler XYZ rotation controller. This is the only controller that separates the X, Y, and Z components of the rotation.

3. To assign this, simply select the object Leg01, the upper part of the first leg, and within the Motion panel, open the Assign Controller rollout and assign the Euler XYZ controller to the leg.

To make the expressions easier to construct, all six of the insect's legs need to have their x-, y-, and z-axes aligned in the same fashion. The easiest way to make sure the legs are aligned properly is to simply clone the first leg to create the others.

4. From the Top viewport, select both leg joints (Leg01, Leg02) and clone them to create the two other legs on the right side.

5. Now create the left legs from the right. Select all the legs on the right side and press the Mirror Selected Objects button. Select the x-axis as the Mirror axis and create copies of the right legs.

6. Position the left legs along the left side of the insect's body. When they are finished, they should look like Figure 5.30.

Now that the legs are in position and properly aligned with the Euler XYZ controllers assigned, they can be assigned individual expressions.

7. Select the upper joint of the second right leg. This joint mirrors the rotations of the front right leg. When the front right leg rotates forward along Z, the second right rotates back. When the front right leg plants itself on the ground, the second right lifts. This is accomplished by multiplying the controlling leg's rotation by -1.

FIGURE 5.30

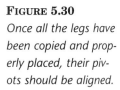

Once all the legs have been copied and properly placed, their pivots should be aligned.

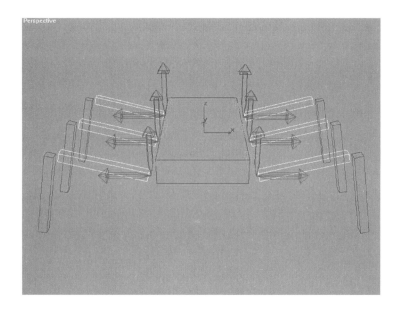

8. Open Track View. Select the track for the second right leg's (Leg04) Z rotation. Change the Controller type to Float Expression. Open the Properties panel to get the Expression Controller dialog.

9. Within the Expression Controller dialog, create a scalar variable named Leg01Z and assign this to the Z rotation controller for the front right leg (Leg01).

10. Enter the expression **-Leg01Z**. This makes the second right leg's Z rotation exactly opposite the front right (see Figure 5.31).

11. Evaluate the expression and close the dialog.

12. Select the front right leg and rotate it around its local z-axis. The second right leg should mirror it exactly.

13. Repeat this procedure for the Y rotation of the second right leg. Create a scalar variable named Leg01Y and assign this variable to the Z Rotation controller for the front right leg (Leg01). Create the expression -Leg01Z in the Expression box and evaluate. The leg's Y rotation will now follow the front right leg.

FIGURE 5.31

The Expression Controller dialog with the expression for the leg rotation entered.

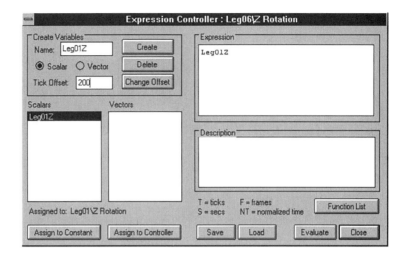

14. Work your way around the body, creating expressions for every leg. Each set of legs mirrors the one in front of it and the left side mirrors the right. Remember that the left legs were created by mirroring the right legs, so their rotations will automatically be mirrored as well, making their expressions the same as their corresponding right legs. The expressions are listed in the following table.

LEG	EXPRESSIONS
Second Right	-Leg01Z ; -Leg01Y
Third Right	Leg01Z ; Leg01Y
Front Left	Leg01Z ; Leg01Y
Second Left	-Leg01Z ; -Leg01Y
Third Left	Leg01Z ; Leg01Y

Once all 10 expressions are written, moving the front right leg moves all the rest in perfect sync. The file BUGEXP02.MAX is included on the CD as a reference. It has all these expressions in place.

Of course, no living creature, including insects, is perfect, so this method does have its limitations when compared to purely keyframing the animation by hand. The limitations are that the legs may seem too perfect, because they move in lockstep. One way to get around this limitation is to add a Tick Offset for each succeeding row of legs. This makes each row of legs move at a slight delay for each step, adding a realistic touch. The Tick Offset is found along with each expression in the Expression Controller dialog, accessed by clicking the Properties panel within Track View. Each variable in the expression created within the dialog can have its own offset.

Recall that each tick is exactly 1/4800th of a second, so a good tick offset would be in the range of one to three frames, or approximately 200 to 600 ticks, depending on the frame rate. Because the tick value is time-driven, the effects only show up when animated. Once the expressions have been set up, animating a walk cycle is quite easy. The front leg simply needs to be moved forward and back in a walking motion, as in the previous section, and the rest of the legs follow.

One other way to create a similar insect walk is to write the expressions so that both front legs are involved. The front left leg controls the second right and the third left, while the front right leg controls the second left and the third right. This forces animation to be created for two legs, but the front legs can have slightly varying motions, which can add to the realism of the shot. Adding a tick offset to each succeeding row of legs can also add another touch of realism. As can be surmised, using expressions to help drive walks has quite a few other possibilities, so the rest is left up to your imagination.

In Practice: Setting Up Characters and Skeletons

- **Geometry Types:** Polygons, patches, and NURBS can be used for creating organic, seamless characters. Deciding on the right geometry depends a great deal on your project's requirements and your own experience. Some plug-ins do not support all geometry types, particularly NURBS. This may force your decision.

- **Using Stand-Ins:** Some animators use segmented characters as stand-ins for increased performance. The segments are linked directly to a skeleton, which in turn deforms a seamless mesh. The seamless mesh is hidden during animation and is brought out for rendering.

- **Inverse Kinematics:** Inverse Kinematics is a great tool, but not for every situation. Many animators use Inverse Kinematics for the lower body only and prefer to use Forward Kinematics for the spine and arms.

- **Expressions:** Expressions can make the most difficult skeleton easy to animate. Complex structures such as wings, tails, and hands can be automated with the proper planning. Experiment and use expressions whenever possible.

- **MAXScript:** MAXScript takes expressions several steps further. MAXScript can be used to write custom animation controllers for even more control over your characters. It can also be used to create custom interfaces to control your characters.

Chapter 6

ANIMATING WALKING

A character's walk conveys a great deal about his personality. The next time you are in a crowded place, notice all the different types of walks that people have. Some people waddle, others saunter, and some drag their feet. It is amazing how almost everyone you see has a unique walk. Mae West, Groucho Marx, John Wayne, and Charlie Chaplin were all characters who had very distinctive walks. If you want to know who a character is, figure out how that character walks.

This chapter covers the following topics:

- The mechanics of walking

- Animating a two-legged walk

- Creating a four-legged walk

- Creating a six-legged walk

- Using animated links

The Mechanics of Walking

Walking has been described as controlled falling. Every time someone takes a step, he or she actually leans forward and falls slightly, only to be caught by his outstretched foot. After a foot touches the ground, the body's weight is transferred to it and the knee bends to absorb the shock. The leg then lifts the body and propels it forward as the opposite leg swings up to catch the body again—and the cycle repeats.

Walks are very complex. Not only do the feet have to move across the ground but the hips, spine, arms, shoulders, and head all move in sync to maintain balance in the system. Though complex, if you break down each of these movements joint by joint, the mechanics of walking become clear.

The Feet and Legs

The feet and legs propel the body forward. To keep your character looking natural, you should always keep the joints bent slightly, even at full leg extension. The walk usually starts with the feet at the extended position—where the feet are farthest apart. This is the point where the character's weight shifts to the forward foot (see Figure 6.1).

As the weight of the body is transferred to the forward foot, the knee bends to absorb the shock. This is called the *recoil* position and is the lowest point in the walk (see Figure 6.2).

FIGURE 6.1

The walk starts with the feet extended.

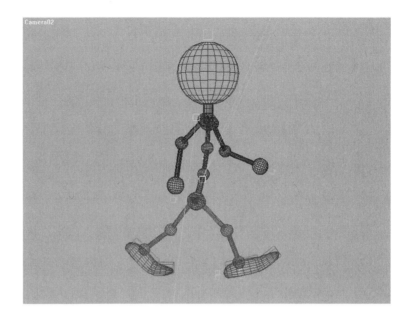

FIGURE 6.2

When the foot plants, the knee bends to absorb the shock.

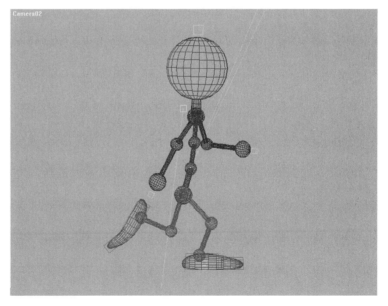

This is halfway through the first step. As the character moves forward, the knee straightens and lifts the body to its highest point. This is called the *passing* position because this is where the free foot passes the supporting leg (see Figure 6.3).

FIGURE 6.3

As one foot passes the other, the knee straightens to full extension, lifting the body.

As the character moves forward, the weight-bearing foot lifts off the ground at the heel, transferring the force at the ball of the foot. The body now starts to fall forward. The free foot swings forward like a pendulum to meet the ground (see Figure 6.4).

FIGURE 6.4

As the weight is transferred from one foot to the other, the body falls forward as the free leg swings forward to catch it.

The free leg makes contact. Half the cycle has been completed (see Figure 6.5). The second half is an exact mirror of the first. If it differs, the character might appear to limp.

FIGURE 6.5

As the weight is transferred from one foot to the other, the body falls forward a bit.

The Hips, Spine, and Shoulders

The body's center of gravity is at the hips—all balance starts there, as does the rest of the body's motion. During a walk, it is best to think of the hips' motion as two separate, overlapping rotations. First, the hips rotate along the axis of the spine, forward and back with the legs. If the right leg is forward, the right hip is rotated forward as well. Second, at the passing position, the free leg pulls the hip out of center, forcing the hips to rock from side to side. These two motions are then transmitted through the spine to the shoulders, which mirror the hips to maintain balance.

When the feet are fully extended, the hips must rotate along the axis of the spine. To keep balance, the shoulders swing in the opposite direction. From the front, the spine is relatively straight. From the top, however, you can see how the hips and shoulders twist in opposite directions to maintain balance (see Figure 6.6).

FIGURE 6.6

From the top, the rotation of the hips and shoulders is apparent.

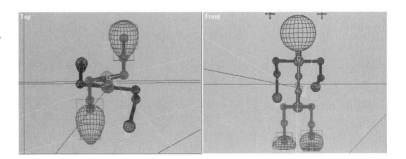

At the passing position, the front view shows the hip being pulled out of center by the weight of the free leg, which causes a counter-rotation in the shoulders. From the top, however, the hips and shoulders are at nearly equal angles to each other (see Figure 6.7).

FIGURE 6.7

As one leg passes the other, the hips are even when viewed from above but skewed when viewed from the front.

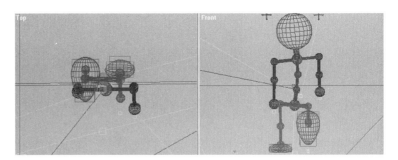

At the extension of the second leg, the hips and shoulders again are flat when viewed from the front. Looking from above, however, you can see that the hips and shoulders have completed their rotation (see Figure 6.8).

FIGURE 6.8

When the weight shifts from one foot to the other, the hips are again twisted when viewed from above— and even when viewed from the front.

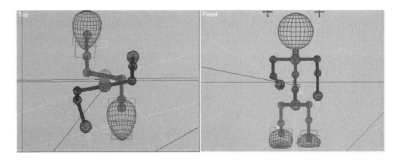

The Arms

Unless the character is using his arms, they generally hang loose at the sides. In this case, they tend to act like pendulums, dragging a few frames behind the hips and shoulders. If the character is running, the arms might pump quite a bit and lead the action by a few frames. Even at full extension, the arms should be slightly bent at the elbows. This keeps them looking natural.

The Head

In a standard walk, the head generally tries to stay level, with the eyes focused on where the character is going. The head then bobs around slightly to stay balanced. If a character is excited, this bobbing is more pronounced. The head might also hang low for a sad character or might look around if the scene requires it.

Body Posture and Emotion

The character's body posture also changes, depending on the character's mood. A happy character arches his back, puts his chest out proudly, and swings his arms jauntily (see Figure 6.9); however, a sad character might slump over, barely swing his arms, and hang his head low (see Figure 6.10). If a character is running scared, he might lean forward quite a bit and push his arms out in front of him, trying to escape the danger (see Figure 6.11). A character who is sneaking around might walk on tiptoe while keeping his hands at the ready (see Figure 6.12). These postures translate beyond walking and should also be used as examples for portraying emotion in non-locomotive scenes.

FIGURE 6.9

A happy character arches his back and sticks out his chest proudly.

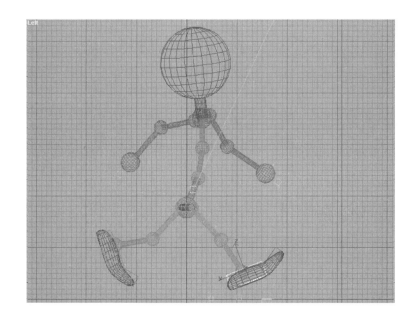

FIGURE 6.10

A sad character hangs his head low and slumps over.

Left

FIGURE 6.11

A character who is running scared leans forward to try to escape the danger.

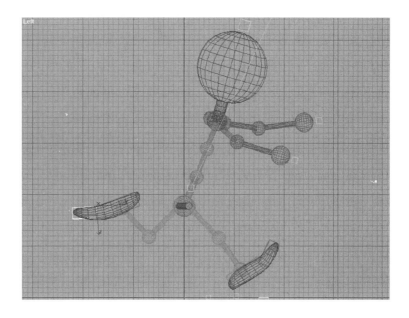

FIGURE 6.12

A sneaky character might walk on tiptoe.

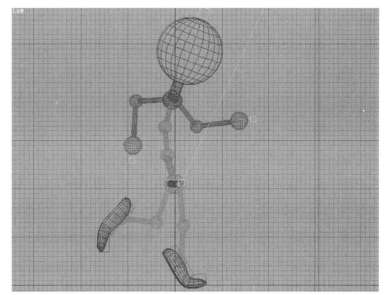

Animating a Two-Legged Walk

For walks, the arms are probably best animated by using forward rather than Inverse Kinematics. This is because the arms usually swing free rather than aim for a specific target (such as when the character is lifting an object.) You can set up Forward Kinematics on the arms using one of two methods. First, the arms can simply be constructed out of simple boxes that are hierarchically linked (see Figure 6.13). These can be animated quite easily by rotating the bones to get the swing of the arms.

FIGURE 6.13

Arms constructed out of simple boxes can be animated by using Forward Kinematics.

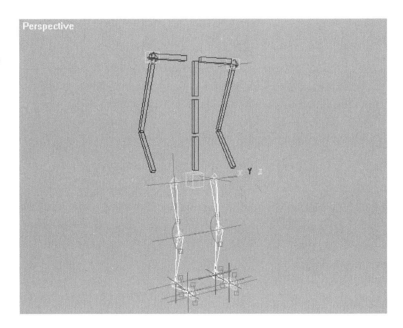

Second, the arms can be constructed out of bones. Typically, bones are geared for IK, but they can also be used for Forward Kinematics. This is accomplished through the Motion panel by deleting the Position end effectors. Because only the ends of the chain can be animated, rotational effectors can be added within the chain to provide the required control (see Figures 6.14 and 6.15).

FIGURE 6.14

*An arm made out of
bones can be rotated
at the root.*

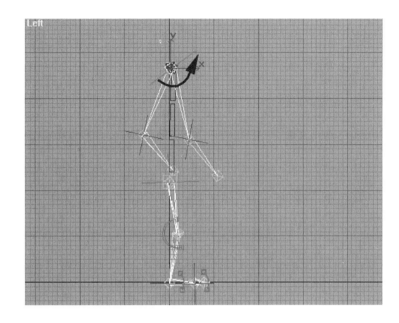

FIGURE 6.15

*A rotation-only end
effector can be used to
rotate the arm at the
elbow.*

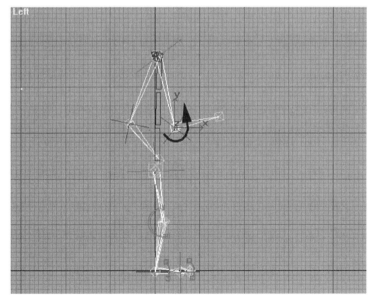

Creating a Two-Legged Walk

This exercise utilizes the new IK features of MAX R2 to animate a simple
walk and relies heavily on the use of end effectors on the legs to keep the
feet locked to the ground. The exercise uses a skeleton almost identical to

the skeleton created in the previous chapter with one minor difference. The arms in this skeleton are configured for Forward Kinematics as opposed to Inverse Kinematics.

Animating the Legs

The legs are usually the best place to start when animating a walk. The positions of the legs and hips will drive the position of the upper body.

THE LEGS

1. Open the file 06max01.max from the CD-ROM. This scene contains a simple skeleton with the legs controlled by IK, the arms controlled by Forward Kinematics, and the spine controlled via a set of expressions.

2. Move the time slider to frame 0. Toggle the Animate button to On.

3. The walk starts with the left leg, which is manipulated at the ankle. Select the effector L_Ankle and move it forward 200 units.

4. The effector moves, but the leg stops short of the target (see Figure 6.16). This is because the hips need to move halfway between the two legs. Select the object Hip and move it forward 100 units and down about 30 units (see Figure 6.17).

FIGURE 6.16

When the end effector is first moved, the leg stops short.

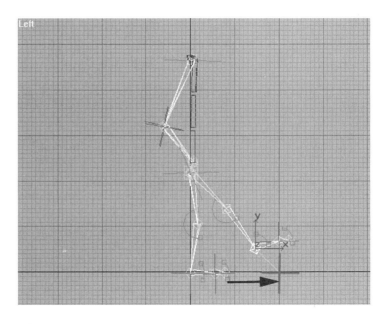

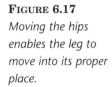
FIGURE 6.17

Moving the hips enables the leg to move into its proper place.

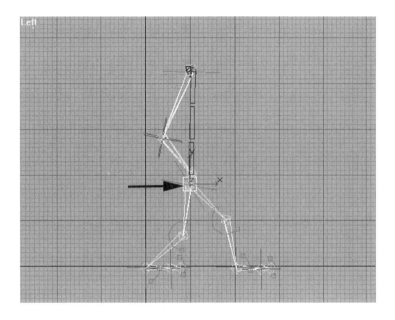

5. This is a good start for the first position of the feet. Continue to sketch out the remaining foot positions. Select the effector R_Ankle. On frame 0, set a key to register the foot's initial position. The key can be set by moving the effector slightly or by right-clicking the Time slider to pull up the Create Key dialog and pressing OK.

6. The walk takes 16 frames per step. Scrub the Time slider to frame 16, which is the start of the right step. Move the R_Ankle effector 400 units forward.

7. Again, the leg stops short of the mark because of the hips. To compensate, move the hips forward 200 units in X.

8. Scrub the animation. The right leg appears to slide across the floor. If your character is shuffling, this might be acceptable, but for this walk, we want the leg to lift off the ground. Move the time slider to frame 8, halfway through the first step. Select R_Ankle and move it up approximately 60 units.

9. At the halfway point of the step, the hips are also at their highest point (see Figure 6.18). Move the hips up approximately 40 units. Scrubbing the animation now gives a very simple step.

FIGURE 6.18

At the halfway point, the hips are also at their highest point.

10. The step can be further modified to add realism. Move the slider to frame 4. This is the recoil position where the left leg fully absorbs the weight of the body and the leg pushes up. The hips are at the lowest position at this point. Move the hips down approximately 50 units at this point. Scrub the animation to notice how the left leg seems to lift the hips off the ground.

11. To lock down the feet for the next step, create a position key for L_Ankle at frame 16.

12. The basics of this first step are complete. Repeat steps 3–10 for the right leg, creating a second step starting on frame 16 and ending on frame 32. The top of this step should occur at frame 24 and the recoil position at frame 20.

Animating the Hips

You can further modify the walk by adding the proper rotation to the hips. The hips rotate forward with the legs and also rock side to side as the free leg pulls it out of center.

HIP ROTATIONS

1. First, animate the forward rotation and go to the first frame of the animation. Select the hips. From the Top viewport, rotate the hips 10 degrees around the vertical, or Z, axis so that the left side of the hip is forward.

2. Move the Time slider to frame 16. Rotate the hips back 20 degrees so that the right side of the hip is forward 10 degrees.

3. Move the Time slider to frame 32. Rotate the hips forward 20 degrees to match the pose on frame 0 (another way to do this would be to copy the key from within Track View).

4. Now get the side-to-side motion of the hips. Move the Time slider to frame 8. This is the top of the left step, where the right leg is off the ground. The weight of this leg pulls the hip out of center. From the Front viewport, rotate the hip along the World y-axis -3 degrees. Move the Time slider to frame 24, the top of the right step. Rotate the hips 6 degrees.

5. Scrub the Time slider to see how the hip rotation adds a more natural motion to the walk.

Animating the Spine and Shoulders

The next motion to animate is that of the spine and shoulders. The shoulder's motion mirrors that of the hips but lags by a frame or two, because it takes a bit of time for the force generated by the hips to traverse the spine and reach the shoulders. The spine also compresses and arches forward as the hips move up and then straighten out as the hips move down.

This particular skeleton has the spine controlled by three sets of expressions that are manipulated by the X, Y, and Z Text objects in the scene (see Figures 6.19, 6.20, and 6.21). The complete setup of these sliders was discussed in the previous chapter. In brief, the X text object controls rotation of the spinal joints around their x-axis. The Y and Z sliders work for their respective axes. Keyframes are set on the sliders, which in turn, control the spine itself.

FIGURE 6.19

Moving the X slider bends the spine forward and back.

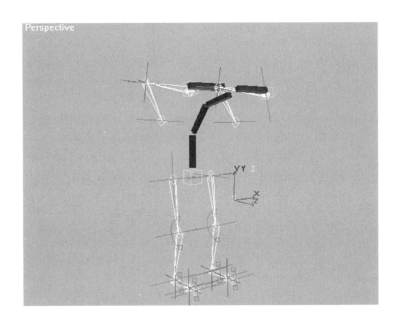

FIGURE 6.20

Moving the Y slider bends the spine side-to-side.

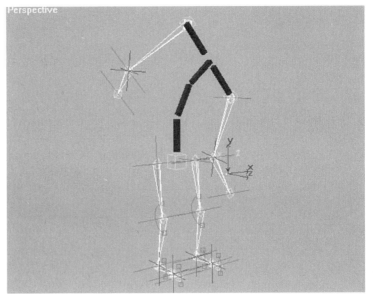

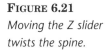

FIGURE 6.21

Moving the Z slider twists the spine.

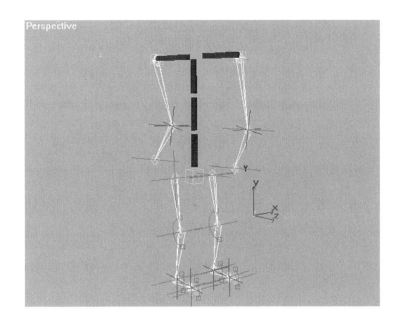

ANIMATING THE SPINE AND SHOULDERS

1. First animate the twist of the shoulders forward and back. Move the Time slider to frame 0. Select the object Spine_Z and move it up 25 units.

2. Move the Time slider to frame 16. On this frame, move the object Spine_Z down 50 units.

3. Move the Time slider to frame 32. Move the object Spine_Z up 50 units. Scrub the animation. Notice how this completes the forward and back twist of the spine.

4. Now get the left-to-right motion. Select the object Spine_Y. Move the Time slider to frame 8 and translate the object down 12 units.

5. Move the slider to frame 24 and translate Spine_Y up 24 units. This completes the left and right motion of the spine.

6. Now animate the arch of the spine. Select the object Spine_X. Move the Time slider to frame 8. Translate this object down 20 units. This bends the spine forward at the top of the step.

7. Move the Time slider to frame 20, the bottom of the second step. Move the object Spine_X up 20 units to straighten out the spine at the bottom of the step.

8. Move the Time slider to frame 24, the top of the second step. Move the Time slider to frame 8. Translate this object down 20 units.

9. Move the Time slider to frame 36, the bottom of the third step. This step will not be animated, but setting the key at this frame is the easiest way to get the proper in-between. Move the object Spine_X up 20 units.

Animating the Arms

The arms of this skeleton are animated by using Forward Kinematics. They are controlled at the shoulder by Dummy objects and at the elbow by rotation effectors added to the chain.

THE ARMS

1. Move the Time slider to frame 0. At this frame the left leg is forward. This means that the right arm is forward. Select the Dummy object R_Arm_Top and rotate it forward 60 degrees.

2. Notice how the arm does not seem to rotate at the elbow. This is because the rotation effector attached to the elbow maintains orientation to world space. Select the effector named R_Elbow and rotate it approximately 10 degrees.

3. Select the Dummy object L_Arm_Top and rotate it back –25 degrees.

4. Again the arm does not rotate at the elbow due to the effector. Select L_Elbow and rotate the effector –45 degrees.

5. Move the Time slider to frame 16 and mirror rotations, using steps 1 through 4 as a guide.

6. Move the time slider to frame 32. Create the forward rotations of the arms to match those on frame 0. This is easily accomplished from within Track View by selecting the keyframes and cloning them by holding down the Shift key and dragging them to the right, positioning the cloned keys on frame 32.

Finalizing the Walk

The basic walk is complete, but it still seems a little stiff. You can tweak the walk by adding a bit of drag to the joints. The spine, for example, takes a bit of time to transfer the force and rotation of the hips to the shoulders, which in turn take some time to transfer the rotation to the elbows. In other words, the further the joint is from the hips, the more it lags behind the motion of the hips.

Normally, this drag is slight, typically on the order of only a few frames. It can be accomplished by selecting the keys for the joints and moving them forward in time by a frame or two.

FINISHING THE WALK

1. From within Track View, select the keys for Spine_X, Spine_Y, and Spine_Z. Move these to the right by one frame.

2. Select the keys for R_Elbow, L_Elbow, R_Arm_Top, and L_Arm_Top. Move these keys two frames to the right.

3. Scrub the animation and continue adjusting it to suit your tastes.

A final version of this animation is on the CD-ROM. It is called 06max02.max.

Creating a Four-Legged Walk

Four-legged creatures are quite common in animation. Unfortunately, a package such as Biped does not help much with this task. Laying down footsteps for two feet is quite straightforward, but the overlapping footsteps required of a four-legged creature can be difficult for an algorithmic package such as Biped to handle.

A four-legged walk is very similar to the two-legged variety, but multiplied by two. The creature's legs still rock back and forth at the hips, but the upper body motion happens parallel to the ground rather than perpendicular to it. Whereas human shoulders rock back and forth in the vertical axis, a dog's shoulders rock back and forth horizontal to the ground as the front paws walk.

The center of gravity is also slightly different for a four-legged beast. Instead of being located at the hips, it is further up on the body, roughly centered between the front and back legs. This may cause you to set up the hierarchy of a quadruped skeleton slightly differently. Because both the front and back legs move equally, the hierarchy can be set up with the center of the spine as the parent.

The location of the root of the hierarchy is important because it represents the *center of gravity*. If the animal were to leap, for example, the entire body's rotation would center around this point, so it is important to place it properly. The center joint of the spinal column makes a good candidate because many four-legged creatures have a center of gravity that is evenly located between the front and rear legs (see Figure 6.22). If the creature has its center of gravity closer to the chest (a cheetah or a greyhound, perhaps) then the shoulders or the first spinal joint may make a better center of gravity (see Figure 6.23). The head also plays a role in determination of center of gravity. A giraffe's long neck places it further up the spinal column, near the shoulders.

FIGURE 6.22

The center of gravity of a dog is centered between the front and rear legs.

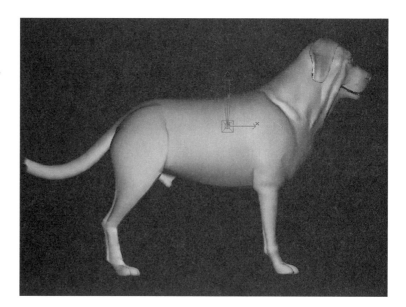

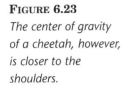

FIGURE 6.23
*The center of gravity
of a cheetah, however,
is closer to the
shoulders.*

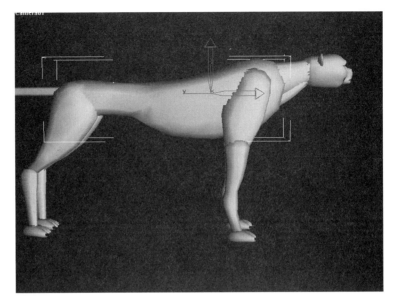

Analysis of a Four-Legged Walk

A four-legged walk is very similar to a two-legged walk in that the hips and shoulders have rotations that mirror each other. When the right hip is forward, the left shoulder is back, and vice versa. This action usually varies a bit in that the front and back legs might be offset by a few frames (see Figure 6.24). Notice how the spine curves much like a human and that the left shoulder and leg are back, mirroring the hip pose. This means that the left front leg, too, is about to plant.

As the legs move forward through the step, the legs that are not currently planted on the ground (the free legs) move forward. The rear legs are fairly similar to a human's, bending at the knee in much the same fashion. The front legs, however, are actually jointed so that they bend forward much like a bird's (see Figure 6.25). This dictates a slightly different lift motion for the front legs. At this point, the spine is straight when viewed from the top, but it may bow or arch a bit more when viewed from the side. This is character dependent; a dilapidated horse's back, for instance, might sag quite a bit.

FIGURE 6.24

This step has the right rear leg forward and about to plant the foot.

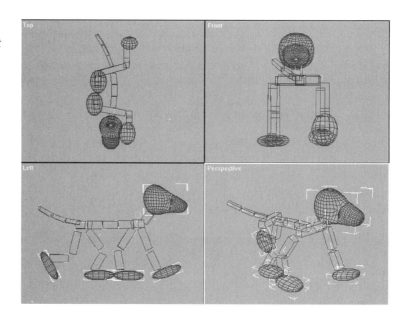

FIGURE 6.25

Halfway through the step, the free legs are moving forward. Notice how the front leg's joint causes a different bend in the leg.

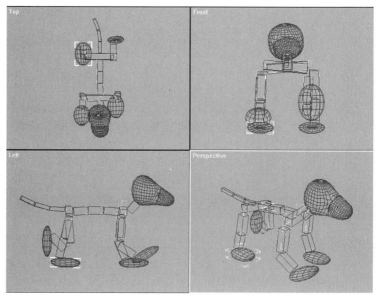

The legs then move through the step and plant the free feet, repeating the first step. In addition to this, a four-legged animal can have several different gaits: the walk, the trot, the canter, and the gallop. The animal varies the timing and rhythm of its steps as it moves faster and faster. In the walk, the animal's legs behave very much like the arms and legs of a human—if the right rear leg is back, the right front leg is forward, with the opposite happening on the left. This changes as the strides change, however. By the time the creature has reached full gallop, the front legs are in sync—going forward and back nearly in unison, with the back legs operating as a mirror to the front.

Animating a Four-Legged Walk Cycle

The new IK that is included with version 2 gives animators a great deal of control when animating a four-legged walk. The legs are manipulated at the feet, which stay locked in place. The spine is animated by using simple rotations. Finally, the head and tail are animated to give the shot a final polish.

Animating the Legs

The best way to start a four-legged walk is to block out the motion of the feet. After the feet are moving properly, the rest of the body can be animated quite easily.

ANIMATING THE LEGS

1. Load the file 06max03.max from the CD-ROM. This file contains a skeleton similar to the one built in the previous chapter. The big difference is that this skeleton has a tail that is controlled through a set of expressions allowing the base of the tail to rotate it.

2. This walk takes 16 frames per step for a total of 32 frames. From the Time Configuration dialog box, set the end time to 32.

3. Now get the first position. Toggle the Animate button on. We start with the right front leg forward, which means the left rear is forward as well. Select the bone R_Front03 and translate it forward approximately 75 units. Do the same for the L_Rear03, the left rear leg effector.

4. Select the object L_Front03. Move this object back about 60 units. Do the same for R_Rear03, the right rear leg. The pose should look like Figure 6.26.

FIGURE 6.26

The legs in the starting position.

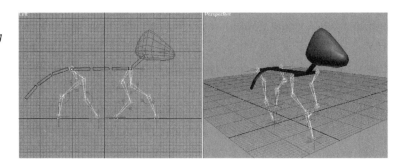

5. Now move the body forward. Move the time slider to frame 16. Select the SpineCent, the center joint of the spine, and the root of the hierarchy. Translate the object forward approximately 125 units.

6. The front left leg and the right rear leg have lifted off the ground due to the translation of the body (see Figure 6.27). Select the object L_Front03. Move this object forward about 250 units. Do the same for R_Rear03, the right rear leg.

FIGURE 6.27

Translating the body forward lifts two of the feet off the ground.

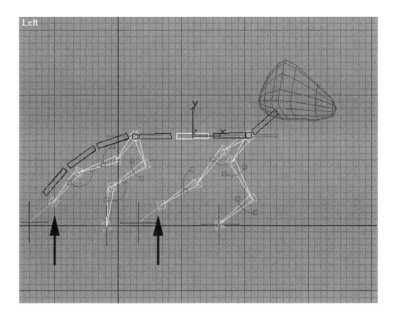

7. From Track View, copy the keyframes for R_Front03 and L_Rear03 from frame 0 to frame 16. This keeps these legs locked in place during the first step.

8. Scrub the animation. The legs that are moving forward drag across the ground. Move the time slider to frame 8. Select L_Front03 and R_Rear03 and translate them up approximately 30 units.

9. This completes the basic blocking for the first step. Use the previous steps as a guide to animate the next step. The second step is a mirror of the first.

Animating the Spine, Hips, and Shoulders

After the feet are moving properly, the next step is to nail down the motion of the spine, hips, and shoulders. Just like in a two-legged walk, the hips and shoulders of a four-legged creature rotate to mirror the motion of the legs. The body of a four-legged creature also bounces up and down as the weight is transferred from one foot to another.

ANIMATING THE UPPER BODY

1. Scrub the animation. Notice how the body moves in a relatively straight line. This might be good for an incredibly sneaky creature, but in a normal walk, the body tends to bounce up and down.

2. Move the time slider to frame 4. This is where the planted legs fully absorb the weight of the body. Select the object SpineCent and move it down approximately 8 units.

3. Move the time slider to frame 10. This is near the top of the first step. Translate SpineCent up approximately 20 units.

4. Do the same for the second step. Repeat the previous two steps at frames 20 and 26, respectively.

5. Scrub the animation. The body should have a more natural bounce and sense of weight.

6. Next get the rotation of the spine and shoulders. Go to the first frame of the animation. Select the object SpineFront. From the Top viewport, rotate it along the vertical axis 5 degrees counterclockwise.

7. Select SpineRear and, from the top viewport, rotate it along the vertical axis five degrees clockwise. The character should look like Figure 6.28.

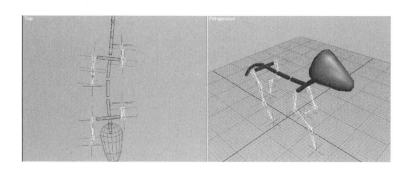

8.   Move the Time slider to frame 16. From the top viewport, select SpineFront and rotate it 10 degrees clockwise. Select SpineRear and rotate it 10 degrees counterclockwise.

9.   Go to Track View. Select the keys at frame 0 for SpineFront and SpineRear. Hold down the Shift key to clone the keys. Drag the clones to frame 32.

10.   Scrub the animation. The spine now has a more natural motion.

11.   The spine can be given another extra motion to add to the sense of weight. As the creature walks, the spine acts much like a taut cable stretched between the hips and shoulders. The weight of the abdomen causes the spine to sag slightly as the weight of the body is lifted. Conversely, as the body moves downward, the weight of the body causes the spine to arch up slightly.

12.   Activate the Left viewport and scrub the Time slider to frame 6, two frames after the lowest point of the walk.

13.   Select SpineFront and rotate it approximately 4 degrees so that the front of the spine arches up in a shallow "U" shape. Do the same for SpineRear. The pose should look like Figure 6.29.

14.   Scrub the Time slider to frame 12, two frames after the top of the first step. This is where the spine arches down. Select SpineFront and rotate it approximately 6 degrees in the opposite direction. This compensates for the original 4-degree rotation and adds 2 degrees of arch in the opposite direction. Do the same for SpineRear. The final pose looks like Figure 6.30.

FIGURE 6.29

Arching the spine helps add weight to the animation.

FIGURE 6.30

The spine at the top of the stride arches up slightly.

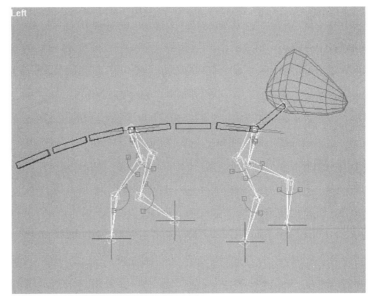

15. Repeat steps 13 and 14 for frames 22 and 28, respectively. This adds the same motion to the second step. Scrub the animation.

Animating the Head and Tail

The final series step is to add a bit of secondary motion in the tail. To finish the animation, the head also needs to be animated. In this case, it will simply be straightened out so that the character looks forward.

ANIMATING THE HEAD AND TAIL

1. Move the Time slider to frame 0. Select the object Tail01. From the Top viewport, rotate it along the vertical axis approximately –5 degrees. Notice how the rest of the tail moves as well. This is because they are controlled by expressions that duplicate the rotation of Tail01.

2. The motion of the tail tends to drag behind that of the spine. Move the Time slider to frame 4. With Tail01 still selected, rotate it another –5 degrees to get the maximum leftward motion of the tail. This is shown in Figure 6.31.

FIGURE 6.31

The tail drags behind the motion of the spine.

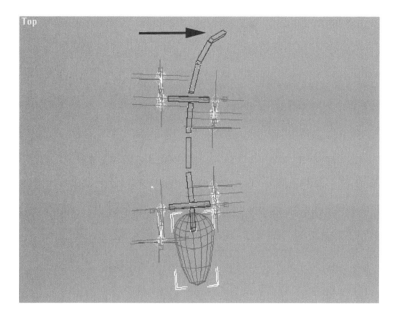

3. Move the Time slider to frame 20. This is also four frames after the maximum bend of the spine. From the Top viewport, rotate Tail01 20 degrees so that it is now to the right of the body.

4. Move the Time slider to frame 32. Rotate Tail01 −15 degrees to place it to the left of the body.

5. Scrub the animation. The tail now has a natural left-to-right sway.

6. The tail also needs to bounce up and down as the character walks (see Figure 6.32). This motion drags behind the up and down motion of the body by a few frames. Move the Time slider to frame 0. From the Left viewport, arch the tail down about 15 degrees.

FIGURE 6.32

The tail bounces up and down as the character walks.

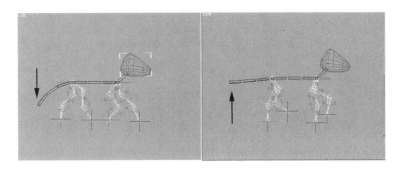

7. Move the Time slider to frame 10. Arch the tail so that it is nearly straight when viewed from the side.

8. Repeat these poses for frames 16 and 26, respectively.

9. Now animate the head. Move through the animation and correct the motion of the head so that it points forward throughout the walk.

The walk is complete. Go back through the animation and tweak the keyframes to suit your tastes. A copy of this animation is saved on the CD-ROM as 06max04.max.

Six-Legged Walks

If four-legged walks seem complex, then six legs might seem intolerably difficult. This, fortunately, is not the case. An insect walk actually follows a definite, repeatable pattern that can be animated on a cycle. A six-legged walk is very similar to the four-legged walk just described—the front two legs move back and forth, while the second set of legs mirror this motion. The insect's third set of legs simply mirrors the second again, closely matching the motion of the front legs. Generally, insects keep at least three legs on the ground, forming a stable tripod at all times.

Because insects are the quintessential segmented creatures, their parts can be put together in a simple hierarchy (see Figure 6.33). Shape animation or bones used to deform a mesh are not needed for such a creature, because an insect's exoskeleton does not change shape. The one exception might be antennae on the insect, which can be animated with bones, or more directly, using a simple Bend modifier.

FIGURE 6.33

As this exploded view shows, Insect legs are naturally segmented, making direct animation of the joints possible.

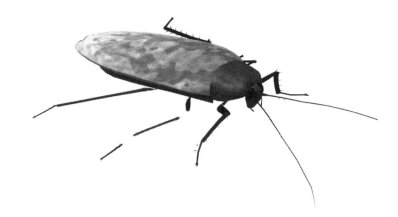

Setting Up an Insect Using Auto Boning

MAX R2's new IK and bones can also be used to animate jointed characters, such as insects. Because insects are usually segmented, the joints can be linked directly to the bones, eliminating the need for a skeletal deformation plug-in. Linking the segments can be accomplished a bone at a time or automatically by using MAX's new Auto Boning feature.

USING AUTO BONING

1. Load the file 06max05.max, which contains a roach model. The roach is already set up in a hierarchy, with the legs attached to the abdomen.

2. Each leg consists of three joints with a dummy attached to the end as an effector. These hierarchies can be set up for IK by using the Auto Bone feature. Select the three objects lmidlegf, llowlegf, lfootf, and dummy01.

3. From the Create panel, select Systems, and then Bones. Make sure all six boxes in the Bone Parameters rollout are checked.

4. Within the Auto Boning box, toggle the Pick Root button. Select the object lmidlegf, the root of the chain.

5. A series of bones is created to match the hierarchy of the linked segments. The segments are now linked to the bones. Select the object Bone04 and translate it to see how the bones affect the leg.

6. The end effector of the leg is now the end effector of the bone chain (Bone04) instead of the dummy. The dummy is no longer needed. Delete Dummy01.

7. Open the Select by Name dialog and toggle Display Subtree. Notice how the root of the bone chain is not linked to the abdomen of the roach. When Auto Boning is applied, the link is not assigned. This must be reassigned manually.

8. Select the object Bone01 and link it to the object Abdomen, the root of the roach body.

9. Repeat the above steps for the remaining five legs. Save the setup once it is complete. An example is provided on the CD-ROM. It is named 06max06.max.

TIP

For easier manipulation when animating, freeze the segments of the roach's leg. This way, they won't be accidentally selected and animated. The segments are manipulated completely by moving the end effectors of the bone chain.

Animating a Six-Legged Walk

Animating this particular insect is accomplished strictly through the manipulation of the abdomen and the bone chain. We need to know how fast the legs will move and how far each step will move the roach.

The rate of an insect walk depends on the species of bug and the bug's demeanor. Generally, bugs move pretty fast compared to mammals, and a quarter or eighth second per step is not out of the question. When walks get this fast, the frame rate of the animation becomes a limiting factor. At 24 fps, an eighth-second stride only takes three frames per step. This is about as fast as a walk can be animated, with one frame each for the forward, middle, and back portions of the step. For this animation, six frames per step gives you a good pace for the insect walk.

For the distance, this is determined by the size of the insect and the length of the legs. Longer-legged insects naturally take longer steps. Insects like the roach have long back legs and short front legs. In this case, the stride length of the walk is usually dictated by the front legs—approximately 120 units per step.

On a side note, when a roach runs, the back legs do all the work and the front four legs actually lift off the ground. The roach actually becomes bipedal.

ANIMATING THE WALK

1. Load the file 06max06.max from the CD-ROM. The roach is modeled at the rest position, with each leg at the halfway point (see Figure 6.34).

FIGURE 6.34

The roach at rest.

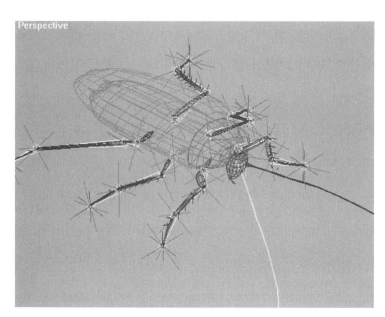

2. Move the Time slider to frame 0 and toggle the Animation button on.

3. On frame 0, move the front left leg forward approximately 60 units. Do the same for the middle right and back left legs.

4. Move the front right leg back about 60 units. Do the same for the middle left and back right. The roach should resemble Figure 6.35.

FIGURE 6.35

The first pose has alternating legs moved forward and the rest moved back.

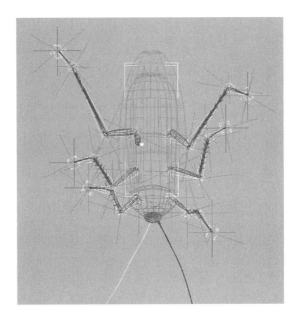

5. Scrub the time slider to frame 6, the start of the next step. Select the abdomen of the roach and translate it forward 120 units.

6. Select the front right leg and translate it forward 120 units. Do the same for the middle left and back right legs.

7. Select the front left, middle right, and back left legs. Set a keyframe for these legs.

8. Now get the middle of the step. Move the Time slider to frame 3. Select the front right, middle left, and back right legs. These legs are moving forward, so they need to lift off of the ground. Move them up about 40 units.

9. The body also lifts during the middle of the step. Select the abdomen and move it up 30 units.

10. This completes the first step. The second step is simply a mirror of the first. Repeat the steps to create the second step (and a third, fourth, and fifth, if desired). The file is on the CD-ROM and named 06max07.max.

Using Link Control to Animate Links

New to MAX R2 is the concept of animatable links. This allows you to reconfigure a hierarchy in the middle of an animation. This new feature is particularly useful to character animators. A good example is when one character hands an object to another character. When control of the object is changed, the link should change as well.

In previous versions of MAX, when transferring an object from one character to another, you would have to use any number of devious little tricks, such as hiding one of two identical objects, or moving one object a frame at a time to the character's hand. With animatable links, however, all of these tricks can be set aside.

Animatable links are implemented in MAX as an Animation controller that is applied to the object. The controller essentially sits on top of the standard PRS controller (see Figure 6.36) and enables the link-controlled object to retain any and all Motion controllers including MAXScript controllers and expressions. After the Link Control controller is applied, the object can be linked to any other object at any frame.

FIGURE 6.36

The Link Control controller is above the standard Position/Rotate/Scale controller.

Link Control Motion Panel

Operation of the Link Control controller is fairly straightforward. The controller simply parents your object's original controller. Most likely, this will be the standard PRS (Position, Rotate, Scale) controller, but Link Control works just as well for Look At or any other controller. The Link Control controller adds one additional rollout—dubbed Link Parameters. As shown in Figure 6.37, this rollout contains a handful of controls:

- **List window.** Displays the links in the order in which they change. Links are added and deleted by using the Add and Delete link button.

- **Add Link button.** Toggling this button and selecting an object assigns it as the parent at the current frame.

- **Delete Link button.** Enables you to select a link from the List window and delete it.

- **Start Time.** Enables you to adjust the start time of a selected link.

FIGURE 6.37

The Link Control Motion panel.

All linking operations must be handled through the Motion panel. This is because Link Control is not accessible from within Track View. An object with Link Control applied appears in Track View as a separate, unlinked object with a cascading Transform hierarchy.

T IP

For the most predictable results, animate the link last—after all of the other objects in the scene are animated. If the animation changes at a later point, delete the links and reassign them.

Using Link Control to Pick Up an Object

This exercise picks up a teapot from a tray and then sets it down again.

USING LINK CONTROL

1. Open the file 06max08.max. It contains a tray, a teapot, and a skeleton along with some animation.

2. Scrub the animation. You will see the tray move up to the skeleton, which lifts an object off the tray and sets it down once again. At this point, however, the teapot, which is the object to be lifted, is not linked to either object and remains stationary. This can be fixed by adding an animatable link.

3. To add an animatable link, select the object named Teapot. Go to the Motion panel. From the Assign Controller rollout, select the Transform controller.

4. Press the Assign Controller button. From the Assign Controller dialog box, select the Link Control. The Link Control motion panel should appear.

5. The teapot can now be linked. Scrub the animation to frame 0. Toggle the Add Link button and select the object named Tray.

6. Turn Add Link off and scrub the animation. Now the teapot follows the tray throughout the animation.

7. Move the Time slider to frame 30. This is where the skeleton picks up the teapot. At this point, the link needs to be reassigned to the skeleton.

8. Toggle the Add link button from the Motion panel. Select Bone03 at the end of the bone chain. If the bone is hard to locate, you may use the Select by Name window to help you. Once selected, Bone03 should be added to the list, with a start time of 30.

9. Scrub the animation. Notice how the teapot follows the skeleton and is lifted off the tray.

10. Move the Time slider to frame 75. Press the Add Link button and select the tray once again. This will now be added to the list.

11. Scrub the animation one last time to see the finished animation. The teapot is lifted from the tray by the skeleton and set back down again. The only attribute on the teapot that was animated was the link itself.

12. The final animation is contained in the file 06max09.max.

In Practice: Animating Walking

- **Walks.** The two-legged walk is like a controlled fall, where the legs catch the body on each step. In each step, the body falls forward and is caught by an outstretched foot, which then pushes the body upward and into another fall. Runs are similar but are more like a controlled leap rather than a fall.

- **Forward versus Inverse Kinematics.** MAX R2 adds an IK system that works quite well for characters. Still, Forward Kinematics should be used for joints that do not need to be locked in place, such as the arms.

- **Walk cycles.** Those animating characters for interactive environments might need to create walk cycles. This can be done by locking a camera to the character so that it matches the forward motion of the hips by copying the appropriate controller. If you use an XYZ controller on both the camera and hips, the X controller can be copied or instanced to achieve this effect.

- **Four-legged walks.** The key to a four-legged walk is the spine, which moves much like the spine of a two-legged walk—with the hips and shoulders of the character following a set of complimentary rotations. In addition to the basic walk, four-legged creatures also can trot, canter, and gallop, which involve differing combinations of footsteps.

- **Six-legged walks.** The number of legs and joints involved with these creatures makes keyframing a bit bothersome. As mentioned in the previous chapter, expressions can be used to assist in the creation of such walks.

Chapter 7

ANIMATING WITH BIPED

Creating and animating your own two-legged skeletons gives you the freedom to customize how they are built. These skeletons typically use Inverse Kinematics to position their limbs, based on the position of their extremities. The position of the arm, therefore, is controlled by the position of the hand. To approach life-like motion of the limbs, the animator must configure the constraints on each skeleton joint to restrict the rotation to the appropriate axis (knees bend but do not twist) and set the appropriate limits for each axis (knees bend backward but not forward). Even with these constraints properly configured, life-like animation can still be difficult to achieve, simply because, when animated, a skeleton still needs to retain qualities such as balance and weight.

Inverse Kinematics knows nothing about the skeleton other than it is a collection of joints. As such, it is easy to have the skeleton in a pose that is quite out of balance. An example of this is the forward rotation of the spine. Unless the hips move backward as the spine is rotated, a bipedal animal quickly goes out of balance and the resulting pose looks unnatural.

Biped is exactly one-half of the Character Studio plug-in. It not only enables automatic construction of "smart" humanoid skeletons with a built-in IK system, it also enables extensive customization of those skeleton's structural details, such as the number of fingers and toes, and whether the biped has a tail. Biped is primarily a footstep-driven animation tool, where the position of the biped is controlled by the timing and placement of footsteps.

The IK system used in Biped is designed specifically for animating bipeds and takes into account the mechanics and restrictions of how bipedal animals move. Integral to Biped is the handling of gravity and the biped's center of mass. This enables Biped to interpolate the position of the biped properly when both feet are off the ground, and to dynamically balance the biped about the center of mass to achieve life-like motions.

This chapter covers the following topics:

- Creating a biped
- Manipulating a biped
- Animating a biped with footsteps
- Performing free-form animation of a biped
- Using animatable IK attachments
- Using libraries of biped animation

Creating a Biped

The Biped Creation button is located under the Systems button in the Create panel. To create a biped, click the button and then on a viewport, and drag. A box appears indicating the size of the biped. Releasing the mouse generates the Biped skeleton.

After the mouse is released, the Biped Creation panel appears (see Figure 7.1). Within this panel, you can configure the skeleton exactly to your needs, including details such as how many segments are in the spine and neck, whether the character has a tail, how many links are in that tail, how many fingers and toes, and whether the character has arms. (A bird, for example, has no arms.) Another important parameter to consider is the Leg Links spinner, which determines how the legs are configured. This has two settings: 3 and 4. A human has a setting of 3 (thigh, shin, and foot), and some birds or dinosaurs have a setting of 4 because the foot bone is extended into their legs and they actually walk on their toes (thigh, shin, tarsal, and foot).

FIGURE 7.1

From within the Biped Creation panel, you can change the structure of the biped.

Once created, the biped can be controlled through the Motion panel (see Figure 7.2). Select any part of the biped and all the controls for manipulating and animating the biped appear. Because Biped is essentially a very sophisticated Animation controller, its controls appear on the Motion panel rather than on the Modify panel.

FIGURE 7.2

Selecting the Motion
tab brings up the
Biped Control panel.

Manipulating a Biped

Bipeds have their own built-in IK, completely separate from MAX's native IK. This system has been configured to give smooth, controllable, predictable motion. Biped's IK always works in real time, and there is no need to apply IK as you might have to within MAX's native IK. The joints of a biped can be manipulated through translation, rotation, and by using footsteps.

With Biped's IK, if you are adjusting a biped's arm by moving the hand, the position of the arm and hand returns to the exact starting position if you return the hand to its original position. An additional feature of Biped is the use of IK Blend to blend between Forward and Inverse Kinematics. This feature enables you to link a hand or foot to another object and have that hand or foot follow the object. The amount of IK blending is animatable, so the hand or foot can effectively be attached and detached from the object over time, enabling you to easily animate the biped catching and throwing a ball, dancing with a partner, or performing other actions where the biped interacts with other objects in the scene. The "Attaching the Hands and Feet to MAX Objects" section of this chapter describes IK Blend further.

Translating a biped's joints is straightforward—grab the joint and move it. The joints moved need not be constrained with end effects or terminators for the joint to move properly. All that intelligence is built into the biped. You can just as easily move the biceps as the pinky and still retain a single, predictable solution for the limb, no matter how many joints the move affects.

To move the biped himself, the Center of Mass object needs to be selected and moved (see Figure 7.3). Rather than a hip-centric model, Biped uses the center of mass as the top of the hierarchy. As such, the pelvis itself is not translatable. The tetrahedral-shaped object found near the center of the pelvis represents the biped's center of mass. Translating this object accomplishes the same effect as moving the pelvis on a hip-centric skeleton.

FIGURE 7.3

To move the biped's body, the Center of Mass object (arrow) must be moved, not the pelvis. The Center of Mass object is represented by a tetrahedron.

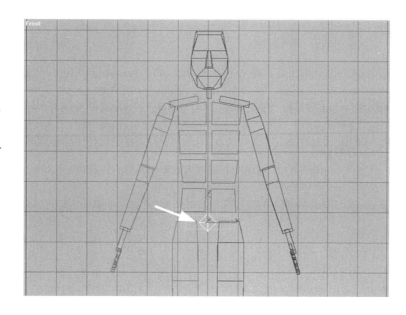

Rotating joints is also possible, giving the animator the flexibility of positioning a skeleton by using any combination of Forward or Inverse Kinematics. Translating joints on the fingers, for example, normally causes a translation of the entire arm. For motions such as hand gestures, rotations are required.

Another thing to be aware of is that not all biped joints can be translated, and not every joint can rotate around every axis. The restrictions on translating joints are that only the Center of Mass object and the leg and arm joints (except for the clavicles) can be translated. The restrictions on rotating joints are more involved. In general, if you cannot rotate a joint in your body about an axis, you cannot rotate the same joint in the biped about that axis. The following are special rotations or restrictions:

- **Elbows and knees.** The elbow and knee joints can be rotated both on their local Z axis (like a hinge) and along their local X axis (along their length). When rotated along their local X axis, the rotation does not occur at that joint. Instead the upper and lower leg/arm are rotated together along an axis formed by the hip/shoulder and ankle/wrist.

- **Feet.** If the foot is planted on a footstep, the foot can be rotated on its local Y and Z axes. The foot remains in contact with the footstep, and the leg joints are rotated to maintain the position of the pelvis. A foot cannot be rotated on its local X axis if the foot is planted.

- **Legs.** If a foot is planted, and a leg is rotated, the rotation may be limited to ensure that the foot remains in contact with the footstep.

When a joint is selected, the disallowed motions are grayed out on the menu bar, which can prove a bit frustrating for the novice. After the restrictions are understood, however, nearly any pose can be effectively attained.

Other Biped Selection and Manipulation Tools

In addition to the standard MAX translation and rotation tools, the Biped Motion panel contains a number of Biped-specific tools to assist in manipulating your skeletons:

- **Center of Mass.** Found under the Track Selection rollout, it selects the biped's Center of Mass object. Sometimes this object can be hard to locate in a complex scene; this button speeds the process.

- **Symmetrical Tracks.** Found under the Track Selection rollout, clicking this button mirrors the current selection on the opposite side of the body. If the left leg is selected, pressing Symmetrical Tracks adds the right leg to the selection.

- **Opposite Tracks.** Found under the Track Selection rollout, clicking this button selects the identical limbs on the opposite side of the body. If the right arm is selected, pressing the Opposite Tracks button selects the left arm and deselects the right.

- **Copy Posture.** Found on the Track Operations rollout, this is a very handy tool that enables you to copy the position of any joint or group of joints.

- **Paste Posture.** Enables you to paste copied postures to another point in the animation or to another biped. Copy and paste posture is also handy for saving the state of a biped if you want to experiment with a pose. If the new pose does not work out, pasting the original pose returns the biped to normal.

- **Paste Posture Opposite.** This is identical to Paste Posture, but this button mirrors the pose to the opposite side of the body, enabling you to take a pose on the right leg, for example, and paste it on the left.

- **Bend Links.** Found on the Track Operations rollout, this tool evenly bends linked joints, such as the spine, tail, or a multi-jointed neck (see Figure 7.4). Activating the Bend Links button causes all the joints in the section (the joints in the spine, for example) to be evenly adjusted by adjusting a single joint.

Animating a Biped

There are many ways to animate a biped. Creating and adjusting footsteps is the obvious method. With version 1.1, however, you can also free-form animate bipeds without footsteps. This, however, is a one-way street—after keys have been added to a free-form animation, footsteps cannot be added to that biped's animation at a later point. If you are in doubt as to whether footsteps should be used in an animation, it is best to assume that they should, and create a free-form area between footsteps. This section takes you through the process of animating with footsteps and free-form animation.

FIGURE 7.4

Bipeds with a single spine joint rotated without and with Bend Links enacted. Bend Links mode even makes rotations of the spine possible.

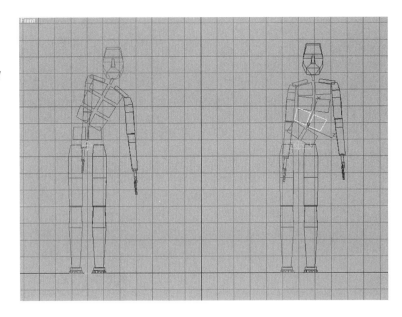

Animating with Footsteps

Footsteps enable you to take advantage of Biped's built-in dynamics to create quasi-realistic motion. The walks, runs, and jumps created by Biped are purposely generic because Biped is a tool that tries not to force a specific style on the animator. The keys automatically generated from footsteps are the minimum required to achieve the motion. This enables the animator to add the desired characteristics without having to delete the many keys that would have to be generated to achieve a realistic default motion. Instead these keys should be thought of as a motion "sketch" that can be easily modified.

To create footsteps, click the Footstep Track button within the Track Selection rollout to activate the Footstep Creation rollouts. Additionally, Sub-Object Footsteps is enabled for the biped. This means that only footsteps may be selected, created, or manipulated while the Footstep Track button is toggled. After this button has been toggled, you are free to create footsteps.

Creating Footsteps

There are two methods of creation (footstep creation and adjustment) along with three types of footsteps: walk, run, and jump. The different types of footsteps represent the different timings for the footsteps. Again, you should think of the footstep timing and placement as an easily modified motion "sketch."

- **Walk.** One foot always remains planted, while the other swings forward. At least one foot is always on the ground. There can also be a section in the walk motion—called Double Support—where both feet are on the ground. Both the number of frames in which each footstep remains on the ground (Walk Footstep) and the number of frames in a double support period (Double Support) are defined by spinners that activate when the Footstep Track button is toggled on.

- **Run.** One foot is on the ground at a time with no double support. There is also a point in the cycle where both feet are airborne. Both the number of frames that each footstep remains on the ground (Run Footstep) and the number of frames that the biped is airborne (Airborne) are defined by spinners that activate when the Footstep Track button is toggled on.

- **Jump.** Both feet are on the ground equally and are airborne equally. The number of frames that both feet are on the ground (2 Feet Down) and the number of frames that the biped is airborne (Airborne) are defined by spinners that activate when Footstep Track is toggled on.

Biped footsteps can be created singly or in multiples. When creating a set of single footsteps, the footstep can be appended in time to the current footsteps, or created starting at the current frame. Each method has its own button, as follows:

- **Create Footsteps (append).** This button enables you to lay down footsteps by clicking a viewport—a good method for creating footsteps over tricky terrain or for complex motions such as dance steps. Footsteps are appended to any current footsteps.

- **Create Footsteps (at current frame).** Same as Create Footsteps (append), except that footsteps are added starting at the current frame. If the footstep being added overlaps in time with an existing footstep, an alert appears, and the footstep is not created.

■ **Create Multiple Footsteps.** This button creates a user-defined number of footsteps with user-specified spacing and timing. Footsteps created in this manner run along a straight line and are best for walking a character through a scene.

TIP

Using the Interpolate option in the Create Multiple Footsteps dialog, you can change the stride length, stride height, and timing of the footsteps over the footsteps being created.

Activating Footsteps

After a series of footsteps has been laid down, the footsteps must be activated. To activate footsteps, click the Create Keys for Inactive Footsteps button in the Footstep Operations rollout. Activation computes dynamics for the biped for any footsteps that have been created, but not yet activated, and it also creates keys within Track View for the biped. Once activated, you can still modify the walk by manipulating the footsteps or keys. If new footsteps are added after activation, those footsteps must also be activated.

Creating a Simple Walk

You can always get instant gratification from Biped by creating a few footsteps and activating them. The following simple task makes a biped walk and gives you a supply of footsteps with which to work.

CREATING A SIMPLE WALK

1. Load 07max01.max from the accompanying CD-ROM. This file contains a biped and a ground plane.

2. Select any portion of the biped. Select the Motion tab to bring up the Biped Motion panel.

3. Footsteps are created and modified from within Footstep mode. Click the Footstep Track button under Track Selection to enter Footstep mode. When this button is toggled on, it enables Sub-Object Footsteps

selection on the biped. While in Footstep mode, only footsteps can be selected and modified.

4. There are two ways to create footsteps: single footsteps manually placed with the mouse, or multiple footsteps automatically placed. Footsteps can be one of three types: walk, run, or jump. Click the Walk button in the Footstep Creation rollout.

5. The fastest way to create footsteps is with the Create Multiple Footsteps button. This creates a number of footsteps with user-specified spacing and timing that can be modified and manipulated later. Press this button to display the Create Multiple Footsteps dialog. Enter **10** for the number of footsteps, make certain that the Start Left option is chosen in the General section, and click OK.

6. Ten numbered footsteps appear, which need to be activated for the biped to follow them. To do this, press the Create Keys for Inactive Footsteps button in the Footstep Operations rollout (see Figure 7.5).

7. Activate the Left viewport with a right-click and play the animation. The biped now follows these footsteps. Instant gratification!

FIGURE 7.5

Activating the foot-steps causes the biped to walk.

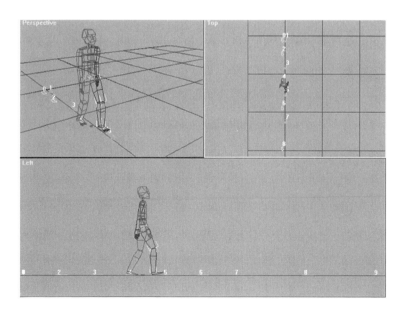

Appending to an Animation

You can append to Biped-created animations quite easily. It is simply a matter of creating additional footsteps and activating them.

APPENDING BIPED ANIMATIONS

1. Click the Run button and then the Create Multiple Footsteps button. Type in **4** for the number of footsteps, choose the Start after Last Footstep option in the Timing section, and click OK. This appends four footsteps to the end of the animation. Activate the new footsteps.

2. Zoom extents the Left viewport and plays back the animation. As you might notice, the biped changes from a walking to a running gait for the new footsteps.

3. Press the Jump button and then the Create Multiple Footsteps button. For the number of footsteps, type in **2**. Activate the footsteps.

4. Zoom extents the Left viewport and plays back the animation. The biped now ends the run with a small jump.

An example of this animation is stored on the accompanying CD-ROM in the file named 07max02.max.

Modifying Footsteps

Once activated, the footsteps can be moved and modified on the fly, with Biped adjusting the biped to match the footsteps automatically.

MODIFYING FOOTSTEPS

1. Using the animation just created, go to the Display panel and click Unhide All. A small platform with a staircase appears. Play back the animation. The biped should walk right through the stairs because Biped just follows the footsteps, which are laid in a straight line across the ground. Biped does not perform collision detection with other objects in the scene.

2. This obstacle can be overcome quite easily by adjusting the footsteps. Zoom in the platform in the Left viewport. Select any part of the biped and, in the Motion panel, toggle the Footstep Track button on. Using the standard MAX selection tools, select footsteps 3 through 15. Move these up so that footstep 3 resides on the first step of the platform. Select footsteps 4 through 15 and move these up so that footstep 4 lies on the second step. Repeat until all the footsteps are properly positioned on the stairs.

3. Play the animation. The biped now walks up the stairs and then runs off the edge of the platform.

4. This can also be adjusted quite easily. Select the biped, go to the Motion panel, and enter Footstep mode. Select footsteps 6 through 8. In the Footstep Operations rollout, adjust the Bend spinner up to 30. The selected footsteps automatically bend. Footsteps prior to footstep 6 are not affected, and footsteps after footstep 8 are rotated to maintain their alignment with footstep 8.

5. Play the animation. Notice how the biped automatically banks as it goes through the turn. A problem still exists, however. The biped still runs off the end of the platform and jumps from and lands in mid-air.

6. In the Front viewport, select footsteps 9 through 13. In the Footstep Operations rollout, uncheck the Width option and adjust the Scale spinner so that footstep 13 resides precisely on the edge of the platform. By unchecking the Width option, the width between footsteps remains the same as the footsteps are scaled downward.

7. Now select footsteps 14 and 15, which are still in mid-air off the edge of the platform. Move these down so that they lie level with the ground plane (see Figure 7.6).

8. Play the animation. The biped now walks up the stairs, rounds a corner, runs, and jumps off the edge. Not bad for a few minutes worth of work.

FIGURE 7.6

Obstacles, such as stairs, can be can be overcome quite easily by repositioning the footsteps.

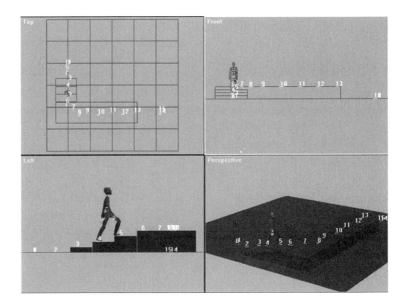

What has this demonstrated? First, by moving the footsteps up the stairs, you saw that footsteps are sub-objects that can be manipulated either individually or in groups. The footsteps can be moved and rotated anywhere in the scene to account for uneven terrain. Also, groups of footsteps can be scaled and bent quite easily by using the Bend and Scale spinners in the Footstep Operations rollout. The final animation is on the accompanying CD-ROM in a file called 07max03.max.

Individual footsteps or a selection set of footsteps can also be rotated using Select and Rotate. Rotating the footsteps this way is different than using the Bend spinner in that the unselected footsteps are not moved or rotated. When a selection set of footsteps is rotated in this way, the rotation pivot point is the pivot point of the footstep that the mouse cursor is over when you click and drag. If you change the Transform Coordinate Center from Use Pivot Point Center to Use Selection Center, each footstep is rotated about its local pivot point. Go figure.

Copying and Pasting Footsteps

Biped enables you to select a set of footsteps, copy those footsteps to a buffer, and splice the footsteps into either the middle or end of the footstep sequence. You can even copy and splice a set of footsteps from one biped to another. The section "Saving and Loading Canned Motions" later in this chapter provides an example of this.

In this example, you copy and splice footsteps on a single biped.

COPYING FOOTSTEPS

1. Load 07max04.max from the accompanying CD-ROM. This file contains a biped walking forward, turning left, and walking a bit farther. For this exercise, you want the biped to turn left again near the end of the animation.

2. Select any portion of the biped and then select the Motion tab to bring up the Biped Motion panel. Click the Footstep Track button in the Track Selection rollout.

3. Maximize the Top viewport and select footsteps 4 through 8. To be able to splice a set of footsteps into the middle of a sequence, the first and last footsteps selected need to be for the same leg.

4. Click the Copy Selected Footsteps button in the Footstep Operations rollout to place the selected footsteps into the Footstep buffer.

5. Click the Insert Footstep Buffer Onto Footsteps button in the Footstep Operations rollout. A copy of the footsteps in the buffer appears in the viewport.

6. Rotate the footsteps 90° about the z-axis.

7. Using the Move tool, click and drag the footsteps so that the first footstep is over the biped's footstep number 12. This target footstep turns red to signify that a splice is possible (see Figure 7.7). Release the mouse button.

   The first buffer footstep replaces the target footstep and the remaining buffer footsteps follow. The original footsteps after the target footstep are automatically copied into the footstep buffer and are now available to paste.

FIGURE 7.7

When you move the first pasted footstep over a valid target footstep, the target footstep turns red.

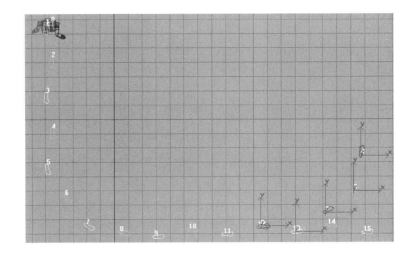

8. Rotate the footsteps 90° about the z-axis.

9. Using the Move tool, click and drag the footsteps so that the first footstep is over the biped's footstep 16. Release the mouse button. The buffer footsteps are now spliced on to the end of the animation.

10. Minimize the Top viewport. Click the Perspective viewport to activate it and play back the animation.

After copying the footsteps into the Footstep buffer and before pasting them into the scene, you can edit the footsteps and associated keys that are in the buffer. To do this, click the Buffer Mode button in the General rollout to toggle on the Buffer mode. The footsteps in the buffer appear in the viewport, applied to the biped. In Track View, the footsteps are shown as the footsteps for the biped, and the associated keys are shown for the biped. These footsteps and keys can be edited just like the normal biped footsteps and keys. To return to the actual footsteps and keys for the biped, toggle off the Buffer Mode button.

Dynamics of Motion

As a biped walks, runs, or jumps, several factors affect the biped's motion: Gravitational Acceleration, Dynamics Blend, Ballistic Tension, and Balance Factor. Each of these factors affects the motion of the biped between keyframes.

NOTE

A walk cycle is the act of falling forward and then catching yourself. To start walking, you extend one leg forward, which shifts your center of mass forward. As your center of mass moves forward past your planted foot, you start to fall forward. The back of your planted foot lifts off the ground, whereas the ball and toes of the foot remain planted. You continue to fall forward until the heel of the moving foot hits the ground. At this point, the momentum of your body starts to pull the back leg forward, and as the back foot leaves the ground, it also pushes you forward. This back leg continues forward until it passes the front leg, and you begin to fall forward again. While one of your feet is off the ground, your entire weight is being supported by the other foot. To maintain balance, the body arcs over the moving foot (the hip shifts toward the planted foot). Biped properly animates the hip to provide this motion (see Figure 7.8).

FIGURE 7.8

Although only supported on one foot, the hip swings over the planted foot.

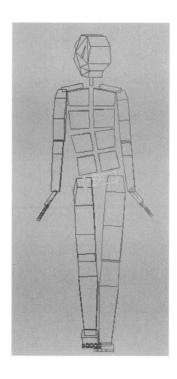

As you walk, the height of your pelvis (and center of mass) from the ground varies. It is at a minimum right after the front foot hits the ground, and at a maximum as back leg passes the front leg.

A run cycle is similar to a walk cycle, except that instead of falling forward, you throw yourself forward. In a walk cycle, at least one foot is always on the ground. During a run cycle, however, there are periods where both feet are off the ground. During these periods, you are airborne or ballistic. You move forward at a constant velocity during this airborne period, and the vertical height of your center of mass is based on how hard you "push off" and also on gravity. Leading up to this push off, your legs are typically bent more than during a walk cycle to generate more power with which to push. As the legs are bent, the center of mass also is lowered.

A jump cycle, in turn, is similar to a run cycle. The only difference is that both feet are in the air at the same time, and both hit the ground at the same time. Again, you move forward at a constant velocity during this airborne period, and the vertical height of your center of mass is based on how hard you push off and also on gravity.

When you land in a run or jump cycle, your center of mass continues downward and forward due to momentum. Your legs act like springs, absorbing this momentum.

Dynamics Blend

Biped stores both Vertical and Horizontal keys for the biped's Center of Mass object. The Horizontal keys are generated at the middle of each footstep's support period and they provide the forward motion of the biped. The Vertical keys are generated at the start, middle, and end of each footstep. The Vertical keys store the extension of the legs and the actual vertical height of the Center of Mass object.

During walking motions, the height is interpolated based on the extension of the legs recorded at each vertical key. This ensures that the supporting leg's knee angle does not change direction between two vertical keys. In effect, when walking, the leg extensions (and the rising and falling foot pivots on the ground) control the height of the body in a natural way.

You can defeat this approach (or selectively blend it) with an interpolation of the actual vertical height by setting Dynamics Blend at each vertical key. At a Dynamics Blend setting of zero, Biped performs a spline interpolation of the vertical heights and ignores the leg extension information at each key. At a Dynamics Blend setting of one, Biped interpolates the leg extension distances and ignores the vertical heights at each key. You can change the Dynamics Blend value only while the Center of Mass object is selected, Move is active, and Restrict to Z is active.

During running and jumping motions, or transitions between them, the height is always determined by the vertical heights at each key because running and jumping are governed by the requirements of gravity, the heights of the body at liftoff and touchdown, and the duration of each airborne period. For running and jumping vertical keys, therefore, Dynamics Blend is grayed-out because it is not applicable.

Gravitational Acceleration

While the biped is airborne during a run or jump cycle, the vertical dynamics are controlled by Gravitational Acceleration (GravAccel in the General rollout of the Biped Motion panel) and the length of time between the lift and landing footsteps. If the length of time between these footsteps is shortened, or the Gravitational Acceleration value is decreased, the maximum height during the airborne period is decreased (on the moon, you don't need to jump very high to cover a lot of ground). The Gravitational Acceleration value is not animatable.

Ballistic Tension

The Ballistic Tension value controls how "springy" the legs are before liftoff and after touchdown in run and jump cycles (see Figure 7.9). The higher the value, the stiffer the legs are, resulting in less leg bending. You can change the Ballistic Tension value only while the Center of Mass object is selected, Move is active, and Restrict to Z is active. This value can only be set at the touchdown keyframe, unless three or more Vertical keys are set during the footprint support cycle. In this case, a Ballistic Tension value can also be set at the liftoff keyframe.

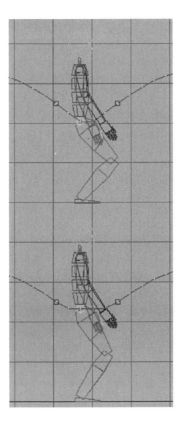

Balance Factor

The Balance Factor value specifies the biped's weight distribution by positioning the biped weight anywhere along a line extending from the center of mass to the head. A value of 0 places the biped's weight in the feet. A value of 1 places the biped's weight over the center of mass. A value of 2 places the biped's weight in the head. The Balance Factor value has no affect on the walk, run, and jump cycle motions; however, it can be used to your advantage when adjusting the rotation of the spine.

Assume, for example, a biped is sitting on a chair and you are animating it so that it leans over a table. With the default value for Balance Factor (1.0), as you rotate the spine forward, the pelvis moves backward to maintain a constant position for the Center of Mass object. If you set the Balance Factor to 0, as you rotate the spine forward, the pelvis remains at the same location. If you attempt to do this while the biped is standing, however, the biped looks very unnatural—like it should be falling over but isn't (see Figure 7.10). The Balance Factor value is set in the Structure rollout while in Figure mode. The Balance Factor value is not animatable.

FIGURE 7.10

The movement of the pelvis back from the center of mass when the spine is bent forward for bipeds with a normal Balance Factor (left) and a low Balance Factor (right).

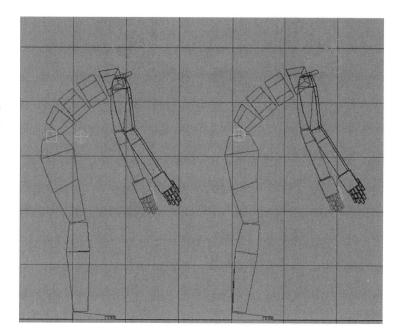

Bipeds in Track View

Although manipulating the footsteps themselves can change the walk quite a bit, the timing of a walk is also very important. A biped's timing can be changed quite radically from within Track View. When viewed as keys within Track View (see Figures 7.10 and 7.11), a Biped animation looks slightly different than ordinary MAX animation. When viewing a Biped animation, notice that the legs, arms, and spine do not have separate keys for each joint—Biped keys span all joints in the limbs (arms, legs, spine, tail). A leg does not have separate keys for the thigh and shin, for example; instead, it has only one key that comprises the position of all the limb's joints. This enables Biped to transfer animation between disparate skeletons quite easily.

FIGURE 7.11

*Biped tracks in Track
View. The footstep
keys are represented
as blocks rather than
dots, and locked Biped
keys are highlighted in
red.*

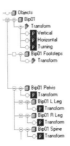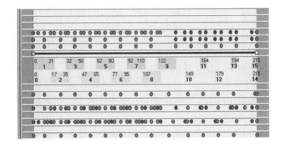

Footstep Tracks

One of the more important tracks is the footsteps track, which has a distinct appearance of alternating green and blue blocks—green are right footsteps; blue are left. The colored blocks indicate exactly when the feet are on the ground. Space between the footsteps indicates that the foot is airborne. If neither foot has a footstep at a given frame, then both feet are airborne, such as in a run or a jump. Walks, by definition, always keep at least one foot on the ground, and if the blocks overlap, both feet are on the ground. Displaying the footsteps this way enables you to know exactly what the feet are doing.

A footstep key actually spans several frames and has a number of components. By default, each footstep is labeled in its center with the footstep number, and each footstep indicates the start and stop frame in the top corners.

To modify a footstep, click the center of the footstep near the footstep number and drag. Clicking the start or stop frame in the corners of the footstep enables you to modify these positions as well, affecting the duration of the footstep. Like any other key, you can also select, move, and resize groups of keys.

Right-clicking a footstep key brings up the Footstep Track dialog (see Figure 7.12), which gives you control over how the footsteps are displayed, as well as some additional selection tools. The top portion of this dialog is for turning off vertical dynamics in free-form areas and is discussed in this chapter's "Free-form Animation" section. The Footstep Number Display section provides options on the frame information shown for each footstep. The Footstep Edge Selection section enables you to change which portion of the previously selected footsteps remain chosen. If you have chosen three footsteps and click the Left button, for example, only the left edges of these three footsteps remain selected. You can then move these edges to increase or decrease the duration for the footsteps.

NOTE

Release 1.1 of Character Studio enables you to select any combination of left and right edges, and generally improves footstep editing in Track View.

FIGURE 7.12

Right-clicking the footstep track displays the Footstep Track dialog.

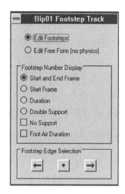

Other Tracks

In addition to the footstep tracks, Biped also has another class of keys not normally found within MAX. These are keys for skeletal objects, such as the legs, and are calculated by Biped and are shown in red. Called *locked keys*, these are keys that Biped requires to perform its calculations. The locked keys cannot be moved or deleted except by changing the footsteps themselves. If you edit a footstep track, the locked keys appear and disappear as the track changes. Finally, Biped also creates normal MAX keys (shown in gray). These are for skeletal elements, such as the arms, spine, and head. These keys can be edited, moved, or deleted, like any other MAX key.

Right-clicking a Biped track other than the Footstep track displays the Change Multiple Keys dialog (see Figure 7.13). This dialog enables you to select keys based on a number of user-defined filters defined as Tracks and State filters. It also lets you apply the last transform performed on a portion of the biped to a selected set of keys.

FIGURE 7.13

The Change Multiple Keys dialog enables you to quickly select and change the values of multiple keys.

The Tracks section defines which tracks in the animation are marked for selection. These can be the Left Leg, Right Leg, Body Horizontal, and Body Vertical tracks. If you want a character's walking body to bounce up and down more, for example, check the Body Vertical box.

State filters define which portion of the step is selected. Biped defines four states that correlate to the major states of a footstep. These are not to be confused with the major poses of a walk described in the previous chapters—contact, recoil, and passing. States define where the foot contacts and leaves the ground, not the pose of the body, and are as follows:

■ **Touch.** The point in the step where the forward foot first touches the ground.

■ **Plant.** Any keys where the leg is planted on the ground. This includes the recoil and passing position.

■ **Lift.** Where the planted leg lifts off the ground.

■ **Move.** Any keys where the leg is off the ground. This includes the recoil and passing positions.

By using a combination of Tracks and State selections, you can select and modify multiple keys. This can change the character of an entire walk quite easily while keeping the walk consistent.

Biped records the last mouse movement and moved body part whenever you do anything with a biped. When you click Apply Increment, Biped applies that mouse move and updates the key for each selected key in Track View that matches the same moved body part type. If you have keys selected on both arms and legs, and you move or rotate an arm and perform an Apply Increment, only the selected keys on the arms are modified.

If you actually set a key when performing the move that is going to be applied to the entire set, the increment of that key happens twice: once for the Set Key and again for the Apply Increment. In general, you should never be in Animate mode or use Set Key if you are attempting to just modify a selected set of keys in a uniform way. The normal sequence of events is to select a set of keys, perform some interactive transform on the body part in question, and click Apply Increment. If you do set a key when the interactive move is performed (either via Set Key or if Animate is on), the key should not be selected in Track View when performing the Apply Increment.

The frame number or keyframe for this "last recorded mouse move + body part" makes no difference because Biped is really just recording the "increment," not the actual posture. It is usually convenient, however, to adjust the increment relative to a particular keyframe.

N OTE

A bug is present in release 1.1 of Character Studio where, if you have keys selected for opposing body limbs (such as both legs), and you perform more than one Apply Increment, the first key on the limb opposing the one transformed is not properly modified. If you perform the transform with Animate on (and deselect in Track View the modified key), Apply Increment properly updates the keys.

You may have noticed in the last example that the biped's feet were passing through the steps as the biped walked up the stairs. In the following exercise, you use the Change Multiple Keys dialog to correct this.

PLANTING THE FOOT ON THE STAIRS

1. Load the file 07max03.max, which is the platform animation created previously.

2. Maximize the Left viewport and zoom in to the area of the footsteps 2 through 6. Advance to frame 40.

3. Open Track View and right-click the Filters button. Choose Animated Tracks Only. Right-click Objects and choose Expand All. Scroll the Track View windows to display the Footsteps track and the left and right leg Transform tracks.

4. Select the right foot. Note that in Track View a key is already present on the left leg track at this frame. Because the foot is off the ground, this is a Move state key.

5. In Track View, right-click one of the leg Transform tracks to display the Change Multiple Keys dialog. In the Select Multiple Keys section, check Left Leg and Right Leg under Tracks, and Move under State Filters. Click the Select button. The Move keys on the right and left legs are selected in Track View.

6. The set of keys selected contains more keys than you want to adjust. Deselect the keys at and before frame 40. Deselect the keys after frame 108 (the right edge of footstep 6 is at frame 108). Deselect the last key currently selected on the right leg (see Figure 7.14).

FIGURE 7.14

The keys on the left and right leg selected when performing the first Apply Increment.

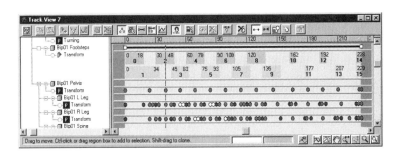

7. Click the Animate button to turn on Animate mode. Move the right foot up two units on the World z-axis.

8. Click Apply Increment in the Change Multiple Keys dialog.

9. Advance to frame 54 and select the left foot. Move the left foot back 10 units on the World y-axis, and up one unit on the World z-axis.

10. In Track View, deselect the second key in each pair of keys currently selected. Deselect the left leg key at frame 54 (see Figure 7.15).

11. Click Apply Increment in the Change Multiple Keys dialog.

12. Play the animation. As the biped walks up the stairs, his feet no longer pass through the stairs.

FIGURE 7.15

The keys on the left and right leg selected when performing the second Apply Increment.

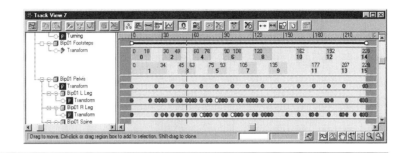

The final animation is on the accompanying CD-ROM in the file 07max05.max.

Manipulating Biped Animation Within Track View

Manipulating a biped within Track View is an easy way to change the character of an animation quite quickly. The timing of the footsteps can be affected just by moving or resizing the footstep blocks.

Walks can also be made into runs or jumps and vice versa. If the footstep keys are placed so that they overlap, the footsteps are *walk* footsteps (see Figure 7.16). If the footstep keys are moved so that they don't overlap, the double support is eliminated and the walk footstep becomes a *run* footstep (see Figure 7.17). If the run footstep is then moved so that both the left and right foot are airborne at the same time, and both are in contact with the ground at the same time, it becomes a *jump* (see Figure 7.18).

FIGURE 7.16

Footstep 9 is a walk footstep because it overlaps footstep 8 by three frames, giving it double support.

FIGURE 7.17

Moving the edge of footstep 9 so that it doesn't overlap footstep 8 turns the step into a run, because double support is eliminated.

FIGURE 7.18

Moving footstep 9 so that it overlaps footstep 10 turns it from a jump into a footstep, because both feet are airborne before the step.

Directly Animating a Biped

Besides animating with footsteps, a biped can also be keyframed directly. The only limits are for a walking biped, because footsteps introduce calculated keys that cannot be deleted or moved outside of changing the footsteps. Outside of this handful of keys, the biped can be keyframed to give a walk more character and life. This animation can be as simple as bobbing the body up and down by animating the center of mass, or as involved as introducing complex leg and arm motions—for a dance sequence or gymnastics perhaps.

Animating a Flip

In this exercise, a gymnastic flip is added to an existing biped animation.

FLIPPING

1. Load the file 07max05.max, which is the platform animation created previously. You are going to make the biped do a flip as it jumps off the platform between frames 213 and 233.

2. To make viewing this action easier, maximize the Front viewport and zoom in to the area of the jump.

3. The biped himself can be flipped 360 degrees by rotating his Center of Mass object. Select any portion of the biped and open the Motion panel. To select the Center of Mass object, click the Center of Mass Object button in the Track Selection rollout.

4. Move the slider to frame 219. Click Angle Snap and rotate the Center of Mass object 140 degrees about the y-axis (see Figure 7.19). Press the Set Key button on the Biped panel.

TIP

The Set Key button sets a key for the selected limb(s). If a limb is transformed while the Animate button is toggled on, a key is automatically generated.

FIGURE 7.19

Rotating the body is a simple matter of rotating the Center of Mass object.

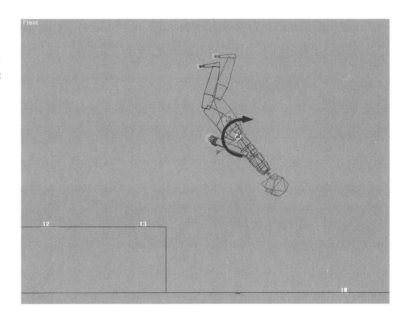

5. Move the slider to frame 225. As you may notice, the biped tries to reverse his rotation to complete the animation because this is the shortest way to interpolate between the rotation key at frame 219 and the key at 233. This can be fixed by further rotating the body back in the desired direction and setting another key. With Angle Snap still toggled on, rotate the biped's Center of Mass object an additional 200 degrees. Then set a key.

6. Notice how the biped automatically extends his legs because the plug-in automatically computes the dynamics of the biped. As you will see later, dynamics can be turned off. For this animation, it is perfectly acceptable.

7. Play the animation. The biped does the flip. Still the animation looks rather stiff. This animation can be given a bit more liveliness in many ways. These methods also employ the various Biped tools.

8. The takeoff step (step 13) is six frames long. To make the takeoff slightly quicker, this can be shortened to four frames. From Track View, locate the footstep block for step 13 and click its right edge. Drag the edge to shorten the step so that it runs from frame 207 to 211.

9. The biped also seems a little light when it takes off. To give it the illusion of weight, the body needs to move lower before taking off because the legs need to absorb the shock of the body and also anticipate the leap. On frame 207, when the foot makes contact, select the Center of Mass object and move it down approximately five units in Z. Then set a key.

10. During the flip, the left leg moves forward and kicks backward to make the body flip. Anticipate the kick motion by bringing the left foot forward at frame 207 (see Figure 7.20). Set a key.

FIGURE 7.20

Move the right leg forward by dragging the foot. This helps to anticipate the flip.

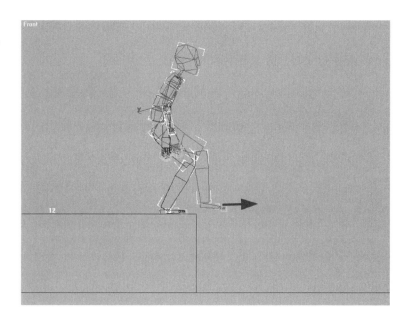

11. Animate the kick of the left foot. Go to frame 200 and drag the left foot back behind the right leg. Set a key here.

12. The body should bend forward a bit more before it takes off. This can be done by rotating the spine around the z-axis. The easiest way to do this is by using the Bend Links mode. Toggle the Bend Links button on and then select a spine segment. Go to frame 207 and rotate the segment about 40 degrees around the z-axis. Set a key.

13. Scrub the animation. Notice that the spine motion pops at frame 209. When Biped creates the original jump, it places a key for the spine at frame 209. With the key just set at frame 207, this key is now extraneous. Delete this key either in Track View, or by advancing to frame 209 and clicking the Delete Key button in the Track Operations rollout with a spine segment selected.

14. Scrub the animation. At the end of the jump, the spine straightens out—which is fine for a standing pose—but the spine straightens out too early. Go to frame 207, where the spine key was set. Select the spinal segments. Click Copy Posture. Move to frame 223, slightly before the landing, and press Paste Posture. The spine bends. Set a key.

15. To anticipate the jump, the arms swing forward quite a bit. Go to frame 205. Select the right hand and move it forward and up so that it is even with the chest and the arm is slightly bent (see Figure 7.21). Set a key. Do the same with the left arm.

16. When the flip begins, the arms pull in toward the body to help give it rotation. On frame 213, move both the right and left hands so that they are roughly even with the hips and the arms are slightly bent. Set keys for both limbs.

17. The head needs to be tucked toward the chest as the body rotates. Go to frame 223 and rotate the head in to the chest. Set a key.

18. Finally, the biped should absorb the impact of the landing a bit more. Go to frame 230 and move the Center of Mass object down about six or seven units (see Figure 7.22). Set a key.

FIGURE 7.21

The arms swing forward before the flip.

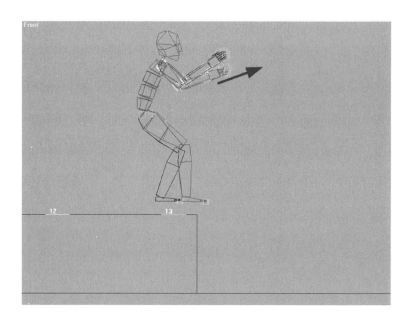

FIGURE 7.22

Upon impact, the body continues moving down to absorb the shock before the character stands.

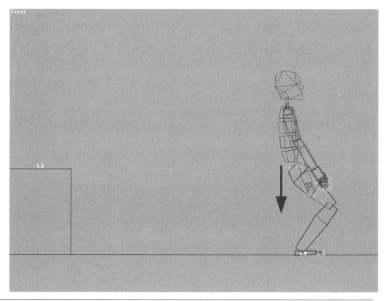

Play the animation. These little tweaks go a long way toward making the flip more realistic and natural. The lesson here is that Biped gives you basic motion only; it is the animator who makes the skeleton come alive. Biped is a very nice tool, but it still needs to be driven by an animator.

This animation can be found on the accompanying CD-ROM as 07max06.max.

Free-form Animation

Not every action in every animation requires footsteps. People also stand still, sit, swim, and sometimes fly. As stated previously, with version 1.1, footsteps are no longer a requirement to animate a biped—making the previously mentioned actions easier to animate. If footsteps are in the scene, the free-form animation must be set up in an area between footsteps. Free-form keys cannot be set before the first footstep, nor after the last.

Free-form Animation Without Footsteps

Free-form animation without footsteps is an all or nothing proposition. After keys have been set, footsteps cannot be added to the shot. If footsteps are required in addition to free-form animation, you can accomplish this by suspending dynamics. This is discussed in the next section.

Animating a biped in Free-form mode without footsteps gives you many advantages, most important of which is that the biped's IK remains active, making it very easy to pose the character. Biped keys are still calculated in the same way, with the keys being assigned to limbs rather than individual joints. The only exception is that vertical dynamics is suspended while in Free-form mode without footsteps. The vertical and horizontal position of the biped's Center of Mass object between keyframes is based on a spline interpolation of the keyframes. Because there are no footsteps, there are also no calculated or restricted keys.

Free-form Animation with Footsteps

Free-form animation with footsteps is very similar to animating a biped without them, but the task requires a few extra keystrokes. The free section must be free of any footsteps. Normally Biped's dynamics want to control the trajectory of the biped, as in a jump. To animate the character completely unencumbered, these dynamics need to be suspended.

FREE-FORM FOOTSTEPS

1. Open Track View, and right-click the Footsteps track to open the Footstep Track dialog.

2. In the Footstep Track dialog, choose the Edit Free Form (no physics) option.

3. The areas between footsteps are highlighted with a yellow box. These are areas where vertical dynamics are being calculated. Clicking a box turns it solid yellow, causing vertical dynamics to be suspended (see Figure 7.23).

FIGURE 7.23

Free-form areas with vertical dynamics turned off are shown as solid yellow boxes in the Footstep track in Track View.

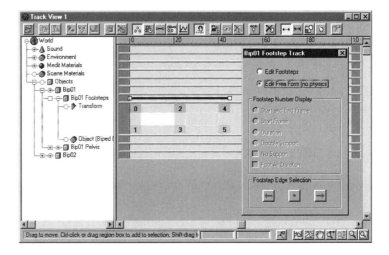

After vertical dynamics is suspended, the biped can be animated in any manner desired—to fly it around the world, for instance, or to mount and ride a bicycle. The only caveat is that the free-form animation must occur between two sets of footsteps, which means that the biped's feet automatically attach themselves to footprints when the free-form section ends.

If the free-form section is at the end of the animation, the end footsteps must be placed a few frames past the end of the animation. The converse goes for free-form animation at the beginning of a scene. In that situation, the footsteps preceding the free-form section are placed before the first rendered frame.

If the character is to resume walking, the free-form animation needs to match up to the footprints at the end of the free-form section; otherwise the biped seems to pop into place.

Standing Still

If your character's feet are firmly planted throughout the animation, you can place only two footsteps in the scene and extend their lengths from within Track View to match the length of the scene. This locks the feet down and gives you the freedom to animate the upper body as desired.

Attaching the Hands and Feet to MAX Objects

Biped has the capability to attach or lock a biped's hands and feet to any object in the scene, which enables Biped skeletons to grip and hold onto things, as well as to keep their feet firmly locked to moving objects (an escalator perhaps). The object attached may be a point in the world space or a point relative to another object (such as the Object Space object).

These attachments can be animated through the use of the IK Blend spinner in the Track Operations rollout (see Figure 7.24). This spinner is the heart of Biped's animatable IK attachments. With it, you can make a biped's hand or foot gradually release its lock. When the IK Blend is set to 1.0, the hand or foot is firmly locked relative to the object space object or at a point in space. If the rest of the biped is moved, the hand or foot remains at the same location. At an IK Blend of 0.0, the motion of the hand or foot is based on the motion of the biped. If the rest of the biped is moved, the hand or foot moves along with it.

Each key for a hand or foot can be set in the Body or Object Coordinate space. If two consecutive keys are set in Body space and the IK Blend value for each is set to 1.0, the location of the hand or foot is interpolated between these keys based on the motion of the object space object. If the Object Space object is moving, therefore, the hand or foot moves along with that object. To attach a hand or foot to an object or a point in space, use the following steps.

ATTACHING HANDS OR FEET

1. Select the hand or foot.

2. Position the hand or foot in its desired position relative to the object to follow.

3. Click the Select Object Space Object button.

4. Click the object to follow. Not selecting an object binds the hand or foot to a fixed position in world space.

5. In the Kinematics section, choose the Object option.

6. Set the IK Blend spinner at 1.0

7. Click Set Key.

FIGURE 7.24

The Track Operations rollout with the Kinematics box. All the operations for animating a lock occur here.

To release an object, spin IK Blend to 0.0 and set another key. As the spinner animates to zero, the lock is gradually broken. If you want to keep a hand or foot locked for a period of time and then release the lock, a second IK Blend key of 1.0 is needed to keep it locked until the release begins. To maintain the position of the hand or foot relative to the object space object, toggle on the appropriate Anchor button in the Track Operations rollout. This action holds the hand or foot in place regardless of the keys set for the hand or foot. Anchors are not permanent; rather they are interactive tools to enable you to set keys with the hand or foot in a fixed position relative to the object space object (or fixed in world space if no object space object has been chosen).

One new feature with version 1.1 is the capability to attach portions of a biped to himself by using the IK Blend function. This enables you to work with closed loops of biped linkages and objects. A sword can be linked to a biped's left hand, for example, and the right hand can be linked via IK Blend to the sword, creating a closed loop of links that can be animated together. As a result, movement of the left hand controls both the sword and the movement of the entire right arm. In addition, you can animate the IK Blend spinner for the right hand to release its grip on the sword during motion.

Using IK Attachments to Dribble a Ball

In this exercise, you experiment with IK attachments and see how changing the IK Attachment parameters affects the biped's motion.

DRIBBLING A BALL

1. From the accompanying CD-ROM, load 07max07.max, which contains a biped and a ball. Activate the Left viewport and play the animation.

    The left hand has been positioned to be on top of the ball at frame 0. It then moves down to the biped's side at frame 16. The ball moves up, then down to hit the ground, and bounces back up.

2. Select the biped's left hand and open the Motion panel.

3. Go to frame 0. Click the Select Object Space Object button and then click the ball. Object Ball appears as the object space object. Select Object in the Kinematics section of the Track Operations rollout. Set the IK Blend value to 1.0 and click Set Key.

    Based on the height of the ball, you want the hand to remain locked to the ball until frame 12. If we just advance to frame 10 though, the hand is no longer in its proper position relative to the ball.

4. At frame 0, click the Anchor Left Hand button to toggle it on. Advance to frame 10, select Object in the Kinematics section of the Track Operations rollout, set the IK Blend value to 1.0, and click Set Key. Click the Anchor Left Hand button to toggle it off and play the animation.

    The hand now remains in a fixed position relative to the ball on frames 0 to 10, and then drops away from the ball and moves to the side of the biped. Now you want to catch the ball on its rise.

5. At frame 0, click the Anchor Left Hand button to toggle it on. Advance to frame 33, select Object in the Kinematics section of the Track Operations rollout, set the IK Blend value to 1.0, and click Set Key. Click the Anchor Left Hand button to toggle it off, and play the animation. The hand now meets the ball as it is rising.

6. Perform an Edit/Hold to save the file and start playing with the IK attachment parameters, particularly on frames 0 and 12. Note that if Body space is selected, or the IK Blend value is 0, the motion of the ball has no effect on the motion of the hand.

The final animation can be found on the accompanying CD-ROM as 07max08.max.

Using IK Attachments to Ride a Bicycle

In this exercise, you see how Biped's animatable attachments can help with difficult animation tasks. Locking objects to a bicycle, such as both hands to the handlebars, can easily cause dependency loops in MAX's native IK. Biped provides a very elegant solution and enables you to lock different parts of the biped's hierarchy to any object or combination of objects.

RIDING A BICYCLE

1. From the accompanying CD-ROM, load 07max09.max, which contains a biped and a simple bicycle (see Figure 7.25).

2. Select the biped's Center of Mass object and open the Motion panel. Drag the biped so that his pelvis is over the seat. Go to frame 0 and set a key for both the Vertical and Horizontal tracks. This can be done by selecting the Restrict to X or the Restrict to Y button, clicking Set Key, then selecting the Restrict to Z, and finally clicking Set Key. Alternatively you can select the Restrict to XZ or Restrict to YZ and click Set Key. This creates keys on both the Vertical and Horizontal tracks. When you set the first key, a warning stating that you are about to create a Biped animation without footsteps appears. This is fine, so press OK.

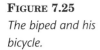

FIGURE 7.25

The biped and his bicycle.

3. Link the biped to the bicycle. Press the Select and Link button on the toolbar. Drag a line from the Center of Mass object to the bicycle seat to make the biped a child of the bicycle, enabling him to move wherever the bicycle moves.

4. Bend the biped over a bit so that the arms can reach the handlebars. Select one spine segment and, using Bend Links, rotate the spine approximately 32° about his z-axis so that the chest is over the pedals (see Figure 7.26). Set a key.

5. Select the biped's right foot. Drag this up and forward so that it rests directly over the right pedal. Select the left foot and drag it to the left pedal in the same manner (see Figure 7.27).

6. Link the right foot to the right pedal. Select the right foot. In the Kinematics section of the Track Operations rollout, choose the option marked Object. Press the Select Object Space Object button. Click the right pedal to select this as the object space object. Set the IK Blend spinner at 1.0. With the Time slider on frame 0, set a key for the foot.

FIGURE 7.26

The Biped properly positioned before linking the feet to the pedals. The spine is bent forward.

FIGURE 7.26

The Biped properly positioned before linking the feet to the pedals. The spine is bent forward.

FIGURE 7.27

The biped with the legs locked to the pedals.

7. Repeat this procedure for the left foot and left pedal.

    Both feet are now locked to the pedals. They will move wherever the pedals move. The pedals have already been linked to the crank, so they rotate as the crank rotates.

8. Scrub the animation. The feet now follow the pedals. Next you need to attach the hands to the handlebars.

9. Select the hands and position them over the handlebars. To get a more natural pose, you should also rotate the arms so that the elbows are slightly out from the body. At frame 0, set a key for each arm to lock in the angle of the elbows.

10. Using the same procedure in step 6, lock each hand to the Bike-Handle object and set a key for each hand's IK Blend at frame 0.

11. Rotate the handle bars. The hands and arms should follow.

12. Adjust the biped's Center of Mass object so that the pelvis rests firmly on the seat. Set a key at frame 0. Figure 7.28 shows the final position of the biped.

FIGURE 7.28

With the hands and feet locked to bike, the biped's animation is driven by the animation of the bike.

13. Experiment with the animation. Because the links are bound on frame 0, any motion of the bike past that point is reflected in the biped. You can extend the animation by copying the cycle of the pedals, and can make the bicycle move by translating it. Rotations to the handlebars are reflected, and if you want to make the biped stand up on the pedals, translate the Center of Mass object up so that the biped stands.

This final animation is on the accompanying CD-ROM in a file called 07max10.max.

Saving and Loading Canned Motions

Biped enables you to save motions from one biped and apply them to another. The motions are applied regardless of the differences in size and structure of the two bipeds. This is very powerful in that it enables you to create canned libraries of motions that can be applied anywhere. Biped has two types of motion files: Biped (.BIP) files, which store the footsteps and associated keyframes of a biped character, and step files (.STP), which store just the footsteps.

The STP file format is rarely used because it merely generates the default Biped motions when loaded. This file format is mainly provided for programmers who might wish to write software that parametrically creates STP footstep patterns (crowds of bipeds walking in a building, for example).

A major feature of Biped is its capability to adapt any BIP file to your character without changing its kinematic structure, dimensions, distribution of weight, and so on. Furthermore, any Physique mapping is also completely independent from the motions. You can load any BIP file onto a biped without changing his Physiqued skin, his pose, kinematic structure, or his center-of-gravity in Biped's Figure mode. The only animation type data not stored in a BIP file are IK attachments to scene-specific objects—because these are, by nature, scene specific. This data is best stored in scenes in the normal MAX file format.

To save a STP or BIP file, select any portion of the biped and, in the Biped Motion panel, click the Save File button in the General rollout. Select the type of file to save, as well as its path and file name, and click OK. All footsteps (and keys for BIP files) associated with the biped are saved.

To replace the entire animation currently applied to a biped with that defined in a BIP file, select any portion of the biped and, in the Biped Motion panel, click the Load File button. Select the BIP file to load and click OK.

A BIP file can also be read into the Footstep buffer and spliced into the current animation. To do this, you need to be in Buffer mode and then load the BIP file. To enter Buffer mode, however, footsteps need to be present in the Footstep buffer. To do this, you need to go into Footstep Track mode, select

Operations rollout. This action copies the selected footsteps into the Footstep buffer and enables the Buffer Mode button.

Frequently, you will not want to apply the entire animation defined in a BIP file, but only a section of it. At the current time, there is not a way to directly do this. Although you can load the animation defined by the BIP file into the Footstep buffer and delete the undesired footsteps, this causes the animation keys to be regenerated. This can also cause a loss of the very animation data you are trying to splice in. The easiest way to get around this is to place another biped in the scene, apply the animation in the BIP to that biped, and copy and paste motions from this biped to the desired one. In the following exercise, you do precisely that.

SPLICING MOTIONS

1. Load 07max04.max from the accompanying CD-ROM. This file contains a biped walking forward, turning left, and walking a bit farther. You want to splice in a motion where the biped walks on tiptoes.

2. Create another biped in the Perspective viewport. This biped will be used as an intermediary, holding the animation imported from the BIP file for application to the original biped.

   Because Biped can properly adjust the animation data while moving between dissimilar bipeds, the details of this biped do not need to match those of the original biped. To prevent the loss of data, however, if the original biped has arms or a tail, this biped should also. As a practical matter, this biped should be roughly the same height as the original biped.

3. With this new biped selected, in the Biped motion panel, click the Load File button in the General rollout. Load creep.bip from the accompanying CD-ROM.

4. Play the animation. As the original biped walks along, the new biped creeps along.

5. With the new biped selected, click the Footstep Track button. Select footsteps 3 through 5, and click the Copy Selected Footsteps button in the Footstep Operations rollout. Click the Footstep Track button to exit Footstep mode.

6. Select any portion of the original biped and click the Footstep Track button. Click the Insert Footstep Buffer onto Footsteps button to display the footsteps in the Footstep buffer.

7. Drag the first buffer footstep over the biped's footstep number 10 and release the mouse. The remaining original footsteps are now shown in their saturated colors. Drag these footsteps so that the first one is over the new footstep 12 and release the mouse.

8. Click the Footstep Track button to exit Footstep mode, activate the Perspective viewport, and play the animation. At this point, you can delete or hide the biped added to the scene.

When you splice in a set of footsteps, sometimes the leg rotation near the end of the splice is noticeably incorrect—the upper leg is pointing toward the biped's head. A single key has been improperly set in these cases. To correct this, perform the remaining steps:

9. Select the leg with the incorrect rotation.

10. Toggle the Key Mode Toggle button on (the Key Mode Toggle button is located at the bottom on the MAX window with the Time controls).

11. Click the Select and Move or Select and Rotate button.

12. Click the Next Frame or Previous Frame button to advance to the keyframe where the leg rotation is incorrect. Note the frame number and the pose of the biped.

13. Click the Next Frame or Previous Frame button to advance to a keyframe where the biped is in a similar pose.

14. Click the Copy Posture button to copy the leg's rotation to a buffer.

15. Return to the keyframe where the leg rotation is incorrect. Click the Paste Posture button to set the leg's rotation from the buffer. Then click Set Key.

By using BIP files, you can set up libraries of motion that can easily be applied to any biped. The capability to share animations between bipeds, regardless of their size or structure, is not found in any other application.

In Practice: Biped

- **Manipulating bipeds.** Using Biped's manipulation tools, such as Select Opposite, can help streamline your work. It is also possible to freeze or hide parts of a biped while working on others.

- **Footstep-driven animation.** Although footsteps certainly take a lot of the drudgery out of creating locomotive sequences, they are only the first step. To truly bring your characters to life, you need to go back over the Biped-generated motions and bring them to life by adding animation.

- **Bipeds in hierarchies.** If your biped is a child of another object, the biped and his footsteps move in relation to the parent. This makes scenes that require moving footsteps—such as ice-skating or walking up a moving escalator—possible by parenting the escalator's stairs to the biped.

- **Free-form animation.** Free-form animation between footsteps defaults to having dynamics turned on, which causes the biped to simulate a jump motion. Typically, it is best to turn dynamics off when starting a free-form animation.

- **Animatable locks.** This is a very powerful feature, so be certain to practice its use and be familiar with the keystrokes. In addition to locking hands and feet to objects or world space, they can be locked in relation to the body itself.

- **Splicing motions.** This is a feature unique to Biped that enables you to apply animation data to bipeds with dissimilar structures. By building and using libraries of canned motions, you can quickly build complex animations for your characters.

Chapter 8

MESH DEFORMATION

In real life, people are made out of a single skin and in MAX, this skin can be a single NURBS, Polygonal, or Patch mesh. This mesh, however, will look like a rigid statue unless you find a way to deform it. Real skin is very flexible and the actions of muscles and bones beneath the skin are all that is needed to bend and flex the skin. In MAX, a number of tools are available to do exactly the same thing. These are known as Skeletal Deformation tools because they take a skeleton—a Biped or a custom-built skeleton—and use that skeleton to deform a mesh much like it would appear in real life.

MAX's open architecture allows for any number of methods for deforming meshes. For the serious character animator, several plug-ins are on the market. Most popular are Character Studio's Physique and Digimation's Bones Pro. Additionally, several methods for deforming MAX geometry use native MAX tools—most notably FFDs and the Linked Xform tool.

This chapter covers the following topics:

- Deformations using FFD lattices

- Basic skeletal deformation

- Preparing meshes for bones

- Fitting the skeleton to the mesh

- Bones Pro

Types of Meshes

3D Studio MAX version 2 provides a number of ways to create a mesh. Geometry can be created as Polygons, Patches, and NURBS surfaces. Additionally, third-party plug-ins such as Clay Studio and Metareyes can be used to create meshes by using metaballs. The type of geometry you decide to use in the creation of your characters depends on a number of factors, particularly the demands of the project at hand. Video game developers might need to use polygons, instead of patches, for example, simply because most game engines accept only these formats. Regardless of type, any type of mesh can be deformed in one way or another.

Polygonal Meshes

Polygonal meshes have been a popular way of creating objects in 3D Studio MAX. MAX's Polygonal Modeling tools are very robust and they make polygons an attractive choice. Deforming a Polygonal mesh, however, can become increasingly difficult as the resolution of the mesh increases.

High Resolution Meshes

High resolution Polygonal meshes can look fantastic when rendered. Unfortunately, they are the hardest geometry type to deform. This is because high resolution meshes have their vertex information so closely packed that the possibility of tearing or creasing the mesh increases geometrically. Additionally, the large number of vertices also bogs down the system at animation time (see Figure 8.1).

One area that can help with the deformation of high resolution meshes are FFD Lattices, which enable a more subtle deformation that lessens the possibility of tearing.

FIGURE 8.1

A high resolution mesh renders well but can be hard to deform.

Low Resolution Meshes

Low resolution Polygonal meshes are typically used to create characters for the gaming community. The limitations of gaming systems demand that the geometry of any scene not exceed a certain polygon count. This limits the resolution of a mesh to limits that most people working in film or video would find inadequate.

Still, with clever texture mapping, a low resolution character can come across as looking quite nice. Most details, such as wrinkles in clothing, hair, and accessories are simply created as highly rendered texture maps.

From an animation standpoint, the advantage of using low resolution characters is increased performance (see Figure 8.2). Just like in a video game, low resolution meshes can animate quite quickly and on a fast system can even be manipulated in real time.

FIGURE 8.2
Low resolution meshes animate very quickly, but they can look blocky and don't render well.

Polygonal Meshes and MeshSmooth

One significant improvement with version 2 of 3D Studio MAX is in the MeshSmooth modifier. MeshSmooth is simply an object modifier that adds detail to a Polygonal mesh and smooths it out. The improvements include the capability to output quadratic polygons for all faces as well as the capability to retain Mapping coordinates.

The quadratic output option converts the entire mesh to four-sided polygons, creating a much smoother mesh. The mapping improvements are a very welcome addition to those who are animating characters, simply because it enables you to animate a low resolution version of a character and render a high resolution version of the character, effectively giving you the best of both worlds.

This technique works simply by adding MeshSmooth to the stack after the Deformation modifier. This interpolates the low resolution mesh into a high resolution mesh (see Figures 8.3 and 8.4). Because this interpolation happens after the deformation, it creates a very smooth looking surface that is reminiscent of a patch-based model. This is because MeshSmooth calculates the interpolated polygons in much the same way as a Bézier patch, essentially turning your Polygonal model into a patch-based model.

Tesselate is another modifier that works in a similar way to MeshSmooth. The big difference is that tesselate does not round off the corners the way that MeshSmooth does and tends to preserve sharp angles, such as corners.

FIGURE 8.3
A very low resolution hand is deformed.

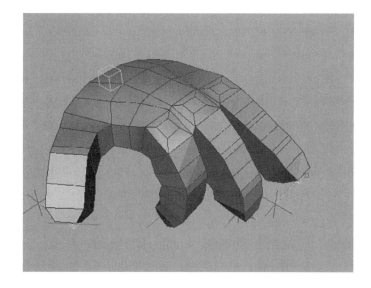

FIGURE 8.4
When MeshSmooth is added after the deformation, the hand smooths out into a seamless, organic surface.

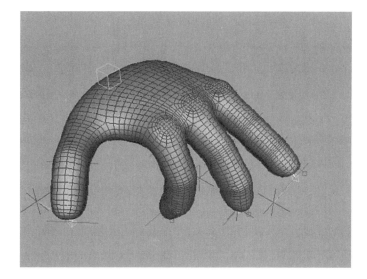

Patches

Because they are a bit more complex to manage than polygons, patches have been overlooked to some degree as an effective modeling tool. They are, however, extremely flexible both from a modeling and animation standpoint. From a modeling standpoint, because patches can be either three or four sided, they don't suffer some of the topology limitations of NURBS surfaces. From an animation standpoint, they are almost as fast as polygons.

One key point with patches is that the resolution of the patch can be dialed in by using the steps spinner in the Topology rollout. The number of steps should be kept low while animating for speed. It can then be dialed up to a higher number for rendering.

NURBS

New to MAX with version 2, NURBS provide a third and welcome option for character animators. NURBS can be used to create extremely smooth and organic surfaces. Most NURBS modeling happens at the Sub-Object level. From an animation standpoint, this enables many different surfaces to be viewed as one object by Mesh Deformation tools. This also provides continuity in mapping as well.

Although NURBS CVs can be animated directly to deform the mesh, Mesh Deformation tools make more sense because many CVs can be animated with a few controlling objects.

One problem with some third-party Mesh Deformation tools is that they do not behave well with NURBS. Some tools tesselate the NURBS surface into a mesh and some simply don't work at all. Most of this is due to the fact that NURBS is new to MAX, and as the offending plug-ins mature, these problems should go away.

Mapping and Mesh Deformation

One problem that many beginning animators face is getting textures to stick to the surface of the character as it deforms (see Figure 8.5). To prevent this, mapping needs to be placed in the stack before the object is deformed (see Figure 8.6). This is the case regardless of the deformation method—a simple taper, bend, an FFD, Bones Pro, or Physique.

FIGURE 8.5

An object is mapped with a simple checker pattern.

FIGURE 8.6

If mapping happens before deformation, the texture sticks to the surface of the object and moves appropriately.

Adding the mapping coordinates can be as simple as generating mapping coordinates when the object is created to selecting multiple groups of faces and adding multiple UVW Mapping modifiers to the stack for each group. The key point is that if the mapping occurs after the deformation, the texture floats across the object (see Figure 8.7).

FIGURE 8.7
*If mapping happens
after the deformation,
the texture does not
stick.*

Deformations Using FFD Lattices

Version 2 of 3D Studio MAX has incorporated some significant improvements to Lattice deformations. The previous version of 3D Studio MAX was restricted to Cubic Lattices with 2, 3, and 4 Control points in each direction. Lattices can now be rectangular or cylindrical and can have any number of Control points in any direction. This gives you much more control when using Lattices as an Object or Sub-Object modifier.

Another important addition are Lattice space warps. These can provide whole new ways of animating. One Lattice can now be used to deform more than one object at a time. This is great for deforming entire hierarchies of objects.

Object Modifier Lattices

Object Modifier Lattices are good overall tools for modeling and their Control vertices can be animated. This makes them a good option for performing mesh deformations. The best way to use Object Modifier Lattices is for local deformations, such as creating bulging biceps or making fat bellies jiggle. To accomplish these sorts of effects, the FFD is best applied as a Sub-Object modifier, usually in conjunction with Edit mesh.

Space Warp Lattices

Space Warp FFDs deform geometry much like Object Modifier FFDs. Space warps, however, can affect many objects, unlike the Object Modifier FFDs, which affect one object or sub-object at a time. You can also animate your objects moving "through" the FFD, so you can create special effects, such as making a car and its occupants fit though a keyhole, for example.

In addition, space warp FFDs behave much like regular objects and have their own stack. The fact that it can have its own stack makes the FFD space warp an attractive option for some character animation tasks because many of the standard MAX modifiers can affect a Lattice. Linked Xform, Physique, and even other Lattices can be used to deform the Space Warp Lattice. The one limitation of Space Warp Lattices is that, because they are space warps, they always float to the top of the stack. This might not be desirable for some applications—for example, when you want to add a modifier such as MeshSmooth to the top of the stack.

Multiple Space Warp FFDs can be applied to one mesh, however. When used in conjunction with bones or dummies and Linked Xforms, a primitive skeletal deformation system can be constructed.

Using a Lattice to Deform a Flour Sack

One of the classic exercises for any character animator is to animate a flour sack. As basic as a flour sack is, a good animator can bring it to life by posing and animating it properly. Not only does this exercise teach you how to maintain character but also about distribution of weight.

Flour sacks are easy to draw, and for 3D animators, easy to model. The problem for 3D animators lies in getting the mesh of the flour sack to deform quickly, smoothly, and easily. For 3D Studio MAX animators, the Space Warp Lattice is a terrific tool for creating such an animation.

Setting Up the Lattice

On the CD-ROM is a file named 08max01.max. It contains a simple mesh resembling a flour sack and five Dummy objects (see Figure 8.8).

FIGURE 8.8

The basic flour sack.

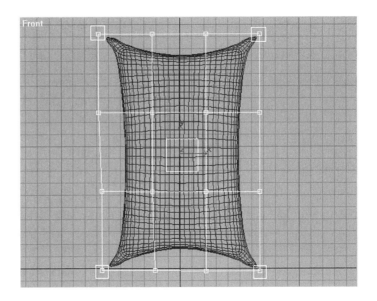

CREATING THE LATTICE

1. From the Create/Space Warps panel, select FFD (Box) and create a 4×4×2 Lattice with a dimensions of 195×135×95.

2. Position this Lattice neatly around the flour sack.

3. Select the object FlourSack and toggle the Bind to Space Warp button from the toolbar. Drag the cursor to the FFD object and release.

4. Select the FFD. Toggle the Sub-Object button to select Control points. Select a few Control points on the Lattice and move them. As you can see, the Space Warp FFD works much in the same way that Object Modifier FFDs operate.

5. Press undo to return the FFD to its original position. Save this file.

Setting Up Dummies to Control the Lattice

Manipulating the raw Lattice by animating the individual control points can certainly be used as a technique to animate the flour sack. The problem with this method, however, is that even a simple 4×4×2 Lattice has a total of 32 Control points. Keeping track of all of these points can prove vexing at animation time.

This dilemma can be circumvented quite handily by employing some Dummy objects to manipulate all the Control points in the Lattice. If you positioned the Lattice properly in the previous exercise, you will notice that the tips of the Lattice line up with some Dummy objects that are also in the scene.

As mentioned before, Space Warp FFDs have their own stack. The Control points of the FFD can be manipulated through the use of good old Linked Xform. This connects the relevant parts of the Lattice to the Dummies. This way, a few Dummies can be animated, leaving the manipulation of the many Control points to MAX.

CONTROLLING THE LATTICE WITH DUMMIES

1. Using the same file you set up in the previous section, select the Space Warp FFD and toggle Control Point Sub-Object mode.

2. From the Front viewport, select the eight Control points at the center of the Lattice (four in the front, four in the back). An image of this is shown in Figure 8.9.

FIGURE 8.9

Selection of the center Control points of the Lattice.

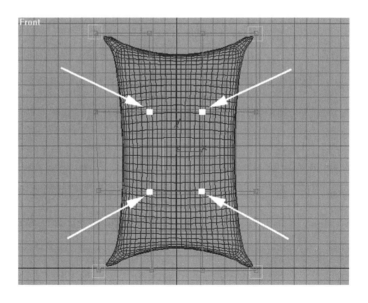

3. Keep the Sub-Object button toggled and add a Link Xform modifier to the stack. Because Sub-Object was toggled, this modifier affects only the selected Control points.

4. From the Link Xform rollout, toggle the Pick Control Object button. Select the dummy named CenterDum, located at the center of the flour sack.

5. Select the Dummy object named CenterDum. Move this object to see how the Control points from the Lattice follow along. Press Undo to return the dummy to its original position.

6. Now attach the outer edges of the Lattice to the remaining dummies. Start with the top-left corner of the Lattice. Add a FFD Select modifier to the stack. This operates much in the same way that the Mesh Select modifier works.

7. Select the six Control points that represent the top-left corner of the Lattice. This selection is shown in Figure 8.10.

FIGURE 8.10

Selection of the top-left corner of the Lattice.

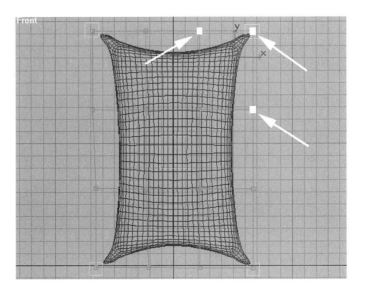

8. Keep the Sub-Object button toggled and add a Link Xform modifier to the stack. Toggle the Pick Control Object button and select the Dummy object TopLeftDum.

9. Repeat steps 7 and 8 to attach the remaining three corners in the same fashion.

10. Once this is done, you have a flour sack that can be manipulated quite simply by using the five dummies. The dummies on the bottom corners represent the feet, the dummies along the top corners represent the arms or shoulders, and the center dummy represents the belly, or center of gravity. Test the assignments by selecting the Dummies and moving them.

11. Once everything works, the FFD Space Warp should be hidden and the flour sack itself frozen. This makes the character easier to animate, because the FFD and the flour sack will not be accidentally selected.

12. When you are done, save your work. A completed version of this file is on the CD-ROM. The file is named 08max02.max.

Animating a Flour Sack

Now comes the fun part—animating the little critter. For this exercise, we will make him jump off of a box. This is a good exercise to learn how distribution of weight works.

ANIMATING THE FLOUR SACK

1. Load the file 08max03.max, which has a flour sack standing on a box. In this file, the Lattice is hidden and the flour sack itself is frozen to prevent unwanted selection of the sack or the FFD.

2. Switch on the Animate button.

3. To make the sack jump, you first want to give the sack a natural pose (see Figure 8.11). Select and position the bottom corners slightly apart and out of parallel. Do the same for the top two dummies, or "arms." Select the center dummy and move it down about 10 units to place the weight closer to his feet.

FIGURE 8.11

An asymmetrical pose looks more natural.

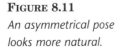

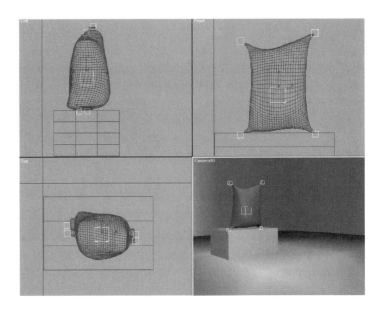

4. To make the sack jump, he first needs to get some momentum. This is done through the age-old animation technique of anticipation—before he jumps up, he needs to bend over to gain the momentum. Move to frame 6, select the top two dummies, rotate them about 20 degrees, and position them slightly in front of the sack and about 20 units down. Select the center and rotate it about 10 degrees (see Figure 8.12).

FIGURE 8.12

Bend the flour sack over at the waist by rotating the upper dummies and moving them forward.

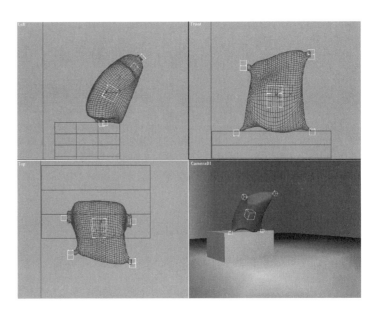

5. Next, create the take-off position. Go to frame 10. Move the two top Dummies up approximately 100 units, forward approximately 70 units, and rotate them −15 degrees. To get some stretch, the lower body should lag by a few frames. Move the center dummy up only about 20 units and forward about 10. Set keys for the feet to keep them locked to the ground at this point (see Figure 8.13).

FIGURE 8.13

Move the top Dummies up and forward to begin the leap while dragging the lower body.

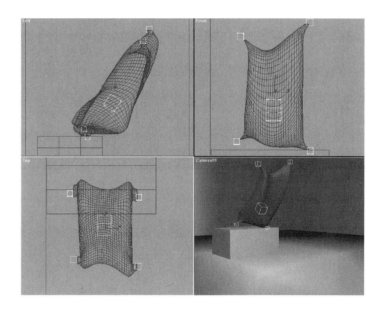

6. Next, pose the top of the leap, which is where the center of gravity hits its peak. Go to Frame 25. Move the center dummy forward about 60 units and up about 20 units. By this time, the upper body is already moving down and the feet have left the platform and moved forward. Move the upper dummies down and slightly behind the center dummy by about five units. Move the feet forward and in front of the body by about five units (see Figure 8.14).

FIGURE 8.14
As the sack hits the top of the jump, the feet have moved forward and the upper body is moving down.

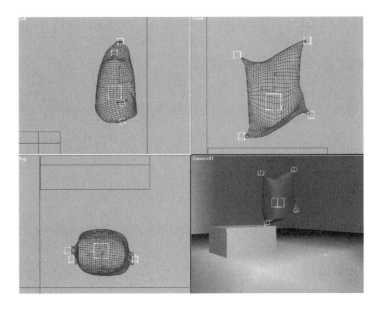

7. As the flour sack begins to touch down, you can stretch the lower body to give a better sense of weight (see Figure 8.15). Go to frame 30. Move the feet down to the ground and forward about 50 units. To create a more natural stance, make one leg hit before the other. Move the center dummy down about 40 units and forward about 40 units. Adjust the top dummies down about 30 units.

FIGURE 8.15
As the flour sack begins to land, you can stretch the lower body to create a better sense of weight.

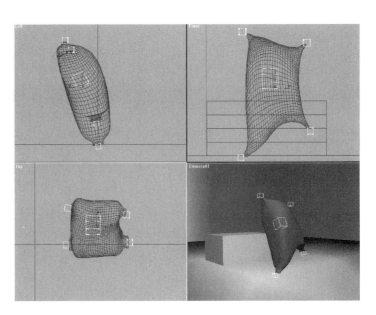

8. The full landing has the flour sack's weight firmly on the ground. Go to frame 35. Move the free foot to the ground and position the center so that the belly touches the ground but doesn't go through the floor (see Figure 8.16).

Figure 8.16

The full landing has the flour sack's weight firmly on the ground.

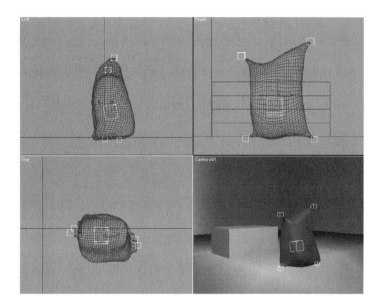

9. The final pose has the weight more evenly distributed. Go to frame 50. Position the center weight up a bit and place the sack in a natural pose (see Figure 8.17).

10. This is by no means the finished animation. You need to go back over the shot several times by yourself to get the timing and the poses correct. One hint might be to add a step or two before takeoff as well as another few steps on landing. A finished version of the animation is on the disk. It is called 08avi01.avi.

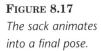

FIGURE 8.17

*The sack animates
into a final pose.*

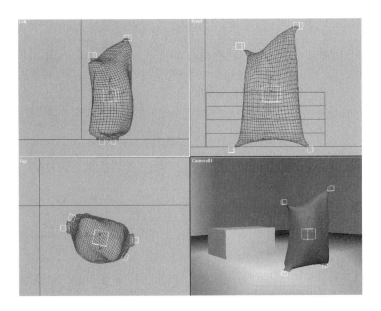

Basic Skeletal Deformation

Although lattices are good for some character animation tasks, most characters need to be deformed by using some form of skeleton. Several methods can be employed to accomplish this. The most popular methods are
Linked Xforms, FFDs, Bones Pro, and Physique. Each method requires a different procedure. To get a comparative overview, therefore, it is best to show
the fundamentals of each procedure on a simple object such as a cylinder,
which is very similar to an arm or leg joint.

Deforming a Cylinder with Linked Xforms

Using Linked Xforms is one method that can be employed without additional plug-ins. The Linked Xform is a very direct manipulation tool that
can be used in a variety of situations. It allows you to link a set of vertices
to a Control object, such as a dummy, a box, or in this case, a MAX bone. This
technique leverages the flexibility of this modifier to attach specific vertices
of the model directly to the skeleton.

XFORM DEFORMATION

1. Load the file 08max04.max from the accompanying CD-ROM. This file contains a simple cylinder with a set of MAX bones inside.

2. Apply an Edit Mesh modifier to the cylinder.

3. From the Front or Top viewport, select the vertices on the right side of the cylinder (see Figure 8.18).

FIGURE 8.18

Select the vertices on either side of the cylinder and apply a Linked Xform modifier to them.

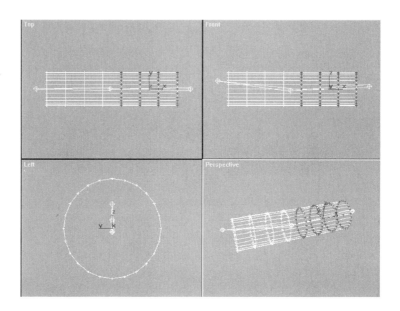

4. Select the Linked Xform modifier.

5. Within the Linked Xform rollout, press the Pick Control Object button.

6. Select Bone01 as the Control object. Select by name to avoid mistakes.

7. Select the cylinder once again. Add another Edit Mesh modifier to the stack.

8. Select the vertices on the left side of the cylinder.

9. Select the Linked Xform modifier.

10. Within the Linked Xform rollout, press the Pick Control Object button.

11. Select Bone03 as the Control object.

The mesh of the cylinder is now deformed by the bones. Turn on IK and translate the end of the bone chain. Because the vertices of the mesh are directly connected to the bones, they move along with them. The one problem with this method is that there is no weighting of vertices, so you can get flat spots in the area between the neighboring Linked Xform modifiers (see Figure 8.19).

FIGURE 8.19

The cylinder's mesh, deformed with Linked Xform modifiers. Notice the flat spots at the joint's "elbow."

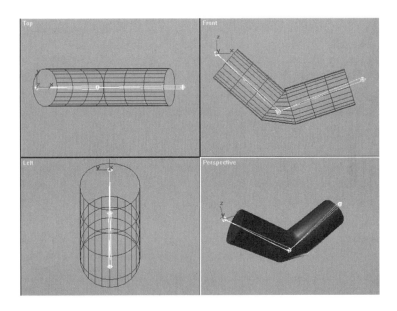

If the Cylinder object was created out of spline patches, the flat spots would smooth themselves over automatically. Not all characters are made of splines, however. One way to sneak around this is to introduce a MeshSmooth modifier in the stack after the Linked Xforms. MeshSmooth actually adds vertices and smoothes out the flat spots in the mesh.

Deforming a Cylinder with Space Warp FFDs

FFDs can be used with bones and Linked Xform in much the same manner as the previous exercise. In this case, however, the bones deform the Lattice, which, in turn, deforms the mesh. For denser meshes, this might be a better method, as the deformation will prove to be smoother (see Figure 8.20).

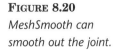

FIGURE 8.20
MeshSmooth can smooth out the joint.

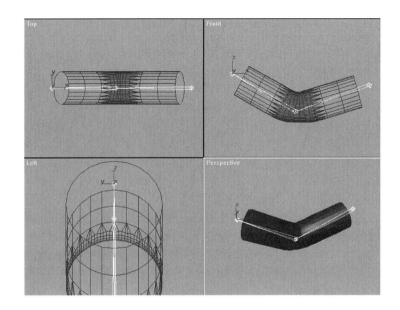

FFD DEFORMATION

1. Load the file 08max06.max from the accompanying CD-ROM. This file contains a simple cylinder with a set of MAX bones inside and an FFD fitted around it.

2. Select the cylinder and bind it to the FFD Space Warp.

3. Select the FFD and toggle the Sub-Object button to enable Control points.

4. From the Front or Top viewport, select the Control points on the right side of the FFD.

5. Select the Linked Xform modifier.

6. Within the Linked Xform rollout, press the Pick Control Object button.

7. Select Bone01 as the Control object. Select by name to avoid mistakes.

8. Select the FFD once again. Add a Select FFD modifier to the stack.

9. Select the Control points on the left side of the cylinder.

10. Select the Linked Xform modifier.

11. Within the Linked Xform rollout, press the Pick Control Object button.

12. Select Bone03 as the Control object.

The setup is now complete. Translating the end effector should now deform the cylinder. Theoretically, this method can also work for complex characters, because multiple Space Warp FFDs can be applied to one object.

Deforming a Cylinder with Bones Pro

Bones Pro is a plug-in sold by Digimation. It enables much more discrete control over the mesh than the previous method. As you will see later in this chapter, Bones Pro enables vertex-by-vertex control over the deformation of a mesh, along with weighting of vertices between bones. A demo version of Bones Pro is on the accompanying CD-ROM.

BONES PRO DEFORMATION

1. Load the file 08max04.max.

2. The Bones Pro modifier has been changed to an Object Modifier for MAX 2. Add the modifier to the stack.

3. Assign some bones. In the box marked Bones, select Assign. A dialog box appears with the names of the objects in the scene. Highlight Bone02 and Bone03, and then press Select.

4. Bones Pro deforms objects that are animated only, and references a "Master" frame (defaulted to frame 0) that indicates the starting position of the deformation (see Figure 8.21). To make the mesh deform, turn Animate on, and move the Time slider a few frames into the scene. Manipulating the bones causes the mesh to deform.

FIGURE 8.21

The cylinder deformed by using Bones Pro.

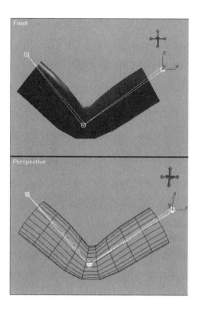

Getting Meshes Ready for Bones

Although deforming a character by using bones might look easy, getting your mesh to deform smoothly can sometimes be a real problem. No matter which plug-in you decide to use, your joints find ways to crimp, bulge, tear, or flatten at the wrong places, making your character look worse than when you started. Every animator runs into these problems, but you can use techniques to help your meshes behave:

■ Build the mesh with the character's arms outstretched.

■ Add extra detail at the bends.

Arms Outstretched

The best argument for building a character this way is that the arms are exactly halfway between the extremes that the arm can take. It is tempting to build a character with its arms at its side. This is one of the more common poses a human takes. Unfortunately, if a character built that way needs to put his arms above his head for any reason, the skin around the underarms has to stretch twice as much as if it were built with the arms outstretched. Centering the arms helps prevent crimping, tearing, and unwanted bulging later on when the character is deformed (see Figure 8.22).

FIGURE 8.22

Building a character with the arms out-stretched allows for a much wider range of motion.

Because the legs don't have nearly the range of motion the arms do, keeping them outstretched is not as critical, particularly for characters that only walk and sit. If the characters are supposed to perform gymnastics, it might give you a bit more control if the legs are slightly apart when built.

Extra Detail at the Bends

Adding detail only where it is needed keeps your models light and easy to control. Many places on the body don't flex as much as others. The elbow and the skin around it flexes quite a bit, for example, but the forearm itself remains fairly rigid. Therefore, the forearm does not need nearly as much detail to retain its shape as the area around the elbow joint. Extra detail also needs to be placed at the knees, the shoulder, the crotch area, and the areas around the wrists and the many joints of the hand. One good reference is the Viewpoint models supplied with MAX and Character Studio, which are built with detail in the proper places.

Eliminating the detail from rigid areas such as the forearm significantly reduces the number of vertices in the model and also reduces the total weight of the model. A lighter model animates easier, deforms more quickly, and renders faster (see Figure 8.23).

FIGURE 8.23
Add detail only where it is needed—at the joint areas where the mesh flexes and bends.

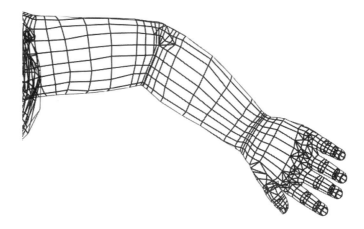

Fitting a Skeleton to a Mesh

After the solid mesh model is built, a skeleton of bones needs to be fit into it for the solid mesh to be deformed. Construction of skeletons was discussed in detail in the previous three chapters. The skeleton can be a Biped, a skeleton of MAX bones, or made from geometry such as boxes. The skeleton is usually tied together in a hierarchy and set up for animation using Forward or Inverse Kinematics.

If you are not using Biped and are building a custom skeleton from scratch, it is best to construct the skeleton with the mesh in mind—even going to the point where you are actually loading the mesh model, freezing it, and then building the skeleton within it, and finally linking the skeleton together in a hierarchy and setting up IK last.

However it is done, the key to fitting a skeleton to a mesh is lining up the joints correctly. Typically, the extra detail modeled in the joints is the guide to use. Line up the joints of the skeleton so that they match up with the joints of the mesh. The key areas to focus in on are as follows:

■ The elbow and knee

■ The hip and pelvis

■ The shoulders

The Elbow and Knee Areas

Placement of bones in the elbow and knee areas is fairly straightforward: center the joint of the bones within the area defined by the joint (see Figure 8.24). If it is modeled properly, the mesh should have a bit of extra detail in this area to help guide the positioning of the bones.

FIGURE 8.24

Placement of bones in an elbow or knee joint.

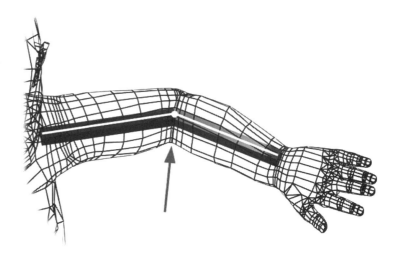

The Hip and Pelvis Area

The hips and pelvis can prove a bit problematic. The hip bone needs to be centered within the hip area, with the leg bones proceeding down through the center of the leg. The detail in the crotch usually flows along an approximately 45-degree angle along the so-called bikini line. Place the joint of the hips and the legs along this line, resizing the hips if necessary (see Figure 8.25).

The Shoulder Areas

These, too, can be problematic. A flexible shoulder joint will aid in placement, particularly if the character is normally sloop shouldered. If this is the case, the shoulder can be rotated downward to match the sloop of the shoulders. The joint between the shoulder and the upper arm should be placed immediately above the armpit (see Figure 8.26).

FIGURE 8.25
Placement of joints in the pelvis area.

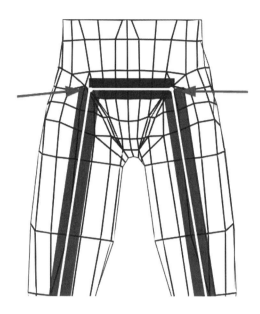

FIGURE 8.26
Placement of joints in the shoulder areas.

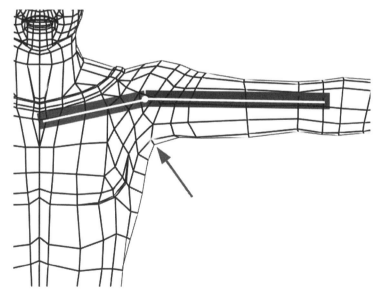

Bones Pro

Bones Pro can use any object as a bone, but it only looks at the bounding boxes of those objects when deciding which vertices to affect. This means that complex geometry used as bones is not necessary. A sphere is still seen by Bones Pro as a cube, because that is the shape of the sphere's bounding box. Because a box's outline is also its bounding box, boxes make for light and easy-to-visualize bones.

Bones Pro Rollout

The Bones Pro rollout is where the bones themselves are selected and assigned to the mesh (see Figure 8.27). You should be aware of a number of controls in this rollout:

- Master Frame
- Bones and Bound Node boxes
- Falloff and Strength spinners

FIGURE 8.27

The Bones Pro rollout.

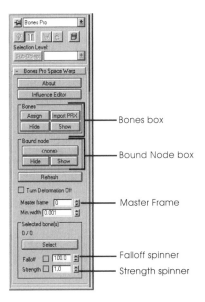

Bones box

Bound Node box

Master Frame

Falloff spinner
Strength spinner

Master Frame

The Master Frame spinner determines on which frame the vertices are assigned to the mesh. Usually, this is frame 0, but any frame can be selected. What is essential is that the skeleton be fitted properly to the mesh on the selected frame.

The fact that Bones Pro requires a Master frame might make it a bit tricky to get it working with a Biped. Bones Pro does not reference Biped's Figure Mode information, so getting the Biped into a stable pose so that it can fit to the mesh can be difficult. If a Biped's animation involves footsteps, the best way to get around this is to create a freeform section in the animation outside the rendering range, and then pose and fit the Biped to the mesh within the freeform section.

Bones Box

Within this box are buttons for assigning the bones to Bones Pro. Bones and meshes can also be hidden or revealed by using the Hide and Show buttons. This is handy for switching off the mesh while animating. On all but the fastest systems, the calculations required to deform the mesh can slow down the system considerably. Hiding the mesh prevents these calculations from taking place and speeds up real-time playback. Conversely, the skeleton should be hidden before rendering and the Hide and Show buttons enable this.

Falloff and Strength Spinners

Bones can be selected from the rollout and assigned to Falloff and Strength spinners individually or in groups. The Falloff spinner determines how much of the mesh is affected by the bone. A larger number means that the bone affects a larger area and more vertices. The Strength spinner determines how heavily these vertices are affected. A larger number pulls the affected vertices closer to the bone.

Influence Editor

This is where vertices are assigned to the skeleton. The Influence Editor has a viewport for viewing the skeleton and the mesh, along with a number of tools for selecting, modifying, and visualizing the effects of bones on vertices (see Figure 8.28). Because the Influence Editor has a viewport, there are the standard navigation controls, along with a pull-down menu to select the standard views (Front, Top, Left, and so on).

FIGURE 8.28

The Influence Editor.

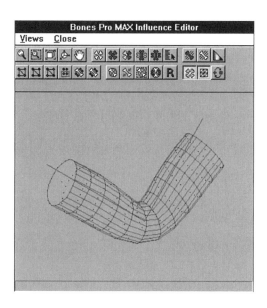

Bone Selection Tools

By default, the Influence Editor is in Bone Selection mode. Clicking any bone selects and highlights it. Clicking again deselects it. In addition, a number of selection controls are provided to assist in filtering the selection. They enable you to select All, None, or Invert the Current Selection. In addition to this are two buttons named Select Unlinked and Deselect Unlinked. These buttons highlight all bones that are not direct parents or children of the selected bone.

In addition to Bone Selection controls, tools are provided for assigning falloff and strength values to any bone or group of bones. These replicate the controls found in the Space Warp Control panel.

Visualization Tools

The Visualize button enables you to see exactly how a selected bone is influencing the mesh. Pressing this button and selecting a single bone produces a rendered image of the mesh. Highlighted on the mesh is a gradient that represents the selected bone's strength and falloff. Colors closer to blue are unaffected vertices and colors closer to red are more strongly affected.

Vertex Selection Tools

Vertex selection buttons enable you to select groups of vertices so that they can be assigned or excluded from the influence of specific bones. These tools enable you to select or deselect all vertices, select them by region, or select and deselect vertices in the range of a specific bone or groups of bones.

Assigning and Excluding Bones to Vertices

By far, the most important group of buttons are the Bone & Vertex Exclusion buttons. These buttons are the heart of the Influence Editor window because they control the assignation and exclusion of specific vertices to specific bones. This is accomplished by selecting a group of vertices and a group of bones and then including or excluding the vertices from the bones.

By default, all Bones Pro vertices are influenced by all bones. The Bone & Vertex Exclusion buttons enable you to alter this. One obvious example might be the head. It should not be affected by bones in the hands or feet. If the character were to scratch his head, for instance, the vertices in the head, by default, would tend to be attracted to the bones in the hand. These buttons enable you to exclude the specific vertices in the head from being influenced by the bones in the hand.

One of the more handy buttons is the Exclude Unlinked button. This enables you to quickly exclude bones that should have no direct influence. A good example of where this might be used is the feet and legs. The right leg should be immune from the effects of the left. Exclude Unlinked assigns vertices between bones that neighbor each other in the hierarchical scheme only. This way, the bones in the right shin are affected by the right thigh and the right foot, but not any other bones.

T IP

Assigning vertices with the Select Vertices by Region tool should be done only as a last resort for packets of stray vertices. It is usually better to select vertices by bone influence rather than by regions, because selection by region invariably produces stray vertices.

Deforming a Body with Bones Pro

One of the more challenging tasks that Bones Pro can be used for is to deform an entire body. This is also a good way to understand the basic tools and procedures contained within the Influence editor.

DEFORMING THE BODY

1. Load the file 08max07.max.

   This file has a simple mesh character with a skeleton fitted to it. The skeleton also has a simple animation. This has been added so that it moves the character through a wide range of motions.

2. Select the object Body and add the Bones Pro modifier to the stack.

3. From the Bones Pro rollout, select "Display Subtree" from the Selection panel. All the bones are parented by the hips. Select these objects.

4. From the Bones Pro rollout, open the Influence Editor.

5. Move the Time slider to frame 30. Notice how the feet are influenced by each other, causing the shoes to distort (see Figure 8.29). Select the bones in the shin, feet, and toes for the right and left side of the body. Press Exclude Unlinked from Selected Bones. The feet should snap into place.

FIGURE 8.29

This situation with the feet can be corrected by selecting the lower leg bones and using the Exclude Unlinked from Selected Bones function from within the Influence Editor.

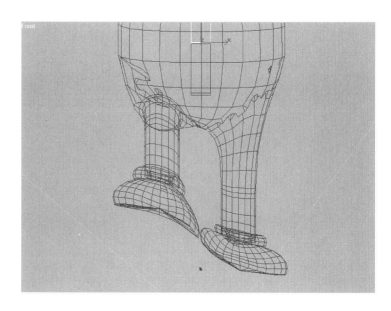

6. Move the Time slider to frame 10. On this frame, the arms are above the head and there is a significant bulge underneath the arms (see Figure 8.30). This is a common problem. To visualize this, select one of the upper arm bones and press Visualize Bone's Influence. This shows a bright area around the upper arm that extends down to the rib cage. Selecting the Spine03 bone and performing the same function shows that the spine has little or no influence over this area.

This lack of Influence is because the spinal bones in this particular skeleton are rather small and their bounding boxes don't extend to the rib cage. Rather than rebuilding the skeleton, you can amplify their Influence by increasing the Falloff—the volume affected. For the three bones in the spinal column, set the Falloffs: Spine01 at 150, Spine02 at 200, and Spine03 at 250. As these are set, notice how the model begins to snap into place. You can further amplify the effect of these bones by increasing their Strength to 2.0. This should pull the model further into place.

FIGURE 8.30

The Visualize tool indicates that the arm's Influence over the rib cage is large, causing a bulge.

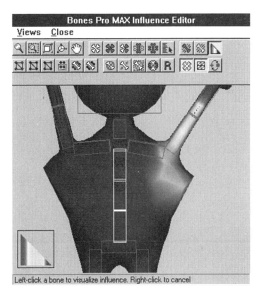

7. The arms, however, are still affecting the rib cage area (see Figure 8.31). Because these bones are supposed to affect the area immediately around the arm only, these bones' Influences can be reduced. Set the bones in the upper arm to a Falloff of 75.

FIGURE 8.31

Adding more Strength and Influence to the spine pulls the bulge into place.

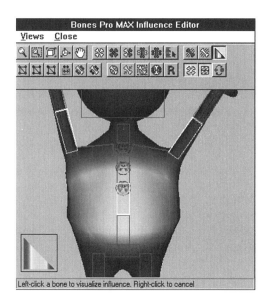

8. Move the Time slider to frame 30. At this frame, you will see the legs distort the lower belly. To eliminate this, reduce the Influence of both thigh bones so that they have a Falloff of 60. Increase the Strength of the hip bone from 1.0 to 1.5.

9. You now see a single vertex being pulled off of the right shoe by the left (see Figure 8.32). From the Front view, zoom into this vertex. Using the Select by Region tool, select this lone vertex.

10. Zoom out slightly and use the Bone Selection tools to select both bones in the right foot. Press the Include Selected Vertices into Selected Bones button. The vertex snaps halfway between the two feet. This is because the left foot is still affecting this vertex.

FIGURE 8.32

This stray vertex can be fixed by selecting it and including it into the proper foot.

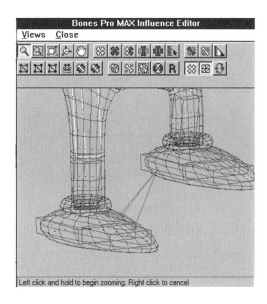

11. Press the Invert Bone Selection button. Now press the Exclude Selected Vertices from Selected Bones button. This frees the stray vertex from any Influences, except for those of the right foot. It will snap into place.

The basic setup is now complete. You can continue to work through the model and fine-tune the parameters within the Influence Editor.

Getting the mesh to deform properly over a wide range of motion might give you some headaches. If you are diligent and test every conceivable body position, however, you should have a rock solid character. Hopefully, you will only have to set up the skeleton one time, and after it is set up, you will have a character that you can use again and again. Even if it takes a day or two to set up the skeleton properly, it's worth it. The time you spend tweaking the skeleton pales in comparison to the time you spend animating your character. Also, having to go back and fix things is never pleasant, so test thoroughly.

In Practice: Mesh Deformation

- **Building the mesh.** Patches work better than Polygonal meshes. Add extra detail at the joints, and model the character with the arms outstretched.

- **Fitting the skeleton to the mesh.** Use the extra detail modeled into the mesh as a guide for placing the bones. If you are creating a custom skeleton, freeze the mesh and use it as a guide.

- **Linked Xforms.** These are a handy way to perform skeletal deformations right out of the box. Although they don't give you as much control as more sophisticated plug-ins, Linked Xforms can work perfectly well on simple objects needing deformation.

- **Bones Pro.** This program gives you more control over mesh deformation than Linked Xforms does because it can assign weight vertices to bones in any combination. When animating with Bones Pro, remember to keep the Animate button toggled on at all times, because manipulating a skeleton without this button on changes the Master frame and affects the way the bones are assigned to the vertices.

Chapter 9

ANIMATING WITH PHYSIQUE

Physique is the second half of Character Studio. It enables some very sophisticated and controllable deformations of MAX objects. Physique gives MAX users the capability to define specific bulging and crimping over a wide range of joint and body types. Combined with Biped, Physique gives MAX users a very robust environment for animating characters. Although Biped is the preferred method for creating skeletons, Physique can be used with any type of MAX skeleton, including custom-built skeletons or, as seen in the previous chapter, simple chains of bones.

This chapter covers the following topics:

- Physique overview

- Using Physique

- Physique and Biped

- Tendons

One of the more vexing problems digital animators face is simulating the realistic flexing and bending of muscles underneath skin. Moving the vertices of an object so that they deform along with the skeletal bones is only the first step. In real life, the bones are actually driven by muscles and tendons under the skin. These muscles relax and contract to pull the bones in the skeleton around. As anyone who has witnessed a Mr. Universe pageant can attest, contracting muscles can change the shape of the skin significantly.

Although not every character animated in MAX needs to be a Mr. Universe contestant, the capability to effectively control and manipulate the shape and appearance of the skin is very important to all characters. Accurate control of the shape of a character enables you to not only bulge muscles but also to eliminate the nasty crimping and tearing of vertices that can be so common in any mesh deformation package.

Physique enables you to store the outlines and bulge angles of any portion of a character's geometry and apply these to the character according to the joint angle. In theory, it works exactly the opposite of actual motion in which the bulging muscle pulls on the joint and causes it to bend. In Physique, bending the joint causes the muscle to bulge. Although opposite in procedure, visually, the effect is identical.

In addition to bulge angles, Physique's tendons feature gives you the capability to maintain a character's shape over many links, to simulate details such as the small web between the thumb and forefinger or the stretching of the skin around the shoulders as the arm rotates.

Using Physique

Physique is an Object modifier. It is applied like any other Object modifier to the object's stack. To be activated, the Attach to Node button must be toggled and the root node of the skeleton selected. After this occurs, Physique takes a snapshot of the positions and orientations of all the bones on the skeleton and uses this to assign specific vertices to specific bones.

The Physique modifier has two types of sub-objects: link and vertex. Link sub-objects are just the bones themselves; vertex sub-objects are the vertices of the mesh.

TIP

Because Physique is an Object modifier, it should be placed in the stack above any UVW mapping or Sub-Object mapping applied to the object because the texture needs to be applied before the mesh is deformed.

Geometry Types and Physiques

Physique supports all three of MAX's geometry types: NURBS surfaces, Patches, and Polygonal meshes. These are also supported in their native mode, which simply means that they are not converted to Polygonal meshes before deformation. NURBS surfaces are deformed at the CV level, while patches and meshes are deformed at the vertex level.

Although any class of geometry works with Physique, it is much easier to deform a Patch or a NURBS surface, simply because patches have fewer vertices. High resolution polygonal meshes are not desired. This is because the large number of vertices simply bog down the CPU, making real-time interaction difficult. Additionally, the density of the mesh makes vertex assignment hard to manage and can cause unwanted creasing and tearing.

Low resolution polygonal meshes, however, can be used quite effectively with Physique. As mentioned in previous chapters, MeshSmooth can be placed in the stack after the deformation takes place to create a very smooth surface. This technique works quite well with Physique, too, and makes for characters that animate fast and render well.

Using MeshSmooth with Physique

As mentioned in the previous chapter, MeshSmooth can be used with Physique to smooth out an object after it has been deformed, turning a low resolution mesh into a high resolution mesh by adding detail. This method works quite well with Physique and the MeshSmooth modifier is simply added to the stack after Physique. MeshSmooth is toggled off while animating and then toggled on right before rendering.

Using FFD Space Warps with Physique

In addition to the three geometry types, Physique can also be used to deform Space Warp Lattices. This enables Physique to manipulate the manipulator, so to speak. The Lattice deforms the actual geometry, but the shape of the Lattice is determined by Physique and a hierarchy of bones.

This technique might be quite helpful when creating softer deformations in areas such as the torso. The FFD is fitted around the desired area and the vertices from this area are bound to the space warp. Physique is then used to deform the FFD space warp, which in turn deforms the vertices, creating a softer deformation.

Hierarchies and Physique

Physique determines its vertex assignments based on the hierarchy of the skeleton. Physique simply looks at the pivot points of the bones and uses that information to create its default vertex assignments.

Physique assigns vertices by placing an imaginary plane at each pivot in the hierarchy and then making a cylindrical projection through the mesh. The imaginary plane is aligned perpendicular to the axis of the joint. Vertices that lie between the two planes are assigned to the joint; vertices residing outside these boundaries are not (see Figure 9.1). The assignment of vertices is strictly controlled by their location in relation to the joints. This makes joint placement of the skeleton of paramount importance.

In case these imaginary planes do intersect and overlap, vertices can be assigned to one joint or the other but not both. A common case would be the vertices surrounding the pelvis area. Because the pelvic bone and the thigh bones are oriented along different axes, significant overlap occurs in the assignment of the vertices. Vertices in these areas typically need to be reassigned during the course of Physique setup. This procedure is discussed in detail in the section "Vertex Control."

FIGURE 9.1

Physique assigns ver-
tices by placing an
imaginary plane at the
end of each joint.

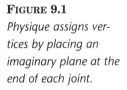

FIGURE 9.1

Physique assigns ver-
tices by placing an
imaginary plane at the
end of each joint.

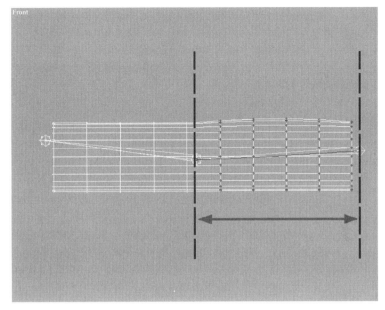

Creating Realistic Bulges

The easiest way to visualize exactly how Physique creates and manages bulges is to use a simple, predictable object, such as a cylinder. This also introduces a number of fundamental concepts, and by using a regularly shaped cylinder, the effects of Physique are made perfectly clear.

APPLYING PHYSIQUE TO THE CYLINDER

1. Load the file bulge.max from the accompanying CD-ROM.

2. Select the cylinder.

3. From the Modify panel, select the Physique modifier and apply it to the stack.

4. Press Attach to Node. The cursor changes to resemble a stick figure.

5. Position the cursor over the root node of the bone hierarchy. This is Bone01. Click the bone.

This is the same procedure that was discussed in Chapter 7, "Animating with Biped," but now that the Physique modifier has been added, it can be taken further by adding a realistic bulge to the cylinder. The file contains a short animation in which the bone in the forearm flexes 90 degrees and then relaxes. Scrubbing the time slider reveals how the cylinder is currently affected—the joint rotates, but the cylinder retains its outline as it deforms with the joints. The joint rotation can be used to create a nice bulge.

The Cross Section Editor

The Cross Section Editor is the heart of many Physique operations and it is one that you will become quite familiar with when using the plug-in. The Cross Section Editor is a floating dialog that enables you to create bulge angles, their cross sections, and, as you will see later, tendons. Its dialog is shown in Figure 9.2, which can be accessed in two ways: by clicking the Cross Section Editor button from within the main Physique rollout or by clicking a specific joint's rollout when Physique is in joint Sub-Object mode.

The Cross Section Editor is modeless, meaning you can use it along with the standard MAX viewports to select and modify parameters on-the-fly. The window has a toolbar with two windows along the bottom—on the lower-left is the Cross Section view, and on the lower-right is the Link view. In combination, these can be used to create and manage the bulge of the skin around the joint.

FIGURE 9.2

The Cross Section Editor. The circular graph on the left is the Outline editor, and the one on the right is the Link editor.

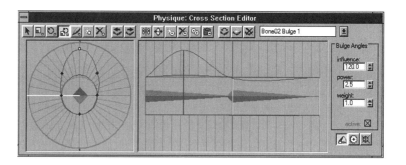

EDITING THE LINK'S CROSS SECTION

To select a specific joint, you need to go into Physique's Sub-Object Selection mode.

1. Using the same cylinder as before, press the Sub-Object button and select the Sub-Object type as Link.

2. From within the MAX viewport, select Bone02. The bone's Link parameters appear.

3. To enable the Cross Section Editor, click the Cross Section Editor button in the Physique Link Parameters rollout.

4. To create a bulge, you first need to tell Physique at what angle the bulge will be defined. The default angle is the angle at which the bone was positioned when Physique was applied. The second angle should be where the joint is rotated the most. In this animation, the maximum rotation is at frame 30. Move the time slider to frame 30.

5. To add a bulge, press the Insert Bulge Angle button. A new bulge angle is created and automatically named Bulge 1.

6. Next, you need to tell Physique exactly where the bulge occurs. This is known as a *cross section*. Press the Insert CS Slice button and the cursor changes. Click the Link view portion of the Cross Section Editor dialog near the center of the left-most link. A red line appears, indicating that the cross section has been added.

7. You can now use the Cross Section Editor to resize the bulge at that angle. Press Select and Scale Ctrl Points and, within the Cross Section view, click the top-most Control point and drag it upward. This movement is reflected in both the Link view and within the normal MAX viewports.

8. Scrub the time slider. The muscle now bulges, as shown in Figure 9.3. When the joint is flat, there is no bulge, but when the joint is flexed, the bulge appears.

9. You can further modify the shape of the bulge by adding more cross sections or by adding more Control points. You can also add more bulge angles to further define how the bulge expands and contracts.

Physique Link Parameters

The bulge can be even further modified by using the Physique Link parameters in the Link Sub-object panel. These parameters give you additional control over how the skin stretches and compresses as the joint bends, twists, and scales.

FIGURE 9.3

A cylinder bulges according to the angle of the joint.

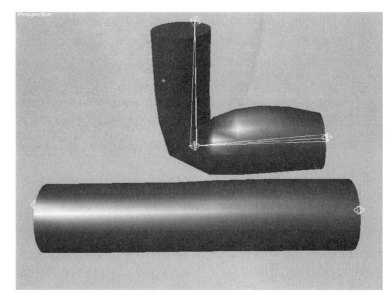

Bend

Bend parameters control the flow of skin over a bending joint, such as a knee or elbow. They apply to hinge-like movement perpendicular to the axis of the bend.

Tension determines the tightness of the crimp at the bend. A higher number produces a more arc-shaped bend, and a lower number causes the joint to crimp more.

Bias determines the angle of the crimp. At 0.5, it is evenly centered between the joints. When it moves higher, the crimp is angled toward the link's child; when it is lower, it is angled toward the link (see Figures 9.4 and 9.5).

Twist

Twist parameters determine how the mesh is affected when the joint is twisted along its length, such as when a hand turns a screwdriver.

Tension determines how much the skin rotates around the length of the joint. A value of 1.0 causes all skin along the length of the joint to rotate evenly. Lower values emphasize the twist closer to the rotating link, and higher values add extra twisting to the skin farther away from the point of rotation. The effects of Twist are shown in Figure 9.6.

FIGURE 9.4

Cylinder bent with different Bias settings.

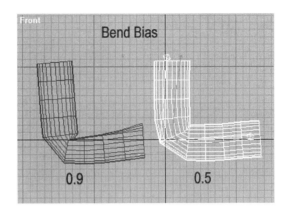

FIGURE 9.5

The figure on the bottom has a high bend tension and the one on the top has a low bend tension.

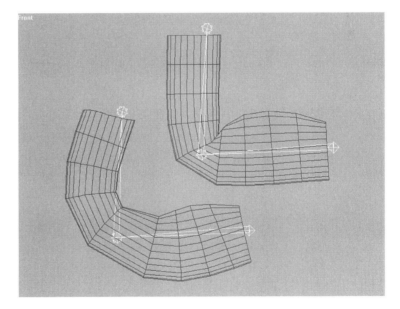

Bias shifts the Twist effect toward or away from the link. A value lower than 0.5 puts more of the twist on the skin covering the child link, and a higher value puts more of the twist on the selected link.

FIGURE 9.6
Checkerboard indicates how twist works.

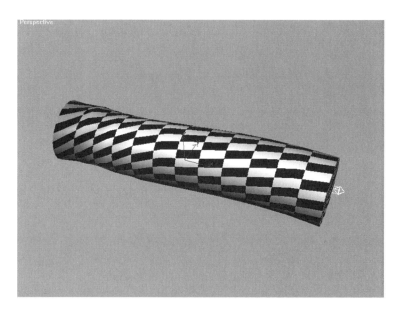

Scale

The Scale parameters affect how the skin and any underlying cross sections are affected by the scaling of the links. Because Physique looks at the hierarchy not the physical bones themselves, the links can be scaled by turning off IK and translating the bones to increase or decrease the distance between the links.

Activating the Stretch and Breathe buttons is one easy way to get Squash and Stretch effects when using Physique. Stretch and Breathe enable you to create this effect automatically by moving or scaling the bone. Stretch pulls out the mesh along the length of the link, whereas Breathe expands the mesh radially (see Figure 9.7). You cannot use this technique with Biped bones, however, because they cannot scale over time.

Physique Joint Intersections

Joint intersections determine how and where the joint creases. Physique tries very hard not to have skin vertices cross over each other because this causes one part of the skin to penetrate another—not something that would happen in real life.

FIGURE 9.7

Bone scaled with and without the Breathe option.

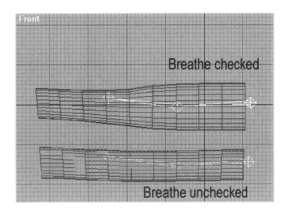

To affect this, Physique places an imaginary plane between the joints and restricts vertices on either side from crossing over. This keeps the skin seamless and can cause a natural crease. A good example is the skin around the fingers. It tends to crease along a nice, flat plane. Sometimes, however, you might want the joint intersections to be less planar, to create a dimple, perhaps.

Typically, the Default Planar joint intersections are fine, but they can sometimes "go flat" before the skin actually touches, particularly when the skin bulges dramatically. This can be tweaked by using the Joint Intersections dialog box. This determines how the plane affects the crease. A bias value of 1.0 means that the plane is fully active, causing a Planar crease; a lower value reduces the planarity of the effect. The From and To spinners determine how much of the skin around the joint is affected by the plane.

Physique and Biped

Although Physique can be used with MAX's native bones or any hierarchy of objects, marrying the two halves of Character Studio enables Physique to be affected by a Biped skeleton. This gives you a very good solution for creating a life-like character.

Fitting a Biped to a Mesh

For Physique to work correctly, the Biped must be properly fitted to the mesh. The joints of the Biped must line up with the mesh's joints. The most critical area is the area where one joint intersects the other. Because

Physique uses the intersection of the joints to define vertex assignment, a misplacement can cause vertices to go astray.

Figure Mode

To facilitate the fitting of a Biped to a mesh, you need to place the Biped in Figure mode, which is a special pose that Biped remembers and can always be returned to with the press of a button. Figure mode also enables resizing and positioning of a Biped freely.

NOTE

You must have an authorized copy of Character Studio installed on your computer to do the exercises in this chapter.

FITTING A BIPED TO A MESH

1. Load your character's mesh file, which is a file on the accompanying CD-ROM entitled 09max02.max that can be used for practice. This particular mesh is a simple, low resolution mesh.

2. Create a Biped roughly the same height as the mesh. In the Biped's Structure rollout, set the number of fingers and toes to match the character. If your character is wearing shoes, one toe will suffice.

3. Select the mesh. Go to the Display panel and press Freeze Selected. This way, the mesh won't accidentally get selected while the Biped is being manipulated.

4. Select the Biped. Go to the Motion panel and place the Biped in Figure mode. In Figure mode, you are free to rotate and scale every joint of the Biped.

5. Select the Center of Mass object and position the Biped over the body so that the hips rest inside the pelvis area. One thing to remember is that manipulating a Biped in Figure mode puts the navigation tools in world space. This means that, from the front, the Biped moves along the XZ axis (see Figure 9.8).

FIGURE 9.8

Proper placement of Biped inside mesh (note that XZ is the front plane).

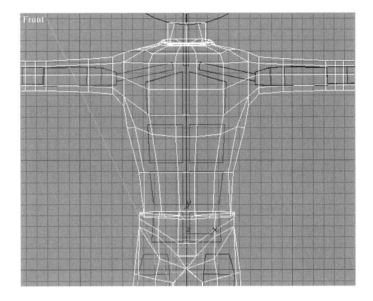

6. Non-uniform scale the pelvis in Z so that the joint between the hips and thighs rests along the V-shaped area, which defines the crease between the tops of the thighs and the crotch (refer to Figure 9.8).

7. Scale the spinal segments so that the shoulders are slightly beneath shoulders of the mesh, and the joint between the shoulder and the upper arm resides above the mesh's armpit.

8. Scale the legs in X so that the Biped's knees are properly aligned within the joint area of the mesh. Rotate the legs to align them with the mesh. The Symmetrical Tracks button can be used to easily select both legs for manipulation. Do the same for the arms and scale them so that the elbows of the Biped line up with the elbow area of the mesh. Rotate the arms to fit into the mesh (use the Top viewport to do this).

9. If your character has fingers that move, adjust the bones in the hand to match the fingers. The Biped's fingers not only can be resized and rotated but also can be moved along the edge of the palm bone to achieve an exact fit.

10. When positioning joints at the end of a chain, such as the head or toes, be certain to place the ends of the bones slightly beyond the edge of the mesh. Because Physique uses the bounding planes of the joints to determine vertex assignment, any vertices not included within these planes will be left behind. In Figure 9.9, the head is too small, so when it tilts forward, the top of the skull remains stationary.

FIGURE 9.9

*If the vertices of the
mesh do not lie inside
the bounding planes
of the joints, the ver-
tices are left behind.*

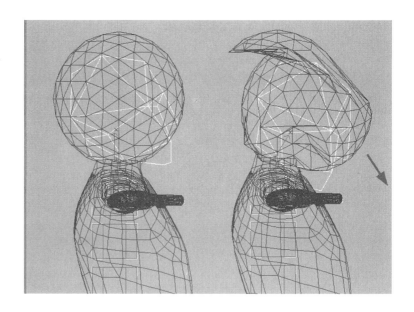

Applying Physique to a Biped

After the mesh has been fitted, you can link the skin to the Biped. The important thing to remember is that the Physique modifier needs to be attached to the pelvis of the Biped, not the Center of Mass object. The Center of Mass object moves on every frame to reflect the changing mass distribution of the Biped. This means that the joint between the Center of Mass and the rest of the Biped stretches and changes shape, causing all sorts of problems.

If parts of the body or clothing are modeled as separate objects, such as a head or a hat, select all the objects and apply a single Physique modifier to them all. Later you'll need to make some of the vertices rigid so that they do not deform (see the next section for a description of how to do this).

Refining How Physique Affects the Mesh

If the character is being used for a wide variety of shots, the model needs to be tested over a wide range of motion to ensure that the skin behaves the way that it should. To test this, it is a good idea to have a test animation that puts the character though its paces. This animation should have the character move its arms and legs through the extremes of motion.

The file 09max03.max on the accompanying CD-ROM is a good example of a test animation to put a Biped and its attached mesh through a wide range of motion. The animation is also saved as a biped file (09bip04.bip) so that you can easily apply it to other models.

Conversely, if the character is being used only for a very specific set of actions, those actions are the only ones that need to be tested. In this case, it might be faster to animate a rough version of the action and then correct any deficiencies in the vertex assignment for those actions only.

Regardless of how you test the motion, if the joint placement of the Biped is correct, most of the vertices in the mesh follow along with the Biped's joints. Unfortunately, nothing is perfect, and there will almost always be stray vertices that cause unwanted bulges.

Vertex Control

If a joint affects an unwanted area of the mesh, the vertices in those areas might need to be reassigned to another joint. To do this, select the Vertex Sub-Object rollout from the Physique panel and reassign the vertices or change their behavior. In Physique, vertices are assigned colors—either red, green, or blue. The specific color of the vertex defines the way the individual vertex behaves. The Vertex Sub-Object rollout is shown in Figure 9.10.

FIGURE 9.10

The Vertex Sub-Object rollout.

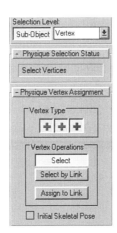

The following list describes the three different types of vertex assignments:

- **Red Vertices.** These vertices are deformable. They flex, bend, and move with the joint to which they have been assigned.

- **Green Vertices.** These vertices are rigid. They move along with the joint, but they do not flex or change shape. This is good for areas such as the head and skull, which remain relatively rigid.

- **Blue Vertices.** These vertices are not assigned to any specific joint and are known as root vertices. They do not move with the skeleton.

By default, each vertex is assigned as deformable, so every vertex in the body should be red. If a vertex is defaulted as root (blue), it means that the vertex did not lie within the bounding planes of any joint within the skeleton and could not be assigned. This is often caused by joints at the end of the chain, such as the top of the head or the ends of the fingers, which did not protrude through the ends of the mesh when Physique was applied. In this case, the Biped needs to be refitted and the Physique modifier reapplied.

One of the most common situations encountered is when the joints in the upper arm affect the area under the arm along the side of the rib cage, causing the skin to bulge as the arm lifts above the head. This happens because the vertically oriented bounding planes of the upper arm intersect the horizontally oriented bounding planes of the spinal bones. In cases in which a vertex can be assigned to more than one joint, Physique just assigns the vertex to the closest joint. Unfortunately, the closest joint is not always the correct joint. One common situation is bulging along the ribcage (shown by the arrows in Figure 9.11), which happens because the vertically oriented bounding planes of the upper arm intersect the horizontally oriented bounding planes of the spinal column.

The Physique Vertex Assignment rollout contains the tools for selecting and assigning (or reassigning) vertices to the correct links.

- **Vertex Type.** This set of three buttons enables you to control which vertices are selected and assigned. These buttons affect the selection set that you create with the Select, Select by Link, and Assign to Link buttons (described as follows). For example, if the red button is depressed, only deformable (red) vertices are selected or assigned.

- **Select.** Enabling this button lets you use the standard MAX selection tools, such as the box or fence, to select groups of vertices.

- **Select by Link.** This button enables you to select all the vertices currently assigned to a single joint. The type of vertices selected depends on the settings of the Vertex Type buttons.

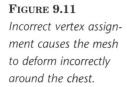

FIGURE 9.11

Incorrect vertex assignment causes the mesh to deform incorrectly around the chest.

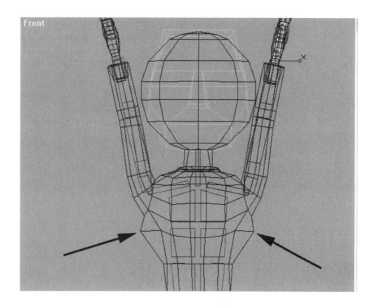

- **Assign to Link.** This button assigns the currently selected vertices to the selected link. The setting of the Vertex Type button determines how these are assigned. If the button is red, the vertices are assigned as deformable, green assigns them as rigid, and blue as root.

T IP

In Character Studio Release 1.1, there is a check box labeled Initial Skeletal Pose in the Vertex Assignment rollout. This check box enables you to toggle between the initial pose (typically with arms outstretched) and whatever pose the figure happens to be in when you enter Physique Vertex Sub-Object level.

MODIFYING THE VERTICES

1. Load the file 09max05.max from the accompanying CD-ROM. This file contains the same character contained in 09max02.max, but with a Biped fitted to it. This is a low resolution Polygonal mesh that will be smoothed out later using MeshSmooth. The Biped also has a short animation to help test the mesh attachment.

2. Select the Biped. From the Motion panel, place the Biped in Figure mode.

3. Select the object MeshMan. From the Modify panel, add the Physique modifier to the stack.

4. From the Physique panel, press Attach to Node. Select the pelvis of the Biped as the root node. Be sure not to select the Center of Mass object. Zoom in so you are sure to hit the right object. By default, the Pelvis object is a yellow-colored rectangular box.

5. Reselect the Biped. Go to the Modify panel and turn off Figure mode.

6. Move the Time slider to frame 10. This is where the Biped moves its arms above its head. Notice the bulge under the arm. This must be fixed by reassigning the vertices within Physique's Vertex Sub-Object mode.

7. Select the mesh. In the Modifier panel, with the mesh selected under Sub-Object vertex, press Select by Link and select the shoulder link. This action highlights all the vertices affected by the shoulder. Notice how the vertices extend down to the underarm area and up into the head.

8. Press the Select button and, while holding down the Alt key and using the Fence Selection tool, deselect the vertices along the upper half of the shoulder, leaving only those along the underarm highlighted (see Figure 9.12).

FIGURE 9.12

The vertices in the bulge are best assigned to the spinal column.

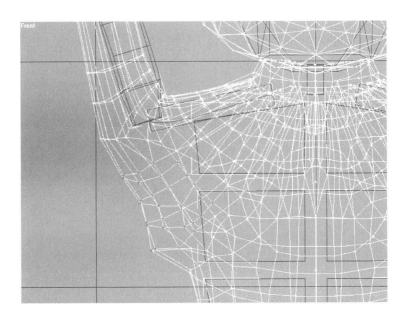

9. Press Assign to Link, select the joint Bip01_Spine3. Most of the vertices pop into place and remain red. A few turn blue, meaning these are out of the bounding plane of the selected joint.

10. To select only the blue vertices, press Select by Link. Within the Vertex Type box, turn off the Red and Green Vertex Type buttons, leaving only the Blue button depressed. Select the joint Bip01_Spine3. Only the blue vertices are selected.

11. Assign these vertices to the spine link immediately below the clavicles. The vertices change color to red.

T IP

Steps 10 and 11 show the "long way" to get the results. In step 10, you can simply Ctrl+click the desired link to assign the root vertices to that link.

12. The head is another area being affected by the shoulders. On this character, the head should be rigid. To accomplish this, make the vertices comprising the head green, or rigid.

    Set Vertex type to all three (red, green, and blue). Press the Select button and using the Box Selection tool, select the vertices in the head.

13. Set the Vertex type to rigid (green) and press the Assign to Link button. Select the head joint. The vertices turn green.

14. Continue through the rest of the body, modifying and reassigning vertices as needed.

15. As soon as the character is satisfactory, place a MeshSmooth modifier on the top of the stack after the Physique modifier. Select quad output and enable smoothing. Notice how the character adds resolution but maintains his mapping.

16. Scrub the animation and you'll notice a performance hit, because MeshSmooth has to recalculate on each frame. Toggle the MeshSmooth modifier off and scrub again. This shows how MeshSmooth can reside in the stack and only be switched on at animation time.

17. Save the file as **09max06.max** (note that this file is also provided on the CD-ROM).

TIP ───

If it is difficult to get vertex assignments exactly right in critical areas such as the pelvis; linking a Dummy object to the offending joint can give you an extra joint to assist in assigning vertices. If this is done, the Physique modifier's default pose must be reapplied.

TIP ───

In Character Studio Release 1.1 and later, you can save the vertex assignments that you've made to one figure and then apply them to another figure, using a file format called .VPH. This can be a great time-saver, assuming that the two models are very similar and start from more or less the same pose. You can use this feature to replace a low-resolution model with a high-resolution version of the same model, for example.

You can use the Cross Section Editor not only for creating bulging muscles but also to fix problem areas of the mesh, such as bulges or creases as well. This is not an obvious use of the Cross Section Editor and it is not described in the Character Studio manual, but it is such a useful technique that an exercise is included to show you how to do it.

As just described, a particularly common problem occurs when the arms raise above the head, the underside of the arm bulges out, and the vertices under the arm tear or cause creases in the body. The Cross Section Editor can be used to further refine the behavior of these joints.

USING THE CROSS SECTION EDITOR TO FIX PROBLEM SPOTS

1. Open the file 09max07.max (this file already has the Physique modifier applied to the mesh). Toggle off the MeshSmooth modifier. Within the Physique panel, go to Link Sub-Object mode.

2. Select the shoulder joint and open the Cross Section Editor from the Physique Link Parameters rollout.

3. Move the Time slider to frame 10 and insert a new bulge angle from within the Cross Section Editor. Name this bulge **Frame 10 Bulge** by using the text box at the top right. Move the slider to frame 20 and insert a second bulge angle. Name this bulge **Frame 20 Bulge**.

4. Move the Time slider back to frame 10 and select the appropriate bulge angle (Frame 10 Bulge). Select default CS slice on the joint between the shoulder and the upper arm. Within the Section view, scale the part of the outline representing the underside of the arm down to reduce the size of the bulge (see Figure 9.13).

FIGURE 9.13

Adjusting the bulge angle by scaling the cross section.

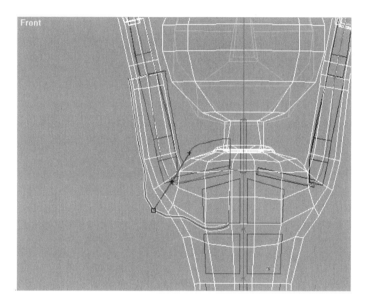

5. Move the Time slider to frame 20 and select the second bulge angle created (Frame 20 Bulge). Select default CS slice on the joint between the shoulder and the upper arm. Within the Section view, scale the part of the outline representing the underside of the arm. This also reduces the size of the crease. Adjusting this bulge angle also reduces the bulge at frame 10.

6. If you need more control, you can add a second CS slice on each arm and scale those appropriately as well.

Figure 9.14 shows the MeshMan model after modification. Even though the vertices have been reassigned, when the arm is raised above the head, a slight bulge still exists. This is fixed by adding a cross section to the Bulge angle on the joint between the shoulder and arm. A second bulge angle on the same joint can also help prevent crimping when the arm is at its side (see Figure 9.15).

FIGURE 9.14

The bulge under the arm is reduced after using the Cross Section Editor.

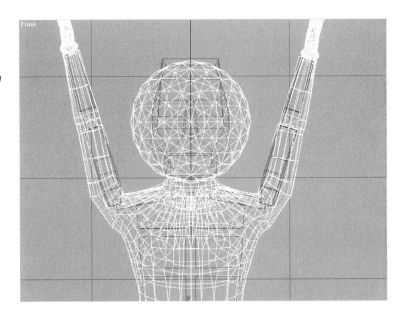

FIGURE 9.15

The second bulge angle is added to the shoulder joint.

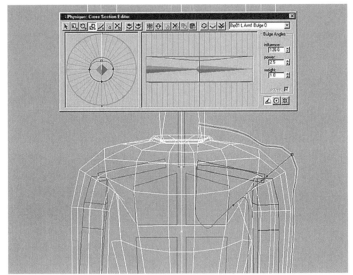

Tendons

Tendons are used to further refine the way the character's skin behaves across many joints when cross sections and bulge angles aren't enough. They enable you to make one joint affect the outline of another joint's vertices over many links. They can be best used in areas such as the shoulder and pelvic areas, where T-shaped branching exists. They can also be used in skinning hands, particularly the fleshy webbing between the thumb and forefinger. A tendon has three main components:

■ **Base.** The base is where one or more tendon cross sections originate. A base may be applied to any link in the skeleton. Usually the base resides in the torso.

■ **Cross sections.** These are much like the cross sections used to create bulges; Attach points are located at radial subdivisions of the outline of the cross section.

■ **Attach points.** These are the points on the cross sections that can be tied to another link. The attached link is usually a shoulder or pelvic bone. Each Attach point may be tied to a different link.

How Tendons Work

For a good example of how tendons affect the skin across multiple joints, use a simple T-shaped mesh and attach a few tendons between the joints as it flexes.

WORKING WITH TENDONS

1. Load the file 09max08.max. This file contains a T-shaped mesh and a set of tendons attached to it. The tendons run from the middle joint of the vertical branch to the middle joint of the right horizontal branch (see Figure 9.16).

2. Move the Time slider to frame 25. Notice how the middle joint on the right limb affects the vertical joint. This is due to the action of a tendon (see Figure 9.17).

3. Move the Time slider to frame 50. As the middle right joint flexes down, it affects the skin on the vertical joint.

4. Move the Time slider to frame 75. Again, the skin on the middle joint bulges, even though many other joints are active.

FIGURE 9.16

This T-shaped object can be used to demonstrate how tendons affect the skin across multiple joints.

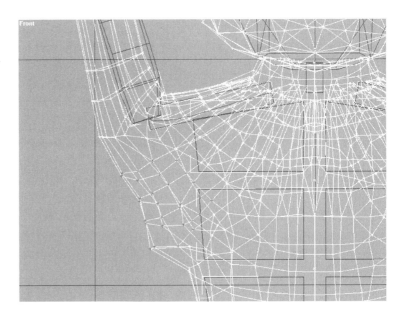

FIGURE 9.17

As the far joints rotate, the skin on the vertical shaft is affected, even though the two joints are not adjacent.

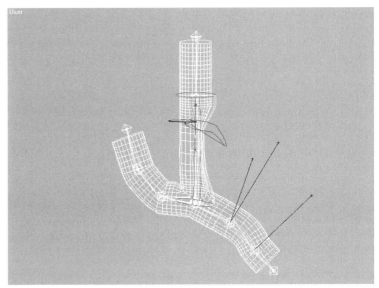

This shows that tendons can give a more globalized effect than just bulge angles, enabling skin to flow across many joints. The T-shaped branch is very similar to the branches that occur in the human body—between the spine, shoulders, and arms; between the spine, pelvis, and legs; and even between the thumb and forefinger. Tendons can be used to the same effect with a Biped or with other types of skeletons, such as 3DS MAX bones.

Creating Tendons

Tendons are created in Link Sub-Object mode from the Physique panel. You just need to select the link that will become the base and press the Create button on the Physique Tendons rollout. This panel has a number of parameters.

- **Sections.** This is the number of cross section bases created for the link.

- **Attach points.** This is the number of radial attach points around each of the cross sections.

- **Resolution.** The radial resolution of the cross sections.

A pair of tendons can be used to help maintain the outline of the belly where it meets the pelvic area. Many times creasing occurs in this area. Tendons can help maintain the shape of the character.

ATTACHING TENDONS

1. Open the file 09max06.max. This file has an animation to test the flexibility of the character. Move the Time slider to frame 50.

2. Select the mesh and go to the Physique Modifier panel select Link Sub-Object mode.

3. Select the central spinal joint (Bip01 Spine 2), scroll down to the Physique Tendons rollout, and set the default Sections parameter to 1. These must be set before the tendon's base is created.

4. Press the Create button. This action creates a base for tendons originating from this joint.

5. Open the Cross Section Editor by clicking Cross Section Editor. Activate the Tendon panel within the Cross Section Editor. Select the Attach point along the front right of the torso, as shown in Figure 9.18.

6. Attach this point to the right clavicle joint. To do this, press the Attach button within the Tendon panel of the Cross Section Editor, and then click the right clavicle joint from within the Front viewport.

7. Repeat the same procedure for the front-left attach point and the left clavicle joint. The tendons are now attached. The tendon, however, does not yet pull the mesh correctly (see Figure 9.19).

8. Save the file. You'll modify the tendons in the last exercise.

FIGURE 9.18

The tendon is in place on the spine link and is ready for attachment.

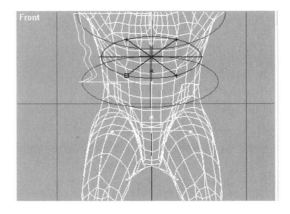

FIGURE 9.19

After the tendons are properly attached, they look like this.

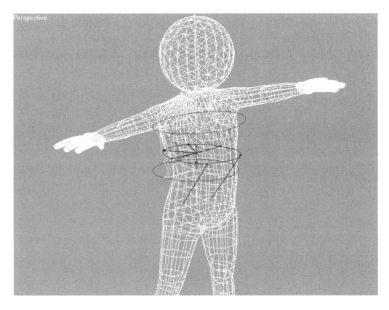

Modifying Tendons

After being attached, the tendons may need to be modified so that they affect the way the skin behaves across the joints. A number of parameters within the Tendon panel of the Cross Section Editor enables you to modify the tendons as needed. These parameters are described here:

- **Radial Distance.** This is how far out the attach points lie from the body. If you look at the tendons from within a MAX viewport, you see a purple outline that roughly matches that of the character's skin. Increasing or decreasing this amount affects the size of the outline.

- **Pull.** This determines how much the skin is pulled by the attached joint. A good example is the chest and shoulder area. As the arms move outward, the skin of the chest is pulled outward along the surface of the skin as well.

- **Pinch.** This determines how much the skin is pushed inward by the action of the tendon attached joint. A good example is the crease that forms in the web of the hand as the thumb moves next to the forefinger.

- **Stretch.** This determines how much the skin is stretched by the tendon attached joint. This gives the skin more or less pliability.

Normally, the values for all these joints are set at 1.0 to give a good skin behavior when the tendons are attached to a nearby link. If the tendons span multiple links, these numbers should probably be reduced somewhat because the effect of a change on a link normally decreases the further away from the link you are. For example, the clavicle should have more of an effect on the upper spine than on the lower spine.

Tendon Boundary conditions are also important for tendons that span multiple links. These determine exactly how far the skin is affected. If these are off, only the joint with the tendon is affected. When the upper bound value is high, the skin on the spanned joints is also affected by the tendon. This is very important for getting a smooth behavior across the skin.

If you enable boundary conditions, it is a good idea to turn off the joint intersection parameters for each of the spanned joints. This action prevents the two features from trying to create different outlines at the joint intersections, and causing unpredictable results.

MODIFYING TENDONS

1. Continue with 09max06.max.

2. In the Cross Section Editor, select the two front attach points. Change Radial Distance to 16, Pull to –0.25, and Pinch to 0.0.

3. In the Tendons rollout, change upper bound to 2.0 and pull bias to 0.0, and then change the lower bound to –1.

4. Unhide the Biped skeleton turn on Animate, and, at frame 10, rotate the clavicles up 30 degrees in the y-axis.

    These modifications have the effect of lifting the skin evenly over the front of the chest as the clavicles raise. The file 09max09.max on the CD-ROM contains the completed tendons. The figure has a Texture map applied so that the effect of the tendons is more visible.

5. Make a preview of frames 0–20 to see the effect.

In Practice: Physique

- **Bulge Angles.** Bulges can be used not only to create bulging muscles, but also to help prevent unwanted effects such as crimping and tearing of the skin.

- **Vertex Reassignment.** Vertices can only be assigned to one joint, and thus must be reassigned to the proper joint from time to time.

- **Using Biped.** Always assign the Physique modifier to the pelvis, not the Center of Mass object. If you need additional control, you may link Dummy objects to the Biped skeleton to get additional joints to help control the skin.

- **Tendons.** Tendons affect the skin across multiple joints and are very helpful in branching areas of the body, such as the shoulder and pelvis areas.

Chapter 10

FACIAL ANIMATION

With Release 2 of MAX, a number of new techniques have emerged for animating the face. These new techniques, along with MAX's NURBS implementation, make the software a very powerful and capable tool for creating and animating realistic faces and facial expressions. With the large number of options available, deciding which approach to take is critical to the final animation. The approach you will take depends on a number of factors—visual style, deadlines, geometry type, and personal preference. Some techniques serve some styles and geometry types better than others. Still, the range of options has been vastly improved, giving animators much more freedom.

This chapter covers the following topics:

- Replacement animation

- Lofted Line mouths

- Direct manipulation

- Using Linked Xforms

- Morphing and multiple-target morphing

Facial Anatomy

Animating the face requires a good eye and a strong knowledge of acting and emotion. You also need to understand the underlying anatomy of the human head and face to understand exactly how they move. The face is by far the most important part of the animation, because this is where the expression of emotion takes place. The face is driven by approximately a dozen muscles that connect the skin to the skull. As with muscles in the body, these muscles affect the shape of the skin by bulging, stretching, and pulling it in a number of directions.

The trick is to understand how these muscles pull and shape the face to create expressions. The groups of muscles fall into two categories: lower face muscles that control the mouth and jaw (see Figure 10.1), and upper face muscles that control the eyes and brows (see Figure 10.2).

FIGURE 10.1

The muscles surrounding the mouth pull the lips outward radially. Another set of muscles compresses and purses the lips.

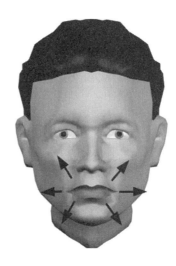

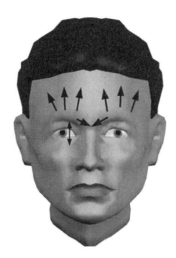

FIGURE 10.2

In addition to opening and closing the eyelids, muscles on the upper half of the face raise, lower, and furrow the brow.

Human anatomy, especially an understanding of muscle action and reaction, provides an exceptionally useful model when you are constructing a face. Human anatomy can also be used as a model for the construction of the face. If the face you create within MAX moves easily along the same lines that these muscles are pulling, you have a much better chance of animating the face.

A good way to learn about facial anatomy and the way muscles move is to buy a portable-sized mirror and use it to watch your own face. Our eyes are extremely skillful in picking out what does not *look* right in an animation. We see people move, talk, and act everyday. This makes the human eye extremely critical of improper facial motions. Any time you need a little help with a facial pose, look in the mirror and use your own face for reference.

Muscles Around the Eyes

There are four major muscles that manipulate the eyes and upper face. The following list describes each muscle and how it affects the face.

- **Frontalis.** This muscle raises and lowers the eyebrows and tends to move most when a person is speaking. Try to look in the mirror and speak without moving your eyebrows. It is not an easy task. A conscious effort has to be made, and then the face looks stiff.

- **Curragator.** A second muscle that assists in brow motion that furls the brow when you show disgust, anger, fear, concentration, and sadness.

- **Levator Palpebrae.** Raises and lowers the eyelids. This muscle is used for blinking and that surprised, wide-eyed look.

- **Orbicularis Oculi.** Used for eye movement and creates the "Clint Eastwood" squint.

Muscles Around the Mouth

Seven muscles work together to move the facial area around the mouth. These muscles are described in the following list:

- **Orbicularis Oris:** Surrounds the mouth and tightens the lips into a pursed, "pout" position.

- **Zygomatic Major:** Works together with the Orbicularis Oris muscle. It is just above the Orbicularis Oris and just below the cheekbone. It pulls the face into a wide grin.

- **Levator Labii Superiors:** Raises the upper lip and the nose to expose more of the teeth. The use of all these lip muscles creates an "EEE" position for the lip synch.

- **Triangularis:** Resides around the corners of the mouth and drives the corners of the lips downward when you are sad.

- **Risorius, Depressor Labii Inferioris, and Levator Menti:** These three muscles control the lower lip by lowering the bottom lip to show the teeth and raising the bottom lip to create a pout expression (see Figure 10.3).

FIGURE 10.3
The muscles of the face.

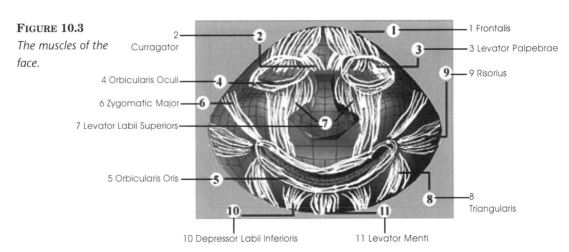

2 Curragator
4 Orbicularis Oculi
6 Zygomatic Major
7 Levator Labii Superiors
5 Orbicularis Oris
10 Depressor Labii Inferioris
11 Levator Menti
1 Frontalis
3 Levator Palpebrae
9 Risorius
8 Triangularis

Simple Facial Animation

For simple animation, or to achieve a highly stylized look in your characters, there are a few methods that can be used. These methods certainly don't attempt realism, but you can use them to create engaging characters. The two systems discussed in this section are Replacement animation and the Lofted Line Mouth, both of which you can use to create a simple lip synch.

Replacement Animation Using Expressions

Replacement animation is a technique that uses several different objects, such as different mouth objects, to appear and disappear as a slider is moved. The slider is simply a separate object, usually a non-rendering Spline or Text object. This is analogous to simple Replacement animation as used by cel animators and puppet animation. Anyone who's watched *The Flintstones* or a Rankin-Bass Christmas special will appreciate simple Replacement animation for mouths.

The technique, however, is not limited only to mouths. It can be extended to also replace eyes, or even entire heads. Disney's stop-motion features *The Nightmare Before Christmas* and *James and the Giant Peach* were animated with replacement heads. Of course, these films were done using physical models filmed with stop-motion cameras, but the same techniques can apply to 3D animation as well.

This technique relies heavily on expressions to get the job done. Expressions are mathematical functions written to control the animation of objects. Creation and management of expressions are performed through the Track View. Those familiar with MAXScript can certainly create the same effect by extrapolating the techniques.

In this example, you will set up an expression that makes an object appear and disappear as a Slider object is moved. There are two ways to make the object disappear—visibility and scaling. MAX's Visibility track makes objects appear and disappear at rendering time, but unfortunately the visibility only affects objects in Shaded view, not Wireframe. To circumvent this, scaling is probably the wisest choice. When the slider is "on," the object is at 100 percent of its normal size. When the slider is "off," the object is 0 percent its normal size—essentially making it invisible in both Wireframe and Shaded view.

To understand how the expression is applied, load the file 10max01.max. This contains a simple head with some mouths that are controlled by expressions to make them appear and disappear as the slider moves.

APPLYING AN EXPRESSION TO AN OBJECT

1. Select the text object that says "Mouth" from the Front View and slide it on the World x-axis back and forth between the two vertical lines. Expressions have been written to make different mouths appear as the slider is moved (see Figure 10.4).

FIGURE 10.4

This simple character uses Replacement animation for the face.

2. Go to Select by Name from the toolbar and select the object called "X-OOO." This mouth still needs an expression to make it appear and disappear as the Mouth slider moves.

3. Expand the tracks under Transform and select the Scale controller and click Assign Controller on the Track View toolbar (see Figure 10.5).

4. In the Assign Transform Controller dialog box, click the Scale Expression controller and click OK.

5. Still in the Track View, select the Scale controller, then right-click and select Properties, or double-click the Properties button on the toolbar. This brings up the Expression Controller dialog box (see Figure 10.6).

6. To save typing, the expression has been stored in a file. From the Expression Controller dialog box, click the Load button and select the expression file 10xpr01.xpr. This expression uses a scalar variable named Mouth, which represents the Mouth slider. In the Expression box, there are three identical "if" statements (one for each of the x-, y-, and z-axes) that tell MAX to scale the mouth to 100%, making it visible when the slider is between 1 and 49 units. Above 50 and below 0 the same mouth shape scales to 0 and becomes invisible.

FIGURE 10.5

The Assign Transform Controller dialog box.

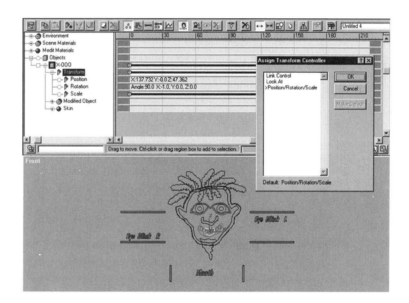

FIGURE 10.6

The Expression Controller dialog box.

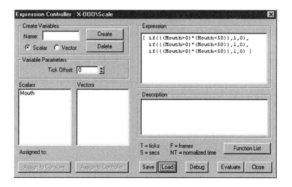

7. Click Mouth under the Scalars window to highlight it, and just below that window the Assigned to: text will say "Constant: 0." MAX must now be told which slider will control the expression. Click the Assign to Controller button.

8. Under the new Track View Pick window, find object Mouth and select the X-position under the Transform/Position controller and click OK. This tells the expression to use the X translation of the slider for the variable Mouth.

9. Click the Evaluate button to make sure that the expression works. If no error messages appear, the formula has been applied correctly; otherwise, go through the steps again to be sure all your syntax in the expression is correct and you have the correct controller selected. Click Close on the Expression Controller window.

10. Using Select by Name, select the Mouth Text object and, from the Front view, move the slider from left to right or, using the Transform Type In, put in an exact value. The mouth should appear within the range and disappear outside of it. You have now set the "X-OOO" mouth shape to appear from 1.0–49.0 and disappear outside of these values.

To be sure you understand the technique for applying expressions to objects, make the eyes blink in the same manner as you just did with the mouth. The technique for the eyes is identical to that employed with the mouth.

For reference, the left eye has already been set up to blink. Move the "Eye Blink L" Text object on the World z-axis to see it blink. The expression covers 0–100 units. From 1–49 units the visible eye shape is "Eye Closed L," and from 50–99 units the eye shape is "Eye L."

The slider for the right eye is called "Eye Right." The open right eye is called "Eye R" and the closed version is called "Eye Closed R." Use the left eye as a guide and the expression file called 10xpr02.xpr. Keep in mind that the values need to be changed on the expression for one of the shapes, or else both shapes appear and disappear at the same time, and that the Eye slider is moving on the z-axis, not the x-axis like the mouth.

These exercises focus only on a few mouth and eye positions, but you can use the technique for as many positions as are required. For an example that has both eyes blinking and all the mouth positions working properly, load the file 10max02.max from the accompanying CD-ROM. To see an example of this character animated to sound, open the file 10avi01.avi. To use the same sound file for your animation with replacement mouths, use the file rasta.wav from the accompanying CD-ROM.

As you can see, this method is very simple, yet quite effective. The techniques of replacement animation can also be used for many other types of situations in which objects need to appear and disappear, or simply be replaced. Replacement animation can free you of the restrictions that shape animation can impose.

The Lofted Line Mouth Technique

Another simple way to create animated mouths is by lofting a line into a lip shape that can be animated. The mouth simply rests on the surface of the face as a separate object. In practice, this setup winds up working like Gumby's mouth, which was a simply a loop of clay. The Lofted Line Mouth changes the shape of a simple piece of geometry to create an animatable mouth. A simple lofted line can be manipulated to look like the many mouth forms needed to make a character talk.

Setting Up a Lofted Line Mouth

The setup of a Lofted Line Mouth animation involves understanding how the Loft, Modify/Scale, and FFD modifiers work. Familiarize yourself with these tools before beginning this tutorial. The following exercise takes you through the steps needed to complete the creation of a Lofted Line Mouth for animation.

CREATING A LOFTED LINE MOUTH

1. Select the line shape and draw the outline of the top and bottom lips with eight vertices.

2. Modify the Lips object at the vertex sub-object level and adjust the line to look like Figure 10.7.

3. Continue editing at the vertex sub-object level. Click the vertex between the two top lip curves and click Make First to make that vertex the first one of the line.

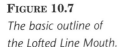

FIGURE 10.7

*The basic outline of
the Lofted Line Mouth.*

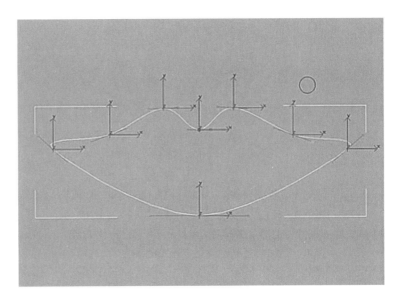

4. Create a circle shape with the radius of 6.0 to be lofted on your line.

5. Click the Select Object button, and select the lip-shaped line you drew for step 2.

6. From the Create/Geometry panel, change Standard Primitives to Loft Object and click the Loft button.

7. Click the Get Shape button under Creation Method of the Loft object and then click the circle.

8. From the Modify/Skin Parameters panel, click Skin and set the following parameters:

Shape Steps = 2

Path Steps = 4

Adaptive Path Steps is set to off

You should now have a Lofted Line Mouth. Continue with the Modify/Edit Spline and Modify/Skin Parameters settings to get the exact shape you want (see Figure 10.8). Adjusting the Shape steps and Path steps under the Modify/Skin Parameters panel can help increase the detail of your loft. You can also add volume to your loft by manipulating the Modify/Deformations/

Scale settings. For the second part of this tutorial, use the Lofted Line Mouth you previously created or open the 10max03.max file on the accompanying CD-ROM.

FIGURE 10.8

The Lofted Line Mouth.

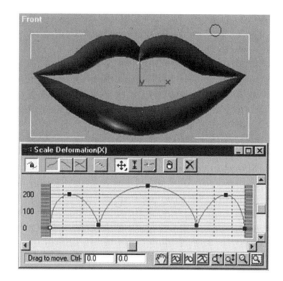

ANIMATING A LOFTED LINE MOUTH "OOO" SOUND

1. Frame 0 of the animation is the mouth at rest. This section will animate it moving into the shape for making the sound "OOO." Go to frame 10 of the animation and click the Animation button.

2. Click the Select and Squash button on the toolbar and manipulate the Lofted Line Mouth to look like an "OOO" sound like in the word "you" by scaling the Lofted Line on the y-axis 135 percent in the Front view.

3. From the Modify/FFD (box) panel, create a Lattice with 4×4×2 number of Control points and select the center Sub-Object Control points of the Lattice.

4. Choose Select and Uniform Scale and scale the Control points to 45 percent (see Figure 10.9).

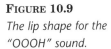

FIGURE 10.9

The lip shape for the "OOOH" sound.

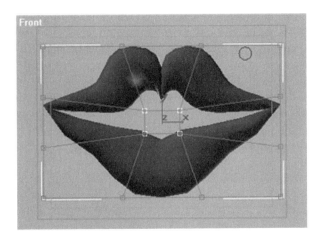

5. Set the total frame count for the animation to be 20 frames under the Time Configuration button on the bottom toolbar.

6. Press Play Animation and watch your lofted line make an "OOO" sound.

The next set of steps shows you how to create the "MMM" sound with the Lofted Line Mouth.

ANIMATING A LOFTED LINE MOUTH "MMM" SOUND

1. Apply an Edit Mesh modifier and, in Sub-Object Vertex mode, select the upper vertices of the Lofted Line Mouth.

2. Apply a FFD (box) 2×3×2 modifier and from the Front view select the Control points surrounding the top arches and middle section of the Lofted Line Mouth (the selection is a T shape) (see Figure 10.10).

3. Make sure the Animation button is on and, in the Front view, move the Time slider to frame 10. Set keyframes for these points by moving them very slightly.

4. Move the Time slider to frame 15. Move these Control points down on the y-axis –35 units.

5. From the Modify/Edit Mesh/Sub-Object Vertex panel, select the lower vertices of the lofted lips.

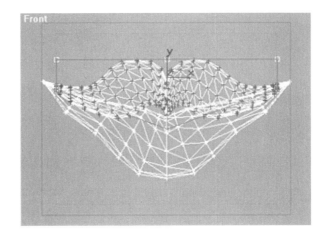

6. Apply a FFD (box) 2×3×2 modifier and select the Control points surrounding the bottom lip and middle section of the Lofted Line Mouth. This will be a mirrored selection of the top lips (see Figure 10.11).

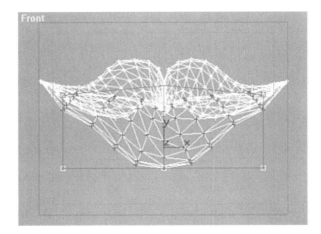

7. Move the Time slider to frame 10. Set keyframes for these points by moving them very slightly.

8. In the Front view, move these Control points up on the y-axis 8 units.

9. Press Play Animation and watch your lofted lips make an "OOO" and an "MMM" sound.

Continue making your different mouth shapes by manipulating the mouth with the Scale functions and Free-Form modifiers. Your Modifier Stack can get quite large with complex phonemes, and the Track View can fill up quickly using the FFD technique.

For even more complex lip synch, the FFDs can be used to model individual shapes that can then be morphed. For more on that topic, refer to the Morphing sections of this chapter.

You can view the final version of the Lofted Line Mouth by loading the filename 10max04.max from the accompanying CD-ROM. To create a line of dialogue, use the sound file from the accompanying CD-ROM called 10wav02.wav. For a reference, open the 10avi02.avi file.

Advanced Techniques for Facial Animation

For more realistic faces, MAX R2 supplies you with two techniques involving its newest modeling tool—NURBS. NURBS modeling is a great way to create smooth organic surfaces.

NURBS (Non-Uniform Rational B-Spline) modeling is very different from the polygonal meshes made with R1 of MAX. CVs, or Control vertices, are a lattice of points created for each curve and/or surface of a NURBS mesh. These CVs are sub-objects of the NURBS object and can be moved and animated to deform the mesh. The placement and refinement of the CVs affect the amount of deformation, making NURBS a very powerful tool for facial animation. Each CV has a rational weight that can be used to adjust the influence of the CV on the curve's or surface's shape. Like most 3D computer tools, NURBS can be made into a complex or simple system.

Animating CVs Directly

One of the nicer features of MAX R2's NURBS implementation is the capability to animate every CV. CVs are simply Control vertices and are very similar to a polygonal vertex. Animating each CV directly gives you the capability to literally "sculpt" the character on any given frame.

Animating CVs works quite well, but it should be approached with caution. When animated, a CV generates its own set of tracks within Track View. A NURBS mesh can have hundreds of vertices, and animating even a few dozen of these can boggle your mind when you open Track View. To learn more about animating CVs directly, load the file 10max05.max and follow these steps.

DIRECTLY ANIMATING CONTROL VERTICES ON A NURBS MESH

1. Select the NURBS head mesh in this file with the Select tool, if it is not already selected.

2. Turn on the Animate button and move the animation to frame 5.

3. Click the Modify/Sub-Object/Surface CV/Single CV button.

4. In the Left view, select the Control vertices that surround the bottom lip, the chin, and the back of the mouth (see Figure 10.12).

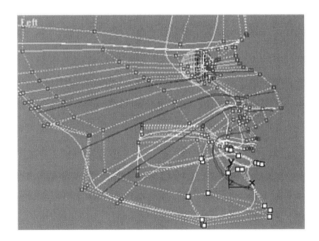

FIGURE 10.12

A selection of the Control vertices surrounding the lower jaw.

5. Pull those Control points down on the y-axis −1 units.

6. Make sure the Animate button is still on and move to frame 10 of the animation.

7. In the Left view, make sure those same Control vertices are still selected from step 4. Pull these Control vertices back up on the y-axis past their neutral position so that the lips touch at approximately 0.5 units (see Figure 10.13).

8. Make sure the Animate button is still on and move to frame 10 of the animation.

FIGURE 10.13

The closed mouth pose.

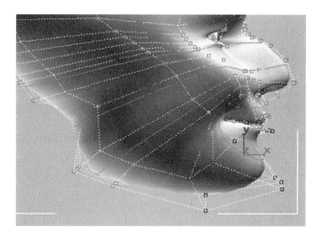

9. In the Front view, select the vertices surrounding the cheek and nose area. Be sure to deselect any Control points on the back of the head from a side view and do not select vertices that encompass the sides of the face (see Figure 10.14).

FIGURE 10.14

Selecting vertices surrounding the cheek and nose.

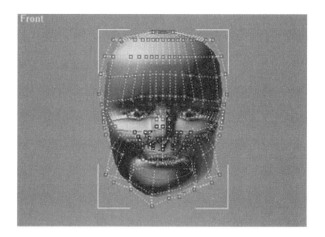

10. Still in the Front view, pull these Control vertices up on the y-axis 0.2 units.

11. Create a preview rendering by using Rendering/Make Preview and watch the NURBS mesh mouth move from an "AH" position to an "MM" position. The cheek and nose motion provides additional overlapping animation of the mouth positions.

12. Open Track View and select the NURBS surface. Expand the tracks and notice how dozens of keys have been created. At this point, you'll understand the problems involved with animating the CVs directly.

To see the final version of this animation, load the file 10max06.max from the accompanying CD-ROM.

The NURBS mesh used is reasonably simple, and still it has over 500 CVs in its Lattice. This means there would be as many as 500 individual CV tracks. The editing of animation on individual CVs in Track View can become cumbersome on most machines, and it can be hard to keep track of which CVs apply to what motion—especially when trying to overlap motion in different parts of the face.

A great little tool that can make this type of animation much simpler is the new MAXScript provided with R2 called Morpher.ms. This prewritten MAXScript takes NURBS meshes and creates a Multi-Target Morph Manager rollout. The Manager can make a "snapshot" of the repositioned CVs at an extreme pose and input that into a Channel slider. Then, using the sliders as a "pose mixer," you can keyframe the poses. This makes the selection of CVs for poses a little more clear, but the keys in Track View are still created for each individual CV and can make Track View sluggish when trying to move keys or adjust eases on function curves. See Figure 10.15 for the Morpher.ms interface.

FIGURE 10.15

The MAXScript Morpher.ms can make sliders for facial animation.

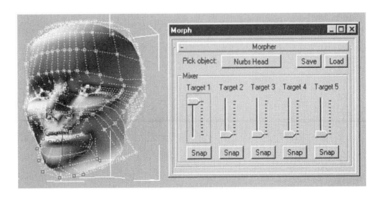

For extremely simple meshes, these methods do work and can be controlled. Still, for a model of reasonable complexity, the large number of keys will give you nothing but headaches. In this case, the CVs should be manipulated in groups using a Linked Xform.

Direct Manipulation Using Linked Xform

The gargantuan task of controlling large numbers of vertices can be made much easier by employing a Helper object to assist in the animation. The Helper object simply controls a large number of vertices through the use of the Linked Xform modifier. This allows you to manipulate one object (the Helper), rather than dozens of individual CVs. Manipulating a Control object also means you have only one set of keys in Track View, rather than the dozens that would be created if the CVs were individually animated.

The use of the Linked Xform method can be quite powerful, giving you very fine control over the shape of the face. You can use any object as your Control object. To see how to animate a NURBS mesh with Linked Xform, load the file 10max05.max and follow the steps below.

DIRECTLY ANIMATING CONTROL VERTICES ON A NURBS MESH WITH LINKED XFORM

1. Go to Create/Text/Parameters and type **Bottom Lip and Chin** in the text window, making the size 1.0. Click in the Front viewport to create the text. Under the Name and Color rollout, name the spline **Bottom Lip and Chin**. The text will not render but can serve as a handy reference. Dummy objects can also be used.

2. Select the NURBS head mesh in this file with the Select tool.

3. Add the NSurf Select modifier to your stack from the Modify panel and click the Modify/NSurf Select/Sub-Object/Surface CV button.

4. Select the Control vertices that surround the bottom lip, chin, and back of mouth (see Figure 10.16).

5. Assign a Linked Xform modifier to the stack from the Modify panel.

6. Under Modify/Linked Xform/Parameters, click the Pick Control Object button to activate it and then click the Text Spline object you made in step 1 to assign it as the Control object.

7. Still in the Front view, turn on the Animate button and move to frame 5 of the animation. Select the Bottom Lip and Chin text spline object and move it down −1.0 unit.

FIGURE 10.16

Selection of the lower lip and chin vertices.

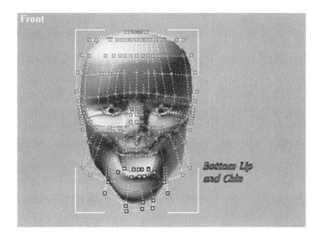

8. To add more Linked Xform modifiers, you must first select different CVs within the NURBS mesh. Add an NSurf Select modifier to your stack from the Modify panel and click the Surface CV button in the NSurf Select Sub-Object rollout.

9. Create a new Control object by duplicating the first. Select the Bottom Lip and Chin Text object and hold the Shift key down while you move it up to create a copy of that object. Go to the Text Parameters panel, change the text to read **Brows** and, in the Name and Color rollout, name this object **Brows**.

10. Select the NURBS head. Select the NSurf Select modifier, and from SubObject/Surface CV, select the CVs that encompass the brow of the head. Do not include the CVs from the side of the head and deselect any CVs from the back of the head (see Figure 10.17).

FIGURE 10.17

Selection of the vertices surrounding the brows.

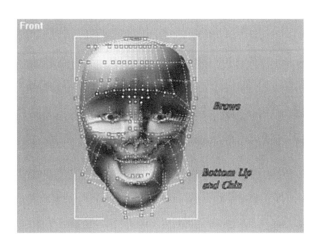

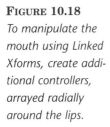

FIGURE 10.18

To manipulate the mouth using Linked Xforms, create additional controllers, arrayed radially around the lips.

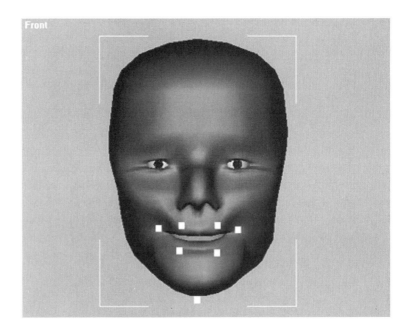

11. Assign a Linked Xform modifier to the stack from the Modify panel.

12. Under the Parameters panel, click the Pick Control Object button to activate it and then click the Text object you made in step 9 to assign it as the Control object.

13. Still in the Front view, make sure the Animate button is on and you are at frame 5 of the animation. Select the Brows Text object and move it up 1.0 unit. The brows now animate up with the open mouth to create a surprised look.

Using this technique, very specific motion can be created and the Track View stays clean. Each Control object you create sets keys for all the selected CVs with one Helper object. Keys can then can be edited with ease and make your overall animation much easier to control and modify.

Continue adding controllers to the mouth area. They should be arrayed around the lips with controllers at the right and left edges of the mouth and along the top and bottom of the lips, for a total of six controllers. This arrangement is shown in Figure 10.18. Additionally, both brows in this tutorial were linked to one Control object, but each could have just as easily been assigned to separate Control objects to make more asymmetrical poses.

Another tool that can be handy with this technique is Peter Watje's Linked Xform+, a shareware plug-in that enables you to weight CVs between multiple Control objects. This can be very useful in areas such as the mouth.

Have fun with this technique and experiment with different clusters of CVs linked to different Control objects using the Linked Xform modifier. To view a final version of this tutorial, load the file 10max07.max from the accompanying CD-ROM.

T IP

Always make sure the Sub-Object button within NSurf Select is on and activated, or that the Linked Xform modifier applies to the whole NURBS mesh and not just the selected CVs you want to move.

Morphing Techniques for Facial Animation

Morphing can create even more complex facial animation while keeping Track View manageable. Morphing changes the shape of the Base object into the shape of other Target objects. MAX R2 offers several ways to create morphing by using Single Morph Target animation and Barycentric morphing or through third-party plug-ins like Mix, Morph Magic, and Smirk.

The Single Morph Target system provided in R1 only allowed for transition between two discrete shapes, which resulted in animation that was stiff at best. The Barycentric sliders that are provided with R2 empower the animator with tools to overlap multiple morph targets, eliminating the stiff feel of straight morphing. The technique can also help control more subtle facial motion and is certainly the preferred method for high-end applications.

Third-party plug-ins like Mix also enable mixing of multiple targets, but they have a more streamlined interface and provide more functions. Examples of these additional functions show their capability to change only the selected vertices on your mesh and the utilization of NURBS meshes for morph targets.

Modeling Morph Targets for Animation

Morph target animation requires that your target meshes have the same number of vertices in the exact same order. This is accomplished by creating a single stock expressionless face, copying it, and reworking the stock face into as many expressions and facial poses as are required.

All the Target methods rely on the creation of individual models that represent the major poses of the face. Because poses can be mixed, all that needs to be modeled are the extremes of the individual muscles. Recall from the beginning of this chapter how the muscles move the face. If an extreme for each muscle is modeled, high quality animation can be achieved with a minimum of sliders. Just as with the problems encountered with animating CVs directly, the more sliders you have, the more information you have to deal with, and the more difficult it is to change your animation.

Creating the Eleven Lower Facial Poses

The mouths used to create lip synch are a good start to creating a library of poses. Because many characters that do facial animation also perform lip synch, some basic phoneme poses always come in handy. In addition to these, a few asymmetrical poses are needed to mimic the action of individual muscles—smile and frown, for instance. These additional muscle poses should be created in separate left and right poses to help bring a natural asymmetry to the resulting animation (see Figure 10.19).

This collection provides plenty of options to achieve almost any dialogue and expression, especially when combining poses for the mouth with the upper facial poses. Each expression and pose is described in the following list:

- **Position 1 (MMM sound)** is the closed mouth, used for consonants made by the lips: specifically, the M, B, and P sounds (see Figure 10.20). In this position, the lips may usually be the normal width. For added realism, you can add an additional closed mouth position with the lips slightly pursed for a cleaner transition to sounds following an "OOO" sound, such as "room."

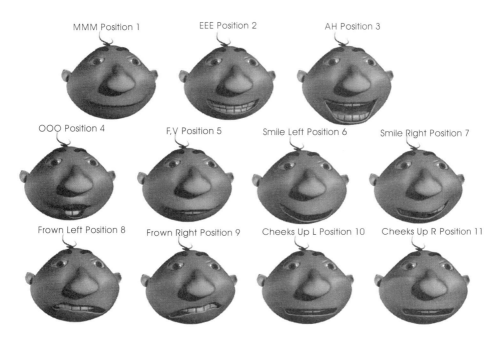

FIGURE 10.19

The eleven basic poses for lower facial animation.

FIGURE 10.20

Position 1 is the closed mouth.

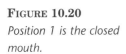

- **Position 2 (EEE sound)** has the mouth open with the teeth closed (see Figure 10.21). It is a very common shape and is used for consonants made within the mouth, specifically those made by E, C, D, G, K, N, R, S, TH, Y, and Z. All these sounds can also be made with the teeth slightly open, particularly in fast speech.

FIGURE 10.21

Position 2 has the mouth open with the teeth closed.

- **Position 3 (AH sound)** is used for the wide-open vowels such as A and I (see Figure 10.22). The tongue should be visible at the bottom of the mouth and the jaw relatively slack. This is basically an open jaw.

FIGURE 10.22

Position 3 is used for the wide-open vowels such as A and I.

- **Position 4 (OOO sound)** has the mouth projected out and in a pursed O shape (see Figure 10.23). It is used for the "OOO" sound, as in "food." This can also be used for the vowel U. When mixed with position 3 to drop the jaw, the "OH" sound is created. This is a good example of using multiple morphs to reduce the number of poses required.

FIGURE 10.23
Position 4 has a projected, pursed mouth.

■ **Position 5 (FF, VV sound)** has the bottom lip tucked under the teeth to make the sound of the letters F and V (see Figure 10.24). In highly pronounced speech, this shape is necessary, but the shape can also be replaced with Position 2 for more casual rapid speech.

FIGURE 10.24
Position 5 has the bottom lip tucked under the teeth to make the sound of the letters F and V.

■ **Positions 6 and 7 (Smile Left, Right)** are the first of a few poses that break up the symmetry of your animation (see Figure 10.25). The smile expression can be combined with the other mouth poses to create a happy character. Mixing in one smile more than the other can make the character seem wry or sarcastic.

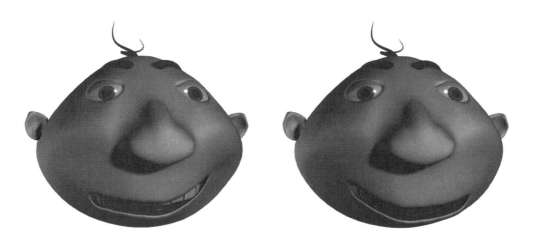

FIGURE 10.25
Positions 6 (Smile Left) and 7 (Smile Right) can be combined with the other mouth poses to create more natural poses.

■ **Positions 8 and 9 (Frown Left, Right)** are two more poses that break up the symmetry of your animation (see Figure 10.26). Mixing in a frown to an existing lip sync can create a feeling of sadness.

FIGURE 10.26
Position 8 (Frown Left) and Position 9 (Frown Right) can be combined with the other mouth poses to create a feeling of sadness.

■ **Positions 10 and 11 (Cheeks Up Left, Right)** are two more poses that break up the symmetry of your animation (see Figure 10.27). You will find it helpful to be able to animate the cheeks separately. These poses can be used with selected vertices in a multimorph program to create even more asymmetry to your animation.

FIGURE 10.27
Position 10 (Cheek Up Left) and Position 11 (Cheek Up Right) can be used to create even more asymmetry to your animation.

Blended together, these basic poses can create almost any facial animation through the use of weighted multi-target morph tools and techniques. The use of additional morphs with the tongue and asymmetrical animation in the brows and eyelids will really make believable motion.

Modeling Facial Poses for Morphing

This exercise will get you started on modeling the required poses for creating facial animation. When you animate faces, be sure to maintain the proper volume in the face. If the jaw drops, the cheeks stretch; if the smile muscle is animated, the cheeks puff up. If the individual models are solid and correct, the animation will follow along and look terrific.

The mesh provided for this tutorial has a high-resolution and a low-resolution mesh that refer to one another. You can also create a similar file by making a Reference object and applying MeshSmooth to the Reference object. The first object is the low-resolution mesh that you modify for your facial poses. The referenced copy keeps MeshSmooth on top of the stack and displays how your changes to the low-resolution model affect the model with MeshSmooth applied. This way you can modify the low-resolution mesh quickly and use the high-resolution mesh for your final animation.

MAKING THE "AH" FACIAL POSE

1. Load the 10max08.max file from the accompanying CD-ROM. Select the mesh called M-Head Lo by using the Select by Name button.

2. Select the Modify panel and open the Modifier Stack to reveal an 8×2×4 FFD on the lower portion of the face. Select the modifier and click the Sub-Object/Control Points button to activate the points.

3. From the Front view, select the bottom two rows of points that apply to the bottom lip. Do not select any points that will deform the corners of the mouth (see Figure 10.28).

FIGURE 10.28

Selection of the lower vertices of the Lattice. These affect the lower lip and jaw only.

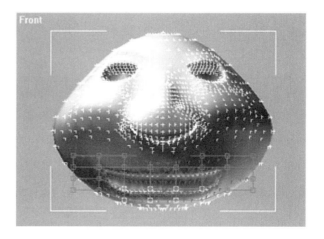

4. From the Front view, pull these points down 13 units.

5. Create a Mesh Select modifier from the Modify panel on top of the FFD (box) modifier and select the Sub-Object/Vertex button.

6. Select the vertices that cover the bottom part of the face and chin while holding down the Control key to include the previously selected vertices. Be sure to deselect any vertices from the back of the head in a side view.

7. Assign a new 8×2×4 FFD (box) modifier on top of the Mesh Select modifier (see Figure 10.29).

FIGURE 10.29

Addition of the second Lattice to the lower face.

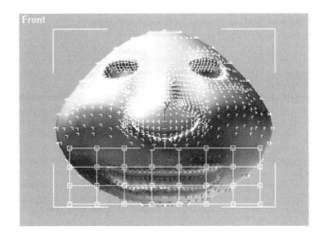

8. Click the Control Points button to activate the points.

9. From the Front view, select the same bottom row of points that apply to the bottom lip as before in step 3. Do not select any points that will deform the corners of the mouth.

10. Pull these points down on the y-axis five units.

11. From the Front view, select only the middle "quad" Control points that apply to the bottom lip and pull down these points 15 units (see Figure 10.30).

FIGURE 10.30

Manipulating the lower jaw.

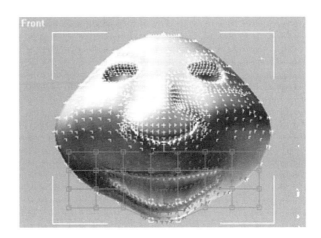

12. Click the Snapshot button on the toolbar and select Snapshot/Single and Clone Method/Mesh. Click OK.

13. From the Select by Name button on the toolbar, select the M-Head Lo01 mesh and move it 300 units to the right.

14. Click the Modify panel and rename the new mesh **M-Head Ah**.

By using FFD modifiers, you should be able to easily create each pose needed for your lip synch. Moving on to more facial poses, the following tutorial shows how you can create asymmetry with your targets and move more than just the mouth vertices of your mesh.

MAKING THE CHEEKS UP R FACIAL POSE

1. This pose will have the right lip and cheeks raised as in a sneer or smile. Select the mesh called M-Head Lo by using the Select by Name button.

2. Select the Modify panel and click the Edit Modifier Stack button to reveal the modifiers you created previously for your "AH" pose. Delete the two existing FFD (box) 8×2×4 modifiers and the Mesh Select that is between them in the stack (see Figure 10.31).

FIGURE 10.31

To return the face mesh to its neutral state, delete these items in the stack.

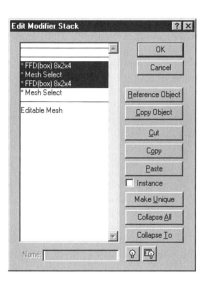

3. Click the existing Mesh Select modifier and select the vertices that cover the cheeks and nose of the face. Be sure to deselect from a side view the vertices from the back of the head.

4. Apply another FFD (box) modifier to this selection with an 8×2×4 number of Control points in the Lattice.

5. From the Front view, select the Control points on this Lattice that cover the right cheek and nose. Do not select the most outside points of the face, only those that cover the skin.

6. Move these selected Control points up eight units (see Figure 10.32).

FIGURE 10.32

Select the vertices surrounding the cheek and nose of the face and add a Lattice.

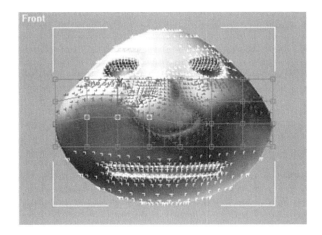

7. Click the Snapshot button on the toolbar and select Single and the Mesh Clone method. Click OK.

8. From the Select by Name button on the toolbar, select the M-Head Lo01 mesh and move it -300 degrees to the right.

9. Click the Modify panel and rename the new mesh **M-Head Cheek Up R**.

Multi-Target Morphing

The single target morphing feature available with R1 was limited in that each pose had to be modeled individually. Without the capability to mix poses, your animation file could get quite large as each additional pose was created. With Multi-Target morphing, this problem is solved by combining different targets to create entirely new poses. Combining targets lessens the need for so many poses and increases the flexibility of your character.

Multi-Target morphing is handled through a number of plug-ins, including Mix, MorphMagic, and Smirk. MAX R2's Barycentric morphing feature provides a solution that is somewhere between straight morphing and full multiple target morphing. With MAX R2's native Barycentric morphing, poses can be combined, but the combined percentages must always equal 100 percent, where in true multiple target morphing, this is not a restriction.

To model the targets for a multiple target morph system, the rules are fairly simple—each model needs to have the same number of vertices in the same order. The easiest way to do this is simply to copy the base, expressionless head and reshape it to the appropriate pose.

MAX supports three different types of geometry—polygons, patches, and NURBS. All these geometry types can be used for creating realistic and effective faces. Each type of geometry has its own problems when it comes to facial animation.

Using Polygons as Multiple Morph Targets

Polygons can be used quite effectively as multiple morph targets. Because all poses are modeled, the possibility of creasing or tearing that normally accompanies mesh deformation is significantly reduced. The one problem that can crop up is with the large number of vertices contained in most facial meshes. This large amount of data can bog down even the most powerful systems.

To circumvent this, good old MeshSmooth can come to the rescue. The face is modeled at a lower resolution to optimize the number of vertices for speed. The morph targets are also modeled at low resolution. This makes manipulation of the face quite easy during morphing. MeshSmooth is then added to the Morph object's stack, adding resolution for rendering time. MAX's Barycentric morphing, Mix, Smirk, and MorphMagic all can be configured in this manner.

Using Patches as Multiple Morph Targets

Patches are sometimes overlooked, but they can be modeled into very realistic faces. These faces can also be animated quite well by using a multiple target morph. The math used to calculate patches is simpler than NURBS, and a patch face of similar detail animates faster. Patches can also provide the modeler with more topological freedom, as triangular and quadratic patches can be incorporated within the same face.

Using NURBS as Multiple Morph Targets

NURBS are great candidates for multiple target morphing. Most morph target programs are offering compatibility with NURBS, now that they are functional in MAX R2. Modeling the target faces with NURBS is as simple as copying the neutral face and manipulating the CVs of the NURBS surface to create individual Morph Targets.

One problem that may arise is that not all multiple target morph programs support NURBS effectively. If you do find that your weighted morph program does not support NURBS, you can create polygonal meshes as your Morph Targets by collapsing the stack to a mesh.

TIP

If you do opt to collapse a NURBS surface to polygons for multiple target morphing, be sure MAX's Adaptive Tessellation is turned off, because this may change the polygon count of the targets, preventing them from being morphed.

Using MAX's R2 Barycentric Morphing

MAX R2 has also created its own version of Weighted Multi-Morph Target animation by adding a Barycentric Morph controller. This controller is automatically applied when a Morph Target is created, eliminating the original single Morph controller. The one catch with this particular form of morphing is that all the sliders must total 100 percent, or else the model changes its scale unpredictably.

Assigning Morph Targets by Using Barycentric Morphing

This exercise assigns a series of Morph Targets using MAX R2's native Barycentric morphing. Although not as robust as some third-party plug-ins, Barycentric morphing can still provide excellent results. When applied,

Barycentric morphing configures your model as a compound object. As with other compound objects, the Morph panel is found under the Creation panel.

ASSIGNING BARYCENTRIC MORPH TARGETS

1. Open the file 10max08a.max. This file has a base head with a number of targets.

2. Select the object M-Head Lo.

3. From the Creation panel, select Geometry/Compound Objects/Morph.

4. Toggle the Pick Target button and select the object M-Head AHH.

5. Toggle the button again and select M-Head EEE.

6. Continue this for the rest of the heads.

7. Once you create you Morph Targets with the Compound Objects/Morph tool, go to the Track View and right-click the Morph controller and select Properties. A rollout menu appears for key info on each target you established and what percentage each target should be displayed at in the animation. See Figure 10.33 for the interface.

FIGURE 10.33

The Morph controller Properties panel.

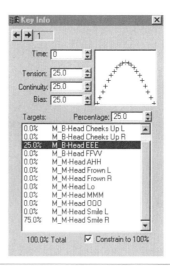

This is not the most intuitive process because the interface must be accessed through Track View, and the panel does not have individual sliders for each shape or a way to create keyframes easily. The only way to create keyframes is to assign them in the Morph Object modifier. The weights are then adjusted in Track View using the Properties panel. This is a lot of jumping around, but the module ships with R2 and does the job.

Using the Morph Manager MAXScript to Control Barycentric Morphing

To help smooth out some of the interface problems, a MAXScript program called Morph Manager is included on the accompanying CD-ROM. It consists of a ZIP file that contains instructions along with two programs. The first is Mrphkeys.dlx, a MAXScript plug-in that adds a bunch of Morph object and Morph controller access functions to MAXScript. This file needs to be placed in your MAX plug-ins directory. The second is Morph-manager.mse, the Morph Manager script. You can either run this when you need it from the MAXScript Utility panel or drop it into the Scripts\Startup folder to make it automatically load when you open MAXScript.

1. From the Utilities panel, select MAXScript/Run Script and then select the script Morph-manager.mse.

2. Once the script is running, use the Utilities pull-down from the MAXScript rollout to select the script.

3. Press the Source Object button and select your base head.

If you load an existing Morph object, its existing targets load in sequence into the sliders. Any as-yet-unassigned targets will show a blank title at the top of the slider and the slider will be disabled.

Pressing the Open Morph Manager button opens the Mixer panel (see Figure 10.34). The Mixer group contains a set of sliders and picker buttons, one for each possible target. You can press Pick under any slider to add a new Morph Target or replace one that has a different target.

The Key Left and Right buttons take you between existing Morph controller keys. If you move the Time slider onto a frame with a Morph key, that key number shows up in the Key field. If you have Auto keyframe turned off, you can only adjust sliders at keyframes; they are disabled on frames without a key. If you have Auto keyframe turned on, you can set sliders at any frame, and a keyframe is created there (whether or not Animate is turned on in MAX). The other items at the bottom of the Mixer work the same as in the normal morph functions in MAX.

FIGURE 10.34

The Morph Manager MAXScript interface.

Using the MorphMagic Plug-In

MorphMagic is a program that takes the Morph Targets you create and provides Channel sliders for you to animate. Each slider can be mixed with others to create an infinite nember of poses. MorphMagic enables you to load up to 100 different targets into Channel control slots (see Figure 10.35). A channel contains a shape, which is pulled from an individual object, a combination of several objects, or selected vertices within an object.

It must be noted that MorphMagic is one of a number of different plug-ins available to perform the task of weighted morphing. Most of the plug-ins available, including Smirk and Mix, use a very similar analogy. All use sliders and have many of the same capabilities. A demo version of MorphMagic is on the CD-ROM.

Setting Up for MorphMagic

For best results, the MorphMagic modifier should be applied to a neutral, relaxed face with the extremes applied to each channel. Your channels can be created in three ways: Morph Target, Compound Target, or Selected Vertices. A Morph Target is a single object used as a target. A Compound Target is a snapshot of a combination of multiple targets, essentially a snapshot of the slider poses. This is good for saving often-used combinations of sliders. Selected Vertices enables you to save modeling time and memory by selecting parts of a model as channels. Keep these options in mind when building your extreme poses for each channel.

FIGURE 10.35

The MorphMagic interface.

By combining values in each Channel control slot, you can morph between any number of your targets at any "weight." For extreme effects, you can overshoot any given channel by using negative values or values greater than 100 percent to amplify the distortion of your main object. Limits on the effects can also be attributed to your Morph channels so you do not go into the negative or overshoot the positive settings of your target. This is achieved by adjusting the Min and Max spinners for each channel in the Channel Settings rollout.

After the targets have been assigned to each channel in the Weighted Morph interface, you must animate the spinners. If you are using the basic muscle extremes as outlined here, you can combine them to create any facial pose desired. Disgust, for example, can be created by increasing the values of the sneer muscle. Happiness can be simulated by adjusting the smile, or Zygomatic Major, muscles. Conversely, by using only the right smile muscle, you can get a smirk. When combined with a left sneer muscle, you get a disgusted smirk. The list goes on forever. You can combine as many channels as you want; all you really need to animate is the relative weights. This process makes it much easier to create the exact pose for the given moment and also requires fewer poses to be modeled.

Upper Facial Poses

Besides the mouth poses, it is important to keep in mind motion and asymmetry with the eyes and brows. Eyes and brows are by far the most important in facial animation. Eyes not only need to blink but also need to express emotion. Many emotions and moods are expressed through subtle changes in the eyes and brows. Stiff unnatural motion in the eyes and brows makes your character look like a doll rather than a living creature. Eye motion as simple as a blink can add a tremendous amount of life to a character, and more subtle changes in the brows can add significantly more dimension to the character. On a broad scale, a shifty character might squint his eyes, a surprised character might open his eyes wide, and a sad character might furrow his brow.

With this in mind, it is essential to have eyes that are controllable in every respect and can be animated asymmetrically. The lids of the eyes need to follow the surface of the eyeball, be able to lower at different increments, and be animated asymmetrically. Eyebrows need to be able to lift and furrow themselves independently of one another (see Figure 10.36).

Brows and eyelids can be modeled as part of the Facial mesh, or they can be modeled separately. If they are separate meshes, it makes the asymmetrical poses more clear in Track View and a little easier to animate.

T IP

The Bend modifier in MAX R2 is a powerful tool to use on a separate eyebrow mesh to change the eyebrow's motion from a defined arch to an angled furrowed brow.

■ **Positions 1 and 2 (Blink Left, Right).** Remember that eyes not only need to blink but also need to express emotion, so two or more poses should do the trick. Spinners with a weighted program can enable many positions between the extremes of a blink, or the eyelids can be separate geometry like you see in Figures 10.37 and 10.38.

FIGURE 10.36
The six basic poses for upper facial animation.

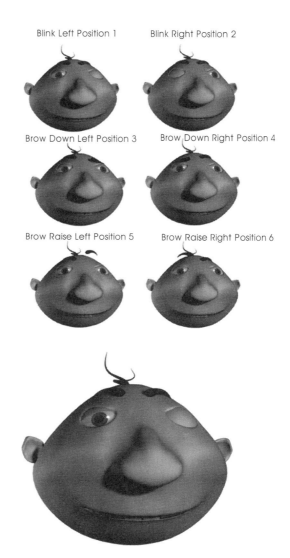

Blink Left Position 1   Blink Right Position 2

Brow Down Left Position 3   Brow Down Right Position 4

Brow Raise Left Position 5   Brow Raise Right Position 6

FIGURE 10.37
Position 1/Blink Left: Position 1 should be designed to be independent of Position 2 and to squint or open wide if needed.

■ **Positions 3 and 4 (Brow Down Left, Right).** Eyes and brows are by far the most important in facial animation, and subtle changes in the brows can add significantly more dimension to the character. Do not forget to provide asymmetrical poses when designing your extremes for the eyebrows (see Figures 10.39 and 10.40).

FIGURE 10.38

Position 2/Blink Right: Eye motion as simple as a blink can add a tremendous amount of life to a character.

FIGURE 10.39

Position 3/ Brow Down and Bent Left: Eyebrows need to be able to lift and furrow themselves independently of one another.

FIGURE 10.40

Position 3/ Brow Down and Bent Right: Subtle changes in the brows can add significantly more dimension to the character.

■ **Positions 5 and 6 (Brow Up Left, Right).** The Bend modifier is useful in creating successful arches and bends in brow geometry. An arch might be used for a surprised or curious character. Do not forget to provide asymmetrical poses when designing your extremes for the eyebrows (see Figures 10.41 and 10.42).

FIGURE 10.41

Position 5/ Brow Up and Arched Left: An arch might be used for a surprised or curious character.

FIGURE 10.42

Position 6/ Brow Up and Arched Right: The Bend modifier is useful in creating successful arches and bends in brow geometry.

Basic Phonemes

Phonemes are the phonetic representation of sounds used to show words being formed. A few examples have been shown previously, like the AH, OOO, and EEE sounds. To animate lip synch, the track of dialogue must be read and understood. Next the sound should be loaded into MAX. An Audio controller tool is provided with MAX R2 that is powerful in working with audio and track reading. Another option is the third-party sound editor called Magpie. This plug-in provides even more flexibility when reading a track and is discussed further in this section.

Reading Tracks

Now that you understand how the basic mouth position operates and how to create it, it is time to break down the track into individual phonemes. This is best done on good old fashioned animator's exposure sheet paper. Otherwise, get a pad of lined paper to read your track on, using one line per frame. If you want, you can also create a spreadsheet for this purpose and do it all digitally. There is an example Excel spreadsheet on the CD-ROM entitled 10xls01.xls. You might use this or print it if you so desire.

Using a Sound Editing Program to Read Tracks

To read a track, many animators use a sound editing program that enables them to view the waveform of the sound and listen to the track a frame at a time. A great sound editing shareware program called CoolEdit is available on the Internet at www.syntrillium.com/cool96.htm.

Once the sound file is loaded into your desired program, the first thing you should do is match your sound editing program's timebase to the timebase you are animating—30, 25, 24 frames per second. After the timebase is set, make your sound file the proper length. If you have silence at the beginning or end of your shot, slug the same amount of silence into your .WAV file. This way you can load it into MAX and use it as reference.

Once the file is cut to length, you can start reading the track and writing down the phonemes. This is done by selecting the active part of the sound file's dialogue or waveform, which should enable you to listen to the snippet and read the exact length of that dialogue on the editor's information window.

The visual readout of the sound file gives you clues as to where the words start and end. Work your way through the track a frame at a time and write down each sound as it occurs on your exposure sheet, frame by frame. It is a tedious but necessary chore.

T IP _____

It is best to create a lower-resolution sampled version of your sound file for use in MAX. This way when you do scrub through the dialogue, the sound file is small and won't bog down the interface as much. A good low-end sample setting is around 22MHz. Use your higher frequency sampling for the final render and test renders.

3D Studio MAX enables you to play back audio in synch with your animation. This is particularly helpful because you might be able to skip the step of track reading and just eyeball the lip synch. This can work only if your system is fast and your models light. Otherwise, you will not be able to scrub your animation interactively.

Using Magpie

Third-party sound editors can provide flexibility when reading a track, but there is no immediate feedback as to how your character will animate. Many animators have turned to third-party lip sync applications to help, particularly if they cannot scrub audio interactively within MAX because of system limits.

A good example of one of these third-party packages is Magpie. The shareware is available on the Internet at http://thirdwish.simplenet.com/magpie.html. Magpie enables you to load a series of bitmap files that represent the key mouth poses as found in your library of poses. These bitmaps can then be timed to the track on a frame-by-frame basis; the final result output is a text file that looks very much like an animator's dope sheet.

T IP

In MAX, real-time playback must be checked in the Time Configuration dialog for sound to play back correctly.

Track Reading and Accuracy

When reading the track, be certain to represent the sounds accurately. In human speech, most consonants are short and usually do not take up more than one or two frames. Vowels, however, can be of any length. If a person is shouting, for instance, you might have vowels that top 30 frames in length.

In these cases, it is important that you do not hold the mouth in the exact same position for very long—it would look unnatural. Instead, adjust the slider for the jaw, so that it relaxes slightly through the vowel. This keeps the mouth positions and the mouth moving between them so that the character looks alive.

READING A TRACK

1. Load 10wav03.wav from the accompanying CD-ROM into your favorite editing program. The dialogue says "Euuuuwah...I don't like that." At 30 fps, the dialogue measures 78 frames.

2. Highlight the first 18 frames of the sound file. This is the word "Ohhhhh." Play this section back. Highlight smaller sections to get the individual phonemes.

3. The next sound, from frames 18–27, is an inhale. Usually you don't worry about inhales, but because this one is so prominent, mark it down.

4. Work through the entire track, writing down the positions of each phoneme. A graphic representation of where phonemes fall is shown in Figure 10.43. On paper you should have something similar to Table 10.1.

5. As a final note, be careful about reading the track too literally. Concentrate on the sounds, not the script. In this track, the character doesn't pronounce the "T" in the word "don't." Instead he goes right into the "L" sound in "like."

FIGURE 10.43

The phonemes as they appear in relation to the waveform.

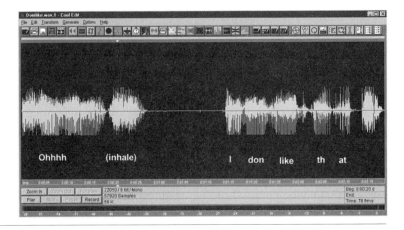

TABLE 10.1

Corresponding Frame and Phoneme

Frame	Phoneme	Frame	Phoneme
1	H	37	(SILENCE)
2	H	38	(SILENCE)
3	H	39	(SILENCE)
4	OH	40	(SILENCE)
5	OH	41	(SILENCE)
6	OH	42	(SILENCE)
7	OH	43	(SILENCE)
8	OH	44	(SILENCE)
9	OH	45	AH
10	OH	46	AH
11	OH	47	I
12	OH	48	I
13	OH	49	D
14	OH	50	D
15	OH	51	O
16	OH	52	O
17	(CLOSED)	53	N
18	(CLOSED)	54	N
19	(INHALE)	55	L
20	(INHALE)	56	L
21	(INHALE)	57	I
22	(INHALE)	58	I
23	(INHALE)	59	I
24	(INHALE)	60	K
25	(INHALE)	61	K

continues

TABLE 10.1, CONTINUED
Corresponding Frame and Phoneme

Frame	Phoneme	Frame	Phoneme
26	(INHALE)	62	TH
27	(INHALE)	63	TH
28	(SILENCE)	64	A
29	(SILENCE)	65	A
30	(SILENCE)	66	A
31	(SILENCE)	67	T
32	(SILENCE)	68	T
33	(SILENCE)	69	T
34	(SILENCE)	70	UH
35	(SILENCE)	71	UH
36	(SILENCE)	72	UH

Loading Sound into MAX

MAX has the capability to load sound directly into the Track View, which makes it excellent for lip-synch applications. Sound is loaded by right-clicking the Sound Track object and selecting Properties from the pull-down menu that appears.

MAX then displays the audio waveform from within the Track View, giving you the capability to read the track directly in MAX. Simply sliding the Time slider audibly scrubs the audio, allowing you to read the phonemes of the dialogue frame by frame. This is best done before animation begins because a properly read track serves as a good reference when animating.

Also, reading the track after animation has been added to the shot can prove troublesome due to machine speed, length of animation, and animation complexity issues. If Multi-Morph Target animation is being used, the calculations required to perform this can tax even the most powerful systems, so real-time playback might not be possible.

Using Audio Controllers

One of the easier ways to do lip synch is to use MAX's Audio controllers. These controllers enable you to translate, rotate, and scale objects based on the volume of a standard Windows .WAV file. The lip synch produced by this method is not exceptionally accurate; it produces a simple lip flapping effect, which is not particularly convincing because of its automated and mechanical qualities. However, for more stylized characters, such as a mouth resembling a duck bill, the method can prove more than adequate.

The AudioRotation controller is the one chosen most often for sound applications because it can be used to rotate and flap the lower jaw (though the Translate and Scale controllers can also be put to similar use). These controllers can be applied from the Motion/Parameters/Assign Controller panel or the Track View/Assign Controller button.

Once applied, the AudioRotation controller is accessed from the Track View/Controller/Properties to be edited. The controller's dialog box has a number of parameters (see Figure 10.44). First is the name of the sound file to be loaded. It must be noted that each controller can have its own sound file, and the sound file does not have to match the sound track in Track View. This enables multiple sound files to be used as controllers—perhaps to flap the lips of a dozen people in a crowded room.

FIGURE 10.44

The Audio Controller panel.

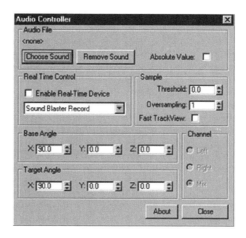

A sound file does not even have to be used, because the controller has a check box to enable a live audio source to be used as the controller. This can be useful for real-time or performance-animation applications.

The Oversampling spinner is critical for smooth operation. A CD-quality audio waveform changes 44,100 times per second, rising and falling constantly. The Audio controller takes the value of the waveform on the given frame and uses that number to calculate the rotation. This can cause jittery behavior because the waveform could coincidentally be at zero, maximum, or somewhere in between when it is sampled.

Oversampling prevents this jittering movement, by smoothing out the waveform seen by MAX. The procedure averages the waveform over a large number of samples (maximum 1,000), giving the effect of a much smoother motion (see Figure 10.45).

FIGURE 10.45

The Audio controller can have a different sound than the sound track in Track View.

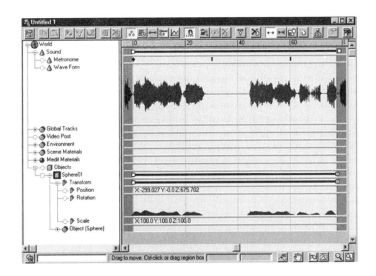

TIP

If your audio sample rate is high (44,100KHz), you might still see some unwanted jitter, even though the Oversampling spinner is cranked up to 1,000. To eliminate this, load the audio file into a sound editing program and convert it to a lower sample rate as described in the previous Tip (11,025KHz, for example). Fewer samples force the controller to oversample over a wider range of time, effectively doubling or quadrupling the oversampling effect.

Along the bottom of the dialog are the limits for the Rotation controller. These limits enable you to set a Base angle, which is the Rotation value used when the sound is silent, and a Target angle, which is the Rotation value used when the waveform is at 100 percent.

Eyes and Other Facial Features

Creating animatable eyes is another important part of facial animation. How the eyes are built determines how they are animated and also how they look to the audience. Eyes fall into two broad categories: internal eyes, which have the lid as part of the surface of the face, and external eyes, which have their own self-contained lids.

Creating Internal Eyes

Internal eyes are akin to more realistic eyes. The eyelids are part of the facial surface, with the eyeball inside of the skull. If your character design dictates internal eyes, you need to plan for this by modeling eye sockets by either modeling the eyelids as part of the entire head mesh or by modeling geometry that is fleshy and separate or attached to the head mesh. This can add a lot of detail, particularly when using patches or NURBS.

The eyeball itself can be either a sphere or a hemisphere because only the front part of the eye ever shows through the skin (see Figure 10.46). The pupil can be made with a simple texture map, or a second hemisphere sitting on the first like a contact lens.

FIGURE 10.46

Because only the front part of the eyes show, the eyeball can simply be a hemisphere.

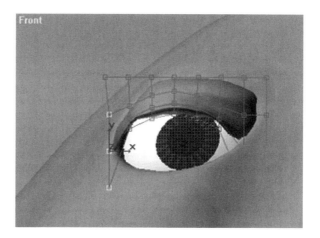

Fitting Internal Eyes to the Mesh

The big problem with internal eyes is that you need to keep the eyeballs locked in the socket while the head moves. This is usually accomplished with a hierarchy—the head being the parent of the eyes. When the head turns, the eyes move with it.

This can cause problems, however, because the eyeballs can be accidentally selected and moved. One way to keep the eyes completely locked in their sockets is to freeze them. This, however, prevents you from rotating them. A more clever tactic is to fit them into their sockets and then add a blank expression to the eyeball's Position track. This keeps the eye from translating but allows for rotation.

Getting the Lids to Move Smoothly

Another issue is the movement of the eyelids. They must move on an arc that is the same radius as the eye. There are three main techniques for movement of the eyelids: Morphing, Linked Xform, and FFD Lattice deformations, or sometimes a combination of these, depending on the detail of motion desired. Keep in mind that the arc of the motion begins with the center and front part of the lid leading the motion; the corners of the lid follow this motion.

Animating Eyelids Via Morphing

To animate by using Morph Targets, the mesh can be designed with lids as part of the mesh, as separate meshes, or as attached objects. The mesh used in Figure 10.47 has attached meshes for eyelids, but the technique applies to all types of internal eyelids. Using the morphing techniques explained previously in the Morphing section, the main mesh has the eyelids in a neutral closed pose.

FIGURE 10.47

An eyelid that is part of the surface of the head can be affected with an FFD.

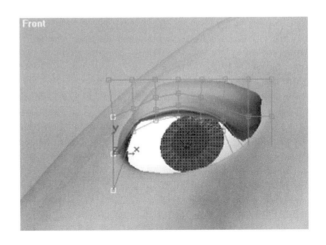

Most meshes work best when the second position of an open eye is created from a closed position, much like a pose of arms outstretched and palms down works best when building the body mesh.

ANIMATING EYELIDS VIA A MORPHING TUTORIAL

1. Load the file 10max09.max and select the mesh called B-Closed Eyes by using Select by Name.

2. Add a Mesh select to the stack and select Faces with a number 3 material ID. This should give you the eyelid selection. Deselect one set of eyelid faces.

3. Select the Modify panel and add an 4×2×2 FFD (box) modifier to the stack. Manipulate the points to simulate the eye opening. Remember that the eyelid closes and opens on an arc over the eye with the center part of the lid leading the corners.

4. Make a snapshot of the closed lid mesh as a copied mesh. Rename that mesh **M-Closed Eyes**.

5. Select the first mesh called B-Closed Eyes, which you added the FFD modifiers to, and delete all the modifiers. This mesh should now appear to have closed eyes again.

6. Apply a MorphMagic modifier to the B-Closed Eyes mesh. Assign M-Open Eyes to a blank frame.

7. Move the animation to frame 5 and turn the Animate button on. Change the spinner in the Mix Bank channel for M-Open Eyes to read 100 percent.

8. Drag the Time slider to see one eye open and close. You can repeat the above steps for the other eye.

You can provide additional positions for the eyes to create specific squinting or surprised poses by manipulating the bottom and top parts of the eye and eyelid. The channels can also be overshot into the positive and negative to create other poses. For instance, to create a wide-eyed look, overshoot the Open Eye channel by 10 percent. The neutral pose of the eyes being open for this mesh can be established as a separate mesh or as 85 percent of the open eye. The choices are endless. To see the Vertex Selection method being used in conjunction with a final version of morphing eyelids, load the file called 10max10.max.

Animating Eyelids with Linked Xforms

Animating eyelids by using the Linked Xform method is the same as the NURBS Facial Linked Xform method discussed earlier in the chapter. Instead of animating the mouth, however, you animate the selected vertices of the eyelids.

By using the Mesh Select or NSurf Select modifiers, you can select the corresponding vertices of the eyelids to be animated. The only problem with this method is that, to get the nice subtle arc needed to open the eye, you need to position the controlling object at the center of the eyeball. Lid motion is animated by rotating the controlling object rather than translating it.

Animating Eyelids with Lattice Deformations

The eyelids can also be animated by using the Lattice Deformation method. For a good reference, look at the previous tutorial entitled "Animating Eyelids Via Morphing." This provides a good example of how to fit a Lattice to a mesh. The difference is that, rather than using the Lattice to create a Morph Target, the Lattice itself is animated. Keep in mind, as discussed before, that the Lattices create a key in the Track View for every single Control point, and this could be too much for you and your machine to keep up with.

Creating External Eyes

Eyes where the lids are not attached to the surface of the face are termed external eyes. This can simplify things considerably when it comes to animation, because separate lids are typically a hemisphere that can be fitted quite easily to the lid. Rotating the lid allows it to move across the surface of the eyeball quite easily.

The best way to model a set of external eyes is to have a hierarchy structure. The first part of this structure is the actual eyeball. To follow along with this description, load the file called 10max11.max and explore the stack of each object to study the settings (see Figure 10.48).

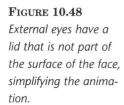

FIGURE 10.48

External eyes have a lid that is not part of the surface of the face, simplifying the animation.

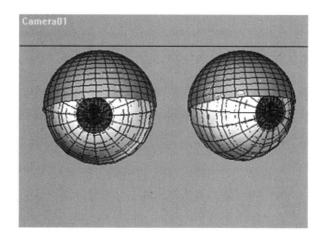

These are very simply constructed eyes that can be used in a variety of situations. The lids of these eyes are not directly attached to the surface of the face, but rather they are separate objects linked to the eyeball itself. This allows for simple construction and gives the lids the capability to change shape along with the eyes, the lids following the surface exactly, even when the eyes are scaled to an oblong shape.

MODELING EXTERNAL EYES

1. From the Geometry Creation panel, create a standard sphere that is 30 units in diameter and has 32 radial subdivisions. Name this sphere **R-Eye**.

2. Select the sphere and then Shift-click the sphere to clone it as a copy. Name this object **R-Eyelid.**

3. Select the copy, being careful not to move it. (If you accidentally jog it, you might want to use Grid Snap to align the two pivots exactly). Within the Modify panel, increase the diameter to 31 units.

4. Remaining in the Modify panel, set the hemisphere spinner to 0.5. This makes the eyelid half a sphere.

5. Clone the object R-Eye again to make the pupil. Name this object **R-EyePupil**.

6. Set the diameter of this object to 30.5 units and the hemisphere to 0.9.

7. Select R-Eyelid and R-EyePupil and link them to R-Eye.

8. Duplicate these three objects to make the left eye.

9. Save the file, for you will use it again later.

Because the objects all rotate around the same center, eye rotation is as simple as rotating the pupil, and blinking is as simple as rotating the lid.

Attaching Pupils via SurfDeform and Conform

Although creating the pupil as a hemisphere, as in the previous exercise, can work quite well, there are other methods for attaching a pupil to an eye. Two of these methods use new features of MAX to create a pupil that moves along the surface of the eyeball, regardless of the eyeball's shape.

SurfDeform is powerful new world space modifier that comes with R2. It works well with a NURBS surface to create a moving pupil across the eyeball surface as an Animation option. Conform does the same thing with polygonal meshes and is a space warp (see Figure 10.49).

FIGURE 10.49

SurfDeform can be used to attach a pupil to an eyeball.

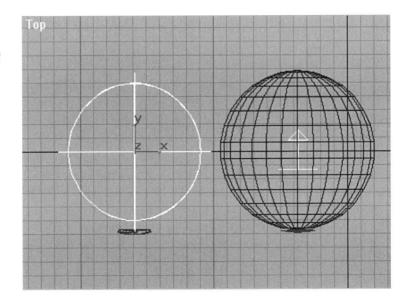

CREATING A PUPIL ATTACHED VIA SURFDEFORM

1. From the Front viewport, create a sphere of radius 50. Place this at the origin (X,Y,Z coordinates 0,0,0).

2. From the Modify panel, turn the sphere into a NURBS sphere by right-clicking the Edit Stack icon and selecting NURBS Surface.

3. At the origin, create a cylinder of radius 15 and height 1.

4. With the cylinder still selected, add a SurfDeform modifier to the stack.

5. From within the SurfDeform rollout, toggle Pick Surface and select the sphere.

6. The cylinder is now deformed to the surface of the sphere. Moving the cylinder in X and Y, move the cylinder along the sphere. You can "dilate" the pupil by adjusting the U and V Stretch values within the rollout.

The second technique uses the Conform space warp to link the pupil to the eyeball sphere and have it rotate on the eyeball's axis. Although SurfDeform requires that the eyeball be a NURBS surface, Conform also works on any deformable surface, including polygonal surfaces.

ATTACHING A PUPIL BY USING CONFORM

1. From the Front viewport, create a sphere of radius 50. Place this at the origin (X,Y,Z coordinates 0,0,0).

2. At the origin, create a cylinder of radius 15, height 1.

3. From the Create/Space Warps panel, create a Conform Space Warp, also at the origin.

4. From the Top viewport, select the Conform Space Warp and orient it so that the arrow points toward the back of the sphere (points up in the Top viewport).

5. With the Conform Space Warp still selected, activate the Modify panel. From the Conform Parameters rollout, toggle Pick Object and select the sphere.

6. Select the cylinder and bind it to the Conform Space Warp.

7. Translate the cylinder toward the front of the sphere. As it hits the surface, it conforms. As you move the cylinder, it stays on the surface of the sphere, but only through a 180 degree range of motion.

These two tools not only have applications for pupils but can be used to stick any object to a face. Because they both take into account the deformation of that surface, they work much better than a simple hierarchy. Some other facial details that can be attached in this manner are eyebrows, the nose, facial blemishes such as a wart, or perhaps a mustache. For reference, examples of both of these exercises are located in the file 10max12.max.

Texture Mapped Pupils

Eyeballs can also have a Texture map assigned to them to create a pupil, but it is harder to create a convincing dilation this way. One tactic to get around this might be to create a mixed material that has one map with a pupil at a normal size and another at a full dilation. Unfortunately, animating between two discrete maps can cause ghosting of the images if it is not over a few frames.

Another option involves creating an animation of the dilation and using that as the Texture map, but be aware that it will loop unless you create it for the whole animation length. If changes need to be made to the timing, a new animation must be created or the offset adjusted. The best idea is to create a separate pupil like the one in the file 10max11.max. Instead of faces being designated with the iris color, you can make a Texture map that is outside of the pupil (see Figure 10.50). Load the 10max13.max file to see a version of successfully Texture-mapped eyes with separate pupils.

FIGURE 10.50

A simple map such as this can be used to create a realistic iris and pupil.

Animating with the UVW Gizmo

Using the Texture mapped method, the animation can be controlled by the UVW coordinates if desired. This way you can create a Texture map and move it on both eyes in synch with one another as long as the same Texture map and the same Mapping coordinates are applied. Referring to the 10max13.max file in the Materials Editor, click the material called Iris. Under the Materials/Maps/Map/Coordinates rollout, you will see spinners for the UV Offset. By moving these spinners you move the Texture map left and right and up and down on the surface of the eyeball. It doesn't take much to move the map. A span of -0.05–0.05 with the U Offset spinner moves the Texture map up and down on the eyeballs. In addition, a span of -0.08–0.08 with the V Offset spinner moves the Texture map right and left on the eyeballs. These controls are animatable and create editable keys in the Track View. This UVW Coordinate motion can be modified in the UVW modifier to get separate motion from right and left eyes as well.

Using the Look At Controller for Pupil Aiming

A very simple way to create synched motion with eyes is by using the Look At controller. By assigning the controller in the Track View or under the Motion panel, you can choose any object as the target of the eyes' motion. To study an example of a successful Look At controller setup, load the file 10max14.max.

This technique has many advantages, including the capability to animate the Look At target with an object that the character's eyes are supposed to be following, such as an insect. Having the eyes move with the motion of another object can be difficult sometimes. The Look At controller, however, gives you timing that is right on the money. Another great advantage to using the Look At controller is when you use a hierarchy with your eyelids as the children of your eyeballs; the eyelids follow the eye motion up as the eye looks up, producing a subtle and more natural motion.

To give even more flexibility to this setup, create a dummy with the same center axis as your eyeball (see Figure 10.51), and link your eyeball to the dummy. Use a Look At controller on the dummy and you still have separate control of your eyeball hierarchy through the parent eyeball, if you need asymmetrical movement or you just want to animate it a different way. You can also easily use this method with Physique if you keep in mind the structure of linking the eyeball parent to the head bone, and not assigning the Physique modifier to the eye hierarchy at all. The eyes continue to stay in the head, move with the deformed head, and follow the Look At controller no matter how the head moves.

FIGURE 10.51

The Look At controller can assist the aiming of the eyes.

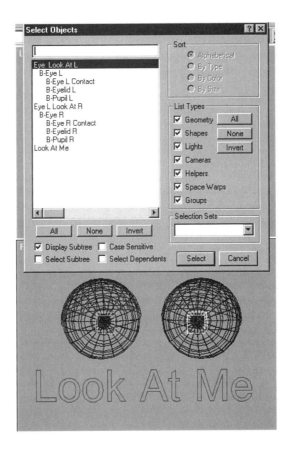

Creating Non-Spherical or Cartoon Eyes

Realistic eyes maintain their shape and always remain spherical. This makes animation of the lids fairly easy. For more stylized characters, particularly those of the cartoon persuasion, it is sometimes desirable to create eyes that are oval or that change shape according to the character's mood. Here are a few methods for creating non-spherical eyes.

Using Scale and Squash on External Eyes

For the external eyes created earlier, the first method for creating non-spherical eyes can be accomplished quite handily by simply making sure the Inherit Scale boxes under the Hierarchy/Link Info panel are checked. Because the eyelid and the pupil are children of the eye, the eye's scaling information will be inherited. This enables you to scale the eyes in any manner possible, including non-proportional scale to make the eyes oblong.

The use of external eyes produces a more cartoon-like appearance, and they are easier to control than internal eyes. Because they don't have to line up exactly with the eye sockets on the face, you have much greater control over how they're placed. They're great for Tex Avery–style eye-popping and afford the animator a variety of stylistic choices.

Furthermore, the scaling can be animated to give the eyes a very flexible squash and stretch effect. This enables you to use the eyes far more expressively on the character. Some examples of this expressive behavior might be as follows:

- During a blink, the eyes can be scaled along the horizontal axis for two or three frames to help give the blink more snap.

- When a character is surprised, his eyebrows rise up. Scaling the eyes along the vertical axis accentuates this even further.

- If a character is loopy or has been knocked senseless, the eyes can be scaled along different axes to produce a crazy or mixed-up look.

- Shifty-eyed characters can have their eyes elongated along a horizontal axis.

Blinks happen all the time, and they are a very useful tool for the animator. Blinks can be used to help shift the direction of the eyes or to convey emotion. They also make your characters come alive—simply blinking the eyes every few seconds makes your characters more believable.

ANIMATING A CARTOON BLINK

1. Using the eyes created in the External Eyes tutorial, turn on the Animate button and use the non-proportional scale tool to make the eyes slightly elongated along the vertical axis.

2. Move the Time slider to frame 6. This is the start of the blink. Within the Motion panel, set the key for the scale of the eyes and rotation of the eyelids.

3. Move the Time slider to frame 9. This is the middle of the blink. Rotate the eyelids 90 degrees so that they cover the eyes. Notice that, even though the eyes are scaled, the lids still follow the surface of the eyes.

4. Select the Squash Scaling tool and squash the eyes down so they are elongated along the horizontal axis (see Figure 10.52).

FIGURE 10.52

To get a more cartoon-ish effect, squash the eyes as they blink.

5. Move the slider to frame 12. Rotate the lids open and use the Squash Scaling tool to return the scaling of the eyes back to normal (for complete accuracy, the keys on frame 6 can also be copied to frame 12 from within Track View).

T IP

Eyes never blink at exactly the same time. Offsetting the blink of one eye by a single frame can add more life to your shot.

Run the animation and notice how the extra squash added to the blink helps make it look more cartoonish. Also notice how the lids stay along the surface of the eye no matter what the shape. For reference, a file named 10avi03.AVI is located on the CD-ROM.

Using FFD Space Warps to Change Eye Shape

A more sophisticated approach to creating non-spherical eyes involves the use of the FFD space warp instead of a scale to create the deformation.

Because a space warp affects all the objects within it equally, the eyes deform and the lids still remain locked to the eyeball.

USING AN FFD SPACE WARP TO ANIMATE EYE SHAPE

1. Load the eyes created in the External Eyes tutorial.

2. From Create/SpaceWarps, create a 2×2×2 FFD box space warp that is slightly larger than the right eye. Position the warp around the eye.

3. Select the eyeball, lid, and pupil of the right eye.

4. Toggle the Bind to the Space Warp button and then drag the cursor to the FFD space warp and release.

5. Select the space warp. Toggle Sub-Object/Control Points. Select one of the Lattice's Control points and move it. The eye should deform. Then toggle Sub-Object mode off.

6. Select the lid and rotate it. It should move smoothly along the surface of the eye.

7. Repeat steps 1–4 for the left eye.

A copy of this file is on the accompanying CD-ROM. It is called 10max15.max.

Creating and Animating Brows

Although the eyes and lids are important, the eyebrows also add a great deal to the character of the face. The brows can be attached as part of the face through a Texture map or as separate objects.

If you're fortunate enough to have a hair plug-in, this also can create brows. The animation procedures, however, are pretty much the same, because the hair created will essentially be either a Texture map (for plug-ins such as Digimation's Shag;Fur, which use textures to define position of the hair) or separate geometry for those that create particles for the hair.

Separate Mix/Morph Targets to Animate Brows

Using separate Mix/Morph Targets enables more motion to re-emphasize brow movement. If you have not designed your eyelids as separate geometry, build several Morph Targets with the eyes in positions like Squinted, Wide-eyed, Angry, and Surprised. This re-emphasizes your brow movement and adds subtle overlap to your animation.

Again, as with the muscles around the face, the best targets to use are those that are the extremes of the muscles controlling the upper part of the face. The two main sets of muscles to consider are the Frontalis, which raises and lowers the brow along the forehead, and the Corrugator, which brings the brows in at the bridge of the nose.

Using SurfDeform and Conform to Attach Geometric Brows

For eyebrows created as separate geometry, SurfDeform and Conform can be used to attach a brow to the surface of the face. The procedure for connecting these is the same as for pupils to eyes. Refer to the earlier discussion under the section "Attaching Pupils Via SurfDeform and Conform." The same techniques apply for eyebrows. This is a nifty way to create eyebrows that stay on the forehead and can be animated at the same time.

Using Texture Maps

Texture maps can be painted to cover the entire face of your mesh and create more realism with blush on the cheeks, painted freckles, warts, or other subtle differences in the skin. The best way to do this if you do not have an external 3D Paint package is to use the Unwrap utility third-party plug-in written by Peter Watje at http://www.blarg.net/~peterw/max2.html. This plug-in extrapolates the mapping coordinates and creates an "unwrapped" version of your mesh, using the coordinates specified. This way you can use the "unwrapped" Wire Texture map as a guide in a Paint program to create your facial Texture map. Remember to check the map in your Shaded mode of MAX to see that the brush strokes you are making fall in the right places on your mesh. Use the Reload Map button when changing the map and reapplying it to your mesh.

TIP

The best mapping coordinates for this technique are those of a cylindrical map with the back of the map (green line) facing the back of the head.

Creating Forehead and Facial Wrinkles with Texture/Bump Maps

Another great option for additional facial animation is the use of Texture Bump maps as wrinkling functions for the skin. If you need the forehead to crinkle as the brow takes on an angry pose, connect the height of the Wrinkle Bump map to the height of a Forehead slider in Mix via an expression. You can also try to animate the Bump map with a Mix material and create the Bump from 0.0–1.0 as the forehead needs to crease.

Tongues and Teeth

The tongue and teeth are particularly important when animating speech. The tongue is a very flexible object. As such, it can be animated with bones, a simple Lattice, or some form of shape animation, such as a morph.

Because we rarely fly our digital camera down our character's throat, the back of the tongue will rarely be seen. The easiest way to build a tongue is by squashing a sphere and putting a dent down its length. Texture and Bump maps can also be used to create a more detailed surface. It's a good idea to fade this texture to black at the back of the tongue so that it remains hidden. The tongue is easily animated by using either morphing or a chain of bones and a package such as Physique or Bones Pro. Using MAX's bones with IK turned off creates a particularly good tongue controller, as the mesh stretches along with the bones as they stretch.

Teeth, on the other hand, remain rigid and do not need to be shape animated. With teeth, only the top teeth are locked to the skull, and the bottom set moves with the lower jaw.

Teeth can take on either a realistic or a cartoonish style. The cartoon-fashioned teeth might be only one cylinder that is scaled for certain mouth positions like the "EE" or the "T" sound. The realistic set of choppers should be upper and lower and can be animated with bones linked to the jaw, tongue, or head. An easy way to keep the teeth inside of the mouth is to attach them to your head for morphing and position them where they need to be in each pose. They will move accordingly as you animate them with Mix or Barycentric morphs.

In Practice: Facial Animation

- **Replacement animation**. Many facial features, such as mouths, can be animated by using replacement techniques. Although it is not realistic-looking, it can be a very effective solution.

- **Animating faces directly**. Direct manipulation of CVs can create good shapes, but the animation can be difficult to control for a complex model.

- **Low-resolution faces**. With a fast machine, a low-resolution face can animate in near real time with MAX. Adding a MeshSmooth modifier after the deformation can turn the face into a high-resolution face at render time.

- **Morph Targets**. The most economical way of creating Morph Targets for facial animation is to model the targets according to the muscles of the face. This creates a much better looking animation while saving on targets.

- **Eyelids**. When modeling an eyelid that is part of the surface of the face, model the default Morph Target as the closed lid. It is much easier to model an open-lid target than a closed-lid target.

Part III

ANIMATING THE ENVIRONMENT

Chapter 11

ANIMATING CAMERAS

When the Lumière brothers made their first motion pictures toward the end of the nineteenth century, they followed a simple principle. They chose one event that they believed was worth filming, mounted their camera directly in front of the person or thing to be recorded, and filmed until the stock footage was completely exposed. They were mostly documents of everyday events that had not been rehearsed and could have also been shown as a series of individual photographs. Using this method, films like the following were made:

- *A Baby's Breakfast* (Le Déjeuner de Bébé, 1895)

- *A Skiff Leaves the Harbor* (Barque Sortant du Port, 1895)

- *Quitting Time at Lumière Factory* (La Sortie des Usines Lumière, 1895)

The camera was used in the same manner as a normal "snapshot camera." The only advantage was that it could record motion.

Even though in the beginning of film history, the audience was astounded by such films, the need for increasingly complex films grew. Within the next years film techniques developed to fulfill these needs. Film language, the capability to communicate very complex processes in only a few scenes with special film techniques, came into being.

Film techniques like the following are all expressions of film language:

- Camera movement

- Picture composition

- Lighting

- Sound

- Editing

Understanding Traditional Film Cameras

Virtuallyany film or television show you have seen has been produced using film language. One of the primary and integral people involved in the production of films is the cinematographer. The cinematographer is responsible for setting the camera shot and deciding what movement is necessary to tell the story. Cinematographers have typically been trained in film school and have many years of experience to be able to capture the film sequences that you take for granted.

As a CG animator you are given the same responsibility as the cinematographer to involve the audience in the scene through the use of a camera. Camera placement and movement is an art that is not easily mastered and should be studied and practiced. All the methods of cinematography that are taught in film school are also valid in CG animation. If possible, take some classes in filmmaking, read books about it, and study the "grammar" of film language.

Computer animation often suffers from the intrusiveness of the camera. This can happen when the freedom of using a virtual camera in a virtual world tempts the animator to get away from the constraints a real-world camera operator faces. When you push the envelope of what is expected, whether it is by moving through a scene at supernatural speed or by being able to fly above, below, and through anything, the audience is more likely to notice the camera work rather than the message of the work itself, if there is any.

You can avoid this by using the camera in ways that people understand. Nearly everyone in today's world has viewed thousands of hours of moving pictures on television and in theaters. Mimicking real-world camera techniques in computer animation gives viewers visual cues they already understand.

One characteristic of computer-generated animation, for example, is the machine-driven precision of the virtual camera. This precision can make the presence of the camera obvious. Computer-animated camera moves often tend to be very uniform in pacing and direction. Working to simulate a human camera operator adds a quality to the animation that brings it closer to the type of camera work people are used to seeing.

A good way to learn about refined camera work is to step back and take an objective look at motion picture and television footage. Ignore the content and focus on what the camera actually is doing. Try turning down the sound while watching TV and analyzing what you see. You are likely to be surprised by the complexity.

The following elements are what cinematographers must consider when recording moving images:

- Zoom lenses

- Camera angles

- Field of view

- Camera moves

- Depth of field

- Transitions

Zoom Lenses

The invention of zoom (variable focal length) lenses made it possible for camera "moves" to be made without actually moving the camera. Orthodox cinematographers use the zoom lens only to change the angle of view between shots and prefer to move the camera itself when a move is called for. (Home videographers love to zoom in and out while making fast pans and tilts to enhance the nauseating effect.)

It is as easy (or easier) to move the camera itself rather than to zoom when creating a computer animation. The zoom, however, can be a very effective tool. Because people are accustomed to seeing zoom effects in films and on television, you can use it to accomplish the same effects in computer space. On the surface, zooming appears to move the camera closer to or farther from objects in the scene. In reality, the angle of view is changing, so perceived spatial relationships also change.

Camera Angle

Varying the viewing angle in a film is done for many reasons: to follow the subject, to reveal or withhold information, to change the point of view, to establish a location, or even to develop a mood. In the '30s and '40s, location shooting was very expensive, so you often see scenes that were photographed in front of projected backgrounds. Also establishing a scene in a wide shot on location and moving to a medium shot in a studio to photograph the subject was often made just to save money.

Then and now many directors consider photography of the actors to be the primary storytelling imagery and continue to separate the subject from the environment, but the truth is that the subject is never separate from the location. By themselves, camera angles have no meaning. It seems clear for most people that a low-angle view of a subject places it in a dominant position, while high-angle views place it in a diminutive position, but that is only valid in a certain situations.

For example, in the motion picture *Citizen Kane* with Orson Welles, low-angle shots are used throughout the entire movie, but their significance depends on the context between subject and environment. In the beginning you see Kane as a young, energetic and powerful man. In these shots, the ceilings are low and Kane—Wells was actually very tall—seems to dominate everything around him. By the end of the film, when Kane is an old man who has lost much of his influence, he is still photographed from a low angle, but now he seems to be very small in comparison to the huge size of his home Xanadu with its high ceilings. Here, the context between subject and environment does not fit the conventional understanding of low-angle perspectives.

Viewer Placement

In film the viewer identifies with the camera. When the camera moves, the viewer experiences the sensation of movement and frequently finds the images onscreen more real than the space around him. This illusion is called transference. Motion rides, for instance, use this illusion to create a successful simulation of physical sensations experienced during a ride through virtual space. Therefore, the viewer can not only watch the action onscreen but also experience it.

Perspective

One way to learn how the change in perspective works from shot to shot in a sequence is to reduce perspective to simple forms. Once the basic forms are understood, you will be able to recognize them more easily when you are visualizing sequences.

FIGURE 11.1

*Linear perspective
(A: Orthographic,
B: one-point,
C: two-point,
D: three-point
perspective).*

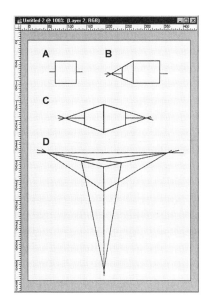

The cube illustrations in Figure 11.1 show the basic forms of linear perspective. Whether you are looking at a room, building, or vehicle, certain viewpoints show depth more than others. In Figure 11.2, you see a building. The View is square to the side and only the vertical lines converge on the horizon. The vanishing point coincides with the center of vision and all other lines do not have a vanishing point at all. These lines do not converge and are parallel to the view and the horizon. It is called one-point perspective because it has only one vanishing point.

If you are not square to the building you have vanishing points for each of the visible two sides. In Figure 11.3, you can see the result of a so-called two-point perspective. The view could be from any side but you have to keep in mind that the camera and the camera target must be level with the horizon to ensure that vertical lines remain vertical.

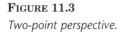

FIGURE 11.3
Two-point perspective.

When you are no longer looking at an object along a level line of sight, vertical lines converge to a vanishing point. This can be seen in Figure 11.4. All three planes of the building now have a vanishing point, which is called a three-point perspective. If you are looking down at a point below the horizon, the building's vertical lines converge downward. They converge upward if you are looking above the horizon. If you again take a look at the building level with the horizon, you have a two-point perspective.

FIGURE 11.4
Three-point perspective.

NOTE

Because of the different perspective projection between the human eye and a camera lens, placing a camera at eye level of a standing person actually looks too high under most circumstances. In an architectural walkthrough, for example, you should determine whether placing your camera above or below (between chest or hip) the subject is appropriate in each situation.

Later in this chapter you will go through an exercise that helps you create an architectural walkthrough. You will then experience the use of one-, two-, and three-point perspective.

Field of View

Field of view is the angle described by an imaginary cone, the vertex of which is at the camera's location. This angle is determined by the focal length of the lens being used.

Short focal length lenses (28mm or 35mm on a 35mm SLR) give a very wide angle of view. Objects in the scene tend to appear far apart from one another. Something appearing on the horizon is nearly invisible, although an object near the camera looks huge. If you take a close-up portrait of someone with a wide angle lens, the person appears to have a huge nose and tiny ears. See Figure 11.5 for an example of different lens sizes.

FIGURE 11.5

The same scene shot with 15, 28, 50 and 135mm lenses.

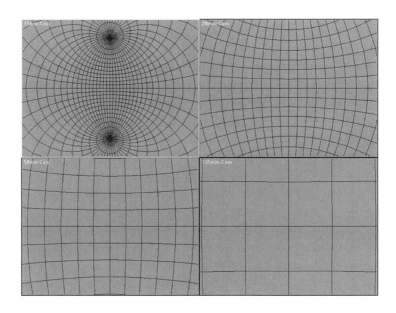

Wide angles of view are useful for showing many objects in a scene simultaneously, establishing shots of buildings and other large subjects, building interiors, and creating emphasis by exaggerating perspective.

Medium focal length lenses ("normal" or 50mm on a 35mm SLR) cover a moderate angle of view. The perspective in the resulting display seems to be about what people "normally" perceive with their own vision. The spatial relationships of objects in the scene look normal.

Long focal length, or telephoto, lenses (135mm to 500mm on a 35mm SLR) cover narrow angles of view. Because objects only at the very center of a scene fill the frame, they appear to be very close to the camera. Spacing of objects in the scene appears to be compressed.

Narrow angles of view are useful when you want to show objects both near to and far from the camera in the same shot, or when you just cannot get close enough to the object to view it with a normal or wide-angle lens.

Because the computer camera can go anywhere and do anything, you won't need a long focal length to get near something, but because people are used to seeing shots using long lenses, you may want to use them anyway. Refer to Table 11.1 for standard lens lengths.

TABLE 11.1

Standard Lens Lengths, FOV, and Names

Lens	Field of View	Type of Lens
10mm	132.01°	Fisheye
15mm	112.62°	Extra Wide-Angle
28mm	77.57°	Wide-Angle
35mm	65.47°	Medium Wide-Angle
50mm	48.45°	Standard/Normal
135mm	18.93°	Long/Telephoto
500mm	5,15°	Extra Long/Supertelephoto

NOTE

In 3DS MAX R2, as well as real-world lenses, the FOV is measured *diagonally* across the frame. This eliminates the discrepancy between the CG lenses and real-world lenses concerning FOV. In 3DS MAX R2, you can also change the FOV degree measuring to vertical and horizontal.

In 3D Studio MAX R2, you have the ability to toggle any camera to orthographic projection, which is necessary if you want to animate text or something that you do not want to have a perspective projection. It is easily done by just clicking the checkbox "Orthographic Projection" in the Modify panel under parameters.

When you observe a scene on film or television, you will notice that it consists of a series of shots, each made from a different perspective, joined together. Even though the shots are distinct and separate, the way they are joined makes each sequence appear seamless. This joining of the individual scenes is accomplished through a technique known as *transitions*.

Table 11.2 shows the basic types of shots and their uses.

TABLE 11.2

Standard Camera Shots and Their Traditional Uses

Shot Name	Visual Composition	Use
Long Shot	Characters are small in frame, all or major parts of buildings appear.	Establishes physical context of action. Shows landscape or architectural exteriors.
Full Shot	All or nearly all of a standing person shows. Large parts, but not all, of a building show.	Shows large-scale action (athletics, and so on). Shows whole groups of people. Displays large architectural details.
Medium Shot	Character shown from waist up. Medium size architectural details show.	Face plays an important role. Two or three people are shown in conversation. Moderate sized architectural detail.
Full Close-up	Head and neck of character shown. Small architectural details. Objects about the size of a desktop computer fill the frame.	Focuses on one character. Facial expression very important. Small architectural details.

| Extreme Close-up | Frame filled with just part of a character's face. Very small objects fill the frame. | Shows small objects entirely. Very small architectural details. Emphasizes facial features in character. |

Transitions

Connections between shots are as important as the shots themselves and usually signify changes in time and place. Here's just a small example to show the importance of film editing. Imagine a scene with a person in a library. This person is looking for a very specific book, finds it, takes it off the shelf, walks back to the table, and reads it. You could shoot this scene in one single shot: a full shot of all the books and the camera moves toward the middle of the board until it reaches the full close-up of one specific book. The person takes it and the camera moves to full shot again, and then to the table. It would be a very dull sequence.

The way to handle this scene would be to describe this little event in maybe three shots. The camera begins with a full shot of the shelf, moving over until a specific book is in the center of the view. Then a cut is made to a medium close-up of the section where the book is and the person taking it. The next shot could be a full close-up of the book lying on a table where the person opens it and starts reading. This example connects some single actions that are continous over a longer period of actual time.

You have many more possibilities to connect or separate shots from another. Today the greatest type of experimentation is going on in commercials and music videos because digital editing systems make it very easy and convenient to compose two pieces of film. All in all there are only six ways to put a film together:

- The Cut

- The Dissolve

- The Wipe

- The Fade-In/Fade-Out

- The White-In/White Out

- Any colored version of the above

The Cut

A cut is an abrupt transition between shots. A cut nowadays has become the most used transition between shots. Sometimes it is used to speed up a plot using a montage sequence. For example, you could use a single camera angle to show the construction of a building with months and years shortened to just a few seconds. Another example is a scene from Steven Spielberg's *Jaws* in which Officer Brody, Captain Quint, and Hooper assemble a shark cage onboard the Orca. The scene is made up of six shots, each lasting about three seconds, for a total of about 18 seconds. These 18 seconds represent about 30 minutes in real-time.

The Dissolve

With the dissolve, you can connect two shots that can be totally disparate in time and place. Dissolves can be any length but are usually between a quarter second (NTSC~12 Frames; PAL~7 Frames) to a full minute (NTSC~1800 Frames; PAL~1500).

Other types of dissolves include the focus in/out or the match shot. When using the focus in/out, one image loses its focus until it is completely blurred and then a second blurred image is focused on. This type of transition could be used to show loss and regaining consciousness. A match shot is a transition between two shots that share one graphic element that is identical in both. Usually a dissolve is used to combine the two shots. For example, you might see a person driving a car during daylight. Then suddenly the background changes from day to night. Car and driver remain at the same position.

The Wipe

The wipe is rarely seen in films today, but it was used a lot throughout the '30s and '40s. It is usually a cross-frame movement of one shot over another like a curtain being drawn. Wipes can move in any direction—vertically, horizontally, diagonally, circles, squares, spirals and any conceivable shape that can be used to remove one shot, and to introduce a new one.

The Fade-In/Fade-Out

The fade to black and the fade up from black has the purpose of separating two scenes from another while the cut and dissolve connect scenes. A typical use would be a scene with a room that ends with the light turned off. You could then make a cut to the next scene that starts with a car coming out of the darkness of a tunnel.

The White-In/White-Out

Fades can also be made using white-in/white-out transitions. You often see this type of transitions when a character has some sort of memory flash coming back or when he is dreaming. It is also possible to let a film end with a camera move onto a very bright light until the frame is totally bleached out.

Camera Moves

Not long after the invention of motion picture cameras, several basic moves evolved, forming the backbone of camera movement technique today. The same techniques apply to the use of virtual cameras in computer animation. You are by no means restricted to these basic moves because cameras are not constrained by time and space. Knowing "real-world" camera techniques, however, is essential because audiences have learned to read moving images through these basic moves.

The fundamental moves (see Figures 11.6 and 11.7) are as follows:

- Pan
- Tilt
- Roll
- Dolly
- Track
- Boom

FIGURE 11.6
Pan, tilt, and roll change the orientation of the camera.

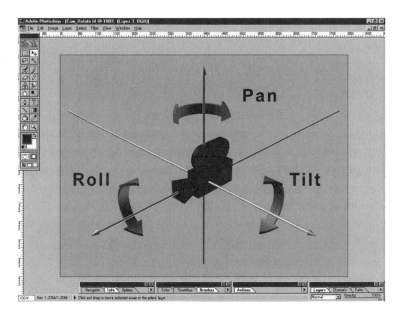

FIGURE 11.7
Dolly, track, and boom change the position of the camera.

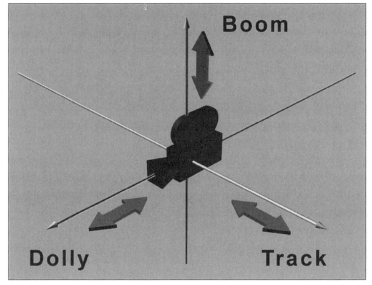

All these moves either create motion by translating the camera's location in space or by changing the rotations around the camera's axis. Another category of moves involves changing the focal length of the camera lens during a shot. It is not really a move, however, in that the camera remains stationary. A move is simulated because the changing angle of view makes objects appear to move closer to or farther away from the screen.

Panning, Tilting, and Rolling

In the horizontal panoramic shot, the camera rotates on its vertical axis as much as 360 degrees, taking in the entire visible horizon. The difference between the pan and any other type of camera movement is that it rotates on one axis in one location rather than being displaced. A pan usually is used to

- Include more space that can be viewed through a fixed frame.

- Follow an action as it moves.

- Connect two or more points of interest.

- Connect or imply a logical connection between two or more subjects.

The most familiar use of a pan is the panoramic shot, a slow horizontal or vertical move. A vertical pan up or down a skyscraper gives a feeling of height and a horizontal pan over a landscape can show the immensity of a location like a valley or mountains. A pan must not always be used as a slow camera movement in one direction; it can change direction completely. For example, the camera follows a subject and then changes into the opposite direction following another subject without a pause. In an airport, for example, this panning from subject to subject could go on forever.

Techniques used in narrative film can also be used in trailer- or logo-animation. Imagine a pan showing the pinboard of a high school. The viewer could learn a lot of what is going on in that school from just panning over the notes. A similar technique could be used in a logo-animation. The establishing shot could be a pan over some images showing what this company actually does. Then you could make a transition and show the logo.

Inexperienced camera operators often make the mistake of panning too fast. You have probably seen home videos that cause motion sickness. When looking from one thing to another, you are panning with your eyes. Panning a camera as fast as you move your eyes just does not work.

NTSC format Video is played at 30 frames per second. Computer animation is often played back at slower speeds, such as 15 or even eight frames per second. Panning too quickly causes the difference between one frame and the next to be so great that the illusion of motion is broken. In cinematography, that effect is called *strobing*. In computer animation, it can also be referred to as *tearing*.

There are two ways of dealing with strobing in computer animation. One is to make certain that pans are not too fast. The following table gives some safe pan speeds for various conditions. Again, observe film and television footage to see just how slow most pan moves are. Refer to Table 11.3 for recommended pan speeds.

TABLE 11.3

Number of Frames Needed for a 45° Pan

Type	15 fps	24 fps	30 fps
Quick turn	11	18	22
Comfortable turn	15	24	30
Casual turn	33	54	66

NOTE

You have to visualize your shot first and then find out the time spent for your turn. Calculate the number of frames needed depending on how many frames you want to use in your animation (NTSC, PAL, and so on). If you still want a very fast pan, consider inserting a straight cut during the movement.

Another way of correcting for strobing is to use Motion blur when rendering. When recording fast moving objects in real-space with video or film cameras, they often appear blurred. This always occurs when the shutter speed of the camera is too slow to freeze that object in motion. This phenomenon is called Motion blur. In addition to preventing strobing, Motion blur allows the computer animator to simulate the effects of real-world cameras. Because virtual cameras do not have a shutter to open and close, this blurring does not occur automatically. Instead, you must explicitly tell the camera to add Motion blur. This small extra step can be invaluable in simulating the realism of real-world cameras. Three kinds of Motion blur are now available in 3DS MAX R2: Object, Image, and Scene.

■ **Object Motion blur:** This produces Motion blur for individual objects in a scene, not the entire scene itself like Scene Motion blur. This technique creates several samples of the moving object during the rendering process that are slightly shifted in time. In the final image, these samples are dithered together to accomplish the Motion blur effect. It can be used to smooth the "strobing" of fast moving objects in an animation.

- **Image Motion blur:** This technique is based on pixel speed and is applied after the frame has been rendered. Because it takes the speed of all pixels of an object into account, it can be used to blur objects and even spherical or cylindrical environment mappings.

- **Scene Motion blur:** This kind of Motion blur shares information between frames. It applies its effect at scene level and takes camera movement into account, which Object Motion blur does not. Most of the information comes from the current frame, but some is from the previous and following frames. The effect is to have less difference between frames, expanding the acceptable limits of camera motion. It is mostly used when creating blurred "trails" behind moving objects.

NOTE

One of the other ways to simulate real-world optics in a computer-generated scene is using depth of field (focus). There are exercises later in this chapter that will cover depth of field and Motion blur.

USING MOTION BLUR

In the following exercise, you will apply Motion blur to a rotating propeller. For better comparison, you will create three different sequences: no Motion blur, Object Motion blur, and Image Motion blur. You will see the benefit of the effect by looking at the resulting films.

1. Load the file 11max01.max from the CD-ROM.

2. Select the Object Propeller and right-click it.

3. Select Properties to open the Object Property panel.

4. You can see three buttons under Motion Blur. Select the Object radio button and click OK.

5. Choose the Render menu.

6. You will see that Active Time Segment under Time Output is selected. Choose an output size, either 320×240 or 160×120.

7. Select Apply under Object Motion Blur. You can leave Duration at 1.0 frames. Set Samples to 14. (Duration Subdivisions will also be set to 14 automatically.)

NOTE

The higher you set the subdivisions, the longer the rendering time will be. Decide if more render time really is necessary for the effect to be accomplished.

8. Render the active time segment to an AVI file.

9. Now you apply Image Motion Blur to the propeller. Go back into the Object Property panel for the object Propeller.

10. Select the Image Motion Blur radio button and click OK.

11. In the Render menu, make sure that the Apply box for Image Motion blur is checked. Leave all values at their defaults.

12. For reference purposes make sure you change the name of the output file. Render the active time segment to an AVI file.

The 11avi01.avi included on the accompanying CD-ROM shows the movement of the propeller without Motion blur, 11avi02.avi shows it with Motion blur applied, and 11avi02a.avi is the final film showing the propeller with Image Motion blur. What kind of Motion blur you will later use in your animations is a matter of taste, but generally Image Motion blur provides the best effect.

Tilting and rolling are functionally similar to panning, except that the camera rotates vertically when tilting and along the z-axis when rolling. The same precautions should be followed when tilting and rolling as when panning.

Dolly and Tracking Shots

A *dolly* is a small-wheeled vehicle used to move a motion picture camera and its operators about in a scene. It is piloted by a *dolly grip*, whose job is to smoothly start and stop the dolly and synchronize its motion with the pans and tilts of the camera operator. When you design camera paths, you take on the role of dolly grip. The most challenging part of the job is achieving smooth, subtle starts and stops. As a virtual dolly grip, you need to recreate the human touch in your camera paths.

When the camera moves in and out of a scene (generally on the same axis as the lens), it is referred to as a *dolly move*. When the move is perpendicular to the lens axis, it is called a *tracking shot*. The same precautions must be observed when tracking as when panning.

Usually the tracking shot is used to follow a subject or to explore a certain space. It can inspect and focus on details of the overall scene. For example, the camera moves slowly away from a door revealing the rest of the house and vice versa. In addition, the tracking shot is not restricted to a straight line. It can also turn corners, move forward and backward, come to a halt and start to move again, change speeds, and cross its own path.

Basic ways to track a subject are the following:

- **Tracking at the same speed as the subject:** The most familiar use of this way to track a subject is to follow two or more persons in conversation. The camera could track them on a parallel path in line or slightly behind or ahead of them. This type of shot is also often used when following a conversation in cars or on any other subject that is moving.

- **Tracking faster or slower than the subject:** This is only a variation of the previous technique. Using this technique, it is possible to see a subject enter or leave the center of the action. In order to show that somebody is winning in a race, the camera would track the subject slightly slower. If we want to show that he is losing, we would track him slightly faster, maybe passing him during the course of the shot.

- **Moving towards or away from the subject:** The camera can also move directly forward or backward. A dolly move towards a subject's face can be used to show a moment of realization. It could also been used as an introductory shot. For instance, the camera pulls back from a picture showing a little forest to reveal that you are not on earth but on a spaceship.

Zoom Versus Dolly

Some people object to the Zoom effect because the viewer is brought closer to (or farther from) the subject without changing perspective. In zooming, the entire image is magnified equally. In a dolly shot, the camera moves toward the subject and the perspective changes. Objects also pass by the side of the frame, suggesting to the viewer that he is physically moving. The moving camera creates a feeling of depth whereas the zoom tends to flatten space, which is better for filming because the moving camera draws too much attention to the move itself.

Because you do not have the ability to get inside your virtual scene, you do not have a very good frame of reference to judge the speed at which you should dolly your camera. The speed of dolly and tracking moves are usually based upon how fast a person moves. Refer to Tables 11.4 and 11.5 for recommended speed tables.

TABLE 11.4
Pedestrian Gaits

Type	Miles per Hour	Feet per Second	Inches per Second
Casual stroll	1.5–2.0	2.2–3.0	26–36
Average walk	2.5–3.5	3.6–5.0	43–60
Brisk walk	4–5	6–8	72–96
Average jog	6–8	9–12	108–144
Average run	8–10	12–15	144–180
All out sprint	12–16	18–24	216–288

TABLE 11.5
Number of Frames Needed to Move 10 Feet

Type	15 fps	24 fps	30 fps
Casual stroll	50–68	80–109	100–136
Average walk	30–42	48–67	60–83
Brisk walk	19–25	30–40	38–50
Average jog	12–17	20–27	25–33
Average run	10–12	16–20	20–25
All out sprint	6–8	10–13	13–17

Boom or Crane Shot

When the camera moves up or down, the shot is traditionally called a *crane shot*, but actually the crane is capable of moving in many directions. It is the least naturalistic move to be made with a camera because you rarely see the world from the high position of a crane. A crane shot draws attention to itself because of the exotic viewing angle and the change of perspective when it moves. Because there is no restriction physically or monetarily of how to move a camera in a 3D environment, CG animators tend to animate most of their cameras as crane shots without even realizing it. Observe the same timing and rendering practices with a crane shot as you would with a tilt.

Depth of Field

One of the problems faced by users of real-life camera optics is that depth of field is limited. When an object in the foreground of a shot is in focus, the background is out of focus. This characteristic is a problem in some circumstances, but it can also be very useful when trying to emphasize an element of the visual composition. Virtual cameras have unlimited depth of field. This leads to computer-generated images that are sharply focused from foreground to background.

You may want to introduce limited depth of field to recreate the "realism" people are used to seeing in film and television. Shallow depth of field enables you to isolate specific objects in a scene. You can also shift the plane of focus during a shot to move emphasis from one object to another. This effect was used to great advantage in *Jurassic Park*, when the game warden was surprised by a velociraptor emerging from the undergrowth.

You can now easily apply such effects to your animations. An Image Filter event called Lens Effects Focus is now included in 3D Studio MAX R2 and can be applied in Video Post. The following exercise uses this new feature to show the technique of how to apply depth of field in 3D Studio MAX R2. You will focus on two points of interest within the scene and also notice that this technique enables you to lead the viewer into the next scene without even showing it. The first point of interest you will focus on is the nine-ball asset and the second point of interest is the white ball and the cue. Because we all know what billiards are about, the most likely thing to happen next is the hitting of the white ball by the cue.

SMALL DEPTH OF FIELD EXERCISE

1. Load the file 11max02.max from the accompanying CD-ROM.

2. Open the Rendering pull-down menu and select Video Post.

3. Add a Scene event to the Video Post queue. Hit Focus Cam from the drop-down list under View and type **Focus Cam** under the label, and then click OK. If the Scene event is selected (inverted), click anywhere within the Video Post queue to deselect it.

4. Add an Image Filter event. Type **Depth of Field** in the label. Then select the Lens Effects Focus filter. Do not click the Setup button here, instead click OK. If you want to use the Video Post Queue Preview feature of the Lens Effects filters, you have to add the event to the queue and then re-enter it for the initial setup.

5. Now re-enter the Image Event panel for Depth of Field and click the Setup button.

6. Select Focal Node as the blurring method.

7. Click select to open the Select Focal Node Object dialog.

NOTE

Any MAX object can be used as the center for this effect: a mesh, a light, a dummy, or the target of a camera.

8. Select the object Focus Dummy and click OK to return. The dummy that is placed at the position of the nine ball is now the Focal object.

9. Focal Range determines how far away from the Pivot point of the Focal object the Blur effect begins. Set it to a value of 20.

NOTE

The values of Focal Range and Focal Limit are based on pixels from the Pivot point of the Focal object, not on MAX units.

10. Focal Limit determines how far from the Pivot point of the Focal object the Blur effect is at full strength. Set it to a value of 300.

11. The horizontal and vertical loss determines the amount of blur applied to the image on the corresponding axis. Set the horizontal Focal Loss to a value of 10. Because Lock is selected, the vertical Loss will also be set automatically to 10.

12. Now click the VP Queue button and the Preview button. After a few seconds, you see the blurred pool table at frame 0 on the Preview screen.

13. Now drag the Time slider to frame 100 (or set the Time to 100 and then hit the Return button). The screen is updated and you see the effect at frame 100.

14. Click OK to return to the Video Post Queue.

15. Insert an Image Output event to render the sequence to disk.

To save some time, you can take a look at the prerendered animation 11avi03.avi on the CD.

In this section, we discussed the use of traditional film techniques, because it is not only important to be technically able to animate a camera but also to understand the ways and possibilities to express yourself when using a camera during the process of filmmaking.

These techniques will help you to realize your idea of the final outcome, be it a logo animation, a character animation, or an architectural walkthrough. The final film will be what you want it to be and not a randomly achieved result. Compare it to the learning of a language—the more elaborate you can handle the language, the better you can express yourself. This is also true for film language.

Using Digital Cameras

Now that you have some grounding in the techniques used in traditional film cameras, it is time to put these techniques to use in the digital realm. This section covers the use of digital cameras in character animation, architectural walkthroughs, previews, and other "abstract" camera effects.

Architectural Walkthroughs

Architectural walkthroughs have been a major selling point for computer animation from the beginning. Imagine the possibility of being able to walk through your dream home before it has been built. Imagine choosing the color of the carpet, walls, all the furniture, and experiencing them in your home before the plans are even finalized. Unfortunately, this has hardly become the norm for building a new home or even for expensive commercial buildings. As an animator, you know all the time and effort that goes into creating an architectural animation on the computer. You also know how much more time and effort goes into creating an environment that would be considered photorealisitic.

After the architectural model has been built, materials applied, and lighting created, your next job is to put the audience into the scene. The camera enables the audience to believe they are moving through the building. They are observers taking part in the animation.

All too often, camera motion in walkthroughs has the objective of showing off everything that the animator has built in one lengthy shot. The animator chooses specific points of interest in the building, chooses a point outside the building to enter from, and then proceeds to draw a spline path that connects all these points. The results are similar to what early moviemakers attempted before the subtleties of editing were discovered. A brilliant 3D model that may have taken weeks or months of work is cheapened by unrefined camera work.

As you work through the next exercises, and as you are composing your architectural animations, keep the following points in mind:

- Analyze sequences created by professional cinematographers for ideas on timing, composition, camera motion, and transitions.

- Don't waste time getting from one point of interest to another. Use transitions to eliminate insignificant material.

- Avoid moves that draw attention to the camera at the expense of the subject.

- Compose and evaluate your camera moves by using the Camera viewport as a viewfinder, not by looking at the top view of the floor plan.

- Avoid camera moves that would not be possible with traditional cameras. Don't do the "death dive" over a railing just to get to the next floor.

- Give the audience time to observe significant objects and points of interest, and then move on.

- Do not move the camera too quickly just because you want to save time rendering or animating. Move at a comfortable pace.

T IP

Use a stopwatch to time yourself walking through a building or other interesting space to give yourself a feeling for how long it should take for certain sequences in a walkthrough. A stopwatch is also useful when examining live-action film sequences and transitions.

N OTE

When you visit a space, you remember the important features of that space. You don't waste memory on the uninteresting walks down the hall or across the parking lot. As an animator, you are responsible for the same selective memory when creating a walkthrough.

Creating the Establishing Shot

The first step in many film sequences is to create an *establishing shot*, which shows the exterior of a building or area in which the action will be taking place. The establishing shot serves many purposes, including the following:

- It associates the building with the environment.

- It enables the viewer to identify with the character of the building. Architects strive to achieve harmony between the interior and exterior of a building. This harmony is essential to the building's character. The establishing shot serves as the audience's introduction to the building.

- It gives the audience a frame of reference to begin their journey. After experiencing the introduction, they feel more comfortable in exploring the interior of the building. The audience understands where their journey will be taking place.

NOTE

It is important to adjust the camera position and rotation while observing the Camera viewport. This is the "viewfinder" that enables you to see what the camera sees. Do not simply place the camera in the Top viewport and aim it at something you want to show. Throughout this chapter, pay particular attention to what is shown in the Camera viewport, and try to match the composition shown in the figures.

The following exercises in this part of the chapter will help you to create a complete architectural walkthrough. In the first exercise, you create and set up the cameras and movement for the establishing shot.

THE ESTABLISHING AND OPENING SHOTS

1. Load 11max04.max from the accompanying CD-ROM. The scene consists of the exterior of a building in a simulated environment.

2. Choose Configure Paths from the File menu. Click the Bitmaps tab and add the path to the CD Maps directory. You may optionally copy the necessary map files to your local hard drive. Also remember to select Draft mode (reflect/refract maps, mapping, and shadows deselected) within the Render menu to ensure fast rendering.

3. Create a target camera at the position and angle shown in Figure 11.8. Name the camera **estab-cam**. While still in the Create panel, change the lens length to 24mm.

TIP

In a walkthrough, you generally want to create a camera that sees more than the standard 48° seen by the human eye. This can help simulate peripheral vision and also enables the audience to feel more involved in the animation.

4. Activate the Perspective viewport and press C to change the view to the current Camera view.

5. Move to frame 90. Use the Motion Control panel to create a position key for the camera and target. Change the Bézier tangents to ease in and ease out for the target and camera. This setting enables the camera to be motionless for the first 90 frames, enabling the audience to become stable and comfortable in the shot before moving.

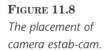

FIGURE 11.8

The placement of camera estab-cam.

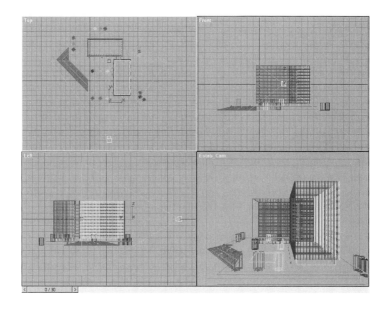

T IP

A great way to set the first key is to go to the preferences and set up a key for the two undocumented keyboard shortcuts called Create Position Lock key and Create Rotation Lock key. These two keys enable you to create a key that automatically changes the tangents of the key you created and the key previous to constant. This enables you to make a camera stop in place from one key to another without the Bézier tangent being applied.

6. Turn on the Animate button and change to frame 420. Move the camera and target to match Figure 11.9. After you have established the camera, turn off the Animate button.

You do not need to show the entire building at this point. The motion in the camera is needed only to enhance the three-dimensionality of the scene and make it come alive to the audience.

If you need to show the entire exterior, create a second animation that follows the walkthrough. A good technique is to introduce facts about the building in this second animation. Facts could include square feet, number of rooms, interior and exterior finishes, and so on. It will also enable you to create a more technically oriented animation using simpler geometry that can release you from the necessity of creating a fully realistic 360° environment.

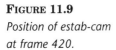

FIGURE 11.9

Position of estab-cam at frame 420.

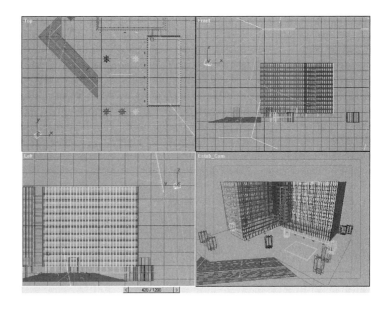

Exterior Detail Shot

The next shot enables you to transition from the initial exterior establishing shot to the inside of the building. You should not just appear inside the building. Each camera shot you create must be a logical progression from the previous one. This progression is called a transition. Often a director focuses on a particular object at the end of a camera shot. This object is then seen at the beginning of the next camera shot, but from a different perspective, enabling the audience to remain oriented throughout the sequence.

For the transition to the interior of a building, it is common to use the main entrance as the transition focus area. Again, you want to add motion to the scene as you did with the last camera. The motion in this case should progress toward the entrance to communicate the feeling of entering the building. After this, the audience knows the next logical place to be is inside.

THE EXTERIOR DETAIL SHOT

1. Continue from the previous exercise. Create a free camera at the position and angle shown in Figure 11.10. Name the camera **extdet-cam**. While still in the Create panel, change the lens length to 24mm and change the Camera viewport to this camera.

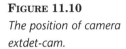

FIGURE 11.10

The position of camera extdet-cam.

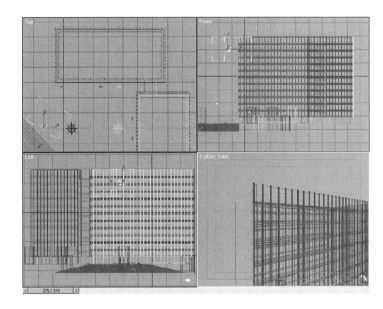

2. Move to frame 375 and create a Position and Rotation key.

3. Turn on the Animate button and change to frame 690. Move and rotate the camera to match Figure 11.11. After you have established the camera, turn off the Animate button.

FIGURE 11.11

The position of extdet-cam at frame 690.

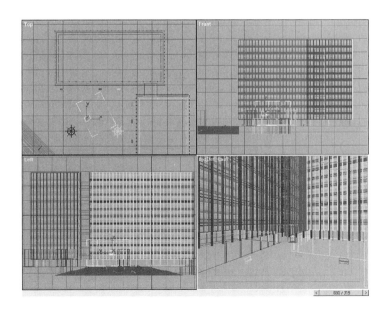

It is important to determine at this point what kind of Video Post transition will be made between cameras. Will it be a fade to or fade from black, or a dissolve from one camera to another? The length of the transition needs to be incorporated into the beginning and ending of each camera move so that the motion does not stop.

For the transition between estab-cam and extdet-cam, you have a 1.5 second (45 frame) dissolve from one camera to the other. In other types of animation, this transition time might be too long, but in the case of an architectural walkthrough, you want to ease the audience from one camera to the other and keep them moving comfortably.

For the transition between extdet-cam and the first interior camera, have the audience pause at the entrance, fade to black, and then fade from black to a motionless camera. This transition helps the audience relate more easily to the change from interior to exterior.

4. Change the in position tangent for the camera to ease in at frame 690.

5. Save your MAX file.

T IP

When using multiple cameras in a scene, animate them at the same time coordinates as will be used in the final animation. Resist the temptation to create all the camera motions at the beginning of the scene. This enables you to compose the timing of your scene more logically, without having to remember exactly how many frames and in what order each camera is to be shown. This also keeps the frame numbers correct when rendering to individual files in the final rendering. It is also possible to create a Note track in the Track Editor for each camera that shows exactly in which frames this camera will be rendered. Place the note key at the first frame in which the camera will be rendered.

You could also make use of time tags. Because it is possible to lock a time tag to a specific frame, you could create one time tag at the frame the camera starts and one at the frame where the transition begins. Now you are able to easily jump between the tags with one mouse click.

Creating the Interior Shot

Before you begin creating cameras for the interior shots, take a few moments to preview the cameras you have animated and save them as AVI files. Keep these files so that they can be examined later as well.

The interior of the building is created by using a separate MAX file. Using separate files can help you in the following ways:

- Lowers polygon count for rendering because you do not have exterior geometry for interior shots, and interior geometry for exterior shots.

- There are fewer objects to sort through in object lists.

- The file size is smaller and more manageable.

NOTE

If changes are made to one file that will affect the other, you must be certain to change both files simultaneously. This can be done easily by making the changes in one file, temporarily merging it into the other, making changes, and then deleting the objects from the merged file.

THE INTERIOR DETAIL SHOT

1. Load the file 11max05.max from the accompanying CD.

2. Create a free camera at the position and angle shown in Figure 11.12. Name the camera **int-cam1**. While still in the Create panel, change the lens length to 35mm and change the Camera viewport to this camera.

3. Turn on the Animate button and change to frame 690. Move and rotate the camera to match Figure 11.12.

The transition between the two interior cameras uses a 1.5 second (45 frame) moving dissolve. This overlap needs to be incorporated into the timing of the cameras as it did in the establishing shots. Also keep in mind that during the dissolve, neither of the camera views will be clearly visible.

Because the composition of each camera shot is critical to the success of the animation, be certain to compose the beginning and ending shots through the Camera viewport, and then adjust the path between them.

4. Change to frame 1005. With the Animate button turned on adjust the camera to the position and angle seen in Figure 11.13.

FIGURE 11.12

Position of camera int-cam1 at frame 690.

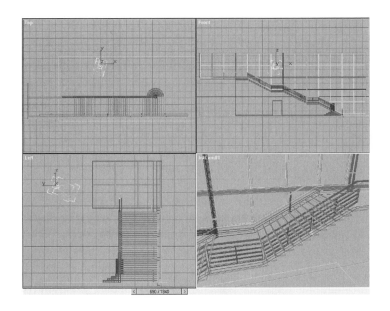

5. In the Motion Control panel, change the Bézier tangents to ease in and ease out for all keys.

6. Play the animation in the Camera view.

FIGURE 11.13

Position of int-cam1 at frame 1005.

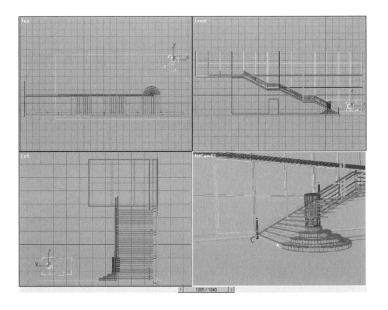

Now you create the second interior shot. The difficulty with this shot is that we do not have a 360° environment within. It is your task to create the illusion that the viewer feels like he is within a room, although we just have a small part of the scenery.

7. Create a Free camera at the position and angle shown in Figure 11.14. While still in the Create panel, change the lens length to 72mm. Name the camera **int-cam2**.

FIGURE 11.14

Position of int-cam2 at frame 990.

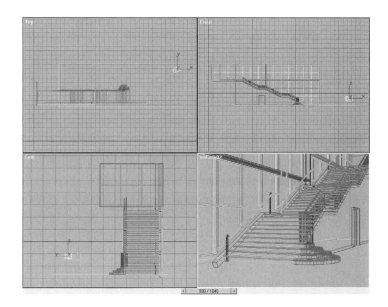

8. Move to frame 990 and create a Position and Rotation key for int-cam2. Change the Bézier tangents to ease in and ease out.

9. Turn the Animate button on and change to frame 1330. Move the camera to match the Figure 11.15. Turn off the Animate button.

10. Create a Preview for both cameras.

FIGURE 11.15

Position of int-cam1 at frame 1330.

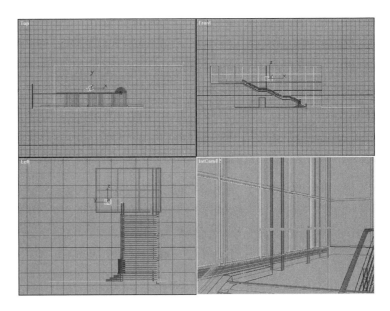

Because camera timing is critical, try to view the animation in as close to real-time as possible with a minimum of strobing. To aid in this, keep the Camera view set to Wireframe. If needed, you can also hide unnecessary objects and change the viewport to Box mode. You may also want to pause at this point and create a preview animation. To keep the animation close to real-time, keep the resolution low. You are only evaluating camera motion, which can usually still be distinguished sufficiently at low resolution.

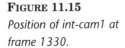

NOTE

If one camera is selected from multiple cameras in the scene, and you change a viewport to a Camera view using the C shortcut, the view automatically changes to the currently selected camera. If you want to select a different camera, either deselect the camera and press C again, or select the desired camera by right-clicking the viewport title.

Closing Shot

The closing camera shot can be the most important one. It is the last picture the audience will see. To aid in determining the final shot, think of the impression with which you want to leave the audience. You may choose to show a wide view of the lobby of the building, or the view of a beautiful sunset from the penthouse. Whatever you choose, be certain that you compose the last frame carefully. Use your knowledge of color, composition, balance, and so forth to help you.

After you have determined the last frame of the closing shot, use the animation of the camera to lead up to it. Swing the camera around the room to enable the audience to discover other interesting details. As they are focusing on the smaller details, they will soon discover the sunset out the window and realize they have come to the end of their journey. As the camera comes to the end of its move, be certain to allow the audience to settle into their last glimpse by using an ease-in on the last key and then pause. After the audience has had a chance to enjoy the last frame, use a slow (45–60 frame) fade to black.

Because we emphasize on the exterior of the building within this exercise, the closing shot will also be an exterior shot.

THE CLOSING SHOT

1. Load the file 11max04.max.

2. Create a Free camera as shown in Figure 11.16. Name the camera **close_cam** and change the lens length as before. Change the Camera view to this camera.

FIGURE 11.16

Position of close_cam at frame 1300.

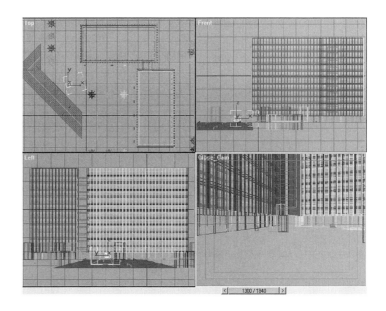

3. Create a position key on frame 1300.

4. Move to frame 1540, activate the Animate button, and modify the camera as shown in Figure 11.17. Change the position Bézier tangent to ease-in.

FIGURE 11.17

Position of close_cam at frame 1840.

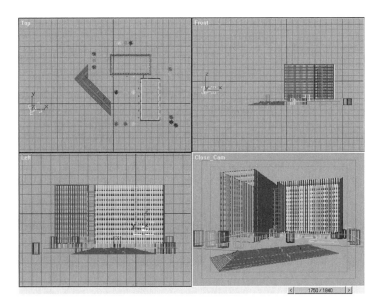

5. Preview the last camera for motion.

Previews

As you complete animating your cameras, you create a preview for each one. These previews can help you determine proper timing for your animation. They also enable you to determine whether the length of the entire animation is correct. To view your preview animations in sequence and to examine the fades and dissolves that are important to the animation just completed, you can use Video Post within 3D Studio MAX. This enables you to put all files you created together so you can view them sequentially. When creating these files, keep the resolution as small as needed to keep the animation playing near real-time.

AVIs should be used for your preview. In comparison to FLIs, AVIs have a larger number of colors, many different possible codecs and drop frames to keep the animation playing at the desired speed. They also tend to be more portable to other systems because they are more popular at this time. Also, standard Microsoft systems can play AVIs without having to install any particular AVI player or codec support.

In the last exercise, many cameras are being used and they must be composited in Video Post. In a walkthrough you do not want to use fast shots or transitions. Straight cuts from one camera to another would be sufficient for a dialogue scene with two subjects but usually not for an architectural walkthrough. We will use dissolves and fades for the transition between the different cameras.

Preview each camera for the frames shown in Table 11.6. As before, save the individual files and script them together to get an idea of the timing of the final rendered animation. After you have verified the timing and made any corrections, render to AVI.

TABLE 11.6

Video Post Setup

Camera	Beginning Frame	Ending Frame	Transition
Estab-Cam	0	420	0000-0090 fade from black
ExtDet-Cam	375	690	0375-0420 cross fade 0660-0690 fade to black
IntDet-Cam1	690	1005	0690-0720 fade from black
IntDet-Cam2	960	1300	0960-1005 cross fade
Close-Cam	1255	1795	1255-1300 cross fade 1735-1795 fade to black

A copy of the Video Post VPX file (11vpx02.vpx) is included on the CD for your reference. You may load this file while in Video Post to render your preview animation.

Digital Camera Animation for Characters

Study almost any movie or television sequence showing people and you will see the basic camera techniques involved for animating characters. Most sequences can be built from basic shots: long, medium, and close-up. See Figure 11.18 for the different framing heights for a character.

FIGURE 11.18

The different framing heights for a character.

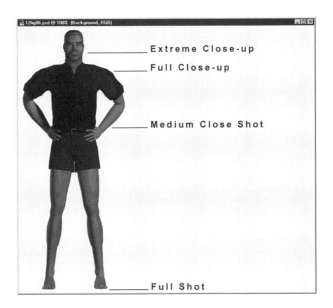

The "long" or full shot shows all or most of the character's body. This is used to show the context in which the character appears or to show large body actions such as running or tumbling. In a full shot, the body is the most important visual element of the character (see Figure 11.19).

When framing a character in full shot, try to avoid centering in the frame. Use the "rule of thirds" to place the character on one of the two axes that divide the frame in thirds. When tracking or panning with a character in full shot, make certain that there is plenty of "nose room" between the character and the edge of the frame he is facing.

A "medium" shot generally shows a character from the waist up. It shows more facial expression. Most conversations in which both speakers appear together in one frame are shot in medium format. The same rules apply regarding "nose room." If a character in a medium shot is facing the side of the frame, allow more space on that side of the frame (see Figure 11.20).

FIGURE 11.19

A figure in a full camera shot.

FIGURE 11.20

A figure in a medium camera shot.

A "close-up" focuses on the character's face. A medium close-up shows the head and neck, where an extreme close-up closes in on the face itself and lets hair and so on go out of frame. It is especially important in close-ups to make certain that the framing is comfortable. Keep an eye on that "nose room" (see Figure 11.21).

FIGURE 11.21
A close-up shot.

Real people have a very difficult time sitting or standing still—only television news anchors have mastered the technique. Most people also move hands and body a great deal to add meaning to verbal communication. One of the challenges a real-world camera operator faces is maintaining a pleasing composition in a frame in which the subject is constantly moving. A skillful operator "floats" with the person, always maintaining appropriate visual relationships in the frame. When studying live action footage, notice that the camera is very seldom locked down when a person appears in the frame. There are constant subtle moves. For computer animation to simulate real life effectively, the same techniques should be adopted. As a character moves from left to right, or turns and faces a different direction in the frame, you should adjust the framing to compensate.

Use the established camera techniques discussed before when animating characters, and thereby move your animation into the realm of "film grammar" your audience understands.

NOTE

Be sure to have Character Studio installed before making the following exercises. You will need it in order to render the movements of the character. You can find the setup on your 3D Studio MAX R2 installation CD, which is a full working version that allows you to open files created with Character Studio and render them. However, it does not allow you to edit any of the Character Studio features.

Camera Placement and Movement

This section covers a basic rule of camera placement and movement, the axis or line of action. The purpose of this axis is to organize camera angles to maintain consisting screen direction and space within a scene or a sequence of shots. With the use of this you are able to make sure that the multiple angles that were shot within a scene can be put together without confusing or disorienting the viewer.

The axis or line of action between two subjects in a dialog scene is usually the line of sight between these two, although it can be almost anywhere in the scene.

Take a look at the following two figures. Figure 11.22 is an example of a basic setup in a dialogue scene. All cameras are within the "work-area."

FIGURE 11.22

Sequence of shots in a dialogue scene. Cameras A, B, and C are all within the "work-area."

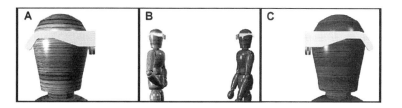

In Figure 11.23, camera D, the close-up of subject 2, however, is not within the permitted area. This setup is confusing because the viewer is not sure anymore of how the subjects are located within the scene.

FIGURE 11.23

Another sequence of shots in a dialog scene. You can see that camera Full-Shot D is not within the "work-area." It seems that subject 1 looks at the back of the head of subject 2.

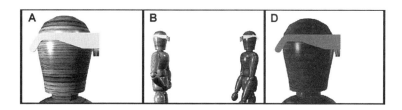

Because the cameras are arranged like a triangle (you can see the setup of cameras A, B, and C in Figure 11.24), this technique is also called Triangle system. Any shot can be joined to any other shot within the Triangle system of setups. You can also employ the Triangle system for other types of situations like single subject and action scenes. Television programs like quiz shows, sitcoms, news, and sport programs use this technique extensively.

FIGURE 11.24

This is the setup of cameras A, B, and C.

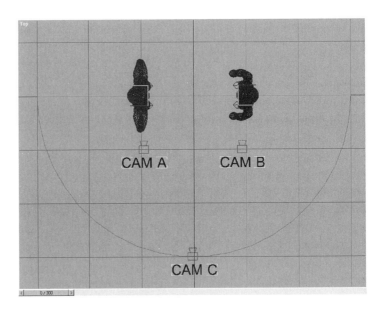

All basic shots possible for any subject can be taken from three points within the 180° working space. Connecting these three points, we have a triangle of variable size and shape. In this figure, you see the three cameras A, B, and C roughly shaping one possible triangle.

Five basic setups can be obtained within the triangle:

- Angular singles (medium shots and close-ups)
- Master two-shots
- Over-the-shoulder-shots
- Point-of-the-view singles (medium shots and close-ups)
- Profile shots

You can find all these basic setups in the named selection pulldown menu.

N OTE

Instead of using three cameras it is also possible to move a single camera to each point along the triangle.

In special cases, the subject or the camera can "cross the line" of action. This is only permitted if the cinematographer wants to establish a new axis. For instance, the camera could pan, dolly, or crane to a new space and therefore establish a new axis that will be further used in the scene.

This could become necessary if a new subject enters the scene from behind the camera. The camera would have to change its position so that the new and the old subjects can be seen.

The following exercise shows you how to apply the triangle system to an actual 3D Studio MAX setting. You will go through the several camera setups that can be used in a dialog scene.

DIGITAL CAMERA ANIMATION FOR CHARACTERS

1. Open the file 11max03.max from the CD.

2. You can see the basic setup of a dialogue scene with two subjects.

3. The x-axis of the world space (the black horizontal line in the Top viewport) is defined as the axis or line of action.

4. Open the pull-down menu for the named selection sets and select Triangle system.

N OTE

A dialog box will pop up, asking you if you want to unhide and unfreeze the selected objects because the selection set you just chose is hidden. Select Yes. Using selection sets, you can unhide and unfreeze objects without going into the Display panel.

5. The three selected cameras build the shape of a triangle where the axis or line of action is the baseline of it. In Figure 11.25, you can also see a half-circle, which is called "work area." You can see that one camera is not within the "work-area" and therefore considered over the line in this setup.

FIGURE 11.25

Basic camera setup for a dialog scene. The horizontal black X axis is the axis of action and the half-circle is the "work-area."

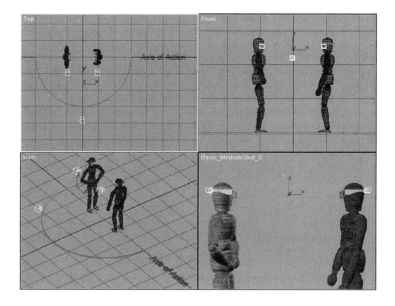

With this half-circle, the cinematographer establishes that in any scene or shot with this setting, only camera positions within this "work-area" are permitted. All shots are then consistent with each other and therefore editable.

6. Select the over-the-shoulder shot named Selection. You will see two selected cameras.

7. Arrange the viewport as seen in Figure 11.26 and take a look at the camera angles used in this setup.

8. Do the same with the other setups to get accustomed to all the different camera angles used in the five basic setups within the Triangle system.

NOTE

If one camera is selected from multiple cameras in the scene, and you change a viewport to a Camera view using the C shortcut, the view automatically changes to the currently selected camera. If you want to select a different camera, either deselect the camera and press C again, or select the desired camera by right-clicking the viewport title.

You will now create a crane shot that "crosses the line" to reveal a third subject.

FIGURE 11.26

Left side of the view-port: Top and Front View: right side: OverShoulderA and OverShoulderB.

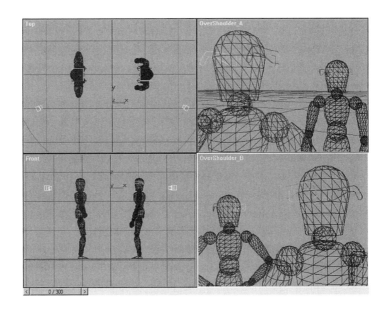

9. Create a target camera with the same position and angle as shown in Figure 11.27.

FIGURE 11.27

Position of the target camera at frame 0.

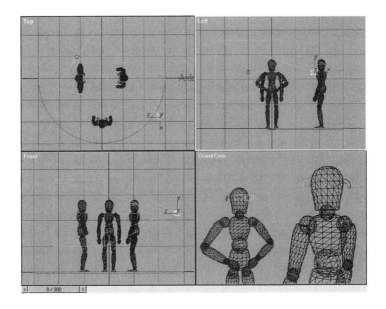

10. Unhide the third subject: the group puppet03.

11. Turn the Animate button on and move to frame 300. Place the camera and target at the position shown in Figure 11.28.

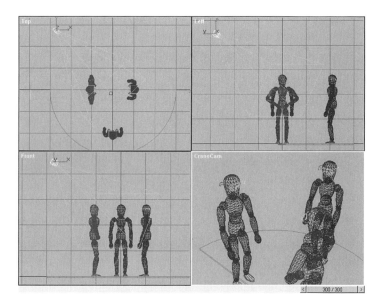

12. Select the camera and click the Trajectories button in the Motion Control panel. You can see the path your camera will take.

13. Change the end time to 300 in the Spline Conversion section and the samples to 2. Click the Convert To button.

14. Access the Modify panel and select the spline you just created. Change the name to **spline-cranecam** and go to Sub-Object vertex and change the endpoints of the spline to Bézier. Modify the spline to approximate the one shown in Figure 11.29.

15. Change the samples to 10 in the Spline Conversion section. Click Convert From and select spline-cranecam.

Using this technique you can maneuver the camera in every thinkable way while still maintaining the beginning and ending frame composition. If necessary, add a few vertices to the spline. You may also adjust the timing of the camera by adjusting the start and end times in the Spline Conversion section of the Motion Control panel.

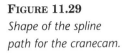

FIGURE 11.29

Shape of the spline path for the cranecam.

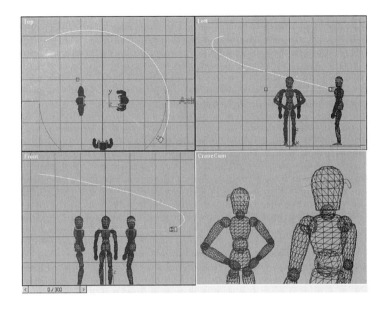

If you add vertices, keep in mind that the more vertices in the spline used for a path, the more radical the camera movement will be. It will also become increasingly difficult to edit the spline and keep it smooth. Keep the fewest possible number of vertices in the spline to ensure smooth motion.

16. To ensure that all subjects are shown in the field of view during the animation, you often have to animate the target of the camera as well. Unhide the spline TargetPath and select cranecam.target.

17. Go to the Motion Control panel and open the Assign Controller rollout.

18. Under the Assign Controller rollout, click position and assign a Path controller.

19. Go to the Path Parameters rollout and click the Pick Path button and then select TargetPath.

20. Play the animation in the Camera viewport.

In the section you just completed, you made practical use of traditional film techniques discussed in the first part of the chapter. Of course, this can just be a quick glance into the wide field of film language, but it should encourage you to get deeper into it.

Additional Effects Using a Camera

In the last part of this chapter, you will be introduced into some additional techniques used in film and TV today. These techniques do not belong to the basic ones introduced in the first part of the chapter, but they can be a valuable addition to your filmwork.

"MTV" Camera Style

In computer animation work, you will likely be asked to generate material for use in what might be described as "MTV-style" footage. Music videos have developed a visual style related to their musical content and youth culture audience. This style has been around long enough that it has spread well beyond just music videos.

The music video style is characterized by camera and editing techniques often just outside the boundaries of the normal and expected. Thus you find unusual camera angles, extreme field of view, unorthodox camera motion, and fast, sometimes jarring, cutting from one scene to another. This style has become a staple in television commercials and other non-music areas.

The best way to adopt the music video style in your animations is to objectively observe the type of footage you are trying to emulate. Visualize how the camera is used, in terms of lens focal length, placement, motion, and so on, and decide what must be done in 3DS MAX to duplicate the effect. Most of the techniques needed can be derived from information and examples given in this chapter.

Shaky Cam

For many years, cinematographers have faced the challenge of keeping the camera steady while moving it through rough terrain. At first, this problem was overcome by building tracks, using cranes and cherry pickers, and using other engineered solutions that generally cost a great deal and chewed up a lot of time.

Of course, a camera operator could just grab the camera and run overland with it on her shoulder. The resulting images would have an unsteady, jerky action that we have come to associate with documentary and television news footage. The implication to the viewer when they see shaky camera images is that the footage is immediate, spontaneous, and somehow more "real" than carefully locked-down and smooth studio shots.

Even though a device was invented several years ago (the Steadicam) that can eliminate undesirable motion in hand-held shots, many contemporary directors and cinematographers deliberately hand-hold the camera to imply spontaneity. You see this most often in television commercials and music videos.

In the real world, achieving a steady image is not easy. In the computer realm, however, perfect steadiness is the default. You may want to use random camera motion to add a "documentary" effect to an animation, in which case you will need to corrupt that perfection with a virtual "shaky cam."

The concept behind creating a shaky-cam in 3DS MAX is fairly simple. You assign a Noise controller to the Position controller of the camera (see "Earthquake!" later in the chapter).

One of the challenges is creating a shaky-cam combined with live-action footage. Luckily, this can also be solved easily in 3DS MAX. Film your live action with a stationary camera. In your MAX scene, create a flat plane object or box in the background of the scene. Create a material for this object that includes the live-action footage as a diffuse map and adjust the mapping so it appears as a "movie screen" to project the live footage onto.

NOTE

The mapping can be accomplished best through the World-Space Modifier Camera map. In the version that was included in the Yost-Funstuff package, it was a space warp, whereas it is now a World-Space modifier.

This setup enables you to have the live footage appear as a background, similar to what you would accomplish in Video Post, but the camera movement is independent of the background. If you shake your computer camera in the scene, the "movie screen" is stationary and achieves the proper illusion. Another valuable benefit of this setup is that it allows Scene Motion blur to be applied to the virtual movie screen and you can add Motion blur to your live footage *after* it has been filmed!

Earthquake Cam

Another effect seen in film, TV, and game cutscenes is the "earthquake cam." This is where the camera shakes to simulate ground motion. This effect can be easily duplicated in 3DS MAX.

EARTHQUAKE!

1. Load 11max06.max from the CD.

2. Select quake_cam and open the Motion Control panel. Apply a Position List controller to quake_cam. A List controller enables you to use multiple controllers on an object at the same time.

3. Apply a Noise Position controller to the available controller slot in the Motion Control panel. The Noise Position controller gives the camera a random position simulating the earth shaking.

4. Open Track View and expand the quake_cam tracks. Select Noise Position, right-click, and select Properties. This action opens the Noise Controller settings. Here you can control specifics about the random-ness of the position.

5. In this Camera effect, you want to have the camera move suddenly at the beginning. This is shown on the characteristic graph as a spike at the left side. You may scan through the seed possibilities to find a suit-able graph, but in this exercise we will be using seed 1.

6. Leave the Frequency at 0,5 and change the X, Y, and Z Strength values to 20 and Ramp out to 90. The ramp makes the camera motion settle down as time passes. To add some "chaotic" movement to the camera, change the Roughness under Fractal Noise to 0,5. Close the Noise Controller box. See Figure 11.30 for a reference of the box settings.

7. Drag the Noise Position Range bar to begin at 96 and end at 150. Minimize Track View.

FIGURE 11.30

The Noise controller settings for the camera position.

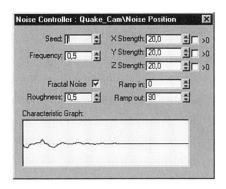

Noise Controller : Quake_Cam\Noise Position

Seed: 1	X Strength: 20,0 >0
Frequency: 0,5	Y Strength: 20,0 >0
	Z Strength: 20,0 >0
Fractal Noise ✓	Ramp in: 0
Roughness: 0,5	Ramp out: 90

Characteristic Graph:

TIP

Because there is no way to type in frame numbers to set the range for this kind of controller, it can be helpful to set the current frame to where you want the beginning or ending of the range. The current frame is represented by a thin vertical line in Track View and can help in the alignment of ranges.

Play the animation in the Camera viewport to see the effect. Play the animation in the Right viewport as well. Notice that the camera position in the Right viewport changes as the animation cycles to the beginning. Generally, you will want specific, predictable control of the camera position before and after the shaking. As you can see, the randomness of the Noise controller placed the camera at a different position at the end of the shaking than at the beginning. The Position List controller assigned earlier will enable you to compensate for this difference in position.

8. In the Motion Control panel, change the Bézier Position controller to Linear Position controller.

9. Move to frame 96 and create a position key.

10. Create a Dummy object around the camera that is aligned with the Pivot point of the camera at its original position. This positioning enables you to realign the Pivot point of the camera to the center of the dummy after the Noise controller has placed it out of position.

11. Be certain that the camera is still selected, move to frame 150, and turn on the Animate button. Align the X, Y, and Z coordinates of the camera Pivot point to the center of the Dummy object by using the Align button on the main toolbar. Turn off the Animate button.

To make the effect a little more realistic, you will also want to add a little random rotation to the camera.

12. Open the Motion Control panel and assign a Rotation Noise controller to the Dummy object. Due to the fact that the camera has oriented its Local coordinate system to the World coordinate system, the camera will be pointing at the ground if you assign the Rotation Noise controller to it. Link the camera to the dummy.

13. Open Track View, select the Noise Rotation, right-click, and select Properties. Set the Seed to **22**, the X, Y, and Z Strength to **5.0**, and Ramp out to **40**. Leave the default settings of Frequency and Roughness. Close the Noise Controller box. See Figure 11.31 for a reference of the box settings.

FIGURE 11.31

The Noise Controller settings for the dummy rotation.

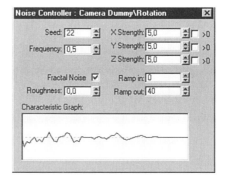

14. Drag the Range bar to begin at 96 and end at 150.

15. Link the camera to the Dummy object and play the animation.

16. To add a little more to the effect, animate the camera to move and rotate as the ground ripple hits.

17. Render to AVI.

NOTE

You can also render the scene in Video Post and turn on Scene Motion blur in the render dialog box. This increases the realism of the effect, because Scene Motion blur takes camera motion into account, as was stated earlier in this chapter.

To view a version of the final animation with the final camera motion, play 12avi05.avi from the CD.

The "Vertigo" Effect

Vertigo is a technique made famous in the Alfred Hitchcock film of the same name. Hitchcock used this technique to visualize the fear of heights of the main character. While the subject was stationary, the camera moved away from him. This changed the perspective of the stairwell that the subject was looking down, therefore creating the effect that it became deeper and more fearful.

The cinematographer takes advantage of the zoom lens' capability to change the angle of view dynamically during a shot. Usually the subject is stationary and the camera moves toward or away from the subject. As the distance between the two changes, the zoom lens' focal length is changed to keep the size of the subject constant in relation to the frame. The effect is that the background appears to "zoom" in or out while the subject stays the same size. This creates a very "eerie" effect that is also used as a variation of the "Moving toward or away from the subject—dolly" (see "Dolly and Tracking Shots," earlier in this chapter).

VERTIGO

1. Open 11max07.max from the accompanying CD.

2. Create a target camera as shown in Figure 11.32. Change the camera lens to 85mm.

3. Link the Bézier tangent to ease in and ease out for each of the three keys.

4. Turn on the Animate button and go to frame 120. Change the lens length to 24mm. Turn off the Animate button.

5. Open the Track View and copy the FOV key from Camera01 to frame 30. Change the Bézier tangent to ease in and ease out for all three keys.

6. Assign a Position Expression controller to the camera. Select and right-click the controller and choose Properties. Load 12xpr01.XPR from the CD.

FIGURE 11.32

The position of the camera for the Vertigo effect.

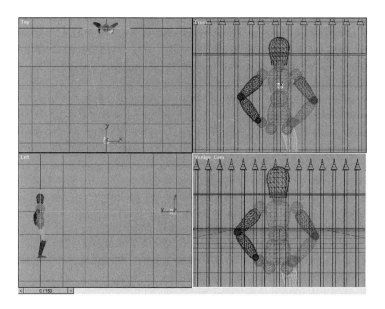

7. Select W in the Scalars box and assign it a constant of 25.

8. Select FOV in the Scalars box and click Assign to Controller. Expand the tracks if necessary and select the FOV : Bézier Float under Camera01. Close the Expression Controller box.

N OTE

The Expression controller evaluated the position of the camera while it was linked to the target. During this evaluation, the motion of the camera is set. After it is set, you can unlink the camera and move the target to a position where the vertigo is enhanced by the viewer seeing the top of the fence come into view. This approach enables you to have the camera move in a horizontal line, while not moving directly toward the target.

9. Render the animation to AVI.

The file 11avi06.avi included on the accompanying CD-ROM shows the completed animation for this exercise. It is also possible to animate the lens in the reverse direction—from 35mm to 200mm. Take a look at the file 11avi07.avi on the CD to see a rendered version of this effect.

In Practice: Animating Cameras

- **Study established camera technique.** Try to learn the basics of the film language. Using the same techniques in computer animation helps the artist communicate effectively.

- **Storyboards.** Always visualize your animations first in the form of a rough storyboard even if you are not an award-winning illustration artist.

- **Depth of Field.** Simulating real-world optics is possible by using LensEffects blur in Video Post. Controlling depth of field enables selective emphasis on different objects in the field of view.

- **Character animation.** "Float" the frame so that there is always a comfortable composition as characters move. Use multiple shots in a scene. Observing existing live footage will help you learn effective camera technique.

- **Architectural walkthroughs.** Effective walkthroughs depend on using multiple cameras and creative transitions between shots. Make the camera's presence as unobtrusive as possible so that the viewer can be drawn into the scene. Use Motion blur where appropriate and pace camera moves such as pans and tilts to avoid strobing, but always keep in mind that the object designed by the architect is the most important thing in an architectural walkthrough, not the narrative abilities of the animation artist.

- **"Shaky Cam" and "Earthquake Cam."** Adding random motion to the camera path can duplicate the kind of motion that disturbs cameras in real life. The effect can be used to dramatically emphasize the force and impact, or to simulate a hand-held camera for a documentary effect.

- **Vertigo.** Dynamically altering angle of view during a shot creates a captivating effect. Use it to dramatize the relationship of a character or object to its background.

Chapter 12

ANIMATING LIGHTS AND ATMOSPHERES

Lighting is an important element in all artwork. Essential in establishing the mood of a scene, it can also focus the viewer's attention on a particular element or area or help separate background from middleground and foreground, thus adding more depth to your work. Highlights can reveal details; shadows can hide or suggest mood.

Depending on how much attention you pay to it, lighting can become your friend or your enemy. Even if, by itself, lighting cannot turn a poorly created scene into good art-work, bad lighting can certainly ruin well-executed images. It, therefore, deserves your attention.

This chapter discusses lighting from a practical standpoint, with particular emphasis on the new features available in 3D Studio MAX R2 and how to animate the various parameters associated with them.

You will begin with a general exploration of lighting in computer-generated imagery, illustrated by simple exercises. Next, you will examine the new lighting instruments and controls available in 3D Studio MAX R2. A series of simple examples illustrates how these parameters affect the flow of light in space. Finally, a tutorial follows in which you create an animated scene, putting in practice the following:

- Setting up lights and adjusting the initial parameters, including volumetric and combustion effects

- Animating lights, including volumetric, projector, and combustion-related lighting

This chapter explores the following topics:

- New lights and features in R2

- Plotting your lights

- Attenuation parameters

- Volumetric lights

Lighting and the Surface Normal

The surface normal is an important concept to grasp, at least in general terms, because all lighting calculations are based on it. Fortunately, you can gain a basic understanding of it without getting into trigonometry or complicated mathematics.

A surface normal is a unit vector perpendicular to, and centered on, a face, which is the smallest possible Planar surface. In 3D Studio MAX, as in most 3D software, the smallest Planar surface is a triangle, defined by three vertices. A vertex is a point, whose position in 3D space is defined by three coordinates: x, y, and z.

The reason for using the triangle is the following: It is possible for a quad (a surface limited by four vertices) not to be planar. A triangle, however, is always planar.

Each face has a normal, which you can visualize as a finger pointing straight out of the face. The finger always has the same length, no matter how big or small the face is (for internal calculations, 3D Studio MAX allows you to scale its representation, so you can see it more easily). Furthermore, because it is perpendicular to the face, the normal can only point "up" (in relative terms) or "down." So the value of a normal is always 1 (if up) or –1 (if down).

GRAPHICAL REPRESENTATION OF A FACE NORMAL

1. Create a rectangle.

2. In the Modify panel, click on the Edit Stack button and choose Convert to: Editable Mesh.

3. Choose Sub-Object Face level.

    Click the Ace icon in the Selection area of the Edit Face rollout. This enables you to choose individual triangular faces.

4. Select a face from the rectangle in the viewport (the face is highlighted in red) and then turn on Show Normals in the Normals area of the Edit Surface rollout. The normal is represented as a blue line. You can adjust the Scale spinner to lengthen the line and improve visibility.

Almost all lighting calculations are related to the angle between the light source and the face's normal. They work slightly differently for diffuse and specular light, which is explored next.

Surface Normals and Diffuse Light

Roughly speaking, the more directly the normal points at the light source, the more brightly the face is lit. As the normal points farther away from the light, either because of modeling or animation, the face becomes darker.

So think of the normal this way: If the "finger" is pointing directly at the light source, the face receives maximum diffuse illumination. As the finger starts to point away from the light source and the angle between the normal and the light source increases, the face receives less diffuse light. If the finger is pointing 90 degrees or more away from the light source, the face receives no light at all. To illustrate this, do the following exercise.

THE SURFACE NORMAL

1. Open the file 12max01.max. You see a rectangular surface, lit by a single Omni light.

2. Select Plane.

3. In the Modify panel, go into Sub-Object/Face mode and make sure that all the faces are selected.

4. Turn on Show Normals in the Normals section of the Edit Surface rollout and change the Scale to 100.0.

In the Front viewport, notice how all the normals are perpendicular to their faces, pointing upward. Mentally draw a line from the Omni light to the base of each normal. The angle created between that line and the normal is what determines how much diffuse light the face receives.

5. Render the Perspective viewport or look at Figure 12.1.

The light seems to fade from the faces that are directly under the Omni light to the rectangles farther away. However, the light does not fade because of attenuation or decay. In fact, the light is not fading *at all*. Instead, each face receives a different amount of light, based on the angle between its surface normal and the light source. The illusion that the light is fading is created by the gradually increasing angle between the normals and the light source.

This is an important concept to understand because it is the basis of all illumination in 3D computer graphics.

The next exercise illustrates that the angle between normal and light source also affects the appearance of a model.

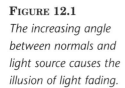

FIGURE 12.1

The increasing angle between normals and light source causes the illusion of light fading.

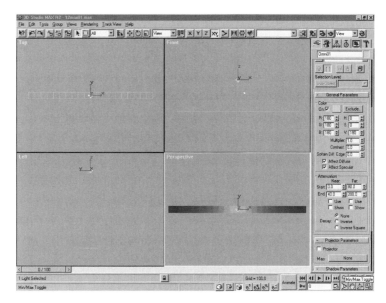

HOW NORMALS AFFECT SMOOTHING

1. Continue with file 12max01.max.

2. Select Plane. Go to the Modify panel and verify that the selection level is set to Sub-Object/Face and that all the faces are selected. Confirm that Show Normals is still checked.

3. Apply the Bend modifier. Increase the Bend Angle to 180 and change the Bend Axis to X.

4. Render the Perspective viewport.

You have taken the same group of faces used in the previous exercise, but this time you added a Bend modifier. Compared to the previous example, see how the light seems to fade more quickly and drastically? Where the object curves away from the light, the faces are nearly black. The rendered object is now curved.

Remember that there are no parameters set for this light, no cone of illumination (it's an Omni), and no ranges. The normals alone are responsible for this; the light itself does not fade. Look at the normals in the Front viewport. They point "away" from the light source more than in the previous example because the faces have been rotated. They also point away in regular increments. This is how curves are created in computer graphics.

This example creates a faceted curving surface. Of course, the more faces, the more normals, the more precise the averaging becomes and, therefore, the smoother the resulting surface.

TIP

By averaging the shading of the normals that you see, the software can create a smooth, continuously curving surface without adding a huge number of faces. MAX uses smoothing groups to instruct the renderer to do this averaging. You can use the Smooth modifier's AutoSmooth feature to automatically create smoothing groups and eliminate the faceted edges in the shading.

Surface Normals and Specular Light

The amount of specular light that a face receives uses similar calculations as for diffuse light, but the process is a little more complex. Without getting into a detailed explanation, the software uses the face's normal to calculate whether the specular light can be "seen" by the viewport or camera after it has bounced off the face.

To visualize this, draw a line from the center of the light source to the base of the face's normal, and then draw another one from the base of the normal, "leaving" the face at a symmetrical angle to the one created by the incoming line and the normal. If the bounce line intersects the viewport or camera's viewing planes, a highlight is visible. If the bounce is going away or is at too great an angle to the viewing plane and does not intersect it, no specular light is visible. This is, in a way, a form of raytracing, limited to one bounce. It's also close to impossible to visualize, isn't it?

1. To aid you, open the file 12max02.max. An object made of a single face, Face_Receiving_Highlight, is lit by an Omni positioned so that the camera can see the highlight. The Omni takes advantage of a new MAX R2 feature and has Affect Diffuse turned off, thus, providing specular light only. Two Tape Helper objects have been set up to show you the path the light follows.

2. Select the Face_Receiving_Highlight object, and go to Sub-Object/Face mode. You now can see the face's normal.

3. Look at Light_Ray and Light_Bounce from both the Top and Left viewports, and zoom in if necessary. The Light_Bounce intersects the Camera Viewing plane at an angle close to 90 degrees; therefore, the highlight is visible and bright (see Figure 12.2).

FIGURE 12.2

Specular light path.

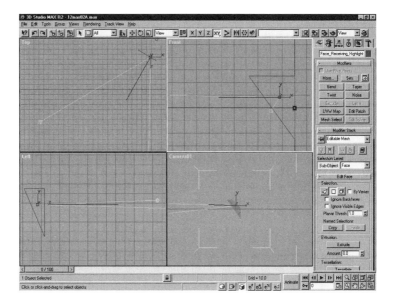

The trouble with this bouncing line is that a very small difference in the initial angle can have a very large impact on the final result. Moving the light source (or the normal) by a small amount can throw the highlight way out of the viewing plane. This is why it used to be very difficult to accurately place highlights on objects and why the Place Highlight tool in the Align drop-down menu can be a great timesaver.

USING "PLACE HIGHLIGHT"

1. Open the scene 12max02a.max. The scene consists of some beveled text, Text01, and a single Omni light.

2. Select Text01. Go to the Modify panel and verify that Sub-Object/Face mode is selected. In the Top view, observe the set of selected faces highlighted in red and their blue normals. Using Place Highlight (next to Array) in the toolbar, we have positioned the Omni light to give a highlight on the selected faces.

3. Click Remove Modifier to delete the Edit Mesh modifier. It was there only to demonstrate the face selection and normals.

4. Select the Omni. Click and hold the mouse button over the Align icon. Move down to the Place Highlight icon and then release the mouse button to select it. The icon should become active in the toolbar and have a green wash indicating it is in a pick mode.

5. In the Top viewport, click the left mouse button and keep it depressed while you slowly move around the X letter of the text object.

You see blue arrows, representing normals, appear as you move, indicating which face would receive the highlight. Looking at the other viewports, you can see that the Omni light is automatically positioned to produce the proper illumination.

Notice how drastically the light has to move to create highlights on nearby faces. This is due to the bounce angle discussed earlier and the fact that it has to intersect the viewport's View plane.

Naturally, as the light is moved, the diffuse lighting is also affected. This can produce a new problem: Placing a light where you need it because your highlights might not give you the diffuse illumination you want. This is the reason why highlights are often created with separate lights, particularly for logos or text. You can verify this by turning off Affect Diffuse in the Omni's Modify panel. The Omni light then becomes a Highlight Only light.

T IP

When precise positioning of highlights and diffuse illumination are required, you can use several lights that each affect either the specular or diffuse components exclusively. Uncheck the Affect Diffuse or Affect Specular check box in the Color section of the light's General Parameters rollout to create a specular-only or diffuse-only light.

As an exercise, you might want to place the Omni where it will give you a satisfactory highlight, leaving it as a Highlight Only light (turning off Affect Diffuse). Then create another Omni, turn off its Affect Specular attribute in the Modify rollout, and position the light to give you a satisfactory diffuse illumination of the text. Of course, you can use any number and combination of lights to achieve the proper result.

We created a file for that purpose: Open 12max02B.max and render the Perspective viewport. We have a blue text with yellow and red highlights. Take a moment to look at the various lights, their colors, and which ones are Highlight or Diffuse lights. Don't move them or adjust them for now. Instead, open up the Materials panel and start playing with Shininess for the Type material. Leave the other settings alone. Start reducing the Shininess value in increments of 10 and render each time. Do you see how the colors blend into each other, creating all kinds of different shades? It starts becoming really interesting around 20 and under. The reason for this is that, as you reduce the Shininess, the highlight becomes larger, and the light spreads accordingly. The shinier your surface, the smaller the highlight. See Figure 12.3.

FIGURE 12.3

The Shininess value of a material affects the size of the highlight.

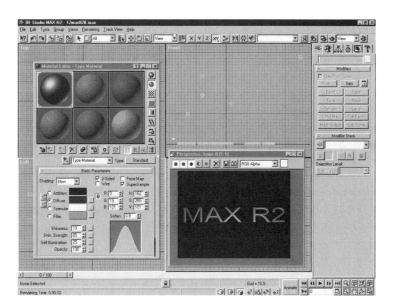

T IP

By using low Shininess values in your material and combinations of Diffuse Only and Highlight Only lights, you can "paint" objects with light.

You should now have a reasonable understanding of normals and how important they are in illumination. The next section explores the lighting instruments in R2 and how they operate.

New Lights and Features in 3D Studio MAX R2

Although users of 3D Studio MAX R1.*x* should feel reasonably at home with the lighting instruments in R2, a number of new features have been implemented.

In R2, there are five types of lights:

- Omni
- Target Direct
- Free Direct
- Target Spot
- Free Spot

Lights can now affect the Diffuse or Specular components of illumination selectively; they also can be softened or hardened. Attenuation has been greatly improved, and Omni lights can now cast shadows and be used as projector lights. You take a look at these new features in the following paragraphs.

NEW TO R2

3D Studio MAX R2 breaks up the old Directional light into two tools, giving you the choice between Free Direct and Target Direct lights.

Because they would require a whole book, all the parameters and lights are not covered in detail. Instead we use the Omni and the Target Direct lights to discuss some new key features in R2 and then briefly examine volumetric lights before proceeding with the tutorial.

Omni Lights

Omni lights do not have a direction. You can think of an Omni as a sphere of light, emanating from the center of the light object and radiating in all directions. If you set up an Omni light in a scene and do not enable Attenuation parameters, all your geometry receives light regardless of where it is located. Obviously the previous discussion about normals and their relative orientation to the light source still applies.

OMNI LIGHTS IN 3D STUDIO MAX R2

1. Open the file 12max03.max, in which an array of spheres is lit by a single Omni light.

2. Render the Perspective viewport or view 12tga01.tga. Notice that the lighting does not vary with distance.

T IP

You can clone your rendered image by using the Clone option in the rendered image window. This enables you to keep the picture for comparison when you render the next one.

NEW TO R2

The Omni rollout is very different from R1.x. Aside from global modifications (common to all lights), Omni lights are now capable of casting shadows and can be used as projectors.

Look at the Attenuation panel. It now includes a Near and Far section with Start and End values for each, as well as a Decay section.

The Near Attenuation parameters can be thought of as a "fade in" type of control for the light, one that operates over distance instead of time.

When turned on, the light increases in intensity from 0 to its maximum value; this ramping begins at the Start value and is in full effect at the End value.

3. Turn on Use for the Near Attenuation of the Omni. Make sure the Start value is 0 and the End value 2450.

4. Render the Perspective viewport or view 12tga02.tga and compare with the previous rendering. The effect is fairly subtle because the fade-in starts at 0, but the light becomes brighter as it moves farther away from the source, toward the Near End value. This is not necessarily realistic, but it is an interesting and useful option.

NEW TO R2

You can now navigate through a series of sequentially numbered images (Using File/View), by using the arrows on the top-right corner of the viewing window.

The Far Attenuation values can be thought of as a fade out for the light. Fading starts at the Start value and is complete at the End value.

5.   Change the Near Start value to 1550, the Near End value to 1920, the Far Start value to 2100, and the Far End value to 2450.

6.   Turn on Use for the Far Attenuation (it should still be on for Near). Render the Perspective viewport or view 12tga03.tga.

The light now fades up from the first row of spheres, reaches full intensity at the middle row, and then fades to dark by the back row. This is not exactly normal lighting, but using only a single light and Attenuation parameters, you have quickly achieved a type of lighting that would previously have been difficult to obtain.

Attenuation is a very useful tool, but it dims the light in linear fashion. In reality, the light diminishes in function of the square of the distance from the object to the source.

In other words, imagine that an object is at a distance of 1 from a light source and receives an amount of light that we arbitrarily call 1, or 100 percent. If you move the object to a distance of 2 and are using Inverse Square Decay, the amount of light the object receives is 1/4 (4 is 2 squared), or 25 percent. If you move the object to 3, it receives 1/9 (9 is 3 to the square), or 11 percent of the light. Using this option, at first intensity drops very quickly over a short distance and then decreases more and more slowly, to an infinitely small value at an infinite distance.

Decay's Inverse Square gives you the option of implementing this realistic algorithm, or you can use a special Inverse option, which dims the light more evenly, using the distance instead of its square. For example, in the preceding exercise, at a distance of 2, the amount of light would be 1/2 or 50 percent. At a distance of 3, the amount of light would be 1/3 or 33 percent and so forth. The light decays more slowly, in regular or linear fashion.

UNDERSTANDING ATTENUATION AND DECAY

1.   Continue with 12max03.max and select Omni01 if it isn't still selected.

2.   In the Modify panel, change the Attenuation Near Start and End values to 0. Verify that the Far Start and End are still set to 2100 and 2450, respectively.

3. In the Decay section, turn on Inverse Square and render the Perspective viewport, or view 12tga04.tga.

The result is barely visible (check the alpha channel) because the inverse square algorithm decreases light exponentially, starting at the Near End value. In this case, the light has dropped drastically to a very small intensity before it even hits the first row of spheres.

4. Change the Near End value to 1550 and the Far End value to 2750. Rerender the Perspective viewport or view 12tga05.tga. The light now realistically fades from the source to the back of the object (see Figure 12.4).

FIGURE 12.4

The effect of Attenuation and Decay.

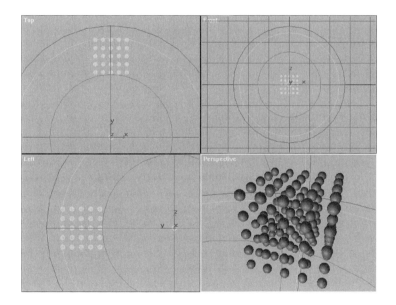

> **N**OTE
>
> When using Decay, bear in mind that the light starts decaying at the Near End Attenuation value, even if you are not using Attenuation. The Near End Attenuation value must always be set when you use Decay. The light then continues to diminish either to infinity, if you are not using Far Attenuation, or until it's cut off by the Far End Attenuation value, if Far Attenuation Use is checked.

Attenuation and Decay parameters might seem a little complicated at first, but they can greatly increase the realism of your scenes and the amount of control you have over lighting. They are definitely worth some practice time.

Two more parameters should be mentioned here. In the Color area of the light's Modify rollout, set the Soften Diff. Edge value to 100. Rerender the Perspective viewport or view 12tga06.tga.

Notice how increasing this value has softened the light by softening the junction between shadow and diffuse light. Now increase Contrast to 100 and rerender the Perspective viewport or view 12tga07.tga. The light is much harsher.

Direct Lights

Whereas the Omni light is a point-type light source, radiating in all directions, the Direct light emits in one direction only—toward the target in the case of a Target Direct or toward the directional arrow in the case of a Free Direct.

Another important aspect of the Directional light is that the source is not a sphere (as in an Omni) or a point (as in a spot), but a plane or surface. You can imagine the light as emanating from the whole Falloff area (as a multitude of parallel rays) and traveling perpendicular to it in one direction. This has obvious implications on what the angle between the geometry's normals and the light will be.

Finally, the Directional light does not spread—it only propagates. This means that the light does not expand in width and height with distance but instead maintains the same proportions.

Directional lights add a new concept to lighting—the cone of illumination. Although this term is accepted for all Directional lights, the name really applies to spot lights, which truly form a cone of light. For Directional lights, think of a "Cylinder" of illumination if Circle is selected in the Directional Parameters rollout, or a "Box" of illumination if Rectangle is chosen. What does this mean?

THE CONE OF ILLUMINATION

1. Open 12max04.max. The rows of spheres are illuminated by a single Target Direct Light.

2. Render the Perspective viewport or view 12tga08.tga. A single column of spheres is lit. This is because the cone of illumination restricts illumination to a cylindrical beam, whose diameter is determined by the Falloff value in the Directional Parameters rollout.

3. Change the Falloff value to 700 and the Hotspot value to 698.

4. Render the image or view 12tga09.tga. All spheres are now lit. This is because all the geometry is now inside the cone of illumination. You can see this in your viewports, where the Falloff is represented in dark blue.

5. Now change the Hotspot value to 0 (it automatically defaults to 0.5) and rerender or view 12tga10.tga.

The light fades from the center of the cone of illumination to the Falloff limits. The Hotspot and Falloff values are essentially similar to Attenuation, but they attenuate the light from the center of the cone of illumination (as determined by the Hotspot value) to its edges (the Falloff value). This attenuation has interesting side effects; it softens or hardens the light, making the junction between dark and light areas smoother or harsher. The closer your Hotspot value is to your Falloff value, the harsher the light is. Conversely, the bigger the difference between your Hotspot and your Falloff value, the softer the light.

One thing to remember is that if you want this effect to appear on geometry, the parameters for Hotspot and Falloff have to be set correctly. If all your geometry is included inside the Hotspot value, for example, you do not see the light fade at all, even if you have a large Falloff value, because the fading would occur outside of the geometry. To verify this, continue with the exercise.

6. Set your Hotspot to 700 and your Falloff to 1500.

7. Rerender or view 12tga11.tga. The lighting is even because all spheres are included in the Hotspot area.

8. Change the Hotspot back to 0 and rerender or view 12tga12.tga. The fading is back and much more progressive because it now occurs from 0.5 (the Hotspot value) to 1500.0 (the Falloff value) (see Figure 12.5).

FIGURE 12.5

Hotspot and Falloff.

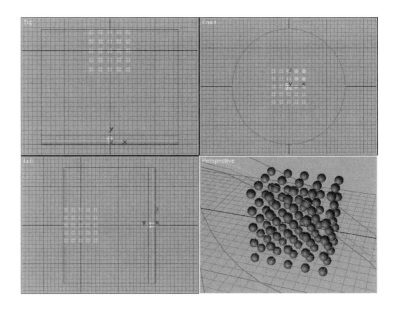

9. Set the Hotspot to 248, the Falloff to 250, and rerender or view 12tga13.tga. You can clearly see the "Cylinder" of illumination in this image.

10. Select Rectangle instead of Circle.

11. Rerender of View 12tga14.tga. You now have a "box" of illumination.

12. The box's aspect ratio can be modified, too, using the Asp. value. Change the Asp. value to 2.0 and rerender or view 12tga15.tga. The "box" of illumination is now twice as wide as it is high.

The proportions of the box can be made to automatically match those of a bitmap. This is done by selecting Bitmap Fit... and then choosing a bitmap. This is very useful when you want to project a bitmap onto geometry and preserve its proportions (also called Aspect Ratio).

Spot Lights

Spot lights are a combination of Omni and Direct lights, in the sense that the light starts from a single point and spreads in one direction, forming a true cone of illumination. This cone can become a pyramid if you change the light from Circle to Rectangle. Beyond this, the Attenuation, Decay, Hotspot, and Falloff parameters operate in the same way as for the Direct light.

You have now explored most of the parameters new to R2 lights. Various combinations of these new and old parameters, including negative multipliers that can subtract light from a scene and the use of the Exclude/Include options, truly give you a limitless lighting palette.

In the following tutorial, you explore a few of these possibilities, but before you start, spend a few moments examining volumetric lights, which play an important role in the tutorial.

Volumetric Lights in 3D Studio MAX R2

This discussion assumes that you have already read the manual's chapters (both printed and online) concerning volumetric lights. If you haven't, please do so.

The term *volumetric lights* is slightly misleading because it seems to indicate a certain type of light. In fact, volumetric lights are an atmospheric effect—fog—controlled by a light. Roughly, a volumetric light is a fog, restricted to a light's cone of illumination. In a volumetric light, however, the Fog parameters are linked to some of the light's parameters.

VOLUME LIGHTS

1. Open the file 12max05.max. The scene is a sphere lit by a target spot.

2. Select Rendering/Environment to open the Environment panel.

3. A volume light has already been set up. Click it to display its parameters.

4. Take a quick look at the Basic parameters. In any of the viewports, select the Spot01 object and go to the Modify panel. Your screen should look like Figure 12.6.

5. Make sure that the Time slider is at 30. (Either scrub to frame 30 or type in the 30 in the Frame Counter window.)

6. Render the Perspective viewport or view 12tga16.tga. The volumetric light is there; it's not exactly subtle, but it's there.

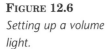

FIGURE 12.6

Setting up a volume light.

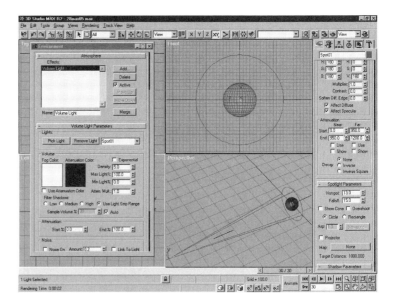

Atmospheric effects are visible only in Perspective or Camera viewports; they will not show in Orthogonal viewports.

The first thing to mention is that you can control the amount of fog in the scene without going to the Environment panel through the light's multiplier.

7. Change the intensity to 0.5 and rerender or view 12tga17.tga. This is equivalent to changing the Density value in the Environment panel from 5.0 to 2.5. (Check if want but don't forget to bring the multiplier to 1 before you lower the Density.) There is one obvious difference: When you lower the spotlight's multiplier, you also affect the object's illumination.

From this exercise, you might conclude that you will often want to use two lights for volumetric and illumination purposes. Although this is far from being an absolute rule, in many cases the adjustments you will want to make to the light for volumetric purposes will not be compatible with good illumination. You will then have to create another, regular light to take care of the illumination that the volumetric light should be casting. Matching the positions for both lights and their targets can facilitate this process.

TIP

Rather than use Exclude to keep the volumetric light from illuminating the scene, uncheck Affect Diffuse and Affect Specular. The light no longer casts any light, but it still casts fog.

Meanwhile, the fog still looks bad. It's much too dense and looks two-dimensional.

8. Bring the light's Multiplier value back to 1 if necessary.

9. Reduce the Hotspot from 13 to 0.5.

10. Render or view 12tga18.tga.

It's an improvement, but something is still wrong. The beam seems to get brighter as it moves away from the light source. This is because you are dealing with fog and fog does increase with distance, but for your purposes, it doesn't look right.

11. Check that the Far Start Attenuation is 950 and the Far End value is 1200.

12. Click the Far Attenuation Use check box.

13. Rerender or view 12tga19.tga. Much better, isn't it?

14. Check that the Near Start Attenuation value is 0 and the End Start Attenuation value 950.

15. Check the Use check box under Near Attenuation and rerender or view 12tga20.tga.

16. Save your work.

You have gone from a very rough, blocky volumetric light effect to a fairly convincing beam of light, without even modifying the Environment parameters at all. This shows how much of an impact the light's Attenuation parameters (and Hotspot/Falloff) have on the volumetric effect.

And, of course, they can be animated.

ANIMATING THE VOLUMETRIC EFFECT

1. Continue with your work from the last exercise or load 12max05a.max. Move the Frame slider slowly from frame 30 back to frame 0.

2. Watch the Attenuation ranges move. If not already open, choose Rendering/Environment. Select Volume Light and check Noise On in the Noise section of the Volume Light Parameters rollout. Noise has already been prepared for animation. Render the animation, or you can directly view 12avi01.avi to see the results.

3. Save your changes.

The animated noise is relatively subtle and doesn't come across too well because of the limitations inherent to the .avi format, but you get a sense of dust moving in the light. You might want to take a look at an easy way to control Noise animation parameters (among others).

CONTROLLING NOISE ANIMATION PARAMETERS

1. Continue with the previous scene or load 12max05b.max.

2. Open up Track View and check that Animated Tracks Only is selected (right-mouse click Filters in the Track View toolbar).

3. Expand Environment/Volume Light and click on Phase.

4. Check that Function Curves is selected in the Track View toolbar. What you see is the curve of the Phase animation for the noise.

Instead of animating the phase by using the Animate button and setting up keys by going to a frame and entering a new value in the Environment panel, we just inserted keys directly in Track View using Add Key and adjusted their positions and values from there.

Tutorial: Inanimate Object

It's time to put what you learned into practice and have a little fun. You are going to set up and animate the lighting for the following scene shown in Figure 12.7.

All the geometry has been built (we thank REM Infografica for allowing us to use their great model of the statue). The scene is fairly heavy, so we have provided most of the rendered images and several .avi files in case you can't afford to spend the time rendering all of this.

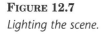

FIGURE 12.7
Lighting the scene.

Establishing the General Lighting

The first step is to establish the general lighting. The goal here is to develop a basic illumination from two standpoints:

- **Artistic.** The general lighting should support the mood you are trying to establish.

- **Practical.** The general lighting should provide you with a base illumination that will be appropriate for all objects in your scene, throughout the animation.

The overall level of illumination will vary from scene to scene, according to your needs or design.

After the general lighting is established, we will proceed to lights that serve more specific functions.

ESTABLISHING GENERAL LIGHTING

1. Open the file 12max06.max. Most of the geometry has been set to Display as Box in the Display rollout to speed up viewport redraws. The statue is hidden for now.

A Combustion system has been set up for the fire. (Go to Rendering/ Environment and select Combustion Fire to look at the parameters, if you want.)

2. Using Select by Name in the toolbar, select the Omni_Fire light and go to the Modify panel. Take a look at the different parameters.

3. View 12tga21.tga or render the Perspective viewport. The scene is very dark; the Omni_Fire lights only the inside of the fireplace and acts as a (very discreet) backlight for some of the geometry. Note that ranges and exclusions have been used (click Exclude… in the General Parameters area of the Modify panel to see a list of excluded objects). Also note that the light is casting Shadow Mapped shadows.

4. Select Spot_Fire_Key and go to its Modify panel. Turn this light on by checking the On box in the General Parameters/Color area. Note the settings for Attenuation and Decay (the Near End Attenuation value, for example, matches that of the Omni_Fire), Hotspot and Falloff values, and the shadow parameters. This light is our key, or main light, and does not use any exclusions.

5. Rerender or view 12tga22.tga. We now have a room that seems to be lit by a fireplace, but the background and the front of the desk and chairs are really too dark. They need some fill light.

NEW TO R2

Most of the lights used in this tutorial use options that are available only in 3D Studio MAX R2.

Select Spot_Fire_Fill and go to its Modify panel. Turn the light on. Again, note the Attenuation settings, as well as Hotspot/Falloff values. In the Shadow area, note that the Smp Range is high, with a value of 16. This is because we want the shadows cast by this light to be softer, more diffuse. This light simulates the firelight after it has bounced off the rooms of the wall. View 12tga23.tga.

A high Smp Range value softens the shadows, making them fade from light to dark more progressively, although this is only true within the limits imposed by the Hotspot/Falloff parameters, which we previously discussed.

Increasing the Size value gives you more detailed shadows, which tends to make them crisper. You can think of the Smp Range value as determining how blurred your shadows will be, whereas the Size value determines how detailed your shadows will be.

Increasing the Smp Range and Size values also increases rendering time.

The Map Bias factor determines how much the shadows are offset from the object that casts them. These three parameters are important, because the wrong values can result in awkward-looking shadows, particularly the Map Bias value. Too low a Map Bias value often results in artifacts—dirty-looking areas or more patterns in your rendering. Too high a value makes your shadows look like they are disconnected from the casting object. Too low an Smp Range or Size value can result in pixelated shadows.

7. To bring the statue in, go to the Display panel, choose unhide by Name, and unhide Statue and Statue_Base. Rerender the Perspective viewport or view 12tga24.tga.

The problem now is a very monochromatic scene, with no clear separation between the focus point (the statue) and the background (the room). Although you can use another warm-colored light on the statue alone to make it stand out, use of a colder light helps accentuate the contrast between foreground and background.

8. In the Display panel, click Unhide by Name and unhide Omni_Daylight_Fill01 and Omni_Daylight_Fill02. In the toolbar, use Select by Name to select Omni_Daylight_Fill01. You can use None and then Lights in the Select by Name panel to simplify your selection process.

9. Go to the Omni_Daylight_Fill01's Modify panel and turn the light on. Repeat the process with Omni_Daylight_Fill02 and turn this light on, too. Rerender or view 12tga25.tga.

The separation between the focus point and the background is much better. Note that you have used low Multipliers on the Omnis to maintain a good range of values on the statue and there is still some of the warm light from the fire on the right side of the statue's face. Attenuation was not used on the Omnis at all because the very small list of objects included in their illumination makes Attenuation unnecessary.

NOTE

There is better separation in the scene now, but where is that colder light suddenly coming from? It could be coming from a window that is out of the shot. But then it would be good to have some "echo" of this in the scene—another source of similar light. The window is a good candidate for this, and you'll give it a volumetric effect.

10. Go to the Display panel and unhide Spot_Volumetric. Select it, go to its Modify panel, and turn it on.

11. Again, take some time to look at all the parameters, bearing in mind this chapter's previous discussions. Rerender or view 12tga26.tga.

Looks pretty bad. Remembering our previous discussion, you might already be thinking about adjusting the Hotspot value. If you are, you're right; we could do this, but not this time.

12. Go to the Shadow parameters for the Spot_Volumetric. Click Cast Shadows to turn it on. Before you render, check the Include… list in the Color area of the light's General parameters in the Modify panel. Notice that only the back wall is casting shadows. Because of the way they're modeled, the windows would cast improper shadows, so we can't include them. You could go in and remodel the windows, but this won't be necessary.

13. Rerender the Perspective viewport or View 12tga27.tga.

14. The fog is too dense overall and it would also be good if it broke up in places, because of the shadows cast by the window's frame.

15. In the Spot_Volumetric Modify panel, under Spotlight Parameters, turn on Projector. The map is a simple checker.

16. Go to the Attenuation area and turn on Use for the Far attenuation. Also turn on Decay/Inverse. Now rerender or view 12tga28.tga.

17. Save your file.

You now have a fairly subtle and convincing volumetric light effect. Check the material used for the Projector in the Materials Editor if you want.

Animating the Lights

The first thing you need to animate is the light cast by the fireplace. It should flicker to some extent, as the flames do. You cannot be true to nature here because a scene lit mainly by a fire would be too dark and become murky, but you can try to re-create the feeling.

ANIMATING THE "FIRE" LIGHTS

1. Open 12max07.max. This is the same scene, but we have hidden a number of the objects and turned off the Render Atmospheric Effects option in the Rendering panel to make things easier to test and faster to render.

2. Unhide and select the Omni_Fire light and open Track View.

3. Verify that Selected Object Only is checked and expand the tracks. Don't forget to also expand the Float list.

4. Select and right-click Noise Float:Noise Float and select Properties. Your display should look like Figure 12.8.

5. Save your work.

You have created a List controller for the Omni's Multiplier. Inside the list is a Bézier Float controller, which gives the light a constant "base" intensity of 0.5 (you can check this by right-clicking one of the keys in the Bézier Float row in Track View; also check the tangent types for the two keys, which are important in maintaining the light at a constant minimum level).

Next in the list is a Noise controller, which makes the intensity of the light fluctuate. Look at the settings and values in the Noise Controller panel that you opened through Properties. Notice in particular that the strength is set at 0.45 and that >0 is turned on. This means that the Noise function generates a random value between 0 and 0.45; this will be added to our "base" intensity of 0.5, making the Omni_Fire's multiplier fluctuate semi-randomly between 0.5 and 0.95. If the >0 option had not been turned on, the Multiplier would fluctuate between 0.05 and 0.95, since the Noise would have fluctuated between 0.45 and −0.45.

FIGURE 12.8

*The Noise Controller
dialog box.*

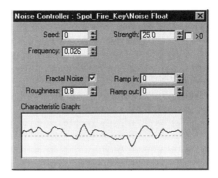

ADDING A NOISE CONTROLLER TO A LIGHT

1. Continue from your previous work or open 12max07a.max. If necessary, close the Noise Controller Properties window and minimize Track View. Select the Spot_Fire_Key and reopen Track View.

2. Expand Spot_Fire_Key and then Object (Target Spot).

3. The Multiplier controller is a list similar to the one that controlled the Omni_Fire's Multiplier.

4. Select the Multiplier controller and then click Copy controller in Track View's toolbar.

5. Go down the list of controllers in Track View until you find Hotspot (third controller down). Click Paste Controller in Track View's toolbar. When prompted for Instance or Copy, choose Copy. We want to modify some parameters.

Your viewports react because the light's Hotspot has just been reduced in size. Select the first key on the Bézier Float row immediately below the Hotspot track in Track View and right-click it.

6. Change its value to 75. Then move on to the next key and change its value to 75, too. Deselect the key.

7. Select and right-click the Noise Float to display its properties. Change the Strength to 25 and turn >0 off. Figure 12.9 shows you what your values should be.

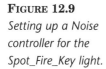

FIGURE 12.9

Setting up a Noise controller for the Spot_Fire_Key light.

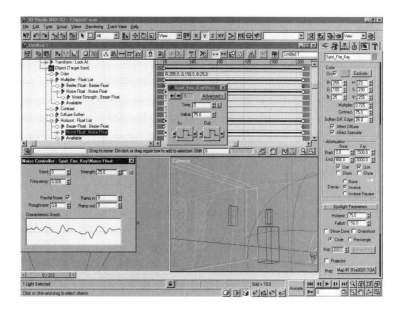

8. Close Track View and all related opened windows.

9. Scrub along the time line (using the Time slider) and watch what happens to Spot_Fire_Key's Hotspot. It shrinks and expands randomly (but the randomness is the same for all parameters, since the timing of the Noise controller has been copied), oscillating between 50 and 100 (75 plus a random number between –25 and 25).

TIP

The Copy controller and Paste controller options make it easy to set up the same or similar animations for various tracks. Think beforehand whether you want the new controller to be an instance (completely the same) or a copy (some modifications are possible) of the Source controller.

10. Render a couple seconds of the scene to check the effect (use Render/Range 0 to 60, and don't forget to save your work as an .avi file, using the File button in the Render dialog box) or view 12avi02.avi.

Fairly convincing, right? You could cut and paste the List modifier to affect the Fire light's Falloff, too, or Attenuation ranges, paying attention to the fact that the "base" keys values and Noise amount would need to be adjusted. There really is a lot of control available.

We now move to setting up and animating the cold light that will stream in from the side window. We will use a Volume Light for this.

ANIMATING THE WINDOW'S VOLUMETRIC LIGHT

1. Continue with your scene from the last exercise or open 12max07b.max. Open Track View again. You can't see any mention of the Spot_Volumetric because it is hidden and Track View does not display hidden objects. On top of that, you are using Selected Only as a filter, so the light must be unhidden and selected to show up. You can animate it, though, because you are animating the Noise's Phase and that is an Environment effect.

2. Expand Environment and then VL Daylight. Go to Phase: Bézier Float and select it. You see that two keys have been set up in that track: one at frame 0, with a value of 0, and the other one at frame 210, with a value of 0.

3. In the Track View's toolbar, click Function Curves. The Track View changes to a different display, showing a flat line joining the two keys.

4. Click Add Keys in the toolbar. Add keys every 30 frames from frame 30–180. Adjust the key's values to get a semi-cyclical type of curve. Figure 12.10 is provided as a guide, but feel free to build a different curve if you like.

T IP

You can type in a key's frame position and value directly in the two white windows at the bottom of the Track View display. This is often more accurate than moving them by hand. A good rule of thumb is to position your keys roughly in the Curve Function display and then type the exact values in the windows. You can also click Show Selected Keys Stats to see the selected frame number and key value displayed in your Curve Function display.

FIGURE 12.10

Setting up the animated noise for a Volume Light.

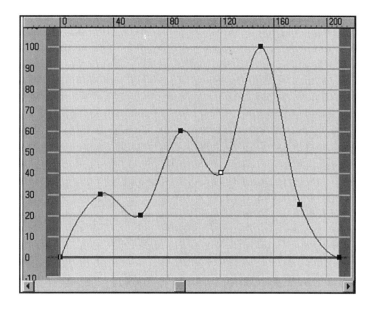

Using Function Curves and Add Keys, you can quickly deal with animating parameters that would otherwise be time-consuming to set up. You can also quickly copy and paste keys in Track View.

The noise of the volumetric light fluctuates over the course of the scene, giving the impression of specs of dust floating in the light. For this effect to be visible, remember to go into Render/Environment, select the VL Daylight and turn Noise on. Do this now, if you want the Noise animation included in your final rendering.

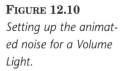

NOTE

Volumetric effects in general and noise in particular increase rendering time.

We now move to the last animated light in our scene. This will be an FX type of light, which will interact with an animated object in our scene and will use both volumetric and projection parameters.

ANIMATING THE UFO'S LIGHT

1. Continue with the scene from the previous exercise or open 12max07c.max. Close Track View.

2. Go to Rendering/Environment, select Combustion Fire, and uncheck Active.

3. Select VL Daylight and uncheck Active. Close the Environment panel.

4. Make sure that nothing is selected in the scene. Go to the Display panel and click Hide Unselected. The scene is now empty.

5. Click Unhide by Name. Make sure that all elements are displayed.

6. Control-click [UFO], Free_Direct UFO and Statue. Click Unhide.

7. In the Top viewport, zoom in on the UFO a little. (It's a group composed of three very simple objects, with a Free Direct light Linked to it.) At frame 0, it is not visible in the Camera viewport. Select the Camera viewport and scrub the timeline (redraws might be slow) to get a sense of what happens.

The UFO comes into frame, notices the statue, and comes closer to it around frame 55. The part we are interested in starts at frame 60 and lasts until frame 120.

At frame 60, the Attenuation values are 0. From frames 60–70, the ranges animate, stay at their full value from frames 70–110, and animate back to 0 from frames 110–120. This means that the light is off until frame 60, and then a beam of light grows out of the UFO from frames 60–70, continues to light the statue's face until frame 110, and then recedes back into the UFO from 110–120. The slight changes of position that you might notice from frame to frame on the UFO object are due to the fact that we added a bit of noise to the UFO's animation to make it less mechanical.

8. Select the Free Direct_UFO light if not already selected and go to its Modify panel.

9. In the Directional Parameters area, notice that the Map slot contains an .ifl (Image File List). An .ifl is essentially a text file, containing a list of maps or images to be used sequentially. Feel free to look up Ufo.ifl in the Maps directory and open it up with WordPad. You'll notice that we repeated some images' numbers because we wanted to slow down the rate of change for the maps.

10. Now open the Material Editor and look at the UFO_Gobo material. We created it as a Bitmap material in the Material Editor and assigned it the ufo.ifl as a map. We then dragged that material's icon from the

Material Editor's window to the Light's Projector Map slot and dropped it there. Note that in the Material's Time rollout, the start frame is 60 (because the light's off until that time) and Loop is an End condition. This makes the .ifl loop over as long as necessary.

11. Close the Material Editor and turn on Projector in the Free Direct_UFO's Modify panel. Now render frames 60 to 120 (don't forget to turn Render Atmospheric Effects back on in the Render dialog first) or view 12avi03.avi. The light comes on, projects some strange signs on the statue's face, and then shuts off.

Final Rendering

That's it. You're finally ready to render the whole thing. You have a choice: You can use the file 12max08.max, which has already been prepared for rendering, or you can go through the trouble of setting everything up yourself, which is not a bad exercise in itself. Unhide all the geometry, check in the Render/Environment that all your atmospheric effects are Active, check that Render Atmospheric Effects is on in the Rendering/Render dialog. You might also want to make sure that all your lights are on, including the two projectors. Then render the Active Range (0–210) or view 12avi04.avi. Don't forget to save your output by clicking Save to File in the Render dialog.

NOTE

At a video resolution of 720×486, this scene took approximately 19 hours to render on a single Pentium Pro machine. It does, however, look much better on video than it does in .avi. If you have a video output board, you might want to consider spending the time.

Because it is not a part of this chapter's focus, the animation of the geometry is not covered here. Feel free to look at the various elements in Track View if you are interested.

In Practice: Animating Lights

- **Plotting your lights.** Plot your lighting carefully and light progressively. Start with just one light, set it up, and then add one more and so on. Remember that lights don't operate in a vacuum; in addition to all their parameters, they also interact with the materials.

■ **Attenuation parameters.** Careful use of Attenuation parameters, as well as the Hotspot/Falloff values, in conjunction with shadows can greatly improve your lighting.

■ **Animating your lights.** Think early on about which lights and which parameters will be animated. Try to evaluate the impact that Shadows and Volumetric Effects will have on your final rendering time.

If your lights are not animated but the scene includes animation, render a series of keyframes to make sure that your lighting works throughout the animation.

If your lights are animated, when you render test segments, hide non-essential geometry and/or lights, and turn off effects that don't impact the light(s) you are currently testing. This speeds up rendering time considerably.

■ **Stand-in Geometry.** A method we use to shorten our rendering times early on is Stand-in Geometry. Very basic shapes (boxes or spheres) are scaled and positioned appropriately to represent more complex objects (like the statue, for example). We use these stand-ins to rough out our lighting and line up Projections, Volumetric Effects, Attenuation, and so on. The final geometry is only used at a later stage for fine-tuning.

Chapter 13

PARTICLES, DYNAMIC SIMULATIONS, AND SPACE WARPS

Particle systems create the defined motion of a multitude of particles that are calculated by procedures inherited by the Particle systems. The particles themselves do not have a specific shape, but they are used to control other objects that can be defined by the Particle system's properties. Commonly, Particle systems are used to represent dynamic objects—for instance dust, smoke, or fire—that have an irregular and complex shape and that can also exhibit their own behavior. It is also possible to use these Particle systems to simulate natural phenomena, such as rain, snow, flowing water, or even flocks or swarms of animals or insects. To further enhance the effect created by this procedural type of animation, you can control the motion of these Particle systems by applying external forces like gravity or wind. For example, it is possible to animate a short circuit that produces some glowing sparks emitting from a broken cable. They will fall down because of the gravity applied to them and then bounce off the floor before disappearing.

This chapter introduces you to the new Particle systems included in 3D Studio MAX R2 and its vast number of new features. In this chapter's exercises, you will learn about the different uses for several Particle systems and how and under which circumstances to apply these new features.

Sometimes it is necessary to control the motion of Particle systems to add more realism to the final look of your animation. To do that, in the exercises, you will use space warps that apply external forces such as gravity to your Particle systems, adding motion to the particles that would be impossible to achieve by normal means.

The last part of the chapter explores the new Dynamic Utility in 3D Studio MAX R2. With this tool, you can automatically create a simulation of real-world motions of geometrical objects, which was nearly impossible to accomplish in previous versions of 3D Studio MAX. When creating such a simulation, often called Dynamic Simulation, the program utilizes algorithms to calculate the motion path of a geometrical object originating from an initial position to a final position by applying forces such as velocity and gravity or other external forces such as wind and properties like mass, friction, and air resistance.

The following topics are covered in this chapter:

■ Particle systems in 3D Studio MAX R2

■ Applying external forces to Particle systems

■ Constraining particle motion

■ Applying image effects to Particle systems

■ Dynamic simulations of geometric objects

Particle Systems

Whenever a 3D animator wants to create or simulate natural phenomena, he normally makes use of a procedural concept known as a Particle system. With such a system, it is possible to create real-world effects like waterfalls, rain, fire, or imaginary effects like fairy dust. A Particle system consists of a multitude of objects that can be planar shapes, little spheres, or any other shape. Their movements are controlled by algorithms defined by a myriad of properties. Here's the basic sequence of using a Particle system:

- **Birth.** A particle is created at a specific frame at a specific rate. You can either create a fixed number of particles per frame or use a total number of particles during the animation.

- **Move.** The particles move along a defined path, which is determined by system-specific algorithms. It is possible to control these algorithms by adjusting and even animating the parameters inherited by the different Particle systems.

- **Death.** Particles die after an adjustable amount of time. If you want to see all created particles during the whole duration of your animation, you must set the lifetime of the Particle system to a higher number of frames than your animation.

It is possible to apply additional effects to Particle systems, such as physical properties like gravity, wind, shape, color, and motion blur, or image effects like Glow and Hilight.

Usually Particle systems will not be the main effect in your animation, but they will be the special effect that adds the final realism to your animation. For example, imagine a launching rocket without trailing exhaust or how difficult it would be to animate falling snow or rain without the use of procedural objects like Particle systems.

Particle Systems in 3D Studio MAX R2

Currently there are six different Particle systems included in 3D Studio MAX R2:

- **Spray** and **Snow.** These two represent the old Particle systems that were included in the previous release of the 3D Studio MAX. They are kept for compatibility reasons and will not be discussed further in this chapter.

■ **Super Spray.** This is an enhanced version of the Spray Particle system and contains the new Particle system features. It can be considered as the basic system that can be used for most effects an animator wants to achieve.

■ **Blizzard.** This is a new version of the old Snow Particle system. Like all new Particle systems, it contains new features that were added in this release of 3D Studio MAX 2. It also has parameters to define the tumbling of the emitted particles to create more realistic snow and confetti effects.

■ **Particle Array.** The unique feature of this Particle system is that it uses a geometric object as an emitter for its particles. This is the Particle system to choose when creating advanced explosion or bursting effects.

■ **Particle Cloud.** If you need a Particle system that is used to create volume effects like a box filled with particles or a gas cloud, this system would be your choice.

Space Warps and Particle Systems

Space warps can be compared to modifiers, except that they influence world space by applying force field–like effects instead of modifying object space. Space warps have no effect unless they are bound to an object. When an object is bound to a space warp, the binding appears at the top of the object's Modifier Stack. This also shows that Space Warp effects are applied after any transforms or modifiers. Some of the space warps in 3D Studio MAX R2 apply external forces to particle motion, which makes it very easy to simulate natural forces or explosive shockwaves.

Currently 10 different space warps are available for use with Particle systems. Five of these can also be used with the Dynamic Utility, which is discussed later in this chapter. The following can be used with Particle systems and the Dynamic Utility:

■ **Gravity.** This space warp creates gravitational effects on Particle systems. It can be used in either a planar or a spherical fashion. If used in a spherical fashion, the particles are always drawn to the center of the sphere; if used in a planar fashion, the particles accelerate in the direction of the arrow of the Gravity icon.

- **Wind.** Wind is much like the Gravity space warp, but you can also add turbulence to the effect. When animated, this space warp can produce a very realistic simulation of wind.

- **Push.** This space warp applies a force to the Particle system in the direction of the pointing arrow of the icon. In addition, you can add a feedback mechanism from the velocity of the particles. When used with the Dynamic Utility, Push provides a point force that can be compared to a finger pushing in one direction.

- **Motor.** This space warp applies a rotational force to the Particle system, whereas the Push space warp applies a linear force to it.

- **PBomb.** The Particle Bomb is used to blast Particle systems apart. You can choose from several blast symmetries—for example, planar, cylindrical, or spherical.

NOTE

To add some extra variation to the PBomb space warp, it is possible to set a value for the Chaos parameter. This will add some randomly created numbers to parameters, such as Strength or Spin, and will give the explosion a more realistic look. If you want to use the Chaos value in the Particle Bomb properties, you have to set Duration to 0.

The following space warps can be used only with Particle systems. Because it is not possible to use them with the Dynamic Utility, they will not be taken into account when calculating a simulation.

- **Path Follow.** This space warp forces a Particle system along a spline. You can control things like the speed at which the particles move, the rotation of the particles around the path, and how fast the particles converge or diverge from the path.

- **Displace.** With this space warp, you can apply forces to the Particle system based on a bitmap or map. Low-luminance areas apply low or no force, and high luminance areas apply high forces to the Particle system. It has the same parameters as the Displace space warp for geometric objects.

- **Deflector, SDeflector, and UDeflector.** These space warps are used to detect collisions with Particle systems. It is possible to either bounce the particles off the deflector or kill them when colliding.

These three deflectors all make use of the same parameters—the only difference among them is that the Deflector uses a planar icon, the SDeflector uses a spherical icon, and the UDeflector can use any geometric object as a deflector.

NOTE

The Deflector and the SDeflector are the fastest to calculate. You should always consider using these before using a mesh as a deflector, especially when it is bound to an object with a high polygon count.

Using Particle Systems

You will now go through some exercises that have been set up to further teach you how to use Particle systems and their associated space warps.

- **Creating Fairy Dust.** The first exercise introduces you to the new Super Spray Particle system and how it can be used with Video Post Image effects.

- **Creating a PArray Particle System.** The second exercise introduces you to the new PArray Particle system and its features.

- **Creating Object Explosions.** The PArray Particle system exercise utilizes the Gravity and Deflector space warps to create an object that explodes into a multitude of fragments.

- **Sending Particles Along a Path.** By using a Path Follow space warp, you will create a Particle system that simulates swarm or flock effects.

- **Creating Bubbles.** In this exercise, you will use some of the effects such as Particle system features and space warps to create a tablet that emits bubbles in a glass.

Creating Fairy Dust by Using Super Spray

In this exercise, you will create a Super Spray Particle system to animate an effect that could be described as fairy dust, which normally emanates from magic wands and the like. You will also link the Particle system to a dummy that moves over a defined path, and finally, add some image effects to the particles to give them a better look in your final animation.

SETTING UP THE SUPER SPRAY PARTICLE SYSTEM

1. Load the file 13max01.max from the accompanying CD-ROM. The scene includes a camera and a circle.

2. In the Front viewport, create a Super Spray Particle system at the center of the World space. The icon size should be 10.

3. Create a Dummy object at the center of the World space. The Particle system should be inside the dummy. See Figure 13.1 for reference.

FIGURE 13.1

The placement of the objects in this scene.

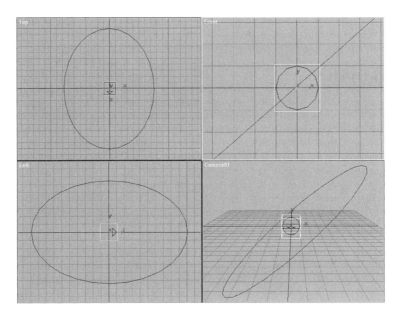

4. Link the Particle system to the dummy.

Now you will set the values for the different properties of the Particle system. You will later assign a Path controller to the dummy. For now, it is better to leave the Particle system at the World center to better see the changes in the emitting pattern when setting different values for the Particle system's parameters.

5. Drag the Frame slider to frame 15. You can now see some particles in the Top viewport where it is easier to observe the effects that the different parameters will have on the Particle system.

6. Make sure you have selected the Particle system. Enter the Modify panel and open the Basic Parameter rollout. Under Viewport Display,

you can set the number of particles displayed in the viewport. Set it to 100 percent to see all the particles emitted by the Particle system.

7. In this rollout, you can also set the spread of the emitting particles. The Off-Axis controls the emitting angle and spread along the plane of the x-axis. Set the Spread for the Off-Axis to 10 degrees.

8. The Off-Plane affects the emission on the z-axis. It is affected only if one of the Off-Axis values is not set to 0. Change the Off-Plane degrees in any way you like, and you will notice that the particle emission is rotated around the z-axis. Set the Off-Plane back to 0 degrees and the Spread to 90 degrees. Figure 13.2 shows the Basic Parameter rollout for the Super Spray Particle system.

FIGURE 13.2

The Basic Parameter rollout for the Super Spray Particle system.

Next, move on to the Particle Generation rollout. Because Fairy Dust is a continuous stream of emitting particles, you will use Rate instead of Total under Particle Quantity. Total, for instance, would be used when simulating bursts or explosions. Rate is used when creating a continuous stream of particles to create bubbles, smoke, or the exhaust of a rocket.

9. In the Particle Generation rollout, type **12** under Rate, so that 12 particles are emitted every frame. Use a Speed of 3 and a Variation of 30 percent. Because Fairy Dust is not a hectic effect, you will use a rather low setting for the speed of the emitting particles.

The next element to define is the Particle Timing, which is also part of the Particle Generation rollout. The Timing determines in what frame a Particle system is born, when it dies, and for how long it is visible in your animation.

10. Because it takes the Particle system 300 frames to move along the path, set the Emit Stop value to 300.

11. Set the Display Until value to 300 so that the Particle system is displayed until the end of the animation.

12. Set the Life value to specify how many frames a particle lasts after its creation. You can also use the Variation value to specify the number of frames by which the life of a particle can vary. Set the Life and Variation values to 30. Leave the Particle size at its default values.

FIGURE 13.3

The scene so far. On the right part of the figure, you can also see the Particle Generation rollout.

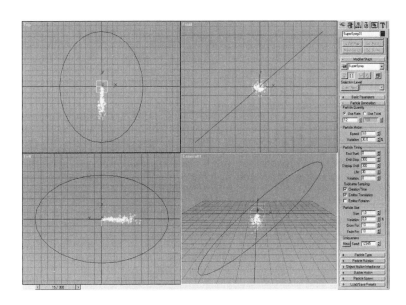

After finishing this part of the exercise, the scene you just created should resemble Figure 13.3 on the previous page. You now have set up the Particle system. The next part of the exercise will be the definition of the particle type and material.

Setting the Particle Type

In 3D Studio MAX R2, you now have several possibilities when setting the shape of the emitting particles. Normally it is sufficient to choose one of the Standard particles:

- **Triangle.** Used with Noise opacity or other Procedural mapping, it can create dust, steam, or smoke.

- **Special.** Each particle consists of three intersecting 2D squares. This particle type is very effective when using a face-mapped material along with an opacity map to create the effect of a three-dimensional particle. It can be used to simulate bubbles, snowflakes, or ticker-tape.

- **Facing.** Each particle is rendered as a square that always faces the view. This particle type is very good to use to save rendering time when simulating the movement of a multitude of objects. For example, if you want to create an asteroid field but you do not want to render hundreds of rock objects, you can create some rock objects for the foreground and a Particle system with the Facing particle type for the background. The only extra work you have to do is create some rock textures for the particle material. You can even create an animated texture of a tumbling rock and create a multitude of moving asteroids.

- **Tetra.** Good for raindrops, sparks, or fairy dust.

You can also choose metaparticles, which are almost identical to metaballs. They consist of small spheres that possess properties such as viscosity and surface tension. These properties control how the particles are merged together, and they can be animated. This particle type can be used for spraying or liquid effects, although it is not very effective to use in a production environment because Particle systems are not multithreaded, and metaparticles, especially lots of them, take a long time to render.

The third and last way to shape your particles is to use Instanced geometry, which you will explore in a later exercise in which you animate a Particle system that creates a swarm of bees flying along a path. For now, you will continue to create fairy dust, using standard particles.

SHAPING THE EMITTING PARTICLES WITH STANDARD PARTICLES

1. Open the Particle Type rollout and make sure Default Standard Particles is selected. Under Standard Particles, select Tetra. Tetra is rendered as a mapped tetrahedron, whose tail points toward the normal vector of the emission and whose head points away. Notice that most of the other rollouts are disabled. They are used only with the other Particle types.

2. Open the Material Editor and select the first samples slot (64 color fairy), if it is not already selected. It is a multi-sub object material consisting of 64 different colored, self-illuminating standard materials. The Material Effect Channel is set to 0 by default. Because you will later apply a highlight effect to the Particle system by using Video Post Image Effects, it is necessary to designate the material for use in the video postprocessing by changing its value to 1. Click on the 0 and change the value to 1 in the flyout.

TIP

When using multiple sub-object materials, each particle is assigned a different Material ID number according to the number of Material IDs in the multiple sub-object. Each particle that is emitted gets a new material and cycles through in a loop.

3. Make sure the Super Spray icon is selected. Click the Assign Material to Selection button to assign the material to the Particle system icon and close the Material Editor.

4. Under Mat'l Mapping and Source, click the Get Materials From: button to update the particles to the newly assigned material. All other parameters can be left at their default values.

5. Save the scene.

NOTE

Any time you change the Particle material in your scene, you must click the Get Materials From: button to update the Particle material selection.

You have now set up the particle type and assigned the material to the Particle system. Now it is time to send the dummy on its way along the path.

Sending the Dummy Along the Path

In this part of the exercise, you will animate the Particle system. You will link the Super Spray Particle system to a dummy that will be animated over a circular path.

SENDING THE DUMMY ALONG THE PATH

1. Continue with the previous scene. Select the dummy and go into the Motion panel. Open the Assign Controller rollout and select Position. Assign a Path Position Controller to the Dummy object.

2. Click the Pick Path button and select circle01.

TIP

Use the H key to select the object.

3. Check the Follow and Bank boxes. Leave all other parameters at their default values and align the y-axis of the dummy to the path by checking the Y box under Axis. Make sure that the scene looks like the one in Figure 13.4.

4. Save the scene.

Adding Highlights

Take a look at the prerendered file 13avi01.avi. It does not look very spectacular at all. Therefore, it would be good to add a final effect to the Particle system. Because we want to accomplish Fairy Dust in this exercise, it seems only logical to add highlights.

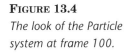

FIGURE 13.4

The look of the Particle system at frame 100.

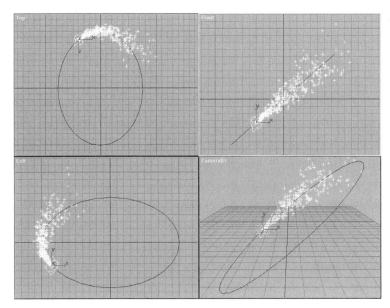

ADDING HIGHLIGHTS

1. Continue with the previous scene. Open Video Post.

2. Add a Scene event of camera01 with the range of 0–300 and click OK.

3. Add an Image Filter event and select Lens Effects Highlight. Do not click the Setup button here; instead click OK. If you want to use the Video Post Queue Preview feature of the Lens Effects filters, you have to add the event to the queue first and then reenter it for the initial setup.

4. Now reenter the Image Event panel for Lens Effects Hilight and click the Setup button.

5. Click the VP Queue and Preview buttons. After a few seconds, you see your scene on the Preview screen.

6. Drag the Time slider to frame 250 (or set the time to 250 and then press Enter). The screen will be updated and you will see the Particle system at frame 250. Press the Update button, and you will see the scene after a few seconds in the Preview screen.

7. Under Properties, select Material ID 1 as the source. The Effects
Channel of the material you previously assigned to the Particle system
(64 color fairy) has already been set to 1. By default, it is set to 0.

8. Under Geometry, click the Vary Size and the Rotate Distance buttons.
This guarantees that the routine will vary the size of the applied highlights. The Rotate Distance results in spinning highlights when the
particles move away from the camera.

9. Under Preferences, make sure that the Effect size is set at a value of 10
with four points. The Color must be set to Pixel. Because the Particle
system is sometimes moving away from the camera, it is good to set a
value for Distance Fade. Click the Size button and set a value of 500.
You can also load the file 13lzh01.lzh by clicking the Load button. See
Figure 13.5 for reference.

FIGURE 13.5

*The Setup window for
the Lens Effects
Hilight.*

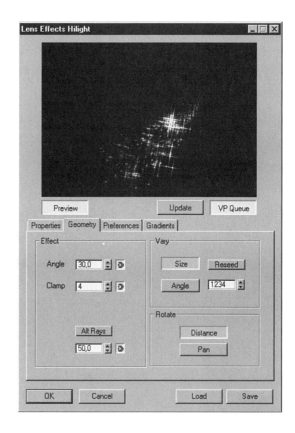

10. Click OK to return to the Video Post queue.

You can either render the queue to AVI or load the 13avi02.avi file from the CD-ROM.

Creating a PArray Particle System

The PArray Particle system is a new feature in 3D Studio MAX R2. Its power lies in its capability to use any geometric mesh object for the distribution of the emitting particles. The new Spawn Particle feature will also give you more enhancement to the final visual effect of the Particle system. This feature gives you the capability to set parameters for the creation of even more particles. For example, it is possible to create new particles when the original ones die or collide with deflectors.

In the following exercise, you will create a PArray Particle system to produce the explosion of a firework rocket and also explore the new Particle Spawn feature to create trails of moving particles. In addition, you will see the effects of gravity bound to the Particle system. As in the previous exercise, you will finish the scene by applying the Glow effect onto the Particle system.

CREATING AN EXPLOSION WITH A PARRAY PARTICLE SYSTEM

1. Load the file 13max02.max from the CD-ROM. It already contains a camera and two spheres that will be used later as emitters for the Particle systems.

2. Create a PArray Particle system in the Front viewport.

3. Select PArray01 and open the Modifier panel to change its parameters.

4. The first thing you have to do is select an emitter for the Particle system. Particle arrays always need a geometrical object as an emitter. Click the Pick Object button and select sphere01.

5. Under Particle Formation, you can determine how Standard particles are distributed over the surface of the object-based emitter. Select At All Vertices.

6. Set the value of Percentage of Particles to 100 percent.

NOTE

To see the different particle emission patterns, set all three spinners under the Particle Motion area to 0. Select Region Zoom and zoom onto sphere01 in the Front viewport. Drag the Frame slider to frame 1 and then choose the various Particle Formation options.

7. Open the Particle Generation rollout. This time you will animate a burst of particles. Under Particle Quantity, select Use Total and set the value to 100. This specifies that the Particle system emits a number of 100 particles during Emit Start and Stop.

8. Because the burst should be rather slow, set a low value of 1 under Particle Motion Speed. To add a little variation to the speed, set the Variation value to 50 percent. Leave the divergence at the Default value.

9. Next set the Particle timing. Because you want to animate a short burst, leave the Emit Start value at frame 0 and set the Emit Stop value to frame 15.

10. Leave the value for the Display Until on 100 and set the Life to 101. The lifetime for the Particle system is now exactly 100 frames.

11. The last thing you have to set within the Particle Generation rollout is the size of the particles. Set it at a value of 2 and leave all the other parameters at their default values.

12. Make sure that the Particle type is set to Standard particles and choose Tetra.

13. Under Mat'l Mapping and Source, select the Picked Emitter option and click the Get Material From: button to update the Particle system material. A predefined material is already assigned to the emitter sphere01.

NOTE

Always remember to click the Get Material From: button whenever you choose a different source, assign a new source, or change the old material to the specified source.

14. Under the Particle Rotation rollout, leave the Spin Speed Control values at 0. Select the option Direction of Travel/Mblur to make sure that the Tetras always face the traveling direction.

15. Open the Load/Save Presets rollout and type Firework into the Preset Name: text box. Now click the Save button and the previous given name appears in the Saved Presets area.

For reference, take a look at Figure 13.6. The scene you just created should resemble this image.

FIGURE 13.6

In this figure, you can see what the scene should look like at frame 30.

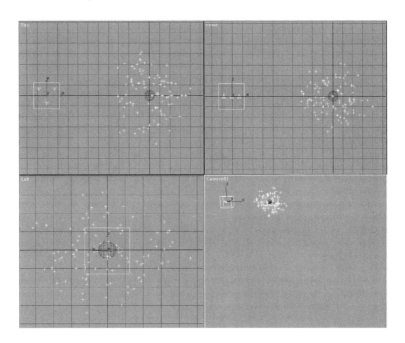

The Particle Spawn Feature

In the Particle Spawn rollout, you can specify what will happen to your particles when they die or collide with a deflector. It is possible to create new generations upon collision or death. In this exercise, you will create trails of the parent particle.

CREATING TRAILS OF THE PARENT PARTICLE WITH THE PARTICLE SPAWN FEATURE

1. Continue with the scene from the previous exercise.

2. Open the Particle Spawn rollout. Under Particle Spawning Effects, select Spawn Trails.

3. Set the Affects spinner to 50 percent. Selecting 100 percent would create too many particles.

4. Under Speed Chaos, check the Inherit Parent Velocity check box. Now the spawned particles inherit the speed of their parents.

In Figure 13.7, you can see the Particle Spawn rollout after setting the parameters for this PArray Particle system.

FIGURE 13.7

The Particle Spawn rollout for the PArray Particle system.

5. Create a second PArray Particle system and enter the Load/Save Presets rollout. Under Saved Presets you see your previously saved Firework. Double-click it and the saved parameters will be loaded. Now this Particle system has the same parameters as the first one, but without the trails.

6. Open the Basic Parameters rollout and click the Pick Object button. Select sphere02 as the emitter.

7. Open the Particle Generation rollout and change the Particle timing so that Start equals 30, Stop equals 45, and Display Until equals 130. To get a slightly different look, click the New button under Uniqueness. Finally, do not forget to update the PArray material.

8. Save the scene.

Now select the Camera viewport and play the animation. The trails are straight lines moving in the initial direction of their emission. Because this looks pretty unrealistic, it would be good to add a gravitational effect (see Figure 13.8).

FIGURE 13.8

The two Particle systems at frame 75 without gravity.

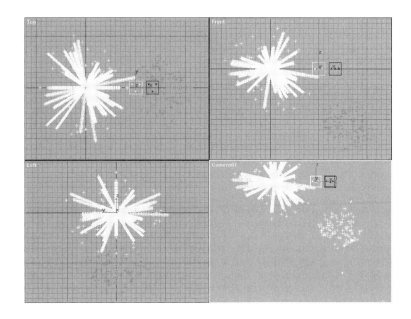

Adding a Gravitational Effect

The Gravity space warp can be used in two ways. If you want to simulate a gravity like you experience on earth, you assign it as a planar gravity force that will pull everything toward the arrow of the Space Warp icon. A spherical Gravity space warp pulls everything to the center of the Space Warp icon; this resembles the force that is experienced in space when you approach a heavenly body.

In this part of the exercise, you will add a little more realism to the explosion by binding the Particle system to a Gravity space warp.

BINDING THE PARTICLE SYSTEM TO A GRAVITY SPACE WARP

1. Continue with the scene from the previous exercise.

2. Create a Gravity space warp in the Top viewport. It is necessary to create it in that viewport because we want the arrow of the icon pointing down the y-axis. If you create the Gravity space warp in any other viewport, rotate the icon until the arrow points down the y-axis.

3. Set the strength of the Gravity space warp to 0.01. We just want to have a slight gravitational effect on the two Particle systems.

4. Select the two PArray Particle systems, click the Bind to Space Warps button, and select the Gravity space warp.

NOTE

You can bind any number of Particle systems to a space warp simultaneously by selecting them all and dragging to the space warp.

Once again, select the Camera viewport and play the animation. This looks better and more like two firework explosions (see Figure 13.9).

FIGURE 13.9

The two Particle systems at frame 75 with Gravity applied to them.

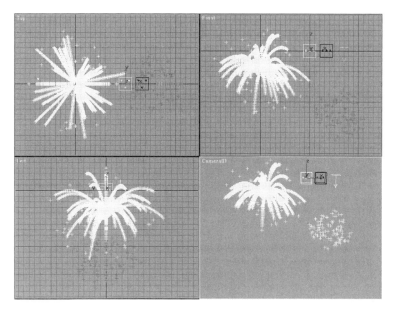

Okay, let's return to the materials that are assigned to the Particle systems.

5. Open the Material Editor and select the second material (Firework 2). Under Maps you can see that a Particle Age map is assigned to Diffuse. With the Particle Age map you can alter the color (or map) of a particle based on its life duration. Particles begin with one color and start to change at a specified age (by interpolation) to a second color. Finally they change again to a third and last color before they die.

6. Open the Track View and expand the Medit Materials—Firework 1 label and its parameters. You can see that the Diffuse color is animated over time in the same manner as the Particle Age map of the material Firework 2. You have to do it like this because spawned particles are not affected by the Particle Age map. For reference, take a look at Figure 13.10, which shows the Track View for the PArray Particle system Firework 1.

7. Save the scene.

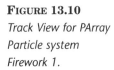

FIGURE 13.10

Track View for PArray Particle system Firework 1.

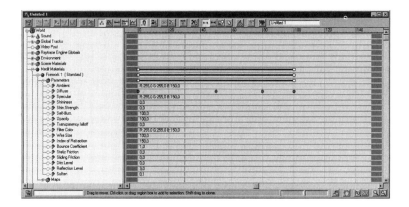

Adding a Glow to the Video Post Queue

You will add a final effect to the two Particle systems: a Glow in the Video Post queue. Glow adds a glowing aura around any assigned object and will make the exploding Particle system in this exercise appear to be brighter and hotter.

ADDING A GLOW EFFECT

1. Continue with the scene from the previous exercise.

2. Go into the Properties panel of PArray01 and set the G-Buffer Object channel to 1. Do the same for PArray02 and set the Object channel to 2.

3. Open Video Post.

4. Add a Scene event of camera01 with the range of 0–150 and click OK.

5. Add an Image Filter event and select Lens Effects Glow. Do not click the Setup button here; instead click OK. If you want to use the Video Post Queue Preview feature of the Lens Effects filters, you have to add the event to the queue first and then reenter it for the initial setup.

6. Now re-enter the Image Event panel for Lens Effects Glow and click the Setup button.

7. Click the VP Queue and Preview buttons. After a few seconds, you will see your scene on the Preview screen. In Figure 13.11, you can see the Lens Effects Glow Setup window after defining the parameters for the PArray Particle system Firework 1.

FIGURE 13.11

In this figure, you can see the scene you just created at frame 50. You can also see the Lens Effects Glow Setup window for the PArray Particle system Firework 1.

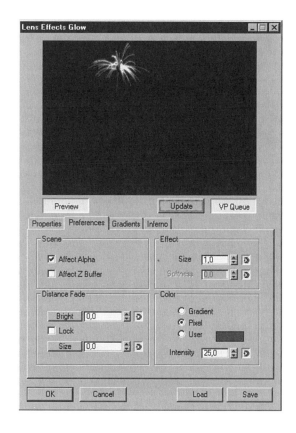

8.   Drag the Time slider to frame 50 (or set the time to 50 and then press the Return button). The screen is updated and you see the Particle system at frame 50.

9.   Under Properties, select Object ID 1 as the source.

10. Under Preferences, set the Size value to 1. Make sure that Color is set to Pixel and Intensity is set to 25. You can also load the file 13lzg01.lzg by clicking the Load button.

11. Click OK to return to the Video Post queue.

12. Add a second Image Filter event and again select Lens Effects Glow.

13. Click the Setup button.

14. Click the VP Queue and Preview buttons. After a few seconds you see your scene on the Preview screen.

15. Drag the Time slider to frame 75 (or set the time to 75 and then press the Return button). The screen is updated and you see the Particle system at frame 75.

16. Under Properties, select Object ID 2 as the source.

17. Under Preferences, set the Size value to 1. Make sure that Color is set to Pixel and set a value of 100 for Intensity. You can also load the file 13lzg02.lzg by clicking the Load button. Take a look at Figure 13.12. It shows the Lens Effects Glow window for the PArray Particle system Firework 2.

FIGURE 13.12

The Lens Effects Glow window for the PArray Particle system Firework 2.

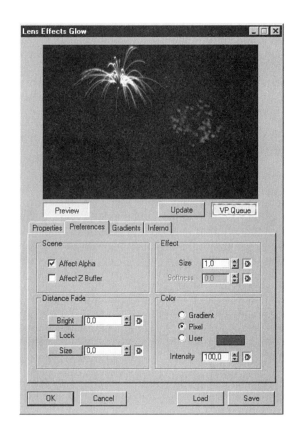

18. Click OK to return to the Video Post queue.

You can either render the Video Post queue or load 13avi03.avi that comes with the CD-ROM.

Creating Object Explosions

In the following exercise, you will learn how to create object explosions. You will use Particle arrays, gravitation, and deflectors. You are also going to apply some workarounds to avoid some PArray limitations in the Particle Fragment Collision Detection and the missing Particle Spinning Decay.

SETTING UP THE PARTICLE SYSTEM

1. Load the file 13max03.max from the CD-ROM. This file contains a camera, an exploding egg, a logo (inside the egg), and a floor. If you play the animation, you will notice that some animations are included as well. The egg disappears at frame 5 and the logo grows until frame 15.

It will be your task in this exercise to animate the bursting of the egg and control the falling, rotation, and collision of the object fragments during the animation.

2. Create a PArray Particle system in the Front viewport.

3. Enter the Modify panel.

4. Under Basic Parameters Object-Based Emitter, click the Pick Object button and select the egg.

5. Select the Mesh option under Viewport Display. After choosing the right Particle type, you will be able to see the object fragments in the viewport display.

6. Before you set the Particle Generation parameters, you first define the Particle type. Open the Particle Type rollout and select Object Fragments.

7. Now you set the Object Fragment controls. Set Thickness to 10 and Number of Chunks to a value of 35 minimum. The object egg is now broken into irregular fragments with a minimum of 35 fragments.

8. Under Mat'l Mapping and Source, select the Picked Emitter option. The Particle system gets the Chrome material from the egg. Click the Get Material From: button to update the Particle system.

NOTE

You can even set different material IDs to Outside, Edge, and Backside of the fragments. It is then possible to assign a Multi-Sub Object material to the Particle system. For instance, if you want to animate the bursting of a spaceship, you can assign an outside and inside material to represent the inside and outside of the ship. It is also possible to assign a material to the edges that can be glowed in Video Post to produce the effect of the heat of the explosion.

9. Open the Particle Generation rollout. You can leave Speed at a value of 10. Make sure that the fragments do not move at the same speed by setting Variation spinner to a value of 30 percent.

10. Set Emit Start to frame 5. The original object becomes invisible at this frame. Also set the Life of the particles to a higher value than the length of the animation to make sure that the fragments do not disappear. Set Life to 101.

11. Open the Particle Rotation rollout. Under Spin Speed controls, set Spin Time to 20 and add a Variation of 30 percent. This defines that it will take a fragment 20 frames to rotate plus/minus 30 percent.

Leave the Spin Axis control at the default value Random. The spin axis for each fragment is now randomly chosen, which will look more realistic. Save the scene.

You have created the setup for the Particle system. The scene you just created should resemble Figure 13.13.

FIGURE 13.13

The scene at frame 10. Under the Modify panel for the PArray Particle system, you can also see the Particle Type rollout with the Object Fragment Control parameters.

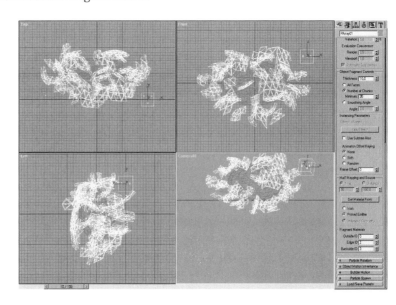

Adding Space Warps to Enhance Realism

To make your explosion scene obey the physical laws of nature, you need to add space warps. The following exercise continues from the scene in the previous exercise, adding the Gravity and Deflector space warps for greater realism.

ADDING SPACE WARPS

1. Continue with the scene from the previous exercise.

2. Create a Gravity space warp in the Top viewport. Because you want the fragments to fall down, the pointing arrow of the gravity icon has to point down the y-axis.

3. Also create a Deflector space warp that has the same planar size as the floor. Move it to a position that is roughly like the one in Figure 13.14. Change the Bounce parameter to 0.5. The object fragments then bounce off the Deflector at half the speed they struck it with.

FIGURE 13.14

The position of the Deflector in your scene. Here you can see the fragments at frame 75. Notice how they pass through the Deflector.

NOTE

It does not matter which way the Deflector is facing because particles bounce off either side of a Deflector. You can witness this by rotating the Deflector 180 degrees.

continues

Because the object fragments are deflected based on the particle's location, which is the center of the object fragment, it is possible that fragments sink into the floor. It is not possible at the moment to correct this, but by lifting the Deflector slightly above the floor, you can correct it a little.

4. Select the PArray Particle system and bind it to the two space warps in the scene—Gravity and Deflector.

Select the Camera viewport and play the animation. You will notice that the fragments continue to spin around after they come to a rest. Because Kinetix did not provide a Rotation Decay parameter, you will animate this effect yourself in the following part of the exercise.

5. Open the Track View and expand the PArray01 track. Now expand the Object (PArray) track. Almost every parameter of the PArray Particle system can be animated, but you are only interested in the Spin Time parameters.

6. Set keys for Spin Time as follows: frame 0 = 20, frame 30 = 20 ease-out, frame 75 = 200 ease-in, frame 76 = 0. Set the keys for Spin Time Variation as follows: frame 0 = 25, 30 = 25 step out, frame 76 = 0 step in.

7. Close the Track View, select the Camera viewport, and play the animation again. You will notice that the fragments come to rest after 76 frames.

8. Save the scene.

   You just completed the animation, but before you render the animation you might want to add a little spice to the final image with Motion blur.

Adding Motion Blur to the Animation

Motion blur can add quite a bit to your final animation, and in 3D Studio MAX R2, it is now a very fast and easy process to add to Particle systems. There are two ways to add Motion blur to Particle systems that are fast to render:

■ Under the Particle Rotation rollout, check Direction of Travel Direction/Mblur. Stretch must then be set to a value higher than zero.

It is also necessary to add the Particle Mblur map to the Opacity mapping of the Particle system's material.

■ The other method is Image Motion blur. Right-click the Particle system and enter the object properties. Under Motion blur, select the Image Option button. In the Render Scene dialog box, make sure that Apply Image Motion blur is checked.

In the next exercise, you will use Image Motion Blur to add Motion blur to the animation. Image Motion blur is easy to apply and provides excellent results. For more information about Motion blur, see Chapter 11, "Animating Cameras."

ADDING MOTION BLUR TO THE ANIMATION

1. Continue with the scene from the previous exercise.

2. Select and right-click the PArray object and enter its Properties panel.

3. Under Motion Blur, select the Image option—leave the Multiplier value at the default and click OK to close it.

4. Now enter the Render Scene dialog and make sure Image Motion blur is applied. You can leave the Duration (Frames) value at 0.5.

Render the animation to AVI. You can also load the prerendered file 13avi04.avi from the CD-ROM.

Sending Particles Along a Spline

In the following exercise, you will use a Particle system together with a Path Follow space warp to send particles along a spline. Used together with Instanced geometry, this creates the image of a swarm of bees flying along a certain flypath. The Instanced geometry is neither kept "upright" nor banked along the path, which means that it will not always face in the direction of travel. You have to apply a workaround to correct this. The workaround utilizes the technique of animating a dummy with a Path Controller and applies the movement of the dummy to the Mesh object that will be used as Instanced geometry by the PArray Particle system. As a result, the Mesh objects—in this case the bees—will always face the direction in which they are traveling.

Creating a Path Follow Space Warp

As you learned earlier, a Path Follow space warp forces a Particle system along a spline. You can control things like the speed at which the particles move, the rotation of the particles around the path, and how quickly the particles converge or diverge from the path.

In the following exercise, you will use the Instanced geometry particle type. When using Instanced geometry as a particle type, you are using identical instances of selected objects in your scene. It is used when animating a multitude of the same object, such as flocks of birds, swarms of bees, or even spaceships when animating effects like the ones seen in the film *Independence Day*.

USING A PATH FOLLOW SPACE WARP TO SEND PARTICLES ALONG A SPLINE

1. Load the file 13max04.max from the CD-ROM. Take a look at the included objects in the scene. You will see a spline, a circular object at the start of the spline, and a "bee."

2. Create a Path Follow space warp.

3. Under Basic Parameters, click the Pick Shape Object button and select the spline Path01.

4. Leave the Unlimited Range box checked. With this, you determine that all particles are bound to the path, regardless of their distance from the Path spline.

5. Under Particle Motion, make sure the default option Along Parallel Splines is selected. The particles now follow a copy of the selected path, parallel to the Particle system. The position of the Path object is not important, but the orientation of the path alters the movement of the particles.

6. If you want the particles to move at a constant speed along the path, you have to check the Constant Speed box. You also have to make sure that you later check the Constant Velocity box in the Path controller of the Dummy object you create later in this exercise. Leave the other Particle Motion parameters at their default values.

7. Set the Motion Timing. These parameters determine how fast the particles move along the Path object. Leave the Start Frame at 0 and set the Travel Time to 150. Now it takes a particle 150 frames to move from the start to the end of the path. Leave the Variation at 0 and set the Last Frame to 150.

Now it is time to create the Particle system.

8. Create a PArray Particle system.

9. Under Basic Parameters Object-Based Emitter, click the Pick Object button and select Emitter01.

10. Leave the Particle Formation at the Default option Over Entire Surface.

11. Select the option Mesh under Viewport Display. The particles now are displayed as Mesh objects, and after you choose the bee as Instanced geometry, you will be able to see the swarm moving along the path.

12. To see all particles, set the Percentage of Particles spinner to 100 percent.

Make sure your scene resembles Figure 13.15.

FIGURE 13.15
Make sure your scene resembles the scene shown in this figure before you continue with the exercise.

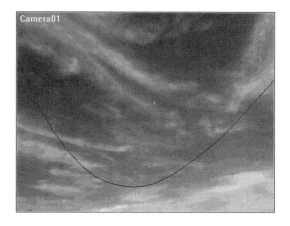

Before you set the Particle Generation parameters, you first set the Particle type.

13. Open the Particle Type rollout and choose the option Instanced Geometry.

14. Under Instancing Parameters, click the Pick Object button and select the object bee01. Because the objects LeftWing01 and RightWing01 are linked to Bee01, you want these objects to be included as well. Therefore, check the Use Subtree box.

It is also possible to use animated objects as Instanced geometry. With Animation Offset Keying, you can specify the timing of the animation for the particles. This is also imperative regarding the rotation of the bee that you will apply later.

15. Choose Birth as Offset Keying. Because the animation of the Source object is a rotation from 0 to 90 degrees along the z-axis and the first particle is born at frame 0, when the wings are in an upper position, then that particle and all subsequent particles are born starting with this position and rotation.

Figure 13.16 shows the Particle Type rollout for the PArray Particle system.

FIGURE 13.16

The Particle Type roll-out for the PArray Particle system.

16. To guarantee that the mappings are taken from the object, make sure that the option Instanced Geometry is selected under Mat'l Mapping and Source. To update the Particle system's material, click the Get Material From: button.

Next, return to the Particle Generation parameters.

17. Set the Use Total value to 50 under Particle Quantity. Now a total number of 50 bees is emitted by the Particle system.

18. Leave the Particle Motion speed at the default value of 10 and change the Variation to 50 percent.

19. It is necessary to set the Particle Timing to the same values as the moving parameters along the Path Follow space warp. Therefore, set Emit Stop to 150, Display to 150, and Life to 150. Leave the Variation at 0.

20. Set Particle Size to 2 and Variation to 50 percent.

21. Leave all other parameters at their default values.

22. Now select the PArray Particle system and bind it to the Path Follow space warp.

23. Select the Top viewport and play the animation. You will see that the bees move along the path, but they will not keep looking into the traveling direction (see Figure 13.17).

FIGURE 13.17

The orientation of the bees with Random selected under Spin Axis Control.

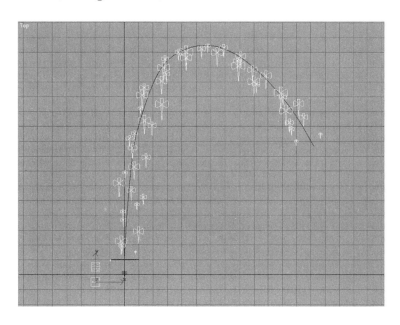

Go back to the PArray parameters and open the Rotation rollout. Select the Direction of Travel/Mblur option under Spin Axis Control. The effect that you see is not quite what you would expect from a swarm of bees (see Figure 13.18).

Save the scene.

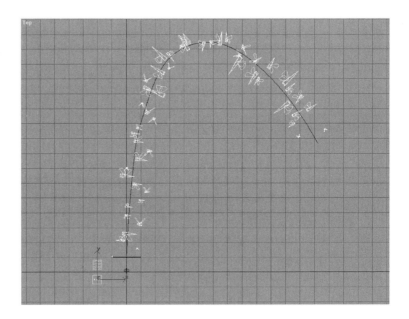

Because it is not possible to tell the particles to look in the "right" direction by normal means, we have to apply a little workaround.

Before you move to the next part of the exercise, however, it is very important that you reset the Spin Axis Control to Random.

Making the Particles Face the Traveling Direction

In this part of the exercise, you will apply a workaround to make sure that the particles always face the direction in which they are traveling. The trick is to animate a dummy that is linked to the source object you previously selected as Instanced Geometry Particle Type. The transforms of the dummy will be inherited by the linked object and will use the Bank and Follow features of the Path Controller of the dummy, which cannot be applied to the Particle system by using only the Path Follow space warp.

USING A WORKAROUND

1. Continue with the scene from the previous exercise.

2. Create a dummy in the Front viewport.

3. Enter the Motion panel and open the Assign Controller rollout.

4. Select Position and assign a Path Position controller to it.

5. In the Path Parameters rollout, click the Pick Path button and select the spline Path01.

6. Check the Follow and the Bank box. Also check the Constant Velocity box if you checked the corresponding box in the Path Follow space warp.

7. Select the Bee01 object and open the Hierarchy panel.

8. Click the Link Info button. Make sure that all boxes are unchecked under Inherit Move. The bee stays at the World center and only inherits the rotational translation of the dummy.

9. Link the object Bee01 to the dummy.

10. Select the Camera viewport and play the animation. The bees are now always facing in the right direction (see Figure 13.19).

FIGURE 13.19

The orientation of the bees with the inherited animation of the linked dummy.

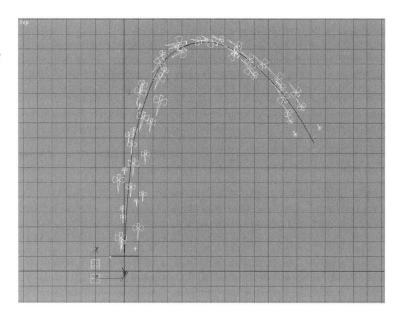

Before you render the animation to an AVI, you can merge more swarms of bees.

11. Merge the file 13max04a.max and select All. A dialog box appears, asking you if you want to use the Scene or the Merged materials. Leave the options alone—the materials are exactly the same in both files—and click OK.

T IP

To speed up your work when creating a scene in the viewport, make use of Named Selection sets. It is also possible to control the percentage of visible particles in the viewport.

When selecting Hidden Named selections, a dialog box will come up, asking whether you want to unfreeze/unhide the objects in the Named Selection. If you answer yes, the Named Selection is unhidden and selected. By answering no, the Named Selection remains invisible but is selected.

Add Image Motion blur to the scene. It is also possible to add Object Motion blur to the wings, but that would consume more render time.

12. Select all PArray Particle systems, right-click the selection, and enter the Properties panel.

13. Under Motion Blur, select Image. Leave the Multiplier at the default value of one. Click OK.

14. Enter the Render Scene panel and make sure that the Apply box under Image Motion blur is checked. Leave the Duration (frames) at 0.5.

Render the animation to AVI. You can also load 13avi05.avi from the CD-ROM.

Creating Bubbles

In the following exercise, you will create bubbles emitting from a tablet in a glass. To add more realism to the scene, you will make a little excursion into the wonderful world of Dynamic Simulations, which you will learn about in the next section, to add movement to the tablet.

CREATING BUBBLES

1. Load the file 13max05.max from the CD-ROM. The following objects are already included in the scene: the glass, the liquid, and the floor.

2. Create a cone with the following values: Radius 1 = 25, Radius 2 = 50, and Height = 100. You can leave all other values at their defaults.

3. Place the cone at the same position as shown in Figure 13.20.

FIGURE 13.20

The placement of the collision cone in your scene.

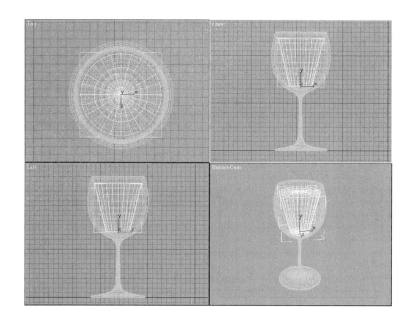

4. Add a Normal modifier to the cone and check the Flip Normals box.

NOTE

Because you will use the cone as a Deflector and the bubbles will be inside the cone, you have to flip the normals so that the collision with the Particle system will be detected.

Do not forget to hide the Deflector object cone01 before you finally render your scene.

5. Create a cylinder in the Top viewport with the following values: Radius = 20, Height = 10. Position the cylinder as shown in Figure 13.21.

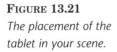

FIGURE 13.21

The placement of the tablet in your scene.

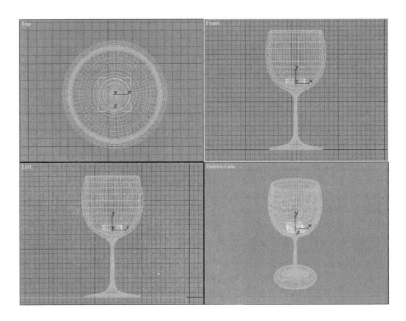

6. Open the Material Editor and select the first slot if it is not already selected (Tablet). Assign it to the cylinder.

7. Create a UDeflector space warp.

8. Click the Pick Object button and select Cone01. Leave all Particle Bounce parameters at their default values.

9. Create a PCloud Particle system.

10. Open the Material editor and select the second material slot (Bubble Substitute). Assign it to the PCloud Particle system.

11. Under Particle Formation, select Object-Based Emitter. Then click the Pick Object button and select the object Cylinder01 as emitter.

12. To see all particles that will be emitted by the Particle system, set the Percentage of Particles to 100 percent.

Now define the parameters for the Particle Generation.

13. Because bubbles are a continuous stream of particles (until the tablet is used up), choose Use Rate under Particle Quantity and set the value to 3.

14. Under Particle Motion, set the Speed value to 5 with a Variation of 50 percent.

15. Select Enter Vector and enter the following values: X = 0, Y = 0, and Z = 1. With this, you have determined that the particles emit along the z-axis, which in this case is upward.

NOTE

The Pivot point of the PCloud icon is taken as reference, but it is also possible to use a Reference object.

16. Define the values for the Particle timing. The Emit Start value should be set to 0, the Emit Stop to 200, Display Until set to 200, and Life set to 201.

17. Set the Particle Size to 1 with a Variation of 50 percent.

18. Now it is time to set the Particle type. Choose Standard Particles and Constant Type. For this animation, you do not need to use a special mapping for the bubbles.

TIP

If you want to animate bubbles nearer to the camera, you can use Facing Standard particles and map a Bubble texture onto it.

19. Under Mat'l Mapping and Source, make sure that the Option icon is selected. Press the Update Material button to assign the Bubble material to the Particle system.

20. Leave the Particle Rotation and the Object Motion Inheritance values at their default.

21. Open the Bubble Motion rollout.

22. Set the Amplitude to 5 with a Variation of 30 percent. Set the Period to 50 with a Variation of 50 percent. Set the Phase to 10 degrees with a Variation of 50 percent.

23. Open the Particle Spawn rollout and select the Die on Collision option.

24. Bind the PCloud Particle system to the UDeflector space warp.

25. Select the Camera viewport and play the animation.

26. Save the scene you just created. You will continue with this file in the next part of the chapter.

You can see that the movement of the Particle system is okay, but because the tablet is not moving at all, it looks rather unrealistic. The next part of the chapter introduces you to the Dynamic Utility, which is now included in 3D Studio MAX R2. After the short introduction, you will continue with this scene to create the movement for the tablet.

NOTE

Notice that there are no sampling controls for the different Deflector types in 3D Studio MAX R2. Therefore, it is possible that some particles might pass the Deflector (see Figure 13.22).

FIGURE 13.22

Here you can see a particle pass the Deflector. If you really need to, you can create a second, slightly bigger Deflector to catch the passing particles.

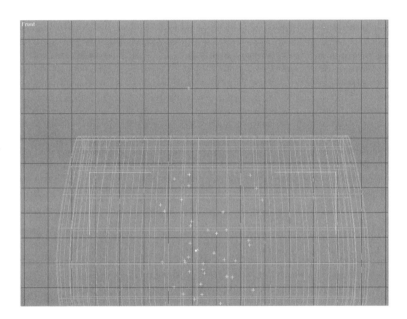

Dynamic Simulations

It takes a great deal of time to create a classic keyframe animation of physical motion for objects, and often the results are unsatisfactory. With the help of Dynamic Simulations, however, it is possible to automatically create realistic motions of geometric objects by simulating their physical properties and applying the natural laws of physical motion. The calculations of these Dynamic Simulations take object properties such as mass, weight, and flexibility into account, as well as external forces such as gravity, friction, and collisions between objects. It is also possible to combine these simulations with other animation techniques such as Inverse Kinematic or basic keyframe animation, which makes it very easy to manipulate the animations or motion trajectories of the objects created by the simulation. Basically, a Dynamic Simulation calculates the position and rotation of an object with a specific mass as it is influenced by an external force.

Note

Dynamic Simulations in 3D Studio MAX R2 are calculated based on a certain length of time at the NTSC frame rate of 30 frames per second. It is possible to solve the animation by using, for example, the PAL frame rate of 24 frames per second, but remember that it will create sub-frames.

Physical Properties of Objects

Due to the existing physical laws, the mass of an object is the property that influences a Dynamic Simulation the most. In the Dynamic Utility of 3D Studio MAX R2, it is sufficient to change the density of the object, because the mass is calculated by the values of the density and volume.

Although it is only possible to solve simulations of rigid objects, you can simulate physical object characteristics like elasticity and stiffness by assigning a Bounce coefficient. This value influences the calculation whenever the object collides with another.

If you want to animate two balls, for instance, one made of steel and one made of rubber, the one made of steel is extremely stiff and heavy and, when colliding with the floor, does not bounce very high. This represents a low Bounce coefficient. The ball made of rubber is also stiff but more elastic. It bounces higher and, therefore, has a high Bounce coefficient. If you want to simulate objects that can deform or have special physical properties, however, you still have to use plug-ins like HyperMatter or ClothReyes:

■ **HyperMatter.** HyperMatter controls the deformation of objects by applying the external forces onto a flexible Lattice that controls the objects' vertices. Theoretically, it would be possible to animate a drop of liquid that collides with an object and—due to its physical properties and its acceleration—bounces off of it again. HyperMatter can calculate the deformation of the object and the absorption of the applied forces due to its physical properties.

■ **ClothReyes.** It is possible to assign fabric properties to objects with this plug-in. Therefore, it is possible to cover a car with a blanket. This blanket is mapped with the last-year version of the same type of car.

A character, virtual or real, now pulls the blanket off the car to reveal the new-year model. It is also possible to assign an external force like wind onto the blanket to blow it off the car. Under normal circumstances, it would be impossible to animate an object like this. With the help of ClothReyes, however, it is possible by setting a few Object and Dynamic parameters.

Different Types of Forces

Several types of forces can be applied to objects in a Dynamic Simulation. It is possible to put them roughly into the following three categories:

- **Linear Forces.** These forces have an effect in only one direction. Gravity, for example, is a linear force.

- **Radial Forces.** This corresponds to the PBomb space warp, which applies a force from one point, like rays in all directions. You can compare this force to an explosion.

- **Conic Forces.** This corresponds to forces that are high at their starting point and decrease as the distance increases. An example of this type of force would be the Wind space warp with a Decay value either lower or greater than 0.

These forces can be applied to objects globally or locally. A Gravity space warp that affects all objects included in the simulation is a global force. A collision between two objects and the forces that are applied during this collision is a local force, because it is only locally affecting the involved objects at the time of the collision.

Other physical properties like friction and air resistance can also affect the outcome of a Dynamic Simulation. Friction is always happening when two surfaces rub together. It is also important to take the air resistance into account, because objects under water are affected by a different type of resistance than objects moving in a vacuum.

Collision Detection

Detecting collisions between objects involved in a Dynamic Simulation is a very powerful technique that is applied to an animator's scene by a Dynamic Utility. Real-world objects react in a natural way to collisions by deforming and changing the direction of speed and motion. However,

Collision Detection consumes a lot of processing time because it has to constantly check the Position and Dynamic properties of all involved objects in order to avoid intersections between objects.

ADDING MOVEMENT TO THE TABLET

1. Continue with the file you created in the last part of the chapter or open the file 13max07.max.

Because you will utilize gravity to create the motion for the tablet, it is important to create a Gravity space warp in this scene.

2. Select the Top viewport and create a Gravity space warp to make sure that the arrow of the icon is pointing down.

3. Open the Utilities panel and select the Dynamics button.

4. In the Dynamics rollout, click the New button and name the new simulation Tablet Simulation.

5. Under Objects in Simulation, click the Edit Object list. In this dialog box, you can either include or exclude objects from your simulation. Include Cone01 (the object you previously used as UDeflector for the Particle system) and the Cylinder01 (the tablet).

Now assign some physical properties necessary for the Dynamic Simulation.

6. Click the Edit Object button.

7. Under Object, select Cone01. Make this object immovable by checking the This Object is Immovable box under Misc Dynamic Controls.

NOTE

If there are no objects to be selected, it is possible that you forgot to include or exclude your objects in the simulation. Close the Edit Object dialog box and go back to the Edit Object list to select some objects to be included in your simulation.

8. Because there is no appropriate standard collision test shape, select the Mesh type.

9. Under Assign Effects/Collisions, click the Assign Object Effects. Here you can include or exclude Object Effects, like Gravity and Wind Push. Exclude the Gravity warp.

NOTE

You do not have to bind space warps to the objects when using them in a Dynamic Simulation. Just assign them in the Dynamic Utility under Edit Objects.

10. The next thing to do is to define the objects that are included within the collision calculations. Click the Assign Object Collisions and include the Cylinder01 object.

NOTE

It is also possible to assign Global collisions. This results in longer calculation times because the program has to test positions and intersections of all objects at all frames defined for the Dynamic Simulation. If there are objects within your scene that never collide, use the method in which you can define the colliding objects separately.

11. Select the Cylinder01 to define its physical properties.

12. Under Misc Dynamic Controls, leave all parameters at their default values.

13. Make sure that Recalculate Properties is set to Never. Because the shape of the object is not changing during the animation, it is not necessary to recalculate them.

14. Set the Collision Test type to Cylinder. It is possible to test the collisions with standard type shapes like box, sphere, or cylinder. During Collision Detection, MAX only approximates the shape of the object, which results in faster calculation times. You can also use the Object mesh for Collision Detection. Although this process is more accurate, it is also more time consuming.

NOTE

Collision Detection fails if an object intersects another at the beginning of the simulation. If you want to set an object on top of another, which is a type of collision, you have to first align them so that the objects sits exactly on top of each other.

15. Open the Assign Object Effects dialog box and include the Gravity warp.

16. Open the Assign Object Collisions dialog box and include the object Cone01.

The Mass of the tablet will be at 205 kilograms (about 450 pounds). You have to check the Override Automatic Mass box because a tablet of about 200 kg is rather hard to move. Set the value to 0.05 kg. Close the box by clicking OK.

Save the scene.

Figure 13.23 shows the Edit Object dialog box of the Dynamic Utility with the parameters for the Tablet object in your scene.

FIGURE 13.23

The Edit Object dialog box of the Dynamic Utility.

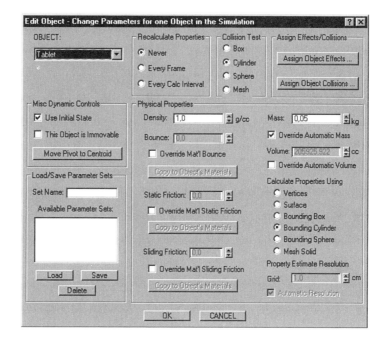

Defining the Timing of the Simulation

The next thing you will do is define the timing of the simulation. There are two important Control parameters:

- Calc Intervals Per Frame

- Keys Every N Frames

As a default, MAX calculates the simulation once per frame and creates keys for all objects included in the simulation at every frame. It is possible that, although you use meshes for Collision Detection, they will pass through each other. The only way to correct this problem is to increase the number of calculations per frame to get more accurate results.

In some simulations, the interactions of objects do not occur at every frame and a high accuracy is not necessary. Therefore, it is sufficient to change the value of Keys Every N Frames to a higher value than 1.

DEFINING THE TIMING

1. Continue with the scene from the previous exercise.

2. Open the Timing and Simulation rollout to define the start and end times of the simulation. Set the start to 0 and the end of the simulation to 200.

3. Click the Solve button to calculate the animation. You can also check the Update Display w/Solve box. You are then able to see the calculation results in the selected viewport.

TIP

If you think that the result of the simulation is either too fast or too slow, you can slow down or speed up the overall effect of the animation by applying a Linear Scale factor to the external forces that affect the objects in your Dynamic Simulation.

It is possible that the Collision Detection behaves incorrectly after speeding up your simulation. To correct this, you just have to increase the Calc Intervals Per Frame.

4. After the utility has finished solving the animation, click in the Camera viewport and play the animation. This looks more realistic.

Figure 13.24 shows the scene after solving the Dynamic Simulation.

Because the Dynamic Utility creates by default a key at every frame of the simulation, the last thing for you to do now is to reduce the keys that were created by the Dynamic Utility.

FIGURE 13.24

This is what the scene should look like after solving the Dynamic Simulation.

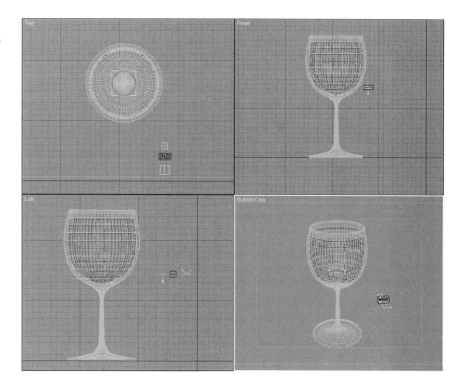

Reducing the Keys Created by the Dynamic Utility

When creating a complex Dynamic Simulation with the Dynamic Utility, the result leaves you with one key per frame for the position and rotation tracks. Often, the same animation can be produced with fewer keys. Not only is it easier to change the animation of the objects when you have fewer keys in a track, but it will also decrease your scene file size. This task can be accomplished by using the Reduce Keys tool in the Track View. Reduce Keys under Edit Time Mode analyzes the pattern of keys in the block of time and creates a new pattern of fewer keys that will result in nearly the same animation. By setting a threshold value, it is possible to specify how closely the tool will match the original animation. For instance, if you apply the key reduction to a position and a rotation track with a threshold value of 0.5, which is the default value, positions will be held within 0.5 units of the original position, and angles will be held within 0.5 degrees of the original rotation.

In the following exercise, you will reduce the keys of the animation previously created by the Dynamic Utility.

REDUCING THE NUMBER OF KEYS

1. Continue with the scene from the previous exercise.

2. Open the Track View.

3. Click the Filters button to open the Filters dialog box. Check the Animated Tracks box under Show only.

4. Right-click the Objects label and select the Expand Objects option.

5. On the Track View toolbar, click the Edit Time button.

6. While holding down the Ctrl key, click the Position and the Rotation labels of the object Cylinder01. The background color of the selected tracks becomes white.

7. Select a block of time by clicking frame 0 and then dragging the mouse to the right. While dragging, you will see two vertical yellow lines. The first line indicates the start of the selected time block; the second one follows the cursor and marks the end.

In Figure 13.25, you can see the Track View window with the two selected tracks for the Tablet object. As you can see in the Track View window, there is one key for every frame, which will be reduced in the next steps of the exercise.

FIGURE 13.25

The Track View window with the two selected tracks.

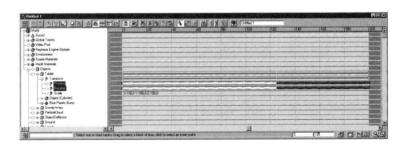

T IP

You can also set the values in the status bar of the Track View. Just click them and type the Start and End values.

8. Now click the Reduce Key button in the Track View toolbar. Accept the default threshold of 0.5 in the dialog box that comes up.

9. Close the Track View and play the animation in the Camera viewport. The animation looks like the one before the reducing of the keys. In Figure 13.26, you can see what the Track View window looks like after reducing the keys.

FIGURE 13.26

The Track View window with the tracks of the Tablet object after applying the Reduce Keys tool.

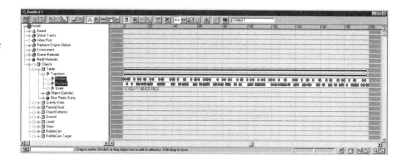

At the moment, the Dynamic Utility included in 3D Studio MAX R2 is very nice for animating effects like balls bouncing on floors or other very simple simulations. If you want to simulate more complex scenes, such as somebody playing billiards or a roulette table, the Dynamic Utility will not work because of the following:

■ **Erratic Collision Detection.** This is also a type of collision in which you set an object on another and make it stay there for the duration of the simulation—assuming that you assigned Gravity as external force to the involved objects. To make this type of collision work, you have to align the objects.

For example, pretend you have a table and three piled-up boxes. You want to push the lower object away and make the upper ones fall down and collide with the table. When the upper ones fall down and the lowest box moves over the table, all three will not be aligned with the table surface. If your simulation is long enough, depending on the assigned Bounce coefficient, the boxes will come to rest and, after a number of frames, will start to move through the table surface. This problem will persist even if you increase the value of Calc Intervals Per Frame or set the Collision Test Shape to Mesh. To better understand this problem, open the file 13max07.max and play the animation in the Camera viewport.

To avoid the problem encountered in this example, it is possible to make some sort of visual Collision Detection or to delete all the keys after the object comes to a rest and before it falls through the table. Unfortunately, this approach is not very realistic if you want to simulate a more complex scene with a multitude of colliding objects.

■ **Slow Calculation.** When developing complex simulations with the Dynamic Utility, the calculation for a multitude of objects used in the simulation, especially the calculation for collision detection between these objects, can greatly increase the time for the solving of the simulation. The Dynamic Utility provides you with several solutions to decrease calculation time. For instance, you can avoid calculating collision detection for every vertex of a complex object by substituting it with a simple object, like a box or a sphere. It is also possible to explicitly select the objects that can collide with any other object instead of using global collision detection between all objects included in the simulation.

In Practice: Particles, Dynamic Simulations, and Space Warps

■ **Particle systems can simulate a multitude of objects.** As these exercises show, Particle systems are very versatile and can be used to create the illusion of all sorts of natural and unnatural phenomena. Smoke, dust, jet exhaust, rain, laser blasts, and welding sparks are all possible with particles. As you explore them further, you will find many more uses.

■ **Each of the Particle systems has similarities, but each also carries its own particular strengths for a given effect.** Each Particle system has some similar parameters, but it is the differences between them that make them versatile. Use each particle's differences to your advantage.

■ **Particle systems can be used alone but are often used in combination with Particle space warps.** Depending on what is called for in the shot, a space warp can usually be added to change the particles' original path or to give the particles a more realistic look. Particles that behave more believably result in a better looking scene.

- **Space warps.** Space warps are a great way to control particles. The speed and direction particles take is solely dependent on the Particle parameters and emitter orientation at the time of birth for that frame in time. The only way to change this is to affect the particles with a space warp like Wind, Path Follow, or Gravity.

- **Always consider calculation time when working with particles.** When using Particle systems, you must keep in mind that the preparation of the particles at render time is not multithreaded. This can result in very long render times, especially when using meta-particles or complex Instanced geometry.

- **Motion Dynamics.** Although it has some serious limitations, the Dynamic Utility is a great tool for creating simple simulations of objects that move in a realistic way concerning physical laws. If dynamic simulations are needed in a production environment, however, it is imperative to use programs like HyperMatter or ClothReyes.

Chapter 14

DEFORMABLE OBJECTS AND THEIR SPACE WARPS

In the previous chapter, you learned about the space warps

that are categorized in 3D Studio MAX 2 as particles and

Dynamic space warps. In this chapter, you learn about the

other space warps included in MAX that affect geometric

objects and also learn about a new concept called the World

Space modifier.

Any mesh object in 3D Studio MAX is considered to be a deformable object. Almost all objects that can be created in the Create Panel under Geometry can be bound to space warps for deformable objects. Only Particle systems have their own category of space warps, as discussed in the previous chapter. All other objects under this section have one thing in common: You can modify them in 3D Studio MAX, either by using Modifiers or space warps. All space warps apply an external force to the world space of 3D Studio MAX. Whereas space warps for particles apply forces to the Particle system to further control the motion of the myriad of particles used in an animation, space warps for objects use their force to deform and therefore change the original shape of the object.

This chapter covers the following topics:

- Coordinate systems in 3D Studio MAX

- Space warp uses with deformable objects

- Other uses for space warps

World Space Versus Object Space

In 3D Studio MAX 2, you distinguish between two different Spatial coordinate systems:

- **Object space.** Each object in your scene has its own Local coordinate system that tracks all the translations and modifications that are made directly to the object. For example, Creation parameters, changes made by modifiers, position or rotation changes, Mapping coordinates, and assigned materials are all parameters defined in object space.

- **World space.** The second Spatial coordinate system in 3D Studio MAX 2 is the constant and immovable system that is called world space. If you look at the different viewports, you will see the Home grid, which is a visual representation of the world space coordinate system.

All objects in a scene are located within the world space coordinate system by their transforms (position, rotation, and scale). The Pivot point and any modifications made to an object by modifiers are defined within the object's unique object space.

Different Kinds of Space Warps

Along with Particle and Dynamic space warps, additional space warps are included in 3D Studio MAX 2 that can be categorized as the following:

- **Geometric Space Warps.** A space warp is a non-renderable object that must be bound to a geometric object to have an effect on it. Although geometric space warps are similar to modifiers, their effect on objects acts more like a "force field" that lies in world space, acting on objects that enter their range of influence. With the help of this kind of space warp, you can apply ripple- or wave-like deformations to objects and even explode them into their individual faces.

- **Modifier-Based Space Warps.** This kind of space warp duplicates the effects of standard object modifiers. The main difference is that they influence the bound objects within world space. For example, let's say you want to animate cattails that are situated along the virtual edge of a quiet virtual pond. You can accomplish this by adding and animating a Bend Object Space modifier. But instead of adding and animating a modifier for each cattail, you can also bind the Modifier-based Bend space warp to all cattails in your scene and animate it. In this case, using a space warp will save you a lot of time and effort.

- **World Space Modifier (WSM).** The major difference between a space warp and a World Space modifier is that the WSM is carried within the object's object space like modifiers. Like space warps, however, the WSM uses world space rather then object space, which makes them convenient for modifying a single object or a selection set.

Geometric Space Warps

At the moment, seven different space warps categorized under Geometric/Deformable are available to the animator. All types of deformable objects—meshes, patches, or splines—can be bound to the space warps and, therefore, are influenced by their force. Of the seven space warps described in the following list, the Bomb space warp is the only one that is available solely as a space warp. The Conform space warp is also a Compound object and all the other space warps can be added to deformable objects as modifiers.

■ **FFD (Box) and FFD (Cyl).** These two space warps are almost identical. The FFD enables you to create a Free Form deformation that is a box or a cylindrical-shaped Lattice Freeform object. By adjusting the Control points of the Lattice, you can control the deformation of the bound object. It is possible to affect a whole object, a part of it, or even a sub-selection of vertices or faces.

The FFD (Box) space warp can be used in conjunction with the Character Studio Physique modifier to get better results when deforming a character around the hip or in the armpits.

■ **Wave.** The Wave space warp creates a linear wave through world space, which is determined by a resizable Planar object. You can use this space warp instead of the Wave modifier if you want to affect a large number of objects with the same force. It is also possible to set a Decay value to limit the range of the effect.

This space warp can be used when animating waves of water or when animating the "wavy" movements of snakes or fishes.

■ **Ripple.** This space warp sends a concentric ripple through world space. It also creates a space warp object—much like the Wave space warp—that affects all bound objects. Use the Ripple space warp if you want to apply the same force to a large number of objects. As with the Wave space warp, it is possible to set a Decay value to limit the range of the effect.

With the Ripple space warp, it is possible to animate the ripples in a water puddle created by rain.

NOTE

It is even possible to bind lights, cameras, or helpers to the Ripple and Wave space warps, which gives you additional possibilities to animate the above-mentioned objects along with other objects that might be affected by these external forces in your animation. For instance, it would be very easy to apply a sine wave motion for a group of lights in your scene by binding it to a Wave space warp.

■ **Displace.** The Displace space warp acts much like a force field that is able to push and reshape the bound objects. The Displace space warp applies forces to objects in two ways:

Apply a bitmap to the space warp, and the gray scale will be used to deform the object. High luminance areas apply a high force, whereas low luminance areas apply a lower force or no force.

Apply a force to the bound object by setting Strength and Decay values and applying the force directly through a gizmo.

It is possible to use the same Mapping parameters and its gizmo, than the ones you use when applying an UVW Mapping in the Modify Panel. If you want to send a ball down a tube, for example, you would choose no bitmap, select spherical under Map, make the space warp object (that would be spherical in this case) slightly bigger than the ball you want to animate, and bind it to the tube. You will later go through an exercise to create such a scene.

■ **Conform.** This space warp modifies the object bound to it by pushing its vertices in the direction of the pointing arrow of the space warp icon. The vertices, all or only a selection of them, move until they either cover a specified distance or hit a selected target. One of the many uses for this technique is gliding one object over over the surface of another object.

■ **Bomb.** This space warp applies a radial force that emanates from its icon onto geometric objects that are exploded into their individual faces. Some parameters have been added in the new release; it is now possible to set a Fragment size for the faces of the object, but it is still the easiest and fastest way to explode objects into their individual faces. Used with Video Post Image effects such as Glow or Highlight, you can still create very nice explosion effects, instead of using the new PArray Particle System, which was introduced in the previous chapter.

It is still not possible to set a fragment thickness with this space warp. You have to use a PArray Particle system instead.

Modifier-Based Space Warps

Not all modifiers are available as space warps, but the ones that are available can be used for almost the same tasks as the Object Space modifiers. When animating a multitude of objects, it is often more convenient to use the Modifier-Based space warps instead of the Object Space modifiers. Just remember the previously mentioned example of animating cattails that move in the wind: You would have to apply a modifier to each object and then animate them. It is definitely easier and less time-consuming to bind one space warp to all the cattail objects in the scene and animate only the Bend space warp to achieve the desired effect. Currently there are six different space warps that you can choose from:

- **Bend.** This space warp can bend deformable objects up to 360 degrees about a single axis. When applying a uniform bend to the object, you can control parameters such as angle and direction of the bend. It is also possible to limit the affected area of the space warp to a specified section of the object.

- **Taper.** The Taper space warp affects an object by scaling one end to create a tapered contour. It is possible to control the amount and the curve of the taper on two axes. By transforming the space warp object in various ways, you have additional options to affect the deformation of the bound object.

- **Noise.** With the help of this space warp, you can modulate the position of the object's vertices along any combination of three axes of the coordinate system. You can create amazing deformation effects with this space warp, like floating liquid in a zero-gravity environment. Using this space warp would also be the best choice when animating the liquid in a lava lamp.

- **Twist.** This space warp twists the geometry of an object. The process resembles the wringing of a wet rag. You can control the angle of the twist on any of the three axes or set the bias that controls the compression of the effect relative to the Pivot point. It is even possible to limit the effect of the space warp to a section of the object's geometry.

- **Skew.** This space warp produces a uniform offset in an object. The amount and direction of the skew on all three axes can be controlled. It is also possible to limit the effect on a section of the geometry.

- **Stretch.** This space warp simulates a traditional animation effect—squashing and stretching of objects. When using this space warp, a scale effect is applied along an axis that has been determined, and an opposite scale is applied along the remaining two minor axes.

For instance, it is possible to create an animation of a bouncing ball. You can create Stretch space warps at all positions where the ball bounces on the floor to create the squashing effect when the ball hits the ground.

World Space Modifier

Camera Map, PathDeform, and MapScale were included in the previous release of 3D Studio MAX as space warps. Although WSMs are carried by objects within their local space, they affect the world space coordinate system. After applying it to an object, you will notice that it's listed in the Modifier stack under Binding, like space warps. Because all WSMs are World Space rather than Object Space modifiers, the object is affected in world space coordinates and also affected by the relative position of the path to the object when using a PathDeform WSM. The main difference between the WSM PathDeform and the Object Space Modifier PathDeform is that the WSM modifier leaves the path in place while moving the object to the path, whereas the PathDeform modifier leaves the object in place while moving the path to the object.

The following list will provide you with a brief description of all currently available WSMs in MAX R2:

- **Camera Map.** This WSM applies Mapping coordinates to the assigned object based on a specific camera. Note that it has to be a Target camera. By doing this, you assign the same Screen Environment map to the background and to the object. The result is that the object is not visible. Because the Camera map WSM is using the world space coordinates of 3D Studio MAX 2, the objects bound to the WSM will not become visible, even when moving the camera.

  You can create "cloaking" objects in your scene with the help of this WSM—for example, a Klingon Battle Cruiser that becomes visible or invisible during a shot.

- **PathDeform.** This WSM deforms an applied object based on a spline or NURBS curve path. The PathDeform WSM moves the object to the position and orientation of the path because it uses the 3D Studio MAX 2 world space coordinate system. By using this WSM, it is very convenient to deform any kind of object along a path.

  You will go through an exercise later in this chapter to better understand this World Space modifier.

- **PatchDeform.** This WSM works exactly like the PathDeform WSM, except that it deforms the applied object by the contours of a Patch object instead of a spline path. This WSM is much like the PathDeform WSM discussed before. The only difference is that instead of using a spline or NURBS curve, it uses the surface of a patch grid to deform an object.

- **SurfDeform.** The SurfDeform WSM works in the same manner as the PathDeform WSM, except that it uses a NURBS or CV surface instead of a spline path. The SurfDeform is similar to the PathDeform and PatchDeform WSMs, but this WSM uses the surface of a NURBS object to deform an applied object.

- **MapScale.** This WSM maintains the scale of a map applied to an object. If you rescale an object in any way, the map maintains its size.

  Originally MapScale was created for vertically oriented walls in architectural models, mapped with tiled textures.

Using Object Space Warps

The real power of using space warps is the capability to bind a multitude of objects to the same space warp; these objects are then affected by the space warp in different ways, depending on their distance from and orientation to the space warp icon.

Another major difference between space warps and modifiers is the different evaluation position within the dataflow. 3D Studio MAX 2 evaluates an object in the following ways:

- **Apply modifiers to the object.** The first thing 3D Studio MAX 2 applies is the changes made to the object by Object Modifiers, such as Bend, Taper, or Twist.

- **Apply transforms to the object.** Next, all transformation changes, such as Position, Rotation, and Scale are applied to the object.

- **Apply space warps to the object.** The last modifications to the object are made by the Bound space warps.

In the Object Modifier stack, the space warp bindings (and also the World Space modifier) are listed last in the stack. Sub-Object bindings are displayed with an asterisk before the binding name.

NOTE

In the previous release of 3D Studio MAX, it was necessary to make the modifier for a sub-selection last in the Modifier Stack in order to bind it to the space warp.

In R2, this is not the case. For instance, you can add a Mesh Edit modifier to an object and add all other modifiers that are necessary for the creation of the object. Next you go back to Mesh Edit modifier, select the vertices, faces, or edges you want to be affected by the space warp, click the Bind to Space Warp button, and select the space warp you want. Now only the sub-selection will be affected.

The next part of the chapter takes you through some exercises that explore the use and affects of the following space warps:

- **Displace space warp.** In this exercise, you will learn about the "force field" effect that is applied by a space warp to world space.

- **Bomb space warp.** Here you will use the Bomb space warp to explode an object into its individual faces. And because it is always good to know how to repair things, you will use the same space warp to put all the tiny faces back together.

- **PathDeform World Space modifier.** In this exercise, you learn about the technique of deforming objects, especially text, along a path. This technique is often seen in animated credit lists and logo animations.

The Displace Space Warp

The following exercise shows you how to use the Displace space warp. This type of space warp applies a force to the bound object that deforms and reshapes it. It is comparable to a Bump map with one major difference: it actually deforms the mesh, whereas a Bump map only affects the final rendering and not the object itself.

In the first part of this two-part exercise, you will see the effect of the Displace space warp when it applies its deformation force to the world space by using a bitmap. In the second part of the exercise, you will send a sphere down a half-tube that will be deformed by a type of "force field" that surrounds the sphere.

USING A SPACE WARP TO APPLY A DEFORMATION FORCE FIELD

1. Load the file 14max01.max from the accompanying CD-ROM. There are no objects in the scene. Only the White Plastic material has been added to the Material Editor for your convenience.

2. Create a box in the Front viewport with the following parameters: Length = 100, Width = 100, and Height = 1.

3. Because you will deform the object with the help of a space warp, it is important to give the object a high resolution. Therefore, set the Length and Width segments to 25.

4. Open the Material Editor and assign the White Plastic material to the box.

5. In the Front viewport, select the box and click the Array button. You will now create three more boxes.

6. In the Array Transformation dialog box, select the Move Totals and set the Z value to 50.

7. Select Reference under Type of Object and under Array Dimensions, set the 1D value to 4 in order to make three more copies of the original object.

There are some advantages to using a Reference object in this case. All modifications to the original will be passed through to the child, but modifications to the Reference object—such as adding modifiers and transforms—are not passed in the direction of the original. This is important because later you will move the object to the path spline, changing its original position and rotation.

In this situation, it is a good choice to make referenced copies so that at a later time it is possible to change the resolution of the root object and, therefore, change all other objects to get better deformation results.

8. Create a Displace space warp in the Front viewport with a Planar map Length and Width of 100. Make sure that the scene looks like Figure 14.1.

9. Select the four boxes and bind them to the Displace space warp.

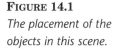

FIGURE 14.1

The placement of the objects in this scene.

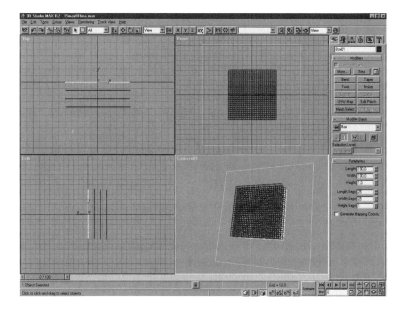

10. Because the Displace space warp has no Strength and no bitmap assigned to it, nothing will be deformed after the binding. Select the Deform space warp, enter the Modifier panel, and select a bitmap under Image. Click the None button to open a File dialog box. Select the file 14tif01.tif from the CD-ROM. It is a modified version of the displace.tif file included in the 3D Studio MAX R2 maps. After accepting the selection, you will notice that the button now is labeled with the name of the bitmap.

11. Set the Strength value to 20.

To get better deformation results, you can select box01 and increase the Length and Width values—for example, to 50. Because you made references to the box01 object, it is necessary to change only the values for the root object. All changes made to the root object are passed to the references. The higher you set these values, the better the deformation effect to the object will be.

Now you will animate the boxes to see the effect of the space warp applying its deformational force to world space in your scene.

12. Select the Displace space warp and open the Modifier panel.

13. Go to frame 0 and enter 0 for the Strength value.

14. Turn on the Animate button and set the Frame slider to frame 100.

15. Set Strength to 40 and turn off the Animate button.

16. Open the Motion panel, select object box01, and go to frame 30.

17. Click the Position button under Create Key. By creating a key at frame 30, you make sure that the object starts to move at this frame.

18. Go to frame 100, turn on the Animate button, and move the object to the position, as shown in Figure 14.2.

FIGURE 14.2

The position of box01 at frame 100.

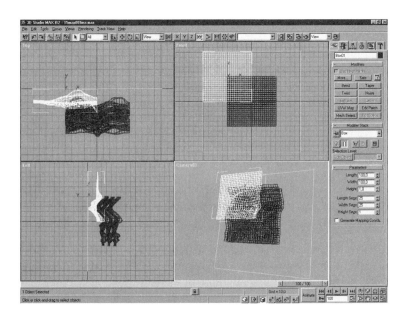

19. Repeat this procedure with the other three boxes. Make sure that your scene resembles Figure 14.3.

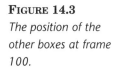

FIGURE 14.3

The position of the other boxes at frame 100.

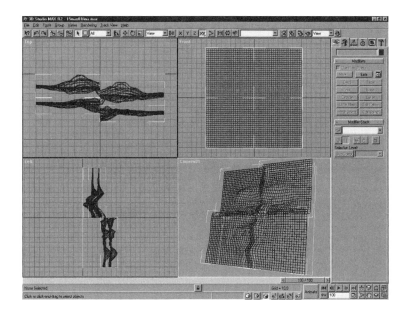

20. Render the animation or play the file 14avi01.avi from the accompanying CD-ROM.

In the next exercise, you will discover other uses for the Displace space warp. You will animate a sphere rolling down a half-tube. Because the sphere has a slightly higher radius than the half-tube, it is necessary to deform the half-tube so that the sphere fits into it.

Before you begin, load the file 14max02.max from the accompanying CD-ROM. The scene contains a half-tube and a sphere. The sphere is animated along the half-tube with the help of a Path controller. Notice that the sphere does not fit into the half-tube because of its greater radius. The task is to create a space warp that emits a kind of displacing force field from the sphere in order to deform the tube while the sphere rolls down. It is very similar to the effect seen in cartoons when a mouse enters a garden hose and deforms the hose because the mouse is slightly bigger.

DEFORMING THE TUBE

1. Create a Displace space warp in the Front viewport. Figure 14.4 shows the rollout.

FIGURE 14.4

The rollout for the
Displace space warp.

2. Select Spherical under Map. The sphere has a radius of 15, so make the Spherical space warp the same size. Enter 15 for Length, Width, and Height.

NOTE

All space warp Distance parameters are based on MAX units, so their scale and detail will affect variously sized objects in different ways.

3. Select and link the space warp gizmo to the sphere.

4. Now you have to align the gizmo to the Sphere object in order to maintain the same position over the animation. Press the Align button and click the sphere. In the dialog box, select Center under Current and Target Object. Then check the X, Y, and Z Position boxes under Align Position (World). The space warp gizmo will now be aligned to the starting position of the sphere and will follow the object down the half-tube. Figure 14.5 shows the settings in the dialog box.

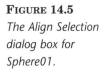

Figure 14.5

The Align Selection dialog box for Sphere01.

With the help of the Align tool, you can align the position and/or orientation of an object's bounding box to the bounding box of a target. It is possible to apply the alignment in various ways. For example, to align the center of an object to the center of a Target object complete these steps:

5. Select the half-tube and bind it to the Displace space warp.

6. Select the space warp in order to enter the parameters that affect the half-tube. Set Strength to 15. Notice that the entire half-tube is affected by the deformation. Set the Decay to 1.5 to make sure only the area around the space warp gizmo is affected. Your scene should look like the one in Figure 14.6.

7. Render the animation to AVI or load the 14avi02.avi file from the accompanying CD-ROM.

The main problem with this kind of deformation is that the deformed objects have to have a very high polygon count in order to assure smooth deformations. Without the high polygon count, the deformed objects look very bumpy.

The Bomb Space Warp

In this exercise, you will learn about several uses for the Bomb space warp. This space warp emanates a radial force into world space, which influences all objects in the specified range by exploding them into their individual faces.

FIGURE 14.6

The scene you just created at frame 65. See how the Displace space warp deforms the half-tube at the position of the sphere.

This exercise is divided into two parts. In the first part, you learn how the radial force that is emitted by a Bomb space warp into world space affects an object that is bound to it. In the second part of this exercise, you will see that this Bomb is indeed a very special one. Not only is it possible to explode objects into their individual faces, but it can also reverse its destructive capabilities by setting exploded faces back together.

CREATING AND EXPLODING A GEOSPHERE

1. Begin by resetting your 3D Studio MAX and loading the file 14max03.max from the CD-ROM. The scene of the file you just opened is empty, but in the Material Editor there are two saved materials that you will assign to the objects created later in this exercise.

2. Create a geosphere in the Front view with the Geodesic Base Type set to Icosa. The radius should be set to 100 and the Segment value to 8. Now you have lots of faces to explode.

3. Add a UVW Map modifier to the geosphere and under Mapping, select Spherical. Click the Sub-Object button and rotate the gizmo –90 degrees along the x-axis.

4. Open the Material Editor and assign the material Explode Out to the geosphere.

5. Create the Geometric/Deformable Bomb space warp. Place it inside the geosphere. Figure 14.7 shows how the Bomb is placed within the sphere.

FIGURE 14.7

The position of the Bomb space warp within the sphere.

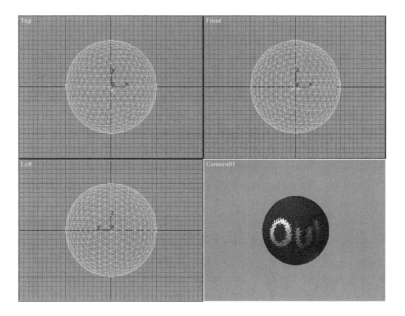

The force originates from the position of the Space Warp object and emanates in all directions into the world space coordinate system. Therefore, the position of the objects and the position of the Bomb icon are very important for the effect. By placing the Space Warp icon in the middle of the object, the effect is like an explosion from within the object.

6. Now you have to bind the space warp to the object. Select the geosphere and click the Bind to Space Warp object. Then bind the object to the Space Warp icon.

7. Scrub the Frame slider up and down the Active Time Segment. You will see the explode effect start at the default frame 5 (see Figure 14.8).

The effect you see is symmetrical and does not look realistic. To improve the effect, you must change the Bomb parameters in order to get a better looking effect for the animation.

FIGURE 14.8

The uniform explosion of the object looks rather unrealistic.

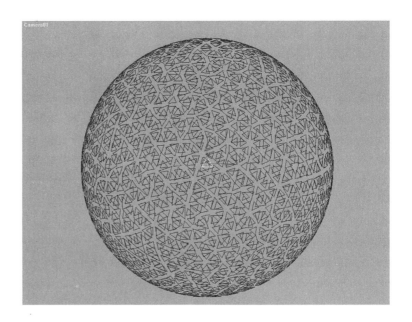

8. Select the Bomb space warp and open the Modifier panel to change the space warp's parameters.

9. Under the Explosion parameters, set the Strength value to 10 to make sure that the object bursts a little harder.

Two more interesting parameters are within this section: the Spin and the Falloff setting. The Falloff parameter determines the range of the effect in world space units. When the Falloff box is checked, the fragments that pass the Falloff are not affected by the Strength or Spin value. The Spin parameter determines the rotational speed of the exploded faces. Note that it determines the revolution per second defined by the Frame rate of your animation.

10. Set the Spin value to 1.

11. A new feature introduced with 3D Studio MAX 2 is the capability to change the Fragment size to a minimum and a maximum value. Change the minimum value to 2 and the maximum value to 10. Now scrub the frame slider up and down the Active Time segment. Notice that the geosphere now bursts into several chunks rather than all its faces.

NOTE

Because it is not possible to set the thickness of the fragments, you have to use the PArray
Particle system to use the Fragment Size feature.

12. Locate the General parameters and set the Gravity value to 0 to simu-
    late an explosion in zero-gravity space.

13. By setting the Chaos value you can add some extra variation to the
    movement of the exploding faces. A random number will be created and
    then added to the parameters, which also affects Strength and Spin.
    Set the Chaos parameter to 4.

14. Set the detonation to start at frame 20.

15. Select and right-click the geosphere to open the Properties dialog box.
    Select Image Motion Blur and set the G-Buffer Object channel to 1.

Because you want the object to hide during the course of the animation,
you have to add a Visibility track to it.

16. Open the Track View.

17. Add a Visibility track to the object geosphere01.

18. Select the Visibility Track label and click the Assign Controller button.
    Assign a Bezier Float controller.

With the help of the Visibility track, you can control whether you see an
object or not. But first, it is necessary to create this track, because it is
not included in the Track View properties of an object by default. This
track cannot be animated by the Animate button. You have to add all
the keys by yourself in the Track View.

When first assigning a Visibility track to an object, an On/Off controller
is automatically assigned to it. If you want to use the effect of an object
slowly disappearing in the animation, you have to assign a Bezier Float
controller to the Visibility track. This effect is called Gradual Visibility.

19. Insert the following keys into the Visibility track: Frame 0 = 1, Frame
    50 = 1, and Frame 65 = 0. The geosphere will be visible from frame 0–50
    and start to hide from frame 50–65.

20. Preview the scene (see Figure 14.9). You can also load the file 14avi03.avi from the accompanying CD-ROM to take a look at the created animation so far.

FIGURE 14.9

The sphere explosion at frame 25.

You have just finished the first part of the animation. In the second part of the exercise, you will create a sphere that implodes and then is put back together.

IMPLODING THE SPHERE

1. Continue working with the scene from the previous exercise, or load the file 14max03a.max from the accompanying CD-ROM.

2. Set the Frame slider to frame 0. Select geosphere01 and meshbomb01, and create copies of them. Then hide geosphere01 and meshbomb01.

3. Open the Material Editor and assign the second Material (Explode In) to the object geosphere02.

4. Select the space warp meshbomb02.

Now you set the values for the meshbomb02. The task is to make the space warp implode the object and then rearrange it later in the animation. You can set the parameters to almost the same values as meshbomb01. Only the Strength, Detonation, and Seed settings should be different. The reason why the Strength and the Spin value should be different will be explained in the following part of the exercise. These values have to be animated to make sure that the effect of putting the object back together looks right. The Seed value makes sure that the explosion does not look uniform. Therefore, it is important that the second explosion has a different Seed value than the first one.

5. Set Strength to –10. Leave all other parameters at their set values.

6. Set the Detonation to 0. To give the explosion a different value than meshbomb01, set the Seed value to 1.

When changing the Seed parameter, you change all randomly created values. When using a copy of a space warp like MeshBomb, it is always a good idea to set the Seed to a different value than its root object. Doing this helps you avoid effects that look too similar.

Next you animate the Strength value in order to rearrange the fragments of the object. You also have to animate the Spin value and the visibility of the object.

7. Open the Track View and expand the tracks for meshbomb02.

8. Animate the Strength value of the meshbomb02 by setting three keys: Frame 0 = –10, Frame 65 = –10, and Frame 99 = 0.

9. Because you will use Image Motion blur later, it is necessary to set the last animated key to frame 99. It seems that the Pixel speed at the last key (in this case 99) is not zero. Although there are no moving fragments at all in this frame, there will still be a Motion blur effect around the sphere. To avoid this, you can extend your rendered animation about one frame or set the last key for Strength and Spin to frame 99.

10. Animate the Spin value by inserting three keys as follows: Frame 0 = 1, Frame 65 = 1, and Frame 99 = 0.

11. Change the values in the Visibility Track keys for geosphere02 as follows: Frame 0 = 0, Frame 50 = 0, and Frame 65 = 1.

12. Unhide all objects.

13. The last thing to apply before rendering the scene is to apply the Image Motion blur to the two spheres. Select both spheres and right-click them to open the Object Properties dialog box. Under Motion Blur, select the Image option. You can leave the Image Motion blur settings in the Render dialog box at their default values.

14. Render the animation or load the file 14avi04.avi from the accompanying CD-ROM (see Figure 14.10).

FIGURE 14.10

The animation at frame 96. Whereas one sphere is just in the process of getting put together, the faces of the first sphere that were exploded are still moving away from the initial starting point.

Play around with the different settings like Falloff, Fragment Size, and so on. It is also possible to play around with the function curves of the keys to change the timing of the animation. You can also bind a Wave space warp to the object to give the exploding objects a "wavy" movement. It is very easy to achieve simple bomb effects, but if you really want to create interesting burst or explode effects, you should use the Particle systems that come with 3D Studio MAX 2. They are discussed in detail in Chapter 13, "Particles, Dynamic Simulations, and Space Warps."

The PathDeform Space Warp

In this exercise, you will use the PathDeform World Space modifier, which was a space warp object in the previous release of 3D Studio MAX. It enables you to deform an object along a spline or NURBS curve. It is a great tool to make fast deformations of objects by just defining a path. Not very long ago, animation of text including a deformation along its path of travel was considered a special effect in 3D animations, whereas it is now simpler and more commonplace because of the tools provided in 3D Studio MAX.

Before you begin the exercise, load the file 14max04.max from the accompanying CD-ROM. Some objects are already included in the file. You will see two spline paths and two Text objects in the scene. The first thing you have to do is to make a copy of the text. It is always a good idea to keep the original of the objects deformed in order to maintain the original parameters and transformation.

DEFORMING TEXT ALONG A PATH

1. Select the two Text objects and the cone. While holding down the Shift button, drag the selection down the y-axis. When you release the mouse button, the Clone Option dialog box appears. Under Object, select Reference and click OK to accept the settings.

There are some advantages to using a Referenced object in this exercise. All modifications to the original are passed through to the child, but modifications to the Reference object, such as adding modifiers and transforms, are not passed in the direction of the original. This is important because later you will move the object to the spline path, changing its original position and rotation.

2. Select the Text01Ref object and open the Modify panel. Click the More button and select PathDeform and World Space modifier. Because WSMs are carried in the local space of the object, they are assigned in the Modify panel instead of the Create Space Warp panel.

3. When the Parameter rollout for PathDeform opens, click the Pick Path button and select the spline Path01.

The object reorients itself, as can be seen in Figure 14.11. The object is using the World Space modifier to deform, but the deformation takes place in the local space of the object.

FIGURE 14.11

The text bound to the World Space modifier after the reorientation.

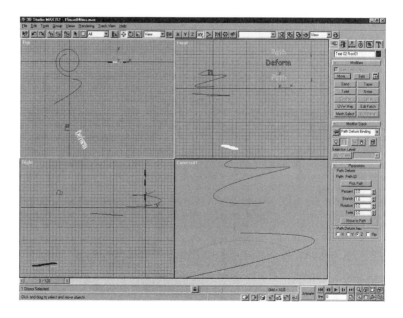

4. Move the object to the spline by clicking the Move to Path button. Now the Pivot point of the Text object is aligned at the first vertex of the spline.

WARNING

Because the Move Object to Path option is animatable, you should use caution when toggling this option while the Animate button is turned on.

5. Select X under PathDeform Axis to place the length of the Text object along the path.

6. Click the Animate button and drag the Frame slider to frame 100. Set the Percent parameter to 105 and the Rotation spinner to 25 to make sure the object faces the camera.

    It is possible to assign a value lower than zero or higher then 100 percent. The object continues to move along the last assigned direction vector.

7. Turn off the Animate button.

Play the animation in the Camera viewport. You will see how the object goes around the bends of the path. You always have to make sure that the object that is deformed by the path has enough faces so that it always can be deformed smoothly (see Figure 14.12).

FIGURE 14.12

The scene at frame 75. See how the Text object is deformed by the path. You will also notice the PathDeform rollout in the right part of the screen.

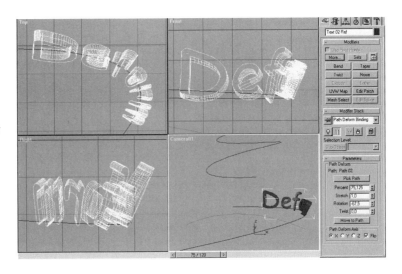

NOTE

The PathDeform WSM can be used as an animation tool as well as a modeling tool. For example, it is sometimes better to use this deformation tool than to use a loft, because with PathDeform WSM you do not discover the non-uniformly scaled shape problems when lofting around bends. When creating signs or logos, the PathDeform WSM can be used for a wide range of tasks.

8. Now assign the second text object, Text02Ref, to the second path by applying a PathDeform WSM to it.

9. Click the Pick Path button and select Path02. Do not forget to move the Text object to the path by clicking the Move Object to Path button.

10. To place the length of the Text object along the path, select x under PathDeform Axis.

Now you see part of the object in the Camera viewport. To avoid this, you have to change the starting point of the object a little.

11. Go to frame 0 and change the Percent parameter to –15.

12. Turn on the Animate button and drag the Frame slider to frame 100.

13. Set the Percent spinner to 105 and the Rotation to –90. Turn off the Animate button.

14. Notice that the Text object is facing in the wrong direction. Check the Flip box under PathDeform Axis to make the direction of the PathDeform gizmo flip 180 degrees.

NOTE

Although you can assign transformations to the object, it is better and more convenient to use the parameters offered by the WSM itself. If you want to apply transformations, such as Rotate, to the object itself, select Local in the Transformation Axis coordinate system list. All transformations are then made by using the Local coordinate system that is carried by the object's Pivot point.

To give the animation a final touch, you underline the text with the help of the PathDeform WSM.

15. Select the Cone01Ref object and assign a PathDeform WSM.

16. Under the PathDeform parameters, click the Pick Path button and select Path03.

17. Move the object to the start of the path by clicking the Move to Path button.

18. Leave all other parameters at their default settings.

The underlining is accomplished by animating the Stretch parameter. It is a very powerful tool and is comparable to a Loft object with an animated scale deformation applied to it. This approach, however, is much easier and faster to achieve. You can animate objects by growing and shrinking them while moving along the path.

19. Open the Track View and right-click the Cone01Ref object label to open the context menu. Select Expand All Tracks.

20. Click the label for ConeRef01 and add a Visibility track by clicking the corresponding button.

21. Add a Visibility key at frame 0 and one at frame 105. With this set up, the object is invisible until frame 105.

22. In the Space Warps tracks, create a key at frame 105 under Stretch. Add another key at frame 120.

23. Right-click the first key you created in the preceding step to open the Key Info dialog for this key. Set the Stretch value to 0, and then click the right-pointing arrow in the dialog box to step to the next key and change the Stretch value to 13. Close the Key Info dialog box to accept the changes. The cone is now stretched along the whole length of the path.

24. Close the Track View.

Select the Camera viewport and render the animation. You can also load 14avi05.avi from the CD-ROM (see Figure 14.13).

FIGURE 14.13

The last frame of the animation you just created, utilizing the PathDeform World Space modifier.

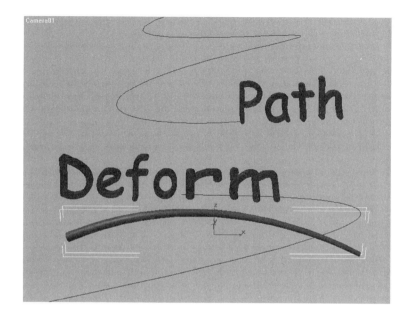

In Practice: Deformable Objects and Their Space Warps

- **Space warps influence world space.** Whether you are using space warps that deform geometry or influence Particle systems, always remember that they affect the scene in world space and not in object space.

  A space warp is much like a black hole in deep space. It has such a high gravitational force that it actually bends the space around it. The further you move from the space warp, however, the less the bending effect will be, until the gravitational influence disappears.

- **Space warps are always evaluated last in the stack.** 3D Studio MAX 2 uses a predefined data flow to evaluate objects in your scene. Space warps are evaluated after the object modifiers and the transforms.

- **Geometric/Deformable space warps.** This type of space warp can be applied to any deformable object—such as meshes, splines, or patches. It is also possible to bind lights, cameras, and helpers to the Ripple and Wave space warps to distort their position transformation.

■ **Explosive effects.** When creating explosive or bursting effects, it is better to use the Particle systems and their space warps. Because of the new Particle features included in 3D Studio MAX R2, it is now possible to use a geometric object as an emitter. With a Geometric space warp, it is possible to explode an object only into its faces, whereas the PArray Particle system can explode an object into a specified number of chunks that have a defined thickness.

Part IV

VIDEO POST EFFECTS

Chapter 15

COMPOSITING AND EDITING

3DS MAX contains a powerful editing, compositing, and special effects tool set: the Video Post module. At its most basic, Video Post (VP) is a way to cut or transition together several animations or stills to create one larger sequence. VP is useful for editing an element's duration or direction and compositing many elements as layers, on top of each other or end-to-end.

Video Post also functions well as a limited batch renderer to simultaneously render (or composite), for example, multiple camera views of the same scene. Video Post is home to MAX's many special effects filters, most of which can only be implemented within a 3D environment, and which are covered at length in the next chapter, "Video Post Effects."

Video Post, however, is no substitute for full-featured, standalone 2D image editing and compositing tools such as Adobe Photoshop or MetaCreations Painter. It's also no replacement for desktop video editing and compositing tools such as Adobe Premiere and After Effects, 4D Vision's Digital Fusion, or Speed Razor Pro, or full-blown editing suites such as Avid or Media 100. 3DS MAX R2 incorporates much of the functionality of the foregoing, including support for Adobe Photoshop- and Premiere-compatible plug-ins. Further, R2 anticipates that you may use these or similar tools.

In Video Post you can edit or splice together animations, composite your scene with pre-rendered stills or animations, or simply splice together stills with stills or animations. This chapter covers the compositing and editing features available in Video Post. Chapter 16 addresses VP special effects.

More than just familiarizing you with the Video Post tools set, these chapters suggest you approach Video Post as an integral part of MAX's creative space and process, and that you use Video Post as another dialog box for building your scene. Just as you wouldn't create materials without considering the effect of your lighting and atmosphere on them, you shouldn't design scene elements, lighting, or materials without considering whether or not you'll render everything together or separately for VP compositing or composite other elements with this scene, or how these elements change when you apply special effects, either in Video Post or in an external environment.

This chapter covers the following topics:

■ Understanding compositing basics

■ Using the Alpha Compositer

■ Understanding shadows and compositing

■ Masking

■ Bluescreening

■ Editing your animations

Improvements to Video Post in Release 2.0

 Those familiar with the Video Post module should be comfortable with the improvements contained in R2, because the interface design has not changed, and the enhancements derive from fixes and "wishlist" items submitted by MAX users to Kinetix since the initial release. The following is a list of the improvements made to Video Post in MAX R2:

- You can now rename entries in the VP Queue and highlight and delete events in the Queue list with the Del key, regardless of whether the event is enabled or disabled.

- Now the 3DS MAX application window remains open (not minimized during rendering), and you can elect to have the Progress dialog box remain open after rendering is completed.

- Similar to the main renderer, rendering in VP supports Scene Motion blur, Object Motion blur, and Image blur. VP rendering also blurs frames and sub-frames as necessary. This corrects a bug in R1 involving rescaled time duration with blurs. The documentation suggests that if you've been using Scene Motion blur or Object Motion blur together with Scaled Output ranges in R1, you will get a different result in R2 and should re-render portions to arrive at new, accurate settings.

- R2 supports Adobe Premiere plug-in filters (including third-party filters), allowing you to use both compositing, transition, and special effects filters compatible with this architecture, including third-party packages such as MetaCreation's Final Effects AP. (This is addressed more fully in Chapter 16.)

N OTE

At this writing R2 does not support Adobe After Effects plug-ins, although this has been requested, and the two companies announced their intention to work together toward making the two products compatible.

If the foregoing appears technical, esoteric, or confusing, fear not, for the remainder of this section discusses the mechanics of using Video Post in compositing and editing.

Compositing Basics

Compositing refers to the act of combining two or more images together to make one image or sequence. Video Post enables you to perform this action, as well as to extend it by performing a composite of two images a multitude of times. Because an animation is just a string of images, Video Post enables you to composite animations. Video Post also enables you to composite a single image with an animation.

Consider the two uses for compositing: image compositing (by layering image information on top of other image information) and sequence compositing (trimming and placing one sequence after another in time with a cut or transition in between). In Video Post you can do both, and in one operation.

A good discussion of the art and technique of image compositing computer graphics and animation occupies volumes. This subject is fundamental to the computer arts, animation, and special effects. If you lack expertise in this area, you should review the many texts on compositing in 2D applications such as Photoshop, Painter, or After Effects. You've previously encountered the use of alpha channels ("masks," "transparency masks," or "alpha masks") in 3D Studio MAX R2 when you created materials with Opacity maps or Bump maps or used a Displacement modifier to modify the geometry of a mesh.

This chapter presumes you understand the basics, including the most basic rule of image compositing: All layers on top of the background layer must contain some masking information to allow some, but not all, of the information underneath to show through. In other words, the background image can be a 24-bit graphic (RGB), for instance, but the next layer up must contain an alpha channel (transparency information in the form of an additional 8-bit grayscale image), making it a 32-bit graphic (RGBA).

Without alpha information, the top layer covers the bottom completely—no composite. Therefore, only certain file formats work for compositing; the oldest and most widely used with 3D Studio is the Targa file format, with its 32-bit options checked. Note that you have two options for an alpha channel in a Targa file: You can keep it part of the file or split it from the original, giving you a 24-bit RGB Targa and a separate 8-bit grayscale file named *A_filename.tga*.

System Performance

System performance is one of the strongest arguments for compositing in Video Post. You might find that when you animate a small scene, it is nice to have all your objects in the scene simultaneously. This way you can animate them and see them in relation to one another.

As your scenes become larger and you begin to tax your system resources, however, you might find yourself yearning for a faster machine (or taking a lot of coffee breaks). Even if you have the fastest machine money can buy, a serious face count coupled with some special effects can make it extremely painful to animate with everything in the same scene. The more complex your scene, the slower MAX responds to your commands. Even fast 3D acceleration hardware does little to help out when you have extremely complex scenes.

If you use Motion blur or Volumetric lighting or render at a high resolution, you also gobble up a lot of RAM at render time. If you use up all your RAM, your computer is forced to use Virtual memory, which is not good. Compositing enables you to break up your animation into pieces. Because each piece is a fraction of the total face count, the computer handles the file much more efficiently. You might find that an animation you create through compositing might otherwise be impossible.

NOTE

Virtual memory is memory allocated on your hard drive to store information that your computer cannot fit into its RAM. Because hard disk drives access data much more slowly than RAM does, using Virtual memory in a scene can dramatically slow down render times. In many cases, buying more RAM can be a more effective upgrade than a faster processor for 3D work.

Modular Design Approach

Splitting up your animation into layers or time segments facilitates a modular design approach. Working with the pieces frees you to concentrate on individual areas. If you are working on character animation and have an elaborate 3D background, compositing enables you to concentrate on your character animation exclusively. You can get the motion you want for your characters and then composite on top of a background prepared separately.

This modular design approach also enables you to use that same background for any other animation while simultaneously freeing you from the headache of merging the MAX files together and re-rendering.

Furthermore, many animators find that approaching animation from a modular point of view works well because it enables them to focus on one element of the animation without getting confused or distracted by other elements. Compositing also enables multiple animators to tackle the same scene without stumbling over one another. After you get used to compositing, you might find yourself using it even when memory and hardware constraints are not an issue.

Compositing has its pitfalls, however; if objects are not rendered together, they are not picked up in reflections or shadow casting. Ways to get around the shadow problem exist and will be discussed later in this chapter.

Modularity also forces the animator to be a little bit more organized. It is important to create subdirectories for your file renders, for example, to avoid cluttering up one directory with long lists of sequential files.

Using the Alpha Compositor

The native Alpha Compositor is the easiest way to composite your animations in R2. The Alpha Compositor is an Image Layer event that composites two images based on an Image alpha channel. The images are combined based on the alpha data present in the second image. This means that to see the top child, the bottom child of a Layer event must contain alpha data (see Figure 15.1).

FIGURE 15.1

The bottom child covers the event above it. It requires alpha data to composite correctly; otherwise, it obliterates the image underneath.

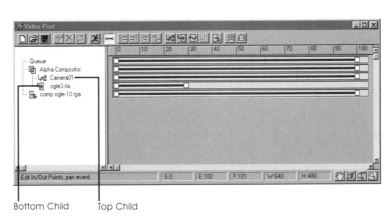

Bottom Child   Top Child

Layer events are like plates that cover one another. The alpha data provides a method for seeing through one plate and on to another. If the bottom child of your Layer event is a Scene event, MAX renders that image and automatically provides transparency data wherever nothing obstructs the background in your scene. If the last layer in the Video Post queue is a Scene event, such as a Camera viewport for example, that viewport is rendered as if it had an alpha channel, and the blank areas become transparent automatically.

NOTE

Transparency data adds an extra 8 bits of information to the file size. You need to anticipate when you need transparency information so you don't waste disk space on 32-bit files when 24-bit files will suffice.

You need to understand certain aspects of MAX directly related to compositing, but not necessarily part of the Video Post module. Therefore, Image Setup parameters, the Virtual Frame Buffer window, the Graphics buffer (G-Buffer), and the Image File List (IFL) are explained prior to diving into some compositing examples.

NEW TO R2

The Alpha Compositor has been improved in the way it reacts to G-Buffer data, after a bug was fixed in the R1 version that produced a black edge around a composited Image event.

Image Setup Parameters

When you have your scene ready to render and you specify a file in the Render Scene dialog, you are given options specific to a particular file type. If you render a JPG file, for example, you can specify the level of compression versus the quality of the image. With TGA files, you can specify whether you want the rendered file to have an alpha channel. You can also include notes about the image (sequence) and set the bits-per-pixel to 32 in the Image Setup dialog (see Figure 15.2).

FIGURE 15.2

By setting the Bits-Per-Pixel to 32, you tell MAX that you want to include an alpha channel in the rendered image.

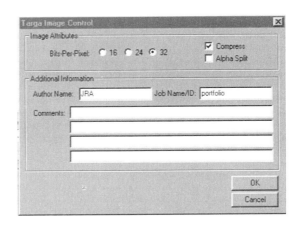

The parameters and notes set for an image file type stay that way until you change them again. If you set the bits-per-pixel for TGA images to 32, for example, all TGA images you render from then on are automatically saved with alpha data even if you close and reopen MAX. With this in mind, be certain to check the Image Setup dialog to update notes and image settings properly.

This Image Setup dialog also gives you an option called Alpha Split. An Alpha Split creates a separate 8-bit image, in addition to the 24-bit rendering. This 8-bit separate image contains the alpha data only. Alpha Split is useful because you can then use this 8-bit Alpha Split image or image sequence in masking operations (see the section on masking later in this chapter). You can apply lossless compression to the Targa file by checking the Compress check box. The disk space saved with this feature more than makes up for the minimal time it adds to opening the file.

The Virtual Frame Buffer Window

Figure 15.3 shows an image of the Virtual Frame Buffer (VFB) window. Notice the eight buttons at the top of the window:

- **Red, Green, Blue, Half Black, and Half White Circles:** Represent the red, green, blue, and alpha channels in an RGBA image.

- **X:** Clears the current frame buffer.

- **Disk Icon:** Enables you to save the image to a file. This is useful when you do test renders and don't necessarily want to specify an output file in the Render Scene dialog box.

- **Grayscale Button:** Allows you to view the image in grayscale.

- **Clone VFB Buttons:** (represented by two figures) Allow you to compare test renders by cloning and keeping any number of VFB copies on the desktop as you work.

- **Dropdown Box:** Enables you to view information saved with the file. If you use a Targa format, your choice is RGB Alpha. If you use other formats, however, such as RLA (discussed later), you can view the other channels stored with that format.

- **Color Swatch:** Right-clicking anywhere in the VFB image brings up an Eyedropper tool and a window providing real-time image and pixel information. The Color Swatch updates with the Eyedropper color as you move it around, giving you a Color Swatch to drag and drop to any other part of the interface.

- **Zoom and Pan:** Ctrl-left-click zooms in on any image in the VFB; ctrl-right-click zooms out. Shift-left-click pans about the image in the VFB (if the magnified image size exceeds the VFB size). These tools are excellent for examining image detail or moving in close to retrieve a particular color with the Eyedropper tool.

FIGURE 15.3

R2's improved Virtual Frame Buffer window.

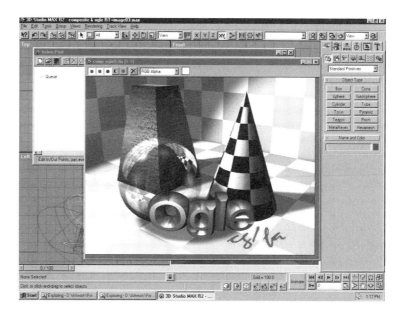

If you press the Alpha Channel button, the image in the window changes and reveals the alpha channel (see Figure 15.4). The white areas represent opaque sections of the image and the black areas are transparent. Notice that the alpha channel for this image provides an area of transparency where no geometry is present. In this image, the transparent area is present in the area revealed by the opening door. The space beyond the door can be a background that you composite in later.

FIGURE 15.4

The Alpha Channel button enables you to visualize your areas of transparency.

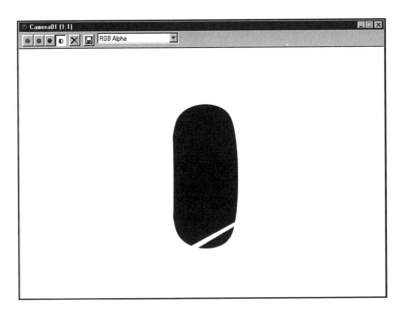

The Alpha Channel button proves particularly useful when doing compositing because it enables you to visualize your areas of transparency. The buttons with the red, green, and blue circles toggle the corresponding channel in the image. If you press the Red button, for example, the Red channel of the image no longer displays in the Virtual Frame Buffer window. By clicking the various buttons, you can toggle the corresponding channel on and off. Visualizing the individual channels that use these buttons is useful when you want to perform masking operations (see the section on masking later in this chapter).

The G-Buffer

The term G-Buffer (graphics buffer) refers to a method of storing geometric information about objects in 3D images. The geometric information is stored so that it may later be calculated and used by image processing programs (Video Post plug-ins). The information is stored in various channels, similarly to the way an alpha channel is stored. Within a G-Buffered image, for example, there might be data that describes how far a pixel is from the camera. This information can then be used to calculate Fog or Distance blur effects (like Lens Effects focus).

3D Studio MAX implements G-Buffer technology. If you specify a Material Effects channel or an Object channel, for example, you set data within the G-Buffer. The Virtual Frame Buffer window enables you to view this data by selecting the appropriate channel from the pull-down list. If no G-Buffer data is available, no channels are listed in the pull-down menu.

MAX supports 10 total possible channels, but not all are added automatically. Not all image types support G-Buffer information. The G-Buffer information recorded by MAX is in a format unique to MAX's renderer. This format is public, but it is not extensible. For this reason, MAX uses Silicon Graphics' popular RLA image format for saving images with G-Buffer information. Figure 15.5 shows an example of the RLA Image File Format dialog box and a view of what information is stored in each channel (Figures 15.6–15.13). Note that using the RLA format with all channel options enabled increases the 640×480 file size to about 3800KB, as compared to about 900KB for the 32-bit Targa file.

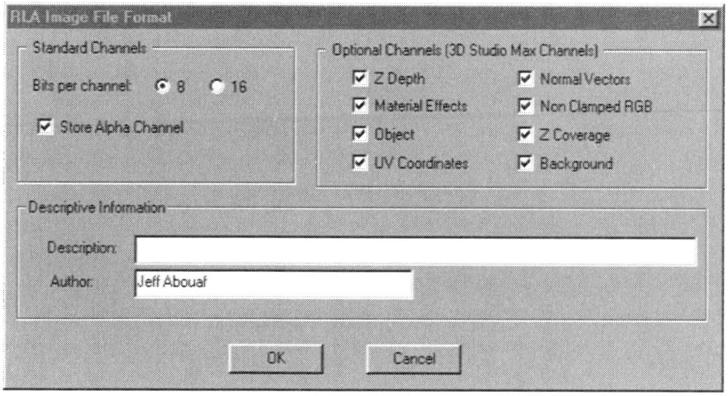

FIGURE 15.5

The RLA Image File Format dialog box.

FIGURE 15.6
The RGB alpha
channel.

FIGURE 15.7
The Z-Buffer channel.

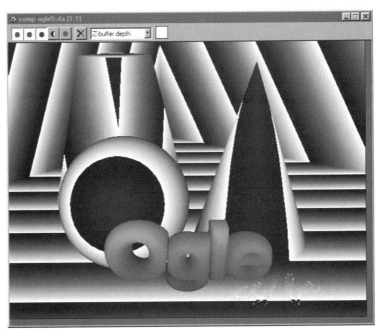

FIGURE 15.8

The Material Effects channel and the Object ID channel appear identical.

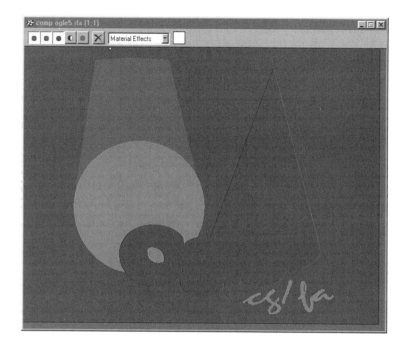

FIGURE 15.9

The UV Coordinates channel.

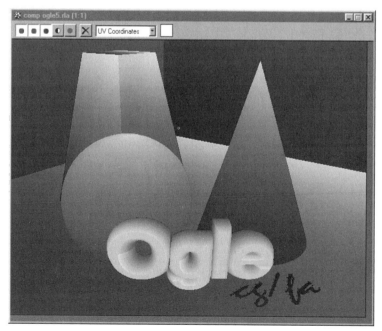

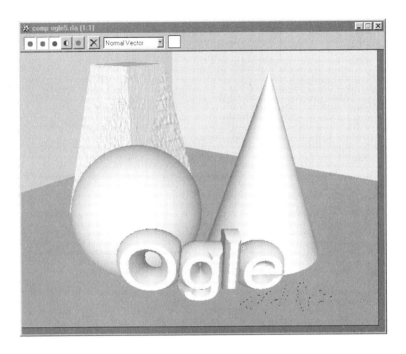

FIGURE 15.12

The Z-Coverage channel.

FIGURE 15.13

The Background channel.

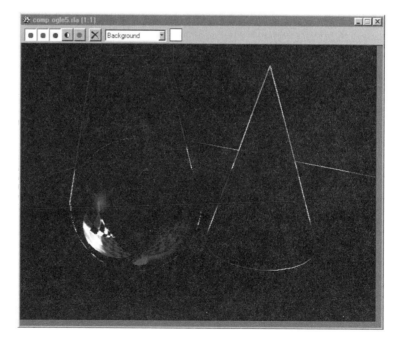

If you save composite content to an RLA format, you'll be restricting your choice of compositing tool to MAX or some other 3D package that specifically supports RLA. After Effects, Premiere, and Photoshop cannot see RLA files.

The Image File List

IFL stands for *Image File List*. An IFL file is a standard text-only file that contains a list of images that you can view and edit in any text editor. Each image in the list corresponds to a 3D Studio MAX frame. MAX reads the file line by line and loads each listed file for a particular frame of animation.

Creating IFL files is easy. You must first have a sequence of images. If you render an animation to sequential TGA files and call the output file Figure.tga, for example, the sequence of files would look like the following:

Figure0001.tga

Figure0002.tga

Figure0003.tga

And so on...

To create this particular IFL, in the File Selection dialog, navigate to the directory that contains the sequential images and type **Figure*.tga** as the input file. The list continues until it reaches the last file in the numbered sequence. MAX automatically creates a file with an IFL extension. The file contains the list of sequential files that match the Figure*.tga wild card.

Note that the IFL file only includes files named exactly the same way and in numerical sequence, so if the number list is broken or you have disparate file names, you must edit the list. You can do this by hand in any text editor, but you will be better served if you use one of the IFL editing or renaming utilities available free of charge at several Web sites mentioned earlier in this chapter. One of these, Resequencer by David P. McCullough, which is included on the accompanying CD-ROM (reseq.zip), works very well to batch-rename a file sequence. The value of such utilities lies in their capability to help you construct IFL files for non-similar or non-consecutive file sequences.

MAX creates the IFL file in the directory that contains the list of images. You cannot, therefore, create an IFL file if the images you intend to use are on CD-ROM. Because CD-ROM is read-only media, MAX cannot create the IFL file because MAX will try to write the file to the CD-ROM. The IFL driver in R2 doesn't support multi-word filenames, such as my file*.tga. These create an IFL that cannot be read into Video Post. You must use a single short filename, such as figure*.tga, for MAX to create a readable IFL.

WARNING

If you are on a network or if you plan to network render, IFL files can slow down your renders significantly. This slowdown occurs because the network needs to send each file specified in the IFL over the network for every frame being processed by Manager. 100BASE-T networks seem to handle this increased traffic without too much difficulty. 10BASE-T or coaxial networks bottleneck, however, if they must send large TGA files around on very limited bandwidth.

Now that you are familiar with some of the core concepts important to compositing, you should discover the power of Video Post's Alpha Compositor. The following exercise illustrates how to perform a composite using the Alpha Compositor and how to perform multi-layered compositing by making one Layer event the child of another (nesting Layer events). This exercise involves compositing a simple logo for a design studio into an existing scene to make a new company logo that suggests the work the company performs. The scene source is a lighting and materials test made for another purpose. The logo consists of two words, ogle and cg/fa, previously rendered separately to still images. Presume you can't redo the logo data and you don't have time to rework the scene. The task is to rescale, reposition, and add special effects to the old logo data so that inclusion into the new scene appears natural and intended.

NESTED COMPOSITING USING A SERIES OF IMAGE INPUT EVENTS

1. From the accompanying CD-ROM, load 15max01.max. The scene consists of a floor and two perpendicular panels forming a cutaway room, mapped with a light gray-white checkered reference pattern. You cannot see beyond the floor and panels. Arranged on the floor are three primitive shapes: a cone mapped with black and white checkers, a polished transparent/translucent sphere, and a tapered box with a pronounced Bump map and gradient.

In the Material Editor for this exercise, you will find two different materials for use on the sphere, one with raytracing and one without. The Raytraced material adds substantially to the render time and is used for the final plates; for purposes of this exercise, you're better served by with the non-raytraced, which is the current material assignment.

2. From the Rendering pull-down list on the MAX main screen, select Video Post (or press V for the keyboard shortcut).

Notice the buttons along the top of the window. Some of the buttons are grayed out, meaning they are inaccessible. Certain buttons are only accessible when events on which they can perform an action are within the Video Post queue.

3. Click the Add Scene Event button, and its dialog box appears. Select Camera01 and click OK.

4. Click the Add Image Input Event button. The Add Image Input Event dialog appears (see Figure 15.14). This dialog enables you to specify a file, a sequence of files, or a device. An example of a device you might use is the Accom WSD Digital Recorder. For this exercise, it is assumed that you are using standard images.

FIGURE 15.14

The Add Image Input Event dialog.

5. In the Image Input section of the dialog, click the Files button.

6. Navigate to CD-ROM and highlight 15rla01a.rla. Click OK.

7. Click the Options button in the Add Image Input Event dialog. You need to resize the top layer image: set Size equal to Custom Size, W equal to 320, and H equal to 200. Click the icon that represents the bottom center position (see Figure 15.15). Click OK twice to return to Video Post.

FIGURE 15.15

The Image Input Options dialog (available from Add or Edit Image Input Event) allows you to rescale and reposition the file to be composited.

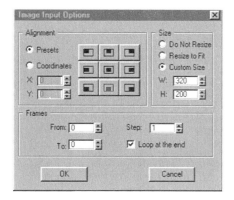

8. Click anywhere on the white area of the queue other than a name to clear your selection. Then click the Add Image Input Event button and load the file 15rla01b.rla. Click Options, set Size equal to Do Not Resize, and under Alignment set the coordinates X equal to 30 and Y equal to 0. (The reason to use the RLA format is to access the Material Effects and Object ID information saved to this format.)

9. Click the Add Image Output Event icon and create a file named **15max01.tga**. (If it isn't at the bottom of the queue, drag it down to the bottom.)

10. Ctrl-click to highlight Camera01 and 15rla01a.rla in the queue and then press the Add Image Layers Event icon. From the drop-down, select the Alpha Compositor. There are no settings for this tool. Click OK. The Scene event and the Image events become the top and bottom children of the Alpha Compositor.

11. Ctrl-click Alpha Compositor and 15rla01b.rla, and click the Add Image Layers Event icon again. Again choose the Alpha Compositor. The first composite is nested in the second; the second composite is on top of the first. Note the order of events in the queue.

12. Click the Video Post Render icon (the runner) and render a single frame 640×480. (If you render to a size other than this, you will need to adjust the size and position of the Image events.)

You have now nested composites using a Scene event and two Image events. RLA file formats are used here so you can continue to add special effect filters to the Image Event objects as well as any of the Scene objects, which is the subject of the next chapter. To see the composite rendered with Raytracing materials and with Glow and Hilight applied to the lettering, see Figure 15.16 or view 15tga01a.tga, included on the CD-ROM. The final Video Post queue should be as it appears in Figure 15.17.

FIGURE 15.16

The final image.

FIGURE 15.17

Final Video Post queue with nested composites. Note the children of an Alpha Compositor Layer event can be Alpha Compositor Layer events themselves.

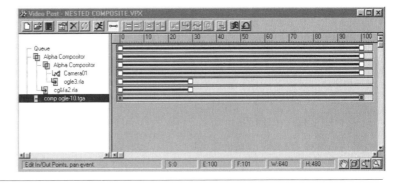

TIP

Notice that if you render the Camera view in step 1 to a 32-bit file, the alpha channel is blank. This is because the Floor and Panel objects occupy the entire frame; there is no visible blank or "negative space" around the objects to be recorded in the alpha channel. If you hide these objects and render only the primitives against a blank background, the background information is recorded in the alpha channel. If you have a scene where there is inadequate alpha information and you require this, you can selectively hide objects, render to a file format that supports alpha channels, and composite the results. You can also render to a format such as RLA, which supports Z-Buffer, object, and material information, as well as RGBA.

Compositing this way in MAX sets you up to easily reestablish your still output for the client's animated logo. You might add a camera move to the scene, ending at the final position, or use special effects filters on Scene objects. You can fade in the bitmap images (together or separately) or animate the Glow or Hilight you applied to part of the logo. (Note that you cannot use Video Post to animate the scale or position of the bitmaps in this exercise.)

Up to this point this chapter has talked about compositing 2D material into a 3D scene and making it appear seamless. The more common situation, however, involves the reverse: placing 3D content on top of a 2D backdrop or animation to produce the illusion-integrated 3D shot.

Understanding Shadows and Compositing

Sometimes an animation requires certain elements that make compositing a little more difficult than just laying images on top of one another. If you use the Alpha Compositor to composite a character on a background, for example, it might look like the character is floating in space while the background is pinned up behind her. In other words, it might look like a composite. A good composite should not give away the fact that it is composited.

To avoid this dilemma, you need to "ground" your composited objects in their backgrounds. You need to make an object feel like it is a part of its environment and that it could interact with the background if it wanted to. To accomplish this, the object should cast a shadow. Shadows give the illusion that an object is present in its environment. For a long time, a strong argument against compositing in many animation studios was the fact that it was difficult (if not impossible) to achieve realistic shadows in a composite. While compositing in MAX, however, techniques enable you to achieving realistic shadows. These techniques are outlined here. Furthermore, lights that might be present in your foreground should affect the background and vice versa, and there is a method for achieving this effect as well.

Screen Mapping and Compositing

Using Screen Mapping to achieve realistic shadow effects in a composite is considered by many to be a "hack" or a workaround. It is only useful in certain situations but is worth discussing and understanding, because it does work for particular situations, and it can work in conjunction with other compositing methods.

The main limitation of the Screen Mapping method is that the camera in the scene must be static. The general term "Screen Mapping" might sound familiar if you have ever used a background image for an environment map. Essentially, a screen-mapped background remains in a direct facing orientation to the camera and fills the screen. If you are using a background and you use Screen Mapping, you would not want to animate camera movement because the background would move exactly with the camera. If you moved the camera 45 degrees, for example, it would still be looking at the same exact background scene. The result would be a foreground that moved against an unchanging background. This is a quite unrealistic and unwanted effect.

For this reason, if you use an environment map and you have camera movement, you need to use one of the other Mapping methods, such as Spherical. If you use the Screen Mapping method to perform a composite, you encounter the same problem with camera movement. If you have a stationary camera, however, Screen Mapping can be used to fake shadow and light effects.

The Screen Mapping method entails setting up a background image in your Camera viewport. You then create geometry and move it so that it matches the perspective of the part of the background image on which you want to cast a shadow. By applying a material that contains the same image as the background in the Diffuse channel and specifying Screen Mapping as the Mapping type, the object is mapped with the background image. Because the Mapping type is Screen, the object has only a section of the map visible. The section of the map visible on the object is exactly the part that the object obstructs from the background. The effect is that the geometry disappears into the background. The geometry, however, is still present and can receive shadows and lighting. Confused? The following example illustrates exactly how this works.

COMPOSITING USING SCREEN MAPPING

1. From the CD-ROM, load 15max02.MAX.

2. Make certain that the Camera viewport is active, select Views from the MAX pull-down menu, and then select Background Image.

The background image feature can be useful for referencing what is happening in a composite. A Shaded viewport with a background image displayed can give you a good idea of what to expect from your final render. The background image can be a single image or an animation. You can specify an IFL file (discussed previously in this chapter) or you can specify an AVI file. When using Screen Mapping for compositing, it is important to display the background image or animation because you need to match the image's perspective with geometry you create in the viewport.

3. Click the Files button and select 15jpg01.JPG from the accompanying CD-ROM.

4. Under Aspect Ratio in the lower-left corner, check the box titled Match Rendering output.

5. Click the Display Background button in the lower-right corner to enable it, and click OK to dismiss the dialog (see Figure 15.18).

You should also turn off the Viewport grid by right-clicking the Viewport label and selecting Show Grid to toggle it off. The grid can obstruct your view of the background image and consequently make Perspective matching more difficult. Notice the object in the scene named Ground. This geometry is a simple box that has been aligned to match up with the ground plane in the image. By applying a material with Screen Mapping, you can make the object seem to disappear into the background image.

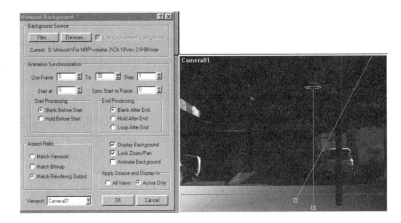

FIGURE 15.18

*The Viewport
Background dialog
enables you to display
a background in the
viewport.*

6. Open the Material Editor, select a Material slot and name it Screen Map 1.

7. Click the Diffuse Map button and select a Bitmap from the Material/Map browser.

8. Under Bitmap Parameters, click the long gray box next to the Bitmap button and select the same file that you selected for your background image, or 15jpg01.jpg from the accompanying CD-ROM.

9. Under the Coordinates rollout, select Environment Mapping, and then from the list box, change Mapping to Screen.

10. Make the object named Ground in the scene the currently selected object, and then click the Assign Material to Selection button from the Material Editor toolbar.

11. Render the scene to the Virtual Frame Buffer window (see Figure 15.19).

You should now see an object in the scene with a material applied that matches the background image. Notice, however, that the background image doesn't show up. Setting the background image in the viewport is not the same as setting a background image for rendering. To set up the background image for rendering, follow this procedure:

12. Open the Material Editor, select a Material slot and name it Background Map 1.

13. Click the Get Material button and select Bitmap from the Material/Map browser.

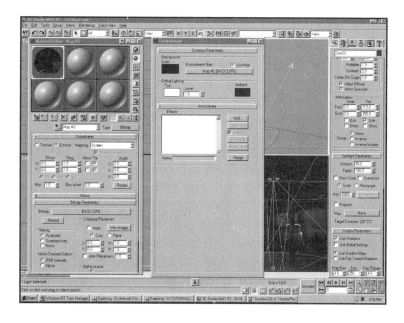

14. Under Bitmap Parameters, click the Bitmap button and select the image you want to use for the background. Again change the Coordinates to Environment Mapping and set the Mapping to Screen.

15. Open the Environment dialog (Rendering/Environment). Drag the Environment map from slot 2 in the Material Editor to the Environment Map button in the Environment dialog, and when prompted, select Instance.

16. Make certain to check the Use Map check box.

Now when you render the scene, you should see the background image and the CG telephone pole. The Ground Plane object has almost disappeared into the background image. One problem you might notice is that the ground plane is not lit correctly to match the lighting in the background image. Next you'll introduce lighting and shadow to the 3D geometry in a manner to blend it with the background plate.

17. Select the Spot01 spotlight that is above the telephone pole, open the Modify panel, and adjust the multiplier to approximately 0.5 to correctly match the lighting.

18. Check the Cast Shadows check box in the Shadow Parameters section.

19. Make certain that the Camera viewport is active and re-render the scene.

You should now see that the telephone pole is seemingly casting a shadow on the background image. The shadow makes the object seem as if it is present in the scene. You can also use this method for lighting effects.

20. Select the Spot02 spotlight, open the Modify panel, and check the On check box that is next to the Color selector. You might also adjust the color of the spotlight to match the color of your typical pale yellow street light.

21. Render the scene (see Figure 15.20).

FIGURE 15.20

The final scene.

Notice that the light appears to affect the ground in the background image as well. To add to the realism of the scene, you might create some telephone wires connecting the CG telephone pole with the real one in the image. Using Screen Mapping in this manner can be quite useful for creating shadow and light effects over real images or CG backgrounds.

This Shadow effect is not limited to ground planes, however. You can cast shadows over buildings or other objects by making simple boxes and Perspective-matching them to the objects. The backgrounds that you use can be animated, but remember that Screen Mapping is not the way to go if there is camera movement.

If there is camera movement and you need shadow effects, you should use the Shadow/Matte material (discussed in the "Matte Shadow" section later in this chapter). The Display Background feature proves very useful for all types of compositing because it gives you an idea of what to expect from the background and enables you to place foreground objects in relation to the background.

Camera Mapping

The Camera Map modifier and space warp works similarly to the way the Screen Mapping method does. Camera Mapping maps the background image onto an object by using a modified planar projection from the camera's point of view. The result is that the object with Camera Mapping applied disappears into the background image the same way that it does with Screen Mapping. You could use Camera Mapping to achieve shadows in a composite. The plug-in contains two parts: a modifier and a space warp.

The modifier sets the object's mapping to the background image for a specified frame. The modifier doesn't work properly if there is camera movement for the same reason that Screen Mapping doesn't. If you use the modifier, the background image is mapped properly only for the current frame you are on when you choose a camera to use for the mapping. If the camera moves, the other frames disorient the mapping from the background.

Essentially the Camera Mapping modifier is another way to do Screen Mapping. Screen Mapping has some advantages because Camera Mapping relates to the tessellation of the geometry. For the mapping to be accurate, the object needs to have a high number of faces. Screen Mapping works with the minimum number of faces.

The second part of the plug-in, the space warp, recalculates the mapping for every frame of animation. The result is that the object is mapped with the correct background perspective for each frame, enabling you to move the camera. You could use this to composite an animation that has a moving camera with a static or moving background. It can be difficult, however, to match the background camera movement with the foreground camera movement. Typically, you must merge the same camera you use in the background MAX file into the foreground MAX file.

Furthermore, using this method to match the lighting in a file that has camera movement can be tough. If you want to composite an animation that has a moving camera with shadows, it is easier to use the Matte/Shadow Material described in the next section. This plug-in is quite useful, however, if you are doing special effects. You can blend an object into the background with the space warp, for example. You can then animate the self-illumination of the material or use a morph material to make the object "cloak" in and out of the background.

Matte/Shadow

There are ways to composite with shadows that get around the static camera problem that limits Screen mapping and the Camera Map modifier's functionality. Shadow Matting is one such method. The Matte/Shadow material has been extended from its R1 incarnation to include the features added by Peter Watje in his Shadow Matte plug-in for R1, which is, namely, to be a material that doesn't visually render, but instead receives shadows and can store that shadow information in the alpha channel (see Figure 15.21).

The following exercise illustrates how to use the Matte/Shadow material to composite an animated character into a pre-rendered architectural walkthrough animation. Why would you do this? First, following an object or character through an environment can add visual interest, clarity, or commentary that you won't find with a camera moving through an environment. Second, you might otherwise want to render the architecture with a Radiosity/Raytrace renderer, such as Lightscape or Radioray, which you wouldn't use for an animated character. Finally, you could also decide you want multiple versions, with or without a character, or with an entirely different character. For all these reasons, if you render the background architecture animation once, you can save substantial time by rendering and compositing ancillary characters or objects.

Note that Video Post permits you to save settings as a VPX file, but the Queue events point to file and path locations specific to the computer you use when you set up the list. So if you use files created on another machine with a different path configuration, you need to edit the events individually to address the correct paths. The accompanying CD-ROM includes saved VPX examples; if you intend to use them, you need to make these corrections.

FIGURES 15.21

The Matte/Shadow material makes an object that will not render in the scene but can receive shadows cast from other objects and save these in the alpha channel for compositing.

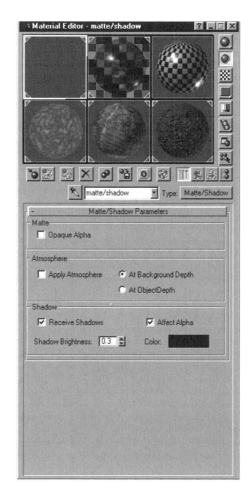

In this exercise, you review how to set up the scene to render image sets to use as layers for compositing. Then you composite and edit pre-rendered material. The animation of the camera and character has been completed for you; because this part can be tricky and time consuming, the steps are explained as part of the exercise.

COMPOSITING AN ANIMATED CHARACTER INTO A WALKTHROUGH ANIMATION

1. Open the file 15max03.max. The building has a main floor and a loft. The walkthrough begins upstairs and proceeds down the staircase to reveal the lower floor. A free camera with a Look At controller (camera-biped) follows a Dummy object (biped-camera) assigned to a Spline path with a Path controller (path-biped).

2. Unhide the biped figure by clicking the Saved-selection set drop-down, selecting Biped All, and clicking Yes at the warning box. This reveals a biped object created and animated in Character Studio. Notice that biped footsteps traverse the loft, go down the stairs and walk toward the back of the building, following a path nearly identical to that used for the dummy. The 50 footsteps occupy about 735 of the 830 frames in the animation and move at a rate set by Character Studio. The footsteps are saved as 15bip01.bip, included with your file.

3. As set up, although the dummy and biped move along the same path and end at the same point, they are not always synchronized. In order for the camera to always keep the character in frame, the biped and the dummy must always be at the same place at the same time. You correct the pacing by clicking the Animate button, selecting the dummy, and animating the Path Options-% Along Path spinner over the length of the animation.

4. From the Named Selection Sets drop-down, select "bip + mesh" and then hide the Biped and Figure objects. Rendering the scene of the camera moving through the space takes many hours. The pre-rendered AVI files are included on the CD-ROM: 15avi01.avi for frames 0–400; 15avi02.avi for frames 401–830. This will be the background.

5. Next you prepare the character to be composited on top of the background. Save the file as 15max02.max.

6. From the Named Selection Sets drop-down, select the "Furniture" and hide these objects (only the building's walls, roof, and staircase remain visible).

7. From the Named Selection Sets drop-down, select "matte/shadow obj."

8. Open the Material Editor. Select the upper-left slot and click the Standard Material button. This brings up the Material/Map Browser; select a Matte/Shadow material.

9. Under Matte/Shadow Parameters, make sure only Shadow/Receive Shadows and Affect Alpha are checked. Set Shadow Brightness to 0.3. (Note: the lower the value, the darker the shadow, with 0 equalling black and 1.0 equalling no shadow). Set Color to black. Assign the material to the selected objects in the scene. These Matte/Shadow settings result in the Scene objects not rendering, while shadows cast by any other objects (the moving figure) are saved to the alpha channel.

10. Open the Environment dialog box (Rendering/Environment) and uncheck Use Map.

11. Unhide the figure named "painted torso." The figure is an athletic male wearing bicycle pants (which depending on your client's sense of humor may or may not be appropriate). The figure has been assigned to the biped using Physique and animated. You can alter the character's movements in Character Studio using the exiting biped that is part of the file.

12. Go to frame 120. Render the camera view to a single 320×240 32-bit Targa file. You should see a color render of the figure against a black background with nothing else visible. Click the Display Alpha Channel button on the Virtual Frame buffer. You will see the figure (white) and its shadow (almost white) cast against the floor and the wall (the wall shadow is almost invisible).

Again, to save rendering time, pre-rendered Targa files are on your CD-ROM in two subdirectories: figure0000.tga through figure0400.tga, and figure0401.tga through figure0830.tga. The time it takes to render the figure against the Matte/Shadow objects is about 10% of that for the background frame in step 4.

NOTE

Make sure you do not hide any shadow-casting lights when rendering against a Matte/Shadow material. You won't see what shadows are being cast during the render because the figure is against a black background. To test this, render single sample frames at various times in the sequence and examine the alpha channel in the Virtual Frame buffer.

13. Open the Video Post dialog. Click the Add Image Input Event button. Click Files and load 15avi01.avi. Click the Options button. By default, Size is set to Resize to Fit, and Frames are From 0 To 400, stepping 1 at a time, and looping at the end. In this instance, the background and composite figure files match, both in size and number of frames. This dialog permits you to resize and reposition the image, as well as change its range and length. Click OK twice to return to Video Post.

14. Before you perform the next operation, copy the Targa sequence figure0000 to 0400 to a directory on your hard drive. Click Add Image Input Event again. Click Files and go to the directory containing figure0000.tga through figure0400.tga you just made on your hard drive. In the Filename box, enter figure*.tga. Click OK twice. A new entry appears in Video Post, figure0338.ifl (actually it comes up as figure0000.ifl on my machine). MAX makes an *ifl (image file list) file and stores it in the same directory as the Targa files. For this reason, you must have the composite images located on a readable drive, not on CD-ROM.

15. Click the button labeled Add Image Output Event. Click Files, set the file type to AVI, and create a file called 15avi02c.avi. Click OK. Set Video Compression to Cinepak Codec by Radius and Compression Quality to 75. Click OK. In the Add Image Output Event dialog, leave Video Post parameters at Start Time = 0, End Time = 400. (You have the option at render time to set the length of the segment.)

16. Click 15avi01.avi and Ctrl+click figure0338.ifl in the Video Post queue. Then the Add Image Layer button becomes active. Click this and from the drop-down list, select Alpha Compositor. Because you use the mask saved in the Targa file, leave Mask/Enabled unchecked (see Figure 15.22).

If you render the VP queue in this state, the masked figure appears to walk in the environment, but he will appear to walk through any object that appears in front of him. This is because the figure is composited on top of the background layer, which contains imagery that belongs in front of the figure. You need to make a new Composite layer on top of the figure, consisting of just those objects that belong in the foreground—in other words, the upstairs railing. On the accompanying CD-ROM, you will find Targa files railing0120.tga through railing0200.tga. If you examine these files, you will see they contain only that portion of the railing you need in front of the figure rendered against a black background.

17. Click anywhere in the VP queue to deselect all events. Click the Add Image Event icon. Locate and enter railing*.tga. Set the VP Start to 120 and End to 200.

18. Ctrl-click railing0120.ifl and the Alpha Compositor events, and then click the Add Image Layer Event icon. Select the Alpha Compositor from the drop-down menu. This gives nested composite events.

19. Click anywhere in the Queue white area to deselect all events. Click the Add Image Output Event icon and create an AVI file named 15avi03.avi. Your Video Post queue should appear as in Figure 15.22; a sample file is included on the accompanying CD-ROM at 15vpx02a.vpx.

FIGURE 15.22

Video Post queue setup for a nested composite of three animation layers. Note you can render a segment of the animation without disturbing these ranges.

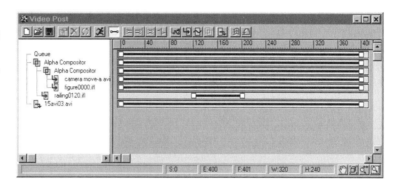

20. Click the Runner icon to render Video Post. Set the range to frames 120 to 400 and render. Video Post composites the figure walking down the staircase, casting a shadow as it goes. On a dual Pentium Pro 180, the entire render process takes about 14 minutes. The final animation appears on your CD-ROM as 15avi03.avi.

Suppose you've decided you want to render frames 350–450. The background AVI files go from 0–400 and 401–830. You need to add the additional background file to the queue.

21. Click in the white area of the Video Post dialog (nothing is selected and the Add Image Input Event button becomes active). Click Add Image Input Event/Files and load 15avi02.avi. Click OK.

22. Under Video Post parameters, set VP Start Time to 400 and VP end time to 830. Click OK. If you need to return to this dialog, you can double-click the name in the queue, the VP Range bar, or the Edit icon on the VP toolbar.

23. Delete the Alpha Compositor event from the queue (use the Delete icon on the toolbar or the Del key).

24. Copy figure files 0401 through 0830 to another directory on your hard drive. Add another image input event with the new range of Targa files. Set VP Start Time to 401 and End to 830. MAX creates a new *.ifl file for this range.

25. Highlight 15avi01.avi and figure00338.ifl, click Add Image Layer Event, and select the Alpha Compositor. Highlight 15avi02.avi and figure0814.ifl, click Add Image Layer Event, and select Alpha Compositor.

Even though you are only compositing two layers, you are compositing four events. The Alpha Compositor only accepts two. The solution here is two unnested Alpha Compositor events. (The Video Post file for this portion of the exercise is on your CD-ROM as 15vpx01.vpx.)

26. Double-click the Image Output Event. Render frames 350 to 450 to an AVI format. You have now spliced the two composited animations together. View the final animation, 15avi04.avi, on your CD-ROM.

By double-clicking any Image Input event and then the Options button in the dialog, you can choose to step frames or loop the animation. In this way you can rescale animation timing. Be careful, however, because changing the timing of some elements and not others can sabotage the composite. If you do this, test render short segments for accuracy.

Even though you've only worked with portions of this sequence, you could have worked with the entire walkthrough or just selected portions. Video Post is an easy place to edit and thereby clean up problems in otherwise salvageable footage. You may not want to simply composite two complete synchronized animations in their entirety; you may opt for something more interesting, such as selecting a few portions of the sequence and cutting it together with a transition.

Using a Matte/Shadow material for shadow effects is usually the best way to go because it saves render time. You can create a "dummy" scene composed of simple primitives that represent your complicated background. Suppose, for example, you have a scene that calls for characters to chase each other through the aisles of an intricate junkyard. Stacking up bunches of junked-up car meshes, barrels, and other miscellaneous objects could create an incredibly complex scene quickly. Trying to concentrate on character animation within this scene would be futile. You should, therefore, create the complex background and render it on its own. Then you can animate your characters and use simple geometry to stand in for the complex background.

First apply the Matte/Shadow material to these simple primitives, render, and then composite your character animation over the complex background that you rendered previously. Matte/Shadow offers the best choice here because you would likely have lots of camera movement in a chase scene. As long as the dummy background and the real background are laid out in the same manner, the shadow effects should be accurate enough to fool the eye.

You can also combine the different methods outlined so far. Although Matte/Shadow enables you to move the camera, you cannot use it to receive lighting. For example, you might combine Screen Mapping with Matte/Shadow to create this effect.

Masking

Sometimes the images you need to composite are 24-bit and have no alpha channel. If you hope to composite such images, you need some way of creating areas of transparency. You can use a program such as Adobe Photoshop to create an alpha channel in your source images, but this can be difficult if the colors in the image are not distinctive. In certain situations, you may need to use a mask to obtain good results in a composite.

A mask enables you to use a separate file to get your transparency data and create your areas of transparency. You can use a separate file's alpha channel for your transparency data, for example. Commonly, the alpha channel is used to create the mask, but MAX enables you to use any of the image channels, as well as G-Buffer information, to create a mask. You can use G-Buffer channels, such as Material Effects or Object channels, to mask out certain objects. If you intend to use G-Buffer information for masking, be certain to use the RLA image format to save your files (see previous section in this chapter on G-Buffer).

If you had one object in an animation that you wanted to mask out, for example, you can set the object to have an Object channel and then render out to RLA. You can then specify Object as the Mask type and, wherever that object is present in the scene, it shows up transparent or opaque. It would be opaque by default and transparent if you checked the Inverted button next to the mask type.

Using the Red, Green, or Blue channel to create a mask is often useful and functions similarly to the way an Opacity map works. When you use these color channels to create your mask, the intensity of each pixel (0–255) controls the level of transparency. Because different channels have different intensities in different images, you can pick and choose which Color channel you want to use for your particular needs. The following example illustrates how you might use one of the Color channels to composite flames over an animation. The flames used come from the Pyromania CD-ROM available from Trinity Enterprises (http:\\www.trinity3d.com). These flames make a good illustration for masking because they ship without an alpha channel. Furthermore, you can experiment with which channel to use to get varying levels of transparency.

USING COLOR CHANNELS TO COMPOSITE FLAMES

1. Open MAX or Save and Reset. Open Video Post.

2. Add 15tga07.tga from the accompanying CD-ROM as an Image Input event. Be certain to check the Cache check box so that MAX doesn't load and rescale the same file for every frame of animation. This is going to be the background that you will be compositing flames over.

3. Add another Image Input event and navigate to 15tga08.tga from the accompanying CD-ROM. With the image highlighted in the directory list, click View to view the image. Click the Display Alpha button and notice that the file has no alpha channel. Click the Red, Green, and Blue buttons in turn to see the different channels of the image. Accept the image and return to the Video Post window.

4. Select both Image Input events by holding down Ctrl and clicking both events. Add the Alpha Compositor Layer event. The Flames event should be listed below the Engine Room event in the hierarchy. Because 15tga08.tga does not have an alpha channel, a straight alpha composite does not work. If you render this sequence, only the flames appear because they have no transparency information yet.

5. Double-click the Alpha Compositor event to bring up the Layer event. Under the section labeled Masking, click the Files button, navigate to the CD-ROM, and select 15tga08.tga. Notice that the Enabled check box becomes checked automatically. Check the Inverted check box to invert the mask. Figure 15.23 provides an example of how to configure the Alpha Compositor.

FIGURE 15.23

The Mask feature enables you to use the different channels in an image to create custom areas of transparency. Notice that you order the Video Post queue as in any other composite, but use the Mask section of the Alpha Compositor to use the RGB image as the mask.

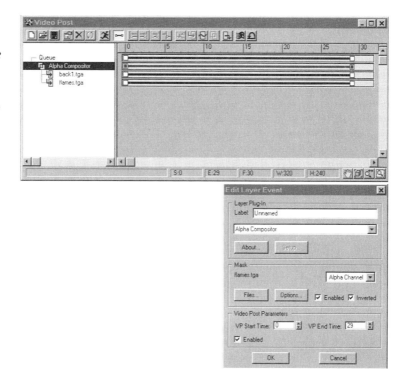

6. In the pull-down list box, select the Green channel from the list. You use the Green channel of the 15tga08.tga image as a mask for your composite. Areas containing information other than black in the Blue channel represent varying levels of opacity.

7. Render a single image to the Virtual Frame Buffer window.

You should see the flames over the image of the engine room and can view the composite as 15tga05.tga. You might experiment with using different channels in the image for the mask. The image can be rendered by using the Red, Blue, or Luminance channel instead of the Green, for example. Generally speaking, the Green channel tends to hold the most detail, Red the most warmth, and Blue the most noise. Fire makes for a particularly tricky composite because the flames need to be semitransparent themselves. It comes down to taste, because each channel option produces a slightly different result. Masking is a powerful way to composite animation because it enables greater flexibility than the standard alpha channel.

Bluescreening

Bluescreening is a widely used method for compositing and is a chromakey technique. Chromakeying is a process whereby a foreground image is shot against a mono-colored screen. The mono-colored screen represents a background that can be replaced by film, video, or computer graphics.

Chromakey techniques such as bluescreening are commonly used in film and television to composite different layers of action together. An actor filmed against a bluescreen in a small studio, for example, could seemingly be placed anywhere on earth or beyond. The method involves shrouding the background in a particular color, commonly blue or green, and then keying the area filled with that color in the image to be the transparent area.

To successfully bluescreen, you need to use a material with a little or no shininess or luster. Special blue or green screen material is available from certain mail-order outlets and specialty stores, but you can also use standard color board available at any art store if you are careful with how you set up and light it. The background must be solid and consistently lit for the computer to successfully find every instance of the color. Inconsistencies, such as shadows or crumples, can cause the computer to miscalculate the areas you intend to be transparent.

Probably the most difficult part of setting up a successful bluescreen is lighting. You need to place high-powered lights behind your subject and point them at the bluescreen material, but you should be careful not to create a hotspot on one part of the material. The light you use to illuminate your subject cannot be brighter than the lights used to illuminate the bluescreen material or you create a shadow. The color you choose for the bluescreen material should also be a color that doesn't conflict with what you intend to be the foreground. You do not want to key a color close to the color of skin, for example, if you want to have an actor in your foreground. This is why a bright solid blue color is normally used. You can, however, theoretically use whatever color you desire.

3D Studio MAX itself does not provide tools necessary to perform chromakey operations. A company called Photron (http:\\www.photron.com), however, makes a plug-in for MAX called Primatte, which performs this function. A demo version of Primatte is on the CD-ROM. The following example illustrates how you might use Primatte to perform a simple chromakey composite of a person shot against a bluescreen background over a background that comes with MAX. Before doing this example, you need to install the demo version of Primatte into MAX. Copy the PRIMATTE.FLT file from the accompanying CD-ROM to your \3dsmax\plugins directory, and then restart MAX.

COMPOSITING A LIVE SUBJECT INTO A VIRTUAL SET

1. Reset and load 15max06.max. Open Video Post.

2. Add 15tga09.tga from your accompanying CD-ROM as an Image Input event in the Video Post queue. This is a still frame of part of the building you worked with in the earlier composites (15max03.max), which you will use as the background (see Figure 15.24). You can alternatively enter Camera-painting in the VP queue as a Scene event. The only drawback is you must wait for Primatte's setup to render the scene before you can see the result. It's generally quicker to position the camera, render the viewport, and composite two bitmaps in Primatte.

3. Add 15tga10.tga from the accompanying CD-ROM as an Image Input event. The image of the model (Elizabeth Stone) was shot on 35mm film against a swatch of bluescreen background fabric that shipped with Primatte. The photo was then scanned into Photoshop, where the bluescreen was sampled and extended to fill the 640×480 frame (see Figure 15.24). This image has no alpha channel.

4. Highlight both Image Input events and add the Primatte Chromakey Compositor as an Image Layer event. Click OK to return to the Video Post window. You must have the Layer event set in Video Post before you can change the setup for the filter.

5. Double-click the Primatte Chromakey Compositor Layer event and then click Setup. In a few moments, the Primatte plug-in window appears.

6. Click-drag the mouse cursor from the left side of the background area to the right side without dragging over the person. This function tells Primatte what area you intend to be transparent. Notice that part of the person has also become transparent. You need to give Primatte some more information.

FIGURES 15.24

The virtual set can be rendered and composited with a model shot against bluescreen by using the Primatte plug-in.

7. Click the button labeled FG (Select Foreground Pixels) on the button bar and click-drag around the torso of the person. You may also need to click-drag around the head area or any area that you see is transparent that shouldn't be.

8. Click the button labeled with the black/white man (View Matte) to see the matte. You can now activate the FG and BG buttons, and then click-drag within the matte display to modify your chromakey settings with this view active. This view can help you visualize what your final Matte object will look like (see Figure 15.25).

FIGURE 15.25

The Primatte interface previews the final composite.

9. Click the View Composite button to return to the Composite Preview window. You have now set up Primatte to chromakey accurately. The result of this composite is Elizabeth standing in front of the painting in the virtual building rather than in front of a bluescreen (see Figure 15.26). By choosing OK from the Operation menu, you can accept this composite and render. The demo version on the CD-ROM, however, is functionally crippled to render Demo across the screen.

Primatte can be used to composite Scene or Image events with other Image events and is flexible enough to fix irregularities you might run into with an uneven bluescreen.

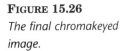

FIGURE 15.26
The final chromakeyed image.

Other Methods of Compositing

So far in this chapter, you have used the Alpha Compositor exclusively when using the tools MAX provides to perform compositing. The reason for this is a simple one. The Alpha Compositor is the best tool that MAX provides for compositing purposes. You should be aware, however, that the following compositing functions are available in MAX, as well:

■ Pseudo Alpha

■ Simple Additive Composite

Pseudo Alpha

Pseudo Alpha is a method of compositing that obtains the color value of the first pixel of the image and uses it to make all other pixels with the same value in the image transparent. The first pixel in the image is the pixel in the upper-left corner. This method has limited functionality, so you might use it if you want to use a particular image for transparency and the image has no alpha channel.

In practice, however, you can only use images that you render with MAX or some other computer program. The reason for this is that the exact value of the first pixel is used to locate all other transparent pixels throughout the image. If you tried to use Pseudo Alpha to do chromakeying, for example, all the blue would not have the exact same value (even with great bluescreen material).

The tiny variations in the color that occur as a result of film or video transfer and compression render Pseudo Alpha useless. You end up with many random holes where the values happen to have exactly the same value as the first pixel. If you use computer-generated images, however, this is not as much of a problem because you can set the background color to be exactly one solid color and one consistent HSV value.

Pseudo Alpha can be used as either a Layer event or a Filter event, and it performs the same function in either instance. A useful plug-in would be to rewrite Pseudo Alpha so that you could pick the color you want and then set a threshold to determine the tolerance of the HSV value.

Simple Additive Compositor

The Simple Additive Compositor composites the two images by using the second image's intensity or HSV value to determine transparency. Areas of full intensity 255 are opaque, areas of 0 intensity are transparent, and areas of intermediate transparency are translucent. This method also has limited functionality. In practice, the only time you would want to use it is if you want to do a funky blend of two images.

Transitions: Editing Your Animations

You have now seen how to layer content with image compositing within Video Post. The next step is stitching together these sequences to form a coherent presentation. You can choose third-party solutions such as Adobe Premiere and After Effects, Speed Razor Pro with PVR hardware, Digital Fusion, Illuminaire, Media 100, and Avid. You could also use Video Post to lay your still/animated modules end-to-end with either a transition or a cut (no transition) between them, and render them to final form.

In making this choice, consider the following:

■ The availability of third-party products, not just for your initial editing, but later on if you want to revise or re-edit. (Some choices require dedicated hardware, such as Speed Razor, Media 100, and Avid, and while substantially more capable, they require a sizable investment.)

■ Will you add sound to your animation? You can position and render a soundtrack with an animation within MAX, but you cannot edit the sound clip in MAX, nor can you composite sound in VP.

■ Does your composite include single or multiple Scene events? You can render multiple camera views in VP, for example, with each having different frame sequences, while performing image or sequence compositing in the same operation. Where compositing is incidental compared to scene rendering, VP is superior.

■ If your scene includes Glows, Hilights, or other special effects that can be implemented only with MAX's VP filters or specific plug-ins, or if your source materials are in *.rla format, your only option is to use VP. Then the question narrows to if you want to initially render your scene with the Effects filters in MAX and composite that result using a third-party solution.

■ To what extent does your piece rely on 2D special effects? For example, After Effects offers more superior titling, chromakey, bluescreen, 2D motion tracking, and special effects filters than are available in MAX. Like After Effects, Premiere has become a software-based cross-platform desktop video editing environment.

■ Are you collaborating with other studios, and if so, what hardware/software do they prefer and have available?

■ If you are working with others in the production process using third-party editing or effects tools, will your MAX "modules" made for compositing cause problems in the other environment? For example, R2 uses a pre-multiplied alpha channel; Photoshop does not. After Effects supports this, but you must make changes to the Import settings for compatibility, and even then, you have problems implementing Lens Effects.

The bottom line is which choices deliver your finished piece the most quickly and cost effectively. MAX ships with a few filters that enable you to do fades and wipes, and there are many third-party plug-ins that enable you to extend MAX's functionality as an editing system. In addition to using the Filter events that ship with MAX, you can use the Alpha Compositor with animated masks to create great transitions. The MAX CD-ROM comes with 50 .FLC files (see R2's World Creating Toolkit, \maps\wipes directory), which can be used as luminance masks to create great transition effects. The following examples show how you can use Filter and Layer events as well as masks to edit your animations and create transitions.

Video Post Event Transitions

This example illustrates how you might arrange a Video Post queue by using layers, filters, and range bars to string together two of the animations used in previous examples in this chapter and do transitions between them. You will use rendered segments from the last exercise.

15avi05.avi, used in the following exercise, is a rendered composite made using the techniques shown in the exercise. The only difference is that single frame images were cached and composited with the animation files, and because the animation files are sandwiched between two layers of still images, there are two "nested" composites.

15avi05.avi was made from the same 15max03.max and 15max01.max files used to prepare the main rendering and composite figure animations. Only this time, the animated figure was rendered to single frame Targa files (against the Shadow/Matte materials) as seen from the Camera-Stairs camera view. Then Camera-Stairs was merged into 15max03.max (the file without Matte/Shadow Materials) and two Targa files were rendered; the background was rendered with the foreground still life hidden; the foreground still life was rendered with the background hidden.

The background image was entered as the first Image Input Event and cached with VP time of 0–300. Then the figure Targa files were entered at 0–300. Last, the foreground still life was entered as an Image Input event, cached over the range of 0–300. The background and animated figure files were composited using the Alpha Compositor. Then the foreground image and the Alpha Compositor Layer event were composited using a second Alpha Compositor. The scene was rendered to an AVI file. The Video Post file is entitled 15vpx02.vpx, included on your CD-ROM for your reference.

The Cache check box instructs Video Post to load the image into RAM and then to use that same information throughout the sequence. This should always be checked if you are using a single image in an Image Input event. By loading the image information into RAM, MAX does not reload or scale the image for every frame. Reloading and scaling takes time, and that makes the render take longer. If you are using a single image, checking the Cache check box saves a lot of time. Do not use this option if you are using a sequence of images. It is necessary to load each image for each frame if you want your background animation to correspond with your foreground animation.

USING TRANSITIONS TO CUT ANIMATION CLIPS TOGETHER

1. Load MAX or Save and Reset.

2. Add 15avi06.avi, 15avi04.avi, 15avi05.avi, and 15avi07.avi (in that order) as Image Input events in the Video Post queue.

3. Create an Image Output event and label it transition.avi.

4. Select 15avi06.avi to highlight it and then click the Add Filter Event button. Select Fade from the list of filters, click the Setup button, and make certain that IN is currently checked active. Set VP Start time to 0 and VP End time to 20. Double-click 15avi06.avi and advance the Start and End times 10 frames each. The first 10 frames will be black and then will fade into the animation.

5. Move the slider to align 15avi06.avi so it overlaps 15avi04.avi by 10 frames. 15avi04.avi begins 20 frames before 15avi06.avi ends. Your transition takes place in the space of this overlap. Without this overlap, part of your transition will appear black.

6. With both events highlighted, click the Add Image Layer Event button and select Simple Wipe from the pull-down list box. Click the Setup button to bring up the Setup dialog for Simple Wipe (see Figure 15.27).

7. The Simple Wipe control lets you set the directions for the wipe (right to left or left to right) and whether this should push or pop. Set the direction you want and click OK. Specify frames 90 to 110 in the VP Post parameters as Start and End times for the event. Click OK to return to the Video Post window.

FIGURE 15.27

Simple Wipe enables you to create Wipe transitions between animations.

8. Align 15avi04.avi and 15avi05.avi so they overlap, as in step 5 (you can drag the range bars from their center, or double-click the bar or the Scene event in the queue to bring up a dialog that allows you to type in precise ranges).

9. Highlight 15avi05.avi and Simple Wipe, click the Add Image Layer Event button, and add a Cross Fade Transition Image Layer event. In the Video Post parameters, set the VP Start time to 170 and the End time to 190.

10. Control highlight Cross Fade Transition and 15avi07.avi, and add a second Cross Fade Transition Image Layer event. In the Video Post parameters, set the VP Start time to 450 and the End time to 470.

11. Highlight 15avi07.avi and add a Fade Filter event (see Figure 15.28) with Fade Image Control set to Out. Set the VP Start time to 541 and the End time to 561. Click Setup and make certain that Out is specified. Click OK to accept this event. Save your Video Post file to 15vpx04.vpx. Save your MAX file.

FIGURE 15.28

Video Post can be used to provide transitions between your animations.

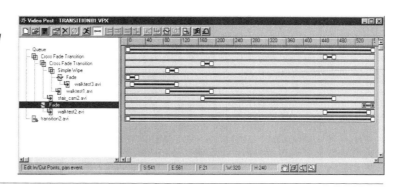

You can render this sequence to your hard disk or view the final rendered 15avi08.avi from the CD-ROM. If you are uncertain whether or not you set up the Video Post queue correctly, you can load Video Post from the accompanying CD-ROM.

The Adobe Premiere Compatible Plug-in in Video Post

New with R2 is the Adobe Premiere Plug-in, which you can access as a map through the Material Editor, or as either a Image Filter event or Image Layer event in Video Post. The creators ill-named this plug-in; it only works with Adobe Premiere-compatible filters, not the filters native to Premiere. This means only third-party filters based on Adobe's SDK work within MAX R2. Apparently the problem arises from an incompatibility between Adobe's SDK and the Adobe filters as written and implemented in Premiere; a similar limitation exists for both Adobe Photoshop and After Effects.

Consequently, most Adobe-native Photoshop filters are not available in MAX through the Photoshop Filter plug-in; presently, R2 contains no After Effects plug-in compatibility. The transitions contained MetaCreations Final Effects AP function properly in R2, although their Premiere-compatible filters cannot be accessed through MAX. (A save-disabled demo copy of MetaCreations Final Effects AP is included on the accompanying CD-ROM.)

USING TRANSITIONS FROM FINAL EFFECTS AP

1. Install MetaCreations Final Effects AP on your hard disk. (If you have the product and have already installed it, ignore this step. If not, a demo version is included on the CD-ROM.) For MAX purposes, you should assign it to its own directory, but for purposes of this exercise, installing it to your Premiere plug-ins directory will suffice.

2. Load your completed file from the previous exercise (if unavailable, use 15max04.max on the CD-ROM).

3. Open the Video Post module. Within Video Post, load the VPX file saved from the last exercise. (If unavailable, load 15vpx03.vpx.) Your queue should resemble that in Figure 15.29.

FIGURE 15.29

Video Post Queue con-figured with transitions between scenes using native MAX R2 transi-tions.

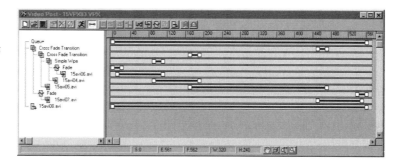

4. Highlight the Simple Wipe entry in the queue and double-click it. This brings up the Edit Layer Event dialog. Click the drop-down (now contains Simple Wipe) and select Adobe Premier Transition Filter. Click Setup. The Adobe Premiere Transition Filter Setup dialog appears.

5. Click the Add Path button and locate your Final Effects AP directory. Four transition types appear in the Filter Selection box (see Figure 15.30). Note you can add a path, but once added you cannot remove it from the list.

FIGURE 15.30

The Adobe Premiere Transition Filter Setup showing Final Effects AP setup choices and options.

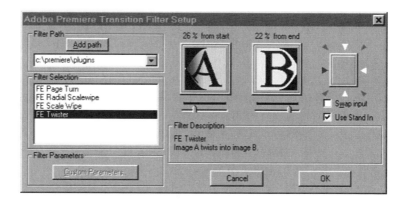

6. The Setup dialog allows designation of percent from the start of the transition, percent from its end, its direction, and an option to swap the A-B rolls.

WARNING

Do not uncheck the Use Stand In check box unless your source files remain in the directory you designated with their queue entry. This feature provides a real-time view of the file footage you are transitioning. If it cannot find your file, you cannot turn back—it will crash R2.

7. Set the transition by clicking OK twice. Edit the Image Output event to give it a new filename. Render a segment of the footage that contains the new Final Effects AP transition.

8. Save the revised Video Post queue to transition02.vpx.

Video Post Masking Transitions

You can use masks (see the section on masking in this chapter) within the Alpha Compositor to do transition effects as well. The accompanying CD-ROM comes with many useful images and texture maps. There is a directory of 2D black-and-white animated .flc files that serve very well as masks. The following example illustrates how you might set this up.

USING AN ANIMATION AS A MASK IN THE ALPHA COMPOSITOR

1. Load or reset MAX and open Video Post. Load the 15vpx05.vpx Video Post file from the accompanying CD-ROM.

2. Double-click the Alpha Compositor Layer event. In the Masking section, click the Files button to bring up the file selector. Navigate to the accompanying CD-ROM, highlight tide.flc, and click the View button to view the animated mask.

3. The tide.flc file is one of 50 files in the \maps\wipes directory on the World Creation Toolkit that ships with R2. Because this file is made up of either absolute black (0) or white (255), you can use the luminance of the image for the mask. Luminance indicates that a value of 0 is transparent, 255 is opaque, and intermediary values are translucent. Because the .flc is only solid black or white, it works well for transitions. In the list box for the mask, select Luminance.

4. Add an Image Output event and render the first 116 frames of the sequence. View the rendered 15avi09.avi file from the accompanying CD-ROM.

    Feel free to experiment with the other .FLC Wipes that come on the accompanying CD-ROM to achieve other interesting transition effects.

Video Post with Other Renderers

Video Post enables you to render different scene elements with different renderers and composite them together for maximum effect. This is particularly valuable if you use radiosity renderers, such as Lightscape by Lightscape Technologies or Radioray by Kinetix.

Radiosity calculates surface illumination by calculating the amount, strength, and character of light emanating from a surface. If a red apple is placed near a white wall and both are illuminated, the wall is directly lit by the light and indirectly lit by the red light reflecting off the apple. You can approximate the effect of radiosity with strategically placed Omni lights of varying colors with positive and negative multiplier settings. Dedicated radiosity renderers produce a physically accurate result, with fewer lighting objects. The results look photographic and are especially suited to design visualization situations. There are several excellent examples of radiosity renders in Lightscape on the Lightscape Technologies site (www.lightscape.com).

Lightscape is a standalone rendering environment. Like R2, the latest release implements Open GL rendering. You can import a MAX scene, with or without a Camera path (or you can create a Camera animation path entirely within Lightscape). When the radiosity solution is complete, you can output a single frame or series of frames based on the Camera path. Lightscape includes the Raytrace Rendering capability and can be used to add specular highlights to images rendered from Lightscape.

Radioray, developed by Lightworks for Kinetix and released during the summer of 1997, performs many of the functions of Lightscape, only as a plug-in integrated and accessed entirely through the MAX application interface. At this writing, Radioray for R2 is in beta with no significant additions from its R1 version and no announced release date. It will likely be available when this volume is released.

Lightscape and Radioray are competitors in the marketplace. Lightscape had the advantage of being in its third public release when Radioray made its first appearance, boasting good documentation, online support, and a strong track record with its clients. Radioray is specifically tailored for use in MAX and is supported by Kinetix. For more information on Radioray, check the Kinetix site, www.ktx.com.

Radiosity renderers calculate the lighting data and store it with the models vertices. This results in a "radiosity solution," which is calculated once. Because the information is stored in the model, with an appropriate viewer, you can move through a model in real time and see the effect of the radiosity solution from any angle. There are two principal drawbacks to working with radiosity renderers: The file size increases exponentially, and the render time can be exceptionally long (hours, days). If you have animated elements in your scene and you use a radiosity renderer, you must recalculate a radiosity solution for each frame, which is not practical.

Alternatively, you can render the *static elements* using radiosity for use as the background: A single radiosity solution works, even if you animate the camera moving through the model. Then you can render the animated scene elements, using R2's default Scanline renderer or a Raytracing renderer, with appropriate masking information, for compositing on top of the radiosity-rendered background. Although the animated elements and their shadows are not as accurate as the radiosity solution, any discrepancy will likely go unnoticed due to the nature of animated movement and animation's comparatively low-resolution output.

Animation Output for Film and Video, Real-Time, and the Web

As an editing/compositing/special effects module, Video Post imposes no additional limitations other than those imposed by the renderer you use. This chapter assumes you are making pre-rendered stills or animations and your Scene Output event is destined for film or video by means of a movie format (*.avi or *.mov) or a series of single frames (*.tga or *.rla). Just as R2's renderer was enhanced to support output to standard film and video resolutions, with more control over image aspect ratio, pixel aspect ratio, and a new Aperture Width Value, you can set these parameters for output events through Video Post.

VP has no particular function in real-time graphics, except to pre-render images, composites, or special effects that are later mapped onto 3D models produced for real-time graphics engines or to produce sprite animations. In either case, any special requirements become specific to the game engine you'll be working with. For example, if you are producing real-time content for Animatek's Caviar system (a real-time game-authoring environment), you can create high-polygon content in MAX in very much the same way you would for film and video. The Caviar compression technology will render the graphics and animation in real time.

Likewise MAX R2 VP contains no special features for VRML output or GIF animations. In these cases, you can use VP to access the renderer's output resolution; the number of frames rendered/skipped by the render; and to edit, composite, or add special effects to images that you will later use as Texture maps. For example, if you are working on an online VRML-based game, you can author your VRML models, create animations, and design/assign animated or still texture maps within R2. You can then import them into New Fire's Catalyst and Torch environment where this content can be enabled with Java applets and compressed/accelerated with New Fire's technology for real-time performance.

R2 does not directly output GIF animations, but it is excellent for generating the source material; you can set the proper resolution and skip frames in Video Post, output to an AVI file or sequence of Targa files, and compile the result into an animated GIF with third-party software. There are several good products, such as GIF Construction Set (shareware available for download), Microsoft's GIF animator, or the GIF generating plug-in released by Adobe for Premiere (available for download to registered Premiere users at the Adobe site, www.adobe.com). You can set R2's Rendering preferences to output 256 colors, but I find little reason to do so, because the third-party software dithers the palette when it outputs the GIF, and color degrades noticeably when this occurs more than once.

In Practice: Compositing and Editing Animations

- **Alpha Compositor:** You can use MAX's Alpha Compositor to combine images or animation. The ordering of Image Input events is important because it relates to which files need to contain alpha channels. Alpha channels provide a way to create areas of transparency, which are necessary for seeing through one Layer event and on to another. Multi-layer compositing enables you to combine as many layers of background and foreground images as you want.

■ **Working with other editing and special effects tools:** Video Post can operate as an effective compositing, editing, and special effects tool to be used liberally as an integrated part of the MAX R2 creative environment. Frequently, however, you will not work alone or only work in the MAX environment. In planning and using Video Post, you should consider other tools and environments that will be used to make your final project. For example, in compositing images, only an RLA format type bitmap saves Material Effects or Object ID information necessary to applying filters in MAX. Yet this file format cannot be read by popular 2D compositing and editing tools such as Photoshop, Premiere, or After Effects.

■ **Shadow and Light:** You can composite and retain shadow and light effects by using the Screen Mapping method, the Camera Map plug-in, and Peter Watje's Shadow/Matte material.

■ **Masking:** You can achieve complex compositing effects by using MAX's powerful masking feature. With masking, you can use any channel in the image to create a custom area of transparency. This includes using alpha data or even using any of the channels specific to 3D (G-Buffer).

■ **Chromakey:** You can use chromakey techniques to composite live action with CG. The Primatte plug-in provides a method of doing chromakeying within MAX.

■ **Other Methods:** MAX provides methods other than the Alpha Compositor for doing compositing. Pseudo Alpha and Simple Additive Compositor are both limited in their functionality. They do, however, provide an opportunity for a creative programmer to expand and improve. Thanks to MAX's open architecture, this is a likely possibility.

■ **Editing:** You can edit your animations in Video Post by using the Range bars and Filter and Layer events. You can also use masking to create transitions and achieve new effects that add impact to your animations.

Chapter 16

VIDEO POST EFFECTS

Special effects in CGI deserve their own volume because the digital wizardry that attracts us is made in both 2D and 3D packages. By narrowing the survey of special effects to 3D Studio MAX R2 alone, you find both geometric (animated deformations, Hypermatter, particles, and so on) or non-geometric special effects (materials, Atmospheric effects, Flares, Highlights, Glow, Blurs, and so on). This chapter examines the latter, in particular the special effects capabilities available through the Video Post module (VP) and the extent to which they are similar, interrelated, or tangential to VP and other non-geometric special effects available elsewhere in R2.

Please refer to Chapter 15, "Compositing and Editing," regarding MAX's compositing capabilities, and for any compositing issues related to special effects in R2.

Don't underestimate R2's Video Post. You can produce some startling effects within your animations, and often you can efficiently use VP without having to use an outside package. Certain stock effects can be produced only by filters within Video Post, such as Lens Effects Glows and Highlights, Blurs, and Flares. They often require specific reference to an Object ID or Material Effects ID. Others interact with Helper objects and/or materials in R2 proper, such as Real Lens Flare or Glow Baby. Then there are effects that you can apply either in VP or in post-production by using other applications— for example, Adobe Premiere-compatible filters, such as MetaCreations Final Effects AP. Last, there are effects that cannot be applied in R2 but that require a different application. These include After Effects or Digital Fusion.

Most effects are used as standard Video Post filters that you add to the Video Post queue. R2 ships with a few Video Post effects as part of the standard package, including Digimation's Lens Effects software, which is a substantial improvement over R1, and for R1 users, this by itself is almost worth the upgrade price.

Plug-in developers have also fleshed out Video Post capabilities with some superb special effects software. Some of the plug-ins discussed are freeware and the fully working versions are included on the accompanying CD-ROM. Other plug-ins are commercially available from their respective vendors for various prices and some have demo versions included on the CD.

The sheer number of plug-ins available today is surprising and most that were created for R1 have now been recompiled for R2. New plug-ins are becoming available on a daily basis and many can be obtained online from the following addresses:

- **CompuServe** Kinetix Forum
- **Kinetix** http://www.ktx.com
- **Kinetix Support** http://support.ktx.com
- **MAX Center** http://3dsmax.3dreview.com/frame.shtml
- **MAX 3D** http://www.max3d.com/main.html

- **Bobo Land**   http://modeling.3dreview.com/bobo/

- **3D Café**   http://www.3dcafe.com/asp/default.asp

- **MaxMatter**   http://www.glyphx.com/maxmatter/

- **Trinity Animation**   http://www.trinity3d.com/index1.html

- **SF 3DS Users' Group**   http://www.sf3dsug.com

Many more effect-oriented plug-ins are likely to be available by the time this book goes to print.

This chapter covers the following topics:

- Glows and Highlights

- Lens Flares

- Blurs

- Adobe Photoshop and Premiere plug-in filters

- Miscellaneous Video Post effects

Glows

Glows are achieved with MAX's Video Post Filter events. They are useful for heat effects such as glowing coals, exhausts, surrounding lights in a soft halo, planetary space scenes, lasers, sparks, lit windows in night scenes, candlelight, and much more. Often Glows take the place of atmospherics, such as volume lights and fogs. When appropriate, Glows can dramatically reduce render times.

MAX ships with Lens Effects Glow (LE Glow), an extremely powerful, versitile filter to add glowing luminosity to objects in your scene. The effect is that the objects in your scene, which appear as though they give off light, will glow near the source as they would in reality. LE Glow behaves differently from the basic Glow (Frame Only) filter, which shipped with R1, or Glow Plus, which is similar, with the added capability to animate Brightness Threshold and size. Glow Plus is included on your CD and used in the first exercise below for two reasons: to acquaint you with how to use effects filters in VP and to emphasize that a simple filter event is preferable to a complex one when all you require is the simplest glow effect.

The Glow effects are based on G-Buffer information (see Chapter 15) and are applied to either a Material Effects Channel ID or an Object Channel ID. Some Glow filter plug-ins enable you to choose either Material Effects Channel ID or an Object Channel ID, and some enable you to use one or the other without giving you a choice. You assign an Object Channel ID number by selecting the object in the scene, right-clicking and choosing Properties, and setting the G-Buffer setting Object ID spinner. Alternatively, you can select the Scene object and select Edit/Properties from the menu bar. You assign a Material Effects Channel ID in the Material Editor by selecting the Target material and choosing a Material ID number other than 0 (see Figure 16.1).

NOTE

If you use a multi-layered material, the Material Effects Channel ID is assigned to the layer (including sub-layers) at which you make that choice. For example, if you use a multi-layered map in one of the Material Map rollouts and are at the layer to edit that multi-layered map when you assign the material effects channel ID, the ID applies to that multi-layered map, not to the entire material.

FIGURE 16.1

When you apply a Material Channel ID number to a Multi-Sub-Object Material, it applies only to the specific sub-object material, and then only to that material's sub-layer downward. You can, therefore, assign different IDs to different parts of the same material.

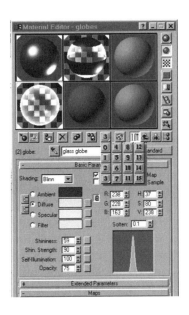

You can spread the same effect across multiple objects in two ways:

- Use the Material Effects Channel ID when you want to apply the effect to many objects assigned the same material.

■ Assign the same Object Channel ID to one or more objects you want to reach with the effect.

The Standard Glow filter that comes with MAX is simple but very useful. In many situations, it is all you need. A freeware plug-in that is an extension of the Standard Glow is available. This plug-in is called Glow Plus and it enables you to cycle the Glow to produce interesting animated effects. Arguably the most powerful and flexible Glow utilities are available in the commercial packages: Digimation's Lens Effects (included with R2), Cebas' Real Lens Flare (RLF), and Positron's Genesis VFX. The following sections outline and use the various Glow filters to illustrate how they are similar and how they differ. The last section outlines some Glow tips to help you achieve more effective Glow effects.

Glow (Frame Only) and Glow Plus

The Glow (Frame Only) filter is the most basic special effects filter. It shipped with R1, and is available free for download for R2. This Glow affects only the current frame and, therefore, cannot be animated, and cannot be used to render to fields.

Glow Plus is a variation on the Glow (Frame Only) filter. Written by Choi Moon-Sun for Effect Ware, this free plug-in is included on the CD (glow-plus.zip). If it's not on your computer, install it prior to doing the next exercise. This plug-in adds the capability to Glow the entire image and control the size and brightness of the image glow.

Glow Plus functions similarly to other Glow filters. You can affect objects in your scene in two ways: by specifying in the Glow Plus Setup dialog a Material Effects Channel ID or Object Channel ID number. The Video Post filter then finds instances of that Material Effects channel in your scene and glows the corresponding material or sub-material (in a multi-material). If you use the Object Channel ID, the filter glows objects in the scene that have instances of that ID number.

SETTING UP THE GLOW PLUS FILTER

1. Open the Video Post module.

2. Add a scene input event.

3. Highlight the scene input event in the queue and click Add Image Filter Event.

4. Choose the Glow Plus filter from the dropdown box and click OK.

5. The Glow Plus filter should be in the Video Post queue, above and to the left of the scene event. Highlight the filter in the queue and double-click (or click the Edit icon on the VP toolbar to open the Edit Filter Event dialog box).

6. Click Setup. This gives you access to the Filter parameters.

The Color section determines the color of the Glow. You can make the Glow color the same as your material by selecting the Material radio button, or you can choose the color of the Glow by selecting User and choosing a color from the Color Picker. The Size spinner determines how large the Glow effect will be in pixels. The higher the value, the larger the effect—both inside and outside the object. (This might appear to intensify the Glow inside the object.) If you choose a color, the Glow weakens as you slide the color's Value slider away from full saturation toward black. In other words, a very dark red gives a gentle red Glow, whereas fully saturated red gives a very intense red glow. The higher Brightness Threshold setting, the less intense the glow, with 255 producing no glow at all.

The following example provides a scene containing a chandelier with transparent globes, each containing light bulbs. The globes are a single mesh consisting of a glass cover and metal arm, already mapped for you with a Multi/Sub-Object material. Likewise, the light bulbs are single meshes mapped with a Multi/Sub-Object material. In this exercise, you apply a simple glow to the chandelier.

ADDING A SIMPLE GLOW TO THE CHANDELIER

1. Load or reset MAX and open the 16max01.max file from the accompanying CD-ROM.

2. Open the Material Editor. Select the "globes" material. Under Basic Parameters, select Material 2, "globe." This takes you to the Standard material for the glass globe. Click the Material Effects Channel icon and assign Number 3. This material is already applied to the Light object, so you do not need to apply it.

3. Open Video Post. Add a Camera01 Scene event. Hilight the Camera01 scene event and add the GlowPlus) filter. Click OK.

You can click Setup at the time you first choose a filter in Video Post and set Filter parameters—in other words, before clicking OK. Some filters are substantial applications in their own right, but with their own render previews. On occasion they do not operate correctly if you attempt to set their parameters before adding them into the VP queue. The safest practice is to add the filter to the queue fir. t, then double-click it, and go into Setup.

4. Double-click Glow Plus in the VP queue and, in the Edit Filter Event dialog box, click Setup to set the Glow Plus parameters (see Figure 16.2). Notice that the Default Source value is a Material Effects Channel value of 1. You can set this to any positive integer. In the Material Editor, you just set this value to 3. Because the Glow filter is set at 3 also, the filter causes the corresponding material to glow.

FIGURE 16.2

The Glow Plus Control dialog permits you to assign a glow by Material Channel Effect ID of the Object Channel ID.

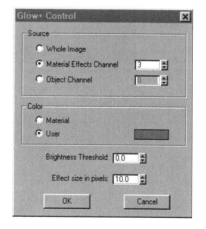

5. Leave Color set to Material and set the Effect size in pixels to 10. Accept the Glow Control values and return to the Video Post window. Execute the sequence to render a single frame to the Virtual Frame Buffer window. Notice the Glow applied to the globes makes the light bulbs appear to glow as well (see Figure 16.3).

6. With the Virtual Frame Buffer window displayed, click the G-Buffer pull-down and change the value from RGB Alpha to Material Effects.

The Virtual Frame Buffer window displays a representation of the Material Effects channel that you activated in your scene. This representation displays the area on which the Glow acted. Figure 16.3 shows the final scene.

FIGURE 16.3

Applying Glow to the globes makes the light bulbs appear to glow as well.

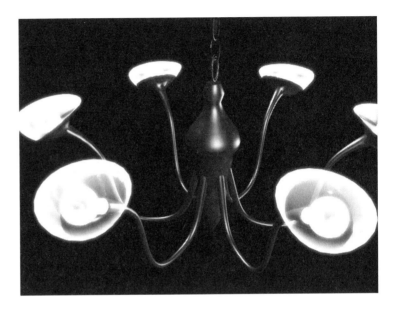

7. Return to the Material Editor and select the "light bulbs" material. This is also a Multi/Sub-Object material. Select the glass material (material 2) and verify that it has been assigned Material Effects Channel number 4.

8. Return to the Video Post queue, double-click Glow Plus, Setup, and change the Material Effects Channel spinner from 3 to 4. Leave the other settings unchanged. Execute a single frame in Video Post. The light bulbs don't glow because the effect is blocked by the surrounding globes' geometry.

NOTE

Be careful when adding Glows or Hilights to objects within other objects (transparent or translucent). You don't see a Glow because it is blocked by interceding geometry. (There is an exception for Raytraced Materials or Maps, which permit glows to show through blocking objects. Also, at the time of this writing, Digimation released Xray, a plug-in specifically designed to address this problem.) There are, likewise, problems with mirrored surfaces—the object glows, but the reflected object does not, unless a Raytraced Material or Map is applied.

Glow Plus settings can be animated, so it works well for simulating flashing lights. You can accomplish this either by setting keyframes or by using a specific controller, such as the Waveform controller in the next exercise. Animating a light bulb requires animating three objects in sync: the light (for scene illumination), the self-illuminated material on the bulb surface, and the glow emanating from the bulb.

Waveform Controller

The Waveform controller is an animation controller that sets animation values based on a mathematical Waveform. You can use the Waveform controller on the Brightness Threshold track of Glow Plus to control the intensity of the glow over the animation cycle, and then copy the controller settings to the multiplier track of the Omni light(s) and to the Self-Illumination value of the light bulb material. This results in the Glow, the surface of the light bulb, and the illumination of the room animating in sync. The following example introduces you to using the Waveform controller.

Using a Waveform Controller to Animate Glow Plus

1. Open or reset MAX. Load the file 16max02.max file from the accompanying CD-ROM.

2. Open Video Post. Select the camera01 event in the VP queue, click Add Image Filter Event, and from the dropdown, choose Glow Plus. Click OK. Double-click the Glow Plus filter event. Click Setup. Notice the Filter dialog contains a Brightness Threshold spinner. We will animate this setting, but with the Waveform controller. Accept the settings and close the Video Post window.

3. Open Track View. Expand the Video Post Track and the Glow Plus track underneath it. Select the Glow Plus Threshold Track.

4. Click the Assign Controller icon on the Track View toolbar. Notice the Bézier Float controller has a > next to it, indicating this is the current controller. Select Waveform Float and click OK. The Waveform controller now controls the behavior of the Threshold setting.

5. With Threshold highlighted, click the Copy controller icon on the Track View toolbar.

6. Expand the Scene Materials tree in Track View and locate lightbulb glass/Self-Illumination track. Click the Paste controller icon on the Track View toolbar, and when prompted, select Paste as Instance. Notice the track information changes when you paste in the different controller.

7. Expand the Objects Tree in Track View and locate Omni01 above/Object(Omni Light)/Multiplier. Paste the Waveform controller as an instance. Repeat the procedure with Omni-lightbulb04/Object (Omni Light)/Multiplier. Now changing the Waveform controller parameters for the Glow Plus filter changes Scene Illumination values and material Self-Illumination values as well.

8. Go to the main interface, check to make sure Camer01 viewport is selected and set to Smooth + Highlights. In Track View, select the Glow+/Threshold track, right-click, and choose Properties to bring up the Waveform controller dialog box, which enables you to control parameters based on a mathematical waveform (see Figure 16.4). Set Period to 25.0, Amplitude to 1.0, Vertical Bias to Auto > 0. Use the Default Sine Waveform and set Effect to Add. Scroll the Phase spinner between 0.0 and 1.0. Notice the effect in the Camera01 viewport: The light and material dim/brighten through the cycle. As you increase Amplitude, the range exaggerates; as you shorten the period, the cycle repeats across frames.

FIGURE 16.4

By instancing the controller in the Glow effect, Omni light multipliers, and material Self-Illumination tracks, you can synchronize all three. You can preview much of the effect in the viewport by moving the Phase spinner value between 0 and 1.0.

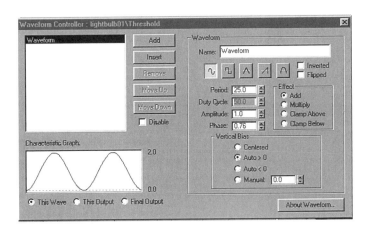

9. Return to Video Post. Check to make sure the selected tracks change in sync and that the values suit you by executing a series of sample frames between 0–50. If acceptable, render the final animation. The final rendered animation is 16avi01.avi on the accompanying CD-ROM.

The Waveform controller and Glow Plus have severe limitations: Although you can adjust and combine Wave types in the former, you can't insert your own expressions. With the latter, only the Glow Brightness threshold, color, and Effect size can be animated. Although you can use this combination in a limited circumstance, their value is truly illustrative. As we progress through the other filter environments—several full-blown applications in their own right—consider how you might animate the effects, lighting, materials, and objects by using different and/or shared controllers.

To create effective dimming or flashing lights, carefully synchronize three animating components:

■ Adjust the lighting object to cycle the illumination over the frames you want, either by animating the light's multiplier or by adding Visibility tracks in Track View.

■ For light bulbs or glass lighting fixtures, map the geometry with a static or animated material containing a high Self-Illumination value. This casts no light, but it makes the object appear to be a light source.

■ Last, in Video Post, add and animate Glow(s) by using either the Material Effects channel or the Object ID channel.

Make sure all three steps are synchronized over the same frames. Synchronizing this might be easier said than done, especially with repeating cycles and multiple lights. The Waveform controller is a useful alternative for this problem.

Lens Effects Glow

R2 ships with Digimation's Lens Effects (LE) special effects filters, which include Lens Effects Glow, Highlight, Flare, and Focus. As their names suggest, they add glows, sparkle highlights, lens flare effects, and depth of field effects through Video Post. The filters were a commercial plug-in for R1. Built into R2, these filters alone nearly cover (and are worth) the price of an R2 upgrade. Each filter is truly a separate application accessed only through Video Post. They share a common "modeless" interface design that enables you to work back and forth between filter settings and the main interface; understanding how one LE filter works goes a long way toward understanding the others.

You load LE Glow in the same manner as Glow Plus. The upper half of the interface contains an interactive Preview window, inactive by default. Clicking the Preview button loads a stock scene with several objects. Pressing the VP Queue button loads the scene as it will render in the VFB. The Preview windows updates automatically with any change to the filter settings. The Update button re-renders the preview image—use this only when you have advanced to another frame in the main interface, which results in a different camera view, and you want that view in the Preview window.

TIP

Rendering a Preview of the VP Queue takes almost as long as rendering the similar size frame to the VFB, and LE Glow retains its current preview settings when you close the filter. If your scene otherwise requires substantial rendering time, re-opening the filter results in re-rendering the Preview frame (whether you need it or not) before you can access any set-tings. To avoid this delay, uncheck the VP Queue and/or Preview buttons before you close it— in other words, it won't render a preview the next time you open it.

To animate effects with any Lens Effects (LE) filter active, you turn on the Animate button in the main interface, advance to the desired keyframe, and make changes within Lens Effects.

Any setting with a green bullet at its right can be edited in Track View (see Figure 16.5 for editable options available in Track View). By default, each is green and depressed, which means it will make an entry in the Track View. Depressing the green bullet turns it red, meaning it doesn't appear in Track View, which enables you to limit the filter's track entries to those you might later adjust. You can save preset still or animated effects as separate files; any animated effect with LE is saved with the MAX file, but if you attempt to save an animated effect as a VPX file, you will be prompted that this will wipe out any animation.

You can save LE Glow settings (including animated effects) or any LE filter file to a separate file for later use. Unfortunately, you can't reuse gradient settings from one LE filter in another. Distinguish this from saving the Video Post file (VPX), which does not save animation data, or the MAX file, which does save animated Video Post filter data.

FIGURE 16.5

All settings in Lens Effects accompanied by a green bullet make an editable entry in Track View. Gradient entries (such as Radial Color) are subdivided by Flag.

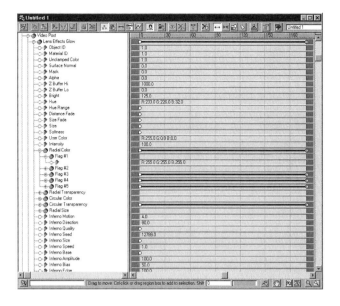

The lower half of the interface is organized under four tabs: Properties, Preferences, Gradients, and Inferno (see Figure 16.6). Each of the LE Glow settings is described in R2's online help.

Using the Properties Dialog Box

The LE Properties tab sets your choice of which objects receive the effect (in other words, Source) and how that effect is filtered as it's applied to the object. Technically, the filter responds to image data stored in the G-Buffer, not to scene geometry. The Source specifies the pixel attributes (image channel data) that will cause the pixel to generate a glow, which is then applied to surrounding pixels. The filter controls how the glow is applied to the surrounding pixels, based on the attributes of those pixels. Most often you'll assign effects according to the Material Effects Channel ID or Object ID. You can't choose more than one Object or Material ID per filter application. This requires either using multiple LE Filter events or selecting other Source options, such as Whole, Unclamped, SurfNorm, or Mask. You can elect the Glow Source based on the following:

■ **Whole:** Everything in the scene.

FIGURES 16.6

The Lens Effects Glow interface is organized under four tabs, designed for you to move back and forth between them and observe the effect in the Preview window.

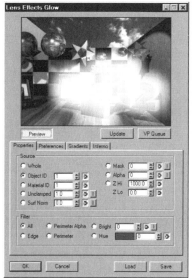

■ **Unclamped color:** Good for highlights and explosions. An Unclamped color is brighter than pure white (255,255,255). The spinner determines the lowest value that will be glowed; the button to the far right inverts the value.

- **SurfNorm:** SurfNorm glows a part of the object based on the angle surface normal to the screen, with 0 = coplaner with the screen.

- **Mask:** Glows the Mask channel of an image. Mask is the Mask image, which can be set in the Add/Edit Filter Event dialog before going into the LE setup. Based on a grayscale value of between 0 and 255, when this option is set, any part of the Mask image larger than the spinner value will glow in the final image. This can be inverted.

- **Alpha:** Glows the alpha channel of an image. The transparency of an Alpha channel is interpreted opposite of the Mask channel.

- **Z-Buffer Hi and Lo:** Glows an object based on its distance from the camera. The glow is applied to any object located between the Hi and Lo range values. This setting can be animated in Track View.

After you choose a Source, you elect a filter, which controls how the Glow is applied to the Source pixels. Your options include All, Edge, Perimeter, Perimeter Alpha, Bright, and Hue. Bright glows only those source image pixels above the specified brightness setting (0–255). If you use Gradients as your color source (under the Preferences tab), the Bright Filter gives good flexibility to control the total amount of Glow; in other words, once you've set all other options, you can use the Bright setting as an animatable master switch. (Alternatively, if you use Pixel or User as your color source under the Preferences tab, you can use the Color/Intensity spinner as your brightness control.) The Hue option lets you pick a single color on the object surface and glow only that color, becoming more restrictive as the value reduces from 255 to 0.

Using the Preferences Dialog Box

Under the Preferences tab, you specify whether the glow affects the Alpha channel and/or Z-Buffer, as well as how it fades over distance (in brightness, size, or both). The Effect settings contain Size and Softness controls. Size measures the size of the glow in pixels. Softness softens and blurs the glow effect and is active only if Gradient is your color choice. For color, you can use the Pixel color, User (in other words, user-defined color), or a Gradient. The Color Intensity spinner is active only for Pixel and User color choices. In flexibility and control, Gradient is the most powerful Color option.

Using the Gradients Dialog Box

There are three gradients: Radial Color and Transparency, Circular Color and Transparency, and Radial Size. Radial gradients change colors in a linear fashion. For example, if the Glow object is spherical and the gradient encircles it, the Linear gradient controls color changes from the center outward. The Radial gradient covers color changes as you move around the gradient circle. The Radial Size gradient modifies and is limited by the Size and Softness settings under the Preferences tab.

Left-clicking anywhere in the gradient sets a Flag at that point. If you then right-click the Flag, you have options to copy, paste, delete, or edit the Flag properties. If you choose Edit Properties, the next dialog, Flag Properties, enables you to adjust the Flag color or position and cycle through and adjust each of the flags in that gradient. As you continue to click the gradient, you add more flags. To delete one, you can drag it off the scale or right-click/delete. Note that you can copy and paste Flag values within or between gradients throughout the Lens Effects interface. If you right-click a gradient where there is no flag, you find additional options, including the capability to save and load gradients. This can become very useful if you use multiple LE filter events, because each includes similar gradient options.

NOTE

Glows generally render much faster than atmospheric effects, and a softened glow can often prove an adequate substitute for atmosphere. In LE Glow, the primary settings are Size and Softness, with noise effects simulated under the Inferno tab.

ANIMATING GLOWS WITH LENS EFFECTS GLOW

1. Load 16max03.max. Open the Video Post and in the queue, click Add Scene Event, Camera01. Click to highlight Camera01 and then click Add Image Filter Event, Lens Effects Glow. Click OK. Highlight and double-click the Lens Effects Glow entry, and then Setup. Click Preview.

2. Notice that several objects appear in a sample scene, with the Glow applied to the 3D lettering. Under Properties/Source, Object ID 1 is checked by default. Incrementally increase the value and note how the

Glow moves to different objects in the sample scene. Next check Material ID, Unclamped, SurfNorm, and Mask and notice the shift in effect for each. Click the VP Queue button; the VP queue is rendered to the Preview window.

3. Open the Material Editor and select the "globes" Multi/Sub-Object material. Within that, click material 2 (globe), and verify that it is assigned Material Effects Channel ID 3. Return to the LE Glow interface. Set Source = Material ID 3. The chandelier globes glow.

4. Turn on the Animate button in the main interface.

5. Click OK to close LE Glow and return to the VP Queue. Double-click each event and set VP End time to 15.

6. Deselect all in the VP queue by clicking anywhere on the white area. Click the Add Image Output Event icon on the VP toolbar. In the Add Image output Event dialog, click Files and create an AVI file called 16avi02.avi. Click render VP icon and render Range to 0–15 frames.

7. Double-click the Lens Effects Glow entry, and then click Setup to return to the LE Glow interface. Under Properties/Filter, check each option and note the effect. Last, select Bright and set the value to 200.

8. Click the Preferences tab and set the following:

   Color = Gradient

   Effect Size = 15.0

   Softness = 30.0

9. Click the Gradients tab. Click the right flag under the Radial Color Gradient (it turns green). Right-click the flag and choose Edit Properties. Click the color swatch in the Flag Properties dialog. Choose a yellow color (H = 44, S = 255, V = 245). Note the color updates in the preview.

10. Without closing the Color Selector, click the center of the Radial Color gradient. This adds a new flag; the Flag Properties and Color Selector update. Change the color to orange (H = 15 S = 208 V = 245). Slide the flag right, then left, noting the effect on the gradient and in the Preview window. Remove the flag by dragging it sideways off the gradient.

11. Make sure the Animate button is on in the main interface, and that you are at frame 0. Click the Properties tab, select and set Brightness to 0. Click the Preferences tab and set Size to 5.0.

12. Move the Frame slider to frame 15. Set Brightness to 255. Close the LE Glow dialog. Render the scene; the glow diminishes as Brightness increases from 0 to 255.

The final version of the MAX file is included on your CD-ROM as 16max04.max. Review the animation. A pre-rendered version of the animation is contained on the accompanying CD-ROM as 16avi03.avi. Glow Plus gives you a dimmer switch for your lighting fixture. Experiment by changing Glow colors and Effect Size in Pixel settings over time.

You can achieve the same animation result by choosing Properties/ Filters/Edge and animating the left flag of the Radial Transparency gradient from white to black. Although LE Glow is extremely flexible and adaptable, its greatest strength lies in its gradients. You can have any number of flags on any gradient, cut and paste flag colors within and among gradients, and animate any changes. This characteristic is the heart of the four Lens Effects filters shipping with R2.

Using the LE Glow Inferno Dialog Box

The Inferno tab adds black and white fractal noise effects to the glow. To enable the effect, you must check the Red, Green, and/or Blue boxes in the Settings panel. If you don't check all three, the noise color will be different from the glow color and might overpower it altogether. If you desire different color noise, you can control its interaction with the glow color(s) under the Parameters settings and Radial Density gradient.

You have three types of noise effect settings: Gaseous (default), Fiery, or Electric. Motion animates the Inferno effect. Direction specifies the direction of the Inferno effect in degrees. Quality (0–10) determines the detail and subtlety of the noise, with the higher, more detailed noise resulting in slightly longer render times.

The following happens under the Inferno parameters:

- Size controls the size of the noise pattern within the glow, a small number resulting in a grainy pattern.

- Speed sets the overall speed of the turbulence.

- Base controls color brightness of the Inferno effect.

- Ampl controls the brightnes of the portions of the fractal pattern.

■ Bias shifts color, such that > 50 results in brighter colors and < 50 results in darker, softer colors.

■ Edge controls the contrast between light and dark areas in the fractal pattern, with a high value resulting in clear patterns and a low value resulting in more subtle effects.

■ Radial Density setting controls how the noise is masked across the effect by using a gradient, with white masking the effect entirely and black letting everything through.

How these parameters can be combined is best shown by example. The following exercise involves a star dissipating gasses prior to going nova. First you'll explore LE options by using a sphere mapped with a reference checkerboard; then you'll substitute an animated fiery material and combine that with the Glow.

SIMPLE ANIMATED GLOW USING LENS EFFECTS GLOW

1. Open 16max05.max. This file contains a simple reference sphere mapped with a checkerboard map. Right-click the sphere and assign Object ID number 1 to the sphere.

2. Open Video Post and click the Add Scene Event icon on the Video Post toolbar. Choose the Camera01 view and click OK.

3. Highlight the Camera01 event in the queue and click the Add Image Filter Event icon. Select Lens Effects Glow from the drop-down list and click OK.

4. Double-click the Lens Effect Glow entry in the queue and click Setup in the Edit Filter Event dialog. This brings up the Lens Effect Glow interface.

5. Click the Preview button (in other words, don't click VP Queue yet). This loads a reference scene with several objects. Notice that Object ID is checked, and the 3D MAX lettering glows. Under Filter, check Perimeter Alpha. The Glow applies to the outline of the lettering. Change the Object ID to 2. The Glow shifts to one of the reference spheres. Cycle through Object IDs 1 through 8. Note that you cannot select more than one Object ID or Material ID per Lens Effects Filter Event. Next set Source to Whole, Unclamped, or SurfNorm, and note how these settings affect groups and areas in the scene. Once you choose a Source, you can then further restrict how the effect is applied with the Filters settings.

6. Set Source at Object ID to 1. Click each of the different options under the filter section and note the effect on the Glow. Lastly, set Filter to All.

7. Click the Preferences tab and set Color to Gradient. Lens Effects' greatest power lies in the Gradient section, which covers not only Gradient colors, but Masking capabilities as well.

8. Click the Gradients tab. Click in the Radial Color gradient to set a Flag, then right-click the Flag, and choose Edit Properties. Click the color swatch, and choose a new color. The gradient should have a third color and you should see the effect updated in the Preview window.

9. In the Material Editor, assign the sun material to the sphere. Return to the LE Glow dialog and click the Gradients tab.

10. Return to the LE Glow interface. Within the LE Glow interface, click Load and load 16lzg01.lzg. This is the animated Glow sequence; a pre-rendered version is included on your CD-ROM as 16avi03a.avi.

11. Check to see you are at frame 0. Make sure the VP Queue and Preview buttons are active. Advance to frame 200; notice the complex effect applied to the sphere. Examine the settings in the Properties, Preferences, Gradients, and Inferno tabs. Because the interface is modeless, you can advance frames and turn the Animate button on/off while working in LE Preview mode.

12. Experiment further by varying the settings.

When you think about adding Glows, think about the effect of the Glow on the camera lens—think about lens flares.

Glow Tips

Many animators live for subtlety. Some have found that Glow effects go a long way toward improving the visual impact of images and animation. This is especially true when Glows are coupled with good lighting. Consequently, you can spend many hours tweaking with Glow settings and trying different methods to achieve specific Glow effects. Consider the following tips when you use Glow in a scene.

Glowing Behind Objects

In certain instances, you might want the Glow effect to come from behind your object. One way to achieve this effect is to render the scene with a simple glow filter (in other words, Glow Plus) applied to the whole object, saving the file or files to disk. Then render the same scene with no Glow applied, saving the file or files with Image Alpha data. You can then composite (see previous chapter) the no-Glow rendering over the Glow rendering. This results in a Glow-behind-object effect. The GLOWCOMP.TGA file on the accompanying CD-ROM is an image rendered using this technique. Alternatively, with LE Glow, you can achieve the same effect by setting Properties/Filter to Perimeter or Perimeter Alpha.

Using Glow with Animated Parameters

You can achieve certain animated effects using any of the Glow procedures outlined in this section by applying Glow to a *material* that has animated parameters. If a material uses an animated map or procedural texture such as Noise, for example, the Glow effect changes based on the state of the material. You can also animate a material's Self-Illumination, and the Glow effect changes based on the Self-Illumination value. This technique works well for flashing lights or objects.

Glowing Text

Sometimes it is better not to glow an entire object. If you want to create a glowing logo and you apply the Glow to the entire object, for example, you might find that the Glow appears to slightly shroud and fade out your text. This happens because the Glow is being applied to every surface in the text. The surfaces on the inside of the text are glowing inward, slightly obstructing the geometry. In this case, it's usually best to apply the Glow only to the faces normally to the camera. This way only the surfaces facing the camera are glowed. The following exercise illustrates this.

APPLYING GLOW TO TEXT FACES

1. Load the 16max06.max file from the accompanying CD-ROM.

2. Select the Extruded Text object and apply an Edit Mesh modifier.

3. In the Sub-Object list box, change Vertex to Face, click the Window Selection button at the bottom of the screen under the Time slider, and select only the faces facing the camera. This is easily done from the Left or Top viewport.

4. With the faces selected, go to the Edit rollout and change the Material ID spinner to 2.

5. Open the Material Editor. The first slot in the Material Editor contains an animated Multi/Sub-Object material. Because you just activated Material ID 2 for the front faces, Material Number 2 is assigned to those faces. Therefore, Material Number 2 is the one you want to glow. Notice that Material 2 animates from green to cyan over the 100 frames and is a different color from the orange Material 1.

   Another advantage to glowing only certain faces in an object is that you can change the color or texture of those faces to obtain different Glow results. Set Material 2 to Effects Channel from 0 to 1 to enable Glow to act on it. Assign this material to the selected text.

6. Return to the Modify panel. Uncheck the Sub-Object button (in other words, return to the Object level), click More, and add a Ripple modifier. Set Amplitudes 1 and 2 to 2.0. Turn on the Animate button, advance to frame 100, and change Phase to 1.0. This gives the text slight movement over the animation.

7. Go to frame 0. Turn on the Animate button.

8. Open Video Post. Click Add Scene Event and add Perspective to the queue. Highlight Perspective and Click Add Filter Event. Select Glow+. Click OK. Double-click Glow Plus in the VP queue and click Setup. Set Source to Material Effects Channel 1. Set Brightness Threshold to 50. Set Effect Size to 6.0.

9. Turn on the Animate button. Advance to frame 100. Set Brightness Threshold to 10.0 and Effect size in pixels to 10.0. Click OK.

10. Click the white area in the VP queue to deselect all events. Click the Add Image Output Event icon and add an AVI file.

11. The text appears to ripple and glow, as shown in the final animation, 16avi04.avi.

Notice that by setting the Glow Plus Brightness Threshold high in the early frames, we've added a negative Glow (the text is dimmed), which slowly brightens as it progresses. If you delete the Ripple modifier and don't animate color or Glow changes, you can simulate a neon sign (see Figure 16.7). Applying a Visibility track in Track View makes the sign appear to flash on and off.

As a supplement to the above exercise, substitute LE Glow for Glow Plus, with the following settings.

Properties: Material ID = 1

Preferences: Effect Size = 2.0; Softness = 30.0

Inferno: Setting = Gaseous (Red, Green, Blue); Size = 7.0; Ampt = 10.0; Edge = 20.0; Radial Density: left = mid gray; rt = white

This places the lettering in an apparent fog. If you combine the Glow Plus from the exercise with LE Glow, delete the Ripple modifier, and apply a Visibility Track to Glow Plus, the letters appear to flash on and off within an "atmosphere" generated entirely by glow filters.

FIGURE 16.7

Using the Glow filter adds realism to a sign.

Animating Glow Location

You also can animate the location of the Glow on an object to achieve interesting special effects. You can have a ring of Glow travel down the arm of a magician character, for example.

To achieve this effect, you use the Volume Select modifier. The Volume Select modifier selects a volume of vertices or faces without using the Edit Mesh modifier. The key aspect of Volume Select is that it enables you to animate the movement of the gizmo. You can, therefore, animate a Selection volume moving around an object. After you apply the Volume Select modifier, you apply a Material modifier and set the Material ID value to 2. This results in an animated Selection volume that changes the Material ID value of the faces it selects while moving around on an object. If you then assign a Multi/Sub-Object material in which a Material Effects Channel ID is assigned to Material #2 and then assign a Glow filter in Video Post set to the same Material Effects Channel ID, the animated Selection volume on the object will glow as it moves. The following example illustrates this procedure.

ANIMATING A GLOW ACROSS A SURFACE

1. Load 16max07.max. This scene consists of a ground plane and a cylinder with a Taper modifier applied.

2. Select the cylinder and apply a Volume Select modifier.

3. Under Stack Selection level, click the radio button labeled Faces. Click the Sub-Object button, and in the Front viewport, non-uniform scale the gizmo down to 10 percent along the Y axis.

4. Move the gizmo so that it is just above the cylinder. Click the Animate button to activate it. Move the Time slider to frame 100. Move the gizmo so that it is just below the cylinder. Click the Animate button to deactivate it.

5. The gizmo should now be animated moving down the faces of the cylinder and selecting the faces that fall within its volume. Add a Material modifier. Change the Value Next to the Material ID spinner to 2.

6. Open the Material Editor. Create a Multi/Sub-Object material. Set the number of sub-materials to 2. Click the Get Material button and then the Mtl Library Button. Select the "proc. Old Glass" material and drag it to the top (first) Material button. Open the Maps rollout and reduce the Opacity Map Amount to 50. Drag-copy Material 1 to Material 2. (Do not make an instance.) Click the button for Material 2 and change the material's Material Effects Channel from 0 to 1.

7. Open Video Post. Add a Perspective or Camera Scene event, highlight it, and add a Glow Plus Filter event. Double-click Glow+, click Setup, and set the Glow Plus to Material Effects Channel to 1, Brightness Threshold to 10.0, and Effect size in pixels to 12.0.

8. Click anywhere in the VP queue to deselect all events and then add an AVI Image Output Event. Render frames 0–100 to see the results. Save your MAX file. Your finished file should resemble 16max08.max on the CD-ROM. (Also see 16avi04a.avi on the CD-ROM.)

Lens Effects Hilight

Lens Effects Hilight looks and behaves very much like Lens Effects Glow. The main difference is the effect, which is a brilliant star shape you might see coming off glass or chrome, especially if seen through glass or a lens (see Figure 16.8). The top half contains the interactive Preview window; the bottom half is organized by Properties, Geometry, Preferences, and Gradients tabs. The Properties and Gradients tabs are the same as in LE Glow. There are no Inferno settings.

FIGURE 16.8

The Lens Effects Hilight interface closely resembles that for LE Glow.

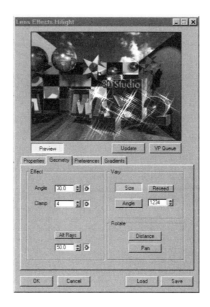

Geometry settings allow you randomize the highlights:

- Angle sets the angle for all stars.

- Clamp spinner lets you minimize or maximize the number of overall highlights across the image.

- Alt Rays setting enables you to choose whether all rays are the same length or if they should vary by the percentage value set in the spinner.

- Vary controls enable you to size and randomize the angle of the stars.

- Rotate controls enable the highlights to rotate automatically, based upon distance and/or the pan from the camera. (Note: All stars have the same number of points, notwithstanding the other randomness you can build in.)

LE Glow and Hilight work very well together—stars nicely punctuate a glow, and they themselves can create a glow.

Lens Flares

Lens flares result when rays from a point light source strike a camera lens. The Glows, rings streaks, star shapes, and so on come from a combination of imperfections in the lens itself and the optical coatings applied. Originally considered a mistake and sign of bad technique, lens flares for the last several years have been a mainstay of special effects.

Lens flares, however, like so many special effects, have been overused to the point of cliché. Your task, then, is to make flares so spectacular as to be unforgettable, or alternatively, so natural as to go unnoticed. Each of the three principal packages discussed in this chapter has potential to deliver either; each takes a slightly different approach to creating flares and consequently each has individual strengths. Lens Effects Flare ships with R2 and incorporates many of the interface conventions of Lens Effects Glow.

Lens flares are optical effects that occur in the lenses of real cameras, but not in MAX's virtual cameras. The effect occurs when light bounces around inside the glass material of a camera's lens. The image is captured while the light beams are in this state of flux, resulting in a photograph containing a bright star-like flare. The term *lens flare* is often used when referring to blemished photographs taken with low-quality camera lenses. If you see a light source through glass in daily life, or if you squint at a bright light source, you should also see a lens flare. If you look at oncoming traffic through the windshield of your car at night, for example, you will see a lens flare.

In 3D animation, lens flares are often used to create added realism in a scene. If you are creative with how you use a lens flare, you can use it to simulate many other interesting special effects. You can use a lens flare to simulate the bursting of a bright star in the galaxy, for example, or to create more realism in car headlights or streetlights. If you have an object in your scene that gives off light, adding a slight lens flare to it can go a long way toward adding visual impact and realism. Essentially, any time you want to make the viewers of an animation know that a specific light is particularly bright, you should consider using a Lens Flare.

Lens Effects Flare

Lens Effects Flare, included with R2, re-creates optical lens flares brought about by shining different light sources into the glass lens of a real camera. LensFX was the best-selling special effects package ever for 3D Studio DOS (for good reason). It enabled 3D Studio animators to add beautiful special effects to their animations while providing great flexibility. The LensFX legacy migrated from DOS to 3D Studio MAX with Lens Effects MAX (for R1).

Using Lens Effects Flare

Like all Lens Effects filters, Lens Effects Flare is accessed as a Video Post Filter event. The interface suggests its status as a full-fledged application with several specialized capabilities. For example, the Auto Secondaries feature automatically creates any number of secondary lens reflections.

For specialized flash effects, Lens Effects provides a feature that enables the user to control the amount that the flare will brighten the entire scene. This feature proves useful when creating explosions and other effects that require a bright burst of light. Lens Effects also has special commands that enable you to control the positioning of secondary flares in your scene, enabling you to have secondary lens reflections that follow different paths and change size based on the camera's field of view. Lens Effects also has a Channel Soften feature that enables you to blur your scene based on G-Buffer Channel information.

You set up the scene by working from the general to the specific. First you must include at least one Point light source in the scene from which the effect emanates; you then tie the effect to the light and to any other objects by clicking the Node Sources box (center-left), and selecting the light(s) and any number of other objects from the Select Flare Objects dialog (see Figure 16.9). If you want objects to interact with the Flare effect, you must include them as source nodes. The left side of the interface includes the Preview window, as found in LE Glow, LE Hilight, and LE Focus. The Lens Flare Properties and Lens Flare Effects globally control the sub-effects. The Properties controls work together. The Squeeze function scales the effect non-uniformly, with 100 being the maximum vertical squash and –100 being the maximum horizontal squash. Note that you see the effect only if you separately enable Squeeze for each effect.

FIGURE 16.9

The Lens Effects Flare interface.

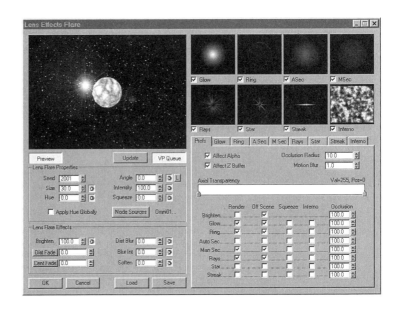

The Lens Effects Flare interface is organized to work from general effects (left) to specific individual effects (right). The right side of the interface gives controls for all sub-effects, which include Glow, Ring, Auto-secondary Flares (ASec), Manual Secondary Flares (MSec), Rays, Star, Streak, and Inferno. The eight windows atop this section give separate previews of each isolated effect—turning off the windows turns off the sub-effect preview but has no effect on its presence in the scene.

You start with the Prefs tab. The check boxes filling the bottom area determine which effects are active in the scene (Render), whether Flare sources outside the scene affect the image (Off Scene), whether the global Squeeze setting is enabled for that sub-effect, and whether Inferno (noise) is enabled for that effect. The settings in the upper half of the Prefs tab specify options—in other words, whether the Flare affects the image alpha channel or Z-Buffer information (distance from camera). The Motion Blur control determines whether Motion blur is added to an animated flare; adding Motion blur smoothes the effect but adds rendering time. The Occlusion Radius controls the area around the center of the flare. It determines when the Lens Flare effect begins to fade as it passes behind another object (measured in pixels). The Axial Transparency gradient affects the transparency of the Lens Flare along its main axis.

Once you've chosen Source Nodes, set up Lens Flare properties and Lens Flare effects, and specified which effects will be active in the Prefs tab, you address settings for each sub-effect. The tab interfaces for each feature follow the same gradient layout as LE Glow. Similar to Lens Effects Glow, every section within the Flare module has at least one color selector for the corresponding part of the Lens Flare. Each color selector can be set to a solid color or a gradient range of colors. The range for the gradient can contain an unlimited number of flags. The flags set the color for the gradient at the location of the flag (see Figure 16.10). The result of these gradient selectors is unparalleled control when choosing a color combination for your Lens Flare. For example, you can have a gradient that cycles from blue to red to green for the Glow radial color of the Lens Flare.

Lens Effects also has a special new feature called Inferno, which is a fractal noise procedure similar to RealLensFlare's Fractal Fury module. Inferno adds realistic fire and smoke effects to Lens Effects. Although Lens Effects is still currently in beta, the indications are that it will be a solid Lens Flare package when it ships.

Generally, you can use only one entry per sub-effect, with the exceptions of Automatic and Manual Secondary Flares. These permit you to add any number of artifact sets. Thus, you can have only one ring. You can "subdivide" that ring, however, into two or more pieces by increasing the thickness and adding flags to the Radial Transparency gradient that oscillates between black and white.

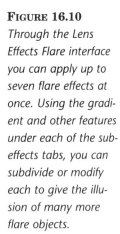

FIGURE 16.10

Through the Lens Effects Flare interface you can apply up to seven flare effects at once. Using the gradient and other features under each of the sub-effects tabs, you can subdivide or modify each to give the illusion of many more flare objects.

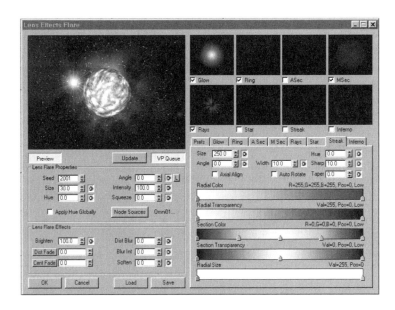

This exercise begins a planet scene. A single Omni light has been added behind and to the left of a planet. The Lens Effect Glow effect has been toned down to work in concert with the flare, and for simplicity, all animation is deleted.

LENS EFFECTS FLARE

1. Open 16max09.max from the accompanying CD-ROM. The scene consists of a single sphere, an Omni light, and a camera. Open Video Post.

2. Highlight the Lens Effects Glow entry in the queue and click the Add Image Filter Event icon. In the dialog, highlight Lens Effects Flare and click OK. Double-click the Lens Effects Flare entry in the queue and then setup in the Edit dialog.

3. Click the Node Source button and select Omni01 and Planet as Flare Objects. In Lens Flare Properties, set Size to 30.0, Angle to 90, and Squeeze to 50.0.

4. Under Lens Flare Effects, click and set Dist. Fade to 10000.0. Leave other settings at the default.

5. Under the Prefs tab, check Affect Alpha and Affect Z-Buffer. Set Occlusion Radius to 10.0.

6. Adjust the Axial Transparency gradient so the left flag is black and the right flag is white. Click the gradient to add an additional flag (you can adjust this nebulae effect caused by the MSec setting later).

7. Check each of the Render boxes (this activates all effects). Uncheck each Off Scene box (there is no light source outside the Camera view). Check Squeeze for the Glow sub-effect, and Inferno for Man. Sec.

8. Click the Glow tab. Click the center of the Radial Color gradient to place a flag. Right-click the flag and choose Edit Properties. Click the color-swatch box to bring up the Color selector. Choose a bright blue (set H to 165, S to 245, and V to 243). You should see the Glow thumbnail preview change (only visible when checked).

9. Click the Ring tab. On the Radial Color gradient, create two flags—one centered and the other halfway between center and right. Make the latter pale-yellow. Change the center flag color to make it less saturated.

10. The Radial Transparency gradient has four flags evenly spaced. Add a fifth in the center and make it black, so that left to right you see black, medium-gray, black, medium-gray, and black. Set Thick to 20. The ring thumbnail should show two concentric rings.

11. Click the ASec tab (that is, Automatic Secondaries). Check the ASec thumbnail preview. Notice the <, >, Add, and Del buttons, which let you cycle through the current flares and add/delete more secondary flares as necessary. Click the Add button. Add a flag to the center of the Radial Color gradient and set it to bright yellow. Click the > button to cycle through the flares and notice the result in the ASec thumbnail box. Notice that you have the option to turn on and fade each effect.

12. Click the MSec tab. Make no changes here; cycle through the six examples.

13. Click the Rays tab. Notice how the Radial Transparency gradient is used to create a dramatic fade. Notice also the control you have over the size, angle, and number of rays. Sharp specifies the sharpness of the ray, as hue specifies the color. Group forces the grouping of rays into smaller groups, giving a symmetrical flower effect. The Autorotate check box rotates the rays around the center of the flare. Make no changes to the default for this exercise.

14. Click the Star tab. Set Size to 125, Angle to 15.0, Width to 10, Qty to 8, and check Random.

15. Click the Streak tab. Set size to 100 and Angle to 15.

16. Click the Inferno tab. Click Gaseous and set Quality to 3.

17. Click the Save button and save your LE Flare settings. Click OK. The final LE Flare settings are included on the accompanying CD-ROM as 19lzf01.lzf.

18. Click the white area of the Video Post queue so no event is highlighted. Click the Add Image Output Event icon. Create a targa file. Click the Execute Sequence icon and render a single file.

The LE Flare effect overlaps with Glow and Highlight. In this exercise, you used LE Glow and Flare together on a solitary shot. The next exercise combines many of the foregoing techniques into a completed space scene—a passing shot of a freighter moving around a planet in the foreground. In the background, the planet glows as it is about to explode. Various Glows have been applied to the ship: LE Glow is used on the Material Effects Channel ID on a portion of the Multi/Sub-Object material, making the windows appear to radiate light. LE Glow (with Inferno) is used together with combustion to glow the ship's engines. The planet uses the animated LE Glow from the previous exercise.

ADDING LE FLARE TO THE COMPLETED SPACE SCENE

1. Open 16max10.max from the accompanying CD-ROM. Open Video Post. Notice several filters have already been added and each is labeled—this is important as you build complex VP queues. Starfield Blur is used to create the background, an animated LE Glow is applied to the sun, and separate LE Glow filters are applied to the ship's engines and windows. (The free ColorCorrect2.dlm plug-in was used to make one of the ship's materials; it is included on the accompanying CD-ROM.)

2. Highlight the LE Glow Engines entry, click the Add Image Filter Event icon, and choose Lens Effects Flare from the dropdown list. Click OK. Now double-click the Lens Effects Flare entry and click Setup.

3. Click Preview and VP Queue. Click Node Sources and select (Space Ship), Omni - Flare, Planet, and Sun and click Update. The default LE Flare effect appears. Click Dist. Fade and Cent. Fade and set each to 5000.0. Set Brighten to 5.0.

4. Click the Prefs tab. Turn on the Render check boxes and Preview thumbnail checkboxes for each effect. Uncheck all Off Scene boxes except for Man. Sec. Click Inferno for Man. Sec.

5. Click the Inferno tab. Check Gaseous. Click the Man. Sec. tab. Click the > button to cycle through the layers. For Man. Sec. 1, check Fade. The flare obliterates the sun.

6. You can either use the gradients to tone down the flare sub-effects or, during the course of the animation, change flare settings so that they do not persist. The animation is on the CD-ROM without the flare effect as 16avi05.avi and with LE Flare as 16avi06.avi.

7. Experiment with the settings. The LE Flare settings for the first 100 frames are on the accompanying CD-ROM as 19lzf02.lzf.

LE Flare also works well in a natural-based scene such as the one in Figure 16.11 to add artistic impact. Figure 16.11 is a scene of a fishing boat on a bay in bright sunlight. The scene uses fogs, as well as a raytraced water surface. The bright lighting and reflective water surface obscure much of the fog and the fact that the water contains several ocean-green colors. Also much of the boat detail is lost in this bright scene. Lens Flares offers easy image enhancement and doesn't add much rendering time. Working with LE Flare Automatic and Manual Secondary Flare options, you can add back the soft glows and missing sea colors, while at the same time giving more character and punch to the subject of the image.

FIGURE 16.11

LE Flare works well to add back colors and softness to an image that is otherwise overwhelmed by reflections.

RealLensFlare 1.5

Cebas' RealLensFlare 1.5 for R2 (RLF), a commercial plug-in that competes directly with Lens Effects, contains many modules for Flare, Glow, Highlight, Depth of Field, Motion blur, Glow Edges, Luma Object and Luma Particles (see Figure 16.12). Unlike Lens Effects, which operates as a series of Video Post filters, RLF uses six Helper objects—Lensflare, Distance blur, Edge Glow, Highlight, Glow, and Motion blur. RLF does an excellent job of creating realistic-looking lens effects and flares. The accompanying CD-ROM contains two images from the planet scene in which RLF is substituted for the Lens Effects Glow and Flare filters (see files 16tga01.tga and 16tga02.tga).

You access RLF settings through the Modify panel and access all of RLF's parameters from the standard MAX rollouts. With the Modify panel open, you can also right-click the Helper object and select Properties. This action brings up the RLF graphical user interface, or you can access the Properties menu from the bottom of the Lensflare Globals rollout. This GUI is where RealLensFlare's biggest strength lies. The interface is intuitive and fun to use. It provides a Preview window where you can see a fully rendered image of the lens. When you change the settings in RLF, the Preview window updates to show the result of the change. The update rendering is extremely fast.

FIGURE 16.12

The RealLensFlare 1.5 interface for R2 competes with Lens Effects, but locates effects in the scene by using proprietary Helper objects. It can be run from within R2's default renderer or as a Video Post plug-in.

FIGURE 16.12

The RealLensFlare 1.5 interface for R2 competes with Lens Effects, but locates effects in the scene by using proprietary Helper objects. It can be run from within R2's default renderer or as a Video Post plug-in.

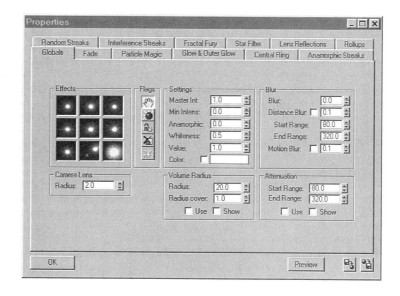

Once these are placed, you have the option to use RLF as a Video Post filter or to use it from within MAX's Scanline renderer. The dialog box is identical for each and allows you to turn on or off features you might have enabled with Helper objects.

The Starfilter module re-creates the star-shaped sparkle that might appear close to extremely shiny materials such as chrome. You can also add twinkling highlights to objects or Particle systems to create sparkly fireworks and other special effects.

The Starfilter module enables MAX's virtual camera to blur objects that are a specified distance from the location of the camera. This effect can give your animations the cinematic realism of a real camera by focusing the viewer's attention on the foreground action. The module is optimized to handle the borderline between foreground and background objects seamlessly and without jagged lines.

As with Lens Effects, you can save and recycle setups with RLF. In the new R2 version, RLF 1.5 adds Fractal Fury, a procedure that distorts the Lens Flare and the glow halo that RLF generates. The procedure uses fractal noise, which is a mathematical procedure that produces random perturbations based on fractal mathematics. The distortion results in gaseous clouds of intense color and variety, wispy electrical arcs, and fire tendrils. Fractal Fury can generate realistic looking space nebula, science fiction-type explosions, and other special effects. Fractal Fury is close in capability to Lens Effects Inferno.

Like the other modules in RLF, Fractal Fury renders very quickly, and its parameters are fully animatable. Because Fractal Fury is a distortion, the setup of your original flare affects your result. You can, therefore, get a different Fractal Fury result by adjusting the basic Lens Flare parameters. The Fractal Fury module contains three basic types of effects:

■ **Electrical:** Randomly generates thin electrical arcs.

■ **Glowing clouds:** Creates globular and swirling gaseous systems.

■ **Burning flames:** Creates twirling, thread-like flames.

Figure 16.13 illustrates some of the effects you can generate with Fractal Fury.

FIGURE 16.13

Effects generated with Fractal Fury.

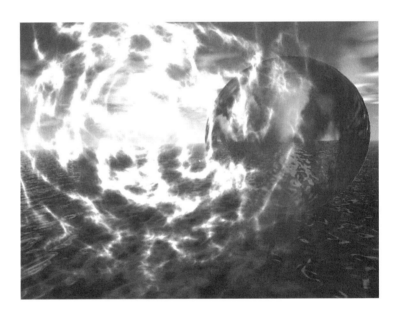

Also new to RLF version 1.5 are Anamorphic Streaks. Similar to the Star sub-effect in Lens Effects Flare, Alpha channel blur, and a Glow Edges function, Anamorphic Streaks gives you greater control over where the Glow appears on an object. This is particularly useful for glowing text and logos because it saves you from needing to set the Glow for certain faces only.

Another new feature to RLF 1.5 is the added support of Motion blur, which you can use to simulate realistic special effects. One way to create interesting smoke, for example, is to apply Motion blur to a Particle system made up of Lens Flares. This might sound scary if you have used Motion blur in the past because it achieves the blur effect by performing multiple offset renders of the object. RLF, however, handles Motion blur very quickly. Adding it to Lens Flares with RLF only adds approximately 30 percent to your render time. Motion blur with Lens Flares is also useful for doing trailers—trailing fast moving objects with motion-blurred Lens Flares.

RLF is also fog aware. As you move the Lens Flare into the fog, the Lens Flare fades and eventually dies out. This proves useful for underwater scenes where an object, such as a submarine, slowly disappears into murky water. The Lens Flare also inherits the color set for your fog.

When you work with Lens Flares, it is often useful to attach, or *bind*, the Lens Flare to an object or a light. If you have a light with a Lens Flare in your scene and you want to animate it, for example, you need the Lens Flare to move with the light. One of RLF's coolest features does this and is called the Automatic Analytical Binding System (AABS). Despite its complicated name, AABS is extremely simple to use and is extremely powerful. AABS is seamless and invisible to the user. To activate AABS, you need only create the Lens Flare helper on the object, light, or Particle system you want to bind it to. The RLF helper detects and attaches itself automatically.

RealLensFlare Glow

RealLensFlare Glow procedure is roughly three times faster than the basic Glow filter (Glow (Frame only) or Glow Plus). RLF Glow adds flexibility as well. In addition to being able to control the size of the Glow and animate it, you can also adjust the density and luminance and animate those aspects of the Glow. You can even choose to glow the edges if you want. These additional options give you finer control than other Glow plug-ins. You might, for example, want a really subtle Glow around an object. With Standard Glow, you might find that a size setting of six is too little, and a setting of seven is too high. The additional controls that Real Lens Glow provides enable you to make subtle changes to different aspects of your Glow.

Of course, the parameters you set for the RLF Glow are fully animatable. As with Lens Effects, you have access to the parameters in Track View. In other words, you can sync RLF values with other controllers, such as the Wave controller, so that one animation cycle drives others.

Binding RealLensFlares to Particle Systems

Binding Lens Flares to Particle systems is great for creating special effects. You can bind an RLF Helper object to Basic and Advanced Particle systems or to Digimation's SandBlaster or Animation Science's Outburst Particle system. When you bind a Lens Flare helper object to a Particle system, each particle becomes an individual Lens Flare. Release 1.5 extends the power of AABS and particle capabilities with Particle Magic. This system enables you to generate variation on each particle. The result is a Particle system that generates non-identical light particles, useful in burning effects, meteor showers, and so on. Particle Magic is also capable of analyzing the rotational position of each particle in 3D space, enabling you to make your highlights rotate with the spin of the particle.

The difference between the Lens Effects that ships with R2 and RealLensFlare 1.5 for R2 lies in how their interfaces work—in other words, using helper objects versus Object and Material IDs—and their relative claims of speed. These differences, of course, affect how you work with the tools. RLF has the distinct advantage of permitting you to work and preview your work from within MAX's main interface, instead of the Video Post module. Lens Effects, on the other hand, is largely gradient driven—many spinners have been replaced with gradients, which enable smooth control between settings and which themselves can be saved and reused.

Blur Effects

Blur effects are useful in a number of situations. They are commonly used to create a depth of field. When your eyes focus on an object, that object comes into focus and objects on the periphery of your field of vision become slightly blurred. The effect occurs in real cameras and is often exaggerated in motion pictures. When viewing a scene, the effect serves to focus the viewer's attention on a particular spot. By using depth of field in your MAX scenes, you can force your viewers to focus their attention on the action. This technique can also save modeling time. Because certain areas of your scene are blurred, you don't need to spend a lot of time detailing those areas. The effect can give your animations the cinematic realism of a real camera. Blurs are also used for special effects, such as the atmospheric distortion created by heat. By using blurs, for example, you can re-create a jet engine's exhaust system and be faithful to reality. This section outlines four methods you might choose for depth of field or other Blur effects.

Blur Plug-In

The Blur plug-in is a freeware plug-in written by Johnny Ow. The plug-in blurs the scene based on a Material ID channel or an Object channel. Because the plug-in blurs the scene based on G-Buffer information and not on computational physics, it is better suited for special effects than it is for depth of field. The Blur plug-in is accessed as a Video Post filter event. Figure 16.14 shows the Blur Control dialog box.

FIGURE 16.14

The Blur plug-in lets you blur a scene based on the Material ID or Object ID.

The Source section enables you to specify the particular Material ID or Object ID you want to use. The Radius parameter controls the level of the blur. A higher radius results in a blurrier area. The Radius parameter also controls the size of the soft edge that surrounds the blurred portions of the image. The Constrain to Shape checkbox instructs the blur to limit its effect to the exact pixels occupied by the specified Material ID or Object channel. If Constrain to Shape is checked, the Radius parameter no longer controls the size of the soft edge because the soft edge is eliminated. The Affect Alpha checkbox instructs the Blur filter to blur the alpha channel, which enables seamless compositing of blurred images. The Overlap checkbox instructs the Blur filter to computationally overlap the pixel sections that it blurs. The effect is usually an increased blurriness, but it also tends to distort and smear the affected regions.

TIP

You can also use the Blur filter to create a faux depth of field effect. Essentially, you leave your foreground object focused and blur your background. By setting the object channel to 0 in the Filter Setup dialog, everything in your scene is blurred unless you change the default value on your objects to a number other than 0. You can blur everything except specific objects, or you can blur everything and then composite a focused foreground.

By enabling you to locate the Blur, based on the location of the object by Object or Material ID, Blur serves a purpose not addressed by Lens Effects Focus, in which you locate the Blur node by object name, by a center radius, or by applying it to the entire scene.

Lens Effects Focus: Distance Blur

The Lens Effects Focus Filter in R2 enables you to do depth of field effects. Unlike the other Lens Effects filters, LE Focus is a simple interface with few controls.

If you select either Radial blur or Focal Node, every object in the scene blurs according to the Focal Range (near) and Focal Limit (far) range settings. Focal Range (near) and Focal Limit (far) have no effect if Scene blur is on: Scene blur creates an even blur throughout. Radial blur places a focused area at center frame, with a blur radiating outward. Selecting Focal Node provides an option for any object to act as a Focal Node; in other words, it remains in focus while objects at a greater and lesser distance are blurred. If you select Focal Node but fail to select an object, you get the same result as with Scene blur. You don't select by Object or Material ID. The settings are sensitive—small adjustments to Horizontal and Vertical Focal Loss result in a noticeable fall-off in clarity as objects recede from the picture plane (see Figure 16.15). Alpha channel support is available for seamless compositing of focal blurred scenes and a Preview button enables you to generate a preview of how your settings affect the Video Post queue. LE Focus enables you to set values for Horizontal and Vertical Focal Loss, which adjusts the overall level of blurriness. You can lock these values so that they adjust symmetrically, or you can create streaking blurriness and other effects by making the horizontal and vertical blurriness values different.

The Lens Effects Focus dialog, like all Lens Effects filters, is a modeless window, meaning you can access other parts of MAX. Any entry with a green bullet on the right creates an entry in Track View.

FIGURE 16.15

The Lens Effects Focus interface. If you choose Scene Blur, an adjustment of 1.0 is sufficient to blur a foreground object as it recedes from the picture plane.

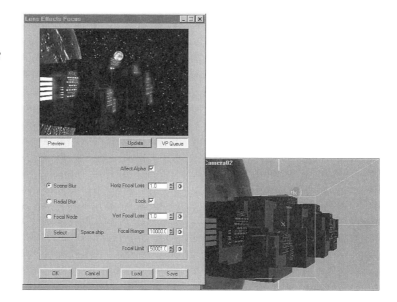

RealLensFlare: Distance Blur and Motion Blur

RealLensFlare's uses a Distance Blur helper object to create Depth of Field effects. You place Distance Blur helpers in your scene, which has the advantage of being a free-floating focus point. Similarly, RLF contains a Motion Blur helper object. However sparse the settings, the capability to move them around and to implement them either in the Scanline renderer or through Video Post can be very useful.

Distance blur can blur the background and adjust focal depths, and it has an auto-focus feature for quick and easy Blur effects. You can access the Blur parameters in Track View, and you can animate the position of the Helper object. This is useful for creating rack focus effects, where blurred objects in the background suddenly come into focus and vice versa.

In version 1.5 of RLF for R2, the Distance blur supports alpha channel processing for seamless compositing of blurred images. Another added feature, 3D Space Blur Radius, enables you to set near and far ranges for the Distance Blur Helper object. You can then animate the Helper moving smoothly through your scene to create realistic fly-through and other effects. A Fancy blur option enables you to blur specified objects only, based on their distance from the camera. This feature enables you to create object-based Distance Blurs.

Adobe Photoshop Plug-In Filters

Release 1.1 and later of 3D Studio MAX includes a Video Post filter that enables you to run Adobe Photoshop-compatible filters on images and renderings from within Video Post. Hundred of filters are currently available for Photoshop and other image processing, editing, and enhancement programs. You can create all kinds of interesting effects by using Photoshop-compatible filters with your MAX renderings. Almost any image processing effect you can think of probably has a corresponding Photoshop-compatible filter. You can use Photoshop-compatible filters, for example, to make your rendering look like a painted fresco, to add a film grain look, or to tweak out the colors in creative ways.

The MAX Photoshop Plug-in Filter event works only with 32-bit Photoshop-compatible filters. Consequently, not all the available Photoshop filters work with MAX. Older 16-bit filters will not be recognized. Furthermore, some of the plug-ins that ship with Adobe Photoshop are programmed to work only with Photoshop. Figuring out which ones work and which don't is a matter of trial and error. If you attempt to use a Photoshop filter designed to work only with Photoshop, MAX will crash. You should save or hold your file if you intend to experiment in this manner.

TIP

The following is a list of fun and useful filters you might try applying to your animations. All the filters in this list are included with Adobe Photoshop 4.0 and have tested well with the Adobe Photoshop MAX plug-in.

- Diffuse Glow
- Glass
- Ocean Ripple
- Film Grain
- Smudge Stick
- Watercolor
- Plastic Wrap
- Rough Pastels
- Paint Daubs
- Sponge

The MAX plug-in uses the native interface of the Photoshop filter to give you an interactive preview of the effect. In most cases, the parameters you set for the filter are saved with the .MAX file and the Video Post .VPX file. This feature enables you to return to the filter to make modifications to the parameters.

Some plug-in filters do not allow MAX to access the settings and, therefore, MAX cannot save them. The Kai's Power Tools third-party Photoshop plug-in utility pack, for example, does not allow MAX to save settings. If you intend to use filters from this product, you should make certain that they are set correctly before exiting the setup, or you should write down the settings for use in future sessions. The Adobe Photoshop Plug-in Filter event can be nested, enabling you to use multiple filters on one image or rendering. You cannot animate the effect, however. If you apply the filter to animation, for example, the filter is applied with the same settings to every frame. Figure 16.16 shows the Adobe Photoshop Plug-in Setup dialog. You must first add the filter to the Video Post queue. You can then double-click the event to bring up the Edit Filter Event dialog and then click Setup to bring up the Setup dialog for the filter.

FIGURE 16.16

*The Photoshop Plug-in
Setup dialog box.*

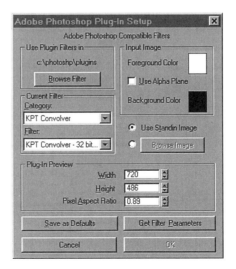

The Use Plugin Filters in section is where you specify the directory where the Photoshop-compatible plug-in filters reside on your hard disk. Click the Browse button and navigate to the directory to select it. After a directory containing filters is specified, select the category you want from the

Category list box in the Current Filter section. The category is encoded in the plug-in file and typically is the name of the developer or the filter package.

Beneath the Category list box is the Filter list box, where you specify the specific filter you want to use. The Input Image section enables you to specify a foreground and background color, which is needed for some Photoshop filters to function correctly. The KPT Page Curl filter, for example, curls the corner of the image like a turning page. To work properly, this filter needs to know the background color because it places the background color into the area revealed by the upturned page.

The Use Alpha Plane checkbox determines how the filter handles the alpha channel in an image. Typically, if an alpha channel is available, the Photoshop filter affects only the opaque areas of the image. If the Use Alpha Plane checkbox is unchecked, the alpha channel information is discarded and the filter affects the entire image. If you are using a mask, for example, the mask is still used and serves to replace the alpha channel. If the Use Alpha Plane checkbox is checked, only pixels designated as opaque in the alpha channel and pixels that are not masked are affected by the filter.

The Use Standin Image radio button sets the background for the Preview window to a standard checker pattern. You can specify an image to use instead by activating the Browse Image radio button and clicking the Browse Image button to select an image.

The Plug-In Preview section sets the size of the image that you want to use in the Preview window. These settings determine how faithfully the Preview window will represent what you see in your final rendering. You should set these parameters to correspond with the image you are using for the preview. Clicking the Get Filter Parameters button brings up the Interactive Preview window and enables you to adjust the settings to use for the selected Photoshop-compatible filter.

Fractal Flow MAX

Digimation's Fractal Flow 1.5d for R2 has its roots in the 3D Studio DOS image processing IPAS routine. Fractal Flow uses fractal mathematics to distort an image or specific parts of an image in various ways. The process involves placing a virtual grid over an image, distorting the grid, and moving the pixels according to the grid distortion. This distortion capability is coupled with extensive masking options: The distortions, waves, and ripples can be restricted or confined by gradient, bitmap, and/or G-Buffer masks. Because most distortions can be animated, Fractal Flow is useful for simulating cloaking spaceships, creating heat distortion, or creating realistic fire, smoke, clouds, water, and other special effects.

Fractal Flow is a Video Post filter. As with Lens Effects, the modeless dialogs enable you to access other parts of the program while they are open. You can minimize or move the Fractal Flow Setup dialog and continue to work in MAX. Like the Lens Effects filters, the Fractal Flow Setup dialog has a Preview window that updates interactively as you change settings, and an Update button to re-render the scene if you advance MAX's Time slider in an animated scene (see Figure 16.17). Likewise, any setting with a green bullet button will make an editable entry in Track View. Fractal Flow is divided into five main panels: Fractal Distortions, Waves, Ripples, Origins, and Masks. You can save your settings to a separate FLO file for later use.

FIGURE 16.17

The Fractal Flow dialog box.

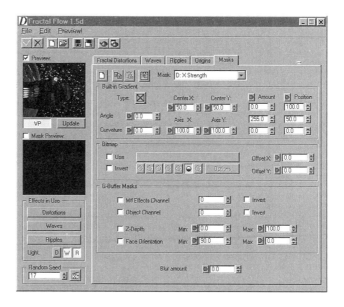

The Fractal Distortions Tab

The Fractal Distortions tab is where you set the general Fractal Noise parameters that distort your images (see Figure 16.18). The buttons on the left activate the corresponding effect (Distortions, Waves, or Ripples). The Light buttons beneath determine which of these effects should receive lighting. Below that is the Random Seed box, which generates the seed number for the effect. After you activate a parameter, you can adjust the value on the right side of the interface and view the results in the Preview window. You can animate the parameters by turning on the Animate button and moving MAX's Time slider in the main interface, and settting checked parameters to different values at different frames.

FIGURE 16.18

The Fractal Distortions tab is where you set your general Fractal Noise parameters.

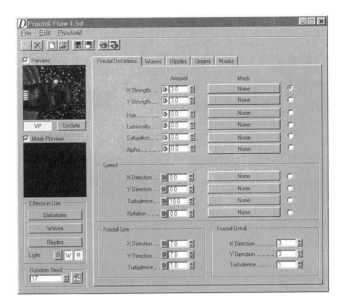

The Preview window at the left gives you a preview of the effect against NTSC-type color bars background. You can also preview any masks in use in the Preview window immediately below. You can set up and render larger preview frames within Fractal Flow: The Preview Setup dialog can be accessed either by Edit/Preview or from the icon on the toolbar. You can set both preview size and aspect ratio and opt to render either the entire VP queue or just up to the Fractal Flow event. Fractal Flow can then render the Video Post queue and show you a rendered preview of your settings.

The Mask buttons next to the various animatable parameters enable you to create a mask for the effect (see "The Masks Tab" section, later in this chapter).

After you select a mask, the Mask Preview window updates to show what your mask looks like. Fractal Flow has very powerful masking features. You can mask using Linear or Radial gradients or you can create a mask by using bitmaps. Seven buttons enable you to specify the alpha channel, the RGB color channels, the M channel (Maximum luminance) or the Y channel (Chrominance value) to use as your mask. You can also specify a specific Material ID or Object channel, and you can limit the mask to a depth range or face normals. A Blur parameter softens the edges of your mask.

The Waves Tab

The Waves tab enables you to create a wave distortion across an image. You can set the number of waves, the X and Y strengths of the wave, the angle at which the waves cross the image, and the speed at which they move across the image (see Figure 16.19). You can animate and mask these parameters in the same manner as those in the Fractal Distortions tab. The Waves tab also enables you to specify the highlight and shadow color, as well as the direction and intensity of the light that accentuates the waves.

FIGURE 16.19

The Waves tab enables you to create a wave distortion on your images.

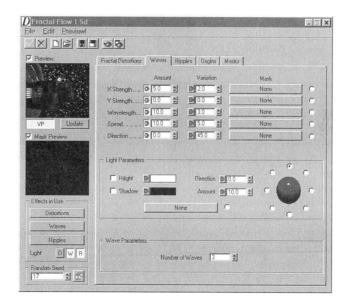

The Ripples Tab

The Ripples tab enables you to create circular ripples across an image. The options for ripples are similar to those of waves (see Figure 16.20). You can also control how the ripples decay as they move away from their origin. You can set the origin of the ripples and use a mask for the origin.

FIGURE 16.20

The Ripples tab enables you to create a ripple effect on your images.

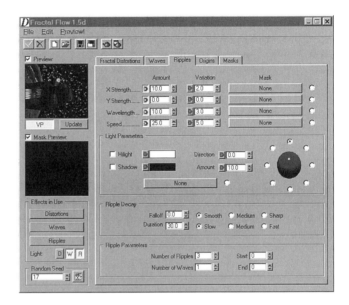

The Origins Tab

The Origins tab controls the alignment of all of the grids for the Fractal Distortion tab and expresses the alignment as a percentage of screen for both the x-and y-axes. Each part of the Fractal Distortion is based upon an imaginary grid. This tab enables you to adjust 6 parametric settings for each X and Y, independent of the others, and of course, animate the changes. This is not for every use, but can work well for certain special effects, such as layering clouds and offsetting alpha channels. This tab also contains adjustments for the Ripple-Origin. It's not as extensive as that for Fractal Distortions, but performs a similar, animatable function for Ripples.

The Masks Tab

Fractal Flow's most unique and powerful offering is its masking capability. The Masks panel lets you tailor the type of transparency (Strength, Hue, Luminosity, Alpha, and so on), make the effect subject to a gradient mask, and limit the mask to a particular Object or Material ID. The interface design encourages you to flip back and forth between the fractal effect and the Masks tab. Within the Fractal Distortions, Waves, and Ripples tabs are Mask buttons. Clicking the radio buttons next to the Mask buttons activates the corresponding mask.

Clicking a Mask button takes you to the Masks tab; when you finish setting mask parameters, a Go To Effects Page icon takes you back to the effects tab you were working on. At the top of the Masks tab you choose which mask you will work on (Distortion, X-strength, Ripple, Speed, and so on). You can cut and copy between masks. The next portion of the Masks tab is divided into three sections: Built-in Gradient, Bitmap, and G-Buffer Masks. The built-in gradient can be either linear or radial. You can locate the center and set the angle, curvature, amount, and position. And, of course, you can animate these settings. The Bitmap section lets you choose a map, choose any one of its RGBA channels, or use its luminosity or yellow component as a mask, position and resize it, and animate any offset of it. The G-Buffer section lets you restrict the mask to the Material Effects Channel ID or the Object Channel ID (or invert the effect) and further modify that selection by Z-Depth and Face Orientation. Most important, you can use the three sections together on each mask.

Almost every parameter in Fractal Flow can accept a mask, and each mask can be different (up to 21 entries). The mask can be a bitmap, modified by built-in gradients, and further restricted by G-Buffer masking. You cannot build multi-layered masks within Fractal Flow, but of course you can use animated masks and further animate changes to any mask. In this way you can add Fractal effects either to a scene or to an RLA bitmap image and position.

Fractal Flow is a very interesting tool because it gives you the capability to liquefy solid objects without modifying or space-warping geometry. This can be done entirely in Video Post. For example, the sidewalk can be singled out, tinted red, and made to flow like lava. Often this type of solution renders more quickly than deforming geometry or creating atmospheric effects and gives the added bonus of giving you more precise control over the final lighting effect than if you tried to re-create it in a 3D environment.

Chameleon

Digimation's Chameleon is a specialized Multi/Sub-Object type of material that provides unique special effects possibilities in Video Post. Chameleon materials are assigned to gizmos, not geometry. Every object with a Chameleon material has a base material assigned to the geometry, with additional materials assigned to each of any number of gizmos (sphere, cylinder, or box-shaped). As the geometry passes through the gizmo position, its surface takes on the material assigned to the gizmo. The Gizmo parameters include an inner and an outer radius, which Chameleon uses to calculate an outward fall-off effect. Setting the radii close to each other creates a ring-shaped material (see Figure 16.21).

FIGURE 16.21

The Chameleon interface.

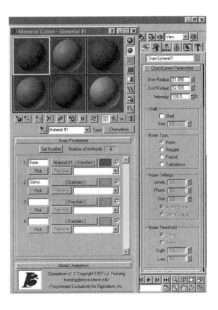

The Chameleon material takes precedence over any underlying material and accepts a Material Effects Channel ID, which makes it amenable to Glows, Highlights, Lens Flare, and other special effects. The accompanying CD-ROM contains a large sphere passing through a narrow, transparent tube, using a spherical Displace space warp to stretch it along the way. A Glow assigned to the sphere is lost once the sphere is inside the tube, even though the tube is transparent. Assume the tube is a character and you want to show the character's distress by having the sphere "glow" as it passes through. You can accomplish this with a spherical Chameleon gizmo moving in concert with the sphere and the Displace space warp. You can then assign and animate one or more glows to the gizmo's Material Effects Channel ID.

You can see this technique applied in 16avi07.avi on the accompanying CD. In this example, the tube is transparent and the Chameleon material is different from the base metallic material on the sphere, and both animated Glows and Highlights have been applied in Video Post.

Chameleon gizmos have both inner and outer radius parameters, which can be used to create a fall-off effect on a Chameleon material or, if set close together, an outline or circular effect. The latter works well for shockwave effects in a space scene:

1. Place the exploding object at the center of a large rectangular plane to which you assign a Chameleon material.

2. Animate a spherical Chameleon gizmo growing outward from the center of the exploding object, with values for the inner and outer radii remaining close to each other throughout the sequence.

3. Use a Matte/Shadow material for the rectangle and Noise for the Chameleon gizmo; then the circular material illuminates the rectangular plane as it expands in the animation.

With Chameleon you can create convincing images without additional atmospherics, Particle system, or geometry.

UltraShock

UltraShock by Digimation is a Video Post filter for adding volumetric effects to Particle systems. It works with MAX's Basic and Advanced Particle systems, as well as third-party offerings such as Sand Blaster. It's valuable because of the quality of volumetric effects and because you need very few particles to simulate a dense effect.

UltraShock uses a Helper object and all controls are accessed through the Modify panel. You set up parameters by addressing three aspects of the Particle system: Shape, Color, and Compositing method. UltraShock ships with seven default shapes, including Noise, Circle, Smoke, Plasma, Flame 2D, Spark, and Fire Ball (see Figure 16.22).

FIGURE 16.22

The UltraShock inter-face is divided into three sections in which you choose the shape, color, and compositing method for the volu-metric particle shader effect.

As to colors, you can use the default Color controller, which is gradient-based and lets you set a range of particles, from birth to death or from inside to out. (The only other controller shipping with UltraShock is the Pandora controller, which works only with the Pandora Particle system, also from Digimation.) Finally, you have one default compositor, but it permits you to composite volumetric Particle effects according to alpha channel, Glow, Darken, or Blur.

Once you've set the Shader parameters, create the effect by using one or more Video Post filters: UltraShock Shader, the basic shader to give the volumetric effect; UltraShock Motion blur; and UltraShock Shadow, if you want the UltraShock Particle system to cast shadows (this requires adding an UltraShock light to the scene).

The accompanying CD-ROM includes an animation of a fishing boat on a bay (16avi08.avi). The smoke effects were created by using UltraShock; the Lens Flare effect was created by using RealLensFlare 1.5.

Genesis VFX

Genesis VFX by Positron is a relatively new entry and a direct competitor in special effects with Lens Effects and RealLensFlare. Like its competition, it is an entire environment for creating special effects. Genesis is built on the idea of combining multiple effects within a single filter entry. The interface is multi-layered and multi-moduled (see Figure 16.23).

One Genesis entry in the Video Post queue is truly a batch order of filter events. The interface is a little different from what we normally see in MAX. It includes a rough general Preview window that gives a graphic description of the location of each effect. Selecting an element by name and dragging in the window moves that element. Right-clicking the window produces a render of the effect. Shift-right-click and you can reposition the entire effect in the rendering window.

FIGURE 16.23

The Genesis VFX interface invites creating, positioning, and editing a series of effects, which can be linked to the scene by object, Object or Material ID, color, or surface and then animated/morphed.

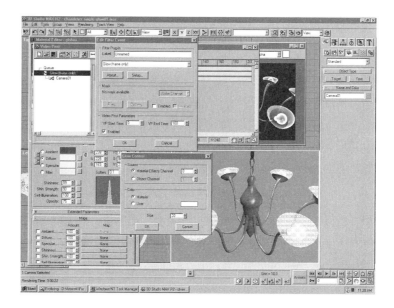

The interface is divided into three sections:

- **Operations folder:** In this folder, you load, save, keep track of elements, and make settings to tie the effects to the scene.

- **Position folder:** In this folder, you address the location of the element and how they will be rendered.

■ **Shape folder:** In this folder, you make new elements, edit old ones, morph between shape elements, and add Noise. You then add these elements to the queue in the Position folder.

Each and every element can be animated separately. At its heart, Genesis tends more toward a creative special effects/animation environment than a reality-based environment. The CD-ROM includes two shots from the LE Flare exercise, which have been re-rendered, substituting Genesis VFX (see 16tga03.tga and 16tga04.tga).

Genesis, by virtue of its interface design, lends itself toward creating the components of an effect, rather than the aspects of an effect as you create them in RLF or LE Flare. To some extent, this appeals more to painters than cinematographers. The CD contains a still of the space scene discussed earlier with a predefined Genesis effect substituted for LE Glow and LE Flare (see Genesis.tga). Here Genesis was used more for fantasy illustration than cinematic realism, which was a use inspired by its design. Genesis also has great potential to be used as a video transition tool in compositing with Video Post. A demo version of Genesis VFX is included on your CD.

Miscellaneous Effect Plug-Ins

Whereas some of the plug-ins mentioned earlier are free, the major offerings are available commercially from Digimation, Cebas/Trinity, and Positron. Many plug-ins are available free for download at MAX-oriented Web sites, in addition to the ones discussed so far. Some are quite useful, and expect many more to follow. This section outlines a few miscellaneous plug-ins that haven proven most useful.

Negative

The Negative filter ships with MAX. This filter inverts the colors of an image. The result looks like the negative of a color photograph. You might use this filter if you need to model a film reel. You can render a frame through the Negative filter and use that image as a tiled map on some celluloid film geometry. You might also use this filter in an abstract or psychedelic animation. Negative requires no setup parameters.

Rotate

Rotate, a free plug-in by EffectWare, takes the picture plane and rotates it in 3D space with six degrees of freedom. It gives the look of a bitmap on a flat plane, except the source can be an image event or a scene event. Although you might be able to animate the angle, you cannot animate the axis or pivot orientation. This can produce very interesting effects in compositing situations.

Gray

Gray, by EffectWare, substitutes a grayscale render of either the whole image or a portion according to Object or Material ID. It's a simple effect and in the right circumstance can save a trip to Photoshop.

Mosaic

Mosaic, by EffectWare, pixelates the image, in whole or according to Object or Material ID. You can control pixel height and width. It has a use for an artistic effect, especially if coupled with other filters.

Contrast

Contrast is an image contrast control filter that performs much like the Brightness/Contrast filter in Photoshop. There are separate spinners for Contrast and Brightness, and each accepts positive and negative values. The settings can be either Absolute or Derived (relative to the image.) This filter works well to give a final adjustment and might save you from having to retouch an image in Photoshop. Its biggest limitation is having to render the VP queue to see the effect.

Ishani Filters

Ishani Graphics has provided the MAX community with four Video Post plug-in filters, as well as four sets of preset effects for the Genesis VFX system: Ambient Scene Tint, Crunch Compressor, Lossy Compressor, and Object Outline.

■ Ishani Ambient Scene Tint works much like Photoshop's Hue controls, in that you can tint the entire scene according to averaged scene colors, RGB value, or single color tint, or you can tint only certain objects according to Object or Material ID. Likewise you can set Tint settings of Brightness, Color Fade, and Solid Opacity, which can be either Additive or Subtractive.

■ Ishani Crunch Compressor is a graphic compression utility.

■ Ishani Lossy Compressor is a graphic compression utility, similar to the Crunch Compressor, but it loses image information as part of the compression process.

■ Ishani Object Outline lets you choose an object by Object or Material ID and place a colored outline around it. This can be useful when combined with other artistic filters, such as Photoshop-compatible filters, or to add emphasis to objects that have had a Glow applied to them.

Starfield Generator

Starfield Generator is a Video Post filter written by Tom Hudson. It is useful for creating realistic space scene backgrounds. The plug-in ships as part of R2. There are many ways to create star fields in MAX. You can create them with environment maps by using bitmaps or procedurals such as Noise.

Starfield Generator's advantage over other methods, however, is Motion Blur. If your scene requires camera movement, the Starfield Generator enables you to control the amount that the stars blur in relation to the movement of the camera. Motion Blur is great for creating added impact in space scenes. It can also be useful for creating special effects such as warp speed star streaks and other effects. Starfield Generator works off of a camera in your scene. You should apply the filter to a Camera Scene event. Access the Setup parameters by clicking the Setup button in the Edit Filter Event dialog (see Figure 16.24).

FIGURE 16.24

Starfield Generator setup parameters.

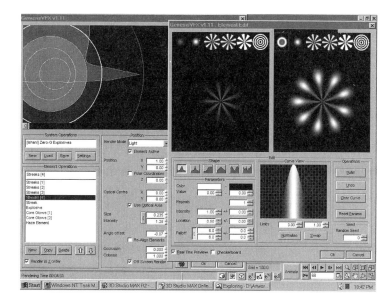

The Source Camera section enables you to select a camera for Starfield Generator on which to base its calculations. If you have multiple cameras in your scene, you should specify the same camera that you add to the Video Post queue. If you specify another camera, the stars will not match the motion of the camera that you render.

The General section enables you to specify the general parameters that determine how your starfield will look. The Dimmest Star and Brightest Star spinners range from 0–255, with 0 being completely black and 255 being solid white. If you want your starfield to be composed completely of dim stars, for example, you can lower the value of the Brightest Star spinner.

The Linear and Logarithmic radio buttons mathematically determine how the brightness changes from dim to bright. The Star Size spinner determines the size of the star dots in pixels.

The Motion Blur parameters determine how the streaking effect occurs when the camera moves. The Use checkbox turns Motion Blur for the stars on or off. The Amount spinner determines how much Motion Blur to use and ranges from 0–100. The Dimming spinner sets the amount that the motion streaks will dim as their trails get longer. This value also ranges from 0–100. The default values for Amount and Dimming work fine in most cases.

The Star Database section determines how many stars appear and where they are generated. The Random button uses the number in the Seed spinner to generate a random number of stars and to place them. The Custom radio button enables you to read in a star layout from a specified file. There is currently no way to save your own star layouts.

Starfield Blur

 Starfield Blur builds on the capability of Starfield included with R2, but adds a new Motion blur algorithm, lets you set up to four colors for the stars, and provides real-time preview across frames (see Figure 16.25). Note that the space scenes in this chapter use this Starfield Generator, which is included on your CD as starblur.zip.

FIGURE 16.25

Starfield Blur is a free plug-in that expands the capability of R2's standard Starfield plug-in to include color choices and real-time previews.

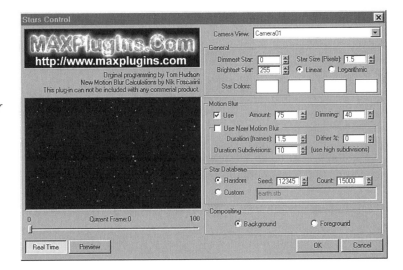

In Practice: Video Post Effects

- **Special Effects:** Special effects go a long way toward adding visual impact to a scene. By using Video Post filters, you can include a variety of effects in your images and animations. Most of the special effects-oriented filters available today are plug-ins. Keeping track of all the new plug-ins can be both a daunting and exciting task. The Internet and CompuServe are both great resources for obtaining new MAX plug-ins.

- **Glow and Highlight:** Glow and Highlight effects are useful in many situations. Basic Glow, Lens Effects Glow, and Lens Effects Hilight ship with R2 and offer as much functionality as any other third-party commercial plug-ins. RealLensFlare and Genesis VFX contain equally powerful and flexible Glow and Hilight modules, but each takes a different approach to how you work with the tools. Lens Effects offers flexibility through a gradient-based interface; RealLensFlare uses Helper objects to allow object-independent movement of the effect within the scene. Genesis offers an artistic alternative and is designed to facilitate batch-processing many effects with only one entry in the Video Post queue.

- **Lens flares:** Lens flares can be a striking addition to any scene. The most common criticism of lens flares has been their gratuitous overuse. You should make certain that your scene warrants using a lens flare before you start tossing them into scenes. Subtle use of lens flares will take your images further. Slight or barely noticeable flares around light sources give extra realism to your scenes. Remember that lens flares can also be used for special light effects. The Fractal Fury module of RealLensFlare 1.5 and the Inferno module of Lens Effects each add the capability to create realistic special effect phenomena.

- **Blur:** Blur effects are useful for creating special effects and reproducing Camera Focal Blur. You can use Blur effects to reproduce atmospheric heat distortion, for example. You can use Depth of Field Blur to more faithfully reproduce the look of a real camera.

- **Adobe Photoshop plug-in filters:** These filters enable you to modify your images and animation in a great variety of ways. The Internet is a great resource for obtaining Adobe Photoshop–compatible 32-bit filters, and a variety of third-party commercial collections are available.

- **Fractal Flow MAX:** This makes special image processing effects possible from within Video Post. You can create general fractal distortions, waves, and ripples within your images and animations.

- **UltraShock:** UltraShock is a specialized volumetric shader for Particle systems that works remarkably well to simulate smoke, fog, and fire effects without resorting to Atmospheric Effects and by using very few particles.

- **Genesis VFX:** Genesis VFX is a third-party special effects plug-in for creating Flares, Glows, and Highlights. Genesis VFX, largely by interface design, suggests fantasy application and additional functions for generating unique scene transitions in Video Post.

Index

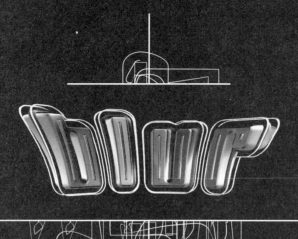

digital effects, animation and design for
film, television, commercials and games

310 581 8848 • www.blur.com

1130 abbot kinney blvd venice ca 90291
constantly looking for great animators
send us your demo reel